masses of new arrivals, the America[n]
found themselves suddenly lifted to a position of leadership of world Jewry. The
creative contributions of both the new
immigrants and the older settlers during
the decades before the First World War
are narrated here in great detail and with
extensive documentation.

Once established, the large Jewish
community faced ever new challenges generated by the growing mobility of its members, the effects of the two World Wars,
the rising tide of anti-Semitism, stimulated
especially by the Nazi propaganda, and
the enormous tasks, economic, political,
and cultural, connected with the rise of
the State of Israel. In this connection the
author analyzes the impact of the World
Wars on religion in general and on the
Jewish community in particular. He then
discusses the various contemporary aspects
of the Jewish communal responsibilities
for philanthropy, education, and Jewish
survival. He dispels especially the frequently voiced doubts about the ability
of American Jewry to be culturally creative in the Jewish sphere.

One of the keynotes of this collection
of essays is that much of the despair now
gripping many Jews might be alleviated
by the realization of the previous "ages
of anxiety" through which their ancestors
had lived and to which they responded
courageously and creatively. There appears to be no reason why such courage
and creativity should be absent from the
present generation.

Steeled by Adversity

edited by Jeannette Meisel Baron

The Jewish Publication Society of America

Philadelphia   5732 / 1971

Steeled by Adversity

Essays and Addresses
on American Jewish Life
by Salo Wittmayer Baron

U.S - Ethical relations
Jews - US - history
Halukkah

(ופ)

To Our Grandchildren
SARA, MANUEL, SHARON, CATHERINE,
ELISABETH, CYNTHIA, JEFFREY

Contents

viii | Contents

Preface

It is with a sense of nostalgia that one looks back on essays and
addresses written over a period of more than thirty years during
one of the stormiest periods in human history. As expected, some
more technical essays, like that referring to Palestine relief, required little reorientation. True, even that essay graphically illustrates the dramatic changes which have taken place in both the
Palestinian and American communities in the century since the
four visits of the three Palestinian messengers it describes. From
small, often struggling communities living, so to speak, on the
periphery of Jewish life, which was then concentrated in Europe
and its Mediterranean extensions, the Jewries of Israel and the
United States have gradually grown into focal centers carrying
major responsibilities for the destiny of the whole Jewish people.

Yet a perusal of these essays and addresses also shows how little
the world has changed in essence. Much of what agitates the minds
of men, and particularly of youth today, of what appears "relevant"
to our generation, in contrast to the alleged irrelevancies of the
traditional lore, is in fact old hat. On closer examination some of
the more basic and permanent ideas of the Renaissance man
which led Columbus, his crew, and backers to discover America
retain more of their freshness than last week's editorials in our
daily papers. Most significantly, the pessimism pervading large
segments of our society today appears far less justified when considered in the framework of long-range historic processes and in
comparison with the earlier "ages of anxiety," surveyed in our
introductory essay.

Unavoidably, nevertheless, in many significant details *tempora mutantur, et nos mutamur in illis.* If anything, it was astonishing to see how little the author's basic outlook on human and Jewish life has changed in the face of the tremendous transformations which have taken place in our time. In fact, in most cases we found no need to update radically the materials here presented. Occasionally we inserted some specific corrections and additional bibliographical references in order to aid the reader in bringing certain factual data into greater consonance with the existing state of our knowledge. But no consistent effort was made to investigate anew all the aspects covered in the respective articles and to present all the new data made available by more recent discoveries or interpretations. However, we feel confident that we are not guilty of any serious omissions and distortions.

Similarly, we found that certain repetitions became unavoidable. While in most cases it was possible to summarize and otherwise to abbreviate statements more fully developed in other essays or addresses, we often realized that too radical an elimination of repetitive statements might seriously undermine the inner consistency of an argument and the logical development of a thought presented in each particular context. We trust that the few readers who will be bored by the sporadic repetitions will bear with us.

In many ways more troublesome were the formal divergences in essays written and speeches delivered on different occasions and addressed to different audiences. The editor made a conscious effort to maintain the stylistic peculiarities of writing by the author, for whom English was the fourth literary medium (after Polish, Hebrew, and German, in which he wrote during the first thirty years of his life). To see his gradual adjustment to America's linguistic usages and modes of expression seemed more instructive than a mechanical leveling of all differences in time and outlook.

No less difficult was our attempt to introduce a measure of consistency into the chaotic stylistic variety employed by the respective editors of the journals, jubilee and memorial volumes, and pamphlets in which these essays and addresses originally appeared. Each of these editors had a style sheet of his own; sometimes the same editors or their successors in the same publication altered particular forms, as did the successive editions of the Chicago *Manual of Style* and Webster's dictionary. To establish a rigid uniformity would have required an unconscionable amount of time and effort and would have diverted even more of the author's and editor's energies from more constructive tasks. We have decided that it made absolutely no difference to the reader whether "nonetheless" or "insofar" is written as one or three words, whether "1880s" is written with or without an apostrophe, and whether "No." is written with a capital "N" or one in lower case. We simply decided not to bow down to the American editorial idol of consistency beyond reason. While in a vast majority of cases consistency has been established, we hope that reasonable readers will pardon us for the relatively few remaining exceptions.

In conclusion we wish to thank the various publishers for granting us permission to reprint these essays and addresses (see the list of acknowledgments) and the staff of the Jewish Publication Society for its vigilance and ready cooperation in seeing this at times rather complicated manuscript through the press. The careful indexer, Mrs. Paula Kasper, has likewise earned our sincere gratitude.

Yifat Shalom   *Salo Wittmayer Baron*
April 19, 1971   *Jeannette Meisel Baron*
Canaan, Connecticut

Acknowledgments

We are grateful to the publishers of the books, pamphlets, and periodicals listed below for their generosity in granting permission for the republication of the following essays and addresses:

Academy of Political Science, Essay 11
American Association for Jewish Education, Essay 17
American Jewish Historical Society, Essays 3, 7, 13, and 18
Conference on Jewish Social Studies, Essays 4 and 9
Council of Jewish Federations and Welfare Funds, Essay 20
Eretz Israel—Israel Exploration Society, Jerusalem, Essay 5
Federation of Jewish Philanthropies of New York, Essay 14
Independent Order of the B'nai B'rith, Essay 19
Jewish History Publications Ltd. (Masada), Jerusalem, Essay 10 (unpublished)
National Jewish Welfare Board, Essays 12 and 15
North Shore Congregation Israel, Glencoe, Ill., Essay 16
Rabbinical Assembly of America, Essay 8
Rutgers—The State University, Essay 6
Synagogue Council of America, Essay 2

I

Introduction

1

Introduction

1 *Ages of Anxiety*

Living as we do in a very turbulent age—one of the most turbulent, indeed, in the history of the United States and the modern world—it is not surprising to find a great many Americans deeply worried over the future of their civilization. The constant encroachments of communism over the area of the Free World, the unending war in Vietnam, the recurrent Middle-Eastern crises, and the general decline in influence and prestige of the United State in world opinion are greatly aggravated by the domestic unrest. There seems to be no prospect for genuine racial peace, for any satisfactory solution of the urban crisis, the untold ecological dangers, the disturbances on the university campuses, and the abysmal poverty of millions, side by side with the affluence of the majority and the extravagant wealth of a minority. Certainly, the growing crime wave has made life in this country both insecure and uncomfortable. According to pessimists, none of these phenomena are transitory and only a total revamping of society along lines as yet uncharted is likely to put an end to them.

It is small wonder, then, that a growing number of expatriates has abandoned this country of their birth and sought relative peace and quiet in other lands—for the most part to little avail. The vast majority remaining behind has been stunned by the unprecedented outbreaks of violence, burnings of the American flag, and other manifestations of a deep hatred for the United States on the part of segments of our youth. While real progress has been made in recent years in the area of civil rights, many individuals feel that they have lost their own civil rights, in fact, even their natural rights of freely and fearlessly strolling through the streets and parks of their cities at any time of the day or night.

For Jews these difficulties have been compounded by the specific complications of their struggle for survival. The resurgence of antisemitism, now often disguised under slogans of anti-Zionism and anti-Israelism, its spread into new large groups of black and white activists, has again raised the specter of deep insecurity in many Jewish circles. The most immediately threatened groups such as the small shopkeepers and craftsmen in the ghetto areas, or the teachers and other workers facing displacement by new-comers, look forward with deep apprehension to an uncertain economic future. They are not even sure of full backing by their own community which faces the dilemma of either helping its coreligionists or their underprivileged competitors. Moreover, for several generations some Jewish pessimists were predicting the speedy disappearance of the Jewish people under the impact of Emancipation. They now feel doubly justified by the communist attacks upon Jews and Judaism and the rise of a genuine "Jewish antisemitism" among the alienated minority of Jewish intellectuals and students. Some of these Cassandras even dismiss the evidence of a certain revival of Judaism in the Soviet Union after decades of sharp governmental repression, which was accompanied by loud predictions of the forthcoming end of Russian Jewry.

Perhaps a few indirect, if minor, answers to the perplexities of our age might be found in the following essays and addresses. Although written over a period of more than thirty years and for the most part aimed at particular narrowly defined themes, they might nevertheless give pause to some readers in their bewilderment today. Without suggesting any panaceas, they might offer some parallels and convey certain lessons which, however remotely, may appear applicable to the contemporary situation as well. In this respect, disjointed as they are and originally written under different impulses and addressed to a variety of audiences and situations, these chapters may have an underlying unity.

The very first essay, celebrating the 450th anniversary of Columbus' discovery of America, shows what happened in the sequel of one such age of great anxiety. The beginning of the modern era was one of crucial transition and deep upheavals. The discovery of the New World was accomplished under the aegis of Spain and coincided with one of the greatest tragedies of Jewish history, the expulsion of the Jews from that country to which they had so mightily contributed and which in return had enabled them to live through several centuries of relative peace and glorious cultural achievement.

This coincidence augured badly for the future of the Jewish people. Together with the Spaniards, the dreaded Spanish Inquisition made its appearance in this hemisphere. Among its main victims were Marranos who in the secrecy of their homes were trying to preserve some vestiges of their ancestral faith. Yet, under these very adverse conditions some of these secret Jews were able significantly to contribute to the upbuilding of the new American civilization. Often unconsciously, they also laid the foundations for the future development of Jewish communities which, between them, now embrace the majority of world Jewry.

Even in parts of North America outside the grasp of the long arms of Spain and Portugal Jews found themselves in a position of helping to pioneer along uncharted paths for their own and their neighbors' benefit and yet of simultaneously often being resented as unwelcome aliens. Those who wished to preserve their Jewish way of life had to struggle against tremendous odds, external and internal. If in Britain's North American colonies they achieved a measure of equality without specific legal enactments, this was largely due to their very small number and the frequent inadvertence of the ruling groups which were preoccupied with much more serious divisions within the colonial societies (see Essay 5). Yet, in the long run the widely felt need for European manpower and the deep denominational and ethnic divisions in the population prevented any single group from attaining a clear majority. Together with the growing effectiveness of its democratic ideology, this emergent "nation of nations" was led to proclaim liberty of conscience, separation of state and Church, and equality of all citizens as major fundamentals of its societal and governmental structure.

None the less, despite the mental affinity to Judaism created by the Bible-mindedness of a large segment of the colonial population and the rapprochement between Jews and Christians generated by the growing interest in the Hebrew language and culture (see Essay 6), the colonial and early American age must have bred much anxiety among those Jewish settlers who wished to cultivate their historic heritage. The approximately 2,000 Jews living in this country at the outbreak of the American Revolution formed only six organized communities in the vast territories of the new federation, all struggling to maintain their identity without any government support—to which their ancestors had become inured in the European world—in fact, often in defiance of a hostile administration. We need but remember that it took New York, the first North American Jewish community, almost eighty years before it was able to erect in the 1730s the first synagogue on this continent. Even then the plot of land could not be acquired in the name of the community, but only through a private transaction in the name of three individual trustees. The funds for this modest building had to be raised through an appeal to coreligionists as far away as the West Indies and England. Yet undaunted in spirit, the Jews persevered, and, often pioneering along new paths, they were able ultimately to construct a magnificent communal structure which has since served as a model for many other Diaspora Jewries as well (see Essay 7).

None of this could be accomplished without great anguish and many doubts. Nor was the swelling Jewish immigration into this country beginning in the 1830s and reaching its climax in the East-European mass immigration at the turn of the century, accomplished without much suffering and the overcoming of untold obstacles. Perhaps a word of warning is in order here. If below (Essay 10) our review of the mass immigration and the ensuing adjustments relates to the period of 1880 to 1914, this long-accepted chronological delimitation is entirely owing here to the fact that the essay was originally composed for inclusion in a large volume devoted to the history of world Jewry during that period. However, I have long been convinced that the march of East-European Jews to the Western Hemisphere had been fully under way before the Russian pogroms of 1881. If a specific year must be singled out for the beginning of that tremendous migratory movement, which in the brief span of 24 years between 1890 and 1914 transplanted almost a third of the whole people from one continent to another, perhaps 1869 would serve as a better starting point. In any case, when the masses of downtrodden Jews from the East-European *shtetls* began arriving on these shores, the American Jewish leadership was overwhelmed by the enormousness of the task of helping these masses to establish new homes. It was not mere prejudice of one kind or another which determined the American representatives at the international Jewish conference in Paris in 1878 to warn their European counterparts that the United States had but limited room for additional Jewish immigrants. Nevertheless, when the floodgates opened and ever swelling waves of migrants landed in the American harbors, the earlier settlers with an almost superhuman effort extended a helping hand to their incoming brethren.

This period of mass migration certainly was another great age of anxiety for both the new arrivals and their Jewish hosts. However, despite their own deep cleavages in ideology and religious outlooks and their leaders' serious misgivings about the agitation of the numerous non-Jewish opponents of that immigration, with its nativist and racialist undertones, and what it might portend for the status of the Jews already settled in the United States, the masses' creative élan overcame all obstacles and within a relatively short time injected its own novel elements of vitality into both the Jewish communities and the American society at large. We must never lose sight of the fact that this entire process was accomplished without any government aid, indeed in the face of an increasingly restrictive anti-alien legislation. I. M. Rubinow, an informed observer on the scene, correctly pointed out that, notwithstanding all their grievous sufferings, so eloquently described by contemporary poets and publicists, these poverty-stricken slum-dwelling Jewish immigrants in New York and other major cities were relatively better off than their Irish or Italian opposite numbers because "it is their diligence and self-discipline which prevent the Jew[s] from sinking to the lowest depths." Rubinow might have added the element of self-help and self-reliance, as well as the mutual assistance extended by relatives, friends, even mere acquaintances from the Old Country, whether or not they belonged to the same *Landsmannschaften,* workmen's circles, lodges, or congregations. Most remarkably, during this very period of agony these immigrants created a magnificent Yiddish press, literature, and theater, brought about a revival of religious orthodoxy in this country, and laid the foundations for American Zionism which, a few decades later, was to play a great historic role in the establishment of the new State of Israel.

This role was in consonance with the millennial yearnings of the Jewish people for its return to Zion. To be sure, early American Reform Judaism tried to repudiate the traditional interpretation of Jewish messianism and to seek ultimate salvation in the lands of the Diaspora, especially the United States. But the majority of believers always clung to the hope of Israel's restoration to its ancestral Holy Land. This was also demonstrated by the great emotional appeal of Palestine relief to the American Jewish public. As shown below (Essay 9), on practical grounds, the American Jewish leaders concerned objected to the dispatch by the old Palestinian *Yishuv,* of messengers to collect donations for the support of the poor Jewish settlers in Jerusalem, Tiberias, Safed, and Hebron. They considered the expenses of the messengers much too high in proportion to the possible yields of their fund raising. Yet time and again, as during the messengers' four journeys of 1849-79, neither the leaders nor the rank and file of American Jewry could resist the call to extend a hospitable reception to these envoys and to collect contributions from rich and poor alike (many gifts were as small as 50 cents) for Zion's sake.

Jewish mass migrations were suspended during the First World War. But by that time the new arrivals had already developed a leadership of their own. Through the Zionist Federation and the newly formed American Jewish Congress, they shared with the older settlers in the task of helping to rebuild the shattered European communities, securing the British Mandate over Palestine with its pledge of developing a Jewish homeland there, and in cementing a measure of unity within American Jewish life itself.

The First World War, followed by the Communist, Fascist, and particularly the Nazi Revolutions and ultimately clinched by the Second World War—a case could be made for considering the period of 1914-45 as that of a second Thirty Years' War—created much new anguish for thoughtful Jews. Apart from the general conflict between the war itself and their traditional love for peace, as well as their concern for whatever relatives or friends they had on the fighting fronts (sometimes even in the mutually opposing armed forces), they were greatly worried over the impact of the war and the revolutions on the Jewish community. We now know that the outcome of that sanguinary thirty-year period was not only the physical destruction of thousands of Jewish communities by the Nazis and the spiritual ruin of Russian Jewry, but also much questioning about the prospects for the survival of the Jewish people altogether. Yet, in the two papers, written during or soon after the Second World War (Essays 11 and 12), I was trying to show that the war had generated many, more or less permament, impulses for a revival of religion, Jewish as well as Christian.

Such return may in part have been the result of personal experiences of soldiers facing momentary death. But more significant was the widespread reaction to the relativism of the preceding age and the quest for absolute verities. The growing disenchantment with the various "isms" of the interwar period and the observation that, while the universities, the press, and the labor unions speedily surrendered under the Nazi onslaught, religion alone remained to offer some resistance, likewise induced many perplexed individuals to rethink their fundamental assumptions. It may indeed be noted that, at least among the Jews and Christians in the free countries, there has been a moderate return to religious beliefs and practices and that even the Soviet Union has given up its once formidable "godless" agitation and made peace with the Russian Church, if not with the Jewish religious establishment. In the United States the three major branches of Judaism have each more than doubled the membership of their congregations and greatly enlarged the scope of their religious, educational, and social activities.

This progress has by no means reduced the concern of Jewish thinkers about the future of American Jewry, however. Despite their inherent conservatism, most Jewish institutions have been under constant review. The area of Jewish philanthropies, for example, so basic in the period of mass immigration, has since been largely preempted by governmental social welfare, which has assumed truly grandiose proportions. Nevertheless, there have existed sufficient "challenges," old and new, to Jewish philanthropic endeavors, to stimulate constant reevaluation of the scope and methods of Jewish social service. Some of these challenges are discussed below (Essays 14 and 20). Certainly the rise of the State of Israel and the task of resettling hundreds of thousands of Jewish refugees from the displaced persons camps, the Arab countries, and other lands, have generated calls of unprecedented dimensions on American Jewry's resources and dedication.

The educational and cultural apects of American Jewish life now became the overriding issue for Jews concerned about their people's survival in the dispersion. In several essays (15-19) I have tried to show that the frequent questioning of any genuine creativity by American Jews in the field of Jewish culture by skeptics of all kinds is not wholly justified. Historic evidence proves that it has taken many centuries for all the great centers of Jewish learning in the past to arise. One must, therefore, realize that American Jewry, whose real cultural history did not begin until little more than a century ago, still is in the early stages of its evolution. Yet it already has great achievements to its credit.

At the same time we must concede that the communal organs

as such must play a more active role than hitherto in fostering Jewish education. Nor is it enough for the community to concern itself with primary and secondary education. Much more has to be done in promoting basic research and teaching on the highest academic levels. All other forms of adult education must also be lovingly nurtured if the Jews are again to deserve the honorific title of a "People of the Book." At the moment they certainly are not a people of *the* book, that is, the Bible. But as I have tried to show (in Essay 16), they are not even a people of other books of serious Jewish content. None the less, this area of communal activity appears to be undergoing much self-assessment and we may be nearing the time for appropriate communal action. Of course, the ultimate outcome of such efforts will depend on the interest and cooperation of a multitude of individuals. The frequent delegation of the entire responsibility for the education of children and adults to the school and community is an easy way out which must end in utter futility.

One aspect of such cultural activity is the preoccupation with American Jewish history. The time has long passed since American Jewry could be much more interested, if at all, in the history of past generations in their native lands than of those who preceded them on the American soil. Below (Essays 3-4) I have tried to examine some of the problems and methods pertaining to the research and writing in the field of American Jewish history and to point out how much has yet to be done to remedy the neglect of generations and to prevent its continuation. It must be stated, however, that since these papers were originally written, American Jewish historical research has made considerable strides. The publications of the last two decades indubitably exceed in quality, quantity, and range of subject matter all that has been done in this field by the preceding generations. (This fact will become apparent to the reader perusing the bibliographical notes appended to Essay 3 in its revised form.) It may be hoped that this progress will gather further momentum.

In conclusion, one may also express the hope that the present age of anguish will be overcome by the pioneering spirit of

American Jewry, as have the earlier eras of crisis. Although some disgruntled American Jews, like their non-Jewish confreres, may give up their residence in the United States, and some others, prompted by idealistic or family considerations, may decide to settle in Israel and help to build up the Third Jewish Common-wealth, the vast majority will doubtless continue living in this country. When imbued with the will of self-preservation as heirs of a millennial tradition, they will be facing the future with many apprehensions but also with an ardent desire to serve. If historic lessons of the preceding three centuries are to provide any guid-ance at all (see Essay 13), one may predict that, despite the greatly diminished number of Jewish immigrants into this land, that of expatriates will continue to be smaller still. As was shown, for instance, in the years 1931-35, all major ethnic groups showed a surplus, often a very substantial one, of émigrés from, over immigrants into, this country. The sole exception were the Jews, who even in that dark era of the Great Depression came to the United States in larger numbers than were ready to leave. Evi-dently, most of them had come here to stay. This trend is most likely to continue into the foreseeable future.

II

Gradual Unfolding, 1654—1879

2 *American and Jewish Destiny: A Semimillennial Experience**

The middle of the Second World War does not seem to be an appropriate time for celebrations. Untold millions of Jews and non-Jews are suffering from brutal maltreatment, starvation, and downright murder. Our country is in danger of foreign domination as it never had been since it achieved its national independence. The fate of the Jewish people is being decided now for generations to come. No one is in that somewhat detached, festive mood today which is the prerequisite for the joyous commemoration of past events, however great and profound their influence may have been on the destinies of mankind.

A time like this may undoubtedly be used to great advantage overtly to demonstrate, and thus help to cement, the inherent unity of the American people. However, there is evidently little need today for patriotic prodding. American Jewry, especially, which from the early days of its settlement on this continent has always given tangible expression of its deep-rooted loyalty and sacrificial devotion to this country, requires no exhortation to serve it now in its hour of greatest peril. Whatever one may think about the much-debated "complacency" of the American public, long before Pearl Harbor many Jews had been deeply awake to the great menace of Nazi world domination. There

* Address delivered at the Observance of the 450th Anniversary of the Discovery of America sponsored by the Synagogue Council of America on October 12, 1942 and published by it.

certainly are but few Jews today who fail to realize how intimately their own destiny is tied up with the victory of the United Nations, in a measure unparalleled in the long history of their people. In fact, not overconfidence and complacency, but irrational fears bordering on hysteria have for years affected large sections of American Jewry and may yet constitute the major drawback to the much-needed calm and rational appraisal of the existing dangers and to the adoption of remedial measures. A patriotic call to Jewish self-sacrifice in the defense of the United States and the American institutions may under these circumstances appear as superfluous as an exhortation to the sun to rise in the morning.

If such celebrations, therefore, are to have any meaning at all they ought to give us pause to consider the great historic experiences of the past and to help us derive from them a lesson and perhaps comfort in our present perplexities. Whatever one thinks about the old adage of history as the *magistra vitae* one cannot deny that only a broader historic perspective may enable us to obtain an approximation of that Archimedean point which would lift us out of the complexities and confusion of our own environment and make us feel the beat of humanity's progression through its present winding and precipitous road.

I

In the age of discovery the western world was in a state of unrest and upheaval in many ways similar to that of our own age. Its leading minds were fully conscious of the epochal transition it was undergoing then. Hardly a century passed from the discovery of America, when they began clearly to differentiate between the "Middle Ages" and "Modern Times" and thus consciously to shut the gate behind the great historical epoch which had drawn to its close in the fifteenth century. Typically medieval though many phases of Columbus' thinking may appear to us today and much as it undoubtedly was tinged with the spirit of fanatical adventure of the medieval Crusaders, it nevertheless bears the unmistakable imprint of those great scientific and artistic explorers, of a Toscanelli, Zacuto, and Galileo, a Pico, Reuchlin, and the two Abravanels, a Leonardo, Valla, and Erasmus, who went out in quest of new truths and a new feeling for beauty and looked for the self-realization of the individual, if necessary in defiance of all established authority. The century of Columbus was one of the most turbulent periods in human history, a period of interminable clashes of interests and emotions. It marked the complete breakdown of the established feudal order and Church supremacy, the rise of an increasingly unrestrained competitive spirit in economics and a secularist, rationalist approach to life and knowledge. At the same time it witnessed those sanguinary Wars of Religion which until their abatement after the blood bath of the Thirty Years' War in 1648 were to keep Europe and the newly discovered lands in a state of constant warfare.

Out of this turmoil and upheaval was born a new world which, far from realizing the specific hopes of the main protagonists of that drama, nevertheless fulfilled the deeper yearnings of humanity in a way which no one, not even a man of such fantastic vision and daring as Columbus, could have foreseen. In fact, the outstanding lesson to us of that great historic experience, perhaps the greatest since the rise of Christianity and Islam, may consist in that very realization of how little the conscious desires and ambitions of a particular generation are reflected in the ultimate effects of its actions. Call it the inscrutable ways of divine guidance in history or call it the inexorable, though almost equally inscrutable, sociological laws of human development, the discovery of America has produced results entirely at variance with the wishes of the conscious agents behind it. It is no aspersion on the shades of the great man whose memory we are celebrating today if I assert that, whatever may have been his private aspirations and mystical dreams, he, perhaps involuntarily, became the exponent of forces and the representative of groups and personalities whose ambitions were ultimately materialized in a way contrary to their expectations.

When Ferdinand and Isabella finally consented to equip Columbus' expedition, they not only accepted his mistaken notion of the short western route to India, but acted primarily because of the great European hunger for gold and silver, the life-blood of the rising mercantilist economy. In the 1940s the gold of the world was being drained in its flow to America where it was ultimately buried in the soil of Fort Knox, while the production of American silver had to be stimulated by the artificial price pegging of the United States Congress. In fact, during the Great War the poor and despised relatives, iron, copper, and tin, appeared so much more precious than their celebrated superiors, in search of which Columbus and his crew, and many after them, were ready to sacrifice their lives.

The age of discovery was also the age of the first great expansion of European imperialism. It marked the beginning of that great European colonization which was to convert increasing areas of this globe into "dependencies" of mother countries. As colonies exploited for the latter's exclusive benefit they were to become instruments for the satisfaction of still greater imperial appetites. Little did the Spanish conquistadores dream that, within half a millennium, the leadership of mankind would slip out of the hands of their Old World descendants and gradually shift to the inhabitants of those newly discovered colonial territories. It is perhaps too early yet to chant the *El male raḥamim* over European imperialism, but if there be any meaning whatsoever to the present international crisis, if there be any fulfillment at all to the great promise of the Atlantic Charter, the present epoch must mean the end of the colonial age and the reconstitution of mankind as a family of self-governing nations. No one in Columbus' day could have dreamed that it would be the newly discovered American colonies which, by the law inherent in their own evolution, would ultimately point to the possibility of an effective, peaceful federation of intrinsically egalitarian states.

The men behind Columbus or, for that matter, Cortes or Pizarro, sent out their fleets across the Atlantic in order to buttress the growing absolute power of monarchy and to secure the weakening hold of the then dominant classes. They certainly could not foresee that they were setting in motion forces destined to overturn monarchial absolutism everywhere and to establish new forms of political democracy undreamed of in the previous experience of mankind. Without being unmindful of existing shortcomings which show that, even here, much is to be striven for before complete democracy in its ideal form will have been attained—if it be attainable at all considering the imperfections of human nature- -no one can deny that the American constitution, the Civil War, the First World War "to make the world safe for democracy," and the Second World War under the aegis of the Atlantic Charter, have revealed this great nation standing up in periods of major crisis in the name of the democratic ideal in a way which has absolutely no parallel in the earlier history of mankind.

II

Most striking of all is the contrast between intention and realization in the field of religious toleration. Most of the discoverers went out as crusaders for their religion and Church. Columbus himself, reflecting the intolerant mood of the age and appealing to the bigotry of his royal patroness, Queen Isabella, whose support he was then soliciting, insisted that his voyage, if successful, would help to spread the control of the Catholic Church among the pagan peoples. He even held out the hope that the gold to be brought from the new Ophir would help redeem the Holy Sepulcher from the domination of infidels—a throwback to the crusading ideals of a Peter of Amiens, made more realistic by the menacing expansion of the Ottoman Empire. It was more than a coincidence that the age of discovery was synchronous with the spread of the Spanish and Portuguese Inquisitions. It was more than a coincidence—and you have all heard this thrice-told tale—that the decree of the expulsion of the Jews from Spain was broadcast through the peninsula on the same April 30, 1492 on which the royal order was issued to equip a fleet for Columbus, and that the execution of this decree came on August 2, exactly a day before Columbus set sail on his first voyage of discovery. Absolute religious uniformity, the unification of Spain on the basis of the same creed and nationality and, incidentally, the expropriation of the accumulated wealth of Spanish Jewry seemed to the powers that were an intrinsic part of the same policy which determined them to send out their fleets in search of new countries where they would establish the same strict Church-State control as prevailed in the motherland. Little did they dream that one of the countries they discovered was destined to serve as mankind's pathfinder on the road of religious toleration, liberty of conscience, freedom of speech, and even complete separation of state and Church. One can easily visualize the shock they would have received, were they to be told that, within three centuries, the founder of that new nation would conclude a letter to the *Jewish* community of Savannah, Ga., with the expression of the fervent religious hope:

> *May the same wonder-working Deity, who long since delivered the Hebrews from their Egyptian oppressors, planted them in a promised land, whose providential agency has lately been conspicuous in establishing these United States as an independent nation, still continue to water them with the dews of heaven and make the inhabitants of every denomination participate in the temporal and spiritual blessings of that people whose God is Jehovah.*

Indeed, the men behind Columbus would have been deeply disconcerted had they foreseen that the new countries were to become havens of refuge for the persecuted of their own and their successors' tyrannical regimes. The great exodus of Spanish Jewry, followed by a progressive dispersal of those Jews who remained for a time on the Iberian peninsula as professing New Christians, added a considerable element of fermentation to undermining the old order. Like the later Puritan or Huguenot exiles the great Sephardic-Marrano Diaspora became in many ways the "yeast" of the new era.

The contribution of both Jews and Marranos to the very age of discovery has, despite Kayserling's highly meritorious pioneering efforts, yet to be told in full and illuminating detail. We are not in a position, for instance, definitely to answer even the intriguing question as to whether or not Columbus himself was of Jewish descent. I can merely say that the weight of evidence still seems to tend toward a denial of such Jewish antecedents. But neither have the positive assertions of such antecedents, insistently repeated for more than half a century, been definitely disposed of. However, there can be no question about the assistance Columbus received in carrying out his epochal plans both from the Hebraic tradition and from a great many individual Jews and Marranos. The biblical narratives and their ramifications in the rabbinic-patristic tradition may have discouraged some timid souls. But by depicting the fabulously rich land of Ophir reached by the crews of King Solomon on a three years' journey, they stimulated the creative imagination of great explorers. A century after Columbus some scholars, Jewish and non-Jewish (Azariah de' Rossi and the German geographer, E. Schmidt, for instance) still believed that the New World was the land of Ophir and that Solomon's sailors had circumnavigated the globe some three millennia before Magellan. We also know of a number of influential Jews who extended to Columbus a helping hand at critical junctures. What is more, most of them seem to have acted out of a genuine interest in his startling discoveries rather than for immediate personal gain. The celebrated astronomer, Abraham Zacuto, for example, while expressing himself in favor of the "hazardous enterprise," did so out of the same scientific curiosity which had guided all his mathematical and astronomic research, the results of which, partly communicated orally to the explorer in Salamanca, were to render him such invaluable services on his journey. Don Isaac Abravanel, the renowned statesman, philosopher, and Bible commentator, was one of the very few Spanish grandees who at a time when the project seemed doomed to failure helped to subscribe the crucial amount enabling Columbus to contribute his required share to the equipment of the fleet. The famous Marrano Luis de Santangel, as is well known, put in the decisive word which averted the Spanish Crown's final refusal and personally advanced much of the money necessary to finance the expedition. It was a matter of historic justice that his name was inscribed on Queen Isabella's monument in Granada in commemoration of his great contribution to the success of Columbus' undertaking. It is most remarkable, I repeat, that there is no evidence whatsoever that Santangel, Diego de Deza, Gabriel Sanchez, and most other patrons of Columbus of Jewish descent acted in any but a wholly disinterested fashion. That, on the other hand, Columbus' crew included several Marranos (among them Luis de Torres who had relinquished his Jewish faith only a short time before his journey and who, as a prospective interpreter, was destined to be the first to land on American soil, finally becoming one of the first permanent European residents of the Western Hemisphere) was a part of the same general spirit of creative enterprise and alertness which characterized Spanish Jewry in the days of its great crisis.

Even these men little knew what they were doing for their descendants' future. Whether or not guided by motives of personal gain or ambition, they wrought better than they knew. Certainly their overweening rulers could not possibly have realized then that the Marranos whom they persecuted and the Jews whom they expelled were to contribute a significant share to the rise of a new civilization which was ultimately to overshadow their own.

III

When our mind turns from the turbulence of the fifteenth and sixteenth centuries to the perplexities of the twentieth century we may perhaps derive some comfort from the thought that we, too, may not yet have an inkling of what our generation is really suffering for. We, too, seem to be living in a cataclysmic era of transition and, like the contemporaries of Columbus, we cannot possibly divine what type of world will emerge from the present turmoil.

Today, the age of geographical and physical discovery on earth seems to be over. As far as one can see the area of human settlement encompasses all habitable regions of the globe. While the future may yet convert present-day deserts and polar lands into centers of some sort of human civilization, one cannot possibly anticipate any discoveries of new countries at all parallel to the epochal explorations of Columbus or his confreres. Only interplanetary discoveries could nowadays rival or exceed their achievement, but these are still in their infancy.

To be sure, the widespread belief that mankind has practically reached the limits not only of its geographic, but also of its numerical expansion has turned out to be just as erroneous now as when a century and a half ago Malthus first depicted the horrors of overpopulation then threatening mankind. These apprehensions may appear just as exaggerated to future generations, as many arguments of the cosmographers in the days of Columbus appear to us today. They may be the object of derision no less legitimate than that which has since been heaped upon the objection raised by a fifteenth-century savant that, even if Columbus actually succeeded in descending the Hemisphere westward, how would he ever hope to ascend it again. Did not the Superior Court of Rhode Island in 1762, in setting aside the naturalization of two prominent Jews, contend that the colony was already full and could not allow for any further increase in population? In the period of imperialist clashes and national isolationism between the two World Wars even we here in America have been all too prone to forget that "generous policy," to quote James Madison, "which offering an asylum to the persecuted and oppressed of every nation and religion, promised a lustre to our country and accession to the number of its citizens." I feel confident that there are yet untold possibilities for the increase, in both numbers and well-being, of humanity in the Americas and elsewhere.

Indeed, a new age of discovery is on! There exists today an even greater need for unprecedented discoveries, not so much in the geographic field, as in the social and spiritual realms. As a matter of fact, we have allowed our physical and technological discoveries to outstrip our ability for social and psychological readjustment. At no time in the long history of mankind could enough goods be produced to satisfy the wants of everybody. Hence the scramble for the limited opportunities with the minority getting more than their due share and the majority living far below a subsistence level. Today for the very first time the long-term productive capacities of this country and of mankind as a whole tax the imaginative faculties of man. This trend, enormously beneficial in itself, has nevertheless created so many new problems as to be in part coresponsible for the present breakdown of human morale. However, we must let it sink profoundly into our consciousness that it is for the first time in history that mankind is potentially able seriously to consider the practical realization of the Four Freedoms, and especially, of the freedom from want and the freedom from fear. Perhaps the old biblical assertion "for the poor shall never cease out of the land" (Deut. 15:11) will have to be reinterpreted, if real poverty and want are able to be banished from the surface of the earth. This seems definitely feasible now. But it will require men of even greater daring and wisdom than Columbus to chart humanity's course through the unexplored oceans of such new social coexistence.

Freedom from want might remove a major cause of human friction and thus help eliminate a perennial cause of fear. Not that economic rivalries are the sole reason for group conflicts and mutual intolerance. Even here in America, where we have enjoyed for over a century and a half the legal safeguards of a most democratic and egalitarian Constitution, we have witnessed in recent years disturbing manifestations of a new spirit of intolerance and discrimination. What Thomas Jefferson had written to Major Noah about the insufficiency of legal safeguards is unfortunately still true today. It is still true that

> more remains to be done, for although we are free by the law, we are not so in practice; public opinion erects itself into an Inquisition, and exercises its office with as much fanaticism as fans the flames of an Auto-de-fé.

There is room indeed for endless exploration before true peace and amity among men is firmly established and fear as the dominant factor in group relations is banished from the world.

The breakdown of mankind's morale, of which Nazi tribalism and Japanese nationalism run amuck are merely an expression, will be remedied only if new spiritual worlds will beckon to distraught humanity. The great achievements of the 450 years which have passed since Columbus, uncontestable as they are on the material and rationalist plane, have failed to satisfy the deep emotional and spiritual yearnings of mankind. It was in part this gap between material achievement and emotional disaffection which has more than any other single factor undermined the consistency of our present civilization. We shall have to find new paths also for a spiritual rejuvenation of the human race.

It may not be too venturesome to conclude these remarks on the hopeful note that some new giants will arise in our midst or in the midst of our children's children who will find the answers to these deeply felt perplexities and offer solutions for which mankind has been groping for ages through bloody trial and error. It is perhaps the most glorious task of our own generation, through suffering and agony, to bring somewhat closer the ultimate fulfillment of those great ideals which were first so beautifully formulated by Israel's prophets and for whose final realization the Jewish people has persevered despite millennial hardships.

3 American Jewish History: Problems and Methods*

An annual meeting of the American Jewish Historical Society may indeed be a fitting occasion for a reconsideration of the basic problems of American Jewish historical research and writing. Judaism has long been cognizant of the great value of a periodic "searching of the soul" by individuals and groups. From time to time, we may, indeed, profitably pause collectively to think over some of the fundamental approaches, methods, and needs peculiar to our chosen field of studies.

Awakening Historic Interest

One of the main difficulties facing Jewish historical scholarship in this country has been the weakness, and at times total absence, of historical interests in the Jewish public at large. There are many valid reasons for this striking contrast between the more historically minded Jewish communities of Germany, Poland, and other European countries and the lack of interest in their own past on the part of the majority of Jews in the Western Hemisphere.

In the first place, American Jews have had few practical needs for preserving, accumulating, and examining records. Throughout

* Address delivered at the forty-seventh annual meeting of the American Jewish Historical Society, New York, February 19, 1949. Reprinted from *PAJHS*, XXXIX (1950), 207-266.

human history records were often kept and investigated merely in order to prove certain legal contentions by individuals or groups. It was more than sheer accident that the rise of the great Jewish historiography in the nineteenth century coincided with the struggle for Jewish Emancipation. Time and again champions of Jewish equality as well as its opponents resorted to historical arguments to prove some particular points. The more heatedly the Jewish question was debated, the more sharply certain Jewish disabilities were attacked or defended, the more stimulus was given for the accumulation of evidence concerning the origin of these disabilities and their effects in the light of previous historic experience. As is well known, some of the greatest works of Jewish historical scholarship, like Zunz's *Gottesdienstliche Vorträge* or Frankel's *Der gerichtliche Beweis*, owed their origin to political and communal controversies.[1]

In America, even in the colonial period, there were few such incentives. The very story of the admission of Jews to individual colonies was, as a rule, speedily forgotten. Even where it had aroused much controversy, as in New York and Georgia, it was allowed to go into oblivion as soon as matters were settled and had to be dug up from archival records by historians of recent generations. The only more detailed story by a Jewish eyewitness, namely, Benjamin Sheftall of Georgia, saw the light of day more than a century after the event. Once admitted, the Jews practically disappeared from the public eye and attracted the attention of visitors, much more than of native recorders. Rare, indeed, was the case when a particular disability affecting Jews aroused public discussion. Jacob Lumbrozo's ominous accusation of "blasphemy," which might have endangered the future status of all American Jews, was allowed to peter out into total forgetfulness. We must actually be grateful for the electoral controversy in the colony of New York in 1737 which raised the problem of Jewish franchise. On some early occasions (Jacob Lucena in Hartford, 1670-71, or Rowland Gideon in Boston, 1675) a Jewish defendant himself pointed out to an American court the fact of his belonging to this "scattered nation" as a reason for *reducing* his penalty. Otherwise Jews were, as a rule, incorporated in the American body politic, so to say, in complete absent-mindedness.[2]

The very emancipation, established as a matter of general principle, through the federal and states' constitutions, was achieved with practically no reference to the Jews as such. In fact, George Washington's famous letters to the communities of Savannah and Newport reveal, through the very care in their wording, how indefinite the constitutional safeguards of liberty of conscience were with respect to the full political and civil equality of Jews.[3] Even such extralegal problems as appeared from time to time in public view, for example, the Jewish participation in American wars or contributions to American civilization, gave only slight impetus to the rise of an apologetic literature based upon historic documentation. Were it not for the autisemitic attacks, for the most part rather mild until Hitler's rise to power, even those apologetic mainsprings of a large part of early American-Jewish historiography would doubtless have dried up and, for example, much of the valuable work of Simon Wolf would have remained undone.

Pride in one's family and locality has been another frequent source of the public's historic interests and, at times, an inspiration for scholarly research. Such pride, however, has long played a rather insignificant role among American Jews. In periods when ever-new waves of immigrants reached these shores, the exaltation of one's family antecedents could be meaningful only to very small groups. A German Jew whose ancestors had lived for centuries in a Rhenish community, a Polish Jew who could point with pride to some of his forefathers who had played a great role in the history of Poland's old capital, Cracow, could expect little response from Jews stemming from other countries and regions to whom these grandees of the Rhineland or Galicia meant little or nothing at all. Moreover, emigration, except in rare emergencies, was largely recruited from classes which even in their own country did not belong to the aristocratic groups, possessing particular family pride or reliable genealogical records. The impact of the new "capitalistic" values and the shift of communal leadership to economically successful classes and individuals regardless of their ancestry likewise reduced appreciation for *yiḥus* (noble parentage); it destroyed whatever interest might have survived in the glorification of one's descent from some man distinguished by piety or learning.

Nor should one lose sight of the other deterrents emanating from the American environment. The more the melting-pot idea gained ground—and it was subconsciously in existence long before the term was coined, probably in a 1907 sermon by Rabbi Samuel Schulman—the more did the immigrant groups look up to the older, long established communities. It may still have been of some interest if a Jew could trace his ancestry back to some prominent Anglo-Jewish or Dutch family. Just as some of their non-Jewish neighbors organized those self-glorifying societies of Sons and Daughters of the American Revolution and began construing genealogies, authentic or spurious, in order to satisfy the ambitions of some *nouveaux riches*, their children, or grandchildren, an occasional Jew, particularly a Sephardi, was interested in emphasizing his descent from a colonial family. But since only about two thousand Jews lived here before the Revolution and many of their descendants had changed their faith, only a tiny fraction of the Jewish community belonged to this group. The overwhelming majority could expect no particular response among its Gentile neighbors, if it traced its descent back to some distinguished rabbi or communal leader in the Old World. On the contrary, the assimilatory forces were so strong that wealthy Jews often preferred to tone down, rather than to emphasize, their prominent Jewish ancestry.

Local pride was not altogether absent among American Jews, but it often was pride in the locality from which each of them had come, rather than in that of his new residence. At least in the first, sometimes in the second, generation, immigrants were inclined to remember nostalgically their home communities, whether or not they formally joined particular *Landsmannschaften*, and generally to maintain a certain historic attachment to them. By the time they became really settled and began developing certain emotional involvements in their new places of residence, they often found themselves outnumbered by newer arrivals who had to go through the same process. Within the country itself there also was extreme mobility. This is, indeed, a major characteristic of the American people which was a nation on wheels long before the discovery of the automobile. Like their non-Jewish compatriots, only more so, Jews moving from one American city to another had in each case to make a fresh start. If, for example, during the 1940s the Jewish population of Los Angeles seems to have increased from some 85,000 to more than 225,000, or that of Miami from 7,500 to 40,000 (it has since reached approximately 535,000 and 140,000 respectively)[4] their majorities largely stemming from the Eastern seaboard could hardly be expected immediately to develop deep emotional interests in the past of their adopted communities.

Even more fundamental have been the barriers erected by the traditional approaches to Jewish history. Modern Jewish historiography owes much of its origin to Europe's Romantic reaction to Enlightenment. Eighteenth-century Enlightenment had also produced distinguished historians of the rank of Voltaire or Gibbon, but theirs often was history for a purpose, written in order to buttress some preconceived notion, some general philosophic principle derived from reasoning, rather than to produce evidence for the specific and unique in the life of each group, for the local or national peculiarities. Enlightened historiography, especially on the Continent, was interested in leveling down differences, rather than in underscoring them. Under these circumstances, emphases on the peculiarities of Jewish history were, on the whole, discouraged even among those who did not share Enlightenment's general aversion to the accepted religious doctrines themselves. For example, the writers of the Mendelssohnian circle were inclined to stress similarities, not differences, and to argue in the name of philosophic principles, and not of historic decisions. Only when France, Germany, and the Slavonic countries experienced that deep-seated romantic revival which glorified all ethnic and cultural peculiarities and generated the various "historical" schools in jurisprudence, linguistics, and so forth, the ensuing great upsurge of historic interest and quest for peculiar national mores as the lofty expressions of various "national spirits," furnished the proper background for the rise of a new Jewish historicism as well. Even England was somewhat touched by this historic and romantic upsurge. America, however, had gone through the nineteenth century with no deep-rooted reaction to the spirit of Enlightenment which had permeated our Founding Fathers. The basic decisions made during the Revolutionary era have not only permanently shaped the United States' constitutional and political life, but have also deeply colored all aspects of American culture. At least until the recent emergence of strong socialist trends the dominant forms of liberal thought have all been direct offshoots of the philosophy of Enlightenment.

This "enlightened" heritage has retarded, but not completely discouraged interest in American Jewish history *per se*. But until recently it has strongly operated against any emphasis on ethnic peculiarities. Like American society at large, American historiography was and, in part, still is permeated with the melting-pot ideology. Consciously or unconsciously its most representative spokesmen have tried to level down the peculiar historic traditions and interests of America's manifold ethnic and religious groups. Interest in Jewish history was either condemned as "parochial" and segregationist or at least discouraged as a side issue more or less irrelevant to the mainstream of American history.[5]

American historiography has also been extremely pragmatic. In his review of the various attitudes to history expressed in the presidential addresses delivered at annual meetings of the American Historical Association during its first sixty years, Herman Ausubel has pointed out that the most important single issue consistently under debate was that of the practical lessons which the study of history might convey to each generation. Even the few advocates of "pure" and detached historic research could not quite escape paying lip service to the pragmatic values of history.[6] In the case of American Jewish historiography there appeared to be little in the past record which could teach practical lessons to successive generations. Except for the few rather restricted areas of apologetical interest very little seems to have happened in the colonial and early American periods which still was of practical relevance to the life of American Jews at the end of the nineteenth and early twentieth centuries.

A most significant deterrent to both public and professional interest also was the long prevailing view of Jewish history. Graetz did not invent the conception of Jewish history as that of an uninterrupted succession of scholars and martyrs. The entire Jewish historiography of the Middle Ages and early modern times consisted of chronicles recording dramatic events, mostly persecutions, massacres, or expulsions, and of such chronological lists of scholars as are exemplified in the works of Sherira, Ibn Daud, or Zacuto. American Jewish history, unable to produce a succession of riots and discriminatory laws, could hardly fit into this traditional pattern. Nor did most Jewish students of the late nineteenth century find much interest in the literary history of a country whose first original Hebrew book (the *Abne Yehoshuʻa ʻal Pirķe Abot* by Joshua Falk b. Mordecai Cohen of Kurnik) appeared in 1860 (previously only prayerbooks, grammars, and the like had been printed in America). Suffice it to remember that not only were the masses unfamiliar with Hebrew lore, but even such communal leaders as Bernard Gratz and Haym Salomon, themselves born in Silesia and Poland, respectively, could hardly write a Hebrew letter without many errors. Some elders had to refer Hebrew epistles received from abroad to Christian translators.[7]

It is small wonder, then, that even the Jewish institutions of higher learning found little interest in teaching American Jewish history. Yeshiva University, the Jewish Theological Seminary, and Hebrew Union College have appointed special instructors in this discipline only in the last few decades. If I may be allowed to cite personal experiences, I found it very difficult thirty years ago to persuade graduate students to choose dissertations in this field, because they did not find it "interesting" enough.

These serious obstacles to history-mindedness among American Jews have fortunately begun to disappear during the last years. We may deeply regret the growth of American antisemitism since

1933 and debate the practical effects of the various methods of anti-defamation. But there is no question that the Jew has become a conspicuous figure on the American scene and as such a far greater problem to both himself and his neighbors. With ever larger numbers of Jews moving up from the status of segregated immigrants into that of integrated American citizens, they may have lost some of the attraction of exotic creatures but increased the curiosity of serious students in the processes of their adjustment and their growing contributions to American life. The dramatic evolution which led to the rise of Israel has further heightened interest of friend and foe. This intensity of interest translated itself also into intellectual curiosity in the past of the Jewish group. Such curiosity is likely to persist even if antisemitism were to vanish completely from the surface of American life. Jewish historic research, therefore, need no longer be conducted in such a vacuum of lack of public interest as it was in the past.

With the cessation of large-scale Jewish immigration and the ensuing greater continuity of Jewish life in each community there has also been a certain revival of family and local pride. Jewish communities begin to view their own past far more seriously. While their attempts at accumulating records and securing genuine scholarly materials still leave much to be desired, there has been at least growing awareness of that need and realization of existing shortcomings.

Our basic approach to Jewish history, finally, has also undergone a vital transformation. Just as in general historiography dramatic events, like battles and treaties, and great personalities, the "heroes," no longer monopolize present-day historic narratives but are given their proper place within the broad stream of social, economic, political, and cultural history, so has Jewish historiography begun to abandon its exclusive concern with the dramas of persecution and learning. In these wider socioeconomic areas the American Jewish community of the last three centuries does indeed offer important problems of research, as noteworthy as any in the long history of the Jewish people in other lands. Moreover, even the traditionally hallowed history of intellectual endeavors now has before it an increasingly significant record of scholarly and literary achievement. For during the last hundred years there have arisen a great literature in Yiddish, Hebrew, and English, a Yiddish theater and press, Jewish schools of higher learning, publishing firms, and new approaches to Jewish education, the impact of which is felt far beyond the confines of this country. Together with the story of the magnificent communal and philanthropic efforts the socioeconomic and intellectual evolution furnishes all the drama that one might look for.[8]

Preservation and Sifting of Records

For many years past historians have legitimately complained of the paucity of extant sources for the earlier periods of American Jewish history. I have sometimes uncharitably spoken of our having, to all intents and purposes, obliterated the memory of entire generations and communities of American Jews. *Quod non est in actis non est in mundo* was a much-quoted saying of the medieval glossators. Greatly derided as a legal maxim, it certainly did reflect the historic fact that where there are no extant records there exists practically no known history. We have lost the basic evidence for many vital links in the historic evolution of Jewish life in this country, much of it probably beyond retrieve. I may be allowed, perhaps, to quote a recent personal experience. At a time when in one of my classes I discussed colonial Jewish history I happened to be also working on certain phases of Jewish history during the Hellenistic period. I was struck by the great similarity of the extant sources. In both periods the researcher depends on whether he can dig up here or there a scrap of papyrus (or paper), discover on it a Jewish-sounding name and then proceed to draw therefrom conclusions for Jewish economic activities, culture, and political status in a particular community. In fact, in some respects we are better informed about Egyptian-Jewish history of two thousand years ago, for in addition to the papyrological sources we have some literature written by contemporary Hellenistic-Jewish historians, philosophers, and poets. Josephus has also preserved for us a number of other records, frequently adding his own and other contemporary interpretations of controversial issues. In contrast thereto, we suffer from the almost total literary inarticulateness of American Jews in colonial America and long thereafter. More, while the ancient world offers the compensation of a closed historic era which can be viewed with the necessary detachedness and from a long-range historic perspective, American Jews live in the midst of a gradually unfolding historic process and their historians are necessarily afflicted by the relative lack of perspective and unavoidable biases of persons who are simultaneously actors and onlookers, parties and judges.

What is even more serious, this neglect in the preservation of vital records is far from remedied today. Many important documents originating from synagogues, schools, or philanthropic organizations, as well as countless private and family papers are being discarded daily, and no one cares. Of course, there are valid explanations. Space is at a premium in large and crowded cities, and the great majority of American Jews live in such cities. The aforementioned mobility of the American people is not only interurban, but also suburban and intra-urban. More than any other people Americans constantly change their residences from one neighborhood to another, thereby causing the replacement of even seemingly permanent monumental structures, like synagogues, Jewish centers, and the like. Private individuals, except in periods of temporary "freezing" of housing as after the two World Wars, have often moved from apartment to apartment every few years. The effect of all this on the preservation of records is obvious. There is a popular saying among archivists that moving archival records twice is worse than a fire. Of course, conflagrations, so frequent in earlier periods, have caused further incalculable damage, directly and indirectly. I have been told that until the middle of the nineteenth century a New York fire ordinance required business firms to dispose of their accumulated papers, considered a serious fire hazard, once every five years.

Once again, however, lack of genuine interest on the part of owners or would-be custodians is probably even more important.

Without pointing an accusing finger I may mention that, for example, back in 1937 I made strenuous efforts to persuade the authorities of the Joint Distribution Committee in Paris to secure their accumulated archives, which had already then been moved once from Berlin, by shipping them to the United States. These documents, containing some of the most valuable data for the history of the Jewish people both in the Old and New Worlds since the First World War, could be utilized for a regularly functioning archive open to scholarly research; if necessary, after the screening of data still considered confidential. However, the leaders of the Joint could legitimately point to the meagerness of their resources, always insufficient for the staggering tasks confronting their great organization, and the need of husbanding them for immediate relief and reconstruction. Viewed from that angle every other national Jewish organization has had its share of responsibility and its equally valid excuses. The American Jewish Committee has only recently begun reorganizing its valuable archival collections on a rational, scientific basis.

One of the main reasons for this continued neglect is, ironically, the plethora of records. If we all legitimately complain of the great paucity of sources for the early periods, any historian working on events or trends during recent decades is often swamped by the excess of available materials. It is clearly impossible for national organizations, local communities, or even individuals to keep permanently on file all papers accumulating in their respective offices. Hence some destruction of records is a daily necessity. Many of these records, moreover, possess from the outset little intrinsic or permanent value. It is commonly known that officials working for the American government during the war survived merely because they did *not* read all the mountainous heaps of paper placed on their desks every day. Even so the National Archives has been allotted a share of that documentation which, for the seven war years of 1940-46 exceeded in bulk all previously accumulated records. At the end of 1939 the Archives held a total of some 200,000 cubic feet of records. By June 30, 1947, the accumulation rose to 813,280 cubic feet, of which 82,967 cubic feet represented the accessions of the one year 1946-47. These accessions nearly doubled those of the preceding year (44,951) and represented almost two-fifths of all the records assembled before the outbreak of the war. Clearly this is an impossible situation. Historians, archivists, and librarians have been working for many years on methods of sifting records properly so as to destroy the documents which are not likely to be historically significant, while leaving those needed for future research. The National Archives themselves not only disposed directly of an increasing number of "unimportant" records (some 17,000 cubic feet in 1946-47 alone), but also prepared and widely distributed a manual for government officials instructing them how to dispose of records wisely, even before they are ready to be dumped in the Archivist's lap. Private corporations have been confronted by the same problems on a lesser scale and I understand that the National Records Management Council in New York has for some time past worked on plans for the proper preservation and disposal of documents by business firms.[9]

On a lesser scale, this is also the problem of Jewish organizations and business firms. In selecting documents for filing the decision is usually made with no reference to future historic research. Even after discarding papers of no apparent practical value an office manager often finds that his accumulation has become so overpowering that no one is able to locate an extant document but a few years old and, finally, in sheer despair, he orders whole truckloads of documents to be dumped indiscriminately. Only in rare cases he goes to the trouble and expense to microfilm such, to him, rather "useless" materials.

The time has come for the American Jewish Historical Society to take the initiative in appointing a commission of scholars to look into the problem of sifting and discarding as well as of the preservation and listing of documents. Intelligent disposal of the irrelevant is, in fact, a most eminent means of salvaging what is really important. Utilizing the ever growing experiences of general bodies in this country and abroad, this commission ought to formulate detailed, flexible plans for the guidance of at least the larger and more historically conscious Jewish communal groups. After a period of experimentation, it might also develop certain novel techniques particularly appropriate to the peculiar needs of Jewish historical research, with its understandable emphasis on religious and cultural imponderables.[10]

To make the accumulation of records more effective, it would seem advisable to have, in addition to the central depositories such as already exist in the library of the Society and at the American Jewish Archives in Cincinnati, some regional depositories. One might readily think of branches of the Society established in Boston, Chicago, Atlanta, Dallas, and Los Angeles, maintaining such regional collections of documents, newspapers, and books. Such decentralization would have the advantages of not only relieving the central agencies from supervising operations from a great distance and, perhaps, also from misjudging the true relevance of certain materials, but also of awakening and maintaining the continued interest of regional groups in their own history—both matters of no mean significance. It would also enhance the quality of historic research, inasmuch as many of these regional accumulations would actually belong to the soil from which they had sprung. Anyone working in such a regional archive would be more likely to catch the spirit of that region, have at his disposal materials accumulated in local non-Jewish archives and libraries, and establish better contacts with specialists working in his field. Even Denmark, for example, which because of its small size and long-range historic interests, has one of the most efficient archival administrations in the world, has nevertheless willingly retained, partly for these reasons, five regional depositories which, before the Second World War, were visited by some 30,000 researchers consulting over 100,000 documents annually.[11]

Such regional depositories would have to be serviced by the central administration, if for no other reason than the constant exchange of information and the retention of uniformity in organization and cataloguing. If organized under the direct auspices of the Society, these depositories would be less likely to put up even that modicum of resistance to visiting inspectors which has often interfered with the smooth running of public archives under general state supervision. But these are some of a great many details which may readily be adjusted, if and when the time comes for the organization of such regional branch offices.

Biblio-Biographical Aids

American Jewish history covers so vast an area and is connected with so many aspects of secular and religious life in the country at large that good bibliographical aids are doubly imperative. Such bibliographical efforts should, in my opinion, aim at two targets: 1) reconstruction of publications accumulated by past generations; 2) constant surveys of current publications. Dr. Rosenbach's volume is a good example of the former category, as is, for England, Cecil Roth's *Magna Bibliotheca Anglo-Judaica;* supplemented by Ruth F. Lehmann's *Nova Bibliotheca Anglo-Judaica ... 1937-1960.* For books and pamphlets, however, which appeared during the last hundred and twenty years this is a gargantuan task and one ought to begin rather with full and annotated bibliographies relating to more specialized fields. For example, a complete listing of Jewish newspapers and periodicals in all languages which have appeared since the 1840s—and, if we include missionary organs addressed to Jews, since the early 1800s—would still serve a useful purpose, despite the valuable work done in this field by F. M. Brody, Jacob Shatzky, and others. Such a list would have to supply whatever information might be secured for circulation figures and editorial policies, as well as the more obvious facts of format, size, and editorial personnel.[12]

Complete bibliographies of Hebrew, Yiddish, and Ladino books published in America would also be very useful. Unfortunately, even the general bibliographical handbook for Hebrew letters by B. Friedberg is almost half a century behind our time. Nor is E. Deinard's American list up to date. Similarly, a comprehensive bibliography of articles in scholarly journals, jubilee volumes, etc., both Jewish and non-Jewish, bearing on Jewish history in America would also serve a very useful purpose. A glance through Jacob

Marcus's and Albert Bilgray's listing of articles which appeared in Jewish *Festschriften* alone gives an inkling of what might be accomplished by a thorough-going review of the periodic, as well as sporadic publications of this kind.[13]

Current surveys are still more imperative. A student of American Jewish history may, on the whole, be expected to be familiar with the more important older publications. Even a beginner is likely to find at least some references to them in the existing literature. But new publications often escape the attention of the most expert researchers. Moreover, there is some inherent element of preservation in the mere listing of a bibliographical entry. In compiling a bibliography for two prewar years, I came across quite a few worthwhile, though apparently ephemeral, publications. Many of these writings may no longer be readily available even in libraries and their mere recording may help dig up some stray copies which might otherwise be definitely lost.[14]

True, this is a very large undertaking. The American Historical Association which published some annual lists of books and articles pertaining to American history has long fallen behind.[15] Moreover, even that undertaking is now imperiled by the vastness of the task and lack of funds. Should this publication be permanently discontinued, it would seem doubly imperative for the various historical societies having a more limited range, to endeavor to list current publications in their own fields.

Another major desideratum is a number of biographical aids. In view of the vital role which accidental mention of a Jewish-sounding name plays in the study of Jewish life on the American continent to the middle of the nineteenth century a good biographical dictionary listing *all* known Jews up to 1840, would be of great assistance to the student. Other volumes should cover in ever more selective fashion Jewish personalities since that time.[16] In choosing the latter entries compilers should be guided by considerations not only of "greatness"—we want to know about men and women of all walks of life as well as about the historical "heroes"—but also of the representative character of the persons concerned. They should offer material for the understanding of the totality of Jewish life and, on the whole, belong to various social groups like fraternal orders, lodges, unions, charitable organizations, political parties, as well as to big business, science, and arts.

From this point of view it seems regrettable that there has appeared no recent edition of *Who's Who in American Jewry*. Although for various reasons it would not seem appropriate for the Society to assume direct responsibility for the compilation of such a new handbook, it could perhaps informally stimulate this undertaking and offer its well-considered advice. Published as a pure business venture such a *Who's Who* would necessarily reflect commercial considerations, but it would nevertheless ultimately serve as at least a partial source of information for contemporary and future historians.[17]

I should like to go a step further and actually suggest the preparation of *new* biographical materials. Some years ago the Yiddish Scientific Institute collected autobiographical sketches of East-European immigrants living in this country. As a result of a public invitation the Institute assembled some 250 autobiographical records, which have already been consulted to some advantage by two or three of my own pupils and others. A more comprehensive inquiry of that type might well be initiated by the American Jewish Historical Society. Once again social and communal importance should not serve as the exclusive criterion. Detailed and lengthy autobiographies, for the most part not intended for publication in full, might be assembled from some five to ten thousand persons representing a variety of interests and different social strata in larger and smaller communities all over the country. A general survey might evaluate the historic importance of those records, but the originals might remain in perpetuity in the Society's archives for consultation as primary historical sources. If such an inquiry were to be repeated every decade or two the value of this material might be enhanced not only quantitatively, but also by offering comparative data and shedding light on the prevailing trends.

Finally, it may not be too early to think of the preparation of an

America Judaica along the lines of *Germania Judaica* or, to a lesser extent, of *Gallia Judaica*. According to the census of religious bodies conducted in 1937, there were 967 "principal" communities in the United States having one or more Jewish congregations, while some 130,000 Jews were estimated to have lived in additional 9,579 "subordinate" communities, for the most part embracing less than 100 Jews each.[18] Since 1937 some new communities have doubtless been added. On the other hand, we also know of communities in many parts of the country which once had Jewish settlers but now have Jews no longer. A complete listing of these thousands of communities in alphabetical order, with a brief description of their Jewish population, past and present, of Jewish organizations and institutions which existed there at any time in the past or still exist today, of their leading Jewish personalities and, particularly, also giving brief bibliographical references, would prove invaluable to every research student, stimulate new research in local archives, and help spread the interest in local Jewish history. The first edition of such a handbook would doubtless reveal a great many imperfections. But with the co-operation of local historians, sociologists, and communal leaders, Jewish as well as non-Jewish, the files might be periodically revised and new improved editions published from time to time.

Population and Migrations

Jewish population studies in this country, as is well known, have thus far been very inadequate. Even our immigration statistics which, between 1898 and 1943, could approach a certain degree of accuracy because of the racial designation, "Hebrew," entered by most Jewish immigrants, have become less reliable ever since this practice was discontinued. Laudable as was the intent of Earl Harrison and his associates in dropping a classification which everyone agreed was scientifically false and, through Nazi propaganda, fraught with anti-Jewish overtones, the elimination of that category has further complicated the work of statisticians wishing to ascertain the number of Jewish immigrants to and émigrés from this country.[19]

If the situation is unsatisfactory today it was, of course, worse in the earlier generations down to the end of the nineteenth century. Even contemporaries used rather crude estimates. The figures usually quoted in our literature, like Isaac Harby's estimate of 1826 or that by Isaac Markens in 1880 are at best "guestimates." Since the census of religious bodies (taken every ten years from 1850-90 together with the general United States census and from 1906-36 by a separate effort of the Bureau of Census in collaboration with respective religious organizations) until 1916 applied to the Jews the criterion of congregational membership, the figures so produced were not sufficiently indicative of the total number of Jews in the country or in any particular community. The 1926 and 1936 censuses, on the other hand, which tried to count all Jews, rather than those affiliated with congregations, have sharply been criticized by experts. Their main shortcoming was that they were not based on local enumeration, but largely on local estimates. While in very small communities such estimates may have closely approximated reality, they proved unreliable in the case of medium-sized communities and still more so in the case of New York City. In 1946 the expected census of religious bodies failed to materialize because Congress, in one of its rare economy moods, cut out the entire appropriation.[20]

At the same time, however, there has been a general awakening within the Jewish community to the need of knowing accurate statistical facts. Such practical considerations as fund-raising, the projected establishment of old-age homes and orphanages, the adjustment of educational policies to the expected size of the Jewish school population in the light of changing birth rates and shifting neighborhoods, or the ascertainment of the number of Jews serving in the armed forces, has led practical communal leaders to devote some of their attention to the accumulation of satisfactory statistical data. For the last few decades various methods have been tried, especially the so-called *Yom Kippur* method, that based upon death records, and so forth. Experts have long since pointed out the shortcomings of all these methods, but it is hoped that a number of convergent hypotheses arising from the application of different methods might ultimately produce an approximation of truth. In the meantime, moreover, statistical science has made great strides by developing, in particular, ever more accurate sampling techniques. On the basis of whatever partial information was locally available B. Seligman and H. Swados submitted detailed estimates in Volume L of the *American Jewish Year Book*. Their findings show that the total number of Jews in the country was by some three-quarter million smaller than might have been expected on the basis of the 1936 religious census. By indirection we may have to revise many older estimates as well.[21]

In 1950 a number of leading Jewish organizations in this country were engaged in creating a new central body for Jewish statistical information which, it was hoped, would be in a position to utilize to the full the latest techniques, as well as to enjoy the wholehearted cooperation of the American Jewish communities. Regrettably, this undertaking did not fully materialize and it was left to the efforts of individual communities to do the best they could in surveying their own membership—with a variety of methods and approaches. However, in 1970 the Council of Jewish Federations has adopted a comprehensive project to survey the entire Jewish population in the country. Combined with the results of the simultaneous official United States Census, this project appears to be quite promising. If successful, this new undertaking should marshal accurate data concerning not only the total number of Jews living in a particular community or in the country at large, but also with respect to such important demographic factors as age and sex distribution, birth and death rates, present and prospective number of schoolchildren, and so forth. Once these data are more fully established and the techniques further refined, it may not be too venturesome to expect that historical studies may likewise benefit. By projecting some contemporary trends backward rather than forward, checking them against every bit of available historical information, and sifting them in the light of most advanced techniques, it may be possible to ascertain with somewhat greater precision the true demographic situation in the past. Fuller data on the natality and mortality among colonial and early American Jews would go very far in helping to explain their partial disappearance from the Jewish communities of later days which seems to have been the result of biological, as well as of assimilatory, factors.[22]

Such demographic researches may also shed new light on the history of Jewish immigration to this country. This aspect of Jewish history has long been intensively studied, partly because of its intrinsic significance for the growth of the Jewish community and, partly, because of the numerous debates on the merits and demerits of immigration. These controversies raged particularly at the turn of the century during the heyday of Jewish migrations. Notwithstanding the large available literature some of it of high quality, our information becomes fairly reliable only after 1898, when the government began inquiring about immigrants belonging to the "Hebrew" race. Since the elimination of this classification in 1943 we are again bound to resort to estimates which, however, in view of their importance to agencies concerned with the care of immigrants, seem to be fairly adequate.

The need of some such new approaches is, indeed, very great. To cite but a few typical illustrations, it is generally known that already some time during the eighteenth century the number of Ashkenazim exceeded that of the Sephardim in most American communities, despite the fact that most congregations still adhered to the Sephardic ritual. We know practically nothing, however, about the size of these successive waves of immigration from Germany and Poland even at a time when they began assuming mass character after 1836.[23] With its penchant for the dramatic, American-Jewish historiography followed the popular misconception concerning the effects of the Revolution of 1848 and the Russian pogroms of 1881 on Jewish mass migrations from central and eastern Europe, respectively. Popular exaggerations are well illustrated by a German writer of 1849 (Friedrich Gerstäcker) who believed that "not one-twentieth of German immigrants in

America were Christians," whereas the inverse ratio seems far nearer the truth. Closer investigation has shown, however, that these dramatic events merely reinforced already existing powerful trends. Although no more definite evidence is available, it is possible, perhaps even likely, that, like German immigration to America generally, that of German Jews actually dropped during the two revolutionary years of 1848-49 in comparison with the preceding European depression year of 1847. By 1850 the trend doubtless was resumed to reach climactic proportions in 1853-55. Only a small number of genuine Jewish "forty-eighters" seem to have reached this country after the breakdown of the Revolution, while most of the other central European Jews arriving in the 1850s or 1860s were recruited from among the ordinary migrants in quest of a better livelihood. As a matter of fact their legal and political status in their native lands had considerably improved under the impact of the Revolution, since some states, including the large kingdom of Prussia, continued to adhere to the principle of full Jewish equality established during the tidal wave of the "Spring of Nations."[24]

Similarly, Russian and Polish Jewish immigration to America had already been in full swing in the 1870s. Like every other migratory movement it would have increased and perhaps ultimately reached the same staggering proportions, had there never occurred any basic change in the Tsarist policies after Alexander III's accession to the throne. Certainly, the non-Jewish émigrés from Russia had suffered from neither pogroms nor May Laws and yet their actual ratio in the total of Russo-Polish emigrants increased from decade to decade. For the same economic reasons, unheralded by any conspicuously dramatic events, Galician Jewry left its age-old communities in proportionately even larger numbers.[25]

Much is yet to be achieved, therefore, by rigorous reinvestigation of all available data for Jewish immigration to this country, Jewish emigration from European lands and temporary or permanent Jewish settlements in such countries of transmigration as England or Canada. A careful examination of both long-range and short-range economic and cultural developments on either side of the Atlantic Ocean would also place the available figures in the broader framework of general evolution which has hitherto been hardly touched upon. Further studies on immigrant adjustment in this country are likewise indicated. Oscar and Mary F. Handlin's pertinent essay only whetted our appetite for more detailed and exhaustive studies of what happened to Jewish immigrants after their arrival in this country.[26]

Still another area of fruitful investigation may be found in the study of changes in public opinion and its attitude toward various immigrant groups with particular reference to Jews. A closer examination, for example, of the antisemitic ingredients, as differentiated from general xenophobia, which came to the fore in the vast anti-immigration literature whether scientific, popular, or fictional, and even in hearings before congressional committees, would merit special attention.[27] It would be significant not only for the history of Jewish immigration, but also for that of the anti-Jewish trends in this country, as well as for many aspects of Jewish community life. Nor would a careful analysis of the mutual influences of the British and American debates on the Alien issue at the beginning of the century and the different attitudes toward Jewish immigrants reflected in these debates be merely of antiquarian merit today. Despite the enormous literature available on the so-called refugee problem since 1933 scholarly investigations of the newer aspects of Jewish immigration before, during, and after the Second World War, if treated from the viewpoint of the general history of Jewish and general migrations might yield new and valuable clues for the earlier periods, too.

Economic History

Unlike the area of population and migrations which have certain conspicuously Jewish facets, that of economic developments must begin with the fundamental question: What is American Jewish economic history? Certainly the Jews active in the American economy are not acting as Jews, but as businessmen, workers, farmers, professionals, and so forth, on a par with Americans of other faiths engaged in the same occupations. Nor is their success or lack of success materially affected by their being Jews. If the country at large is prosperous, as it was in the 1920s and 1940s-1960s, Jews are likely to prosper, too. A sudden depression, like that of 1929-32, engulfs the Jewish citizens in this country, indeed all over the world, without any "fault" of their own or because of anything their community did or failed to do.

Nevertheless, there are certain aspects of economic life which are of particular relevance to Jewish history. To begin with, public opinion has never asquiesced in dealing with the Jewish "economic man" as merely a part and parcel of the general economy. Such indiscriminate condemnation of an entire group as characterized by General Ulysses S. Grant's well-known order No. 12 of 1862 may have been a rare exception.[28] But the issue of the role of Jews in commerce, banking, or the professions has often been in the public eye; at times, a subject of extended controversy. In the period between the Civil and the First World Wars, when American business was generally appreciated, it was an apologist, like Isaac Markens, who played up the Jewish share in various branches of commerce. The Jewish businessman appeared as one of the pioneers of the American economy. Like other pioneers, he may have been appreciated in theory much more than in practice, in abstract glorification much more than in personal relations, but, as least, his general function seemed to be highly valued. No sooner, however, did the climate of opinion change during the years of the Great Depression and bankers and businessmen found themselves under attack, than antisemites began concentrating their assaults upon Jewish big business and "international" banking. In sharp contrast to 1888 when Markens wrote, the editors of *Fortune* in 1936 considered it a great favor to the Jewish community that they proved, on the basis of detailed though scattered evidence, that Jews played but a relatively minor role in America's leading business establishments. The Jewish ratios in the medical and legal professions have likewise long been an embattled area.[29]

Apart from these public relations aspects, Jewish occupational distribution has also had a considerable internal, even ideological, significance. For the last two centuries economic restratification has been a major watchword of communal action. Ever since the middle of the eighteenth century societies were springing up in many lands trying to help Jews to abandon the traditional ghetto occupations and to find more "useful" employment in the "productive" areas of agriculture and industry. Among the greatest ideological trends dominating Jewish emigration from Russia to America was the *Am Olam* movement of the 1880s and 1890s which sought to colonize Jews on American soil just as its contemporary and rival, the "Lovers of Zion" movement, tried to settle them in Palestine.

More detailed data, therefore, on the changes in the occupational distribution of Jews in the various stages of their history in this country would to some extent serve as a measuring rod for the successes and failures of these manifold communal efforts. Unfortunately, even our knowledge of present-day conditions is still rudimentary. Despite such materials as are embodied in the Sophia M. Robison volume, the work of the Jewish Occupational Council, the vocational services of the B'nai B'rith and other agencies, we have but a smattering of accurate knowledge concerning the number of Jews in various occupations. What can be achieved by patient research in older directories, when used in combination with available more recent data, painstakingly assembled and analyzed, has been shown by a pilot study undertaken by Henry J. Meyer for the city of Detroit. More such studies with directories going back much further than 1890 would both increase the amount of our information and refine the methods employed.[30]

Agriculture is the major exception inasmuch as the Jewish Agricultural Society has carefully watched the processes of Jewish settlement on land ever since the beginning of this century.

Hence, Gabriel Davidson, long-time director of that Society, has been able to produce not only a readable account of the history of Jewish farming in this country, but also one based upon more or less ascertainable facts, even in regard to the earlier periods. In view of the interest aroused by the public debates on the subject and the ensuing special investigations, one may also speak with some confidence about the number of Jewish physicians or dentists in this country, or that of Jewish students at schools of higher learning.[31] Far less reliable are the data for other professions or for the Jewish ratio among workers, while the much talked about but little studied problems of the Jewish businessman, big and small, are statistically almost completely in the realm of fancy. A thoroughgoing contemporary effort, coupled with the reinvestigation of all available records of the past, might yet yield some valid approximations which, even if not wholly satisfactory to the statistician, will give the historian at least some basic data to go by.

The role played by the Jewish peddler in the successive stages of Jewish settlement in this country, particularly in the mid-nineteenth century, is another intrinsically Jewish aspect of American economic history. In many respects a Jew became a peddler not because he happened to be an American in search of a livelihood, but because as an immigrant, and particularly as a Jewish immigrant, he saw in this occupation his major opportunity.

Quite apart from the predominantly Jewish character of this trade in certain periods and areas, it also had many significant Jewish communal and social aspects. In recommending a Palestinian messenger Isaac Mayer Wise, then in Albany, wrote on February 5, 1850, "Since many of our members are absent from the City, nothing could be done in his favor until Pesach next." Evidently this was but one of many instances when communal action in many parts of the country was impeded by the prolonged absence of perhaps the majority of congregants who were traversing the villages with their wares. The social implications of families deprived for long periods of their adult male members and children growing up without close paternal supervision have yet to be investigated. So have the effects of peddling upon the weakening of Orthodox observance and the necessary adjustments in ritual and work on the Sabbath, as well as on the shaping of Judeo-Christian relations when the peddler frequently was the only representative of his faith personally known to countless Christian customers or competitors. In view of this great importance of peddling for the internal as well as external history of the Jewish communities, we may doubly regret the paucity of detailed investigations in this field. Rudolf Glanz's, Lee M. Friedman's, and Maxwell Whiteman's essays have served to open it up for further research, but much is yet to be done before we shall acquire the necessary exact knowledge of the gradual transitions within the various categories of peddlers (such as were enumerated by Isaac M. Wise in his *Reminiscences*), their general economic status, the average duration of each phase, and the relationships between peddling, traveling salesmanship, and the ultimate development of the mail-order houses.[32] All of these problems, significant for American economic history in general, are doubly significant for Jewish history.

Of considerable importance also is the Jewish share in American labor and labor movements which belongs to the relatively best studied areas of American Jewish economic history. Although the ambitious investigation of the Yiddish Scientific Institute has thus far not progressed beyond the end of the nineteenth century, there is a considerable literature, some of it of fine quality, pertaining to individual labor unions with a greater or lesser Jewish membership or to biographical accounts of important labor leaders. Nevertheless much has yet to be done in ascertaining in detail the rise and decline of Jewish employment in various industries, both "light" and "heavy," the effects on Jewish workers of the successive business cycles and the two world wars, the relationship between the size and kind of employment and the rate and type of immigration, etc. The enthusiastic comment of two writers in 1930, stating that,

*these Jewish tailors have immeasurably enriched America. For
while their fellow workers—diggers of coal, forgers of steel,
weavers of cloth—are still widely denied a collective voice, the
masses in the needle trades have been revealing what free, responsible citizens can contribute toward the development of life
and industry,*

has largely been superseded by the New Deal labor legislation
and the new position of labor in the United States' economic and
political structure. But the influence of Jews as individuals and
still more as members of organized, predominantly Jewish groups,
on the great historic achievements of the American working
classes during the last 90 years is yet to be told in full and
illuminating detail.[33]

From another angle a searching analysis of the role played by
Jews in the real estate trade would shed some new light on both
Jewish and general American history. As early as 1891 the *New
York Sun* commented, "Of late years also they [the Jews] have
become conspicuous for investments in landed property. Some
of the most notable of the purchasers at the Real Estate Exchange are Jews." Writing on conditions in Boston at the
beginning of this century, Robert A. Woods stated that "the
increase of Jewish ownership in real estate during the past ten
years has been amazing. . . . In the North and West Ends in
1900, estates with a total assessment valuation of $6,544,700
were charged to persons of names unmistakably Jewish."[34] Since
that time the Jews have entered the real-estate market in New
York and many other cities in expanding numbers and with increasing resources. They have done so, however, not only as buyers
and sellers, but also as large- and small-scale builders and archi-
tects. The names of Albert Kahn and Erich Mendelsohn are likely
to remain memorable in the history of American monumental
architecture for both public and private use. Bearers of lesser
names have in the aggregate likewise made tremendous contributions to the development of American cities.

To be sure, in this phase of the real-estate industry Jews acted as individuals, rather than as Jews. At the most one may assert that the long tradition of their urban life and their centuries-old experience in mortgage loans and other aspects of the trade in real estate had predisposed them to play a significant part in the upbuilding of America's metropolitan centers with all their ugly as well as fascinating features. There is one facet, however, which has affected them as members of the Jewish group, namely the discriminatory real estate covenants and other restrictions on the sale and renting of residential space. These forms of discrimination, highlighted in 1877 by the notorious Hilton-Seligman affair, became an increasing social as well as economic problem in view of the growth in numbers, greater diffusion and, paradoxically, the progressive integration of Jews in American society. Apart from outright discriminatory agreements, there have developed in recent years many more insidious forms. Jewish efforts may, in part, have been coresponsible for the May 1948, decision of the United States Supreme Court which declared such real estate covenants legally unenforceable, but the court has nevertheless "sanctioned a host of other 'gentlemen's' devices that are enforceable extra-judicially." Charles Abrams from whom this quotation is borrowed has analyzed a number of such devices which have the same socioeconomic, if not quite the same legal effects. They operate in a realm, where law itself is often powerless. For Thomas Jefferson's remark in a letter to Major Noah is even truer today than it was in 1818: "Although we are free by the law," commented the sage of Monticello, "we are not so in practice; public opinion erects itself into an Inquisition and exercises its office with as much fanaticism as fans the flames of an *Auto-de-fé*."[35] Careful analysis of the period and the circumstances under which such discriminatory practices began to be aimed at Jews and seriously to affect their economic as well as social life and what, if any, efforts were made by the Jewish community to combat them would shed some new light on a significant, still unfinished chapter in American Jewish economic history.

Discrimination in housing is far overshadowed in importance by discrimination in employment. Most of the immigrants coming from countries, which at the time of their emigration, offered the Jews few if any opportunities in public service, took it almost for granted that they would not be admitted to any appointive office. Moreover, their unfamiliarity with English, local mores, and laws made them, as a rule, little qualified for civil service. No sooner, however, did they become Americanized and they or their children had gone through American schools than they began seeking opportunities for earning a living in the employ of federal, state, and local administrations. This happened in the period of the "spoils" system, as well as after the establishment of a regular civil service based upon competitive examinations. To the surprise of many more recent arrivals it was easier for well-qualified American Jews to secure public than private employment—the exact reverse of conditions in central Europe. After Franklin D. Roosevelt's election and particularly during World War II when the nation had to strain its manpower resources, both physical and intellectual, Jews found a great many new opportunities to serve their country in administrative as well as military posts.

This entire story, fairly familiar in general outline, has never been told in any well-documented monographic studies. There has been much publicist discussion, particularly in antisemitic and apologetic literature, concerning the alleged equation of the New Deal with a "Jew Deal" and the reputed overcrowding of wartime Washington with Jewish officials, but no one has bothered to assemble any body of reliable evidence and to ascertain the solid core of fact, rather than of legend. At one time when funds were made available for a careful study of this significant aspect of Jewish life, the war effort had preempted all qualified personnel. Everybody has heard of Jewish Cabinet members or of the four Jewish governors who served concurrently as the chief executives of four important states. But the really important *economic* facts, such as whether and to what extent a candidate's Jewish faith proved an obstacle to the securing of, or advancement in, office, the ratio of Jews in various branches of civil service, the extent to which there were regional differences between various parts of the United States, or the general relation between Jewish population density and the proportion of Jews in a particular area of service—all these and many related problems have not even begun to be explored. For example, the popular New York saying during World War II that the enforcement of price controls was left entirely to "Mike and Ike," that is an Irish policeman and a Jewish clerk of the Office of Price Administration, could in no way be statistically confirmed or denied. The further back we go the task may be facilitated by the lesser numbers of persons involved but it is aggravated by an increasing paucity of extant records.

Discrimination in private employment, admission to private schools, colleges, medical institutions, and so forth, are even more ramified and complex. Suffice it to refer again, for example, to the report of the B'nai B'rith Vocational Service Bureau which has not only compiled extensive data on Jewish students enrolled in the American schools of higher learning in 1946, but also attempted to compare them with a similar report submitted for 1935. The trends during the intervening decade are in some respects even more significant than the actual findings. It has been shown that the percentage of Jewish students taking up the traditional studies of law or medicine has greatly decreased, while that of the students of engineering has nearly doubled. Even the large teaching profession, as a rule underpaid and often dependent on appointment, has attracted a somewhat larger ratio of Jewish students in 1946 than in 1935, while that of non-Jewish students has sharply declined. The further growth of Jewish participation in, and partial leadership of, the teaching profession, as demonstrated during the teachers' strikes in New York and elsewhere in 1968-69, actually had sociopolitical effects far transcending the immediate economic issues. Perhaps it is not too late to trace back some of these trends to the earlier decades of this century by utilizing whatever material may still be extant. On the discriminatory practices in private industry our knowledge is even more fragmentary despite efforts of such agencies as the American Jewish Congress and the American Jewish Committee, and the data quietly accumulating in such public bodies as have been established in the several states possessing fair employment practice laws of one kind or another.

The historically highly significant question as to when such discrimination began seriously affecting Jews, what forms it has taken, and what its economic as well as social effects have been in the respective periods, cannot be answered even by remote approximations. Nor do we know much about the history of various communal efforts to combat discrimination either by suasion or by some FEPC legislation on a federal and state, or municipal basis.[36]

Communal History

Another important borderline aspect of economic and communal history is the problem of communal financing and its relation to what might be called communal wealth, or the total wealth of the communal membership. In our days of stupendous fund raising we often fail to realize how poor the early Jewish communities really were. Unlike in the Old World, Jewish congregations here, as a rule, could not afford to build their synagogues from local resources. When Shearith Israel decided to erect its Mill Street Synagogue in 1728 it went far afield in soliciting contributions from the Jews of the West Indies and the English homeland. "We have already purchased an appropriate site," its elders wrote, "for the edifice and another for a cemetery, but for want of sufficient means, the Yehudim here being but few, we have not been able to carry out our intention and until our hopes are realized, we must continue for the present to congregate in a synagogue rented from a Goy." It is difficult to imagine what would have happened to American communal history if benefactors like Abraham de Mucata in London, an Ashkenazi Jew of Boston (which was not to possess a synagogue of its own for another century), and other Jews from Barbados, Jamaica, and Curaçao had not contributed a lion's share to the building fund. In 1759, the famous Newport synagogue, today a national shrine, was completed in time only because its leaders "resolved to crave the assistance of the several Congregations in America" and thus succeeded in raising the necessary funds. As late as 1826 the newly

formed B'nai Jeshurun in New York issued a Hebrew appeal "to
our Jewish brethren near and far to ask them for a donation to
the sacred work in accordance with their financial ability and good
will." It also promised the donors that their names would be inscribed in the record book for perpetual remembrance.[37]

One cannot help feeling, however, that these difficulties arose,
in part, from the fact that the Jews had not yet been educated
to giving "until it hurts." Often coming from communities endowed with powers of taxation, they had been accustomed to
offer purely voluntary donations only for such supplementary
causes as charities and the education of poor children, while the
basic needs of synagogue and cemetery were covered by taxation or
loans secured by future tax revenues. As early as 1664, Asser Levy,
who had started life in New York ten years earlier as a manual
laborer and since 1660 was allowed to practice the licensed profession of butcher, was able, as "one of the wealthiest inhabitants,"
to lend the city 100 florins. The signers of the Newport letter of
solicitation included Aaron Lopez, a budding shipping magnate
in the country. Certainly a great many Continental communities,
as well as later American congregations, succeeded in erecting
houses of worship without outside assistance, even if their members had lesser financial resources.[38]

The situation changed in the nineteenth century, however, with
the influx of new immigrants. The nascent communities, particularly of the Middle West, were now confronted with the difficulty
of securing qualified personnel, rather than of raising the necessary
funds. In fact, they were prepared to pay their synagogue officials
what at the time were munificent salaries. A characteristic letter,
written by the Rev. S. M. Isaacs of New York in 1851 to the
editor of the *Jewish Chronicle* in London, may be reproduced
here in full:

*When last I had the pleasure to converse with you, when in
London, I expressed my regret that time did not permit my delivering a lecture on the condition of the Jews in America, feeling
convinced that it would tend to remove much misconception*

which at present exists in England on that important subject. Since that time I have seen much of their condition which even astonished me, although a resident in the States for twelve years. I allude to my journey to the West. Having been invited to consecrate a synagogue 1100 miles from here, I expected to find some few families in Chicago, one of the leading cities in Illinois; but I certainly was not prepared that, after leaving Buffalo, I should see any of our race: yet it is remarkable that not a village on my route was without an Israelite, much less the towns such as Detroit and Ipsylanti [Ypsilanti] each containing twenty families, Ralmazoo [Kalamazoo] and Marshahte [Marshall] and, others in proportion; and all these are destined to be congregations; but where are the ministers to be found to guide them in the way they should go? This is indeed a vital question. At Chicago they offer a salary of 500 dollars for a חזן (reader) and teacher, which is equal to 1000 dollars in New York, as the living there is very cheap; beef threepence per pound; houserent a fourth what we pay; poultry—a pair of fowls for three shillings—and other things in proportion; yet I fear it will be long before the situation will be filled, as they require one conversant with English, and alas! where are they? If our educational establishments in England would but train young ministers, such as I proposed when steward at the Jews' Hospital, the supply would equal the demand, whilst now there are some five or six vacancies not likely to be supplied. Of the חינוך at Chicago you have already been advised by the paper; suffice it to say, that it was all that a Jew could wish to realize; his co-religionists—emigrants from Bavaria, most of them —obtaining an excellent living, and respected by their fellow-citizens. I regret to state, that the synagogues at St. Francisco have received a severe check by the late conflagration.[39]

From that time on, budgets of the Jewish communal groups have increased by leaps and bounds until in recent years they have reached the tremendous proportions of the United Jewish Appeal, various federation campaigns, and other drives.

These financial aspects of Jewish community life, important everywhere, are doubly important in the United States where the financial contribution has often been the main criterion of communal allegiance. In fact, the gradual shift of the center of gravity of Jewish community life from the synagogue and school to the charitable organization is one of the most intriguing facets of American Jewish history. The reasons for this transformation have often been discussed, but its individual stages since the middle of the nineteenth century still await elucidation. The amazing growth since World War I of the federation and welfare fund movements, and the unparalleled success in marshaling the resources of American Jewry for Jewish relief and reconstruction abroad and the building of Zion, has led to further concentration of fund raising efforts and increasing emphasis on the individual contribution as the major form of affiliation.

This "checkbook Judaism," as it was sometimes uncharitably called, has had many important effects on the whole structure of the Jewish community. In the early American communities, and even in some small communities today, sentimental attachments were often reinforced by the "moral suasion" of a powerful public opinion. In its first By-Laws, adopted in 1706, Shearith Israel expected to be able to enforce its will on recalcitrant members, for "the whole Congregation shall assist the said Parnas and assistants to recover the same [fine]." Communal will was further strengthened by the serious threat of refusal of religious burial and, less effectively, of withholding synagogue honors. The Rodeph Sholem Congregation in Philadelphia could in 1810 still impose a fine of 25 cents for a member's unexcused failure to attend Friday evening or Sabbath morning services or withdrawal from services before their completion. But already, in 1878, in a letter to the editor of a New York weekly we find the following comment: "It has justly been observed, that of the large number of Jews in this city, only a small per cent join regular constituted synagogues." The writer explained this deficiency by the relatively high congregational dues as well as by sudden changes in ritual. He also stressed the fact that being a member of a congregation gave one little direct advantages. "Mutual Benefit Societies provide burial

ground and funeral expenses, besides other benefits, and cost less."
Since rabbis were prepared to officiate at any wedding for a small
fee there was no direct incentive for joining a congregation except,
perhaps, for the services rendered by the congregational school to
members' children.[40]

It is astonishing but true that we have no detailed, fully documented monographs on any major philanthropic or other communal institution of recent generations. Samuel Joseph's aforementioned study of the Baron de Hirsch Fund is clearly the exception confirming the rule. Only recently have there appeared the
first general historical reviews of such outstanding Jewish organizations as the American Jewish Committee and the National
Jewish Welfare Board. On the occasion of its fiftieth anniversary
plans were afoot for the publication of a comprehensive history
of the National Conference of Jewish Social Welfare. The Joint
Distribution Committee was likewise planning to prepare its own
history.[41]

Such institutional autobiographies, Jewish and non-Jewish, however, written under the sponsorship of the respective organizations,
necessarily have all the disadvantages of personal autobiographical
records, with few of the compensatory features of psychological
directness and "human interest." As a rule conceived as a part of
general information to be conveyed to their respective constituencies and the public at large, they can rarely be as candid and
detached as are some of the best individual confessions. Often
they merely combine certain features of regular annual reports,
enlarged so as to cover the organization's entire history, with
attempts at greater popularity. Like other semi-popular literature
they crave to satisfy that mythical creature, "the general reader,"
and hence refrain from "overburdening" their presentation with
too many facts, figures, or documents. Useful as some of these
writings are to the historian and grateful as we ought to be to
these organizations for expending their time and energy on producing them, in contrast to many other groups which do not
bother about supplying even that minimum of information, they
are by no means definitive. Much of that material will some day

have to be reinvestigated by students with exacting requirements for fully documented historic information.

The fiscal aspects of community life have another significant bearing on the totality of American Jewish history. Since so much of communal life depended on contributions by wealthy individuals, it was but natural that communal control should rest with the wealthy classes. This transfer of control from the traditional "aristocracy" of learning, piety, and descent to the communal plutocracy had been under way even in European countries since the rise of modern capitalism. But there the community had, for the most part, the legal powers of compulsory taxation and hence depended far less on purely voluntary offerings. In this country the generally high appreciation of the businessman served to underscore the financial dependence of all communal groups on the goodwill of wealthy donors. While employing a communal official it was not even necessary to insert such candid contractual stipulations, as are recorded in Surinam in 1783, namely, that "if differences arise between the congregation and the parnassim he [the rabbi] is always to take sides with the parnassim and to help them with advice."[42]

During the depression years of the early 1930s, to be sure, the size and quantity of large contributions sharply declined and the community depended chiefly on the popular support of numerous small and medium-sized donors. There also was a general decline in the prestige of wealthy leaders among Jews and non-Jews, "economic royalist" having become a term of opprobrium. But when after World War II the urgent needs of foreign relief and reconstruction called for the highest. intensification of Jewish fund raising, dependence on large contributions, and with it the power of the purse, had been partially reestablished.

The bulk of funds raised [comments an informed observer] was derived increasingly from large givers. The average contribution was approximately $163 in 1947 as compared with $130 in 1946. Contributions of $100 and more were credited with 92.6 per cent of the funds secured (90.1 per cent in 1946). Six per cent of the contributors in 1947 (giving $500 and over) were the source of 75 per cent of the funds raised. (In 1946, 5.4 per cent of the contributors gave $500 and more and were responsible for 70.4 per cent of all funds raised.)[43]

A certain counterpoise has developed, however, in recent years through the establishment of an ever larger communal bureaucracy. Long accustomed to having its rabbi and teacher set the tone in communal affairs, the Jewish community now has added to these officials a vast body of administrative personnel in charge of both the raising and distribution of funds. The sheer size and ramifications of the communal structure had become so vast and complex that the older part-time wealthy leadership had to delegate its responsibilities, in an increasing degree, to the full-time professional group of communal administrators and trained social workers.

These overshadowing developments in the American Jewish community, in sheer quantity transcending anything known in previous communal history, have never yet found their historical analyst. Some basic statistical data have been supplied in Linfields's and Karpf's studies for 1927 and the mid-1930s, respectively.[44] A great many sources are also available in the studies issued by the Bureau of Jewish Social Research, the Council of Jewish Federations, and other groups, as well as in such periodicals as *The Jewish Social Service Quarterly* and the *Jewish Community*. Apart from factual data we also possess a considerable body of thought and interpretation in the annual *Proceedings* of the National Conference of Jewish Social Welfare, the *Yearbook* of the Central Conference of American Rabbis, and other groups. Only a body of trained historians, however, equipped with a good knowledge of the workings of the Jewish community, can hope to cope adequately with this vast body of published and unpublished material. Although most of these investigations would naturally turn to developments of the last half or three-quarters of a century, their results, if projected back into the earlier periods, would doubtless also greatly enrich our understanding of the more limited source material relating to the earlier communal ventures.

Of course, I am not suggesting that we should discard the hitherto traditional approach to communal history, namely the study of individual communities and congregations. Even in this field a great deal has yet to be done. New York has been extensively treated in the aforementioned works by Grinstein, De Sola Pool, Goldstein, Rischin, and others.[45] The early story of Philadelphia Jewry has been told by Wolf and Whiteman. For Easton, Pennsylvania, Joshua Trachtenberg has assembled much significant historical as well as sociological material. Charleston, South Carolina, too, where Barnett Elzas's work early in this century has been supplemented by a volume from the pen of Charles Reznikoff, has an adequate up-to-date history.[46] But our knowledge of most other communities still leaves much to be desired. One wishes that American rabbis, teachers, and social workers would see their way clear to emulating their Central-European confreres who often considered it incumbent upon themselves to bring to light the records pertaining to the past of their respective communities. Perhaps, in time, one or another official of every important community, though small in size, will consider it a moral obligation to accumulate, through patient research extending over many years, all significant records from local and state archives, the archives of his own congregation and other communal bodies, as well as from private sources (including reminiscences of some older surviving members which may thus be first confided to writing). If a number of these or other communal leaders, equipped with the necessary local knowledge, including that of active personalities, their family backgrounds, and the relations with non-Jewish neighbors, were to utilize the sources thus accumulated for the writing of shorter or longer narratives describing the growth and evolution of their communities, we would in the aggregate achieve that much-needed large collection of basic monographs which alone will warrant useful generalizations. The mere fact that local communities and national agencies would evince interest in such works and guarantee publication of worthy books and pamphlets of this type would in itself be an inducement to many scholars to undertake these labors of love.

At the same time, we must encourage the pursuit of studies of such specialized groups as the *Landsmannschaften*, fraternal orders, labor unions, and the like, as well as of such institutions as the Jewish centers, Jewish hospitals, orphanages, and homes for the aged. We must be grateful to the WPA research staff for having produced the first worth-while study of Jewish *Landsmannschaften*. That it has the shortcomings of any pioneering effort, somewhat aggravated by the difficult circumstances under which the study was conducted, goes without saying. It is even more amazing that a great fraternal organization like the B'nai B'rith, now more than a century and a quarter old, with ramifications in many lands has been given such scant consideration by historians. Our knowledge of the other fraternal orders is, of course, even more rudimentary. We are fortunate, on the other hand, in having Benjamin Rabinowitz's history of the Young Men's Hebrew Associations from their inception to 1913. This study ought to be continued beyond 1913 and comparable studies encouraged for other communal institutions.[47]

Only after the accumulation of much more detailed, sound, and well-interpreted information shall we be able to reach reasonable conclusions concerning the successes and failures of that great voluntary enterprise going under the name of American Jewish community. Most other Jewish communities in the world started with some recognition, even backing, by the powers that were. Especially the medieval and early modern communities under both Christendom and Islam had a fully recognized status as corporate bodies under public law, endowed with powers of taxation and other forms of enforcement of the communal will. Even in recent generations the Central-European, as well as the oriental, communities have enjoyed the backing of public law. In contrast, from the outset American Jewry had to build its communal structure without the cooperation of government and in the face of tremendous inner difficulties. In the early years the community had to fight inch by inch to secure even such elementary rights as those of building a synagogue or establishing a cemetery. With the separation of state and Church even the most sympathetic governments could extend little more than moral encouragement by tax exemptions for communal institutions, the licensing of ministers for the performance of marriage ceremonies, the appointment of army, navy, hospital, and prison chaplains and the like, while the successive waves of immigration from many lands and internal ideological divisions threatened to disrupt all communal bonds and to engulf the Jewish community in utter anarchy.

That American Jewry succeeded in overcoming these staggering handicaps and achieving as much singleness of purpose and unity in action, if not in outlook, as it did—if, in the face of tremendous adversity, it built the imposing structure of its philanthropic, educational, and social institutions which have already served as models for many other countries—this may be a source of legitimate pride for American Jewry.[48] But it does not free us from the obligation of trying more fully to understand the strength and weakness revealed in this evolution. This is the more important as the destruction of the old European centers and the shift of Jewish Diaspora life to newer countries has in many ways made the American community a pacesetter for world Jewry outside the State of Israel. More comprehensive and penetrating investigations of the entire range of American Jewish communal history, therefore, are of fundamental importance for the understanding of the entire history of modern Jewish communal organization as well as of the future trends now shaping up the world over.

Cultural and Religious History

Perhaps our most serious lacunae are to be found in that very area which, next to the history of persecutions, has loomed largest in Jewish historiography, namely, the *Gelehrtengeschichte* or, more broadly, the history of Jewish thought, culture, and religion. Unbelievable though it may seem, some phases of that evolution are historically almost a *terra incognita*. It would far transcend the bounds set for the present discussion, if an attempt were made here to block out even remotely the important fields of investigation. Suffice it to say that, for example, we have no adequate history of Jewish letters in America (in Hebrew, Yiddish, and Ladino as well as in English or German). A century ago Francis Lieber already expressed his amazement at the fact that "the German Jews in America gain in influence daily, being rich, intelligent and educated, or at least seeking education. They read better books than the rest of the Germans, the booksellers tell me." We have a few studies of the Yiddish theater but even those are not up to date. One must bear in mind that in its early stages the Yiddish theater was more than an artistic institution. As noted by the distinguished German historian, Karl Lamprecht, who had attended several New York performances in 1904, it was a crusading semi-religious force in the community. "In ancient Hellas, too," Lamprecht reminisced, "they must have played theater with such religious consecration." We know still less about the Jewish theatrical arts in English in the double sense of plays of Jewish content performed by Jewish theatrical groups and the role which Jews have played in the general American theater. The biographies of Adah Isaacs Menken of an earlier period can merely whet the appetite for more knowledge about the artistic achievements of the recent decades when Jews began playing such a remarkable role as playwrights, actors, producers, and promoters on the legitimate stage, the movies, television, and the radio.[49]

Similarly the Jewish role in graphic arts and music has been sadly neglected even in areas which directly impinge on Jewish life like synagogue decorations, Jewish sacred music, folksongs, etc. The achievements of Jewish men of science have been treated in the interesting monographs by L. Gershenfeld, S. R. Kagan, and others, but their traditional approach to such "Jewish contributions to civilization" may properly be supplemented by studies of their effects on the internal evolution of the Jewish community. The very science of Judaism, which now can look back with pride upon several generations of solid accomplishment in this country, has never been adequately described. Once again the biographies of individual leaders like Mordecai Manuel Noah, Isaac M. Wise, Solomon Schechter, Louis Brandeis, Louis Marshall, Judah L. Magnes, Stephen S. Wise, and Abba Hillel Silver can merely underscore the absence of detailed and systematic treatment of the major historic trends in the various branches of religion and learning.[50]

Unbelievable though it may seem, it is a fact that we do not possess any comprehensive studies of the great religious movements among American Jews. Even Reform Judaism, otherwise highly articulate for almost a century and fortunate in finding in Rabbi David Philipson an able historian of some phases in its evolution, has never been analyzed with adequate detail and comprehensiveness. For the time being Beryl H. Levy's Columbia dissertation and some essays by the alumni of Hebrew Union College offer partial data and insights. The papers and discussions recorded in the volumes of the *Yearbook* of the Central Conference of American Rabbis, the vast array of published sermons, articles, and books by Reform rabbis and laymen certainly offer, together with archival sources, an almost inexhaustible mine of information.[51] Moshe Davis's and Marshall Sklare's volumes on Conservative Judaism, dealing with its earlier representatives to the end of the nineteenth century and the sociology of the movement are pioneering efforts in this field.[52] It is to be hoped that they will stimulate further monographic studies, particularly of the last seven decades of greatest flowering of the Conservative movement. Orthodoxy, the largest and most variegated group, is not only almost completely unorganized, but its history in this country is as yet a practically uncharted sea. Many serious investigations will be required, some in the nature of "pilot studies," before satisfactory methods for dealing with these crucial developments will be evolved since in various areas we already begin to suffer from a disproportionate plethora of documentation on certain phases combined with its great paucity in other phases. Such disequilibrium in the source material is likely to throw off balance any but the most disciplined historian with a fully developed sense of proportion. Apart from uncovering the more obvious biographical data of some outstanding leaders these studies will have to penetrate the core of the ideological conflicts and ritualistic variations as well as of their underlying social causes.

Connected with such studies of Jewish religion would be a fuller examination of Judeo-Christian relations in the religious field. In the first place one may think of the more or less continuous efforts on the part of various churches to convert Jews. Cotton Mather's prayer, "This day from the dust, where I lay prostate before the Lord, I lifted up my cries: for the conversion of the Jewish Nation, and for my own having the happiness, at some time or other, to baptize a Jew," reflected the basic attitude of the Colonial church-men to Jews and Judaism. That conversionist interests dominated the thinking of even such a friend of Jews as Ezra Stiles is evident from many pages in his diary. Despite several incipient studies we are only on the threshold of a really adequate knowledge of the history of Christian missionary efforts amongst Jews in this country. Their ramifications in the intellectual history of America, their influence on the spread of the knowledge of Hebrew and Jewish history, as exemplified in the early career of Judah Monis or the historiographic endeavors of Cotton Mather himself, and the stimulus they gave to the apologetic and polemical writings of both Christians and Jews are yet to be examined in fuller detail.[53]

The history of both antisemitism and interfaith movements, even if limited to their strictly religious aspects, in the twofold sense of religious fanaticism or tolerance on the one hand, and of the growing recognition among Christian leaders of the essential interdependence of Judaism and Christianity on the other, is a wide open area for extensive research.[54] Once again it would not do to limit such studies to the upper reaches of Christian and Jewish thought, but rather, in order to secure fuller understanding, one would have to examine the manifold forms of both popular religious prejudice and popular good will. Last but not least, one ought to look forward to a careful reexamination of both the similarities and the dissimilarities in the evolution of Jewish *versus* Christian religious thought in this country. It may be too rash to speak of a history of American Jewish theology—its relative absence is in itself an intriguing historical problem deserving careful elucidation—but there were enough bridges built between the religious outlook and practices of Jews, even of Orthodox Jews, and their Christian neighbors, to require detailed and unbiased analyses by experts.

Even the institutional aspects of Jewish scholarship have been insufficiently investigated. The Jewish Theological Seminary of America, to be sure, published in 1939 a semicentennial volume. But what was said at that time in a review of this work is still true today.

> As a jubilee volume it admirably performs the function of a landmark, giving pause to its leaders and supporters and awakening the interest of the public at large in its past and future. The serious student of American Jewish culture, however, . . . may wish that the Seminary authorities should some day see their way clear to making available the rich stores of information of Jewish cultural and communal interest assembled in its archives in a scholarly, fully documented history of the school and of its influence on the affiliated congregations.[55]

Only Yeshiva University has been the subject of a more detailed monograph by Gilbert Klaperman.[56]

We know less about the other great institutions of learning in this country, the Hebrew Union College-Jewish Institute of Religion, the Dropsie College for Hebrew and Cognate Learning, the Hebrew Theological College, and the various fine Jewish teachers' colleges. Not even the seventy-fifth anniversary of the foundation of Hebrew Union College, the oldest of these institutions, has given sufficient impetus for the publication of a detailed documentary history which would make available to further research many significant documents accumulated in the archives of this outstanding center of learning during a most crucial period in American and world Jewish history. In the spirit of the old talmudic adage that "rivalry among scholars increases learning," it would not be too venturesome to hope that if a comprehensive multi-volume work of this kind saw the light of day, it would set the pace for a considerable number of other ambitious institutional histories. Similarly, The Jewish Publication Society of America, whose very aim is to diffuse information among American Jews, has not seen fit to utilize its seventy-fifth anniversary for a more comprehensive and detailed review of its achievements as well as failures—and there necessarily have been some failures, too—over a period of three-quarters of a century. Joshua Bloch's bibliographical compilation is but a step in the right direction.[57]

All this is not stated here in a spirit of censure. All of us realize how long American Jewry and its leaders have labored in building and expanding the areas of these institutions' fruitful activities as well as in weathering the recurrent crises. At this very moment they have their hands full with the consolidation of the tremendous gains they have made during the last two decades and in adjusting their functions and outlook to a world fundamentally altered by the Great Catastrophe and the rise of the State of Israel. But it seems to me that this very process of adjustment would be greatly aided in our historically ever more conscious generation, if some of the precious time and energy were diverted to a candid and careful reexamination of the earlier stages of growth.[58]

To a certain extent the same observations hold true of the entire field of Jewish education. We have an increasing mass of detailed information on certain specific phases or the more recent evolution. The studies prepared by the research departments of the American Association for Jewish Education, the Jewish Education Committee, and others, as well as the numerous articles published in such specialized periodicals as *Jewish Education* and *Shebile ha-Ḥinnukh* offer a mass of excellent raw material for the historian. However, detailed historical investigations have been sadly lacking—Alexander Dushkin's dissertation on New York during the early decades of this century being a noteworthy exception.[59]

As a subsidiary but no less vital issue one ought to study the impact of the separation of state and Church on the history of Jewish education as well as on that of the general education of Jews. Again, we have many specialized statements by lawyers, educators, and publicists on some phases of the influence exercised by separation on the growth and decline of the Jewish day school, the study of Hebrew and Jewish history in secondary schools and colleges, the "released time" program with its effects on Jews and Jewish attitudes toward it, the effects of tax exemptions on religious and educational institutions, and so forth.[60] But comprehensive studies making use of refined historical approaches as well as of more specialized educational, psychological, and sociological techniques appear to be a major desideratum for the knowledge of both the past and contemporary affairs of American Jews.

The field of social history likewise has untold possibilities. From the outset American Jewry has begun developing certain customs and folkways peculiar to itself. "American orthodoxy," writes David de Sola Pool, himself a leading Orthodox rabbi, "has tacitly almost forgotten the prohibition of shaving, the law forbidding the mixture of materials on one's garments, and hundreds of similar Jewish laws which in other ages and lands had unquestioned authority." On the positive side American Jewry has developed certain customs even in synagogue observance which have no parallel in other countries, such as the particular Bar Mitzvah ceremony as analyzed by Isaac Levitats. Other customs in synagogue, school, home and even business would offer a plethora of attractive fields of investigation to competent students.[61]

Collective Versus Individual Effort

The above enumeration, reflecting an almost random choice of existing lacunae, reveals the *embarras des richesses* confronting the student of American Jewish history. Considering the enormous literature available on other phases of American history, which forces doctoral candidates laboriously to comb the field before they find a desirable, as yet unexplored, dissertation topic, American Jewish history offers a wide open field for a legion of competent research workers. The above illustrations could readily be amplified by any scholar in the field.

In fact, entire branches of American Jewish scholarship have been neglected here. For example, the legal and political history of Jews in the colonial and early American periods has engaged the close attention of jurists like M. J. Kohler, B. H. Hartogensis, L. Huhner, and others.[62] But there is much yet to be done in regard to such specialized legislation as that affecting the Sunday law observance, fair employment practices, the Jewish chaplaincy, and others. While domestic legal history necessarily became very limited with the progress of emancipation, America's role in the shaping of international law affecting Jews is yet to be told in detail. The Adler-Margalith volume is little more than a good beginning, while the National and other archives are bulging with material awaiting careful exploration. Apart from the older phases, the United States' role in the adoption and application of minority rights and human rights and its share in the Zionist movement and the rise of Israel would all bear comprehensive and detailed examination. Only recently have well-documented histories of certain phases of the Zionist movement in the United States appeared in print.[63]

Some of us may object that all these observations may be of interest to individual teachers and students, but that the American Jewish Historical Society as such can do little about encouraging that type of research. No one will deny that ultimately the success and failure of American Jewish historiography will depend on the efforts of creative individuals stirred by the drama of Jewish life in this country. Nevertheless, the mere fact that a society of scholars would stimulate a number of such collective undertakings as the biographical and geographic dictionaries suggested above, that in its journal and separate publications it would offer a permanent forum for the communication of technical studies whose marketability is necessarily limited, and that by its contacts with Jewish communal bodies it would help stimulate the interest of both the leadership and the public in Jewish historic research, should prove an invaluable aid to scholars specializing in this field. Once scientifically valid material is accumulated, it would enable writers and publicists to make use of them for more popular presentation which, in turn, would widen the circle of interested students and add incentive to scholarly investigations as well.

Is not all this transcending the usual objectives of a historical society? It certainly is, if the functions of a society are envisaged within the traditional narrow confines of what is called the "warehouse theory" of custodianship over accumulated source material. Many historical societies, however, have in recent years stepped out of these narrow bounds. "I suspect," says Julian P. Boyd, "that by the policy of concentrating on the past, and what manuscripts fortuitously turned up, such societies have sold their message, on the whole, to those whose definition of history and of the purposes of historical societies is the narrowest, and in so doing have sold their own birthright." Boyd points out that in a statement of policy the Historical Society of Pennsylvania has given up the warehouse theory in favor of serving as a positive force in the community.[64] How much more should this novel approach apply to a society dedicated to the exploration of the past of a religious group which has a deep emotional stake in its very survival! The time seems, indeed, to have come for the American Jewish Historical Society and other national and local Jewish organizations to assume their rightful places as major constructive forces in the cultural life of the American Jewish community.

4 *A Documentary History of the Jews in the United States 1654—1875. Ed. by Morris U. Schappes. A Book Review**

This first comprehensive collection of documents pertaining to more than two centuries of American Jewish life will be of great assistance to both scholars and students. In six years of painstaking research, the author has utilized the resources not only of the great New York libraries but also those of the National Archives, the Library of Congress, and some two-score other libraries. The list of acknowledgments (p. xxiii) is truly impressive. Mr. Schappes has earned the particular gratitude of all serious workers in the field by publishing many documents hitherto either wholly unavailable or extant only in scattered, rare publications. For one example, the report of the American consul in Beirut dated March 24, 1840, concerning the well-known Damascus blood accusation (pp. 202 f.) reveals the almost unbelievable naïveté of some American diplomatic agents in the Near East in the face of entirely incredible stories affecting Jews. Incidentally the British, but not the Austrian, consul proved equally gullible. On the other hand, Washington and the American minister in London succeeded in preserving their *sang froid* in disregarding such biased reports (pp. 204 ff.). All students of American history, moreover, will be grateful to Mr. Schappes for this handy compilation which will greatly facilitate the study of American Jewish history, much neglected in both Jewish schools and general colleges.

* Reprinted from *JSS*, XIII (1951), 77-80. This volume, with a Preface by Joshua Bloch, appeared in New York, 1950 (3d rev. ed., 1971).

Following widespread usage, the collection begins with the oft-reprinted correspondence between Peter Stuyvesant and the Dutch West India Company in 1654, which marked the beginnings of Jewish group life in this country. The author has refrained, in our opinion wisely, from including documents pertaining to the much-debated problem of Columbus' Jewishness, the participation of Jews in the latter's voyage of discovery, and the incidental references to Jewish individuals who appeared in various parts of the American continent before 1654. He concludes his collection with two newspaper items of December 1874. He nowhere explains the reason for stopping at this particular point. However since, contrary to widely accepted historical folklore, East-European mass immigration had been in full swing long before the Russian pogroms of 1881, the mid-1870s are as convenient a break as any other. The author promises, moreover, a continuation of this collection for the subsequent, more turbulent period of American Jewish history, during which this community gradually matured into a position of world leadership.

Well over two hundred documents are reproduced in whole or in part in these 159 entries. Each entry is provided with an informative introduction and is carefully annotated. The author reveals considerable erudition in the vast literature in general American history as well as in the specialized monographs on some of its Jewish phases.

Deeply impressed as one necessarily is with the amount of learning and loving care which went into the preparation of this volume, one must not overlook, however, some of its inherent weaknesses. Certain important phases of American Jewish history are not treated at all. For example, the dramatic struggle of the Jewish community to establish itself as an organized body and to carry on the traditions of the Old World are given but scanty attention. We learn nothing about the protracted conflicts which often preceded the building of a synagogue and the establishment of a Jewish cemetery against the overt hostility of the powers that were. Nor do we hear about the great financial difficulties which New York Jewry had to overcome before constructing the first synagogue on the North American continent. Only by successfully appealing to the generosity of coreligionists as far as the West Indies and London was it able to build in 1728-33 its first house of worship, that of the Spanish and Portuguese congregation. Similarly, the famous Newport synagogue which, by Act of Congress, has since been declared a national shrine, was erected with the aid of many other communities—a sort of reverse UJA. While these facts are not mentioned, a similar appeal of the Cincinnati congregation of 1825 is reproduced in full (pp. 178 f.), because it illustrates "the struggle of Jews in the frontier communities." These internal difficulties, and many other complications arising from the purely voluntary ties of the American communities, which were so greatly at variance with the contemporary European communities recognized by public law, are nowhere recorded in the documentary collection before us.

This omission is by no means accidental. "American Jewish history is always," Mr. Schappes broadly states, "a part of American history, and cannot be scientifically investigated except in relation to it" (p. xi). Although almost a truism, this idea had to be clearly restated. However, American history as such, especially in its earlier phases, includes also much of the history of American religious denominations. Certainly American Jewish history cannot be understood without relation to such internal Jewish factors as religion, education, Jewish folkways, of which the few documents here included (for instance, Nos. 50-60, 75-77) can hardly give an inkling to the most assiduous reader. Moreover, Jewish history on this continent is just as much a part of world Jewish history as it is of American history. The author himself admits in the same context that both Jews and non-Jews had carried over into the New World much of their Old World heritages. But there is hardly any reference here to the continued intimate relationships between American Jews and those of other lands. Even the problem of Palestine relief, which often engaged the attention of communal leaders in this country, as elsewhere, is mentioned only tangentially in connection with Judah Touro's will of 1854 (pp. 333 ff.).

Under these circumstances, Mr. Schappes's volume might properly be considered a collection of documents primarily relating to the political and economic history of the Jews in the United States. The economic phases of Jewish history are particularly well treated. The author rejects the erroneous approach of many previous writers in this field "which takes the exclusion of Jews from any field as relevant, but their inclusion is dismissed as irrelevant to Jewish and relevant only to 'general' history" (p. xiii). He is perfectly right in treating as fully of Jews admitted to industries, professions, or residential sections as he does the story of their exclusion from them. It is doubly remarkable, therefore, that he makes little use of the interesting documentary material on the economic activities of early New England Jews, published by S. Broches from Massachusetts archives. In political history, too, there are some such noteworthy lacunae, as the denial in 1737 of electoral rights to Jews by the New York legislature which evidently ran counter to the earlier more tolerant practice.

More significant than these omissions is a certain basic weakness in the way this documentary material is presented. The author is perfectly correct in assuming that readers would be greatly aided not only by explanatory notes and references to specialized literature—most of his notes are indeed excellent—but also by brief introductory remarks describing the background and general frame or reference of each particular document. However, in order to be valid such introductory matter must explain, not prejudge. As far as possible it must abstain from value judgments. Mr. Schappes, however, makes clear that he does not consider the historian's task completed by the presentation of the various sides of an argument. In his opinion, the historical writer must reach definite conclusions of his own; otherwise he "becomes a useless and merely titillating chronicler" (p. xviii). This sweeping generalization may be debatable even in the writing of history. It is doubly questionable when it relates to a documentary compilation which, because of its inherent selectivity and limitations, cannot possibly of itself justify any such broad conclusions.

In narrating, for example, the story of Jewish participation in the American Revolution, Mr. Schappes realizes that the majority of Jews were patriots. But he rightly also produces an address of loyalty to the British Crown signed on October 16, 1776, by 948 New Yorkers including sixteen Jews (pp. 50 ff.). In his introductory remarks, however, he gives the impression that it was only "some of the richest Jews" who stayed in New York, because "the loyalists were generally found among the rich merchants and landowners who put the class benefits . . . above the national interests of the new state." Such class interpretation, in itself a dubious oversimplification of a highly complex situation, has little bearing on this particular document. It is not only controverted by the numerous wealthy Jewish patriots like Francis Salvador, Mordecai Sheftall, Aaron Lopez, and Haym Salomon mentioned by the author himself, but also by the individuals recorded in this very document. In his own notes Mr. Schappes admits that seven of the sixteen Jewish signers are otherwise unknown, that one was a *mohel* and teacher, another a sexton, occupations not known for the wealth of their holders. None of the other signers, nor for that matter any other Jewish loyalists, were in any way comparable with their leading coreligionists on the revolutionary side. Equally gratuitous in this connection is the author's criticism of two papers on Jewish loyalists by Cecil Roth, whose interpretation is allegedly "dominated not by an interest in international democracy but in the expansion of the British Empire" (p. 578). Such generalizations may have their place in a comprehensive monograph on the Jews in the American Revolution which would marshal and weigh the whole evidence. But they certainly do not belong in a book like the present, in which only a few pertinent documents are excerpted (Nos. 34-44) and which, therefore, does not enable the reader to reach independent conclusions with respect to controversial issues.

In the light of American Jewry's recent active participation in the building of a Jewish state, it is also remarkable that Mr. Schappes mentions Mordecai Noah's Ararat project, one of the earliest modern Jewish "territorialist" enterprises, only in his introduction to an excerpt from Judge Noah's much later *Discourse on the Restoration of the Jews* (1844). This excerpt is cited more fully because it allegedly shows that "even then the strategy of 'Zionism' was linked to that of imperial rivalry" (p. 247). This interpretation is debatable. A careful reading of the whole *Discourse* shows that its author rather took the imperial rivalries for granted, but envisaged the Jewish colonization of Palestine primarily as the realization of the Jewish people's messianic dreams, concurred in by Christian religious teachings. It also was to accrue to the benefit of both the Ottoman Empire and the Muslim populations who "are also the descendants of Abraham." Such introductory remarks certainly are not helpful in bringing home to the uninitiated reader the underlying intentions of the author of that document.

Taken as a whole, however, Mr. Schappes's volume, if used with the neccessary caution, doubtless will stimulate the study of Jewish history on this continent. It certainly is one of the major contributions in this field to appear in recent years.

5 The Emancipation Movement and American Jewry*

Students of Jewish history have long been accustomed to date the beginnings of Jewish Emancipation with the French Revolution. To be sure, with his fine historical feeling Heinrich Graetz perceived that one cannot understand the evolution of Jewish Emancipation without paying close attention to the preceding Haskalah movement in Germany, a movement which introduced the Jews into Western culture. For this reason he started the eleventh volume of his *History* with a description of the Mendelssohnian period. Nevertheless the historians who followed him, "liberating" themselves from his intellectual-biographical approach, turned to the great political event of the French Revolution which not only had changed the general image of political history, but had also formally proclaimed the equality of rights for Jews. They made of this event a cornerstone for the entire structure of modern Jewish history. True, in 1927 Max L. Margolis and Alexander Marx in their well-known historical work started a description of the Emancipation period with the year 1787, that is, after the American Revolution following the Declaration of American Independence on July 4th, 1776. They referred, of course, to the proclamation in that Declaration that all men were born equal and had inalienable rights.[1] But these scholars were suspected of American ultra-patriotism and most of their colleagues

* Revised English trans. from a Hebrew article in *Eretz-Israel*, IV (1956- Isaac Ben Zvi Jub. Vol.), 205-214.

continued to view the events of 1789-91 in France as the starting point for the entire subsequent evolution.

This approach may be justified on two grounds: First, the French Revolution directly influenced 40,000-50,000 French Jews; this number increased several times over by the French conquests in Holland, Italy, and Western Germany, while the Napoleonic armies spread the French revolutionary doctrines to Eastern Europe. In contrast, the number of Jewish residents in the United States at its foundation did not exceed 2,000 persons, that is less than 0.1 percent of the whole Jewish people. Secondly, the basic approach to Jewish as well as general history in Central Europe was predominantly legalistic and documentary. The most important societal developments in those countries found their major expressions in political and legal documents, while historical periods were usually divided according to dramatic events, such as wars and peace treaties, revolutions, and constitutional enactments. The French Revolution dealt with the Jewish question over a period of two years before it formally proclaimed Jewish equality of rights. Under its influence the principle of equality was publicly adopted by other countries. In Holland, for example, the political emancipation of the Jews in 1796 was accomplished under the influence of the French conquerors against the will of the Christian majority of the population. Even many Jews objected to it because they were afraid that as a result of equality they would have to give up their self-determination with respect to legal and cultural affairs. In the fundamental Constitution of the United States, on the contrary, including its first ten Amendments, generally known as the Bill of Rights, Jews were not mentioned. All the rights they had acquired as a result of the American Revolution sprang automatically from its general principles without a thought being given to the Jewish question.

In the last several decades a large change has taken place in the general historical approach. Especially the inhabitants of England and the countries under the rule of English law realized that the greatest changes in their lives were not always reflected in the laws of the state, and that much that arose from custom or oral law exceeded in importance and historical consequences all that was expressed in parliamentary resolutions or court decisions. English Jewry, for example, could develop in the course of two centuries, from the days of Oliver Cromwell and Menasseh ben Israel to the age of Queen Victoria, without finding appropriate expression in any formal law. It was possible for Lucien Wolf to prove that the Jews of his country had in some respects been emancipated as early as 1697, since it was in that year that the Royal Exchange of London had decided permanently to assign 12 of 124 licenses to Jewish brokers.[2] For the same reason, the American lawyer Arthur Kuhn, discussing the negotiations concerning the status of Amsterdam Jewry in 1616, could suggest that the proposals submitted at that time by Hugo Grotius represented the first blossoming of Jewish liberation.[3] On my part, I have long come to the conclusion that one cannot hope to understand the development of legal and political emancipation without a careful review of the basic social forces which brought them about. That is why one must deal at the same time with the impact of both the economic and cultural emancipation which had preceded the legal emancipation by several generations.[4]

From this point of view it may be worth while to consider the status of American Jewry both before and after the Revolution. This must be done not only from the aspect of the few laws dealing with Jews, but in the main from the standpoint of actual practice and social life. These aspects, almost totally neglected by Jewish scholarship, outside the specialized literature dealing with the history of American Jews,[5] may help shed new light on the entire history of the Jews in the modern period.

Before 1740

The beginnings of Jewish settlement in North America are still obscure. Not only are the difficult questions of Columbus' origin and the participation of many Marranos in his epochal discovery still debatable, but we can never be certain of the Jewishness of many new settlers in the sixteenth and seventeenth centuries. Some of their names appear to be Jewish; for example, that of Elijah Legardo who is mentioned in the colony of Virginia as early as 1621. But this is no decisive argument. The problem of Jewish identity in all colonies resembles in some respects the question of Jewish allegiance in Mediterranean countries under ancient Hellenism and Rome. Their Jewishness is derived for the most part exclusively from their Jewish-sounding names mentioned in the sources which happen to be extant today. But it is well known that many Puritan inhabitants of North America chose with preference biblical names for their sons and daughters, while, on the other hand, many Jews adopted English family names. Hence one cannot rely on the onomastic criteria for the identification of Jews.

At the same time it is precisely this difficulty which clearly indicates how unimportant the Jewish question appeared to be in most of these colonies. In general, individuals, or even families, who emigrated to the American colonies and settled there either in a city or a village, appeared to the majority of their neighbors simply as European immigrants who had come to establish themselves in the New World. As a rule the majority paid no attention to their being Jews, except in the rare cases when, for some external reason, the question was specifically raised. Even in New Amsterdam (later New York) the arrival of Jacob Barsimson might have gone unnoticed, were it not for the issues raised by the landing of twenty-three Jewish refugees a few months later. In many instances, when one's Judaism was mentioned at all, it was done to favor the particular Jewish individual rather than to his disadvantage. For example, Rowland Gideon "ye Jew"—later a prominent Jewish businessman in London—was first mentioned among the Boston taxpayers in 1674. In the following year he, together with one Daniel Baruh, perhaps likewise a Jew, became involved in a litigation. In his petition to the court, Gideon tried to captivate the benevolence of the judges by quoting the ancient

Hebrew law which provided for one law for both the citizen and the stranger. He added that he was "praing for the prosperity of your Goverm^n and that you may be further fathers of this scattered Nation."[6]

Five years before a similar occurrence is recorded in the case of Jacob Lucena in Hartford. It appears that this New York Jew was arrested in connection with some sexual transgression. Said to have been "notorious in his lascivious dalience and wanton carriage and profers to severall women," he was sentenced to a fine of £20. When he protested, the municipal court reduced the fine to £10 "considering he is a Jew." In the end, with the help of his New York friend, Asser Levy, he paid only £5, the judges wishing to treat this reduction "as a token of their respect to the sayd Mr. Assur Levy."[7] We must remember, moreover, that most of the New England colonies, especially Massachusetts, were by no means religiously tolerant at that time. Some of them severely persecuted both Catholics and Quakers. None the less, Jews are mentioned there in various documents over several generations.

However, in those years an incident occurred which might have endangered the entire future of Jews in North America. The colony of Maryland was founded by the Catholic Lord Baltimore, whereas the majority of the population was Protestant. Because of the constant friction between the Protestant legislature and the Catholic governor a number of intolerant decrees were enacted. One of these laws, passed in 1649 and reconfirmed in 1656, decreed that

> Whatever person or persons within this Province and the Islands thereunto belonging shall from henceforth blaspheme God, that is curse him, or shall deny our Saviour Jesus Christ to be the Son of God, or shall deny the Holy Trinity . . . or the Unity of the God-head, or shall use or utter any reproachful speeches, words, or language, concerning the Holy Trinity, or any of the said three Persons thereof, shall be punished with death, and confiscation or forfeiture of all his or her Lands and Goods to the Lord Proprietary and his Heirs.[8]

On the basis of this law Jacob Lumbrozo, a Portuguese New Christian, who but two years before had settled in Baltimore, was haled in 1658 before the courts because he had allegedly blasphemed against the Christian God. Lumbrozo apparently had come to America from Portugal and Holland. In the New World he served as physician, innkeeper, farmer, and money-lender. The episode which gave rise to the lawsuit was based upon the testimony of one John Hoffsett that he had had a religious disputation with Lumbrozo. To Hoffsett's claim that Jesus' resurrection had proved that he was superhuman, Lumbrozo allegedly replied that Jesus' disciples may well have absconded with him. On the witness' question as to why no other man had performed such miracles as Jesus, Lumbrozo's ready answer was that such acts could also be performed by magicians. Hence, according to the witness, when it was pointed out to him that he had thus equated Christ with necromancers, Lumbrozo said nothing but laughed.[9]

Had Lumbrozo been condemned on the basis of the aforementioned law, such a sentence might have established a dangerous precedent for all Jews, at least in the colony of Maryland and in some other colonies which had similar provisions on their statute books. In fact, however, he apparently was not sentenced, perhaps because of an intervening general amnesty on Richard Cromwell's assumption of the office of Lord Protector of England. In any case, five years later Lumbrozo is mentioned as denizen of Maryland and a landowner, and in one of the documents as a sworn justice in Baltimore. However, it is not impossible that this man, who was by no means distinguished by his general moral conduct, had in the meantime embraced Christianity. In any event from that time on we hear of no case of Jews being summoned before the courts because of their denial of the belief in the Trinity.[10]

Needless to say, from time to time some churchmen tried to convert their Jewish acquaintances to Christianity. Among them was Cotton Mather, one of the famous Protestant leaders, who had become so deeply interested in Jews and Judaism that in

1714 he completed a six-volume *Biblia Americana* on the history of the Jewish people since the beginning of the Christian Era. It reveals the orientation of that pastor who, according to several entries in his Diary, used to recite prayers for the conversion of Jews. On July 4-5, 1713 for example, he recorded his "Vigil-Prayer: For the conversion of the poor Jew, who is this day returned once more unto New England, and who has now for 19 years together been the Subject of our Cares and Hopes, and Prayers." It seems that on that occasion, too, Mather waited in vain.[11]

Yet some ten years later Judah Monis, the first Hebrew grammarian in America, underwent conversion before he was appointed instructor in Hebrew at Harvard College. More important to us is the fact that two years before, while still a Jew, Monis obtained from the College a Master of Arts degree on the basis of a Hebrew grammatical study, the first of its kind in the English colonies.[12]

There is no doubt that many Jews ultimately were assimilated by the Christian environment and totally disappeared from the Jewish scene. But those who remained true to their ancestral faith for the most part felt no need to fight for their rights. In most colonies European immigrants of all faiths and nationalities were accepted without difficulty, although only the colony of Rhode Island was established on the basis of an avowed design for religious toleration. Roger Williams, its main founder, expressed the opinion that the colony should also admit Jews, "for whose hard measure, I fear, the nations and England hath yet a score to pay."[13] In fact, no sooner was the city of Newport founded in 1649 than Jews began settling in it. By 1677 twenty-seven Jewish heads of families were allowed to acquire their own cemetery, probably the first legally established Jewish burial ground in North America. In 1684 the Rhode Island Legislature resolved more guardedly, that Jews might "expect as good protection as any stranger, being not of our nation, residing amongst us in this his Majesty's Colony, ought to have, being obedient to his Majesty's laws."[14] True, religious tolerance elicited much op-

position in the other colonies, particularly among the clergy.
Cotton Mather, for example, irately called Newport "the common
receptacle of the convicts of Jerusalem and the outcasts of the
land."[15]

None the less most colonies treated Jews as individuals rather
than as members of their specific religious group. In South
Carolina, for which John Locke prepared the fundamental Constitution in 1669, the leaders tried to increase the settlement in
the colony by proclaiming liberty of conscience for all believers
except "papists." In Locke's tract the Jews are mentioned along
with heathens "and other dissenters from the purity of the
Christian religion." In the opinion of the English philosopher,
the new colony had the duty not to reject these infidels but, on
the contrary, to facilitate their getting acquainted with the
Christian religion by contact with their neighbors living in accordance with justice and morality.[16] Because of the frequent
wars between England and Spain, Catholics were not considered
loyal citizens of any colony located close to a Spanish dependancy.
There were many cases in which the courts interpreted regulations
concerning specific disabilities as applying to Catholics but not
to Jews. Generally speaking, Jews benefitted greatly by not being
singled out in the laws as such. From many angles, their legal
status was indeed superior to that of their Catholic compatriots.

Only in two colonies did the Jewish question emerge in
public debates at the beginning of the Jewish settlement there:
in New York and Georgia. These developments have often been
described in historical literature and the story need not be repeated here. Suffice it to mention that the Jewish settlement in
Georgia took place in the very first months of the colony's
foundation in 1733. In that year the two Jewish communities in
Savannah, one Ashkenazic and the other Sephardic, embraced
between them more than 80 persons, and amounted to about
20 percent of the total "white" (non-Indian) population. Notwithstanding the opposition of the organizers of that colony in
London—to the extent that one of the trustees, Thomas Coran,

threateningly predicted to his colleagues that in time Georgia would turn into a Jewish colony—the local administration treated the Jews on a par with the Christian settlers. The great contrast between these conditions and those prevailing in contemporary Europe came clearly to the fore when, in 1734, a ship filled with Protestant refugees from Catholic Austria landed in Savannah. These "Salzburgers" were very well received by the city's German Jews who could communicate with them in their own language. According to their clergyman Bolzius, the twelve German Jewish families on the spot "show a great love for us." Several years later (July 3, 1739) Bolzius informed a correspondent in Germany: "We are close to the Spaniards and on account of such dangerous proximity, care is taken to keep down Negro slaves and Roman Catholics. With these exceptions all sects and all kinds of people are tolerated and are permitted to enjoy all manner of liberty like native Englishmen. Even the Jews of whom several families are here already, enjoy all privileges the same as other colonists."[17]

In New York alone, the most important Jewish community in North America, both chronologically and numerically, the Jews found themselves obliged to fight for their rights. During the first ten years (1654-64) after their arrival in the city, then known as New Amsterdam, they were able to overcome the obstacles placed in their way by their local opponents and to avert the threat of total expulsion only by invoking the assistance of their Dutch coreligionists, especially the influential shareholders of the Dutch West India Company, which was in control of the colony. However, we must remember that the twenty-three immigrants who arrived in the city in September 1654 were impoverished refugees who, upon landing on the North American continent, still owed two-thirds of their fare to the owner of the ship on which they had sailed. In most European countries of that time insolvent debtors were considered criminals subject to imprisonment up to several years. The heads of the Dutch Reformed Church, faced with the obligation of providing for all the local poor, had long objected even to the settlement of penniless Lutherans. Ultimately, the Jews were allowed to remain in the country under the condition that they would take care of their own poor, and would not engage in public worship.

Their penury did not last long, however. One of their leaders, Asser Levy, was not only able to acquire sufficient wealth to be counted among the main creditors of the city in 1644, that is, within ten years after his arrival, but he also constantly defended his rights of citizenship, a struggle which automatically safeguarded the rights of the other Jews as well. He secured a license to open a butcher shop without the customary oath in Christian terms, served as a patroon engaged in the fur trade with Albany, and even acquired real estate in the city. Most remarkably, when the authorities imposed upon him a special tax in lieu of service in the guard against Indian attacks, he roundly refused to pay it. He ultimately forced the officials to allow him to fulfill that duty in person, on a par with the Christian burghers. As early as 1657, four other Jews formally received citizens' rights, be it in the limited sense in which such rights were being granted to Jews in Amsterdam, Holland.[18]

After the English conquest the rights of the New York Jews remained basically unchanged, although the governmental enactments of that period are far from explicit on this point. The reason for this legal ambiguity was the generally equivocal nature of the Jewish status in the contemporary mother country, as well as the often contradictory pronouncements by the first Governors. In his Proclamation of 1665 Governor Mathias Nicolls spoke about religious toleration extended to all "believers in the Christian faith." Yet, nine years later Governor Edmund Andros used the formula of the rights enjoyed by all "persons of whatever religion." In 1683, on the other hand, the colonial legislature mentioned again only "believers in God by Jesus Christ."[19] All this was evidently done in a sort of absent-mindedness. Just as in Jewish sources we read sometimes the word "Jew" when the writer meant "man," so, it appears, these legislators spoke about "Christians" without giving any thought to the presence of Jews in the colony.

In practice the legal status of Jews was determined by their daily relations with their Christian neighbors and by the existing business practices much more than by formal laws. As a rule Jews enjoyed the rights of other inhabitants, except on those rare occasions, when for special reasons some doubts were raised on this score. In such cases the authorities, after consulting the existing legislation, sometimes disqualified Jews from a particular activity. However, even such precedent-setting renewals of certain disabilities were often forgotten within a few years. For example, the main difficulty for the establishment of a regular Jewish community in New York—a major concern in all newly established Jewish settlements—derived from the aforementioned condition placed by Governor Peter Stuyvesant of New Amsterdam on the admission of Jews, that they would not indulge in *public* worship. This restriction principally involved the outlawry of public religious institutions. Indeed, both the Dutch and the English authorities long denied the right of Jews to establish a cemetery of their own. As late as 1685 the municipality of New York rejected their application for the building of a synagogue. None the less, at least beginning in 1682, Jews made use of an independent cemetery,[20] and ten years later a French traveler, Lamotte Cadillac, reported seeing a Jewish house of worship in New York. In 1695 even the location of that synagogue was indicated on the city's map prepared by Pastor John Miller, although formally this building doubtless appeared as but a private home used by Jews for quiet and unobstrusive divine services. As late as 1728, when the Jews decided to build a regular house of worship, they were able to acquire the land only in the name of the three communal elders, not in that of the community as such which was not yet recognized as a juridical person. Nevertheless the building was erected, and from the 1730s on there has existed a public synagogue in New York belonging to the Spanish and Portuguese Congregation Shearith Israel.[21]

Moreover, a *house* of worship was not a basic requirement of the Jewish faith. Even orthodox Jews—and the majority of colonial Jews seem to have been ritualistically observant—could meet in any private home and conduct their divine services without scruples. But under the assimilatory pressures of the free environment some Jews developed considerable impatience with the burden of their law. Abigail Franks certainly was not alone in feeling as she did when she wrote her letter to Naphtali Franks on October 17, 1739:

> I must Own I cant help Condemning the Many Supersti[ti]ons wee are Clog'd with and heartly wish a Calvin or Luther would rise amongst Us I Answer for my Self, I would be the first of there followers for I dont think religeon Consist in Idle Ceri-monies and works of Supperoregations Wich if they Send people to heaven wee and the papists have the Greatest title too.

Such voices were, indeed, characteristic of the Jewish society on the approach of Emancipation.[22]

In contrast to the obstacles placed in the way of the Jewish community at large, individual members hardly felt seriously hampered by their disabilities. There is no evidence, for instance, that the testamentary rights of Jews were in any way curtailed. The extant wills of New York Jews in the pre-Revolutionary period betray no apprehensions on the part of the testators that any provisions might prove unenforceable because the writers happened to be Jews. True, according to the accepted systems in both Holland and England the authorities were able to forbid Jews to engage in retail trade. An instance of such a prohibition is indeed recorded in connection with the application for a pertinent license by Ḥazzan Saul Pardo (Brown) in 1685. But this apparently was an exceptional case. When in 1724 Solomon Myers received the right of a denizen he was specifically regis-tered as a "shopkeeper." Rights of citizenship were also speedily acquired by Jacob and David Robles, who had lived in France as Marranos outwardly professing Protestant Christianity, and had to leave that country after the revocation of the Edict of Nantes in 1685. If Asser Levy had belonged to the guards in the Dutch period, another Jew, Joseph Isacks, is mentioned among the English soldiers fighting against the French in America under the regime of William III (1689-1702).[23]

Most importantly, it appears that some Jews even took part in political affairs. True, when in 1719 Moses Levy was elected to serve as a constable of the South Ward, he preferred to pay a large fine of £15, rather than to accept that burdensome office. Very likely most Jews evinced little interest in political controversies. They must have known that the Spanish and Portuguese Congregation in London, which generally served as a model for Shearith Israel in New York, had in 1668 adopted a resolution forbidding its members to form parties, even for elections within the community. This prohibition remained in force for several generations and was expressly renewed in 1817.[24] No such provision was ever adopted by a New York or any other American congregation. However, this type of thinking may well have served as a deterrent for active participation by the few Jewish residents of the colonies in the political struggles of the day. Only by mere coincidence do we learn about Jewish freeholders undisturbedly voting in elections to the New York Legislature, although Catholics were specifically barred from them by law. No one seems to have raised any objections until 1737, when Cornelius Van Horn complained to the Legislature that his opponent, Adolph Philipse, had been elected with the aid of Jewish voters. On this occasion the Legislature resolved that "it not appearing to this House that persons of the *Jewish* religion have the right to be admitted to vote for Parliament Men *in Great-Britain*, it is the unanimous Opinion in this House, that they ought not to be admitted to vote for Representatives in this Colony."[25]

What is truly important in this connection is not the prohibition for Jews to vote in the future, but the fact that before the controversy of 1737 they had often participated in elections without any protest. It appears that very shortly thereafter this disability went into discard, again not by formal vote of the Legislature but in actual practice. At least in 1761 Jewish voters are again mentioned without much ado in documents from the city of New York. The Swedish traveler Peter Kalm, who visited New York in 1748, simply recorded that the Jews "enjoy all the privileges common to other inhabitants of this town and province." In South Carolina we learn from a protest as early as 1703 that "Jews, Strangers, Sailors, Servants, Negroes and almost every Frenchman . . . came down to elect, and their Votes were taken." This protest was carried all the way to London. Although the protesters won their case and, in 1721, the law specifically restricted the voting rights to free white citizens "who believed in the Christian religion," the well-informed Barnett A. Elzas claims that "there is nothing to show that the Jews were ever subsequently interfered with in the exercise of the franchise."[26]

Naturalization Act

In 1740 a major step was taken toward Jewish Emancipation, when the English Parliament adopted a special Naturalization Act for the English colonies in the New World. Not only were Jews counted among those eligible for citizenship after a sojourn of seven years in any American colony, but they were singled out in Articles 2 and 3 for specific exemptions. As a rule residents wishing to become naturalized had to produce proof that during the preceding three months they had received the Lord's Supper in one of the Protestant churches of England or the Colonies, as well as to take a citizen's Oath of Abjuration "upon the true Faith of a Christian." Together with the Quakers, Jews were exempted from the first requirement, while Jews alone were allowed to omit the Christian formula of the oath.[27]

The basic difference between the new and old provision for naturalization consisted in the Act's automatic extension of the rights of citizenship conferred by one colony to all other colonies as well. Apparently this change was considered more significant by the Jews of Jamaica than by those residing in the Continental possessions. We shall therefore not be astonished that in the list of 189 Jews (five names appear dubious) counted among the newly naturalized citizens in the years 1740-53, compiled by scholars from British archives, no less than 151 resided in Jamaica, while only 24 were New York residents, and but a few individuals lived in the other colonies. Moreover, after 53 of the new citizens had become naturalized in the first year, their number subsequently dropped to 19 in 1741, to 3 in 1742, although it suddenly increased to 30 in 1743.[28] However, this very restraint in applying for naturalization bore clear testimony to the sense of security felt by the large majority of Jewish settlers in the North American colonies and the absence of any urgent need on their part to improve their legal status.

Probably almost all Jews who applied were naturalized without difficulty. Only the applications of two Jews are known to have been rejected by the authorities—of all places in the colony of Rhode Island, which a century before had pioneered in the area of religious toleration. In 1762 the future shipping magnate, Aaron Lopez, who had settled in Newport some ten years before, submitted such an application, together with another Newport Jew, Isaac Elizer. In explaining its rejection the Rhode Island Supreme Court had to resort to utter sophistry. The judges argued that the purpose of the Naturalization Act, as indicated in its Preamble, was to foster an increase in population which the English lawgivers had declared to be "a Means of advancing the Wealth and Strength of any Nation or Country." However, they contended, in the Court's judgment Rhode Island had already become overpopulated, and quite a few of its residents had been forced to emigrate to Nova Scotia. Hence it could not have been the intention of the legislators to apply the law to that colony. This refusal made a great impression not only upon Jews. One of the pro-Jewish churchmen of that generation, Ezra Stiles, then serving as Protestant pastor in Newport (he later became president of Yale University) had derived therefrom the following lesson:

I remark that Providence seems to make every Thing to work for Mortification to the Jews, and to prevent their incorporating into any Nation; that thus they may continue a distinct people . . . [It] forbodes that the Jews will never become incorporated with the people of America, any more than in Europe, Asia and Africa.[29]

This singular Rhode Island refusal may have been prompted by some personal biases, however. We must not forget that in the preceding few years three other Jews, including Moses Lopez, Aaron's elder brother, had been naturalized in Rhode Island. At the advice of a friend, Aaron himself crossed the border to Taunton, Massachusetts, where he was granted naturalization without any difficulty. Thereupon he returned to Newport which could no longer deny him the privileges of a naturalized citizen and, in the following years, he became one of the most successful merchants of his generation. Among his possessions appeared no fewer than 113 ships, whether wholly owned by him or in partnership with others. From a remarkable letter he wrote to a friend in 1767 we learn that at that time Aaron had dispatched one of his ships to Lisbon in order to bring his younger brother, sister-in-law, and their three children, to America. In this way, to cite him, God had delivered this Marrano family "from the reach of the barbarous Inquisition."[30] Aaron and his family also heavily subsidized the building of the beautiful Newport synagogue in 1759-63. This synagogue is still intact, and in 1946 it was declared by the United States Department of the Interior a national monument under the protection of the United States government. Otherwise, too, Lopez proved his generosity, frequently helping needy scholars and other poor.[31]

The impact of the Naturalization Act was perhaps greater on the Jews outside than on those residing in the American colonies. As a consequence, in 1753 the English Prime Minister Henry Pelham reminded Parliament that that Act had been adopted in 1740 "by both Houses without opposition." He therefore demanded that a similar law be enacted for England herself. It is well known that at first Pelham's proposal was readily accepted and, in the so-called Jew Bill, extended the right of naturalization to Jews in the mother country as well. However, the center of the British Empire was not yet prepared for this decisive step. After a few months Pelham himself had to retrace his steps in the face of a widespread anti-Jewish agitation and to propose to Parliament the abrogation of its former decision. Yet a simultaneous attempt by the opposition to use this opportunity to revoke also the law of 1740 was defeated in Parliament by a vote of 208 to 88.[32]

While it brought no immediate change in the status of English Jewry, Pelham's abortive undertaking had many long-range moral effects. Many statesmen and writers in other European countries, especially the numerous admirers of the English constitutional developments, frequently referred to this event, using it as an argument for the abrogation or modification of the numerous disabilities of their own Jewries. Count Gabriel H. R. Mirabeau, in his well-known book on Moses Mendelssohn published shortly before the outbreak of the French Revolution, devoted a special section to the Pelham bill which he reprinted in full. Moreover, the glaring distinction between the status of the Jews in the colonies and that in the mother country at a later date also strengthened the hand of the champions of Jewish Emancipation in England. Sir John Simon, a native of Jamaica who had moved to London and there played a certain role in the struggle for Jewish equality of rights in the mid-nineteenth century, reminisced in 1891 that he himself had been prompted actively to participate in this struggle by the contrast between the freedom he had enjoyed in his native Jamaica and the disabilities which had still existed in England upon his arrival in the 1840s.[33]

In any case, long before the American Revolution the legal status of American Jews was for all practical purposes nearly equal to that of the other inhabitants. In fact, it is difficult to think of important disabilities which seriously affected their daily life and economic opportunities. Although the law formally drew no such distinction, it appears that the Jews in substance enjoyed all civic rights, or what the Germans used to call the *privatbürgerliche Gleichberechtigung*. For example, one of the greatest occupational obstacles confronting European Jews at that time consisted in their exclusion from Christian artisan guilds, a restriction which often made it impossible for them to engage in certain crafts. The history of the guilds' perennial struggle against Jewish competitors fills some of the darkest pages in the history of the European Jews from the Middle Ages to the nineteenth century. In contrast, the American guilds apparently admitted all qualified persons. Hence Jewish guild members are often mentioned in the sources as a matter of course. Myer Myers, for instance, was one of the most skilled silversmiths in pre-Revolutionary New York. Until today American museums highly treasure some of his products considered among the best of the colonial period. Myers was not only accepted as a member of the New York Gold and Silver Smith Society but he was even elected as its president, once seemingly a few years before the Revolution, and for the second time in 1786. Nor did Presbyterian churches hesitate to purchase his silver plates and use them for their offertories.[34]

Even in their political rights (what the Germans called the *bürgerliche Gleichberechtigung*) Jews suffered from few practical disabilities. Where they did, this was most frequently the indirect effect of some general regulations adopted against papists or Protestant dissenters from whichever denomination happened to be dominant in a particular colony (for instance, the Episcopalians in Virginia, or the Congregationalists in Massachusetts), and not because of any specific opposition to Jewish rights. As we recall, after 1737 the New York Jews again voted in elections without objections.

The contrast between the status of North American Jews and that of European Jewry of the time is well illustrated by the career of such a new immigrant as Francis Salvador. In 1773, this scion of a well-known Sephardic family in London, then aged twenty-six, settled in South Carolina. While still in London he had lost most of his fortune (including his wife's dowry), estimated at £73,000, as a result of risky business ventures, an earthquake in Lisbon, and a sharp decline of the shares of the Dutch East-India Company. He managed to salvage, however, a remnant of his possessions so that after his arrival in America he acquired a large estate of some 7,000 acres and many slaves. Most remarkably, within a year after his settlement he was elected to the First Provincial Congress of South Carolina. A year later he was reelected to a seat in the Second Congress which in 1776 became the General Legislature of the new State of South Carolina. In both these bodies he served on many committees and delivered speeches which were well received. Regrettably, the life of this prominent Jewish leader was cut short at the very beginning of his career when, after the outbreak of the Revolution, he fell in a battle with Indian partisans of England. In its eulogy a contemporary newspaper asserted that "the whole army regretted his loss, as he was universally loved and esteemed by them."[35]

The Revolution and Its Aftermath

The changes brought about by the American Revolution in the status of Jews were, therefore, more a matter of principle and psychology than of actual practice. During the Revolution some Jews participated in the struggle on the side of both belligerents. As a matter of record the American commanders paid little attention to the faith of volunteers, and until today we can distinguish between Jewish and non-Jewish servicemen or sympathizers only on the basis of names, or some specific chance information. Even after decades of research American scholars are still unable to pinpoint exactly the number of Jewish volunteers in the revolutionary forces, just as we cannot estimate precisely those who had remained loyal to the king. Between the two opposing camps of patriots and loyalists there undoubtedly also were many indifferent or neutral Jews, just as there were indifferent Christians. But it seems that their number was relatively small.[36]

In any case it appears that Jews participated in the war in a higher ratio than their percentage of the population. In Georgia, for example, we know the names of 6 Jewish soldiers stemming from a community numbering only 100 souls. Among the Jewish volunteers were a number of officers; among them Colonel Isaac Franks, one of George Washington's adjutants. Major Benjamin Nonez had immigrated from France in 1777 and immediately joined the patriot army. He participated in all battles in South Carolina and occasionally he served as an adjutant to Lafayette or Washington. Nor must we overlook the fact that the total number of American Jews at the time was about 2,000.[37]

The most remarkable aspect of the Jewish role in the revolutionary armies was that, after centuries of alienation from military service, Jews dared to take up arms. On the other hand, their neighbors looked at them as officers and soldiers equal in rank to their Christian counterparts. As far as we know there never arose a discipline problem between Christian soldiers and their Jewish superiors. If the Jewish officer David Franks, a coworker of the well-known traitor Benedict Arnold, was likewise suspected of treason, this suspicion did not arise because of his being a Jew, and he was ultimately completely exonerated. In Georgia Mordecai Sheftall, one of the first native-born colonists, served for a time as chairman of the patriotic "Parochial Committee" in Savannah. This Committee ventured to forbid one of the Protestant pastors to officiate because he was known as an English loyalist. After the outbreak of the war, Sheftall was appointed Deputy Commissary-General of Issues for South Carolina and Georgia and held other high offices in the "rebel" administration in Georgia. To be sure, after a short time he and his son fell into English hands. But even then they were treated like other prisoners of war and were released in September 1780.[38]

Needless to say, there also were Jew-baiters who accused Jews of treason in favor of the opposing side, of shirking military service, and of exploiting the existing economic crisis for their own benefit. Among the anti-Jewish writings of the period one might cite the following satirical poem:

Tax on tax young Belcour cries,
More imposts and a new excise,
A public debt's a public blessing
Which 'tis of course a crime to lessen.
Each day a fresh report he broaches,
That Spies and Jews may ride in coach[es].
Soldiers and Farmers don't despair,
Untax'd as yet are Earth and Air.[39]

Accusations of this type were frequently heard in both Europe and America long after Emancipation, too. But from the outset, the psychological attitude and behavior of the American Jews toward their accusers took on new forms. When a writer in a Charleston paper denounced the Jews of Georgia claiming that, "after taking every advantage in trade the times admitted of in the State of Georgia, as soon as it was attacked by an enemy, [they] fled here for an asylum with their ill-got wealth—dastardly turning their backs upon the country when in danger," a Jew challenged him in the same paper by pointing out that only women and children had saved themselves in this way. Jewish men, on the other hand, even if they happened to be in Charleston on business, hastened to return to Savannah in order to take part in the defense of their colony. The author of that anonymous reply signed "A real *American* and True hearted Israelite."[40]

Such an upright attitude in the defense of Jewish human and civic rights characterizes also the answer of four Newport Jews whom the local officers of the Rhode Island Brigade had accused (together with 73 Christian inhabitants) of being "enemical to the United Colonies in America" and of siding with the English regime. Admittedly the decisive majority of the city's Jewish population were sympathizers with the uprising. The seventy-seven accused men were asked to take an oath of loyalty to the Revolutionary cause. Three Jewish loyalists evaded the oath under the excuse that it was "contrary to the custom of Jews" to take such oaths. The communal rabbi, Isaac Touro, presented the additional argument that he still was a Dutch citizen. But the fourth man, Moses Michael Hays, answered in a long and proud letter. He explained his refusal by saying:

> I have and ever shall hold the strongest principles and attachments to the just rights and privileges of this my native land. . . . I decline subscribing the Test at present from these principles first that I deny ever being inimical to my country and call for my accusers and proof of conviction, Second, that I am an Israelite and am not allowed the liberty of a vote, or voice in common with the rest of the voters though consistent with the Constitution, and the other Colonies, Thirdly, because the Test is not general and consequently subject to many glaring inconveniences, Fourthly, Continental Congress nor the General Assembly of this nor the Legislatures of the other Colonies have never in this contest taken any notice or countenance respecting the society of Israelites to which I belong. When any rule, order or directions is made by the Congress or General Assembly I shall to the utmost of my power adhere to the same.

Hays persisted in his refusal until the patriotic command issued an order that all inhabitants without distinction should take that test. From that moment on Hays financially supported the patriots, and after the Revolution became one of the leaders of the city of Boston. He was among the founders of insurance companies, banks, and other important business institutions. For four years (1788-92) he officiated as Grandmaster of one of the Masonic lodges, with Paul Revere serving as his Vice-Chairman in 1791.[41]

This is not the place to analyze at length the impact of the American Revolution on Jewish Emancipation. In the extensive Congressional debates on the new Constitution, the Jewish question was not discussed at all. The Jews themselves referred to the problem of their rights only on special occasions. For example, when the respective Jewish communities sent their well-known letters to George Washington, they added, to cite Moses Seixas' address in behalf of the community of Newport, "Deprived as we hitherto have been of the invaluable rights of free citizens, we now—with a deep sense of gratitude to the Almighty Disposer of all events—behold a government erected by the majesty of the people—a government which to bigotry gives no sanction, to persecution no assistance, but generously affording to all liberty of conscience and immunities of citizenship, deeming everyone of whatever nation, tongue, or language, equal parts of the great governmental machine." In his replies Washington wrote in the same vein, even picking up the phrase of the Government "which gives to bigotry no sanction, to persecution no assistance."[42]

Of course, from the outset the American Constitution was based on freedom and equality of all faiths. It demanded that there should be no distinction between members of the various denominations in appointments to Federal offices (Article VI). The first ten Amendments, the so-called Bill of Rights, which were adopted after long debates in 1789 and became law in 1792, expressly forbade Congress to enact any law whatsoever which might make it possible for one denomination to dominate the others, or to forbid the free worship by any sect. This rule has been basically observed until today, and religious freedom and sectarianism are a most typical phenomenon in the public life of the United States. Even today new Christian sects arise without any difficulty. The two governmental censuses of religious bodies in America prepared in 1926 and 1936 have shown that in the course of ten years the number of religious denominations listed in that census rose from 212 to 256. It is quite likely that today they number in excess of 300.

However, we must not forget that the Constitution originally obligated only Congress and the Federal authorities. In the first decades, particularly, each state pursued its own legislative aims which often were in conflict with the spirit of the Federal law. Not surprisingly, the problem of States' Rights as contrasted with those of the Federal government became one of the most heatedly debated questions in the entire history of the United States. Even today it is a source of many controversies, differences of opinion among parties, and even contradictory judicial decisions. Hence in the first generation after the enactment of the Federal Constitution many quarrels arose in the states of New York, Pennsylvania, North Carolina, and Maryland over laws which directly or by inference, in actuality or potentiality, discriminated against Jews. Some of these questions are very complicated in their juridical import and their underlying social factors, and we need not dwell on them here. Suffice it to mention that as a rule whenever shown by representatives of Jews or other religious minorities that a particular bill might militate against the principle of complete equality, the legislatures were prepared to adopt clarifying or remedial amendments. Only in Maryland did the party struggle on this issue last until 1826.[43]

Nevertheless the general impression made on public opinion in America and other countries was that Jews were completely emancipated by the Revolution which, originally nurtured from French ideologies, now reciprocally influenced that in France. The French "Rights of Man" were to a large extent but an imitation of the American Bill of Rights. When in September 1791 the French Constituent Assembly stopped debating the Jewish issue and decided to grant the Ashkenazic Jews, too, full equality of rights "because they are men," we hear in these statements an echo of the writings of the French *philosophes*, as well as of the practical enactments of American statesmen. On April 20, 1833, at the inception of the struggle for Jewish Emancipation in England, Joseph Hume arose in Parliament and displayed to his colleagues a letter he had received from John Quincy Adams, the former President of the United States (1825-29). According to Hume, in this letter Adams "bears testimony to the advantage of the admission of the Jews to civil rights and declares that no set of men can be better subjects. He also expresses a hope that other countries throughout Europe will follow the example of the United States which have admitted Jews to a participation in the rights of free citizens." The impact on European Jews was even more pronounced. In 1822 Eduard Gans, a careful jurist, and

Leopold Zunz, generally a critical scholar, wrote to Mordecai
Manuel Noah that

> the better part of European Jews are looking with the larger
> countenance of hope to the United States of North America,
> happy once to exchange the miseries of their native soil for
> public freedom, granted there to every religion; and for that
> general happiness which, not the adherents of a privileged faith
> alone, but every citizen is entitled to share.[44]

The Reign of Custom and Public Opinion

Such legal evolution involved certain risks. Precisely because
the principles governing the legal status of religious minorities
were not spelled out in detail, the authorities might have introduced many far-reaching changes in the actual state of affairs
without altering the existing laws. That is why the importance of
courts in countries ruled by Anglo-Saxon legal traditions is much
greater than in those living under the dominance of the more
systematic Roman law. In this respect the Anglo-American legal
system resembles Jewish law, particularly the rabbinic oral law.
Under both systems the law can easily be adjusted to changing
social needs through a new interpretation of the traditional sources,
rather than through special enactments. In the United States
there is the additional incentive not to spell out matters too
clearly because of the potential conflict between Federal and
state laws. For this reason it has been possible, for example, for
the Southern states to preserve for a long time certain laws and
customs discriminating between white and black citizens despite
the principle of complete equality established by the Federal
Constitution and even regardless of some basic laws enacted by
these very states.

Under these circumstances the power of custom and shifting
public opinion is far greater in the United States than in those
countries where specific and detailed laws try logically to regulate most areas of life. Thomas Jefferson, the father of democratic
thought in the United States, fully recognized this fact. In his

interesting letter to the New York Judge Mordecai Manuel Noah of May 28, 1818, Jefferson thanked Noah for the speech at the "consecration" of the new Spanish and Portuguese synagogue in New York. The former President added:

> Our laws have applied the only antidote to this vice [of religious intolerance], protecting our religions, as they do our civil rights, by putting all on an equal footing. But more remains to be done, for although we are free by the law, we are not so in practice; public opinion erects itself into an Inquisition, exercises its office with as much fanaticism as fans the flames of an Auto-de-fé.[45]

From time to time there existed and still exist antisemitic movements in the United States which have sought to curtail the rights of Jews. Nor must one completely discount the danger that, if an avowedly antisemitic party were to seize the reins of government over the United States or even over one of the individual states, the existing laws might not be able to prevent discrimination against Jewish citizens in certain practical areas. But we must remember that even so detailed and outspoken a Constitution as that of Weimar enacted in 1919 could not withstand the basic change in public opinion and was quickly submerged under the Nazi deluge after but fourteen years.

In any case, Jewish historians ought to recognize the primacy of social and cultural factors, and to realize the extent to which even the legal evolution is much more influenced by these underlying trends than it reciprocally influences them which it, of course, also does. In evaluating the history of the legal and political Emancipation of the Jews, we ought to give due recognition to the force of those long-range basic socioeconomic and cultural factors, the slow unfolding of which cannot be precisely dated, and to attribute to them at least as much importance as to the more dramatic events of wars, revolutions, or constitutional enactments which take place before everyone's eyes at particular moments of history.

6 *From Colonial Mansion to Skyscraper: An Emerging Pattern of Hebraic Studies**

Hebraic studies in America date back to the days of the Pilgrim Fathers; their pursuit on a college level began in the first years of American college teaching at Harvard. In fact, few civilizations have been as Bible-minded as was colonial America, particularly colonial New England. True, the sociopolitical aims of the Puritan movement might well have been realized without the backing of scriptural texts. Herbert W. Schneider may be right in stating that "the Puritans, searching the Scriptures for texts relevant to their own particular needs, soon discovered the general similarity between themselves and the ancient Israelites."[1] Yet one must not overlook the inherent autonomy of legalistic thinking. Once set in motion, the chain of conclusions drawn from the law—in this case scriptural authority—always possesses a vitality of its own and generates decisions which otherwise may not be made.

Colonial Hebraists

It is not surprising, therefore, that the colonial divines, like their confreres in Europe, developed a deep interest in both the original Hebrew texts of the Old and the Greek originals of the New Testament, a curiosity long nurtured in Europe from the

* Paper delivered at the Inaugural Convocation of the Department of Hebraic Studies at Rutgers University, April 23, 1963; published 1964.

mainsprings of Protestantism and Humanism. Protestant leaders had always emphasized individual conscience and the obligation of each believer to search for truth directly in the Scripture, rather than to rely on authoritative traditions handed down by the Church. Humanism, on the other hand, had instilled in its devotees a profound reverence for the ancient languages and the recognition that no translation could ever equal the precision of the original. On the British Isles, in Holland, and elsewhere Hebraic studies had, therefore, been extensively cultivated throughout the sixteenth and seventeenth centuries. Many secondary schools as well as such leading colleges as those of Cambridge and Oxford, had sent out pupils versed in biblical Hebrew not only into the ministry but also into many lay walks of life. Some of their pupils settled in the American colonies. While no such towering Christian Hebraists as Pococke, Selden, or Lightfoot in England, Vitringa or Surenhusius in Holland arose on this side of the Atlantic—there existed neither the economic opportunities nor research facilities for such concentrated learning in the American colonies—a number of scholars assiduously labored in trying to penetrate the mysteries of the biblical texts. For them, too, the ideal scholar was, as he had become from the days of Erasmus, the *trilinguis homo,* the man who knew Hebrew, Greek, and Latin.

Curiosity of this type affected even such outstanding laymen as Governor William Bradford (1590-1657), one of the pilgrims on the "Mayflower" who served as governor of the Plymouth Colony. In the Preface to his *History of Plymouth Plantation* Bradford not only quoted a few biblical passages in Hebrew, together with a brief Hebrew-English vocabulary, but he movingly wrote:

> *Though I am growne aged, yet I have had a longing desire to see with my own eyes, something of that most ancient language, and holy tongue, in which the Law and oracles of God were write, and in which God and angels spake to the holy patriarch of old time; and what names were given to things from the*

creation. And though I cannot attain to much herein, yet I am refreshed, to have seen some glimpse hereof; (as Moyses saw the land of Canaan afarr of) my aime and desire is, to see how the words and phrases lye in the holy texte; and to discerne somewhat of the same for my own contente.[2]

Bradford's interest in the Hebrew Bible was not restricted to its religious message. Like the majority of his fellow dissenters from the Church of England, he believed that the new colonies ought to be founded entirely on the basis of biblical law. A classical expression of this trend was given by Reverend John Cotton, particularly in his work entitled *Moses, His Judicials*. Even more graphic was the title of that treatise as published in London, 1641: *An Abstract of the Lawes of New England, As They are Now Established*. The impact of biblical legislation has indeed been felt in almost all American colonies including New Jersey soon after its foundation three hundred years ago. This is true not only of East Jersey but also of West Jersey with its predominantly Quaker community. Even in the eighteenth century Ezra Stiles, President of Yale, believed that the Americans were really "Canaanites, though arriving hither by different routes." President Samuel Langdon of Harvard went even further. Invoking the antimonarchical passages from the Book of Samuel, as did most of the republicans of that period in both the Old and the New Worlds, Langdon exclaimed, "The Jewish government according to the original constitution which was divinely established, if considered merely in a civil view, was a perfect republic." It is small wonder, then, that statesmen like Roger Williams were eager to acquire familiarity with the Hebrew language. During his stay in England in 1643 Williams exchanged lessons with John Milton, the poet-statesman and fine Hebraist (he was even familiar with the rabbinic literature), who taught him several languages including Hebrew. He also claimed in another context, "I have longed after some trading with Jews themselves, for whose hard measure, I fear, the nations and England hath [have] yet a score to pay."[3]

Others, more fortunate, had the opportunity to study Hebrew in their earlier years, particularly after 1638 when the newly founded Harvard College instituted instruction in Hebrew as an integral part of its curriculum. The demands placed upon these early students were quite exacting. If we are to believe Cotton Mather, it was the college president's duty personally to inspect their progress. He daily "joined an *exposition* upon the chapters which they read out of Hebrew into Greek, from the Old Testament in the morning, and out of English into Greek, from the New Testament in the evening."[4] Evidently, students were not expected to offer their own translation from the Hebrew into Greek, a task which would tax the ingenuity of many a well-trained philologist today, but rather to recite passages from the Hebrew Bible, side by side with those from the Septuagint. We need not expect that their knowledge of either language was perfect. But the effort itself showed the intensity with which Hebrew studies were cultivated at a time when high-level instruction in other subjects was still in its infancy.

Similarly in writing theses the Harvard graduates often had to select rather complicated problems in Hebrew linguistics. The very first class graduating in 1642 was offered the choice of writing on the following topics: "Hebrew Is the Mother of Languages"; "The Hebrew Consonants and Vowels Are of Equal Age"; and "The Hatef Vowel Does Not Form a Syllable." The first two propositions are generally repudiated by scholars today. Yet most of these first Harvard students doubtless presented arguments in their support. One wishes one could peruse these examination papers but, unfortunately, none has been preserved.[5]

Serious Impediments

Intensive study of Hebrew at western universities was by no means an innovation. As early as 1311 the ecumenical Church Council of Vienne had adopted a canon demanding the establishment of Hebrew chairs at leading European universities. Such chairs were soon thereafter founded in Bologna, Salamanca, Paris, and Oxford. Rome had had one even earlier.[6] The main purpose of the Council and its spiritual mentor, Raymond Lull, was avowedly missionary. Knowledge of Hebrew, as well as of Arabic, was to enable Christian teachers to convert both Jews and Muslims to Christianity. No such aims could be pursued in seventeenth-century England or her colonies, since until the middle of the century there were no recognized Jewish communities in either area. The *Domus Conversorum* in London, which until 1609 still accommodated a few prospective converts and occasionally furnished Jewish experts in Hebrew to assist English scholars with respect to rabbinic commentaries, accommodated catechumens who required no further persuasion to turn Christian.[7] After the arrival of the first Jews in more significant numbers, to be sure, such conversionist motives reasserted themselves also on the American scene. One of the leading Christian Hebraists of the time, Cotton Mather, often prayed, as he did on July 18, 1696,

> *This day, from the Dust, where I lay prostrate, before the Lord, I lifted up my Cries: . . . For the Conversion of the Jewish Nation, and for my own having the Happiness, at some Time or other, to baptise a Jew, that should by my Ministry, be brought home unto the Lord.*[8]

However, even then the center of Hebraic studies in Cambridge, indeed all of Massachusetts, had but very few Jews who could be subject to missionary pressures.

Today, of course, conversionist aims are hardly ever pursued in the teaching of Hebrew. To begin with, the large majority of possible converts to Christianity neither know Hebrew nor require scriptural arguments from the Hebrew originals for their change of faith. If I may indulge in a personal recollection, I still vividly recall a visit from a young Christian theologian who had earned a Master's degree from a distinguished American university and a similar degree from an equally famous theological seminary. He explained to me that he wished to secure a Ph.D degree in Jewish history, in order to serve as a more effective missionary amongst the Jews. As in the case of other students I inquired about his earlier Hebrew training and told him that, before securing such a degree, he would have to be able to read with relative ease both classical and modern Hebrew. This was the last I heard of him. Evidently the Hebrew requirement now proved to be a deterrent for, rather than an instrument of, missionary ambitions.

Not that all early students of Hebrew were particularly eager to learn the language or were diligent enough in their pursuit of that knowledge. As in all other periods, problems of discipline loomed large in this field, too. As early as 1653, the young Harvard tutor Michael Wigglesworth complained, "My pupills all came to me y^{s}day to desire yy might ceas learning Hebrew: I wthstood it wth all ye reasō I could, yet all will not satisfy y^m."[9] We possess a similar testimony from a Yale graduate of 1788 who had attended Hebrew classes under President Ezra Stiles. Stiles, who had acquired a comprehensive knowledge of Hebrew and other Semitic languages, was able, while minister at Newport, to deepen it through many conversations with several visiting rabbis, including the Palestinian messenger, Haim Isaac Carigal. In his autobiography Jeremiah Mason, the Yale senior of 1788, reminisced that at that time "the President insisted that the whole class should undertake the study of Hebrew. We learned the alphabet, and worried through two or three Psalms, after a fashion; with the most of us it was mere pretense. . . . For the Hebrew he [Stiles] possessed a high veneration. He said one of the Psalms he tried to teach us would be the first we should hear sung in Heaven, and that he should be ashamed that any one of his pupils should be entirely ignorant of that holy language."[10] A similar dichotomy between teachers and students could also be detected at King's College, now Columbia University. Its first President, Samuel Johnson, appealed to the governors of his college "to countenance and encourage the study of Hebrew which I taught as many as would, as being the mother of all languages and eloquence, as well as the fountain of all knowledge and true wisdom." He even tried to persuade both governors and students that familiarity with Hebrew is "a fashionable study and even a gentleman's accomplishment." Yet eighteenth-century Columbia could no more boast of any distinguished Hebraists among its alumni than could Harvard or Yale.[11]

Apart from their normal inertia, the colonial students of Hebrew suffered from the outset from a deficiency of books. They did not even have enough English Bibles despite the huge output in Amsterdam. The Jewish printer, Joseph Athias, who in 1670 had received from the Dutch States-General a protective decree giving him the exclusive right to print English Bibles for fifteen years, boasted in 1687, "For several years I myself printed more than a million Bibles for England and Scotland. There is no plow boy or servant girl there without one."[12] Even in the 1720s when a recent convert, Judah Monis, taught Hebrew at Harvard, the students still had to copy by hand his newly written grammar until, with the aid of the Harvard administration, the book was printed in 1735 in 1,000 copies, every freshman and sophomore being obliged to buy a copy for 12 shillings and 2 pence. This was a relatively high price, considering that the entire fee for a quarter's tuition was just being raised then from 15 to 20 shillings.[13] Yet with their characteristic pioneering vigor, the colonists undertook to help themselves and, in 1640, produced an independent English translation of the Psalter, the so-called Bay Psalm Book. Prepared by Richard Mather in cooperation with Thomas Welde and John Elliot, this so-called "first book printed in North America" (there were, in fact, a couple of earlier insignificant publications) bore the characteristic title:

The/ Whole/ Booke of Psalmes/ Faithfully/ Translated into English/ Metre./ Whereunto is prefixed a discourse de-/ claring not only the lawfullness, but also/ the necessity of the heavenly Ordinance/ of singing Scripture Psalmes in/ the Churches of/ God./ Coll. III./ Let the word of God dwell plenteously in/ you, in all wisdome, teaching and exhort-/ ing one another in Psalmes, Himnes, and/ spiritual Songs, singing to the Lord with/ grace in your hearts./ Iames V./ If any be afflicted, let him pray, and if/ any be merry let him sing psalmes.

In order to be able to insert a number of Hebrew characters (for instance, in Psalm 119 to emphasize the Hebrew alphabetical acrostic), the Cambridge printer had secured in England a small selection of Hebrew font. These letters were large and rather crude; they were not provided with vowels. None the less they enabled the printer to put out a book representing the fruit of Hebrew learning among the early settlers. Such deficiencies in Hebrew fonts were to plague the successors of the Massachusetts Bay printers for many years thereafter.[14]

Scholars also suffered greatly from the lack of library resources. Although a number of generous collectors bequeathed their books to the Harvard College Library (some individual books had stemmed from Lightfoot's personal library, giving rise to the unsubstantiated rumor that the English savant had left his collection to Harvard), it took several generations before even this prime library in the country was able to furnish enough facilities for research students comparable with those available at many provincial colleges in the Old World.[15]

In contrast, we now possess in the United States some of the best printing presses and libraries in the world. True, Hebrew printing still offers some formidable obstacles for scholarly publications. But these arise mainly from the high costs concomitant with America's high standard of living and printers' wages. As to libraries, suffice it to say that we possess in the Jewish Theological Seminary of America much the largest accumulation of rare Hebraica and Judaica anywhere in the world, including well over 9,000 Hebrew manuscripts. Important collections exist also at other Jewish and non-Jewish institutions, including Columbia and Harvard Universities. Their number has been rapidly growing in recent years. For one example, a committee, aiding Professor Leon A. Feldman, has succeeded in assembling in a few years a good working library of Judaica and Hebraica at Rutgers—The State University. Of course, no collection will ever satisfy a librarian or a research scholar. In many cases, Americans may still have to travel to the Old World in the pursuit of archival and manuscript studies, although such researches, too, have been greatly facilitated by the development of microfilming and other advanced techniques. In short, one may indeed look forward to both study and intensive research at this and other great centers of Hebraic learning in the United States.

Broader Horizons

Remarkably, despite two centuries of experience and a still more venerable European tradition, it required persuasion, in 1838, to maintain instruction in Hebrew even at theological seminaries. A characteristic argument in its favor was advanced at that time by B. B. Edwards in his inaugural address as Professor of Hebrew at Andover Theological Seminary. In this speech, bearing the characteristic title, "Reasons for the Study of the Hebrew Language," Edwards advanced five main propositions:

1. An argument for the study of Hebrew may be derived from the fact, that great eminence in the pursuit, on the part of a few individuals, cannot be expected in the absence of a general cultivation of the language. . . .
2. My second argument for the more general study of the Hebrew is, that we may be better prepared to take all proper advantage of the immense stores of erudition on the general subject which have been collected in Germany. . . .
3. The importance of the study of the Hebrew language may be argued from its effect in strengthening the faith of the student in the genuineness and divine authority of the Scriptures. . . .
4. The influence of the study of the Hebrew Scriptures on the imagination and the taste. The imagination is not a modification of memory or of any of her mental faculty. It is an original quality of the mind. . . .
5. Another important consideration is the bearing of the study of Hebrew upon the missionary enterprise. The one hundred and twenty-two ordained missionaries sent out by

the American Board of Commissioners for Foreign Missions, sixty-nine of whom were educated at this institution, have published, with the aid of their assistants, between fifty and sixty millions of pages, a large proportion of which are parts of the Scriptures. The number of languages employed is twenty-nine, nine of which were first reduced to writing by these missionaries. In all this wide department of labor, augmenting every year, an accurate acquaintance with the original Hebrew is, of course, indispensable. . . .[16]

Edwards did not realize the contradiction inherent in his second argument and in those that followed. German biblical scholarship at that time was indeed entering the period of its highest achievement. But this success was predicated on an increasingly radical biblical criticism which was likely to undermine, rather than strengthen, the Christian faith. True, not all criticism was necessarily antireligious or even antitraditional. As a matter of record, one of the earliest classics in this field, Richard Simon's *Histoire critique du Vieux Testament*, published in Rotterdam, 1675, was actually written for apologetic purposes. A pious Catholic, Simon tried to persuade his readers that the Protestant criticism of the Catholic tradition militated against any real comprehension of Scripture, because the numerous contradictions and other puzzling statements in the Bible could be understood only with the aid of the traditional interpretation of the Vulgate and its authoritative commentators. He unconsciously took a leaf from a tenth-century rabbinic author who had in a similar vein argued against the criticism leveled by Karaite sectarians against the talmudic interpretation. Both authors overstressed the difficulties in the existing biblical texts not in order to weaken the faith of believers but rather in order to show the inescapability of relying on their respective religious traditions.[17]

Not surprisingly, other Catholic leaders viewed with alarm this devious way of combating heresy. They observed that many readers more intently pondered over Simon's questions than over his answers. Moreover, not long after Simon, Benedict Spinoza was able to use similar arguments in an opposite interpretation. The great philosopher spoke with contempt of the rabbinic efforts to harmonize the contradictions in the Old Testament books which, in his opinion, had been written in periods different from those ascribed to them by tradition. In the two centuries following Spinoza's *Theological-Political Tractate* biblical criticism became ever sharper; it was also supported by an ever greater accumulation of critical materials, philological, historical, and *religionsgeschichtlich*. Even if written by believers in the fundamentals of revelation, many of these critical works raised the specter of a conflict not so much between faith and reason, as between faith and history. The ever larger body of historical materials providing certain basic facts of ancient Jewish history opened up a deep gap between the scriptural narratives and verifiable historical facts which some contemporary theologians have, rather ineffectually, tried to bridge over by the assumption that religious verities, being metahistorical, cannot be undermined by purely historical data. Other, more secular-minded students, ever since the skeptical Enlightenment age, rejected all such compromises and, beginning with its extremist spokesmen, the Deists, were prepared to throw overboard the entire reliance on biblical revelation. It so happens that French Deism, together with the French democratic ideals, captured the imagination of some leading thinkers in the United States, a trend which necessarily reduced the fervor of American college students for the study of Hebrew. At the same time the rapid growth of American universities, their constant branching out into ever new disciplines, and the increasing pragmatism in the entire system of higher education militated against the continued stress on the study of Hebrew or the other "impractical" classical languages.[18]

On the other hand, the awakened scholarly interest in ancient Israel also broadened the horizons of study of the Jewish past in general. While the majority of devotees of Hebraic lore stopped with the second fall of Jerusalem and the story told by

Josephus—Josephus' works had indeed become a household object second only to the Bible in many colonial homes—some students now evinced interest also in the history of the Jewish people after the first century. Curiously, Jewish historians were not the main protagonists in this branch of modern research. Jewish chroniclers of all kinds, to be sure, recorded major events in their contemporary history. If they turned to the more remote Jewish past, their objective was to narrate primarily the story of anti-Jewish persecutions in the light of the then dominant "lachrymose conception of Jewish history." Others specialized in intellectual history, particularly through offering the record of successive generations of outstanding sages. Only one leading Jewish historian, Azariah de' Rossi, contributed a series of searching studies into various aspects of ancient Jewish history which he analyzed with the critical methods of an advanced Renaissance historian.[19]

However, no comprehensive history of the Jews since the first century appeared in any language until the Protestant minister Jacques (Jacob Christian) Basnage de Beauval, published his distinguished *Histoire des Juifs*, whose revised second edition appeared in fifteen volumes in The Hague, 1716-26. Despite certain faults emphasized by contemporary and later critics, this first modern history of post-biblical Jews and Judaism immediately captured the imagination of the public in England and other countries. Its first edition was soon reissued in an English translation in 1706, and again in an abridged form in two volumes in 1708. This work remained the permanent foundation stone for the whole historiography of the Jewish people written by both Christians and Jews for more than a century.[20]

Basnage's work, supplemented by his various monographs on more specific aspects of Jewish history, found eager readers also on this side of the Atlantic. Cotton Mather, especially, to whose comprehensive work *Magnalia* we owe most of our information about the Christian Hebraists in this country, also undertook to include in his encyclopedic work on the Bible a section devoted to the history of the Jewish people since the beginning of the

Christian era. Entitled *Biblia Americana,* his vast manuscript in six volumes still reposes unpublished in the Library of the Massachusetts Historical Society and only a few excerpts therefrom have seen the light of day. However, it is truly remarkable that an eighteenth-century New England divine should have spent so much time and effort on the postbiblical history of the Jews which generally was of much less interest to Christian students of theology. That Mather was not exclusively animated by intellectual curiosity may be noted from his aforementioned prayer for the conversion of Jews. The scope of this section clearly emerges from the following passage in a 1710 advertisement describing the ninth division of this work:

> A sort of Twenty-ninth chapter of the Acts; or an Elaborate and Entertaining History of what has befallen the Israelitish Nation, in every place, from the Birth of the Glorious Redeemer to this very day: And the present condition of that nation, the Reliques of the Ten as well as of the Two Tribes, and of their ancient sects, yet (several of them) Existing also, in the several parts of the world, where they are now dispersed, at this time, when their speedy Recovery from their sad and long Dispersion is hoped for.[21]

More fortunate was, in 1812, a lady historian, Hannah Adams, who succeeded in publishing a concise history of the Jews up to her own time. She herself described the purpose of her far from original contribution as follows:

> The history of the Jews since their dispersion has been but little investigated even by the literary part of the world, and is almost entirely unknown to the general mass of mankind. The design of this work, including the introduction, is to give a brief sketch of their situation, after their return from Babylonian captivity, to the nineteenth century. . . . The history of the Jews is remarkable, above that of all other nations, for the number and cruelty of the persecutions they have endured. They are venera-

ble for the antiquity of their origin. They are discriminated from
the rest of mankind by their wonderful destination, peculiar
habits and religious rites. Since the destruction of Jerusalem,
and their universal dispersion, we contemplate the singular
phenomenon of a nation subsisting for ages without its civil and
religious polity, and thus surviving its political existence.[22]

Remarkably, the Jewish share in this entire evolution of
Hebraic studies in America to the mid-nineteenth century was
quite insignificant. Here and there a visitor from Europe or
Palestine could offer the Christian ministers some novel interpretation of biblical passages and, more frequently, communicate
to them the fruits of his rabbinic or kabbalistic scholarship. In
his *Diary*, Ezra Stiles, in particular, frequently records the presence of such Jewish visitors in Newport upon whom he, as a
rule, called first, and who subsequently reciprocated his visits.
Understandably, the messianic idea loomed very large in all these
discussions. But Stiles and his Jewish interlocutors also freely
aired other areas of agreement or disagreement between Christianity and Judaism, as reflected in the Talmud or the chief kabbalistic classic, the *Zohar*.[23]

Native American Jews at that time possessed little Jewish
learning. As early as 1712-13, to be sure, Rev. John Sharpe, who
was agitating for a School Library in New York, asserted, "It
is possible also to learn Hebrew here, as well as in Europe, there
being a synagogue of Jews, and many ingenious men of that
nation from Poland, Hungary, Germany, etc." But this was an
evident overstatement. More typical of the intellectual level of
the Jews in colonial America is Ezra Stiles' report of March 27,
1771 that, when Isaac Hart of Newport, R. I. had received a
Hebrew letter from Hebron, Palestine he had to come to him, the
Congregational minister, to have it translated. A number of
letters written by such outstanding Jewish citizens as Bernard
Gratz of Philadelphia or the Revolutionary financier, Haym
Salomon, reveal how deficient their Hebrew knowledge really

was. And both leaders had left Silesia and Poland, respectively, where Hebrew learning was widespread, as adult young men. Even for his Yiddish letters Salomon required assistance from more learned contemporaries.[24] Similarly when Sampson Simson, an early Jewish graduate of Columbia College, had to deliver in 1800 a commencement address in Hebrew, his opus, dealing with "Historical Traits of the Jews from Their First Settlement in North America," though composed with the aid of Gershom Mendes Seixas, minister of the Spanish and Portuguese congregation in New York and trustee of that College, leaves linguistically much to be desired.[25] True, here and there we learn of a Jew tutoring non-Jewish students. An advertisement to this effect was published in five successive issues of the *Pennsylvania Packet* of March 1790 by one Abraham Cohen, son of the Reverend Jacob Cohen of Philadelphia. But there is no way of telling how much Hebrew he himself knew and was able to transmit to his disciples. The same man claimed to teach Spanish as well.[26] An occasional businessman like Israel B. Kursheedt possessed the necessary rabbinic learning to answer certain questions of law. Yet it was not until 1838 that the appointment of Dr. Isaac Nordheimer as professor of Semitic languages at New York University brought forth a reputable Jewish scholar who soon produced a comprehensive Hebrew grammar. His career was cut short, however, by his death in 1842 at the age of thirty-three.[27]

Renewed Upsurge

The change since 1838 has indeed been startling. While the progressive secularization of American life has greatly reduced the Bible-mindedness of the population, and while classical studies in general were constantly losing ground particularly during the first decades of this century, the study of Hebrew at, as well as outside, universities was making speedy progress. The main reasons doubtless were the very large Jewish immigration to this country which brought in its wake a considerable number of well-trained scholars, rabbis, and teachers as well as informed laymen, and, on the other hand, the American people's broadening interests in foreign countries and civilizations. The large Central-European immigration which had gathered momentum in the mid-1830s brought with it a number of students of Jewish lore. True, as late as 1848, when a permit for kosher wine had to be secured from New York, a translation of the particular Hebrew text was prepared by William L. Roy, a Christian professor of Oriental languages. But it is likely that the reason for this particular selection was to persuade some government official of the correctness of that rendition. In fact, by 1846 Max Lilienthal, a German rabbi who had arrived via Russia in New York, allegedly could organize a regular *Hebrah Shas*, a group of members devoted to the study of the Talmud. Some years later a thirteen-year-old boy, son of Rabbi Jacob Silberman, a native of Suwalki, was able to deliver a Bar Mitzvah speech studded with rabbinic quotations along the lines of similar orations delivered by learned thirteen-year-old boys in eastern Europe. The young man's uncle, H. S. Silberman, even included that address in his volume *Or Ya'aqob* published in Jerusalem, 1859. Apologizing for that inclusion, Silberman wrote:

> Incidentally, it may serve to show the world that also in America it is possible to make Jewish scholars of children, for, as the Talmud has it: "Whoever wishes to do a good deed receives divine assistance for its accomplishment." The speaker was born and brought up in America, in Hazelton, Pennsylvania. I may truthfully say, however, that the motive prompting me to publish this address is not a desire to reflect glory upon myself nor my family, but purely and simply the correction of a common error. It is generally supposed that America is no country in which children can be educated in the Jewish lore. This is a grave mistake. While the American custom is to have children take up business, yet, whoever cares to bring up his children as scholars can readily accomplish it. It would indeed be a libel upon that country to presume that America causes an estrangement from our sacred laws.

Finally, in 1860, the first rabbinic book was written and published in New York. Although it merely was a none-too-original commentary on the *Sayings of the Fathers*, it served to open the floodgates of an ever increasing stream of Hebrew and Yiddish publications in this country.[28]

The multiplication of American colleges and universities and the stupendous numerical growth of university-trained intellectuals have also quickened the general interest in Hebraic studies, as in many other fields of cultural endeavor. This growth is now proceeding at an unprecedented speed and it was conservatively estimated that by 1975 America's college and university enrollment would probably skyrocket to more than 13,000,000 students.[29] Undoubtedly, the more recent disenchantment of American youth with the various "isms" and a certain revival of religious feelings during the postwar era have likewise contributed their share to focusing its attention on the study of religion, including Judaism.[30]

At the same time the rise of the State of Israel, concomitant with the United States' new role in world affairs, brought about an intensification of interest in the Middle East as part of the expanding area studies at American universities. Front page news in the daily papers relating to developments in Mandatory Palestine, the Israel War of Independence or the Sinai campaign could no more be ignored than could other important world news which in recent years have begun affecting the daily life and the outlook of the average American in an unprecedented degree. These dramatic events may at times have receded into the background before 1967—I still recall an Israeli visitor at my home speaking with elation of the disappearance of Israeli reports from the front pages—but America's involvement in international affairs and the American public's interests in developments in other countries have become an abiding ingredient of American culture.

It is small wonder, then, that surveys conducted in 1940 and 1950 have shown an increasing number of American colleges, universities, and seminaries offering courses in the Hebrew language and literature, in Jewish history and religion. The latest data available show that, in 1940, a total of 124 American schools of higher learning included such offerings in their curricula. Only 47 of these were theological seminaries. Ten years later the total number increased to 206 institutions, rising again to 245 by 1957. These 245 institutions include 61 undergraduate colleges, 72 universities, and 112 seminaries. Even more noteworthy was the increase in enrollments and course offerings. During the seven years of 1950-57, when the number of institutions increased by 20 percent, that of courses offered, and of students taking them, jumped by 100 percent.[31]

In line with this evolution was the establishment of chairs and even whole departments devoted to Jewish studies (including Jewish history, literature, and religion) at numerous American colleges and universities. According to a survey published in 1966, no less than 92 such institutions gave full-time instruction in this field.[32]

Their number has further increased since. The growing interest in this field has vividly been demonstrated to me personally in the last few years by the number of inquiries from colleges and universities asking for recommendations of qualified instructors in Hebrew civilization. I was often unable to supply a sufficient number of such names. This situation sharply contrasted with that of 1929-30 when I started teaching at Columbia University and when such positions were extremely scarce. The general growth of that profession is also illustrated by the number of professional organizations devoted to the cultivation of biblical and other Hebraic studies. The Society of Biblical Literature and Exegesis, the National Association of Biblical Instructors, and the National Association of Professors of Hebrew now effectively supplement the several important Jewish scholarly organizations which for many years past have cultivated the broad spectrum of Jewish research from the biblical period to the present.

Quantitative expansion has been accompanied by qualitative improvement in methods of instruction and the widening of the subjects taught in these courses. Even the linguistic studies of

Hebrew have undergone a great transformation. Long cultivated exclusively by philologists primarily interested in Hebrew as part of Semitic languages, Hebrew had interveningly become a living language with an entirely new vocabulary and even a good deal of slang. A miraculous evolution of but two generations has changed this "holy tongue" of old into a secular medium of communication in daily affairs, as well as an instrument for the cultivation of various natural and social sciences. For many years past the Hebrew Language Academy in Jerusalem has been kept busy in supervising the usage of new scientific and technical terms in all walks of life. It certainly has not been easy for American teachers of Hebrew to keep up with this constant progress which has but partially been reflected in the highly articulate Israeli press and scientific publications. With their customary humor the Israelis have graphically described this change: When twenty years ago a customer entering a store in Tel Aviv spoke a literary Hebrew, he was asked: "Are you a teacher?" Today such a customer is asked: "Are you a tourist?" This task of "keeping up" has been greatly facilitated, however, by the frequent visits of our teachers to Israel and the corresponding exchanges of Israeli visitors to this country.

Equally significant has been the growing interest in various novel aspects of Jewish and Israeli life in the past and the present. The very biblical studies have achieved new meaning through the ever expanding archeological discoveries and the refined methods of scholarly investigation. The avidity with which were greeted in recent years the discovery and decipherment of a large Ugaritic library dating from approximately the days of Moses and the still more widely heralded Dead Sea Scrolls has demonstrated to the people at large how much the biblical specialist has learned from the diggings in the soil of Israel and its neighboring lands. Simultaneously, great curiosity, both professional and lay, has been awakened about the contemporary life of the new country, its pioneering achievements over the last half century, and the major contributions it was making to the art of building a new state in limited space and with even more limited natural resources. The great tragedy of European Jewry under the Nazi regime, its causes and effects, including such outstanding episodes as the Warsaw uprising or the Eichmann trial, have likewise attracted wide attention among the general public and scholars alike. Psychologists, psychiatrists, and social scientists have pondered over the problems of the enduring character of antisemitism and the means of combatting it under different civilizations. From other angles, demographists have tried to ascertain the number, age and sex distribution, and other population aspects of the Jewish minority which, with still other approaches, has been analyzed by sociologists, economists, and students of religion. Anthropologists found great interest in studying such exotic Jewish groups as the Ethiopian Falashas, the Cochin Beni Israel, the Caucasian Mountain Jews, or even the more familiar ethnological manifestations which had arisen from the long-isolated life of the Yemenite, Bokharan, and Kurdish Jews. Linguists of all nationalities had a field day in studying the peculiarities of the Jewish dialects of Yiddish, Ladino, Judeo-Arabic, or Judeo-Persian.

Between these increasingly ramified researches in biblical antiquity and contemporary Jewry the eighteen centuries of Jewish life in the dispersion have also been receiving increasing attention. General American scholarship is realizing more and more that medieval and modern Jewish history is not merely a theological discipline relating to the history of a Church or a religion, but part and parcel of the history of western as well as Islamic civilization. What the founders of the "Science of Judaism" in the early nineteenth century had dreamed of as their ultimate desideratum, has come true in the United States and other parts of the world. Leopold Zunz, Ludwig Philippson, and others yearningly looked forward to the time when Jewish studies would be cultivated not only at theological seminaries but also through special chairs and departments established at universities and treated there on a par with other humanistic or social science disciplines. Such departments and chairs are now in full operation at a number of American, British, and other universities, in addition to the schools of higher learning in Israel. The Hebrew University in Jerusalem alone has no less than five professors specializing in five different periods of Jewish history. An even larger number has dedicated itself to Bible studies, archeology, rabbinic learning, Jewish mysticism, Hebrew linguistics, modern Hebrew literature, contemporary Jewish life, and other branches of Jewish learning. No American university, not even those operating under Jewish sponsorship like Brandeis or Yeshiva University, can provide such a detailed program of instruction in this field. However, the growth of the academic interest and the increasing availability of qualified personnel augur well for the future of Jewish studies in the United States.

7 American Jewish Communal Pioneering*

The first three centuries of Jewish communal experience on this continent were primarily a period of constant communal exploration and pioneering. True, from its inception the Jewish people has been called upon to perform pioneering services. It first pioneered in the field of religion, introducing the doctrines of ethical and historical monotheism to the far corners of the western world. Twice in antiquity, and once again in our time, it has pioneered in colonizing a state without a mother country to support it. Throughout the history of its dispersion, it had to perform ever new noteworthy economic functions. At the same time, in order to survive under constantly changing external conditions, it had to blaze many a new path in communal co-operation. In our day, when most western men attend churches and mosques, it is difficult for us to imagine, for example, what a major revolution the synagogue represented in the ancient modes of worship.

It is small wonder, therefore, that upon their arrival in this country, Jews found themselves in a most congenial environment. Here the entire nation was a nation of pioneers, not only pioneers of the brawn, but also pioneers of the brain; not only covered-wagon explorers, but also inventors, scientists, efficiency experts, educators. Jews caught the spirit of America and synthesized it with their own heritage. Their new pioneering spirit found an

* Address of the President, delivered at the Fifty-second Annual Meeting of the American Jewish Historical Society held in Philadelphia, February 20, 1954; and published in *PAJHS*, XLIII (1953-54), 133-50.

outlet in many fields of economic endeavor and, from the outset, extended also to their own communal affairs.

Freedom Versus Authority

To begin with, the American Jewish community had to be built along unaccustomed lines. Ever since ancient times the communities of the Old World enjoyed, as a rule, the support of government and public law. Their communal control, to be sure, had often been abused by the powers that were for their own purposes, particularly for fiscal exaction. Yet for that very reason emperors and kings, bishops and municipalities found it to their advantage to strengthen the Jewish communal bonds and the authority of communal organs. In many respects, indeed, the ghetto community resembled a state within the state. In modern times when Emancipation had undermined the structure of Jewish self-government, the Jewish communities of central and eastern Europe still enjoyed a great measure of control over their members. Even in the twentieth century a Jew in Berlin or Budapest, Vienna, Warsaw, or Mussolini's Rome was born into his community. He belonged to it so long as he did not make a public declaration that he did not wish to belong. In many countries, he was required to declare that he was no longer a Jew. If he was a member of the community he was subject to communal taxation, enforced taxation of the kind collected by states and municipalities. In many countries and periods he was also subservient to communal law enforcement and socioeconomic regimentation.

All this was absent in America. The first twenty-three Jews, who in September 1654 arrived on these shores and unwittingly organized the first Jewish community in North America only one generation after the arrival of the Pilgrim Fathers, were allowed to settle in New Amsterdam under the condition that they would not perform public worship. This restraint was imposed by the ruling Dutch Reformed Church not only on Jews but on such other religious minorities as the Lutherans. In 1659, the Lutheran preacher, Johannes Ernestus Gutwasser, was deported because he dared to preach to his congregation. From 1654 on, the Jewish community of New York had to struggle step by step in order to secure the necessary permits for the erection of those basic communal institutions which were taken for granted in any Old World township. It took nearly thirty years before New York Jewry was granted formal permission to establish a cemetery. Not until 1728 could it dream of building a synagogue of its own. In this battle for their own religious freedom, in which they were aided at the beginning by their influential coreligionists in Amsterdam, the Jews helped blaze the path for the ultimate adoption of the principles of liberty of conscience and freedom of association. But from its beginning during the colonial period, and again under the United States constitutional separation of state and Church after the Revolution, the American Jewish community could subsist only because of the voluntary allegiance of its members, and carry out its tasks with their voluntary contributions and their voluntary submission to communal discipline and authority.

This new situation, of course, confronted not only Jews but, to an even greater extent, those Christian Churches which had long been "established"—that is, supported by government fiat, in their home countries. Here, George Washington had to expostulate in his letter to George Mason of October 3, 1785, that,

> although no man's sentiments are more opposed to any kind of restraint upon religious principles than mine are, yet I must confess, that I am not amongst the number of those who are so much alarmed at the thoughts of making people pay towards the support of that which they profess, if of the denomination of Christians or declare themselves Jews, Mahometans or otherwise, and thereby obtain proper relief.[1]

Nevertheless the Churches of all denominations began to flourish after the removal of these governmental crutches. A keen visitor like Harriet Martineau wrote admiringly in 1837,

that the event has fully justified the confidence of those who
have faith enough in Christianity to see that it needs no protection from the state, but will commend itself to human hearts
better without.[2]

One must bear in mind, however, that for more than half of the
three-hundred-year period a measure of Jewish communal control
was safeguarded by the existence in each Jewish community of but
a single congregation, or at the most, as in Philadelphia after 1802,
of one each of the Sephardic and Ashkenazic rituals. Even New
York possessed only Shearith Israel until the formation of B'nai
Jeshurun in 1825. Although founded by Spanish-Portuguese immigrants and always adhering to the Sephardic ritual, it embraced all
professing Jews in the city. In fact, it has been estimated that
by the time it erected its first synagogue in 1728-1733, this Spanish
and Portuguese Congregation included a majority of Ashkenazic
members. So long as there was only one synagogue (or one synagogue of each rite) in town, its leadership could control recalcitrant
minorities by threats of such ecclesiastical censures as the refusal
of synagogue honors, non-admission of children to the Jewish
school, and, in more drastic cases, refusal of synagogue rites at
weddings or burials. Responding to the new ideals of religious
freedom, Shearith Israel's post-Revolutionary constitution of 1786
replaced some of these extreme sanctions by a system of fines,
which ranged to £5 for certain offenses. Even the new constitution
of 1790 still threatened that

any *Yehudi* violating any religious laws by eating *Trafa, Breaking
the Sabbath* or any other sacred day—shall not be called to the
Sepher [recitation from the scroll of law] or receive any other
Mitzva [synagogue function] or be eligible to any office in this
congregation.[3]

Twenty years later Rodeph Shalom Congregation of Philadelphia
adopted a constitution imposing a fine of twenty-five cents on any
member who failed to attend Friday night or Saturday morning

services, without valid excuse, or withdrew from such services before their completion.[4]

Controls of this kind were greatly weakened when a number of congregations began competing for members in the same locality. Together with the general decline of religious observance and the growing struggle between Reform and Orthodoxy, such decentralization, aggravated by the proliferation of various extra-synagogal societies, totally undermined the authority of the religious leaders. It is estimated that by 1860 New York already embraced twenty-seven Jewish congregations. Their number increased in New York State to 1,560 according to the United States Census of Religious Bodies in 1936, and doubtless went up further in the last three decades. Not surprisingly, therefore, we read in a remarkable letter on "The Synagogue Question" addressed by one S. to the editor of the *Jewish Messenger* (published October 11, 1878), that only a small percentage of New York Jews had joined regular congregations. The writer blamed this phenomenon, as we recall, on the high membership dues, and partly on the then fashionable frequent changes in ritual. But he also pointed out that there was little practical inducement in regular membership, since Mutual Benefit Societies were providing burial grounds at less cost. Even rabbis could easily be secured to officiate at weddings at little expense. Perhaps the only tangible advantage, the correspondent concluded, in joining a synagogue consisted in the members' children attending religious schools. Of course, with the subsequent establishment of communal Talmud Torahs, Sholem Aleichem schools, and the like, even this advantage greatly diminished.

Most remarkable in this entire evolution, however, is not the fact that there have been so many unsynagogued Jews, especially in the larger communities, but rather that so many have founded and joined ever new congregations. With great devotion and self-sacrifice they erected thousands of synagogue buildings, many of them monumental structures—the fascinating story of whose architectural evolution has been fully described by Mrs. Rachel Wischnitzer[5]—and pioneered along novel paths of intercongregational and country-wide cooperation. Whatever the reasons, it is truly astonishing that the leadership of the Orthodox, Reform, and Conservative wings in religious Jewry are able to point to the more than doubling of the membership of their respective congregations since the beginning of the Second World War.

Geographic Expansion

Communal pioneering was also kept alive by the necessity for American Jews to found new communities in ever new areas. Like their fellow Americans of other faiths, they have been an extremely mobile group, participating in the great westward migration and other important population movements. No sooner, for example, did the Jews of America learn about the discovery of gold in California, than the gold rush fever seized them, too, and many of them found their way across the continent to the new promised land. Even foreign Jews were so deeply impressed by the novel Jewish life taking roots in California soil, that the letter of authorization issued by Jerusalem authorities to a new messenger who was to visit the United States in behalf of Palestine relief, was addressed to the Jewish communities of the United States of America and California.[6] The new settlers were, indeed, greatly concerned with their religious and communal welfare. A private letter addressed to the *Jewish Chronicle* in London informed that leading Anglo-Jewish weekly in March, 1850, that "a party of Jews had left New York to settle and form a congregation in California taking with them a Shoḥet and Sefer Torah."

New communities of this kind sprang up also in the Middle West and in the South. A year after the aforementioned letter (July 25, 1851), the Reverend Samuel M. Isaacs reported to the *Jewish Chronicle* about his journey from New York to Chicago noting, with obvious exaggeration, that "not a village on my route was without an Israelite, much less the towns." He complained, bitterly, however, of the lack of English-speaking rabbis to serve these nascent congregations.[7] Here Isaacs echoed a warning, sounded more broadly by Isaac Mayer Wise three years earlier.

> We have no system for our worship, nor for our ministry and
> schools, and we are therefore divided in as many fragments as
> there are congregations in North America. It is lamentable, but
> true, that if we do not unite ourselves betimes to devise a prac-
> ticable system for the ministry and religious education at large,
> —if we do not take care that better educated men fill the pulpit
> and the schoolmaster's chair,—if we do not stimulate all the
> congregations to establish good schools, and to institute a reform
> in their Synagogues on modern Jewish principles,—the house of
> the Lord will be desolate, or nearly so, in less than ten years. . . .[8]

We shall presently see how the community, especially under
Wise's own leadership, tried to meet the need of both providing
English-trained rabbis and stemming the process of fragmentation.

Not all the communities established in the nineteenth century
are still functioning today. Many a prosperous community before
the Civil War, particularly in the South, has disappeared, partly
because of economic shifts, and partly because of the strong assimilatory forces of the environment. Yet one must no more see signs
of inner decay and disintegration in such Jewish "ghost communities" than in the innumerable "ghost towns" of the general
American civilization. For each "ghost community" one can readily
mention several communities which had since sprung up even in
the South. Certainly no southern community has ever reached the
size and affluence of contemporary Miami. That Floridian city,
which in 1940 counted only some 7,500 Jews, now embraces a
community of well over 140,000 permanent residents, probably
being the sixth largest Jewish community in the country.

Nor did the westward movement cease with the end of the nineteenth century. It is not generally realized that the decades of the
1940s-1970s were the greatest decades of westward migration in
American history. Jews have participated fully in that movement.
Dallas, Fort Worth, Houston, Phoenix, and Tucson, small communities but thirty years ago, now figure among the more important Jewish settlements in the United States. Los Angeles,
rarely mentioned in the annals of Jewish history at the beginning

of this century—the *Jewish Encyclopedia* did not consider it necessary to devote to that community, numbering in 1904 only some
3,000 Jews, more than 27 lines—is now the second-largest Jewish
community in the country, just as the Los Angeles metropolitan
area as a whole has displaced that of Chicago as the second largest
American metropolis.

Perhaps the most significant recent developments have consisted
in the transfer of many Jews and non-Jews into suburban settlements. This movement, promoted to a large extent by Jewish
pioneers and builders, has already set in motion forces which are
likely to revolutionize the general and Jewish ways of living in
this country. Its strong impact, like that of the growth of the
western centers, has already begun to make itself felt in the Jewish community and created some unprecedented religious and cultural challenges.[9]

Newer Forms

A pioneering community has never been subdued by such challenges, but was rather stimulated by them to new creative efforts.
Confronted with the problem, so despairingly mentioned by Isaacs,
of securing English-speaking rabbis and teachers, the American
Jews proceeded with the creation of the necessary institutions of
learning. Within a few years after Isaac's pessimistic observation,
Isaac Leeser organized the Maimonides College in Philadelphia
(1867-1873).[10] This College was the predecessor of the Hebrew
Union College in Cincinnati, the Jewish Theological Seminary of
America, the Isaac Elchanan Yeshiva, now Yeshiva University, the
Hebrew Theological College in Chicago, as well as of the numerous teachers colleges training instructors in Hebrew and Yiddish. These schools have become part of an educational structure
which has astounded the outside world, even though its effectiveness has often been subjected to sharp criticisms from within.
Insofar as they were constructive, these criticisms themselves were
a sign of inner vitality and led to the perennial quest for new
answers to many an educational enigma.

In general, whenever the community felt a particular need strongly enough it found means of satisfying it without recourse to legal enforcement, through persuasion and the usual minor pressures of public opinion. In a well-known presidential address at the American Historical Association, Professor Arthur M. Schlesinger spoke of the American "passion for associational activity [which] became a sovereign principle of life." He also quoted Will Rogers' quip that "two Americans can't meet on the street without one banging the gavel and calling the other to order."[11] Jews found themselves in this respect, too, in a congenial environment. Even in the Old World they distinguished themselves by their predilection for charitable, educational, and other societies. For example, the community of Rome in the seventeenth century had twenty charitable and educational associations which operated outside the formal community. The official communal organs fully supported these autonomous bodies and, in 1617, even provided that any citizen refusing to stand with a box and solicit donations in public should be punished by a fine. In Amsterdam, two centuries later, the will of a distinguished philanthropist, B. Cohen, included bequests for 210 charitable and educational associations, to which he had more or less regularly contributed before his demise.[12] With such a millennial heritage behind them it is not astonishing that American Jews soon founded innumerable voluntary associations of their own, including some which were wholly unprecedented in character.

In 1850, for example, the Jews of Philadelphia organized the first Young Men's Hebrew Literary Association. The name is characteristic. Evidently it was not a borrowing from the Christian "Y," because the first Young Men's Christian Association was formed more than a year later, in December 1851. However, when Leeser and his associates in Philadelphia felt that there was a need for Jews, at that time particularly German Jews, to band together for literary purposes, they organized an association which quickly transcended the scope of the usual literary circles. This organization was followed by many others in Baltimore, New York, Boston, and elsewhere. The German Jews had long been known as voracious readers and booklovers. So impressed was, as we recall, the well-known political theorist, Francis Lieber, that in 1869 he commented that "the German Jews in America gain in influence daily, being rich, intelligent and educated, or at least seeking education. They read better books than the rest of the Germans, the booksellers tell me."[13]

These literary associations were bent upon cultivating the minds only. They often included in their statutes provisions against purely social activities, such as card playing or dancing. However, there were other Jews, especially among the young, who wished to get together principally on a social basis. As early as 1761, the seven Jewish families then living in Newport organized a Jewish social club. To keep its purely social character intact, members were forbidden to discuss synagogue affairs there, under a fine of four bottles of good wine for each offense.[14] The German and later East-European mass immigration further stimulated the growth of such informal clubs, and especially of fraternal orders.

Among the latter one need but refer to the rise of the Independent Order of B'nai B'rith, organized by Henry Jones and eleven German-Jewish associates in Essex Street, New York, in 1843. From its inception this organization pursued ambitious and highly diversified aims. According to the preamble of its constitution

> B'nai B'rith has taken upon itself the mission of uniting Israelites in the work of promoting their highest interests and those of humanity; of developing and elevating the mental and moral character of the people of our faith; of inculcating the purest principles of philanthropy, honor and patriotism; of supporting science and art; alleviating the wants of the poor and needy; visiting and attending the sick; coming to the rescue of the victims of persecution; providing for, protecting and assisting the widow and orphan on the broadest principles of humanity.[15]

Stimulated in part, as were many other Jewish communal activities, by the negative factor of anti-Jewish discrimination; in this case non-admission of Jews to the existing Masonic lodges, this fraternal order spread rapidly to other parts of the city and the country.

In 1866, the then Grand Sar, Benjamin F. Peixotto, could already address his circular letter to sixty existing lodges, including nine formed in the preceding year. Before long the B'nai B'rith achieved an international following, many lodges being organized in the Central-European heartland of the old communities.

Similarly phenomenal was the development of another typically American Jewish institution: the Jewish center. Since the establishment of the first institution of this kind in 1854 the Jewish Center movement has spread all over the land; in fact to many countries abroad. Not only are there now some three hundred and fifty Jewish Centers in the United States and Canada, but centers have also been established in such distant communities as Johannesburg and Jerusalem.[16]

International Cooperation

Precisely because they had to rely on purely voluntary loyalties, the American Jewish communal organs required constant democratic cooperation within each community and between one community and another. Unlike the European communities which usually started their historic career with the building of a synagogue and cemetery out of their own resources, American Jews erected all their first communal structures through cooperative endeavor. When in 1728, three-quarters of a century after its foundation, Shearith Israel finally found itself in a position to build a house of worship, it issued a call for financial assistance to several groups and individuals residing in the West Indies and England. "We earnestly request you all," the New York elders wrote to their confreres in Jamaica, "as well as your Haham to communicate it to the members of your holy Kahal so they may contribute all they can to the building of a holy synagogue which we have decided to erect, with the help of God."[17] Without the financial support coming from other countries, particularly Great Britain, in a sort of reverse Joint Distribution Committee operation, the first North American synagogue on Mill Street in New York could not have been consecrated in 1733. Two decades later the community of

Newport embarked upon the building of its beautiful synagogue which has since become a national shrine. Although several leaders of the Newport community, including Aaron Lopez, were quite wealthy, they nevertheless felt the need of appealing to Shearith Israel and other communities for assistance. Once again it was interterritorial cooperation of Jews which made possible the erection of this noteworthy structure. Even in the nineteenth century such appeals continued. In 1825, the Hebrew Congregation of Cincinnati addressed to that of Charleston a letter of solicitation which included the following telling passages:

> Being deputed by our Congregation in this place, as their Committee to address you in behalf of our holy Religion, separated as we are and scattered through the wilds of America as children of the same family and faith, we consider it as our duty to apply to you for assistance in the erection of a House to worship the God of our forefathers, agreeably to the Jewish faith; we have always performed all in our power to promote Judaism and for the last four or five years, we have congregated where a few years before nothing was heard but the howling of wild beasts, and the more hideous cry of savage man . . . . It is also worthy of remark that there is not a congregation within 500 miles of this city and we presume it is well known how easy of access we are to New Orleans, and we are well informed that had we a Synagogue here, hundreds from that City who now know and see nothing of their religion would frequently attend here during holidays.[18]

Needless to say, the Jews of New Orleans preferred to worship in their own synagogue and within three years organized an independent congregation. However, as late as 1863, the Jews of Washington, D. C. could build their first synagogue only with the aid of coreligionists from other communities.[19]

Inter-communal cooperation continued in ever new forms, especially in such traditionally hallowed areas as Palestine relief. In those very centuries when the local congregations appealed for outside help for their synagogues, they responded to many calls from the Holy Land, whose memory remained undimmed in the minds of American, as of all other Jews. Ever since Haim (Ḥayyim) Isaac Carigal's visits in America during the colonial period, so graphically described by Ezra Stiles, many Palestinian messengers arrived on these shores carrying on their age-old mission of raising funds for the poor of the four holy cities. Incidentally, however, they injected here, as elsewhere, significant cultural and religious elements into the life of the local communities, and helped cement the interterritorial unity of the Jewish people. In one respect, moreover, the manuscript now located at the Hebrew University Library, which recorded the four journeys of Palestinian messengers to America between 1849 and 1879, and excerpts from which my wife and I published in 1943,[20] seems to offer a unique record. At least I have not come across any other instance in which messengers submitted a ledger to individual donors and asked them to enter there their names and the amounts, however small, which they contributed. For the most part the contributions ranged only from fifty cents to one dollar. This democratic procedure was quite appropriate to the American environment. The incidental gain to American Jewish history certainly could not have been foretold at that time. Now some of these entries represent the only surviving vestiges of many of these early communal pioneers.

American contributions to Palestine Jewry were not to remain limited to financial contributions alone, even when the latter began reaching the staggering dimensions of the United Jewish Appeal, and the numerous special campaigns. It is not generally known, but it is nevertheless a fact, that although its antecedents go back to groping attempts in Odessa in 1905, the first comprehensive Ḥalutz organization, that extraordinarily effective training ground for Palestine pioneers, was established in the United States during the First World War (1917). It was, indeed, fitting that a pioneering organization should spring up in the midst of an ever pioneering community. Similarly, Israel's armed forces owe a great debt of gratitude to American Jewry. While the *Hashomer*, the local militia which kept guard over the early colonies, was a native growth of the Palestinian soil antedating 1914, it was not until

World War I that the first regular army unit manned by Jews was formed, namely the so-called Jewish Legion which fought under General Sir Edmund Allenby in the Palestine campaign of 1918. The organization of the Legion and much of its personnel came from America, including such of its temporary residents as Vladimir Zeev Jabotinsky and David Ben-Gurion.

Human Welfare's Expanding Frontiers

American Jewry's best known pioneering activities have been in the area of charity and public welfare. Not only because of Stuyvesant's well-known injunction the Jewish community always took care of its own poor. This was, indeed, an ingrained habit taken over from generations of Old World Jews who had always prided themselves on being *raḥmanim bene raḥmanim* (merciful children of merciful sires). To be sure, there were times when the number of Jewish poor was exceedingly small. In a letter to Israel Russel dated November 28, 1849, the Reverend H. A. Henry described the life of the Cincinnati congregation. Chiefly composed of German-Jewish merchants, large and small, the minister contended, it included not a single poor man among its members.[21] About the same time a writer in the *Asmonean* observed:

> The Israelites of this country have but a faint idea of their prosperous condition, in comparison with their brethren of Europe. In the city of Amsterdam there are twenty-two thousand Israelites, two thousand of whom are enabled to provide for themselves, without being able to extend any help to others; four thousand who give alms, and the rest, amounting to the number of sixteen thousand, are wholly or partially sustained by their more fortunate co-religionists. Compare this with the city of Boston, in the United States where with a congregation exceeding one hundred members, there is not a solitary Israelite who receives permanent or occasional charity.[22]

Of course, statements of this kind appearing in the European-Jewish press helped create the myth of universal prosperity in

America and added stimulus to Jewish migrations. Idealistic motives, too, added strength to this quest for a better way of life than was possible under the oppressive conditions in the older European communities. Long before the rise of the *Am Olam* movement, an Austrian writer despairing of the success of the Revolution of 1848 wrote that, if not for the sake of the living generation, the Central-European Jews ought to leave their homes for a free country on account of the generations to come. "In my mind I already hail your children, the children of the free. Salem Alechem!"[23]

The arrival in this country of growing multitudes of penniless immigrants totally reversed the previous idyllic picture. Certainly in periods of mass immigration there were a great many new settlers who required assistance in finding jobs, retraining for new occupations and learning the English language and the American ways of life. Many of them required direct relief until they could secure a foothold in the American economy. In such periods the United Hebrew Charities, the National Refugee Service and other organizations performed Herculean tasks in helping newcomers to establish themselves in their new habitat.

Far beyond their purely philanthropic services, the various Jewish charitable organizations performed the highly significant function of unifying the community at large. Since American Jews were recruited from many countries, each group bringing along with it different sets of mores, and a different outlook on life, it was very difficult for them to work together in communal affairs. At times animosities carried over from their respective countries of origin were intensified here. Early in the century, a Russian Jew marrying a Galician Jewess committed what, in the opinion of his fellow-citizens, was almost intermarriage. Discrimination on a social level, even in employment, was not rare. These intense rivalries were reinforced by sharp religious controversies. In the period of radical Reform, led by Isaac Mayer Wise, David Einhorn and Samuel Hirsch, Orthodoxy, constantly on the defensive, deeply resented the new religious movement. Militant Orthodoxy thus clashed with militant Reform in a way making communal cooperation in the religious sphere well-nigh impossible. The newly arising Conservative movement, rather than mediating between these extremes, injected still another force of separation. Culturally, too, the communal bodies were deeply divided by the conflicts between the Zionists, diaspora nationalists and "assimilationists," Hebraists and Yiddishists, Socialists and defenders of the capitalist order.

With religion and culture, those mainstays of Jewish communal life, proving to be a divisive rather than a unifying force, it was necessary for the community to cooperate on another level, principally that of charity and social welfare. No one doubted that sick people required healing, that old persons and orphans required special care. Certainly the successive waves of immigrants required constant attention and help. On the level, therefore, of communal assistance to the poor, the underprivileged, and the newcomers, the Jews of all convictions and all countries found themselves in perfect agreement, as to aims, if not methods. Ultimately, there arose the significant federation movement which combined the fund raising activities of many charitable societies into one communal chest. Beginning with Boston in 1895, such federations sprang up in many communities. In New York, where even more ambitious attempts at uniting all Jewish communal groups under one *Kehillah* of the older type had failed, its Welfare Committee, established in 1912, helped pave the way for the New York Federation organized in 1917.

These federations, without abrogating the autonomy of each constituent organization, nevertheless helped them all in raising larger funds at lesser expense, in reducing unnecessary duplication, and in better planning. True, as Joseph Jacobs observed,[24] the revenue of the federations in their early years remained fairly stationary. But before long it began mounting at an accelerated pace and, aided by the increasing income of the ever newly "Americanized" immigrants, it soon outstripped anything imagined by the founders in their wildest dreams. Fears that federations would lead to the diminution of bequests and other endowment funds by persons, mostly interested in specific causes, likewise proved unfounded, at least up to the time when heavy federal and state taxes, combined with lower rates of interest, began playing havoc with the general traditional system of endowments. The one major problem, still unsolved, is the extent to which federations, by greatly reducing the financial responsibilities of the respective boards of directors, have minimized the latter's creative contributions, and possibly even aided in their undemocratic self-perpetuation. On the whole, however, the federation movement has proved fairly successful in steering a middle course between efficiency and self-government, centralized authority and democratic cooperation. This combination was attempted on an even larger scale since the 1930s when the newly created Council of Jewish Federations and Welfare Funds has been offering its constituent members much advice and guidance, without arrogating to itself any powers of enforcement. After World War II the United Jewish Appeal has become the prime responsibility of the Jewish community, topping all other responsibilities, local, national, and international.

All this required new methods of fund raising and distribution. The Jewish communities have, indeed, pioneered in erecting and perfecting the machinery for the solicitation, collection, and allocation of unprecedented amounts. They also devised ever new methods of putting these funds to more efficient as well as better uses. During the present generation, particularly under the New Deal, the government has taken over many charitable areas previously under the exclusive control of voluntary associations. The Jewish communal charities now had to enter new fields, and pioneer in those residual domains of social welfare unsupported by public funds. Precisely because they have been able to concentrate all their energies on fewer significant undertakings, they could achieve remarkable results with their new approaches to preventing poverty and disease rather than curing them, and generally with their application of the most advanced methods of psychology, psychiatry, and sociology in meeting these social ills. The story of Jewish social welfare in this country is one of the glorious chapters of Jewish communal pioneering for the benefit of Jews and non-Jews alike. We must remember that, for many years past, non-Jews have constituted the majority of patients being cared for in Jewish hospitals.

Quantity Versus Quality

All these major advances, however, also involved a considerable price. As with everything else in life, there are no lights without shadows. One of the greatest dangers to the American Jewish community has always been its frequent emphasis upon quantity rather than quality. Because of its new dependence on over-all communal charities, the size of the funds raised, the number of people cared for, and the sums expended on particular causes loomed larger and larger. Few people have inquired as to what was really accomplished with a particular quantity.

Reliance on quantitative criteria increased in direct proportion to the growing complexity of communal affairs and the relative unfamiliarity with them of responsible communal leaders. Every communal group dependent on voluntary contributions is likely to appreciate more fully the larger donations, and to assign a position of honor and leadership to the large donors. It is a debate of long standing, for instance, among the apologists of the Church of England and their American counterparts, as to whether a Church prospers more when it is "established," that is, dependent on governmental support, or when it is "free," that is, dependent on voluntary gifts and hence often catering to great wealth, or using demagogic appeals to the masses. In the United States the situation has long been aggravated by society's general appreciation of the wealthy businessman, and the widespread belief, especially on the part of the businessmen themselves, that financial success is a mark of over-all competence. All these trends have created, even in the religious sphere, what a Presbyterian preacher has recently so aptly designated as the "ecclesiastical assembly line."

To be sure, few North American congregational leaders were as outspoken as their confreres in Surinam who in 1763 wrote into their contract with the newly appointed rabbi an express provision

that in case of conflict between the congregation and its leaders—
he would always side with the latter. However, no lesser a figure
than Isaac Leeser was threatened with dismissal by Moses A.
Dropsie, because he was suspected of favoring the secessionist side
in the Civil War. After gracing the Baltimore pulpit for many
years, David Einhorn, on the other hand, was not allowed to return to it because of the congregational leaders' Confederate sympathies.[25] In more recent years, too, many a rabbi found himself
in considerable difficulties because his social or political views
ran counter to the views held by influential Board members. If
these conflicts arose far more frequently over sociopolitical rather
than purely religious issues, this was not necessarily a sign of the
lay leaders' recognition of their lesser competence in religious matters, but rather their greater personal involvement in certain sociopolitical ideologies, or their greater fear of unfavorable outside
repercussions.

Voluntarism creates other communal difficulties as well. In the
field of religion, particularly, voluntary association would naturally
lead to differences of opinion, or rituals. Generally speaking, religion is not poorer but richer because of diversity, just as culture is
enriched by differences in cultural strains. We need not agree with
Kierkegaard's evaluation of religion as so exclusively a personal
affair between the individual worshiper and his God that it is a
sign of cowardice for man to band together in congregations. But
we shall not deny the basic validity of the proposition that religious
and cultural diversity has often been a true force of strength and
enlightenment—a proposition so eloquently defined by Thomas
Jefferson. Though personally not a very pious man, the third
president of the United States was not altogether wrong when
he wrote thanking Dr. Jacob de la Motta for the discourse at the
consecration of a synagogue in Savannah:

> It excites in him the gratifying reflection that his country has
> been the first to prove to the world two truths, the most salutary
> to human society, that man can govern himself, and that reli-
> gious freedom is the most effectual anodyne of religious dissen-

sion; the maxim of civil government being reversed in that of religion, where its true form is, "divided we stand, united, we fall."[26]

Divisions of this kind, however, have often interfered with major positive undertakings on a community-wide basis. Accustomed for too long a time to march on crutches supplied to it by its recognition in European and Near Eastern public law, the Jewish community has not yet learned to appreciate fully the intrinsic value of religious and cultural disparity. Those of us, moreover, who have always seen in the Jewish community a welcome substitute for the lack of a Jewish state have also deplored divisions of any kind as undermining that statelike control. But in actual life the American Jewish community has often noted, however unwillingly and hesitantly, that, from the purely religious and cultural point of view, pluralism is not necessarily an evil, but may well represent a gain.

New Challenges

All these and many others are truly perplexing difficulties which have emerged from the three centuries of pioneering in American Jewish communal life. As its strength grew, its numbers increased, and its obligations became more and more ramified, the problems besetting the community became vaster and more complex. However, American Jewry which, under the great strains and stresses of its initial groping for a foothold in America's communal structure and, again, under the tremendous difficulties of mass adjustment in the late 1800s and early 1900s, succeeded in meeting the ever recurrent emergencies, will also find an answer to its present-day perplexities. As it has entered the fourth century of its communal existence, it is certainly prepared to pioneer again along new and uncharted paths of communal collaboration.

8 *The Image of the Rabbi, Formerly and Today**

The rabbinic literature was to a very large extent written by the rabbis themselves, and whatever we read there about the old-type rabbinate has been colored by that authorship. True, from the eighteenth century on, we have had an increasing number of critics of the rabbinate, whether they came from the Ḥasidic wing, who felt that the rabbis were too legalistic, or from the Maskilim. Probably the most outspoken opponent of the rabbinate was Zalkind Hurwitz, a Polish Jew employed by the Paris National Library in the revolutionary period. According to Hurwitz, the only remedy for the Jews, if they wanted to become westernized, was to abolish the rabbinate altogether.

Perhaps our best approach, therefore, might be to look at the differences between the old rabbinate and the rabbinate as we know it in America today.

It has been said that the rabbi has become a jack-of-all-trades. In fact, this is one of the most astonishing developments. In practically every other profession there has been an increasing specialization, whether in engineering, accounting, or law, and certainly in medicine—they say that before long we shall have a doctor who will treat only the right nostril and not the left one. In the rabbinate, however, the opposite has been the case. The

* Address delivered at the Sixtieth Annual Convention of the Rabbinical Assembly of America on May 9, 1960. Reprinted from the *Proceedings* of that organization, XXIV (1960), 84-92.

rabbi, as well as the American minister in general, has assumed the responsibility for a great many functions which were never his.

Even in America up to almost a century ago we had rabbis, or rather reverends as they were called, whose main function was to read prayers, to be the liturgical leaders of the congregation. The old-type European rabbi, on the other hand, rarely, if ever, conducted services. The congregation may have considered it an honor to ask him to lead in the *Ne'ilah* service, or some other very distinguished moment in the liturgy. But this invitation came to him not because nobody else was able to conduct those services—almost everybody else was qualified to do so. In most houses of worship it was a layman who led in the prayers. And if they wanted somebody endowed with a beautiful voice, they looked for a *Hazzan*. But the rabbi of old was as a rule only one of many worshipers.

More importantly, the American rabbi has become primarily a preacher. The sermon has assumed a centrality in American Jewish life which it has never had in the traditional community. Most old-time rabbis were satisfied with two sermons a year. Those were not even sermons in the modern sense, but rather lectures which required a great deal of acumen and learning on the part of the audience, because their halakhic parts consisted of super-pilpul on certain especially difficult problems in Halakhah. It was, in fact, customary for the rabbi to announce in advance which passages in the Talmud or *Poskim* he was going to quote so that the congregants could prepare for that sermon. Understandably, such an interpretive discourse appealed only to the learned minority of the congregation and, delivered only twice a year, it was considered relatively unimportant within the totality of rabbinic functions. The real sermonizing was done for the most part by an outsider, the itinerant Maggid.

Perhaps an even more important difference between the old and the new rabbinate is that the latter has become deeply involved in all aspects of fund raising. This is fully understandable. We are a voluntary community, a community which can be maintained only if the membership is prepared to support it. In contrast, the old-type community had the power of taxation. In the older community, it was possible for the Polish Council, the Va'ad Arba' Ha-arasot, to pass a resolution forbidding the rabbi to participate in deliberations about tax assessments.[1] Today, on the other hand, the rabbi has become a fund raiser, not only for his own congregation but for the whole community, for the United Jewish Appeal, and all other major causes affecting the Jews. He has also largely become the financial manager of his congregation.

A well-known controversy has been conducted for years between the Anglican Church in England and their brethren in America, the Episcopalians. In England the Anglican Church is a state church, supported by the government, whereas the American Episcopal congregations, like the Jewish, are free societies, supported only by the will of their members. The Episcopalians have long argued for the superiority of their system because they have had to appeal to the individual members and to their voluntary association and possessed only their spiritual force behind them. On the other hand, they contended, belonging to a community only because the law required it has rendered the allegiance of a great many members superficial. This is undoubtedly true. (We have witnessed also in the modern European Jewish communities which had the public law behind them, the presence of many purely nominal members who never went to synagogue but nevertheless continued to pay their dues.) To which the Anglican Church answered that any voluntary association has the great demerit of playing into the hands of richer members on whose financial support the society so greatly depends.

Personally, I had to raise this issue in an essay on "Freedom and Constraint in the Jewish Community," which was based upon the following documentation: In 1876 the Prussian Diet passed a law allowing Jews to leave the Jewish community "for religious scruples," without joining any other religious denomination. Until that time a Jew could leave the community only by saying that he was a Christian or an unbeliever. It was an alliance of free thinkers and ultra-orthodox who jointly pushed the law through, allowing Jews, without any further elaboration, to claim that they had "religious scruples" forcing them to leave the community.

A few years later the Austrian government was preparing a new Jewish community law for Austria. Naturally it was interested in finding out how the law of 1876 had operated in Prussia. It addressed a pertinent inquiry to Otto von Bismarck, who was both Chancellor of Germany and Prime Minister of Prussia. I published Bismarck's reply, which was based upon a very thorough investigation. The tenor of this reply was that generally the law was all right, but that in practice it played into the hands of a few wealthy members in each community, since it enabled them not only to withdraw from the community if the communal majority did something they did not like, but also, by the mere threat of withdrawal, to force the community to accept their opinion. Since it was they who contributed most funds and since by a simple declaration that they were leaving the community because of religious scruples—whatever that meant—they would cease to pay the communal taxes, such threats could not be dismissed lightly.[2]

We thus have to reckon with a fact of life, unavoidable under the existing circumstances, that the American rabbinate and the American ministry as a whole have become deeply involved in finances, not only in their own congregations, but in the community at large. This involvement has had the further effect that it has put some of the rabbinical functions, indeed all communal functions, on a quantitative rather than a qualitative level. The measure of success has now consisted in the number of congregants, or the number of children in school, or the number of people belonging to a men's club, or a sisterhood. The quantitative measure necessarily led also to the public relations aspect. Many of the functions and activities began to be designed not so much for their substantive merits, for whatever they would achieve for the Jewish religion, for Torah and education, but for whatever impression they would make on the public mind. It all interrelates. Whether or not one personally deplores them, these are the facts of life, arising from the essence of the separation of Church and state, which we all welcome. The facts are that no governmental enforcement is possible, that we have to have voluntary communities, and that with their voluntary character go quantitative measurements, fund raising, public relations, all of them very vital aspects of service of the American ministry as a whole.

As against that, in the old traditional community the rabbi could stand up and, if need be, repudiate the lay leadership of the community. That struggle between layman and rabbi was going on through the ages. In certain cases the rabbi lost out. Our traditional literature does not reflect it fully, but there were occasional excesses, as in the case of the congregation of Surinam which hired a rabbi as far back as 1763 and, as we recall, wrote into the contract a clause that whenever there would be a conflict between the elders and the community at large, he, the rabbi, would side with the elders against the community.[3] There were other cases in which provisions were inserted that no rabbinic function of major importance would be performed without the consent of the elders. But these were exceptions.

As a rule, the rabbi had enough prestige, enough authority to command genuine respect. Ferdinand and Isabella, the Catholic rulers of Spain certainly were no great friends of Jews. And yet in the case reported to them in 1483, of a rabbi assailed by a fellow Jew because he had placed him under a ban (*herem*), the rulers issued a sentence of death on this assailant because they felt that the rabbinate ought to be protected and enabled to lead the community authoritatively and fearlessly.[4]

Even economically, the rabbinate became a rather desirable occupation. Unlike today, some people spent money in getting rabbinic positions. While not so prevalent as in the Catholic Church, where "simony" had become in the late Middle Ages a major internal issue and target for attack by reformers, the acquisition of rabbinic posts through "pull" and even outright bribery was not quite so rare as we are inclined to think. A most remarkable case occurred in the Vilna community in the eighteenth century; a community which, though not yet as large and influential as in the following century, when it was called the Jerusalem of Lithuania, was, nevertheless, a major center of Jewish learning. In 1750 a powerful elder bribed his way to a point where his son-in-law, Samuel b. Avigdor, an immature youngster, became the rabbi of Vilna. He lacked the necessary qualifications; he did not know enough Torah and had to go back home to study under his father for another couple of years, all the time supposedly officiating as the rabbi of Vilna. To be sure, after his father-in-law's demise a faction in the community protested and the struggle lasted for several decades, but even thirty-five years later the elders still were unsuccessfully trying to depose him.[5]

All this happened in defiance of a resolution passed by the Lithuanian Council in 1694 in order to stem such abuses. It read: "If a rabbi be elected because of a loan or bribe, the amount so advanced shall be confiscated by the province, and he [the rabbi-elect] be forbidden to assume office, and the recipient [of the money] be permanently demoted. Before a rabbi-elect preaches his first sermon, according to custom, he shall be obliged to appear before his [provincial] chief rabbi and shall state under oath that he is assuming his office lawfully." More remarkably, the Prussian government, which took over parts of Poland, issued in 1797 an order for these newly annexed provinces in which it stated that the rabbis "had been used to purchase their positions for extravagant sums after overbidding one another, and hence attempted not only to obtain a comfortable living for themselves and their families, but also to secure from their coreligionists full compensation for their investment."[6]

Those are things which usually do not appear in the romantic historiography about the rabbis. But those were, nevertheless, the facts of East-European life two or three centuries ago. Power in every area of life has often had a corrupting influence. It may well be that the illustrations here cited were only the unavoidable, if rather exceptional, counterpart of the rabbis' great prestige and of the great power exercised by them in all walks of life.

There is another area of difference, and I think it is equally significant: the rabbi today has to perform a great function as a representative of the Jewish community before the non-Jewish world. I am referring, in particular, to his good will speeches before interdenominational groups which, whatever one may think of their effectiveness, have become a part of the American folkways. They are part of the picture of the emancipated Jewish community trying to become integrated into the majority nation and still remaining an identifiable minority. While becoming more and more part and parcel of the large nations among whom they live, the Jews nevertheless face much discrimination, even animosities created by various historical and social factors. Hence it is important that the rabbi, who is a spokesman for Judaism, and also indirectly for the Jewish people, should try to secure some good will. In the old community the rabbi did not perform that function. It was usually left to an influential and well-connected layman, a *shtadlan*, to represent the Jews before the respective governments and public opinion. Here and there a rabbi had to debate religious issues, and even enter some public disputations with Christians. But such instances were quite exceptional, and were usually shunned by both parties. On the whole, the rabbi was far less concerned about what the Christians thought about his community than about what the Jews thought about their Judaism and about how he could most effectively teach its fundamentals to them.

Finally, the rabbi has in recent years often engaged in an activity which has become increasingly popular, but which is always extremely complex and difficult, namely, religious counseling. Although counseling has been considered an integral activity of the Christian ministry for centuries and the Catholic Church in particular, with its confessional, has always practiced it rather intensively, the rabbis performed such functions in a very limited degree. The modern specialization in psychiatry and psychology has made it doubly difficult for the rabbi to try to serve as a religious counselor. Even a professional psychiatrist, well trained though he may be, often is at a loss how to handle a difficult case in human relations. Yet the rabbi is often forced to try his hand because he is expected to; more, because he is at times really in a position to help.

I happen to have served as chairman of a committee which set up at Columbia a university seminar devoted to religion and health. This seminar tried to explore, with the aid of present-day knowledge and techniques, the relationships between religion and health. Curiously, the suggestion for that investigation came, not from our side of the campus, not from the social scientists or philosophers, but rather from the medical men, from members of the Medical School faculty. They felt that the modern medical profession has been deprived of important aids, both diagnostic and therapeutic, when it lost that all-important support which religion used to give to counseling, to helping individuals disturbed in their family relations, and the like. We all agreed that there is much to be achieved by a renewed cooperation of religion, psychiatry, and general medicine, in trying to solve some of these most difficult and elusive problems confronting the health of mankind.

The old-time rabbi, I repeat, as a rule had little concern for these aspects of the ministry. I believe that some of his major drawbacks which gradually led to his downfall lay precisely in his lack of interest in, and qualifications for, religious counseling, as well as preaching. In part these shortcomings of the old rabbinate led to the great Ḥasidic revolt. The masses did not relish the rabbi's pilpulistic sermons, however learned. They preferred the Maggid and still more the charismatic Zaddik with his moralistic stories and parables. Their need for religious counseling was likewise met by the Ḥasidic movement, whose leaders became the great and most effective religious counselors of recent generations.

In short, the old rabbinate was concentrating essentially on two areas of life: Teaching the Torah and judging. Even the sermon, as I said before, was devoted to teaching. Judging related to ritualistic as well as to civil matters. Here the rabbi had to be on his toes all the time because his congregants were learned men, often equal, even superior to him in learning. A romantic, like Nathan Neta Hannover, tells us about the Jews of Poland before the Cossack rebellion of 1648, that out of fifty adult male Jews in an average community, twenty had the title *Morenu*.[7] This is doubtless an exaggeration, but there is no question that a considerable number of Jews, whether or not possessing the title *Morenu*, were very learned. In America the situation is totally different because large segments of the community do not even appreciate learning on the part of the rabbi. There was a time not so long ago when I was hearing frequent complaints from pupils all over the country, from all sections of the rabbinate, that some congregants were actually resentful if a rabbi allotted two or three hours a day to study. They expected him to go around and make speeches or perform other duties, rather than "waste" his time on books. This rejection of learning is, fortunately, declining now but it is nevertheless still lingering in many quarters. There still are far too many influential members to whom the rabbi's function is anything but that of a teacher of his congregation. To salvage some of their educational role quite a few rabbis began specializing in reviewing books. Any best seller which appeared was reviewed "authoritatively." It made no difference to what branch of literature or science the book belonged; as soon as it got on the best seller list, it was considered worthy of a rabbinic review. Both rabbi and congregation readily overlooked the fact that almost by definition most books becoming best sellers must necessarily appeal to a more average taste and hence are not the best books having an impact on the elite. Yet it is these books which the congregations have often expected the rabbi to interpret for them in an authoritative way. But they cared very little about his function as a teacher of Judaism as such.

Even less is expected today of the rabbi's judicial function. With the weakening of the ritualistic concerns in daily life, very few Jews now go to ask the rabbi a *she'elah*. Hardly any Jew nowadays writes contracts with other businessmen in terms of Jewish law, and then goes to the rabbi to adjudicate a litigation. In other words, the administration of Jewish law as a primary function has practically disappeared, except in the strictly religious phases affecting the synagogue and its related branches.

Looking to the future, I wish to say that it appears that the ancient rabbinic function of judging is probably irretrievably lost. As an individual, the rabbi may of course participate in a court of arbitration, such as Dr. Israel Goldstein had been trying to promote for many years. He may take part in voluntary settlements of other kinds. But he has totally lost his authority as a judge, operating on the basis of Jewish law, particularly in the general areas of civil or criminal law. Not even in Israel, where he still performs some judicial functions in the area of personal law, such as marriage, divorce, adoption, and inheritance, is the rabbi considered primarily a judge.

Interrelated with this vanishing judicial function is the problem of talmudic learning. We need but recall the paradoxical argument in one of the responsa of Solomon ibn Adret when he complained that many Jews in Spain were repairing to Gentile courts. Rashba resented this alienation from Jewish tribunals not so much because it entailed the weakening of Jewish self-government, but rather because he feared that, as a result, Jews might forget the Torah.[8] By a curious reversal, Jewish law as such was the essential value; one studied the Torah not in order to be a better judge, but one used the judiciary as a lever for the study of Torah. Like Rabbi Solomon, most old-time rabbis believed in this paradoxical centrality of Torah as a supreme value by itself, versus which even the whole administration of the law was but a secondary function.

Yet I have the increasing feeling that, from another angle, the rabbi is again becoming more and more a spokesman for Jewish learning in his congregation. The more educated its members become, the more numerous among them are those who had not only graduated from college but have become specialists in some branch of science, the humanities, or social sciences, the rabbi is less and less able to afford to be that "jack-of-all-trades." In order to be effective, he will have to become, more and more, a representative of that specialty which is his, namely, Jewish learning. Generally, the role of the amateur is diminishing in our complex world. More and more the road is open for the learned, the effective, and the efficient in the rabbinate as well. Though I may be mistaken, I believe that the role of the rabbi as a great teacher of Judaism is coming back and, before very long, his other functions, which will necessarily remain very diversified, will all become but subsidiary to that basic function.

9 Palestinian Messengers in America, 1849–79: A Record of Four Journeys*

In the annals of Jewish communities and their interterritorial efforts in behalf of their oppressed or needy brethren, the *ḥaluk-kah*, or organized relief for the Jews of the Holy Land, has for centuries occupied a most focal position. Appealing simultaneously to the charitable instincts of the individual, the people's deep yearnings for Palestine, and the widespread belief that the remnant gathered in Zion, through its exclusive devotion to a life of piety and learning, promoted the spiritual interests of the entire people and contributed to the salvation of all individual Jews, this type of relief was generally considered one of the paramount duties of the various communal organs. In many communities special officers were entrusted with the task of collecting regular contributions and of transmitting them to Palestine. Small wonder, then, that the Palestinian Jews themselves, so greatly dependent on such assistance, often sought to promote these local collections and to counteract the natural inertia of communal leaders by sending delegates abroad on their own initiative. The latter were known as *shadarim*, or, in full, *sheliḥe de-rabbanan*, 'messengers of the rabbis' (reminiscent of the ancient *apostoloi*). Often equally distinguished for learning, piety, and diplomatic skill, they usually succeeded both in enlisting the support of the leaders and in eliciting a

* Reprinted from *JSS*, V (1943), 115-62, 225-92. This essay was written jointly by Salo W. and Jeannette M. Baron.

direct response from the masses. Indeed, their authority frequently was so great that they were called upon to settle local disputes, to decide controversial matters of law, and generally to serve as consultants on difficult or disputed questions. Even in the nineteenth century, when their influence was already on the wane, they often served as a significant link not only between the Jews of Palestine and their coreligionists abroad, but also between the Diaspora communities themselves.

It has long been recognized that the records of donations kept by these messengers, their occasional diaries and travelogues, and their reports to the authorities at home constitute invaluable sources of information for the history of both Palestinian and Diaspora Jewry. The extensive travel book of Ḥayyim Joseph David Azulai (1724-1805), the most prominent of the eighteenth-century messengers, has indeed been widely quoted and commented upon even before its complete publication in a critical edition. Other such records have likewise been utilized by scholars,[1] although many are still hidden away in public and private libraries.

The following presentation is based principally upon a manuscript volume in the Hebrew National and University Library in Jerusalem.[2] It is the original record kept by three successive messengers who visited the United States in the years 1849-50, 1861, 1867-69 and 1876-79. Containing not only the original letters of authorization issued by the elders in Jerusalem but also various autograph testimonials by leading British and American Jews and many signatures of individual contributors, it sheds considerable new light on this significant communal activity and on a large number of individuals active in the young or nascent communities of the New World. The data here given, of course, often require elucidation and amplification from other contemporary sources, such as the American Jewish periodicals. Many a detail, however, will of necessity remain obscure and, particularly, many a name unidentified until further material becomes available.

I   The Mission of Aaron Selig, 1849-50

The first Palestinian messenger sent to the New World seems
to have been Moses Malki (1759). In 1771 came the colorful
Haim (Raphael Ḥayyim) Isaac Carigal (1733-77) who greatly
impressed Ezra Stiles. According to the autobiographical
"Memoir," preserved in the appendices to Stiles' MS Diary at
Yale University, Carigal was but 28 years old when he first arrived
in Curaçao for a sojourn of two years (1761-63). Subsequently
he visited the other communities in both the West Indies and
the American mainland, establishing contact not only with Jews
but also with interested Christian theologians and Hebraists.
Considering the very small size of the contemporary Jewish
population in the Americas, his mission seems to have been eminently successful. Apart from covering his expenses and forwarding unspecified amounts to the Palestinian authorities, he is
recorded to have sent from Jamaica, in 1771, the amount of
$1,000 to his wife whom he had left behind at Hebron.[3]

Such free disposal of funds naturally aroused frequent suspicions.
These were aggravated by the occasional appearance of unauthor-
ized messengers, and even of downright impostors who exploited
for their private advantage the sentimental attachment of their
brethren to the Holy Land. Among the recipients in Palestine,
moreover, internecine strife between the Sephardim and Ashkenazim and between the Ashkenazim themselves (insofar as
they had come from different sections of the German-Polish
settlement), as well as pronounced favoritism by local distributors,
gave rise to repeated complaints which discouraged many a
philanthropist abroad. At best, the large traveling expenses and
commissions of the envoys consumed an inordinately large part
of the funds collected. Frequently voiced in European communities, these objections carried double weight in the Western
Hemisphere, the great distance of which from Palestine facilitated
misrepresentation, increased expenses, and hampered any attempt
at adequate surveillance.[4] When, in 1849, an American Jewish

visitor to Palestine, Simeon Abrahams, upon his return to the United States, severely criticized the administration of the *ḥalukkah*, Isaac Leeser (1806-68), the influential Philadelphia minister and editor of the monthly *Occident and Jewish Advocate*, the most widely read Jewish periodical in America, gave succinct expression to prevailing local opinion in the following words:

> All admit that something should be done by which the whole amount raised for these poor people should reach them, without discount, drawback, or commission of whatever kind: whereas by the system of accredited collectors who every now and then come over, a great portion is lost in travelling expenses, besides which, one-third of the net proceeds is retained by them for commissions, and thus nearly the whole amount collected is consumed without the least perceptible benefit to those for whom the donors intended their charitable gifts. This desideratum was in part successfully accomplished about sixteen years ago when the society תרומת הקודש of the City of New York was established under the auspices of the learned and venerable Israel B. Kursheedt, Esq. the principal object of which was the collecting and forwarding of funds to the four cities (Jerusalem, Hebron, Zafeth and Tiberias) of Palestine, but more especially that preventing that complete system of robbery and deception which before that period was so often practised on the Jews of the U.S., by persons pretending to have authority to collect for the Palestine fund, who afterwards were proved to be rank imposters. The funds collected by this society have uniformly been forwarded to the pious and charitable Rabbi Hirsch Lehren, of Amsterdam, who so energetically attends to the relief of the poor of Palestine, and the gifts thus forwarded to the Holy Land to be equally distributed among the inhabitants of the four cities.[5]

Nevertheless, the need for relief was clearly indicated by Abrahams himself in a private letter (dated Dec. 22, 1849) to a friend, Daniel Myers in Liverpool, which was published in full in the London *Jewish Chronicle*. The following excerpts give a vivid picture of the situation of the community of Jerusalem:

The number of our people in the Holy City is about five thousand, most of them in a very abject and impoverished state; this number is much larger than has been here, at one time, for many years. The causes of the great poverty are various; first there is no business to be done here, secondly, there are large numbers of old pious men and women, who come here to finish their day, and repose in קדש אדמת (holy ground), this class is numerous. Thirdly, the dearness of the necessities of life; it may perhaps astonish you, as it did me; yet provisions are as dear here as in New York. Fourthly, the larger number of sick, and above all the very many who are blind of one or both eyes, among our people both old and young, one out of every three has diseased eyes. Another cause of trouble is, they have no hospital to go to, except the one belonging to the English Missionaries, which to the pious Israelite is worse than death itself.

In 1848-49 the revolutionary movements in Europe greatly interfered with the regularity and size of the European donations. Consequently, the eyes of many Palestinian Jews, especially among the members of the newly organized German congregation in Jerusalem, turned hopefully to the growing communities of the New World. Rev. Nicolayson, a resident British missionary, soon reported to his London headquarters a "new scheme" to send a deputation to America, "where large numbers of German Jews have settled," and to solicit their assistance. "The new German congregation at Jerusalem," he added, "has a plan of establishing proper schools, hospitals, manufactories and trades."

The first envoy to arrive was Yehiel Cohen, ostensibly to collect funds for the rebuilding of the Synagogue Beth-El in Jerusalem. He was followed by Yehosef Schwarz, author of the significant Palestinological treatise, *Tebuot ha-areṣ* (which Leeser himself later translated into English), and Zadok Levy, dispatched by the German-Dutch community of Jerusalem. Finally there arrived Aaron Selig Ashkenazi, delegate of the main Ashkenazic *halukkah* district, the so-called Perushim of Jerusalem.[6] It is the latter's mission, recorded in great detail in our MS, with which we are here principally concerned.

The leaders of the Perushim were evidently aware of some of the prevailing suspicions and criticisms. In fact, Aaron Selig himself had years before become involved in a controversy with the Amsterdam officials when he visited Western Europe to collect money for the construction of a new synagogue in Jerusalem.[7] This awareness explains not only the excessive pathos in their appeal but also the careful advance arrangements for a 'fool-proof' record to be kept by the delegate. He was handed a bound volume, the blank pages of which were numbered consecutively. The messenger was to receive no funds without having them entered in the book, preferably by the donors or the local administrators of the charities. If for some reason a folio should be missing (as happened indeed with fol. 8), its loss was to be authoritatively confirmed by the secretary of the *Kolel*.[8] The elders were careful, however, to impose no other restrictions on the movements of their representative. They also refrained from mentioning the commission which he was ultimately to obtain and which, to judge from the above-mentioned statement by Leeser (confirmed also by other sources), probably ran as high as a third of all receipts.

In their appeal, which was to serve simultaneously as the credentials for Aaron Selig, the five Jerusalem elders (Isaiah Burdaki, Nathan Neta b. Mendel, Aryeh b. Yeraḥmeel Neeman, Joseph Zundel Salant, and David Tebele, the son of Chief Rabbi Solomon Hirschell of London)[9] addressed themselves, with the customary grandiloquence of the period, to the rabbis and laymen of "all the lands of America to the borders of East India (!) as well as West India" invoking upon them the Divine blessing of being vouchsafed participation in the messianic restoration to Palestine. They emphasized that Jewish prayers were issuing uninterruptedly from Zion and particularly from the Wailing Wall, and that they, the descendants of Ashkenazic Jewry, who through all the ages of extreme suffering had staunchly adhered to the creed of their forefathers, [10] were now filling the role of the ancient *anshe maʿamad* as representatives of the several tribes to Israel. The obvious implication was that the community of Jerusalem thus performed a great service for their coreligionists in other lands, hence it was entitled to their support. This claim was then advanced under complimentary utterances regarding the well-known charitableness of the American Jews and with the accompanying promise that special prayers would be read in behalf of the donors whose names were to be entered in this book. The merits of Aaron Selig, his trustworthiness, learning, piety, and scholarly descent were also extolled and full powers given to him to act in behalf of the Jerusalem Perushim.[11]

Equipped with these credentials, dated somewhat inexactly as of Sivan 5608 (June 1848), the messenger arrived some three months later at his first destination, Gibraltar (Elul 5—September 3). His stay there did not prove to be particularly profitable, as may be learned from the following entry made on Elul 28 (September 26) by Henry Joseph:

> Rabbi Aaron Selig arrived in Gibraltar on the 5th of the present month, having requested the Parnassim of this ק״ק to accept him as a public Missionary from the אשכנזים of Jerusalem. They refused so to do, it being contrary to their regulated custom. . . . Rabbi Aaron, however, by a limited subscription of private individuals, obtained the sum of Thirty Dollars, which enabled him to procure a Deck passage to England on board a steam packet, in this inclement season of the year he being very anxious to proceed on his mission.[12]

England proved more cooperative. To be sure, our MS contains no English entry before February 26, 1849, but Aaron Selig must have landed in the country some time in the early autumn of 1848. It is not too hazardous to assume that the sudden burst of renewed interest in the affairs of Palestinian Jewry in the British capital during the last months of 1848 and the beginning of 1849 was due, at least in part, to his exertions. Sir Moses Montefiore, the celebrated philanthropist who had consistently proved Palestine Jewry's outstanding champion, once more took up its cause. On December 14, 1848 he addressed a circular letter to all the British congregations urging them to organize Palestine relief on a permanent basis. The *Jewish Chronicle* published this appeal in its issue of January 12, 1849 and followed it up the next week with two strong editorials. It also reprinted in full the *New York Tribune's* report of the Thanksgiving Day address delivered on November 23, 1848 by Mordecai Manuel Noah, the old American protagonist of pre-Herzlian Zionism. To give its sentiments more tangible expression, the *Chronicle* also opened its columns to a public subscription for a "Relief Fund for the Jews of Tiberias." Lists of subscribers were, indeed, printed in several successive numbers.[13]

The silence of our account-book may perhaps best be explained by the fact that no contributions were handed directly to the messenger. Evidently, all sums collected through the *Chronicle* and the various other communal organs were sent directly to Palestine through Montefiore's well established channels. Before departing for the United States, however, Aaron Selig succeeded in enlisting both the moral and financial support of the two other important Anglo-Jewish communities, namely, Birmingham and Liverpool. From the Birmingham Hebrew Congregation he secured not only two pounds for his expense account, but also the following testimonial, signed by its famous preacher, Morris Jacob Raphall (1797-1868), which must have proved very valuable to him in his subsequent negotiations across the Atlantic.[14]

> *These are to certify that Rabbi Aaron Selig Ashkenazi deputed by the Congregns. of* אשכנזים פרושים *in the holy city Jerusalem has submitted his credentials to the Wardens, and has been promised that at the next Half-yearly General Meeting of the Free Members of this Congregation his application on behalf of our suffering brethren shall be taken into consideration, and a sum for their relief be forwarded to Sir Moses Montefiore Bart. In Witness whereof I have hereunto set my hand and the Seal of the Congregation at Birmingham this 26th February 5609.*

In Liverpool, as we learn from an entry by D. W. Isaacs, Minister of the Old Seel Street Synagogue, on March 28, the considerable sum of £10 14s 6d had been collected in the congregation and handed to the messenger, evidently to pay his passage. A second entry by M. S. Oppenheim, another minister of the same synagogue, informs us that he, too, had "Collected from the Old Congregation Seel Street the sum of £4 15s which I intend with the Blessing of the Almighty God to send to Sir Moses Montefiore with the weekly Subscriptions which I hope and trust with the help of God to establish in Liverpool." On the same day one Lazarus Harris, a lay member of the congregation hailing from Lithuania, pledged himself to assist Oppenheim in these weekly collections.[15]

Upon his arrival in New York Aaron Selig found the ground well prepared by the earlier efforts of Yeḥiel Cohen. Even the Christian public witnessed one of the recurrent surges of pro-Palestinian sentiment. The following notice, which first appeared in the *Watchman* and was subsequently reprinted in the *Occident*, bears witness to the depth of this interest:

> There is a new Society now forming, for assisting poor Israelites on their way to Jerusalem, "with bread and water"; this infant society has originated and is supported by a number of the members of the Society of Friends of England (i.e. Quakers): They have a worthy and valuable agent, Mr. Manning, formerly belonging to the English Mission for promoting Christianity among the Jews, but who is now located about an hour's walk from Jaffa, a sea-port town belonging to the Holy Land. He has rented a large house with spare rooms so that indigent Jews can have food prepared according to the Casher manner.

It seems to have taken Aaron Selig little time to secure the following recommendation from Judge Noah:

> The very full and satisfactory documents brought from Jerusalem by the Reverend Aaron Selig recognises him as the only person authorised to make Collections in the United States for the German and Polish Synagogue in the Holy Land. He is entrusted to have the amount collected sent to the agents either

in Amsterdam, or London, all that he requires is a small amount for travelling expenses. It is advisable in order to prevent the Costs [being] increased (?) by Sending Messengers, for the Congregations to appropriate an annual amount whatever each can afford to be sent to the Holy Land—New York 29 May 1849.

Jacques Judah Lyons (1813-77), Minister of the leading New York Spanish and Portuguese Congregation Shearith Israel, likewise entered his indorsement (dated Sivan 13, 5609—June 3, 1849) adding the wish that Ashkenazi's "mission of Benevolence may be crowned with success." Of even greater importance was the whole-hearted indorsement, signed on Sivan 3 (May 24), by Samuel Myer Isaacs (1804-78), Minister of the Shaaray Tefilla Congregation of New York, because Isaacs soon undertook the task of organizing country-wide relief action on a permanent basis, and for many years served as its most active local representative. Similar approval was also registered by Simon C. Noot, Assistant Reader of the B'nai Jeshurun Congregation (Sivan 3— May 24), Ansel Leo, Reader of the same (the Elm Street) Synagogue (June 3), and Simeon Abrahams (Sivan 14—June 4). The latter, although generally critical of the methods applied in the collection and distribution of Palestine relief funds, readily testified that "while at Jerusalem תוב״ב was there informed that Rabbi Aaron Zelig was fully Authorised to collect Money for the benefit of one of the Congregations of the City." Lastly, the Trustees of the Congregation Bné [B'nai] Jeshurun, according to a communication registered by their Secretary, Henry Goldsmith, "after having examined the document of Rabbi Aaron Selig Ashkenasi have appointed two gentlemen of this Congregation to take up Subscriptions and Collection for our distressed brethren in Jerusalem."[16]

Similar action was taken, or promised, on June 17-18, by the three congregations in Philadelphia. The Board of Trustees of the Congregation House of Israel (Beit Israel), according to an entry signed by its secretary, Joseph Rosenbaum, "resolved that a society shall be erected for the purpose of raising yearly subscriptions for the aid of ouer distressed brethern in Jerusalem, which money shall be remitted annually to Sir Moses Montifiore (*sic*)." A more cautious indorsement, confined to a pious wish of success, was also signed by Abraham Hart, President of the Congregation Mikve Israel; and this was subsequently copied verbatim by S. Adler (?), President of the Congregation Rodef Sholem. The last to sign a testimonial was Isaac Leeser of the Mikve Israel Congregation, but his recommendation was both more extensive and definite:

> Having always felt a great interest in the condition of the afflicted Israelites in all the countries, especially those of our ancient home the land of Palestine, I cannot refuse to Rabbi Aaron Selig Ashkenazi my hearty recommendation to all our brethren in America and to request them to aid the cause for which he is sent by forming societies and contributionships to send annually a given sum, however moderate, for the relief of the poor of the Holy Land; since their situation is of that nature that they cannot hope under present circumstances to earn enough for their own livelihood; therefore I express sincerely the hope that a favourable change in their position may soon enable them to support themselves by the labour of their own hands.

We may understand the reason for Leeser's initial hesitation, if we peruse his editorial in the July issue of the *Occident*, partly cited above. Evidently written about the time of Aaron Selig's arrival in Philadelphia, this article contains a number of further references to the newcomer which shed additional light both on his own endeavors and on Leeser's attitude towards him. Continuing the exposition of his views on Abrahams' memoir, Leeser wrote:

> We approve, nevertheless, of Mr. Abrahams' proposition not to give to the Messengers, should they come, anything except gifts for themselves to defray their personal expenses; and to send the donations collected for Palestine through some accredited

friend of ארץ ישראל such as Sir Moses Montefiore or R. Hirsch Lehren. This would soon stop the arrival of Messengers, as they could not get any commissions for collections, and the funds would reach, undiminished, those for whom they were intended.

Since the above was written, we have seen and conversed with Rabbi Aaron Selig Ashkenazi, the accredited messenger from the Polish congregation of Jerusalem. Rabbi Aaron is a native of Lithuania in Poland, but for about 18 years, a resident of the Holy City. He represents that, as usual, great distress prevails among his countrymen at Jerusalem, especially as many of the annual contributions which were formerly sent thither have not been received of late on account of the troubles in Europe. He has, therefore, been sent to America without his own consent, being ordered by the elders to appeal to our brothers on this side of the Atlantic for their aid in relieving them from their sore distress. Rabbi Aaron does not wish to receive the money collected himself but desires it to be sent through Sir Moses Montefiore, and only receive as much as will defray his very small expense account. We were truly pleased with the quiet and proper demeanour of this messenger, and we really trust that he may succeed in impressing on the mind of Israelites all over the country to do something for the poor of Palestine. The best method would be to get up a society in each place, the object of which is to be to collect by small contributions, from 50¢ upwards, a moderate sum to be sent annually to Jerusalem, Hebron, Tiberias and Zafeth, and to designate how much shall be appropriated to each congregation, so as to avoid any misunderstanding respecting the charitable intentions of the donors; and we have every confidence in the integrity of the various heads of the congregation that the directions would be obeyed to the letter.[17]

Leeser's was the most extensive and constructive proposal thus far advanced. If consistently carried out, it would have put the entire *ḥalukkah* system on an efficient and orderly basis. However, neither the recipients nor the donors were as yet ready for such comprehensive regulation.

Aaron Selig's reception in Baltimore likewise left little to be desired. Abraham Rice, Preacher of the Nidhe Israel Congregation, although at that time in the throes of resignation (he announced his withdrawal from office for October 1849), extended to the visitor a hearty welcome and recorded in his book the establishment of a society

> under the name משמרת הקודש יסוד עולם to send every year to Sir Moses Montefiori the sum collected, for our poor Brethern in the Holy City. Witness whereof I have herewith set my name and the Seal of the Cong. at Baltimore 3rd July 5609.

The Fels Point Hebrew Friendship Congregation (Oheb Israel), through its Secretary, M. Polevik, likewise indorsed the envoy's credentials, and pledged affiliation to the new society in order "to send their Mite to our poor Brethren in Palestine."[18]

Aaron Selig's next stop was Cincinnati. His arrival had been somewhat unluckily preceded by the organization a short time before of a society for the assistance of the Jews in the Holy Land, of which Rev. James Koppel Gutheim (1817-86) was President, while Seixas Solomon served as Secretary. The avowed purpose of that society, according to a communication in the *Occident,* was "to collect funds for transmission through mercantile houses to Palestine, without the intervention of messengers." In an (undated) entry therefore in the messenger's book signed not only by Henry Hart Leitz of the Congregation Bene Isroel, but also by five other officials (David Mayer, Daniel Ullmann, Samuel Banee [?], Abraham Harris, and Nathan Malzer) in charge of the communal charities, the cemetery, and the abattoir, the Cincinnati elders could merely record the unanimous decision taken at a meeting of all local congregations "that funds should be collected by subscription and contributions . . . remittances would be made half yearly through Sir Moses Montifour or some other responsible person."[19]

In Louisville, Aaron Selig's credentials were recognized by the trustees of the Congregation Adas Israel (A. Schweat [?], President) who laid the matter before the general meeting of the

Congregation. Then "a subscription was taken from the members to be paid semi-annually and forwarded to Sir Moses Montefiour" (August 13, 5609).[20]

After a relatively long interruption, undoubtedly caused in part by the High Holidays, we find Aaron Selig in New Orleans where, on October 22, 1849, his credentials were attested by Isaac Hart, signing as Parnass-President of the Congregation Shari Chesed [Shaaray Chased], who added:

> I have opened a Subscription List for the Israelites of our City to which many have affixed their names. The object for which is to form ourselves into a Society to enable us to forward Semi annualy to Sir Moses Montefore such Sums as may arise from the above named Supscription. Below I am pleased to add the names of our present members.
>
> N.B. Any sums sent to me from our Neighbouring Cities or Towns I will cheerfully forward in the name of Congregation or Parties sending it.

The appended list of subscribers includes 45 names and the annual amounts pledged by each. The latter, ranging from two to five dollars, totaled $132.50, a respectable sum for those days.[21]

Only two days later Israel I. Jones, Parnass of the Congregation Shaare Shamaim in Mobile, Alabama, certified Aaron Selig's credentials and promised "at the next meeting of our Board of Trustees to lay the same before that body and advocate annual appropriation for the relief of our suffering brethren of the Holy Land." A little later (November 3, 1849) Jesaias Weil, Parnas, Henry Lehmann, Vice Parnas, and Em. Lehman, Secretary of the Hebrew Congregation in Montgomery, wrote:

> A general Meeting was call[d], and it was unanimous agreed "funds should be collected by Subscription, and forward such sums to Sir Moses Montefore."

An appended list includes ten subscribers pledging amounts from $1.00 to $10.00 and totaling $37.50.[22]

On November 11, Aaron Selig was in Charleston, S. C., where

he secured attestation of his credentials from Samuel Valentine, Secretary of the relatively young Congregation Shearit Israel (founded in 1843), and where an aid society was formed to "obviate the necessity of sending any Messengers hereafter to this country." Further, "the Mission of the Revd. Rabby is recommended to such other Congregations as he may visit in this country." Valentine lists the 31 members who "constitute the Society at present," adding that "others may join hereafter." (For some reason Jacob Rosenfeld, Ḥazzan and Lecturer of the Charleston congregation, felt prompted to amplify Valentine's matter-of-fact attestation by a note of blessing for the messenger and his mission.) While no amounts are mentioned, it seems that each member of the society subscribed for only $1.00 per year. This may be deduced from a report in the *Occident* which caused Leeser to urge his readers to emulate the Charleston example, since "fixed annual contributions are the proper mode of giving permanent relief." Nor did the activities of the congregation cease with Aaron Selig's visit; in both 1850 and 1851 we learn of collections totalling $22 and $24 respectively, which were forwarded to the *Occident*.[23]

Having obtained, on November 26, 1849, a similar attestation from the Trustees of the Beth Shalom Congregation in Richmond, Virginia (signed by Jacob Ezekiel, Secretary) and their promise "to submit his Claims to the next annual Meeting of this Congregation" and to forward all amounts collected to Montefiore, Aaron Selig returned to New York.

Before embarking upon another extended tour, which was to take him through the communities of New England and northern New York, our messenger sought to reinforce the moral and organizational status of his undertaking by obtaining renewed indorsements from Raphall, Noah, and S. M. Isaacs. On December 11, Raphall, now in New York, once more certified that "I have known him many years as a pious and learned man and as an honest and faithful משולח [envoy]. And that he personally, and the Mission entrusted to him are fully deserving of every kindness and support." Noah, more concretely, wrote into the book, on January 10, 1850:

> Rabbi Zelag Ashkenazi leaves this city for Hartford, New Haven, Albany, Utica, Syracuse & Buffalo to make an application for aid for our brethren in the Holy Land. Our Congregations have voted twenty-four dollars each per annum for that purpose. The money is to be transmitted to Sir Moses Montifoire from here and will be received here by Morland Micholl Esq., the Rev. S. M. Isaacs or the subscriber.

The reference is evidently to a resolution adopted several months previously by his own congregation, Shearith Israel of New York, which, under date of Tammuz 11, 5609 (July 1, 1849) was reproduced in full in the *Occident*. It consisted of the following preamble and two resolutions:

> Whereas the poor of the Holy Land among our brethren have always been objects of solicitude and attachment among the pious throughout the world, and their support is a duty which devolves on Jews and which should never be neglected,
> and whereas the custom of sending messengers from the Holy Land to collect charity is attended with great expense, and sometimes with great difficulty in relation to the distribution of the funds collected, therefore
> Resolved, that this congregation entertaining such views, do hereby appropriate an annual sum of $25, commencing the 1st of July 1850, towards the support of all poor Jews in the Holy Land, and by this mode avoid hereafter the recognition of any messenger. And to inform the Jewish authorities of the course we have adopted.
> Resolved, that a copy of the foregoing be transmitted to the Parnass and Board of Trustees of all the congregations in this city for their consideration and action, in advancement of a measure of so much interest to our people generally.
> N.B. The Parnass of this congregation (Samuel Lazarus, Esq.) is willing to receive any donations from congregations or individuals in the furtherance of this benevolent object, and will transmit the same to its proper destination.

In his introductory remarks to this communication Leeser warmly praised this type of "annual congregational succour which, with the aid to be expected from the various societies lately established, will go far to do away with the propriety of sending out messengers hereafter to collect personally for the poor of the Holy Land." Further, he urged all other American congregations to follow the example of "the oldest Jewish community in the country." To reinforce Noah's statement, Isaacs expressed his readiness to forward all funds transmitted to him from the various societies to Montefiore "for the sole purpose and use of the Parties in the Holy Land known by the name of 'Parushim' forming a body of Seven Hundred Souls who are reputed to be in great distress."[24]

Equipped with these old and new testimonials and a fairly impressive record of his preceding journey, Aaron Selig repaired to New Haven. From the congregation Mishkan Israel there and from Isaac Strouse, its Rabbi, Ḥazzan and Secretary, he obtained, on January 20, 1850, a pledge of annual collections in behalf of the Palestinian poor, which funds were to be forwarded through Isaacs to Montefiore in London. The first collection, instituted that day, yielded a total of but $22.50, despite the fairly large number of 23 participants (duly listed). The individual contributions, ranging from 25¢ to $3.00, compared unfavorably with the size of the individual donations in the southern communities. The same holds true also of the other communities in the Northeast which, as is also elsewhere attested, were more populous, but on the whole, less wealthy.[25]

Two days later, Hartford joined the procession. The congregation Beth Israel, represented by Jacob Lithauer, its Secretary *pro tem*, and Abraham Hollander, its Parnas, recorded a meeting of its directors at which Aaron Selig's credentials had been approved and an aid society organized "under the name of משמרת הקודש יסוד עולם for the purpose of sending the semi-annually collected sum, through the hands of the Rev. S. M. Isaacs of New York to Sir Moses Montofier in London, to aid our pious, poor brethren in the Holy City."

An appended list of subscribers contains 19 names, with contributions ranging from 50¢ to $3.00 and totaling $19.50.[26]

In Boston independent action was taken by the two congregations Ohabei Shalom and Bat [Beth] Israel. The former, a young and growing community, through its Secretary, Rev. Josef Strauss, entered its attestation on January 27, 1850 and this was repeated, with but minor alterations, by the sister congregation, represented by I. W. Ezekiel, Parnass and Lewis Marks:

> *This is to certify that Rabby Aaron Selig Ashkenazi, has sub-mitted his Credentials to the Presd. and directors of the Con-gregation Ohef Shalom as a Messenger from our Distressed Brethern in the Holy Land, whose Message is for the purpose to establish Societies, whose Contribution are to be transmitted to Sir Moses Montifior in London, to aid our distressed Brethern in the holy City.*
>
> *A Society for that purpose is about to be formed in this City, and whatever Amount can be raised, will be forwarded through the hands of the Rev. S. M. Isaacs of New York to Sir Moses Montifior in London. We will cheerfully recommend Him, to the Sympathies of our Brethern, wherever he meet them.*

Both congregations appended lists of subscribers. The first contains 13 names but mentions no amounts contributed or pledged, while the second enumerates twelve donors, nine of whom list their contributions. These range from one to five dollars and total $19.00.[27]

In Albany, on the other hand, Aaron Selig had to be satisfied with a promise for the future, as we learn from the following entry signed by Rabbi [Isaac M.] Wise D.D. and President F. Shulz of the Congregation Beth El on February 5, 5610:

> *Our worthy Brother Rabbi Aaron Selig Ashkenasi, messenger of our poor Brethern in the holy City of Jerusalem, which the Lord may restore, has come to us to solicit our aid for the poor of our people; but since many of our members are absent from the City, nothing could be done in his favor until* פסח *next I will try to constitute* בעז"ה *a society to aid the poor of Jerusalem. It is a lamantable feature of the total absence of national love among our brethern the remnents of Israel, that even the rich, whom God has blessed with abundance, withdraw their hands*

> from the needy and poor watchmen, that God's mercy allowed
> to remain in the sacred vineyard חרפה שברה לבי ואנושה I hope
> that other Congregations and individuals will do more for the
> house of Israel.

This attestation, written in Wise's characteristic style, incidentally
sheds interesting light on the economic status of Albany Jewry;
the absence from the city of such a large number of the members
was undoubtedly due to their extended peddling over a vast area,
which did not allow them to return even once a week to their
homes. This occupational feature may also help to explain another
phenomenon, rather extraordinary in those days, that a number
of the Jews in Albany belonged to neither the Beth El congregation with its 150 contributing members nor to the Congregation
Beth Jacob, counting only some 30-40 members, but had no
synagogue affiliation whatsoever.[28]

Utica, where our messenger took up a direct collection, introduced a new feature into his record. Instead of merely signing
their names and mentioning the amounts of their contributions,
the Utica donors entered shorter or longer discourses of their
own in either Hebrew or German. Even though their command
of either language left much to be desired, they evidently preferred
them to English which they either knew still less well or else
considered as less appropriate for religious use. Some of them
inserted special greetings to friends living in Palestine, especially
to Asher Lemel, formerly Rabbi of Galin whom some of the
Utica Jews remembered as their revered teacher. (Representative
extracts are presented below in the Appendix.) Only at the end
followed the official attestations of Aaron Herschfeld, the Parnas
(with a personal contribution of $2.00) and Judah Loeb Elsner,
the Minister of the Congregation Beth Israel.[29]

The example of Utica was partly emulated in Syracuse, where
of the 18 signatories pledging amounts varying between 50¢ and
$2.00, the majority were satisfied with a brief note in Hebrew or
German. The longest is the last entry by A. Kühlsheimer, dated
February 18, 1850:

In Erwägung der äusserst dürftigen Verhältnisse in welchen unsere Glaubensbrüder in der heiligen stadt Jerusalem versetzt sind erheischt es unsere Pflicht, die uns durch den würdigen H. Selig gegebene Veranlassung zu benutzen und nach Kräften zu bethätigen ("לא תאמץ את לבבך ולא תקפוץ את ידך מאחיך האביון") *daher freue ich mich, habe ich mich entschlossen zum Zwecke dessen jährlich 1 Thaler zu spenden.*

R. Syracuse, den 18t Febr. 1850 A. Külsheimer[30]

In Rochester, the messenger had little immediate success. In a statement signed on February 19, by S. Treumann, Secretary *pro tem*, and (in Hebrew) by Mordecai Tuska, the Ḥazzan of the B'nai Brith Congregation, we find a verbatim repetition of Isaac M. Wise's indorsement, except for the concluding Hebrew phrase. (We may assume that conditions in Rochester so greatly resembled those in Albany, that the two officials found it most convenient simply to repeat the same statement.) In Buffalo, on the other hand, two days later, Aaron Selig persuaded a gathering of ten citizens, meeting in the private house of Solomon Fridenberg, to pledge weekly contributions of 2¢ each to the society Mishmeret Hakodesh for the benefit "of the Poor Israelites of Jerusalem." These ten members were soon followed by many others, so that the record shows a total of 48 signatures, including those of A. Ansell, ש"ץ ונאמן and of four male and three female members of the Fridenberg family.[31]

Upon his return to New York Aaron Selig tried to wind up his affairs without undue delay. Apart from receiving direct contributions, such as that listed under the name of Heschel B. Joseph Katz of Weltinetz in the amount of $1.00—there is no way of ascertaining how many more gifts of this kind remained unrecorded—he registered receipts primarily from three organizations, those headed by Isaacs, Philip Levi of the B'nai Jeshurun, and one newly established and headed by Judah Hirsch Goldberg, a professional scribe. During the middle days of Passover Isaacs entered two accounts which showed that he had theretofore received the following sums: from Cincinnati $250.00; St. Louis

$62.00; Louisville $50.00; Hartford $11.00 and the Beth Israel Congregation in New York $5.00. Of this total of $378.00 he had given Aaron Selig $10.00 for his traveling expenses, sent $350.00 to Montefiore, and still had on hand $17.00 (the discrepancy of $1.00 was due to a mistaken addition).[32] Levi listed, on May 9, 1850, the names of 29 contributors who had given him sums ranging from 25¢ to $5.00 and totaling $41.75. He, too, advanced $10.00 to the messenger, retaining the balance for transmission to Montefiore. Concerning Goldberg, agent of the third relief organization, we first hear of him in connection with a $2.00 contribution by one Meir Makowe early in Nisan (March). He may, however, also have been the collector of the eight amounts (totalling $7.21) previously listed on the same page. He is again mentioned in a long Hebrew entry, dated Sivan 1, 5610 (May 12, 1850) which reads as follows:

עלינו לשבח ועל טוב יזכר שם הרב המופלג והמפורסם חכם ונבון אי"א
מרבים כקש"ת מו"ה צבי הירש ב"מ יחיאל סופר סתם דפה ק"ק נוא יארק
שהשתתף בצערינו ועמד לימין צדקינו וקבל אותי בצל קורתו ונתאכסנתי
אצלו זה זמן כביר והתנדבו אנשים מנדיבי עמים להתפלל בביתו במנין
בכל שבת ושבת כמקדם ולהתנדב בעד עלית התורה כל אחד כפי אשר נדבו
לבם ועלה סך הכל לערך עד היום דלמטה ששים ר"ט מעות אמעריקא ומזה
קבל הרב המופלג המפורסם שלשלת היוחסין שד"ר מעה"ק תובב"א בחודש
כסליו העבר סך עשרים ר"ט מעות אמעריקא על הוצאותיו. עוד קבל הרב
ר' אהרן זעליג שד"ר הנ"ל ביום דלמטה סך שלש ושלשים ר"ט מעות
אמעריקא והמותר נשאר בכאן. ועלינו אי"ה להתעסק במצוה רבה כזו
ולקבץ עוד נדבות בעד אחינו בני ישראל אשכנזים פרושים הי"ו ולמסור
מהיום והלאה כל הנדבות שיעלה בזה המנין ליד הרב המופלג ומפורסם
אי"א מרבים כקש"ת כמו"ה משה ב"מ יעקב רפאל הי"ו שנתמנה אותו
הרב ר' אהרן זעליג שד"ר הנ"ל לנשיא על כל הבאים אשר בכל מדינות
אמעריקא ומידו יבוא בטח ליד השר וטפסר מו"ה משה מונטיפיאורי הי"ו
וחלק כחלק יאכלו ותיכף (?) לנטילה ברכה אשריהם ואשרי חלקם לחיים
בירושלים ועין בעין יזכו לראות בנחמת ציון וירושלם בב"א ואני הח"מ
וכל אנשי נדיבי עמינו מבקשים לצלות בצלותא דרבנן למען ירבו ימינו
וימי בנינו אצל כל מקומות הקדושים ובפרט אצל כותל המערבי אשר לא
זז שכינת עוזו משם נקבנו שמותינו של כל אחד ואחד בכדי שיעלה
זכרונינו בתפלתם בעד אריכת ימינו והצלחתינו עד ביאת משיח צדקינו
בבהיר"א יום א' ר"ח סיון שנת בך ה' יסד ציון ובה יחסו עניי עמו [ישע'
יד:לב] לפ"ק ואלו הם המתנדבים בעם

While there seems to be a change in the person speaking in the nominative, we may clearly deduce from this entry the following facts: Goldberg not only entertained Aaron Selig at his home during the latter's long stay in New York, but also organized in his residence regular Sabbath services. All monies "offered" during the recitation of the weekly lesson were devoted to Palestine relief. By June (?) a total of $60.00 had thus been collected, of which the messenger received first $20.00 and then $33.00. The congregants further pledged themselves to continue their efforts after Aaron Selig's departure from America, and to hand the funds, for ultimate transmission to London, to Moses ben Jacob Raphael (Raphall) whom the messenger had appointed as the *Nasi* (chief) of all the officials active in behalf of Palestine. The appended list of contributors unfortunately gives the 71 names only in their Hebrew forms, so that identification is difficult. In any case, Goldberg, in whose handwriting all these names are evidently listed, nowhere mentions any connection between his undertaking and that headed by Isaacs, still allegedly the National Treasurer of the entire enterprise.[33]

The shift from Isaacs to Raphall was evidently inspired by Aaron Selig himself. It was the result of a long simmering conflict between the messenger and his chief patron in the United States which had come to a head a few weeks before. Isaacs and his associates, long opposed to the excessive costs of collection by messengers, and perhaps disgruntled over the free use by Aaron Selig of his wide discretionary powers, published in the *Asmonean* of April 26, 1850 the following communication:

> *Notice is hereby given. To the Presidents and Members of the various Societies organized throughout the United States, in support of the mission of Rabbi Aaron Selig for the Poor of the Holy Land, not to pay any monies whatever either to Messengers or through any channel except through the only accredited agents* [Isaacs, Noah, and Micholl].

Aaron Selig countered this move by a diplomatic maneuver, more clever than effective. Without any direct reference to Isaacs's announcement he published in the *Asmonean* of May 10, 1850 a "special notice":

> That the authorities in [of the] Ashkenazim Perushim, have ratified in due form the appointment he made of Chief Treasurer in Birmingham in the person of the Rev. Dr. Raphall, and have further decreed that as the Rev. Dr. is now located here in New York that he holds the same appointment, viz. Ashkenazim Perushim, principal treasurer in America, and request that all those gentlemen who have kindly undertaken to collect funds for the Holy Land, will be so good as pay all such collections to the Rev. Dr. Raphall, who will forward them to their proper destination.

There is no way of ascertaining whether Raphall was previously consulted and, if so, whether he realized that he was being used as a pawn in the messenger's game. It does not seem likely that so soon after his arrival in New York he would have cared willfully to antagonize some of the most prominent local leaders. Small wonder, therefore, that Isaacs, indirectly replying in the following issue of the *Asmonean,* made no reference whatsoever to this personal angle, but rather emphasized what evidently had long been another bone of contention between him and the messenger. The latter naturally represented only the interests of his sponsors, the Jerusalem Perushim. Isaacs, however, and the other American friends of Palestine relief, were little interested in the factional divisions of Palestine Jewry, and wished to see the amounts collected distributed equitably among *all* the needy Jews of Jerusalem, Hebron, Tiberias, and Safed. In his communication to the editor, therefore, after citing a recent letter from Montefiore stating that he had forwarded £72 4s 1d (evidently the equivalent of the $350 sent to him by Isaacs) to Rev. Isaac Cobo and David Herschell Berliner in Jerusalem for distribution "amongst *all* the poor according to the wish of the donors," he added the following lengthy explanation:

The system of encouraging messengers from the East has, for years, been productive of evil; it has fostered mendicancy, it has destroyed harmony, and robbed the poor pilgrims of hope, located on Holy Ground, of a portion of the liberal means the Jews of America contribute towards their support. It cannot be too generally known, nor too widely disseminated, that a fourth part of the sums collected by messengers, swells the pockets of the employed, exclusive of his travelling expenses and what he gathers on his own private account. . . . Urged thereto by some valued friends in Europe, I have devoted my time to the subject, and have transmitted large sums to the houses of Montefiore and Lehren. In all cases requiring the amount to be distributed amongst all the poor, instead of fostering sectional feelings, the result has been highly advantageous to the recipients, no expense is incurred in the transmission, and the poor man obtains the whole of his due. Let us then urge congregations to discountenance all messengers.

It was this point of view which finally induced a conference of New York and Philadelphia congregations (attended by Isaacs of Shaarey Tefilah, Noah and Abrahams of Shearith Israel, Jacob M. Falkenau and Ansel Leo of B'nai Jeshurun, Henry Moses of Anshe Chesed, Jacob Weinschenck of Rodef Sholem, Isidore Raphael of Shaarey Zedek, Abraham Schwarts of Shaarey Hashamaim and by Isaac Leeser, Max Lilienthal, and Abraham Hart of Philadelphia) to allot the following shares in the American collection to the three main branches of Palestinian Jewry: 48 percent were to be distributed among the Ashkenazim hailing from Russia and Poland, 14 percent to those belonging to the German and Dutch congregations, and 38 percent to the Sephardim of the four cities. Probably in the same connection Isaacs decided to join forces with the existing *Terumat hakodesh* organization which had been founded as early as 1833; notice to this effect was published in the *Asmonean* of September 27, 1850. The four directors (I. B. Kursheedt, S. J. Isaacs, S. Abrahams, and S. M. Isaacs) expressed once more their desire to transmit all funds to Palestine "free of any Messengers Feeds [!]," and urged the congregations and individuals to send their contributions for early transfer to Montefiore.[34]

These undesirable complications may have hastened Aaron Selig's decision to end his sojourn in America and to return home *via* England. Within five weeks from the above Hebrew entry our account-book registers his presence once more in Liverpool, where on Tammuz 6 (June 20, 1850) M. S. Oppenheim and Lazarus Harris (who now designated themselves as the *gabbaim* of the Holy City of Jerusalem) again endorsed his mission.

The appended list of contributors includes forty names, with monthly subscriptions ranging from 6d to 2s and totaling £2 1s, a figure which compares favorably even with the largest recorded American collection of $250.00 in Cincinnati. The two officials also report a total collection of £19 5s 6d (from which they gave three pounds to Aaron Selig for his expenses) and the transmission to Montefiore during the preceding January of £21 0 0 from an earlier collection.[35]

A week later Aaron Selig appeared in Manchester, apparently for the first time. Although cautiously worded, the following entry shows that he succeeded in enlisting also the support of this growingly important congregation:

Messrs Simon Joseph & John M. Isaac wardens of the Old Congregation, Manchester having perused the documents produced by Rabbi Aaron Selig & believing in the truth of his Mission, after having consulted with the Sub-Committee—Resolve—To ascertain the willingness of Sir Moses Montefiore to transmit any funds which may be collected in Manchester for the purposes of this Mission & guaranteeing the same shall be distributed among the Ashkenazim community Jerusalem generally and without distinction, pledge themselves to use their best exertions in the furtherance of this object by setting on foot a canvass for Subscriptions among their Coreligionists in this Town & that the amount so subscribed shall be transmitted to Sir Moses Montefiore annually or biennially in order that the Contributions of the charitably inclined may be forwarded to Jerusalem.

This statement is amplified by an interesting Hebrew entry signed by one Naḥman b. Jacob ha-Levi, formerly of Hamburg, and by a communication of I. (J.) Kantrowitz, Minister of the congregation (ש״ץ דק״ק הנ״ל) informing Joachim Levy, Hebrew Master at the Hebrew Educational Society School (very likely identical with the preceding Naḥman) "that I have undertaken to use my energies in furthering the laudable object."[36]

The last recorded stop in his journey was Birmingham, which had also been his first station in England on his west-bound trip. The local congregation once more received him hospitably and, apart from mentioning that as a result of his previous appeal £15 had been forwarded to Montefiore in February 1849, it registered a promise, signed on July 3, 5610 (1850) by Philip Abraham, Secretary and S. M. Marks, Warden:

> that at the next General Meeting of the Congregation which will be held during סוכות הבע״ל his application for relief on behalf of our suffering brethren shall be again taken into consideration and a sum for their relief will be raised in such way as the Meeting shall there and then determine which amount shall be forwarded to Sir Moses Montefiore.[37]

Once more there is no evidence that he visited the British capital, but it would seem no less strange for him not to have attempted to give to Sir Moses a first-hand report of his journey, after he had instructed all communities visited on the road to forward their funds to the London banker, than it would have been for him to issue such instructions without a preliminary authorization by the prospective recipient.

Thus was concluded a journey which had taken Aaron Selig twice through Britain and at least once through all the major Jewish communities in the United States from Boston to Alabama and which lasted, all told, some two and a half years. The results, if we are to judge from the entries in our record alone, could not be regarded as eminently satisfying to the senders, since the amounts mentioned as having been dispatched to Montefiore totalled less than $600.00. On the other hand, the emissary must have received directly considerable sums which did not find their way into the record. To a certain extent he was forced to accept such outside revenue, since his total recorded allocation for traveling expenses from the day of his arrival in America to that of his return to England was only $73.00. Even if we assume that in most places local Jews felt it an honor to extend hospitality to this envoy from Jerusalem (as was indeed the case in Goldberg's house in New York), this sum could not possibly have covered all his expenses. While we do not know how particular he was to render to his sponsors a full account of such unrecorded funds, it may be assumed that, especially in computing his commission, the authorities in Jerusalem took into account these sources of income.

Moreover, far more important than the immediate results of the journey was the stimulus thus given to the British and American communities to organize permanent societies for Palestine relief and to revitalize such as had previously been established. It was, as we have seen, with a view toward such permanent activities that influential local leaders countenanced Aaron Selig's mission.

Unfortunately we lack records showing the progress of the collections during the subsequent years. In the two English communities, Liverpool and Birmingham, efforts were evidently relaxed during the messenger's absence, and more than a year passed between the dispatch of the first collections to Montefiore (in January and February 1849) and his return visit in the Spring of 1850. This slackening of effort probably obtained to an even greater extent in the less well organized American communities which lacked, in the matter of Palestine relief, the stimulus and leadership of such men as Moses Montefiore and Hirsch Lehren. Samuel Isaacs, though far from deficient in devotion and tenacity, seems to have exerted a less enduring influence upon his coreligionists. Only once, in 1853-54, did he succeed, in response to an appeal by Montefiore and Chief Rabbi Nathan Adler, in organizing nation-wide collections in behalf of famine-stricken Palestine, and in raising more than five thousand dollars. It was also undoubtedly due to his influence that his friends, Sampson Simson, Simeon Abrahams, and others founded, in 1853, the North American Relief Society for Indigent Jews in Jerusalem, Palestine, of which he served as Treasurer. Since the society soon secured a legacy of $10,000 from the estate of Judah Touro, it had at its disposal an annual revenue of some $700 from this fund, which it forwarded regularly to Palestine. Otherwise, however, it did little to keep alive the interest of American contributors.[38]

II   The Mission of Abraham Nissan, 1861-62

With the marked decline in American support, it is not surprising that ten years later both the community of Tiberias (which in 1857 had sent one Nahum Cohen to the United States to solicit contributions toward the construction of a synagogue and school building) and the elders of the Jerusalem Perushim found it expedient to dispatch another messenger to the Western Hemisphere in order to reawaken the interest of the ever-expanding communities of the New World.

As a preliminary step to the designation of the new emissary, the Jerusalem authorities decided to put in order the minute-book formerly handled by Aaron Selig, since the numerous attestations and indorsements entered therein were likely to prove very helpful to his successor as well. Yeḥiel Brill, Secretary of the Kolel Perushim, after checking the paginated leaves in the book, stated officially that those still unfilled, beginning with the new title page, numbered 130 folios exclusive of that page.[39]

The state of mind of Diaspora Jewry was not particularly favorable to a new mission. Apart from the severe economic depression which had hit American Jewry, along with the rest of the population, on the eve of the Civil War, the very idea of a messianic restoration to Palestine had been under sharp attack by reformers in Europe and America. With even greater vigor the latter opposed all incipient attempts at secular political action aimed at the extension of the Jewish settlement and Jewish rights in the Holy Land. It was at this juncture that Isaac M. Wise, commenting in his *American Israelite* on the rumor that Napoleon III intended to "make Rothschild King of Jerusalem and open the country again for the Hebrews," took occasion to condemn it as "so absurd that none can believe it; for it is evident that European and American Israelites would not emigrate to Palestine and there fight half-savage Arabs, Druses and Turks, and wild beasts in order to have a king of their own, the vast majority of the enlightened Hebrews being republicans in principle. . . ." The Syrian massacres, in the spring and summer of 1860, which entailed considerable sufferings also for the Jews of Northern Syria, although helping to attract the attention of the western Jews to the status of their coreligionists in the Middle East, diverted many of their charitable endeavors to the relief of the Jews of Damascus and its immediate environs. Even those who had retained their unswerving loyalty to the Palestine ideal were often discouraged by recurrent reports concerning the maladministration of relief funds in the four holy cities. In the *Occident* of October 4, 1860, for example, there appeared a letter from Jerusalem which warned Americans of the projected dispatch of several messengers and counseled

> to give them nothing beyond helping them to return home, if they have not the means themselves. The charities of Palestine can be collected much cheaper by gentlemen residing there. . . . It is time that this constant soliciting for the Holy Land were put a stop to; it seems to be a quagmire into which the treasures of the world could be sunk without producing a visible effect. . . . It is no use to maintain men to study for the salvation of Others which, I fear, will be long delayed, if it depended on what they can accomplish. We say this with due reverence; but it is time to speak and to put a stop to a useless burden.

At the same time the author advocated some form of permanent relief to be administered by the Diaspora Jews themselves.

Rumors of this kind began to circulate also in interested non-Jewish circles, especially in connection with the unceasing controversies between the Palestinian rabbinate and the missionaries sent out by the London Society for the Promotion of Christianity amongst the Jews. Resenting the stubborn resistance of Palestinian Jewry to their conversionist efforts, these British missionaries seized on the evident shortcomings of the *ḥalukkah* system to cast aspersion upon the integrity of their opponents. One such report, sent from Jerusalem on June 20, 1861, was published in the London *Daily News* and, through its republication in the *Jewish Chronicle*, gained wide circulation also among Jews. Referring to the difficulties which had arisen between the rabbis and the British Consul, James Finn, it spoke of the

> Augean stable of corruption here, the system of mendicant messengers for collecting of synagogue alms, which the rabbis make so profitable a business for themselves and a clique of personal dependents, and from which the poor derive so little benefit. It seems that during a law-suit, first begun at the consulate by themselves, the consul found reason to imprison two rabbis of Hebron, who are under his jurisdiction, in order to make them bring out their accounts. Instantly the whole rabbinism of Jerusalem and Hebron took alarm, and in retaliation excommunicated the prosecutor with the most awful solemnities, and repeated it day after day.

Similar criticisms were also voiced by unbiased Jewish visitors like Ludwig August Frankel whose widely-read travelogue *Nach Jerusalem*, published in Vienna in 1858, contained many sharp attacks on the *ḥalukkah* system. The sting of these accusations was not entirely removed by the occasional weak retorts in the Jewish press of England and America. Even the staunchest friends of the *ḥalukkah* had little to say in favor of the messenger system. At best, they concentrated upon organizing local committees to collect contributions without the large overhead expense of a visitor from Palestine. Indeed, it was just at this time that such a central committee was organized in Paris on the initiative of Blumenthal, who had then returned from a journey to the Holy Land. "The rabbis of the Central consistory and of the consistory of Paris," reports a contemporary paper, "are members of the Parisian committee, which has already sent a physician to Hebron." Such reports invited emulation.[40]

Undeterred by these unfavorable prospects, which must certainly have come to their attention, the hard-pressed elders of the Jerusalem Perushim proceeded with the selection of their messenger to the United States. Their choice fell upon Abraham Nissan Ashkenazi (for some reason never called here by his family name Weinstein) whom they had previously employed as a fund raiser for the construction of the Great Synagogue in 1855. The necessary new credentials were issued in Tammuz 5620 (June-July 1860). Once more combining the credentials with a pathetic though less flowery and bombastic appeal, the four elders (Isaiah Burdaki, Joseph Zundel Salant, Jacob b. David Theomim, and Jacob b. Judah Berlin) addressed themselves to the rabbis, elders, philanthropists, and all other Jews "residing in peace in all the States of gracious America and the magnificent State of California." Reminding the recipients of the preceding mission of Aaron Selig and of the indorsements given to him by many American leaders, they appealed to the Jews of America to renew their efforts in behalf of the *Mishmeret ha-Kodesh* for the benefit of their Kolel, the membership of which had in the meantime increased to 1,500. They urged that annual subscriptions be solicited and special collection boxes placed in synagogues and private houses, and promised that every donor entering his name in the messenger's book would be remembered specifically in the congregation's prayers, particularly during the holidays. They also undertook to issue direct individual receipts for each contribution, insofar as local committees might furnish complete lists of donors and subscribers.[41]

To reinforce this appeal, Abraham Nissan also secured the following recommendation from James Finn, dated Nov. 30, 1860:

The undersigned, her British Majesty's Consul for Jerusalem and Palestine, recommends to the consideration of the benevolent, the miserable condition of the Perushim Congregation of Jews in Jerusalem (about fifteen hundred souls) at this present time, on whose behalf Rabbi Abraham Nissan is proceeding to collect alms. The harvest of the country has failed in the South, from natural causes—in the North, has been destroyed by the wicked insurrection of the Mohammedans and Druses, which has also seriously injured the course of trade and currency. I have every reason to fear, that by the time this letter reaches America, the distress will be much greater than it is at present.

Other letters of recommendation, of unspecified authorship and content, included one addressed to the President of the United States. It must have been inspired by Nahum Cohen's apparent success four years before in enlisting the aid of President Pierce.[42]

Upon his arrival in New York Abraham Nissan first turned to the old loyal friends of his Kolel, Isaacs and Raphall. Isaacs was at first deeply puzzled, and in an editorial on the "Distress in Jerusalem," published in the *Jewish Messenger* of Jan. 18, 1861, publicly expressed his hesitation as to what reply ought to be made to these appeals, since "it is but too apparent that the communities are not in a position to respond in a manner commensurate with their feelings." He contented himself with a pious wish for better times. Nevertheless, at the messenger's insistence, he entered a formal attestation in the book (Shebat 23, 5621—Feb. 3, 1861), adding his address (119 West Houston Street), and intimating his willingness to accept contributions. Later, he clarified his position in two editorials in the *Jewish Messenger* of Feb. 15 and March 8, where he spoke of his reluctance to serve again as the Treasurer for the messenger's collection,

but as they would not exonerate us from the duty, and as we love every footstep of our inheritance, we have accepted the office, and hope that we shall be instrumental in raising a large amount for those poor Pilgrims of hope. Candidly speaking, we would have wished that the Rabbi had come in our midst in a

> more propitious time; still, as he is here, let not our troubles in
> the West, lessen our feeling for those starving in the East. . . .
> We shall be glad to receive donations, and forward them direct.
> Acknowledgments from the recipients in Jerusalem will duly
> reach donors.

Raphall, on the other hand, commented but briefly on Isaacs's
attestation: "I certify the correctness of the above Statement. N.Y.
4th Febr., 5621/61."[43]

The contributions soon began to accumulate. Apart from individual donations, such as those of Sampson Simeon Leo (five
dollars) and H. Marks (one dollar), Isaacs registered, on Feb.
12, the receipt of eighty dollars from the Congregation Beth
Hamedrash. Pesach b. Gedaliah Rosenthal, Rabbi of the congregation—which he calls Beth Hamedrash Hagodol—amplifies this
statement by a Hebrew entry saying that an additional $7.13 had
been paid by him on Adar 18 (Feb. 28) for the messenger's expenses. Further light on this action is afforded by a resolution of
the same congregation (located on Forsyth Street) which Isaacs
published in full in the *Jewish Messenger* of Feb. 15. This demanded that all monies offered in the synagogue on the forthcoming Sabbath Shekalim, and all revenue accruing from a special levy
of "half a shekel," be assigned to Palestine relief, and that an
address of solicitation be delivered by Rabbi Rosenthal at the
morning services, to which all members were to be specially invited.
Such action was to be repeated annually at the same season. The
$80.00 which resulted from the collection were handed to Isaacs
by the President of the Congregation, John Boyer. Isaacs also listed
in the book (on March 1) the further receipt of $25.00 from the
New York Congregation Shaary Zedek, on Henry Street;[44] $109.84
from the Congregation Shaarey Tefilla, on Wooster Street; and
$150.00 from the Congregation Rodef Sholem, on Clinton Street.
The latter amount, collected from offerings made at the Sabbath
services of Feb. 23 and handed to Isaacs personally by a delegation
consisting of President Mayer Schutz, Vice-President Hezekiah
Kohn and Treasurer Solomon Hyman, elicited from him the public

tribute that "such liberality emanating from Israelites not so very wealthy, reflects the greatest credit on all concerned." The congregations B'nai Jeshurun and Anshe Chesed, on the other hand, merely promised to take up a collection during the forthcoming Shevuot festival. Isaacs concludes his entry by saying that "several other Synagogues will adopt a like course, and I earnestly hope the Country Synagogues will adopt the same plan." On April 8, the congregation Beth Israel u-Bikur Cholim, through its Parnas Ellis Joseph (of 34 Dey St.), sent to Isaacs $62.25 which, we learn elsewhere, resulted from donations on the last day of Passover following a suitable address by the President. It also repeated verbatim the pledge of Shaary Zedek for future collections. A few individuals likewise entered their contributions. Among them were four gifts from one Dob Eliezer (דוב [?] אליעזר) totaling $4.50, of which $2.00 were to be delivered by the messenger to the children of Rabbi Moses Lilwener, $1.00 to the daughter of one Rabbi Isaiah and only $1.50 to the general fund of the Jerusalem congregation. Other contributions, here unrecorded, included a donation of $20 from the Beth Hamedrash Adas Jeshurun (through its President H. Brody) which was publicly commended by Isaacs in view of its small membership "mostly in humble circumstances," and of $50 from the *mohel* Samuel Hymans in Brooklyn. The latter sum, like the similar amount coming in Feb. 1862 from Hymans's "charity box" (probably the same silver box which had been given to him as a "true friend of the Holy Land," by admirers at a Testimonial tendered to him in July 1861) was very likely handed to Abraham Nissan directly. No wonder that Isaacs, fearing the recurrence of abuses concomitant with such direct collections, used the opportunity of reporting the Hymans contribution in order to remind readers of the *Jewish Messenger* that the Jerusalem authorities insisted upon full and correct accounting, and to add:

> We should, therefore, regard it as a great favor, if parties, forwarding donations, through any other channel, would be kind enough to inform us of the amount, and through whom transmitted, so that we may be enabled to comply with the wishes

of the constituted authorities, and at the same time be enabled
to furnish an historical sketch of the benevolence of the Israelites
in America, as again exemplified in their sympathy for the suffering in the Holy Land.[45]

The relative aloofness of the B'nai Jeshurun and the Anshe
Chesed may perhaps best be explained by the arrival, about the
same time, of a circular letter addressed to the Trustees of the
former congregation by the President of the German and Dutch
Congregation of Jerusalem (abbreviated: HOD), soliciting special
contributions for a "Habitation for Poor and Pilgrim Jews" to be
erected in Jerusalem. B'nai Jeshurun forwarded its copy of the
letter to the Board of Delegates, which, however, seems to have
taken no action except to mention it in its Second Annual Report (July 1861), in referring to similar hospices previously erected
from Montefiore and Touro funds. "Thus identified," it added,
". . . with a system of benevolence so generally approved, it is
reasonably to be inferred that the Israelites of the United States
will watch its development with the greatest interest and in due
season extend a liberal hand towards its support." Before Abraham
Nissan concluded his journey, moreover, there appeared in the
Occident of February 1862 the following lengthy notice which,
together with the report published there two years before, must,
despite the more sympathetic note of Feb. 1861, have sounded
discouraging to many prospective supporters of the mission. It
may, incidentally, also help to explain the otherwise incomprehensible studious avoidance of Philadelphia by our messenger.

It is officially announced, under date of Amsterdam, Cheshvan,
5622, that Mr. Akiba Lehren has accepted the post of Pakid and
Amarkal for the Holy Land conferred upon him. . . . The
Amsterdam committee have succeeded also in settling the differences between the various communities in the Holy Land,
and have resolved in distributing all money destined simply for
Eretz Yisrael in general 67/168 to the Sephardim congregations,
—in Jerusalem (33), Zafeth (14), Hebron (12), Tiberias (8)—
Dutch and German congregations 34/168, and to the Perushim

in Jerusalem 39, Chassidim in Zafeth 35, Volhynians in Tiberias 13½, Russians in do. 4½, the חב"ד in Hebron 9 parts of the remainder 67/168. Should the sums received exceed 1000 florins, then shall half the excess go to the Dutch and German Israelites on account of the moneys coming from their respective countries; of the other half the Portuguese congregation in Jerusalem is to receive one fifth, because they have to pay more taxes to the government than all the other congregations; the other four-fifths are to be distributed in the proportions as indicated above, dividing all in 168 parts, and omitting the Germans and the Hollanders.—The distribution will take place quarterly. No messengers for collecting shall be countenanced, and any community sending such messengers will be excluded from the distribution by the Committee. We call the attention of the public to the above arrangement, and inform them, at the same time, that all letters and moneys for Palestine may be sent to the address of Mr. A. Lehren, Amsterdam, with the full assurance that their benefaction will be properly applied. Any special donations will, of course, be handed over to the parties designated. . . .[46]

Despite these handicaps Abraham Nissan, encouraged also by Isaacs's good wishes which had appeared in the *Jewish Messenger* of April 19, and which bespoke "for him a welcome wherever he may visit," set out for a tour through the States. He proved to be no less successful in Boston than he had been in New York. On May 5, he first obtained from B. Nelson, President of the Congregation Ohabei Shalom a general pledge to "endeavor to do our duty towards amolerioting (!) the condition of our coreligionists of Jerusalem." Individual subscriptions were taken up, among which that of Isaiah Pachter, the congregational sexton, was of special importance. Pachter not only doubled his own contribution of one dollar, but soon thereafter (Sivan 3—May 12) agreed to serve together with B. Nelson and the Reader Benjamin b. Menasseh Jacob as the permanent *gabbaei Yerushalayim* in charge of regular collections. Another member, Simon b. Wolf Zuckerman, subscribed for one dollar, but expressed the hope that he would be able in time to raise his annual contribution to $4.00.

Still another, signing Mendel b. Israel, evidently the local *mohel*, promised from that day on to institute collections at every circumcision ceremony which he might attend. Lastly, a congregant named David Davidson (of 80 Washington Street) entered a long, rather remarkable Hebrew note (Appendix II). These individual contributions having yielded a total of $52.50, the congregation decided, on May 12, 1861, "on motion of Wm [William] Kingsbury Esq.," to appropriate $50 from the congregational treasury. Supplemented by a further $7.50 from individual gifts, the total of $110.00 was sent to Isaacs in New York, who indeed confirmed its receipt on May 14. In his accompanying letter, Nelson, apart from expressing regret "that clouds are gathering over this land and paralyzing its commerce," commented on Abraham Nissan's visit: "Allow me to say, that during his stay in this city, the Rabbi has resided with me, and has been visited by several of the members who were all edified by his excellent conversation. As for my part, I only wish his stay were prolonged."

The Adath Israel Congregaiton, too, acting through its President B. Heineman, Vice-President M. Hofmann and Secretary J. Shoninger, entered its attestation (on May 5) and recorded a decision of its Board of Trustees "to award five dollars towards the relief of our Coreligionists the Congn. Askenasim Perushim, and have appointed two Gentlemen to take up Subscriptions & contributions among our members, the proceeds of which will be duly forwarded to the Rev. Dr. Raphall or Rev. Isaacs in New York."[47]

After a brief stay in New York, to which he seems to have returned in the middle of May, in order "to await the action of the Greene St. and Norfolk St. Synagogues, and also of several others who have not yet responded," we next find our messenger in Schenectady, where the congregation Shary Shomaim through its President, Pfeifer Levy and Secretary, D[avid] Marks, promised him "a jearly contribution to the utmost extend of our power." It seems to have raised immediately $9.50, increased by a contribution of the local "Minyen" in the amount of $5.00. Only $13.00, however, were sent to New York, the balance having possibly been turned over to the messenger for his expenses. There also were a few individual donations. The congregation Anshe Cheset of neighboring Troy resolved, on May 30, to send ten dollars to Isaacs (signed T. Cohen and Levi Laub, Secretary). On June 4, the two congregations in Albany, acting through their respective presidents, Sigmund Adler and S. Levi, entered the following statements:

> At a meeting of the Congregation Beth El of this City the sum of $25.00 was contributed for the alleviation of our destitute brethren at Jerusalem, the present protracted state of our commercial community being the cause of this limited amount. But, we, the undersigned hereby promise, annually to raise means for the same purpose to any possible extent within our power.
> The Congregation Beth El Jacob of the City of Albany contributed for our brethern living in distress at Jerusalem, the sum of $14—to the utmost extent of our power. Above sum was the result of the meeting last Sunday, only for that purpose. Wishing to have much imitation in other congregations we sign. . . .

Both congregations promised to forward their contributions to Isaacs.[48]

The Jews of Utica, as during Aaron Selig's earlier visit, exceeded in their articulateness (or exhibitionism) their coreligionists of the other communities. First the congregation Beth El, through Isaac b. Dob Wakman and Charles Rosenthal, entered at the end of Sivan (June 8, 1861) a Hebrew note explaining why, due to the absence of most members on business, it could furnish the messenger only a small sum for his expenses, but pledged more for the future. Indeed in December 1861 Rosenthal sent Isaacs $20.00 with reference to Abraham Nissan's intervention. The congregation's *shohet*, Elijah b. Solomon Zalman, went further and on Tammuz 3 (June 11) promised to institute weekly collections for this purpose. Not to be outdone, Judah Leib b. Yehoash, another slaughterer as well as scribe, apart from pledging (in an extensive Hebrew entry) his own annual contribution of $1.50, promised, together with another contributor, Meir Freidman, to

gather weekly alms for Palestine and, as soon as the sums collected amounted to ten dollars, to forward them to Jerusalem.
He failed to indicate, however, the connection between his action
and that initiated by his colleague, or whether he intended to use
the good offices of Isaacs or Montefiore in dispatching the contributions to their ultimate destination.[49]

Syracuse, Rochester, and Buffalo followed suit. As regards the
first-named city, apart from individual contributions registered
in the messenger's book, we find there a Hebrew entry by one
Israel b. Michael Herson, dated Monday of the weekly lesson
Balak, and stating that the congregation had forwarded $35.00 to
Montefiore in addition to $15.00 paid out to the messenger. More
permanent collections were to be instituted through boxes placed
in various homes. The local *mohel*, Moses b. Menaḥem Wendel
and the *shoḥet*, Israel b. Dob, in separate entries, pledged themselves to exert all their efforts to collect money for this purpose.
The congregation Berith Kodesh in Rochester likewise resolved
to forward to Isaacs a contribution of $25.00 (according to a state-
ment signed on June 23 by Moses Hays, its President). In publicly
acknowledging the receipt of this sum on September 18, Isaacs
commented: "We are pleased to note, amid the general indifference on religious matters, in view of the more engrossing national
difficulties, this remembrance of the Holy Land and its peculiar
claims to our sympathy. Our Rochester friends lose none of their
characteristic consideration for those who appeal to them for
assistance." The same amount was allotted by the Congregation
Beth El of Buffalo in a resolution registered, on July 1st, by
B. Hyman, President and Isaac Black, Vice-President, and concluding with the wish "may Heaven bless their Messenger Revd.
Abraham Nisson and grant him further Success." In that appropriation were included, however, $10.25, privately collected by
Zevi Hirsch b. Israel Greenberg. That is why on Tammuz 21,
5621 (June 29, 1861), before departing Abraham Nissan appointed
Greenberg together with one Isaac b. Sender ha-Levi as the per-
manent supervisors of Palestine relief. The congregation Scheeris
Israel which, according to a brief entry here, had only been

founded some two months before, likewise decided, on July 3, to "try all what there is in our power to send yearly the Mony what be reset on Purim and Madunas Jad" to Isaacs (signed by President A. B. Rosenthal and Secretary Aaron Westhofen).[50]

From Buffalo Abraham Nissan embarked on a hurried trip through the Middle West. The impetus to this trip may have been given him by Isaacs who, a decade earlier, had had the opportunity to witness the growth of the mid-western Jewish settlement, to which he testified in the aforementioned noteworthy letter to the editor of the London *Jewish Chronicle*, dated July 8, 1851.[51]

In Cleveland Abraham Nissan merely obtained, on Ab 4 (July 11), the promise of Elḥana b. Feiwel to serve as a permanent agent for the Palestine relief and a contribution of $3.50 paid to the latter by one Shalom b. Shraga (possibly his brother). In Pittsburgh, on the other hand, the congregation Rodef Sholem raised by subscription the sum of $40.75. Its President, William (in Hebrew: Alexander b. Eliezer) Frank and Secretary *pro tem*, C. D. Arnthal, stated on July 17, that they had deducted therefrom $10.00 for the messenger's railroad fare and expenses. In Cincinnati, where a committee headed by a certain Melzer and Hyman Moses had long been active collecting contributions and forwarding them to the Central Committee in Amsterdam, Isaac M. Wise signed the following endorsement (July 22):

> *This is to certify that the bearer Rabbi Abraham Nissan of Jerusalem is the accredited messenger of our poor brethern in Palestine to receive donations for them. He is in possession of authentic documents to this effect. I therefore recommend him to our brethren and to all other Charitable men.*

In view of Wise's growing influence even this more moderate endorsement undoubtedly proved very helpful. On the following day came a donation of $15.95 from elders Joseph Holzman and Jacob Hirschberg, the former adding the explanation that "Rabbi Abraham Nissan not having remained long enough, we could only collect the small amount mentioned above, the Gentleman having promised us to return here. We shall do our best for the cause which he so worthily represents." There is no evidence, however, that Cincinnati attempted at that time to duplicate the remarkable achievement of its previous effort.[52]

In Indianapolis the messenger secured from M. Woolf, President of the Hebrew Congregation a recommendation (entered July 29) and nine contributions totaling $7.85. The following day, M. Hallstrin, President of the Congregation Ahvas Achim of Lafayette, registered contributions of its members totaling $6.00. In Chicago, Abraham Nissan personally entered, on Ab 28 (August 4), a receipt for $10.00 collected by the Society of Young Men (החברה קדישא דהבחורים) and for other collections totaling $21.00. He also obtained an attestation (dated August 6, 1861) from M. M. Gerstley, President of the Congregation Anshe Mayrib. Another entry, in German, signed by one T. Henke (Glenke?), stated that the signer not only contributed $3.00 immediately but also

> verspricht jedes Jahr an den dürftigen und nothleidenden Brüder in Jerusalem eine Gabe zur Verfügung an Herrn M. Montefiore in London, sowie von den übrigen Mitgliedern der hiesigen Gemeinde, womöglichst eine Unterstützung beizufügen.

All these contributions were evidently paid directly to the messenger and never reached Isaacs, who makes mention of them neither in his journal nor in his later summary in the messenger's book.[53]

The reason for this rather hurried journey through the midwestern communities was evidently Abraham Nissan's desire to reach California as speedily as possible. The gold rush had attracted Jews in such number as to bring about a rapid establishment of new Jewish communities on the West Coast. This development elicited numerous reports and wide-spread comments in the European Jewish press, while the alleged quick accumulation of great fortunes must have loomed in tenfold exaggeration in the minds of the poverty-stricken masses of Palestinian Jewry.

It was, indeed, on this account that, as we have seen, our messenger was dispatched specifically to that state of the Union. For
some reason, however, his arrival in San Francisco was greatly delayed, and three and a half months passed between his last entry
in Chicago and the first mention of his stay in California. This
delay can be fully explained neither by the intervening Jewish
holidays nor by the still considerable difficulties of travel to the
new frontier. If Abraham Nissan had allowed himself so little
time for negotiations in the Middle West in order to utilize the
more propitious summer months for his trip to the West Coast,
he must have been sadly disappointed. In any case, the first dated
California entry in his book is a note signed by Simon Craner,
Secretary of the Congregation Shearith Israel in San Francisco,
dated November 22, 1861 and stating that the congregation had
appropriated one hundred dollars "per annum towards the relief
of our Coreligionists in Jerusalem, and that a committee have
been appointed to devise ways and means for their further relief."
The Minister of the congregation, H. A. Henry, amplified this
note by the following lengthy attestation, dated December 1861
(Tebet 5622):

> *I have had the pleasure of perusing the documents in the pos-
> session of Rabbi Abraham Nissan which show that he is the ac-
> credited Emissary from the Holy Land, and deputed to solicit
> subscriptions towards the support of our suffering Brethren in
> the City of Jerusalem, viz. the* אשכנזים פרושים וכו' *I also ac-
> knowledge the receipt of Letters of introduction from the Revd.
> Dr. Raphall and Revd. Mr. Isaacs of New York strongly recom-
> mending the Rabbi to my especial notice to aid him in his
> praiseworthy mission. I therefore considered it my duty as an
> Israelite in the first instance, to extend to him that hospitality
> becoming his exalted position and I am pleased to record that
> during his stay at my House, his uniform Conduct as a pious and
> learned Israelite has confirmed him in my opinion as fully verify-
> ing all that he himself states, and what has been said by others in
> his behalf. It shall ever be my study D.V. [Deo volente] to use
> my humble influence for the benefit of my Coreligionists in the*

land of Promise. It is gratifying to me to be enabled to record the ready response which was given to the application of the Rabbi to my Congregation שארית ישראל of this city, who resolved unanimously to award One hundred Dollars p. Annum from its funds for the poor of Jerusalem, with the promise to do all in their power to collect as heretofore and transmit the result of their labors as often as possible.

In addition to the above a Society has been formed in this City called אוהבי ציון "Friends of Zion" for the relief of our Brethren and is now at this time fairly organized, particulars of which will shortly be published, and issued to the world, which will show the feeling of the Israelites of California towards their foreign brethren in distress. It is confidently hoped that a very handsome sum will be annually raised for the Amelioration of the Condition of אחינו בני ישראל באָרץ הקדושה and it will be Constant study of the Board of Trustees to see that the funds so collected shall be applied to its legitimate purpose.

The smaller Beth Hamidrash of the Society Shomre Shabbat through Moses Arye Bian (Biach), first handed the messenger $9.00 from its treasury (Wednesday of *Shemot*) and six days later informed him, through its Parnas Abraham Abba b. Solomon Segal, in a lengthy Hebrew communication that, although most of its members had joined the new society *Ohabe Zion*, it allotted $25.00 from congregational funds to Palestine relief. To this society refers also the following communication addressed to Revd. Abraham Nissan by its Secretary, I. N. Choynski on December 23, 1861-5622:

Reverend Sir
It affords me much pleasure to inform you that a Society for the permanent relief of your needy Coreligionists at Jerusalem has been formed, and that we have at present some three hundred members pledged for this laudable purpose. The Society promises fair to increase considerable in numbers and it will be the height of our ambition to see our suffering brethren well provided for.
The Society Friends of Zion wishes to be remembered to their

> Brethren in Jerusalem, and you may assure them that the Israel-
> ites on this Coast will not forget them in their hours of trial.
> May the God of our pious Patriarchs prosper you in your journey
> is the prayer of the Society "Friends of Zion."

These communications are preceded by a note entered by one
Israel b. Jacob who had given an unspecified amount, in return
for which he asked that every year on Marheshvan 9, a light be
kindled and the memorial prayer recited for his father, Jacob b.
Isaac, deceased in 1848. Another contributor, Moses Aryeh b. Raphael Katz gave eighteen cents for a *mi sheberakh* to be read in
behalf of his daughter, Judith bat Rachel, very likely in connection with some illness.[54]

Back in New York at the end of January 1862, Abraham
Nissan—once again unlike his predecessor—refrained from lingering on in America, and already on Feb. 14, Isaacs announced his
forthcoming departure "on this week's steamer." "He has commended himself," Isaacs added, "to his coreligionists by his ur-
banity, fidelity and learning. May his voyage be prosperous." This
announcement was accompanied by the following translation of a
long Hebrew valedictory "Letter of Thanks from the Palestinian
Messenger to his brother Israelites in America":

> I, Abraham Nissan, appointed messenger from the Ashkena-
> zim Perushim at Jerusalem, to the Israelites of North America,
> beg to place on public record my thanks for the kind manner
> in which I have been received, and for the truly generous way
> in which my mission has been answered. Every footstep I have
> trod from New York to San Francisco, has reminded me that
> Israel has not changed, for in every way have I been received
> with true Jewish kindness. And for this, I beg to tender not only
> my poor words of acknowledgement, but also those of my prin-
> cipals in Palestine. I will entreat them, on my return to Jeru-
> salem, to join with me in prayer to the God of Israel, that it
> may please him to restore peace and happiness to this destructed
> land, where my co-religionists have ever enjoyed the sweets of
> liberty. All the money that has been forwarded to Rev. S. M.

Isaacs, authorized treasurer for our congregation in Palestine, has been faithfully transmitted, and his accounts properly audited.

As it has been deemed inexpedient by the Rev. Dr. Raphall and Isaacs, who have proved themselves lovers of Zion, by the efforts they have made in behalf of my mission, and whose reward will be exuberant—that I should visit many of our congregations, in consequence of internal difficulties, I have yielded to their advice, and return to the East, although half my mission has not been fulfilled. Still, relying on the well-known benevolence of my nation, who will never forget Jerusalem that they will continue to forward their donations to the Treasurer in New York, I bid them all a farewell. Should it please the Disposer of events to commission me once more to visit the Occidental hemisphere I hope it will be to meet them all in peace, when one brother shall address the other in words of kindness, and union and concord guide the general happiness.

Upon his return to Jerusalem, moreover, the elders of the Perushim addressed letters of thanks to their American patrons. Isaacs briefly referred to those letters, mentioning only that "the societies which have been organized in California in behalf of the poor of the East, appear to afford the greatest satisfaction," but refused to publish the thanks for the services of a number of individuals, "as it would neither be pleasing to the donors, nor just to other contributors."[55]

Therewith ends the actual record of Abraham Nissan's journey. It is followed (apart from a small individual entry in New York) by an account of all receipts and expenditures handled by Isaacs as national treasurer. Written in Hebrew and dated Shebat 30, 5622 (Jan. 31, 1862), it mentions the following total receipts (for the most part previously recorded):

Beth Hamedrash, New York	$80.00
Shaary Zedek	25.00
Rodef Sholem	150.00
Beth Hamidrash Adat Jeshurun	20.00

Beth Israel u-Bikur Cholim	62.25
Shaare Tefila	109.84
Ohabei Shalom, Boston	110.00
Troy Hebrew Congregation	10.00
Albany Hebrew Congregation	21.00
Beth El, Albany	12.00
Buffalo	25.50
Pittsburgh	30.75
Adas Jeshurun, Boston	14.17
Shaarey Shomaim, Schenectady	9.25
Rochester Hebrew Congregation	25.00
Utica	20.00

These receipts, totaling $724.76, were balanced by four shipments to Montefiore, amounting to $650.25, nine advances to Abraham Nissan amounting to $64.03 and expenses for mail and messengers of $10.48.[56]

This financial statement could not, of course, include such contributions as the aforementioned fifty dollars from Hyman's charity box, or an additional $13.50 from Congregation Beth Israel Bikur Cholim (through its President, Isaac Levy), received by Isaacs in the following February; nor could it take account of a further $50.00, from S. D. Moss, forwarded to him in 1862. Nevertheless a comparison of the computation with the preceding entries reveals in the first place that all the funds collected by Abraham Nissan on the last part of his trip in Cincinnati, Indianapolis, Lafayette, Chicago, and San Francisco were never sent to the national treasurer, but were handled exclusively by the messenger. Apart from the very likely numerous gifts which had not found their way into the record at all, the latter seems to have had a share in more contributions than is expressly stated (e.g., in Syracuse, which does not figure in Isaacs's account because the funds had been sent directly to London). The Adas Israel in Boston, with its congregational contribution of $5.00 and an unspecified amount resulting from subsequent subscriptions, does not appear at all in Isaacs's record. The difference between the original entries and Isaacs's account concerning the contributions of the two Albany congregations (amounting to $4.00 and $2.00 respectively) may likewise best be explained if we assume that these amounts were deducted for the messenger's expenses. It is more difficult, however, to account for the discrepancy between the $13.00 claimed to have been sent from Schenectady and the $9.25 actually received. It also goes without saying that Abraham Nissan, no less than Aaron Selig, was hospitably received, and perhaps even lavishly entertained by some of the pious Jews in the various localities which he happened to visit. Evidently Isaacs, chafing under this unbusinesslike procedure, exerted pressure on the messenger to leave the country and soon thereafter (on April 11), in fulfillment of his "duty as a public journalist," published an editorial on the "Messengers from Palestine." Having so long refrained from placing his ideas on record, "lest we should injure the cause of those who are on their mission," he felt it incumbent upon himself, "now that the field is clear," to advise his readers "that the Missionaries should be discountenanced for their commissions and traveling expenses consume nearly one-half of the amounts collected." Rather should contributions be forwarded to Montefiore through the North American Relief Society or any of its trustees, with the reasonable expectation that, within two months, acknowledgments would reach the donors from the ultimate recipients.[57]

Nevertheless, it must be borne in mind that if Abraham Nissan's sojourn in the United States was not unprofitable to himself, his sponsors in Jerusalem had no cause for complaint. The amounts collected were easily twice as high as those gathered under the stimulus of Aaron Selig, and well over $700.00 evidently reached the Perushim through Montefiore, apart from their share in the distribution of the $700 sent by the North American Relief Society to the four "holy" cities. Moreover, the permanent societies organized by this messenger in many communities, which were visited for the first time by any Palestinian messenger, and which extended all the way from Indianapolis to San Francisco, gave promise of a substantial regular revenue for Palestine relief.

III   The Mission of Nathan Neta Notkin, 1867-69

The ravages of the Civil War focused the attention of American communities upon sufferings at home and tended to diminish their interest in Palestine relief. None the less, activities in behalf of the Holy Land were never altogether suspended. Not only did the North American Relief Society continue its annual remittances of seven hundred dollars from the income of the Touro bequest,[58] but the Board of Delegates had for some time devoted its attention to the situation and had established a special Palestine Fund. In December 1866 it issued a circular to the Jews of America calling their attention to Montefiore's recent report to the British Board of Deputies and urged them to cooperate "in providing some more enduring and substantial aid for Palestine than simple almsgiving." Further, in presenting its annual report in June 1867 the Board repeated its recommendation:

> Our love for the Holy Land [it wrote] must not take the form of merely momentary help to prevent starvation. We must consult for the time interests of our brethren there, many of whom have not had in view the duty of providing for their own livelihood and, destitute of energy, appeal to us for counsel and substantial assistance. We must encourage industrious habits, the cultivation of the soil, the direction of labor. Agriculture and industrial interests need to be developed.

Again, in pointing out the persecutions recently suffered by the Jews of the Danubian principalities, North Africa, and Persia, the Board emphasized the importance of Palestine as a country of immigration, and sounded the fully Zionist keynote: "It is our glorious aspiration for the future of Israel, that once more shall the sceptre of Judah vindicate the restoration of Jewish nationality in its ancient seat." However, the Palestine Fund as such, showing a balance of over $3,216.83 during the fiscal year, had increased only by the interest of $199.70 on this sum, but had received no fresh donations. The Executive Committee, recognizing the difficulties occasioned by "the general stagnation in business," nevertheless put the problem before the entire Board for further consideration.

It is in connection with earlier appeals of the Board that we learn also of local activities in two such diverse and distant communities as Richmond, Va. and Congregation B'nai Jeshurun, New York, both of which undertook in 1865 to gather funds for the poor of Jerusalem. In Richmond the attempt was even made to put the appeal on an intercongregational basis. On October 8, 1865, S. A. Winstock, E. Goldsmit, and I. Schriver of the Congregation Beth Shalome were delegated to cooperate with similar committees to be elected by the two other local congregations, the Beth Ahabah and Keneseth Israel, in a united action for Palestine relief. Beth Ahabah, however, refused to take part in this common action and, on Dec. 17, replied that, having received an appeal from the Executive Committee in New York, it would forward its contributions directly to the central agency. Neither the amount nor the date of such payments is recorded, but it may readily be assumed that the Committee here mentioned was the group which, in the name of the American Board of Delegates, had in the same year approached other congregations, such as the New York B'nai Jeshurun, which is reported to have contributed $500.00. Whatever the amounts may have been, they evidently did not satisfy the Ashkenazic recipients in Jerusalem, who soon decided to dispatch another messenger to the United States.[59]

The new mission enjoyed wider backing than those of the previous messengers. Realizing that disparate, competitive efforts led not only to a squandering of resources and an increase of expense but also to a lessening of interest on the part of prospective donors, the authorities in Jerusalem organized, at the end of 1865, a "Central Committee of all the Ashkenazic *Kolelim*," with a permanent secretary in the person of Joseph Rivlin and a regular distribution of all revenue.[60] It was this Central Committee and its constituent groups that decided to make a united appeal in behalf of all the Ashkenazic congregations in the city. The letter of authorization handed to the new messenger in Ab 5626 (July-Aug. 1866) was signed by the following congregations: The Ashkenazim Perushim (as before), the Polish congregation of the District of Warsaw, the German congregation Ahabat Zion, the congregation of Ḥasidim and Galiner, and the Austrian congregation of Galicians. Great care was taken to find a worthy successor to Abraham Nissan, who had passed away several months before. As a son-in-law first of Joseph Zundel Salant and subsequently of Isaiah Burdaki, the new messenger, Nathan Neta Notkin (*or* Natkin) was related to the two most influential leaders of the Ashkenazic Jews in Jerusalem. Further to impress American audiences, the Jerusalem elders secured the following letter of recommendation from H. Victor Beauboucher, the U. S. Consul in Jerusalem:

> The condition of the Jews in Jerusalem being such as to require the assistance of their brethren and others in the West on account of their extreme poverty, the bearer of this present is strongly recommended to the Charitable feelings of all Americans.
>
> Given under my hand and the seal of the consulate this 17th day of July 1866.

The brief letter of authorization, duly entered in the messenger's book (in which the donors were urged to register their names), was amplified in a lengthy discourse entitled *Yerushalayim titten kolah* (Jerusalem uttereth her voice) in which the reasons for the mission and the deplorable conditions of Jerusalemitan Jewry were expounded in detail. This description was to be further elaborated by the messenger's oral communications.[61]

Unlike his predecessors, Notkin was very careless in keeping his accounts. Only a few pages are filled with entries in strict chronological sequence. Some are left blank altogether, while a good many contain signatures deriving indiscriminately from different localities and dating from different periods. In one case a belated entry is made in pencil at the bottom of a page which had by chance been left unfilled by Abraham Nissan six years before. A number of entries are altogether undated, and their period cannot always be safely deduced from their position between other dated notices. Neither is there any indication that Notkin was in touch with the existing national or local organizations for Palestine relief, nor any reference to a national treasurer to whom all the funds were to be sent, although a treasurer of a New York Committee for Jerusalem is indeed mentioned in several pledges. In all likelihood, the messenger handled most of the contributions directly, without effective supervision on the American side. It may well be that his reputable family connections gave him greater self-assertion and encouraged his negligence in bookkeeping. In these circumstances the reconstruction of his first journey through the United States, extending over a period of two and a half years, is necessarily a difficult task, and the resultant picture must remain somewhat fragmentary.

Notkin seems to have arrived in New York in January 1867. The incompleteness of his records becomes apparent when we note that he suddenly appears in the company of another messenger, Rabbi Aryeh Leb Cohen, who later just as rapidly disappears from the scene. Moreover, instead of the usual indorsements of the mission by outstanding leaders of New York Jewry, such as had been entered into the record in the case of both Aaron Selig and Abraham Nissan, we find only the brief statement of N. Cowen, President of the Congregation Beth Israel u-Bikur Cholim (dated Jan. 9, 1867) certifying that his congregation "have delivered to the Tre[asurer] of American Reliff Committee for Jerusalem the first instalment of One hundred and forty Dollars." In another entry (dated Jan. 14) M. Danneberg, President of the Congregation Schary Rachmim, merely registers the information that he had "received of the Comitte a Letter for the Bennevit of Jerusalem." Apart from a few small individual contributions, of uncertain date, no further donations from the American metropolis are recorded in any of the years between 1867 and 1869.[62]

An entirely different picture is presented by the reports in Isaacs's *Jewish Messenger*. In the issue of Jan. 18, there appeared an extensive appeal to American Jews by a Committee consisting of Raphall, Isaacs, Rev. Dr. A. Messing of the Chrystie Street Synagogue, M. Danneberg, N. Cowen, J. Rosenthal, and D. Lasky describing "the terrible truth that dire distress is now existing in Palestine." The Committee, organized "at the earnest solicitation of the accredited messengers," referred to the documentary evidence presented by "Rabbi Nathan Natkins [sic] and Rabbi A. L. Cohen, duly delegated Messengers . . . ," and emphasized the distinction between its appeal for contributions toward the feeding of the needy Palestinians and that of the Board of Delegates which—apart from the large sum transmitted to Jerusalem in 1866—solicited new donations for a housing project in Palestine:

> Let every officer of a congregation or society constitute himself a committee to collect and forward annually contributions for the poor of Jerusalem. Where is the synagogue or society that cannot spare at least $50 or $25 from its treasury yearly? Where is the individual that cannot economize a few cents a week for so laudable a purpose? Even little children would gladly dispense with some of their toys, if they knew this trifling deprivation would purchase food for the hungry. All this can readily be accomplished, if you desire it.

The Committee contemplated weekly meetings at the synagogue of Congregation Beth Israel u-Bikur Cholim, on Chrystie Street, "where they will be happy to have every lover of Jerusalem to take part in the proceedings." It finally requested all congregations and individuals to extend to the messengers "a reception worthy of their mission and object," to enter their gifts in the messengers' book, "in which will be seal and endorsement of the Committee," but to forward all "monies and communications" to Isaacs. This Committee evidently intended to cooperate with, rather than supplant the permanent North American Relief Society of which Isaacs was a most active officer. On February 6, 1867 the Society met under the presidency of Dr. S. Abrahams to accept a bequest of one thousand dollars from the estate of Rosanna Osterman of Galveston, Texas. A resolution to this effect was prepared by Isaacs, in collaboration with Louis Levy, and published in the *Jewish Messenger*.[63]

In January and February 1867 Notkin was active chiefly in the metropolitan area or in its immediate vicinity. Apart from a few individual donations from Jersey City we find a statement by M. Hannoch, President of the Congregation Benai Abraham, of 131 Market Street, Newark (dated February 14, 1867), in which the messenger and his colleague A. L. Cohn (*sic*) are mentioned as the transmitters of a letter to the congregation. Hannoch adds "und verpflichte mich alles für Jerusalem zu Thun, und den empfangene Gelder an den Comitte, auf Jerusalem, zu New York zu übersenden." A similar pledge was entered on the same day (likewise in dubious German) by Joachim Stein, President of the Congregation Oheb Shalom of Newark (41 Livingston Street), and on February 15, by Isador Lehman, President of the Congregation Benai Jeshurun, of the same city. About that time a Mr. Bass, President of the "Shool Beith Israel" 43 Atlantic Street, Brooklyn, promised that "we shall try and do all we can," while M. Kessel (?), President of an unnamed congregation at 151 South 8th St., Williamsburg, pledged himself "to do all that lies in my pover for Jerusalem." In Paterson, N. J. the Congregation Benai Jeshurun, acting through its president, Jacob Edelman (of 67 Main Street) and its secretary, Joseph Brown, collected $28.50 from 26 members, who contributed amounts ranging between fifty cents and five dollars.[64]

Notkin and Cohen soon proceeded to Philadelphia, where they first secured an indorsement from the Board of Hebrew Ministers (dated March 31, 1867), signed by M. Jastrow, G. Papé, S. Morais, J. Fränkel, and M. Cohn, with Jastrow adding his signature on behalf of the absent Isaac Leeser.[65] The latter, however, subsequently took occasion to express his own views both in a recommendation entered in the book under the same date, and in a communication to his journal, *The Occident*. The recommendation reads briefly:

It is now nearly eighteen years since this volume was in my hand when I recommended Rabbi Selig Ashkenazi to the benevolence of the faithful in America; and as it is at present handed to me by Rabbi Nathan Notkin who is sent hither after the decease of this just named pious Israelite, I cannot avoid expressing my admiration of the care with which the chiefs in the Holy City preserved all the documents, referring to their messengers. I would, therefore, hope that those who feel for the "breach of Zion" will not withhold their beneficence at the present juncture.

In the *Occident*, Leeser could give freer rein to his sentiments, fed by repeated experiences over a period of two decades. Expatiating on a contemplated pilgrimage to Palestine by one Hyman Moses of Cincinnati and his wife, he commented:

It is needless to say that he travels at his own expense altogether and that any donations entrusted to his care will be expended for the purpose the donors may desire, either paying them over to the private parties who are to be benefited or expending them for general charity, or to build houses, schools or workshops. By-the-by, we saw lately two messengers, Rabbi Nathan Notkin and Rabbi M. [A. L.] Cohen, who had been sent out last year to collect funds in consequence of the losses sustained for a second time by the locusts, that plague of eastern countries. If any messengers were ever worthy of credit it was these two delegates, who are natives of Russian and Prussian Poland. But what is the use of their travelling thus far? They collected about $160.00 in Philadelphia, and fully two-thirds went for necessary expenses. Little, therefore, remains for the charity for which they plead. This is no fault of theirs nor of donors here, but is inherent in the wretched messenger system, the evils of which we have frequently exposed. But it seems that the people of Palestine, whenever any calamity befalls them, at once think that their new messengers will be able to move the charitable feelings of 'the outland' חוצה לארץ as they were never before: but constantly recurring experience will contradict this again and again, and the messengers gather but little above their expenses, waste their time, and send home but sorry returns for so much labor. The better plan would be not to encourage the messengers at all to travel, but to provide them with means at the first port they land, to go back without delay, after depositing their credentials into the hands of some prominent friend of Palestine who would do them better service than they can do for themselves.

Leeser's colleagues fully shared his sentiments, as may be gathered from the following entry of the Board of Ministers, signed by Jastrow and Leeser on April 4th, which fully bears out the published report of the financial inadequacy of the local collection:

> In consequence of the disagreeable weather during the month of March (Veadar) and other untoward circumstances the collections of Rabbis Notkin and Cohen have not resulted as favorably as was first expected, being only fifty Dollars ($50) after defraying their expenses incurred during their stay in this city. The Board of Ministers regret this result greatly; but they intend hereafter to institute annual collections in this city & vicinity without the intervention of messengers, since the expense attending this mode of gathering money necessarily consumes a large part of the funds received from the benevolent.[66]

In May 1867 the two messengers finally set out for their first extended journey through the American communities. Cohen seems to have withdrawn from the mission at an early date since the entries soon indicate the presence of Notkin alone. Undated entries recording four individual contributions in Utica and Rome, are followed by five signatories of members of the Berith Sholem Congregation of Oswega, dated May 23, 1867. During the following three days Notkin secured not only a number of individual contributions and pledges of annual donations from the Jews of Syracuse, but also appointed Abraham Judah Eisenbadt and Israel Hersohn (the latter, as we have seen, previously active in behalf of Palestine relief in 1861) as permanent supervisors of the funds collected for the ḥalukkah. In Rochester he succeeded in securing a number of individual donations ranging between one and three dollars and gifts of ten dollars and two dollars respectively from the Trustees (טרוזטיהם) of the congregation Berith Kodesh and from the *minyan* of Polish Jews (June 2-3). Without delay Notkin next proceeded to Buffalo where (on June 3-4) he collected a number of individual contributions and a collective donation of five dollars from the Congregation Ansche Chesed. One of the largest Buffalo contributors, Israel b. Moses, requested in return for his ten dollars that prayers be recited at the Wailing Wall in behalf of his wife, Frome bat Rote, so that she might be cured of melancholia.[67]

In Cleveland (on June 11) several individual gifts were increased by a contribution of eight dollars from the Polish congregation Beth Israel. One M. (in Hebrew: Schachne) Jacobs, apparently an officer of the Hebrah Kadisha (the seal of which indicates that it had been "organized Shebat 5624" Jan.-Feb. 1864), promised to act permanently as an agent in behalf of Jerusalem, "to collect contributions and to distribute boxes as far as possible." Following a visit to Toledo and Detroit, Notkin arrived in Chicago, where he secured (under the date of June 23) an attestation signed by David Melzer, President, and Phil Adolph, Secretary of the Congregation B'nai Sholom, and a collective donation of twenty dollars. On June 24, Samuel Witkowsky, as Secretary, registered that "die Chebra Kadische Ubikur Cholem hat für die Brüder in Jerusalem eine Summe von $3.00 Dollar [gespendet]." Three days later Notkin received ten dollars from the United Hebrew Relief Association in Chicago, through its Secretary, Julius Rosenthal. These contributions from organizations were increased by numerous individual gifts. Moreover, between June 24 and 27 Notkin seems to have made a trip to Peoria, Ill., where he secured a number of contributions, including one of five dollars from Henry Ulman, signing as President of the local community (קאהל).[68]

The messenger's next stop was St. Louis. There the United Hebrew Congregation, through its President, Michael Spiro and its Secretary, Max Wiener, followed the example set by the Chicago congregation not only by donating a similar amount of twenty dollars, but also by copying almost verbatim the attestation to Notkin (July 1). On July 17, B. M. Garfunkel and a Mr. Liebreich handed to the messenger the amount of $52, the result of their collection of 27 individual contributions ranging between one and five dollars apiece. A month later Notkin received from the affluent community of Cincinnati the considerable sum of $220. This amount had been collected by Asher Heller, Salomon W. Heller, and S. Isaacs (of the firms of Heller Bros. and Co. and Isaacs & Sons, respectively), and was handed to the messenger on August 21. It is noteworthy that there is neither any record of congregational action, nor any indorsement by Isaac M. Wise who, as we have seen, had favored Notkin's predecessors by encouraging recommendations.[69]

The coincidence of Wise's change of mind concerning the future of Palestine and of its Jewish settlement with the exertions of a local resident, Hyman Moses, in behalf of that cause (alluded to in the aforementioned editorial by Leeser) undoubtedly were responsible for this official silence. One may pursue Wise's progressive alienation from the Palestine ideal in his numerous communications and editorials on the subject published in the *Israelite* during the entire period of his editorship of that journal. By 1869, a short time after Notkin's visit to Cincinnati, his opposition to the traditional messianic doctrine reached a stage in which he did not hesitate to invoke a rather dubious statement in the *Jewish Messenger* in support of his thesis. "In 1850," he observed, "the editor of the journal [*The American Israelite*] was threatened with excommunication and persecution, because he uttered publicly his veto against that doctrine, and in 1869 it is admitted in the only orthodox journal of our coreligionists." Going beyond most of his contemporaries and successors in the Reform camp in his theological dogmatism, he even voiced his apprehension lest the continued growth of archaeological evidence undermine accepted views on biblical religion. Referring to a report published in the Boston *Sunday Herald* on recent explorations of the "Palestine Fund Society" he wrote:

> On the whole we think it about as well to let the Old Jerusalem rest under the accretions of ages, as it is described in the Bible and Josephus. If it should be unearthed we have no positive assurance that it would not again be "run into the ground"

and its actual appearance might disturb the faith of some and confound the theories of others. . . . *The Jerusalem we are after, and which alone is of any consequence to mankind, cannot be found under the rubbish of two thousand years.* . . .

Small wonder, then, that he likewise had little use for the struggling communities of the Holy Land, whose main *raison d'être* was their link with the national past and the hope for an ultimate physical redemption of the people through its restoration to Palestine. In an editorial on the "Jews in Jerusalem," on August 13, 1869, he climaxed his description of the community (then numbering some 8,000 Sephardim and Ashkenazim) by delivering the following sharp rebuke:

> They live on the alms of European societies, who sometimes in mistaken zeal, send poor Jews to their ancient land and support them by subscription. . . . The consequence of this artificial colonization is that the Jewish inhabitants of the Holy City are a degraded set of idle paupers. The funds sent from Europe are much abused by the Rabbis, who keep the lion's share for themselves, and the poorer people are content to live on a miserable dole rather than labor for their bread. Schemes have been tried to encourage them to cultivate the soil by obtaining grants of land for them, but the idleness of the Jews themselves has hitherto frustrated this praiseworthy attempt. Sir Moses Montefiore was instrumental in building for them schools and houses and a mill outside the City near Birket-es-Sultan, or Lower Pool of Gihon, but his charitable efforts have been apparently wasted on so ungrateful and lazy a people. . . .

Hyman Moses, on the other hand, so deeply believed in the necessity of Palestine relief that he decided, in 1867, to proceed thither together with his wife, after selling all his belongings. He undoubtedly began his "tour of collection for Jerusalem" in his home city, where, as we have seen, he had already assisted Abraham Nissan during the latter's visit in 1861. His avowed purpose was, upon arrival in Jerusalem, to use the funds collected in America to further Montefiore's "constructive" plan of building houses for the Jewish settlers. It was about the time of Notkin's journey through the Middle West that Moses arrived in Philadelphia and New York. Echoing Leeser, Isaacs, too, reported Moses's projected "Pilgrimage to Palestine," in warm terms, concluding with the recommendation: "We bespeak a cordial reception to Mr. Moses knowing, as we do, the sincerity of his motives and the laudable object he has in view." Considering that Cincinnati's charitable contributions for Palestine had been largely preempted by Moses's efforts shortly before Notkin's arrival and that many donors must have drawn the obvious comparison between the former's wholly disinterested endeavors and the costliness of the latter's travels, the amount of $220 handed to the messenger is a clear testimony to both the deep-rooted philanthropy and the relative affluence of the community.[70]

From Cincinnati Notkin proceeded to Montreal, where, on September 9, he "appointed" S. Silverman "Collector for the poor and distressed of Jerusalem." The relevant entry is signed by Silverman together with one Louis Albert. The very next day, Silverman, acting as President of the "German and Balash Congregation" (German and Polish Congregation), promised to send eighty dollars "to Palestine or Jerusalem," while on Sept. 9, H. Goldberg, signing for the "Purtugus" Congregation, attested that he had given Notkin sixty-one dollars.

Much less successful was the messenger's visit to Boston, sharply contrasting with the effective missions of his predecessors in this leading New England community. B. Nelson, still in office as President of the Congregation Ohabei Shalom, attested merely that the Board of Trustees, at its meeting on Sept. 15, had decided to place Notkin's petition before the general meeting of members. The two other congregations, Mishkan Israel (through Moses Strecker) and Adath Israel (through its Secretary, John Phillips per J. [G.?] Shoninger) donated only five and seven dollars, respectively. Neither were there any individual contributions, except for two of one dollar each by Moses and Judah Leb Strecker. In contrast thereto, the Congregation Beth Israel of Hartford, Notkin's last New England stop, stated, through its President, Henry Lewitts, its approval of his mission and the decision of a special meeting of its members "to forward at once fifty Dlls to the poor of Jerusalem" (Sept. 24). This phrasing seems to indicate that the amount was not handed directly to the messenger but was to be forwarded through other channels to the Holy City.[71]

For several months thereafter our record is silent, until we learn suddenly of Notkin's appearance on the West Coast in February 1868. An entry dated February 2 (Shebat 9, 5628) and signed by J. R. Brandon, President, A. H. L. Dias and A. Blockman, Trustees, and Emanuel Blochman, Secretary, records the establishment of a "Society for the Relief of the Jews of Palestine" in San Francisco, from whose 150 members it was hoped to raise at least five hundred dollars annually. This society was probably identical with the Society *Ohabei Zion* founded by Abraham Nissan in 1861, but now in a state of quiescence. On February 10, Brandon attests that it "remitted to Sir Moses Montefiore at London Fifty pounds (£50) Sterling to be disbursed by him for the objects profared." On the same day, L. Elkus, President and S. Zekind, Secretary of the Congregation Benai Israel of Sacramento, Cal., testified that they had given $75 "for to relieve of our corelegonists in Jeroselem." A similar amount was voted, on the following day, by the Hebrew Benevolent and Congregational Society of Marysville, as attested by its President, Joseph Lask, and its Secretary, Henry Shreyer. There were also two individual contributions of five dollars each in that city. A week later the Nevada Hebrew Society, through its President H. Barut (?), stated that it had given ten dollars to the messenger for his expenses and promised to decide at a regular meeting "what we are going to due for the Distress." This entry is followed by one (dated strangely on the same day, Feb. 18) signed by S. Sanders, President, Lyon Zacharius, Secretary, and Jacob Heyman, Financial Secretary of an unnamed Society at Grass Valley, Cal. It mentions the collection of $18.50 by the Committee and states that the "Society will meet on Sunday next to decide what amount they will donate toward the destrest of

Jerusalem." In Stockton, H. Kullman, President of the Congregation Rahim Ahoovim (Re'im Ahubim) states (on February 24) that a congregational meeting had resolved to institute a private collection, and had handed to Notkin the sum of $45. In Los Angeles, Charles Prager, Secretary and Treasurer of the Hebrew Benevolent Society, recorded (on March 18) that a meeting of its members voted to appropriate $100 for Palestine relief.[72]

Meanwhile there arose on the Eastern border another somewhat embarrassing situation. At the beginning of 1868 another messenger from Palestine, Azriel Selig Hausdorff, equipped with letters of recommendation from a leading conservative rabbi in Central Europe, Azriel Hildesheimer, then of Eisenstadt and from Fischl (?) Hirsch of Halberstadt, who were in charge of the administration of the almshouses in Jerusalem, began collecting donations for the building of such almshouses for the poor in Palestine.

Nathan Adler, Chief Rabbi of England, adhering to a previous promise "not to encourage messengers from Jerusalem . . . in order not thereby to injure the annual subscription of our benevolent American co-religionists," at first refused to give Hausdorff a letter of recommendation. Later, however, at the request of Hildesheimer and Hirsch, he wrote to Isaacs in New York to "observe that Mr. Housedorff's mission and object are quite laudable and worthy of generous aid" (Feb. 19, 1868). Isaacs, with evident reluctance, published this letter in his *Jewish Messenger*, stressing his general objection to messengers on the grounds that "a large percentage is deducted from the gifts of the benevolent for traveling and other expenses," but conceding that Hausdorff's documents were genuine and his mission laudable.[73]

Were it not for a mere accident, Notkin would have found, upon his return to the East, still another Palestinian messenger busy collecting money; one, moreover, endowed with a special appeal to the local patriotism of American Jewry. The tiny American Jewish community in Jerusalem, under the leadership of Benjamin Lilienthal and M. Koppel, decided to establish a

Fund "for the relief and comfort of all such Israelites as are come from the United States and also for the purchase of a piece of ground near Mount Moriah, as near unto the spot where our Temple stood, as it shall be possible; for the building of a Synagogue, a Public School or any other Structure that shall seem advisable for their need." For that purpose they dispatched Lilienthal, "a man aged and pious who undertook at his own cost to make a journey through the United States," to present their claims to the American Jewish public and to solicit contributions. Lilienthal was also provided with a warm recommendation (dated Nov. 1, 1867) by the American Consul, Victor Beauboucher, separately addressed to Isaacs in New York and to Rabbi Max Lilienthal in Cincinnati:

> The number of American Jews residing in Jerusalem is very limited, a dozen altogether; but these unfortunates are the most miserable of all and do not receive pecuniary succor from any one, the German Committees never having given them a cent, and those of America perhaps do not know them at all.
>
> I have done all I could to relieve these poor people ever since two years that I am in Palestine; and seeing their increasing misery, I this day address myself to you, in order that something may be done in their favor by the Committee of which you are a member.
>
> One of them, Benjamin Lilienthal, whom I know as an honest man, left yesterday for the States, and will be able orally to make to you the lamentable narration of the position of his coreligionists and fellow-citizens in Palestine. I have remitted to him the necessary recommendations for the success of his travel, and beg you to receive him with the attention due to a good and honest father of a family. . . .

After embarking aboard the *Harmonie,* however, Lilienthal was forced back to England through a breakdown of the ship's machinery. The Jerusalem representatives thereupon resolved to address themselves directly to Isaacs, on June 12, 1868, sending him a long appeal in English with an accompanying recommendation by

Lorenzo M. Johnson, American Vice and Acting Consul in Jerusalem. "The American Israelites," wrote the Vice Consul, "are few in number but I am sure are as worthy of the assistance of their fellow-men, as any of the Jewish communities in the Holy City." Isaacs published all of these communications in the name of the "Committee on behalf of the American Jews," adding that he would "cheerfully" comply with its request and forward to it all contributions remitted to him. He refused, however, to dispatch a messenger to other communities, because of the outlay which "consumes most of the money."[74]

Notkin, who in his account book completely ignored this twofold competition, seems, on his return trip East to have stopped for a while in Panama (?), where he received from Samuel Piza, on May 6, 1868, the sum of two pounds sterling. The next entries, undated, come from Washington, D.C. The Hebrew Congregation there, apart from contributing three dollars along with $25.50 donated by sixteen of its members, entered an indorsement of Notkin's mission, over the signatures of its President, H. L. Blout, and its cantor (*ḥazzan*), Jacob S. Jacobson. Washington figures also in another entry (dated June 14, 1868) in which the Elijah Lodge No. 50 of the Independent Order B'nai B'rith, through its President A. Otoble (?), Treasurer D. S. Danielman, and Secretary Jacob S. Jacobson, recorded its donation of ten dollars. Three days earlier, however, seven members of the community of Alexandria, Va., entered their contributions ranging between twenty-five cents and two dollars. On June 12, several members of the Potomac Lodge, No. 104 of the I.O.B.B. (D. Barwald, President) in Georgetown entered their gifts totaling $8.05. (It is possible that Notkin made the trips to Alexandria and Georgetown between two sojourns in the American capital.)[75]

These visits marked the beginning of an extended tour through the Southern communities. In Richmond, Va., the Polish congregation Keneset Israel and the Portuguese congregation Beth Shalome (through J. Gundersheimer and Abraham Lazarus) cooperated in donating between them $17.30 (June 20). This sum was increased by $21 collected privately by N. W. Nelson and others and handed to the messenger by M. Millhiser. The modesty of these amounts, considering the size and wealth of the community, can be explained only by the aftereffects of the Civil War and perhaps also by the direct contributions to Palestine relief initiated three years previously by the Board of Delegates, in which Richmond Jewry seems to have taken an active part. In any case, the local leaders realized that a word of explanation was in order; for on Tammuz 3 (June 23) Jacob Ezekiel, Vice President of the Congregation Beth Shalome, found it necessary to enter the following statement:

> The bearer of this Rabbi Nathan Notkin has not met with much success for the cause he is travelling for, on account of the impoverished condition of the South, his mission is fully appreciated and trust our Israelitish brethren in other places will render such aid as their circumstances will admit of, I fully commend Rabbi Nathan to the benevolent.

In Norfolk, Va., the results were somewhat more encouraging. M. Frankfurt, President, and L. Hofheimer, Vice President of the Congregation Oheb Sholom not only collected by June 25 the sum of $56.61, which they delivered to Notkin, but also promised to act in the future as permanent local officers in charge of Palestine relief. In Wheeling, West Va., on the other hand, a mere paltry sum of five dollars was raised on July 1. By way of explanation, Augustus Pollack, evidently referring to the aforementioned Hyman Moses, wrote into the book:

> The efforts made by Rabbi Nathan Natkin bearer of this record, to collect funds for the poor Jews of Jerusalem were here less successful than could have been wished for resulting less from want of interest, than actual home necessities, and the additional cause, that a subscription for charity at Jerusalem had been forwarded but recently from here through a reliable citizen from Cincinnati, Ohio.

In Youngstown, O., D. Theobald, President, and E. Guttman, Secretary of the Congregation Rodef Sholem duly entered (on July 12) a donation of fifteen dollars towards the messenger's expenses and the promise of an annual contribution "provided a proper person, duly authorized and residing in one of our neighboring cities will call on us to that effect."[76]

Several weeks elapsed before our messenger opened his book for further entries. We first find him in Nashville, Tenn., where on August 10, 1868 he secured a pledge from Mical Schwartz, S. Cohen, and D. J. Heyerhardt (?) to serve as the permanent *gabbaim* (treasurers) for Palestine. Two days later a number of donors (including "all Laydis") of Shelbyville, Tenn., contributed a total of $18.25. On August 17, L. H. Alexander, Secretary and Jacob Franklin, First Trustee of the Hebrew Benevolent Congregation of Atlanta, Ga., contributed $15.00, while Samuel Levy, President of the Congregation Children of Israel of Augusta, Ga., registered, the following day, a congregational donation of "Twenty four 35/100 Dollars in Currency and one doll. in silver." The sum was increased by $6.45 subsequently collected by Bernhard Phillips, Vice President of that congregation. The Congregation Beth Israel of Macon, Ga., soon joined with a contribution of $13.25, according to an undated entry of its Vice President, E. M. Brown. Next came Montgomery, Ala., with a dozen individual contributions totaling $18.00 on August 28, and Selma, Ala., where the "Hebrew Association" (M. Marx on Committee), on August 31, donated ten dollars, while ten individual members contributed an additional $13. In Meridian, Miss., A. Wolff and Rosenbaum & Co. made on Sept. 2, a collection among "our few Jewish citizens and aid of other citizens" which yielded $21.10. (This is the first mention of active aid extended to this Jewish charity by non-Jews, although such aid had clearly been anticipated by the American consul at Jerusalem.) The following day 15 members of the Congregation Beth Israel of Jackson, Miss., contributed a total of $10.25. Finally, in Memphis, Tenn., Notkin (whose name was here curiously misspelled Analca or Anacta) received, on Sept. 20-21, several individual contributions as well as ten dollars from the Hebrew Relief Society, represented by its President, Sol Hesse.[77]

Two weeks later we find our messenger in Louisiana, where he secured, on Oct. 4, from Rabbi James K. Gutheim of the Congregation Shaare Chesed of New Orleans an attestation and a congregational subscription of twenty-five dollars. Another rabbi, Benjamin E. Jacobs of the Congregation Temime Derek, commented on Oct. 6:

> I am certain the money will reach its proper channel as I recognize this book having been in the hands of the late Rabbi Abraham Nissan whom I assisted to raise funds for the same purpose.

Lastly, Henry S. Jacobs, Minister of the Congregation Nefuzoth Yehudah of the same city, added his brief "endorsation" on Nov. 1, while a great many individuals recorded their private contributions. William Bendel, of Lafayette, La., entered, on Nov. 23, the record of his collection amounting to fourteen dollars. On Nov. 26, the congregation Shaare Chesed of Baton Rouge, through its Secretary, A. Kowalski, contributed ten dollars, increased by another four in individual contributions.[78]

On the final lap of his journey Notkin returned to Mobile, Alabama, where on Dec. 24, 1868 he not only secured a contribution of $25 from the Hebrew Relief Association, headed by M. Goldsmith, President and J. F. Epstein, Secretary, and on Dec. 28, $10.00 from the Ladies Hebrew Benevolent Society (likewise J. F. Epstein, Secretary) but also a large number of individual donations. In Savannah, Ga., which he undoubtedly had visited during his journey through Georgia in August, he now reaped the benefits of his efforts. Apart from a general attestation, dated Jan. 3, 1869, we find here several individual contributions and a statement by one Simon Gerstmann that he had turned over to the messenger the sum of $35 which had been collected by him in a *minyan* held in his house during the High Holidays. Gerstmann himself figures as one of the donors to the extent of fifteen dollars. In addition to these individual contributions totaling $51 (or rather $52), the officers of Palestine relief, represented by Julius Levkey, entered the following statement under Jan. 12.

Wier נבאים *haben zusammen genommen in der Stadt Savannah ein hundert Dollar für die Armen in Jerusalem, welches wir senden zu die Ehrwürdigen Herrn Meyer Orbach [Auerbach] und Samuel Shalant [Salant] in Jerusalem. Rabbi Natkin hat ein und fünfzig Dollar zusamen genommen alles zusamen $151 Dollar.*
   Die ein fünfzig dollar sind die die an der obigen Seite stehen.

In Charleston, S. C., Notkin obtained a general indorsement of his mission by Joseph H. M. Chumaciero, Rabbi of Beth Elohim, dated Shebat 8, 5629 (Jan. 20, 1869), a contribution of five dollars from the Dan Lodge No. 93 of the I.O.B.B., represented by its President, B. Spring and its Secretary, J. T. Kaplan, and twenty-odd individual donations totaling nearly fifty dollars. In neighboring Marion, too, a dozen members of the Hebrew Congregation not only donated a total of $27 for the benefit of the mission, but also, on Jan. 21, 1869, entered into his book, a formal attestation. Four days later, 23 members of the Jewish community of Wilmington, N.C., personally entered contributions ranging from one to five dollars and totaling $42.00. Moreover, Nathaniel Jacobs, who evidently arranged the collection, added the promise that "I am also willing to give my services as Treasurer to forward yearly such sums as may be contributed for above purposes."[79]

Notkin's activities during the following months are shrouded in darkness, although it seems that he spent February and March 1869 in New York. At any rate during the month of April we find him once more on the road, again traversing the northern section of New York State. But apart from a few occasional glimpses warranted by a number of individual contributions in Elmira on April 20, in Hornillsville on April 22, and in Buffalo on April 25-26 (Iyyar 14-15), we know nothing about the progress of his journey and its financial results.[80] Neither does our record inform us of the conclusion of this first mission to the United States and of the date of his embarkation for Palestine. We also look in vain for a financial summary such as had been prepared by Isaacs at the conclusion of Abraham Nissan's journey. Since Notkin himself collected most of the funds and made little use of the existing national organization, he could confidently delay his report until his return to the Holy Land. Whether such a report was ever submitted and to what extent it filled the evident gaps in our record cannot be ascertained.

In these circumstances, and in view of the evident incompleteness and disorderliness of Notkin's record, no full comparison may be drawn between his visit and those of his two predecessors. It is obvious, however, that he spent more time and covered more ground than either of them. The record of his American sojourn covers a period of nearly two and a half years—it may actually have lasted much longer—whereas the previous messengers spent only about a year each in the United States. While Aaron Selig visited the South, and Abraham Nissan was the first to venture to the West Coast, Notkin spent considerable time in both the Western and the Southern communities. If his collections were at all commensurate with the extensiveness and apparent intensity of his efforts, the sums gathered must have been vastly superior to those obtained during the two preceding journeys. Although the experience in Philadelphia and, to a certain extent, in Savannah cast an ominous shadow upon the ultimate productivity of Notkin's efforts, it seems that enough money remained for distribution in Palestine for his sponsors to regard the mission as at least a qualified success. This alone can explain why, within less than seven years, they decided to send him once again to the United States.

IV   *The Second Mission of Notkin, 1876-79*

Notkin's second mission started under better auspices than the first. If in 1867 the elders of the various Ashkenazic communities in Jerusalem realized the importance of pooling their resources and decided to issue a united appeal to their coreligionists in America, this time they were joined by the Sephardic elders as well. Moreover, the communities of Hebron, Safed, and Tiberias which usually acted independently now placed themselves squarely behind their common messenger. Apparently for the first time in history, Notkin thus appeared before the American contributors to Palestine relief as the accredited spokesman of the entire *Yishuv*. Only the great urgency of relief needs in the constantly growing Palestinian settlement,[81] and the growing realization that disparate efforts were both more costly and mutually competitive, could have induced the ever quarreling elders of the various communities to join hands in this common effort.[82] Better informed about the attitude of the prospective American contributors, they equipped their messenger not only with the customary Hebrew credentials but also with the following translation of both the letter of authorization and the appeal:

> Upon thy Walls, O Jerusalem, I have set watchmen; never will they cease those who make mention of the Lord. Give him no rest untill he establisheth and maketh Jerusalem a praise in the earth: Isaiah LXII 6-7.

> This Book
> invites all benevolent to inscribe—for a memory in Jerusalem— the name of, and free donation which, everyone may be pleased to offer for the sake of the Lord through the bearer, an excellent, illustrious among Israel, Rabbi Nathan Natae Natkin, authorized message by the ecclesiastical Rabis residents of the holy land. He being appointed message from the Sephardic, Ashkenaz, Prushim and Chasidim congregations, residents in the four holy Cities, Jerusalem, Hebron, Safed and Tiberia to appeal before our brethren at the U.S. & California to remind them of their love [of] the land of promise, that they may bestow upon it grace and salvation; to establish committees in every district and town, to affix boxes for gethering money in favor of the holy

land in every house of Israel, and to receive donations either, for the relieve of the poor inhabitants of the holy Land in general or for paying the amount for the property surrounding the cave of Simon the Pious for building dwelling houses, and establishing Service of the Lord at that holy place, as is particularly described in the documents in possession of the revered bearer, Give audience to all his words.

May long live prosperity, peace and concord follow you forever, as are the wishes of the Chiefs of the Congregations of the holy Land, signed this 14th day of Iyar 5636.

With Divine Aid

This is to authenticate and certify that we the undersigned, Chiefs of all Congregations of Sephardim and Ashkenasim residents of the 4 holy Cities viz Jerusalem, Hebron, Safed & Tiberia, having learned the anguish of thousands of Israelitish inhabitants of these holy Cities That as long as the holy Land remains desolate, it profits nothing of its own, but from remotest parts its bread is given, from distributions and offerings of the children of Israel for the relieve of their coreligionists inhabitants of the holy Land. The life of the latter is consequently dependent only on the gifts of their [brethren] abroad, In accordance to the mercy and kindness of these, the good of those increases, and considering that, if there is no one to resuscitate and to animate our benevolent brethren, and their own troubles extinguishes from their heart, the remembrance of this holy deed, Consequently their donations diminishes, and then the poor of the holy Land, their wifes, children, widows and orphans, who lift up their eyes to the benevolence of their correligionists, what shall become of them? Wherefrom shall come their assistance?

Therefore, we have elected from amongst the holy congregations an excellent man, the learned and pious Rabi Nathan Natae Natkin, and in the name of all Sephardic & Ashkenas communities of the four holy Cities, we send him in this mission to the U.S. of America and California to inform our brethren at these countries of the sufferings of our poor, and that they have no means whatever for their maintenance, but the gifts of their brethren abroad, in whose hearts it has pleased God to

plant love and sympathy for their poor brethren in the holy
Land that the name of Jerusalem might not be oblivious from
them.

What has induced us to do so will be related by our friend
the revered Delegate himself. And we hereby ascertain that we
have authorized the revered delegate the bearer to do in favor
of the holy Land and its inhabitants, and his deeds and actions
is as our own, and at his speaking with you, it ought to be considered that he is an appointed messenger by twenty thousand
Israelitish inhabitants of the holy Land, and it might be considered therefore as if we all, our elders, wise men and all our
congregations are present before you entreating your kindness
and mercy, to renevate your love for Zion and Jerusalem the
Land of your ancestors, the place of the holy temple, He who
sympathizes with her anguish, will partake of her rejoicings and
her glory will shine upon him.

Dear Brethern. Chiefs of every district and town be therefore
mindful of that, to do honour to the Lord and to Jerusalem, and
have mercy with your coreligionists.

The Lord that dwelleth in Zion, will magnify your honour
and reputation as are the wishes of your entreators, signing at
Jerusalem in the month of Iyar, 5636.

Both the Hebrew and English credentials were signed on Iyyar
14, 5636 (May 8, 1876) by the Sephardic and Ashkenazic leaders,
including Abraham Ashkenazi (1813-80), the Ḥakham Bashi of
Jerusalem, Moses Benveniste, Raphael Meir Panisel, the President
of the Committee, Meyer b. Isaac (Auerbach) of Kalisz (1815-
78), Chief Rabbi of the Ashkenazic community, and others. An
"attestation of the foregoing Seals and Signatures" by Noel
Temple Moore, the British Consul in Jerusalem, was obtained on
May 9, 1878, while F. S. de Hass, the American Consul certified
two days later "that I am personally acquainted with several of
the parties whose names and seals are appended to the above document, and that the statement given of the condition of the Hebrews
in Jerusalem is correct."[83]

The state of mind of American Jewry was at that time not altogether favorable to such a mission. Although fully recovered

from the Civil War crisis and steadily increasing in numbers and affluence, its constant disappointments over the *halukkah* and its methods had chilled the zest of even some of the staunchest supporters of Palestine relief. In 1876, in particular, a report on conditions in Palestine, submitted to the Board of Deputies in England by two of its influential members, Samuel Montagu (later Lord Swaythling) and Asher Asher, and at first unpublished, had been issued privately by the authors and widely circulated in America, where it had received extensive comment in the Jewish press. As summarized, for instance, in the *Jewish Messenger*, the report stated that

> pauperism has been the curse of the Jewish inhabitants of Palestine; that it is not confined to the aged, the sick or the infirm, but that it has become a positive institution, to which persons of every phase of life, from the cradle to the grave, have recourse; that under the name of Cholucah, or almsgiving, every Jewish child born in Palestine is inscribed in a book as entitled to receive his portion of the alms. One of the results of this disgraceful system is that the most common marriages that take place are between boys of fifteen and sixteen, and girls of thirteen and fourteen, the moving idea being that every child born will produce an additional income from the Cholucah, and hence procreation is regarded as a legitimate means of livelihood! To add to the evil, the report states, that many who receive the Cholucah do not employ it for the purchase of the necessaries of life, but positively lend out the money at usurious interest to the Arabs. Again, the collections which pour in from Europe and America, and more especially the money which comes from Poland and Russia, is vested for distribution with the rabbins, who insist, before disbursing a dollar to others, on apportioning the larger part to themselves. One more fact, and a terrible one it is, may be gathered from the report. The rabbins, who arrogate to themselves the direction of everything that comes under the name of instruction, rigidly confine the instruction to the teaching of Hebrew and Talmud. They rigorously exclude all secular instruction, and instances are cited in the report of persons whom the rabbins have actually excommunicated for no fault

other than that of having allowed their children to be taught Arabic or some European language. It must not be supposed, says the paper that these facts apply to all the Jews in Palestine indiscriminately. A wide line of demarcation must be drawn between the Germans and the Portuguese. The latter have little or no show in the Cholucah, and hence their marked superiority to the Germans in mental culture, industry, and moral and social elevation.

In vain did Moses Montefiore attempt to counteract the painful impression created by this report by contradicting some of its statements on the basis of his own direct observations.[84] In vain, too, did the leading Ashkenazic rabbis in Jerusalem, Meyer Auerbach and Samuel Salant, publish a heated reply, emphasizing the hearsay nature of Montagu's accusations, gathered as they were during a brief stay of but fifteen days. Isaacs himself could do no better than conclude a long expostulation by admitting that "the system of Cholukah is unfortunate in its manner of distribution, and should be changed, but it would be more than misfortune, it would be a calamity, if the well-meant efforts to improve the civilization, culture, and condition of the communities in the Holy Land, should be permanently thwarted." Even the collections for the Montefiore Testimonial Fund which, designed to foster the economic reconstruction of Palestinian Jewry by the promotion of agriculture and crafts among them, had at first evoked a ready response on the part of both the British and the American public, were affected adversely by these criticisms. Many American Jews shared the sentiments voiced by Harry H. Marks in his article, "The Jews of Jerusalem and the Montefiore Testimonial." published in *The Independent* and reprinted in the *Jewish Times*. The author attacked the Board of Deputies for having selected Palestine as the object of the Testimonial Fund without first consulting the public, which was largely opposed to this idea:

Not because they were in any way wanting in that religious sentimentality which identifies Jerusalem with the events of the past greatness and the future hopes of many of their race; but because they believed, and with abundant good reasons that the majority of the Jews of Jerusalem had been fearfully degenerated by the system of pauperism in which generation after generation had been nursed. . . .

While in London some weeks ago I had a conversation with a gentleman who had seen a letter addressed by the heads of the Portuguese congregation in Jerusalem to Mr. Montagu stating that they refused to sign a document contradicting Mr. Montagu's report, notwithstanding the entreaties of one who accompanied Sir Moses Montefiore to the Holy Land, and who absolutely threatened them with the displeasure of the aged baronet for refusing to comply with the request. The consequence of all this is (1) that the Montefiore Testimonial is an unqualified failure (2) that the demoralization and disgraceful condition of the Jews of Palestine has been well exposed, and (3) that the benevolent are likely in future to think twice before they once contribute to the support in idleness and pauperism of the worthless Hebrew population of Jerusalem.[85]

To forestall the evil impression of these criticisms upon the prospective contributors, the Executive Committee of the Fund adopted a resolution on February 16, 1876, "that the Fund be expended in the purchase of ground in the Holy Land, in the building of houses there, and in establishing a Loan Fund, and in aiding the able-bodied inhabitants in agricultural and trading pursuits." The possibility of such constructive aid was emphasized by Montefiore himself in a record of his latest journey, then being published serially in the Jewish press, in which he invoked the unanimous testimony of persons familiar with local conditions "that there would be no difficulty whatever to secure as much land as might be required, either for cultivation or building purposes." Further to safeguard the Fund against possible maladministration, the Executive Committee adopted Montagu's amendment demanding that one or more European agents be dispatched to Palestine to supervise the expenditure.

Despite these safeguards the effect of Montagu's revelations upon the American public was extremely discouraging. The Board

of Delegates, which, in May 1875, had decided to cooperate in
raising the Testimonial Fund, now grew weary of the entire
proposition. Its President, Judge Philip J. Joachimsen (1817-90),
submitted a lengthy report on conditions in Palestine to the annual
meeting of May 20, 1876, warning against taking the line of least
resistance and discontinuing all aid to Palestine Jewry.

> We have contributed for so many years in the belief of doing
> good (without seeming to care how it was done) that we have
> our share of responsibility for the existing state of things, and
> if our aid being withheld, greater sorrow and shame should come
> to the Jews of Palestine, would we not be responsible for as
> great a desecration of the Jewish name as has happened within
> this century.

He therefore argued for the continued support of the Testimonial
Fund and for the allotment of specific subventions to (1) the
modern elementary schools planned by the Alliance Israélite
Universelle, (2) hospitals and orphan asylums, (3) poor widows
especially recommended by the American Consul to the Ḥakham
Bashi, and (4) only an indispensable minimum to the indiscriminate support of men over 21. Curiously, and evidently not
wholly representative of the Board's views, Joachimsen concluded
his report by still another recommendation:

> To say to those who now have charge of the Chalukah, that if
> the tide of emigration can be turned to this part of the world,
> the Jew will find here resources for his intelligence and labor
> which in the end compensate richly for change of home-air, of
> habits and customs, without at all interfering with his religious
> duties.

The Board's committee on Palestine went further, however, and
submitted additional resolutions calling for the suspension of all
future contributions to Palestine relief and the withholding of
monies already appropriated for the Testimonial Fund "until the
Executive Committee shall render a report as to the best means

of achieving the objects herein contemplated." It further urged the Executive Committee to communicate with the other large Jewish bodies, such as the British Board of Deputies, the Alliance Israélite, and the Berlin Committee for Jerusalem Orphan Asylums, with a view to adopting a joint course of action.[86]

It was into this atmosphere of suspicion that Notkin entered upon his arrival in New York. His first business was to secure an attestation from S. M. Isaacs, the veteran treasurer of Palestine charities. Isaacs, who, on June 2, had written an editorial on the decisions of the Board of Delegates, expressing approval of the general intention to investigate this relief problem "with a view to suggestion of a plan for the permanent benefit of Palestine," but regretting the Board's suspension of further payments toward that cause, now stated briefly, under date of Tishri 5, 5637 (Sept. 23, 1876): "This is to certify that I have examined the papers of Rabbi Natkin, and they are correct." A few weeks later Notkin's efforts were rewarded by the following entry signed on Oct. 25, 5637 (1876) by A. Raffel, President of the Grand Beth Hamedrash of New York:

> *This is to certify that the Trusties of the Congregation Beth Hamedrash Hagodel have delivered to Rabbi Nathan Natkin of Jerusalem, Palestine the sume of $133-50/00 the contribution of this Congr. as also of different societies for the benefit of the destitutes of the Holy Land.*

There is no further record of any communal action in New York in behalf of Notkin's mission, but several persons entered individual donations without date. Among these appears a woman, Yente Karo of Titusville, Pa., but there is no evidence that our messenger visited Pennsylvania at that time. She may have joined the contributors, while on a visit to New York. The first record of Notkin's out-of-town activities comes to us from Rome, N. Y., where various entries of individual contributors are dated Nov. 21, 1876. These are followed immediately by a number of signatures from Erie, Pa., but since they are all undated they cannot be definitely ascribed to the same period. In fact, the page preceding these entries from New York City, Rome, and Erie, contains numerous entries from Rochester, dated Nov. 25 and 30, 1876 (one signer, perhaps by mistake, gives the date of December 15, 1878). It seems probable that the Rochester visit followed immediately upon that to Rome. Among the Rochester contributors appear the congregations Beth Israel, with $3.00, and Berith Kodesh, with $5.00, while the individual donors include one Morris Elgutter of Omaha, Neb. In view of the absence of any further references to Notkin's visit to Nebraska, it seems likely that here again we are dealing with a visitor who happened, while in Rochester, to contribute to a cause which appealed to him. The record next takes us back to Elmira, N.Y., where on Dec. 3, 1876 one A. F. Cohen donated twenty dollars to our "poor coreligionists throughout Jerusalem," and to Buffalo, where, on Kislev 24, 5637 (Dec. 10, 1876), the Society *Berith Shalom*, through H. Einoch, entered the specified contributions of 12 members totaling $17.79. Congregation Bnai Israel in Elmira, offered five dollars, while numerous other individual contributions greatly increased the revenue in the latter city.[87]

Notkin soon embarked upon a more ambitious journey of which, unfortunately, we possess only fragmentary, not to say accidental, records. Very often the larger communities which he undoubtedly visited are not mentioned at all, while a smaller congregation, by sheer chance, or through somebody's insistence that a record be kept, occupies a prominent place. Neither is the sequence here any more strictly chronological than are the preceding entries of this somewhat negligent emissary. In any case, according to our record, Notkin visited Indianapolis on Jan. 24, 1877, where, apart from an unspecified congregational contribution, he recorded four gifts totaling $9.50. He then proceeded to Salt Lake City, where the Ladies' Hebrew Benevolent Society (represented by its President, Lotte Popper) contributed $10.00 on Feb. 23. On March 6, the Hebrew Benevolent and Congrega-
Vice President, M. A. Marcuse and its Secretary, N. Schneider)
that it had been founded on July 22, 1855) attested (through its
tional Society of Marysville, Cal. (the seal of which emphasized

that it had donated $25.00. The next entries, according to date but not location, are those of Cheyenne, Wyo. on July 23, 1877 and of St. Joseph, Mo. eight days later. Only three individuals in the former and one in the latter community seem to have subscribed, all for negligible amounts. In the same connection appear two small contributions from Council Bluffs, Iowa, but no date is given. After another intermission of several months we find our messenger active, on Oct. 3, 1877, in Detroit, where, in an attestation surpassing even the oddities of the preceding entries in its picturesque orthography, David Simon, "one of the comite" places on record that

> An general Meeting held by the Congregation Bnei Isral of thes city: and an sead Metting our Worthy Congregation Past to Donated to Rev. Nathun Natkin the same of Ten Doll. for the Poor of Jaroslom to Relife our Worthy Frends and Brotheron.

This congregational gift was, however, largely exceeded by numerous individual donations. From Detroit Notkin seems to have proceeded to Toledo, O., whence we possess the next two (undated) entries of individual contributors. On Oct. 22, he was active in Nashville, Tenn. where he obtained not only contributions amounting to $45.10 (including $5.00 from the Hebrew Ladies' Benevolent Society), but also an attestation from Alexander Rosenspitz, Rabbi of Temple Ohavai Sholom, in the following terms:

> The Bearer, Rabbi Nathan Natkin of Jerusalem, being a legitimate Envoy of the Israelites of the Holy Land to solicit aid for the suffering and distressed of his country; I hereby recommend him to the utmost charity of the people of our State in general, and the Israelites in particular.

Not less successful was Notkin's trip in New Orleans, where on Nov. 24, some fourteen subscribers, in part anonymous, contributed $56.00. Moreover, on Dec. 17, Simon Haspel and Isidore

Levi (giving their private addresses as 142 Decatur St. and 24 Magazine St. respectively) entered a pledge to act as joint treasurers of Palestine relief funds and to remit them annually to the messenger.

In Shreveport, La., Notkin's next recorded stop, seven contributors of a total of fourteen dollars signed up on Dec. 31, 1877. On Jan. 7, 1878 a single donor attested to his presence in Marshall, Texas. A week later he secured both contributions and an attestation from the Jews of Galveston, the latter being issued, on Jan. 14, 1878, by M. Koppert, President of the Congregation Bnai Israel, and following verbatim that previously accorded by the Rabbi of Nashville. But there is no evidence that either here or in Tennessee the appeal to the non-Jewish citizens bore any fruits. Apart from an undated entry from Mobile, Ala., we may further pursue Notkin's journey by his presence in Baltimore on Feb. 11. There, M. E. Sakolski, in behalf of the Chevra Bnai Yisroile Congregation, presented the messenger with five dollars. In two Yiddish postscripts Joseph Heiman, President of that Congregation, promised to follow through with yearly collections. On March 5, Notkin, finally reached Richmond, Va., whence came the contributions last recorded in our minute book. However, several pages back we find a number of individual contributions from Elmira, N. Y., all dated Dec. 29, 1878, which probably were inserted there to fill an empty space.[88]

In view of the specific limitations and the fragmentary character of our minute book we shall not be surprised to find therein no record whatsoever of the broader movements which affected American almsgiving for Palestine Jewry. Not even the passing of the staunchest supporter of Palestine relief, Rev. Samuel M. Isaacs, on May 19, 1878, is mentioned except perhaps indirectly through the absence of his name among the three new Trustees referred to in its final pages. Neither were the exertions of the North American Relief Society[89] nor those of Hyman Moses in Cincinnati considered worthy of reference. We learn, however, from the *American Israelite* of Jan. 21 and Oct. 27, 1876 that Moses had forwarded two substantial sums of 420.27 and 436

Dutch guilders respectively to the Central Committee in Amsterdam, and that he had received numerous communications from Palestine (for instance, from Isaac Prager) hailing him as one of the outstanding benefactors of the poor in that country. Notkin even ignores the undoubtedly far-reaching repercussions of the Board of Delegates' efforts to solve the problem of Palestine relief on a world-wide scale. Not only were the searching replies sent from Europe to the Board's inquiry much debated among the American Jewish public—although the Board itself, confronted by the rise of the newly organized Union of American Hebrew Congregations, was speedily losing ground—but out of this correspondence emerged the memorable Paris Conference of August 1878 with the participation of some of the outstanding Jewish leaders of Europe and America. The Palestine relief problem naturally came up for extensive discussion. The well-known historian, Heinrich Graetz, who as far back as 1872 had addressed to the Jewish organizations an extensive critical report on the conditions of Palestine Jewry, now submitted a proposal for its amelioration through (1) a more efficacious division of offerings made for their benefit, (2) occupational training of Jewish youth and (3) the establishment of effective orphan asylums. Rabbi Mongliano of Bologna, with more direct reference to the shortcomings of the *ḥalukkah*, suggested that "an end be put to the heavy expenses incurred principally by the small communities in Palestine in sending Jewish messengers to Europe, by forwarding direct to their destination the offerings and collections made in behalf of the Jews in the Holy Land." These resolutions, though well received by the attending delegates, could the more readily be ignored by Notkin, since the Paris Conference disbanded without setting up a permanent executive organ to carry out its decisions.[90]

The outbreak of the Russo-Turkish war in 1877 added to the complexities of the Palestinian Jews as well as of their supporters abroad. American Jewish leadership found itself suddenly confronted with the perennial problems of the "protection" of their coreligionists abroad when numerous Russian Jewish subjects in Jerusalem, apprehensive of the effects of the war on the now hostile Turkish authorities, applied to the United States Consul F. S. de Hass, for protection. De Hass, on his own responsibility took over about 100 protégés, thereby putting himself in a rather embarrassing position. On the one hand, the State Deparment in Washington disavowed his action, and in its reply to the Board of Delegates, signed by F. W. Seward, Acting Secretary of State, on June 29, 1877, took a conservative stand on this question of international law. Unlike the British authorities who, since the 1840s, had often successfully assumed a measure of protection of foreign Jews in Palestine and in the other provinces of the Ottoman Empire, Seward contended that the United States could protect only native or naturalized American citizens, and that Russian Jews could be taken under the custody of the American consuls only if the Russian government should apply for it to the State Department and Turkey should consent. On the other hand, the ever quarrelsome Jews of Palestine found fault with De Hass's attempt and soon spread rumors concerning the alleged mercenary motives of the Consul. These ultimately found their way into the *Jewish Chronicle* and the *New York World*. De Hass replied in an extensive communication to the *Jewish Messenger*, dated Dec. 3, 1877 in which he ascribed these rumors to a disgruntled former interpreter who had tried to extort 20 Napoleons from a rabbi and then attempted to involve the Consul. De Hass submitted also a letter sent to him by 193 Jews of Jerusalem (including Meyer Meizel, Levi Isaac Alexander, and Aaron Lipkin) on May 3, 1877 thanking him for his intervention. No sooner did this international complication resolve itself peacefully than a new difficulty confronted De Hass's successor in Jerusalem in regard to the American Jewish citizens residing in the Holy Land.

The action initiated in 1867 having remained without effect, the American community seems to have resigned itself to the discriminatory treatment by the local *ḥalukkah*. The economic crisis, brought on by the Russo-Turkish war, however, forced the Americans to apply once more to the Consul and, through him, to their coreligionists at home. On Oct. 10, 1877, J. G. Wilson, the new Consul, addressed two similar letters to S. M. Isaacs in New York and to Max Lilienthal in Cincinnati:

> I think it proper that the Hebrew people in America should know the conditions of their brethren at Jerusalem, who are in distress, and need assistance. They are citizens of the United States, with naturalization papers and passports. Some of them are Russian, and Polish Jews and, since the war, the aid formerly received from their European friends is no longer received. Some of them are artizans—workers in Olive-wood and, since the war there is no sale for their wares—the travelers are so few. Some of them are drivers, dragomen, servants of travelers from Jaffa to Jerusalem and Damascus; but, since the war, they find no employment.
>
> One of them, a soldier in the United States army four years, a dragoman, says he has had no food for two days, except the garbage picked up from the street. One is an orphan girl, 14 years of age, penniless and dependent on others almost as poor as herself. There are 13 families or perhaps 15 representing 45 to 50 persons who need help and who, without help, must suffer. I have just received a delegation of Jews in their behalf, and a letter, and they beg me to let their brethren in America know their situation. When the war is over, they hope to be again able, by their own labors, to earn a support. Any money for their relief sent to me, will be deposited in a bank as a relief fund, and distributed by a committee, and vouchers will be sent to the donor. . . .[91]

The old international rivalries in the Eastern Question, moreover, now reawakened in enormous intensity by the march of the Tsarist armies, brought once more to the fore the problem of a restoration of Jews to Palestine, thus stirring up the pro- and anti-Zionist passions within and without the Jewish community. Apart from the project, then seriously debated, of handing over to the Pope, dispossessed from his temporal dominions in 1871, the holy places in Jerusalem and of transferring his residence there—

a proposal which aroused only mild opposition among the Jews —more and more voices were heard in favor of Jewish restoration under an English or English-American protectorate. Even before the outbreak of the war, Hebrew journals such as *Lebanon* and *Ha-Maggid* were full of rumors concerning the alleged acquisition of the Holy Land from Turkey by some of their wealthy coreligionists. So serious a journal as the *Monetary Gazette* advocated, in 1876, the exchange of Turkish bonds held by Jewish bankers for land in Palestine. About the same time, the *Hebrew Observer* argued, in an article on "The Future of Palestine," that "the country wants capital and population . . . the Jews can give it both. . . . To England, then, naturally belongs the role of favoring the settlement of Jews in Syria." Similarly, the *Commercial Advertiser* of Sept. 22, 1876 concluded an article on "Jerusalem Rebuilt" with the exclamation: "It is quite possible that we may witness the foundation of a Jewish Anglo-American republic in that country. . . ." At the time of the Russo-Turkish war and the negotiations at the Congress of Berlin, at which all the anti-Russian forces were led by the "Jew," Disraeli, these Zionist expectations were treated seriously in the world press. The following Paris correspondence published in the staid *Pall Mall Gazette* of London in June (?) 1878 may serve as a typical illustration:

> A rumour has got about that Lord Beaconsfield will not return empty-handed and that he is preparing for his countrymen a sensational surprise—not less a thing in fact, than a British protectorate over the Holy Land. . . . But the question is whether Englishmen, if they understood the full extent of the responsibilities in which such a bargain would involve them, would consent to it, and whether the Turks themselves would agree to the bargain unless England assumed every one of the responsibilities attendant upon protectorate.

Most of these utterances were read in America, excerpted in the general and Jewish press, and often produced heated arguments pro or con. The *Jewish Messenger*, for instance, always orthodox and pro-Zionist, reservedly expressed the hope that "now that the

British flag floats from Cyprus, the problem of colonizing Palestine is about being solved." The *American Israelite*, on the other hand, and its editor, I. M. Wise, often with considerable heat, repudiated all such ideas. Thus, in Sept. 1876, the Cincinnati *Gazette* published an extensive communication on "The Jews Return to Palestine," in which the evidently Christian author predicted their speedy return in connection with the forthcoming settlement of the Eastern Question, claimed that the Rothschilds had, through their loans in the Greek war of 1820-21, acquired a mortgage on the Holy Land and flamboyantly declared that "when the standard of Judah, by permission, is raised upon the walls of Jerusalem, the seas will whiten with sails, and steamers and locomotives will lead the march of the scattered Hebrews from all nations to the Holy Land, such as crusaders never saw." Wise believed that he could dimiss all such utopian ideas with sarcasm:

> In all those beautiful words there are but two slight mistakes, viz: the Jews do not think of going back to Palestine among Bedouins and sandy deserts, and the nations in power do not want them to go there. No European country to-day would give permission to the Jews to emigrate with their wealth or even without it; and the European Jews have as little an idea to go as the Rothschilds want to purchase Palestine, or be Kings of the Jews. It is all dream and phantasy. The world goes not backward; its march is onward, and this will expunge the old race prejudices as well as the religious superstitions of the races. We are marching toward Jerusalem, we march toward One God, one law and one human family, and history lies not. . . .

A few months later Wise sharply attacked a Mr. Conway, the London correspondent of the Cincinnati *Daily Commercial*, because the latter ventured to predict a forthcoming partition of Turkey, and the revival of a Jewish Kingdom in Turkey under Queen Victoria.[92]

Not a word about these discussions, which could hardly have fostered his work, appeared in Notkin's record. He went about his task of collection, strong in his faith and in his conviction of the great religious role of the Palestinian settlement in the divine scheme of existence. It was in the midst of these activities, however, that, after his return to New York, he fell ill and died. The account book and perhaps some other records were taken over by the new supervisors of Palestinian relief, with whose attestation, dated June 2, 1879, the volume concludes:

We the undersigned Trustees have examined the accounts of Reverend Nathan Natkin the Collector from Jerusalem and find the accounts of the Book correspond in every particular to the Drafts sent for the same

Isaac Barnett	394 Canal Street N.Y.
J. H. Kantrowitz	31 East Broadway N.Y.
S. Raphel	47 Essex Street[93]

Unless this statement was purely euphemistic and designed to clear the name of a revered visitor, we must assume that Notkin had submitted a much fuller account of his receipts and expenditures than those recorded in our book. Apart from their sporadic and fragmentary nature, the sums entered therein would hardly have sufficed to cover the expenses of the messenger over a period of nearly three years, and certainly would have left no balance whatsoever to be shipped to Jerusalem. These fragmentary records give us nevertheless an inkling of the success of Notkin's mission even in remote and small communities, and it may readily be assumed that he was no less successful in the larger centers of Jewish life, such as Philadelphia, Boston, Cincinnati, Chicago, and San Francisco. It was right, therefore, for the New York Trustees to return the minute book, together with whatever other records and funds were left behind by the deceased messenger, to his superiors in Jerusalem, who in turn guarded it long enough for it to find its way into the National and University Library in the new period of Palestine's upbuilding.

Appendix I   Hebrew Entries in the Messengers' Notebook

A. *Members of the Jewish Community of UTICA, N. Y. (1850)*
   (fols. 17b-18b)

ידו הגדולה וזרוע חנטויה

I
אשר נשבע לאבינו בהר המוריה להרבות זרעו כעפרות תבל וכגפן פוריה,
יקיום שבועתו למשה כשאמר לו אהיה כי הוציאנו מארץ מאפליה וגם שבאנו
באש ובמים ויציאנו לרויה אך אחינו בני ישראל אין איש שם על לב על
בית ה' שהיא גדר הדחויה ומאחר שראיתי בבית ישראל שערורויה שאין איש מת-
עורר על אחינו שבארץ הקדושה אשר מתגוררים בירושלם הולכים בתורה
ובטהרה מעלות מעלות אך המה חונים בגלות והמה עניים מרודים
אביונים ודלים. לכן נדרתי שני דאללער בכל שנה ושנה לחיות לי לזכות לנש-
מתי וחלק בתורתם אברהם פינקוס יאטיקא יום וי'ו עש"ק כ"ו שבט ית"ר לפ"ק

II
בזאת אפתח שער בעד אחינו השרויים ביגון וצער, ואני כסיל ובער ונדרתי
לתן א' דאללער בכל שנה, בשמחה ורנה, ואל יהיה לי לחרפה ולבזיון, כי אנכי
דל ואביון, אך אם יזכני צל חביון לבא לציון, אז אשמח על החזון כשמחת
יונה על הקיקיון.
יאטוקא יום א' כ"ח שבט לסדר ויקחו לי תרומה לפ"ק הק' רפאל מרדכי בן
לאמ"א מ"ה שרגא פייבש ממשפחת פינקוס

III
גם אנכי אתן כפי יכולתי לאהבנ"י הדרים בארץ הקדושה א' ר"ט בכל שנה
בלי נדר הק' ארי' בן לפידום כ"ץ פה יוטיקא. גם בני חק' צבי בן לפידום ארי'
כ"ץ יתן א' ר"ט בלי נדר

Mit innigster Wonne erfülle ich die Heilige Pflicht **ואהבת לרעך כמוך** der
nächsten Liebe um für meine Brüder in der Heiligen Stadt **ירושלים תו"בב** eine
freywillige Gabe von jährlich drey Doller zu diesem wohlthätigen Zwecke zu
spenden. Utica den 10ten Fäber 1850 Mit mein eigenhändig Unterschrift
הק' יוסף בן חיים אלפייא Fogel. Feldmann

Ich freye mich zu diesem obigen mein weniges als eine Unterstützung   IV
beyzutragen und verpflichte mich jährlich einen Betrag von *Ein Doller*
beyzutragen.   **הק' משה בן יצחק סג"ל מסדוקי**
Utica den 10ten Feber 1850

Zur Unterstützung der Armen in der heiligen Stadt Jerusalem sehe ich es   V
als Nächstenliebe und Pflicht an, so viel es meine Verhältnisse erlauben
nähmlich einen jährlichen Beytrag von Ein Doller zu spenden
Utica den 10ten Feber 1850

פורש אנכי בשלום הראב"ד
מ' אשר לעמיל מק"ק גאלין עם אחיו ובני ביתם מקאליש הק' אליעזר בן ר'
שמואל ישראל מקאליש בן אחות ר' זלמן מגאלין.

Ich Endesgefertigter fühle mich verpflichtet eine Spende zum Wohltäti-   VI
gen Zwecke an meinen Brudern in **ירושלים תוב"ב** von *Ein Doller* jährlich an
den hierzu bestimmten Vorsteher zu senden. **הק' מאיר לעוויטצקי אויס קאליש**
Utica am 10ten Faber 1850

Auch ich versage eine Gabe zum Obigen wohlthätigen Zwecke zu VII
spenden, und verpflichte mich jährlich *Ein Doller* zu sämtlichen obigen Cassa
zu geben.
Utica am 10t Faber 1850   הק' חיים בן מרדכי מקאללישר

VIII   גם אנוכי לא אחשך את נפשי ולא אקפוץ את ידי מלידה כפי כחי, מלתן מעט
רכושי אשר הנני ה' לעזור לאחב"י השוכנים בארץ הקדושה עם סך א' ר"ט לשנה
בלי נדר ואתפלל להקוראים דברי אלה שיזכירו את שמי למורי רבי התורני
מ' אשר לעמיל אב"ד דק"ק גאלין עם אחיו ואשתם ובני ביתם כ"ד תלמידו
ישראל בן שמואל מקלעטטשאווע ופרום בשלום חביריו מו"ה משה בן יעקב מגאלין
וד' יראני בבני מקדשינו ויקבץ נדחינו ואז נראה דודים כאהבת חביבים,
חבירו ישראל בן שמואל פה יוטיקא.

IX   גם אני באתי לכתוב על ספר הלז שאני נודד לשארית בני עמי בירושלים שני
דאללער בכל שנה ושנה להיות לזכות וחלק בתורתם הק' יוסף בן כ"ה ר' מרדכי
שווייג   מישוב באללעף אין אונגגארין פה אטיקע כ"ח לחדש שבט תר"י לפ"ק.

X   ממני אחי הבחר יהודא שווארץ אלעף דאללער בכל שנה

XI   מקרבי הבחר יהודה קייזער מק"ק ביבעניץ אלעף דאללער בכל שנה

XII   Ich freye mich eine freywillige Gabe für meinen armen Brüdern in der
Heiligen Stadt Jerusalem beyzutragen mit der Verpflichtung jährlich zwey
Doller zu spenden.
Utica am 10ten Faber 1850

אהרן קערן

XIII   גם אני אודה לה' על שהחייני ליתן מעט מן המעט אשר ניתן לי, לעזור לאחינו
בני ישראל הדרים בארץ הקדושה ואקוה לה' שגם כל אחד אשר מזרע ישראל
הוא יעזור להדרים בא"י, בכדי שלא יסור עבודת ה' מן הארץ והעיר אשר ישבו
בה אבותינו ובזכות זה והתקוה אשר נקווה שירחם הבורא על בניו ויביאם
וינהלם לארצו ויבנה מקדשו במהרה אתן אלף 1 דאלאר אתן לצדקה בעד אנשי
ירושלים בלי נדר צבי בן אברהם הערשפעלד יוטיקא.

XIV   גם אני באתי לבקש מאחב"י לעזור ולסעד לאחינו בני ישראל הדרים בירושלים
בכל מה דאפשר, הן בממונם והן בדבורם, ובפרט לפרנסי קהילה וקהילה לדבר
על לב אנשי קהילתם לנדב בכל שנה ושנה בכדי שלא יסור עבודת ה' ממקום
הנבחר והקדוש, ובזכות זה ה' יקבץ נדחינו ויביאם לארץ הקדושה, נדבתי תהיה
בלי נדר שני דאללער בכל שנה. אהרן בן אברהם הערשפעלד פרנס דק"ק
בית ישראל דיוטיקא.

XV   בעה"י. בזאת יבא אהרן אל הקודש! כי זא"ת בגמ' צו"ם קו"ל ממו"ן דהיינו
תשובה תפלה צדקה וג' אלו בגמ' זא"ת וזאת הרבינו המפואר והתורני היקר
מהו"ר אהרן זעל"יג אשכנזאזי משולח נאמן מעיר הקדושה תותב"ב אמן, והאיש
הנחמד היה ברוב קהלות קהילתינו במדינות אמריקא, אמנם בא גם לכאן
לבקש רחמים בגלל אחינו ב"י היושבים בהר הקודש בירושלים לתפלה ולהגנה,
ונתתי אל לבי לעשות כפי יכולתי וכעצם כחי לתת נדבה לעניי ב"י בארץ הק-
דושה במתנה א' דאללער ב"נ מדי יום בשנה ולהזכיר את ירושלים, כמא'
הנביא זכרה ירושלים ימי עניה י"ו ובזכות זה יקוים בנו מקרא שנ' השיבינו
ה' אליך ונשובה חדש חדש כקדם, ולבנות הוא בעצמו את בית קדשינו ולק-
בץ גלויותנו שנ' בונה ירושלים ה' נדחי ישראל יכנס. היום יום א' כ"ח בשבט
שנת הא"ל יצלי"ל בונה ירושלים ה' נדחי ישראל יכנס. היום יום א' כ"ח בשבט לפ"ק.

נאם יהוד' המכונה ליב עלזר ש"ז ונאמן דק"ק הנ"ל אוב דאס געלט וועט אייון
קומען וועלין ווער עם ב"ה אף שיקין א מיסטערע אייזיק אין נייארק אהרן
בו אברהם הערשפעלד.

B. *David Davidson of* BOSTON *(1861)*
(fol. 32b)

בעזרת האל ק"ק באסטאן במדינה
אמעריקא היום יום א' פרשת במד-
בר, ארבעים יום למב"י תרכ"א
ודוד הוא הקטן מאנשי אוהבי הש-
לום דק"ק באסטאן

אם אשכחך ירושלם תשכח ימיני
תדבק לשוני לחכי אם לא
אזכרכי !
אם לא אעלה את ירושלים על
ראש שמחתי, והנה למען אחי
ורעי אדברה בא
הפנקס פתוח והיד כותבת
וכל הרוצה ליתן יבוא ויתן,
ואל יאמר שוב ומחר אתן

ומה אמר דוד המלך עליו השלום ואנוכי תולעת ולא איש, דבר אין בפי,
ובלשוני אין מלה, הן יהו' ידעת כלה, אני עבדך בן אמתך. ואיך יכנס דג קטן
במים אדירים אשר תנינים גדולים הולכים שם, אדבר יראתי פן אבולע, ואם
אחשה וחטאתי לאלהים ! וחכמינו ז"ל אמרו אחד המרבה ואחד הממעיט, ובלבד
שיכוין לבו לשמים, ואמרתי בלבי, לב מהור ברא לי אלקים ורוח נכון חדש
בקרבי, ובתורתינו הקדושה נאמר, איש כמתנת ידו — ובזה אני בא, אבינו אב
הרחמן, הראינו אות לטובה, מהר קדמוני רחמיך: השב שכינתך לציון עירך
— וסדר העבודה לירושלים — ותחזינה עינינו בשובך לציון ברחמים. ושם
נעבדך ביראה כימי עולם וכשנים קדמוניות — נאום דוד בן כ"ה דוב ז"ל.
במתנת ידו א' דאללאר.

C. *Abraham Abba of* SAN FRANCISCO *(1861)*
(fol. 39b)

בע"ה היום שנכפל בו כי טוב לסדר ואראה אל אברהם שנת וגם הקימותי
את בריתי לפ"ק פה סאנפראנציסקא. אף כי חברת שומרי שבת מעט היא, וגם
רובם ככולם באו בברית יחד חברת אוהבי ציון אשר יסדו וכוננו אנשי חסד
ורחמים עם אלקי אברהם דפה, יהי נועם ד' אליהם ומעשה ידיהם יכונן, חסדם
לא יסור מאתם ויהיו תהלה בארץ: יצו ד' אתם את הברכה חיים ושלום עד
העולם ויקויים בהם תהלת נעים זמירות ישראל (אשרי משכיל אל דל וכו'):
וגם מאמר החכם בספר החכמה (מלוה ד' חונן דל וגמולו ישלם לו): עכ"ז כאשר
ראינו את האיש הרבני וכו' כמו"ה אברהם ניסן ציר נאמן לשולחיו בני ציון
היקרים: לעורר לבות אחיהם המפוזרים בקצות תבל: ושמעינו את שיחתו אשר שפך
לפנינו ברחמים וחנינה: עלי צרת אחינו ב"י המדוכאים בעניות מרודות, נכ-
מרו רחמינו על אחינו: ובאנו גם אנחנו בתוך הבאים בעזרתם ולחיות מן
המתנדבים בעם סך חמשה ועשרים דאלער מדי שנה בשנה, להיות עזרה בעת
צר לאחינו ב"י הבאים להסתפח בנחל[ת] ד' בארץ החיים: היושבים על התורה
ועל העבודה לעבדה ולשמרה בירושלים: אשר משם עולה תפלה כ"ה לשער
השמים: וגדולה צדקה שמקרבת את הגאולה: יהי רצון מלפני אל למושעות:
שיקרב ויראה לנו את קץ הפלאות: ישלח לנו במהרה את הגואל: בימינו תושע
יהודא וישראל: ונזכה לחזות בנועם ד' ובבנין אריאל:
נאום אברהם אבא בא"א מו"ה שלמה סג"ל פרנס מק"ק שומרי שבת.

הרפה שברה לב ואנושה

דק"ק

Appendix II

Unless otherwise specified, amounts of contributions and collections are given in U. S. dollars.
Many readings are tentative.

AUSTRIA-HUNGARY

	1876-79
Francis Joseph, Emperor	

EISENSTADT	1867-69
Hildesheimer, Azriel	

FRANCE

PARIS	
	1859
Munk, Solomon	
	1867-69
Alliance Israélite	
Crémieux, Adolphe	
Paris Conference	

GERMANY

	1876-79
Delegates to Paris	
Conference:	
Graetz, Heinrich	
Levy, Asher	
Levy, M. Gottschalk	

BERLIN	1876-79
Committee for Jerusalem	
Orphan Asylums	

HALBERSTADT	1867-69
Hirsch, Fischl (?)	

GREAT BRITAIN AND POSSESSIONS

Canada

MONTREAL	1867-69
German and Polish	
Congregation:	80.00
Albert, Louis	
Silverman, S.	
Portuguese Congregation:	61.00
Golaberg, H.	

England

BIRMINGHAM	1849-50
Birmingham Hebrew	
Congregation	£2
Abraham, Philip	
Marks, S. M.	
Raphall, Morris Jacob, Rev.	
See also NEW YORK	

LIVERPOOL	1849-50
Old Seel Street Congregation	
Harris, Lazarus	
Isaacs, D. W. Rev.	£10.14.6
Oppenheim, M. S. Rev.	£4.15

Monthly subscriptions:

Aaronson	1/
Abrahams, I.	1/
Abrahamson	1/
Ahlborne	2/
Behrend, D.	2/
Beruch, B.	/8
Coppel, Z.	/6
Goldsmid	1/
Gollin	1/
Goodman	/8
Grant	1/
Harris, Julius	1/
Harris, L.	1/
Hayman, L.	2/
Isaacs, Benj.	1/
Isaacs, John	1/

Jackson, Mrs. Abm.	1/
Jackson, F.	1/
Jacobs, Henry	/8
Josephson	1/
Lazarus, Isaac	/6
Levy, Henry	/6
Marks, D.	1/
Moss	1/
Myers, D.	2/
Nathan, Mozley	1/
Nathan, N.	1/
Nathan, Wolf	1/
Nelson, Mrs.	1/
Nelson, B.	2/
Nelson, Joseph	/6
Oppenheim, M. S., Rev.	1/4
Sampson	1/
Samuel	/6
Samuel, I.	1/
Samuel, W.	1/
Solomon, Jacob	1/
Solomon, Susman	/8
Sweetman	/6
Teaman	1/

LONDON

1850

Hirschell, Solomon, Chief
  Rabbi
Montefiore, Sir Moses

1853-54

Adler, Nathan, Chief
  Rabbi

1861

Montefiore, Sir Moses

1867-69

Adler, Nathan, Chief
  Rabbi
British Board of Deputies
Montefiore, Sir Moses

1876-79

Beaconsfield, Lord (Disraeli,
  Benjamin)
British Board of Deputies
Asher, Asher
Montagu, Samuel
Montefiore, Sir Moses
Montefiore Testimonial Fund

MANCHESTER   1850

Isaac, John M.
Joseph, Simon

Kantrowitz, I., Rev.
Levy, Joachim
Nahman b. Jacob ha-Levi

Gibraltar

1849

Joseph, Henry

Jamaica

KINGSTON   1849-50

Jacobs, Solomon, Rev.

HOLLAND

AMSTERDAM

1849-50

Lehren, Hirsch

1861

Lehren, Akiba

1876-79

Central Committee

ITALY

BOLOGNA   1876-79

Mongliano, Rabbi

PALESTINE

JERUSALEM

1849

Congregation Perushim:
  Burdaki, Isaiah
  Nathan Neta b. Mendel
  Neeman, Aryeh b. Yeraḥmeel
  Salant, Joseph Zundel
  Tebele, David

1861

Congregation Perushim:
  Berlin, Jacob b. Judah
  Brill, Yeḥiel
  Burdaki, Isaiah
  Salant, Joseph Zundel
  Theomim, Jacob b. David
Consul:
  Finn, James,
  British Consul

1867-69

Central Committee of all the Ashkenazic *Kolelim*
Aniksht, Meir b. Asher [Kamaikin]
Berlin, Jacob b. Judah
Biedermann, Isaac David
Eisenstein, Abraham b. Zevi
Eliezer, Nathan (?)
Eliezer Zevi Kab ve-naki
Epstein, Schneur Zalman
Hausdorff, Selig
Isaac [Oplatka]
Isaac Zevi b. Moses ha-Levi
Jacob Judah Levi (or Leb)
Kahanov, Moses Nehemiah
Katz, Joseph [Isaac?]
Moses, Aaron Leb
Ralbag, Moses Eliezer Dan b. Aryeh Leb
Rivlin, Joseph
Segal [Hamburger], Moses
Theomim, Jacob b. David
Wunder, Eisig
Zeeb ha-Kohen
Zevi David
Consuls:
Beauboucher, Victor H., U. S. Consul
Johnson, Lorenzo M., U. S. Vice Consul and Acting Consul

1876-79

Central Committee:
Abraham of Nowemiesto
Aniksht, Meir
Ashkenazi, Abraham [Auerbach], Meyer Isaac
Bax [Berk], Nissan
Benjamin, Yehudah Leb
Benveniste, Moses
Eisenstein, Abraham
Graf (?), Moses
Hayyim Nissim Baruch
Isaac Zevi b. Moses ha-Levi [I. H. Marcus]
Jacob [b. Dober] of Minsk
Joseph Katz
Lewin, Solomon Zalman
Maggid, Elijah Sorasohn

Panisel, Ralphael Meir
Ralbag, Moses Eliezer Dan Behar
Salant, Samuel
Schlank, Johanan Hirsh b. Mordecai
Yafeh, Eisig
Consuls:
Pascal, Austrian Vice Consul
Mocre, Noel Temple, British Consul
Munchhausen, Baron von, German Consul
Beauboucher, Victor H., U. S. Consul
de Hass, F. H., U. S. Consul
Wilson, J. G., U. S. Consul

PANAMA

	1867-69
Piza, Samuel	£2.0.0
COLON	1867-69
Cantoni, Salvatore	5.00

UNITED STATES OF AMERICA

Alabama

MOBILE

1849

Congregation Shaarei Shamaim
Jones, Israel I. [J.?]

	1867-69
Hebrew Relief Association	25.00
Arnheimer (?), M.	10.00
Baerman, A.	1.00
Bauer, S.	2.00
Berheimer, A.	2.00
Bernstein, H.	3.00
Cash	1.00
Cohen, J. [I.?]	1.00
Epstein, F.	
Frohlichstein, H.	2.00
Gans	1.00

Goldsmith, M.	1.00		Weil, Dav.	1.00
Goldstein, M.			Weil, J. & H.	8.00
Goldstucker (?)			Weil, Jac.	3.00
Hahn, S. L.	5.00			
Hartmann, N.	1.00			**1867-69**
Heidelberger	1.00			
Hirschfield, S.	2.00		Cash	1.00
J., B.	2.00		Gerson, A.	1.00
Kaufman, J.	1.00		Gerson, M. L.	1.00
Laser, H.	2.00		Hausman, G.	1.00
Leinkauf, Wm. N.	5.00		Levy, Jacob	1.00
Leinkauf	3.00		Meertief, S. A.	1.00
Levy, M.	1.00		Meyer, Henry	1.00
Lyons	1.00		Munter, M. & Co.	2.00
Marcus, S.	2.50		Natan (?), F. H. & Bro.	2.00
Marx, H.	2.00		Oppenheimer, Louis	1.00
Marx, H.	1.50		Strassberger, A. H.	5.00
Marx, M.	3.00		Weil, D.	1.00
Meigs, (?), D. J.	2.00			
Metzger, S.	1.00		SELMA	**1867-69**
Meyer, L.	2.00		Hebrew Association	10.00
Meyers, L. A.	1.00		Marx, M.	
Moldauer, J.	1.00		Adler, B.	1.00
Mooy, A. & B.	5.00		Goldmann, L.	1.00
Neubrit (?)	1.00		Herzfeld, Albert	1.00
Pake, S.			Meyer, Emanuel	2.00
Pelko, A.	1.00		Meyer, J.	2.00
Pincus, A.	2.00		Meyer, M.	2.00
Reis	1.00		Nagl [Stagl?], Chas.	1.00
Schonfeld	1.00		Oberndorf, Joseph	1.00
Simon, M., Bros.	2.00		Regenstein, Gabriel	1.00
Strauss, S.	5.00		Schwartz, M. Jr.	1.00
Weis, S.	1.00			
Ladies Hebrew Benevolent			*California*	
Society	10.00		GRASS VALLEY	**1867-69**
			Committee	18.50
	1876-79		Heyman, Jacob	
Richard, S.	1.00		Sanders, S.	
			Zacharius, Lyon	
MONTGOMERY				
	1849		LOS ANGELES	**1867-69**
Hebrew Congregation:			Hebrew Benevolent	
Cellner, S.	2.50		Society	100.00
Englander, M.	2.00		Prager, Charles	
Gerson, M. L.	2.50		Ezekiel b. Samuel	1.00
Heim, Isaac	1.00			
Lehman, H. & Bro.	10.00		MARYSVILLE	
Lehman, Em.				**1867-69**
Lehmann, Henry			Hebrew Benevolent and	
Myers, I. [J.?] & G.	5.00		Congregational Society	75.00
Newman, I. [J.?]	2.50		Lask, Joseph	

Shreyer, Henry
Cohen, William 5.00
Peyser, M.W. 5.00

1876-79
Hebrew Benevolent and
Congregational Society 25.00
Marcuse, M. A.
Schneider, N.

SACRAMENTO 1867-69

Congregation Benai Israel 75.00
Elkus, L.
Zekind, S.

SAN FRANCISCO
1861

Beth Hamidrash of Society
Shomre Shabbat 34.00
Abraham Abba
Bian [Biach?], Moses Arye
Israel b. Jacob
Jacob b. Noah
Katz, Moses Aryeh
b. Raphael
Segal, Abraham Abba
b. Solomon
Ohabe Zion (Society Friends
of Zion)
Choynski, I. N.
Congregation Shearith Israel
per annum 100.00
Craner, Simon
Henry, H. A., Rev.
1867-69
Society for the Relief of the
Jews of Palestine £50.0.0
Blochman, Emanuel (Eliezer
b. Menaḥem)
Blockman, A. (Abraham
Yeḥiel b. Asher Lemel)
Brandon, J. R. (Joseph b.
Abraham)
Dias, A. H. L.

STOCKTON 1867-69

Congregation Rahim
Ahoovim 45.00
Kullman, H.

Connecticut

HARTFORD
1850
Congregation Beth Israel
Altman, E. .50
Bamberger, L. 1.00
Baum, I. [J.?] .50
Cahn, P. .50
Fox, G. 1.00
Hollander, Abraham 2.00
Katzenberg, H. 1.50
Lithauer, Jacob 3.00
Mayer, S. 1.00
Raymont, N. 1.00
Rice, I. [J.?] .50
Rosenblatt, H. 1.00
Rothschild, A. .50
Rottenberg [Rollenberg], L. 1.00
Selling, D. 1.00
Stern, M. 1.00
Wallach, F. 1.00
Wallach, S. 1.00

1867-69

Congregation Beth Israel 50.00
Lewitts, Henry

NEW HAVEN
1771

Stiles, Ezra
1850
Congregation Mishkan Israel:
Adler, .25
Auerbach, .50
Bretzfelder, Israel 1.50
Franken, N. 1.00
Harris, .50
Kaufman, A. 2.00
Kern, I. (J.?) .50
Lauterbach, .50
Lengsfeld, .25
Mailander, 1.00
Mandelbaum, L. .50
Markuse, 1.00
Midas, M. .50
Rothschild, Joseph 1.00
Rothschild, Laz. .50
Smith, Jacob 3.00
Strauss, Benj. .50

Strouse, Isaac, Rev.	1.00
Thalman,	2.00
Ulman,	1.00
Waterman, L.	1.50
Williams, Is.	1.00
Williams, Wolf	1.00

District of Columbia

GEORGETOWN 1867-69

Potomac Lodge No. 104 I.O.B.B.	
Barwald, D.	
B., N. W. (?)	1.00
Nordlinger, B.	1.00
Ottinger, D.	2.00
Other members	4.05
Gärnter, J.	1.00

WASHINGTON

1867-69

Elijah Lodge No. 50 I.O.B.B.	10.00
Danielman, D. S.	
Jacobson, Jacob S.	
Otable (?), A.	
Hebrew Congregation	3.00
Adler, H.	1.00
Abraham, Isaac	2.00
Bauer, A.	1.00
Blout, H. L.	
De Wolff, Benjamin	1.00
Gotthelf & Behrend	3.00
Hänlein, J. H.	.50
Heilbrun, L.	1.00
Herzberg, Charles	2.00
Hirsch, M.	1.00
Jacobson, J.	1.00
Jacobson, Jacob S.	
Lansburgh, G.	1.00
Luchs, L. & Co.	3.00
Oppenheimer, Leopold	1.00
Prince, H.	1.00
Solomons, A. S.	5.00
Young & Behrend	1.00

1876-79

Seward, F. W., Acting Secretary of State	

Georgia

ATLANTA 1867-69

Hebrew Benevolent Congregation	15.00
Alexander, L. H.	
Franklin, Jacob	

AUGUSTA 1867-69

Congregation Children of Israel	25.35
Levy, Samuel	
Phillips, Bernhard	6.45

COLUMBUS 1867-69

Ehrman, N.	2.00
(*paid in New Orleans*)	

MACON 1867-69

Congregation Beth Israel	10.25
Abraham, D.	1.00
Brown, E. M.	
Hirsch, M. M.	2.00

SAVANNAH 1867-69

Gerstmann collection:	
Cohen, Morris	1.00
Cottner, Salomann	2.00
Davidson, I. S.	4.00
Gartensteig, I. S.	3.00
Gerstmann, Simon	15.00
Golinsky, A.	4.00
Mamlook, A. L.	5.00
Max, E.	1.00
Cash	1.00
Cash	2.00
Cash	2.00
Gottschalk, Brown	5.00
Levkey, Julius	1.00
Reich, Morris	1.00
Slager, A.	1.00
White, J.	2.00
Wislow, A. B.	2.00
Additional collection by Levkey and associates	100.00

Indiana

INDIANAPOLIS

1861

Hebrew Congregation	7.85
Anonymous	2.00

Anonymous	.50
"	.25
"	.25
"	.30
"	.35
"	.20
Moses,	1.00
Woolf, M.	3.00

1876-79

Israeloff (?), Abraham	
b. Joseph	5.00
Marks, H.	2.00
Mossler, Solomon	2.00
Tobias, Jacob	.50

LAFAYETTE 1861

| Congregation Ahvas Achim | 6.00 |
| Hallstrin, M. | |

Illinois

CHICAGO

1861

Congregation Anshe Mayrib	
Gerstley M. M.	
Henke (Glenke?) T.	
per annum	3.00
Society of Young Men	10.00
Other Collection	
Aberbruhum (?), Joseph	3.00
Anonymous	10.00
Anonymous	5.00
Greenfelder, Isaac	
(collector)	1.00
Silberman, M.	4.00
Wein, Abraham	2.00

1867-69

Congregation B'nai	
Sholom	20.00
Adolph, Phil	
Melzer, David	
(b. Isaac ha-Kohen)	
Chebra Kadishe Ubikur	
Cholem	3.00
Adams, D.	2.00
Perlinsky and Louis	1.00
Witkowsky, Samuel	
Other Contributors:	
Herbst, Hartwig	1.00
Price, Rosenblatt & Co.	1.00
Name blotted	1.00

United Hebrew Relief	
Association	10.00
Julius Rosenthal	10.00

PEORIA 1867-69

Local community	5.00
Ballenberg, Morris	1.00
Bennett, E.	.50
Bennett, I.	2.00
Bennett, S.	2.00
Hertz, H., & Co.	1.00
Schradzki, A., & J.	2.00
Schwabacher, Henry	2.00
Schwabe, Isak	1.00
Schwerzman, D.	1.00
Ulman, Henry	

Iowa

COUNCIL BLUFFS 1876-79

| Eiseman, Simon | 1.00 |
| Newman, B. | 1.00 |

Kentucky

LOUISVILLE 1849

| Congregation Adas Israel | |
| Schweat (?), A. | |

Louisiana

BATON ROUGE 1867-69

Congregation Shaare	
Chesed	10.00
Dalsheimer, L.	2.00
Kowalski, A.	
Rosenfield, A.	1.00
Tendler (?), E.	1.00

LAFAYETTE 1867-69

| Bendel, William | 14.00 |
| Cohen, J. | .25 |

NEW ORLEANS

1849

Congregation Shari Chesed:	
Annual subscription	
Baker, M.	2.50
Benjamin, A.	5.00
Brown, M. S.	2.50
Cohen, B.	2.50
Cramer, J.	2.00
Dalseimer	2.00

Ehlbert, A.	5.00	Congregation Temime Derek:	
Elsassor, S.	2.50	Aaron, S.	2.00
Fabine, M.	2.00	Adler, Edward	2.00
Frank, A.	2.50	Aronstein, M.	1.00
Goldman, M.	5.00	Bloom, H.	5.00
Goldsmith, L.	5.00	Cain, L. B.	3.00
Goldstein, H., Rev.	2.50	Cash	1.50
Haber, A.	5.00	Cerf, D.	2.00
Hart, Isaac	5.00	Cohen, Beniamin	2.00
Hess, C.	2.50	Dalheimer, N.	1.00
Hockstein, E.	2.50	Davis, William	?.00
Hockstein, S.	2.50	Dreyfus, H.	1.00
Hyams, L.	3.00	Ehrlich, S. [Samuel David	
Hyman, M.	2.00	b. Naftali]	2.25
Jacobs, S.	3.00	Epstein, Z. & Co.	2.00
Karpp, Julius	2.50	Fircheimer Bros.	5.00
Krofoski, L.	2.50	Fortheimer & Haber	4.00
Levi, G.	2.50	Friend, A	1.00
Levi, J. S.	2.50	Gerson, Ben.	2.00
Levy, A.	2.50	Goldsmith, F.	3.00
Levy, L. A. Jr.	2.50	Goldsmith, M.	1.00
Levy, Penel	2.50	Goldstam	2.50
Morris, A.	2.50	Haspel, Simon	5.00
Myer, Alex	2.50	Hausman, J.	—
Myer, Jacob	2.50	Heims, H.	5.00
Myer, S.	2.50	Herman, E.	2.50
Newberger, A.	2.50	Heyman, A.	2.00
Prince, J. L.	2.50	Jacobs, Benjamin E. Rev.	3.00
Regensburger, L.	2.50	Kaufman, Chas.	1.00
Regenski, M.	2.50	Kaufman, M., & Co.	5.00
Rose, A.	2.50	Kausl (?), Sam	1.50
Sherwin, S.	3.00	Kern, H.	2.00
Shuler, L.	5.00	L.J. (?)	1.00
Simon, L.	2.50	Landau, J.	5.00
Simon, W.	2.50	Lehmann, A.	5.00
Spero, J.	5.00	Levi, Isidore	20.00
Synon (?), S.	2.50	Levy, J.	2.00
Worms, N.	2.50	Levy, Lionel C.	5.00
Young, A. de	3.00	Mann, A.	1.00
		Moses, B.	1.00
	1867-69	Newhaus, Lehman	10.00
Congregation Nefuzoth		Phelps, Lewis	3.00
Yehudah:		Rennard, M.	1.00
Davis, Henry	1.00	Roos, A.	1.00
D'Meza, H. H.	4.00	Rosenthal, J.	1.00
Jacobs, Henry P. Rev.	3.00	Rosenthal, Nat	3.00
Koch, N.	2.00	Rosenthal, S.	1.00
Liberman, E.	3.00	Scheuer, L. A.	2.00
Phelps, E.	2.00	Schwartz, I. M.	2.50
Congregation Shaare		Schwartz, M. J.	2.50
Chesed:	25.00	Silverstein, S.	2.00
Gutheim, James K. Rev.		Simon, Jos.	2.00

Spiro, Josef	1.00
Stein, Louis, & Bros.	5.00
Thalheimer, T.	2.50
Weil, M.	1.00

1876-79

Bonesser (?), Z.	5.00
Cash	2.50
Cash	2.00
Cash	2.00
Cohen, P.	0.25
Ehrlich, S. [Samuel David b. Naphtali]	7.61
Friedlander, Samuel	5.00
Haspel, Simon	5.00
Levi, Isidore	10.00
Levitt, D. C.	4.00
Levy, E.	5.00
Paid	5.00
Rosenberg, B.	4.00

SHREVEPORT · 1876-79

Fagotston & Ripinski	2.00
Goldberg, L.	2.00
Harris, J.	4.00
Herold, Simon	1.00
Levy, S. Jr.	2.00
Munzesheimer, M.	2.00
Solinsky, L.	1.00

Maryland

BALTIMORE · 1849-50

Fels Point Hebrew Friendship Society
Polevik, M.
Hebrew Congregation
Rice, Abraham, Rev.

1876-79

Hevra Bnai Yisroile	5.00
Heiman, Joseph	
Sakolski, M. E.	
Cohen, N. M.	1.00
Jacobs, A.	0.25

Massachusetts

BOSTON · 1850

Congregation Bat [Beth] Israel:
| Abraham, Lewis | 2.00 |

Alexander, I. [J.?]	2.00
Cohn, Abraham	2.00
Dewis, Victor	1.00
Ezekiel, I. W. [Isaac b. Ezekiel]	5.00
Friedländer, Salomon	2.00
Gruschinski, I.	
Lyon, Chas.	
Marks, Lewis [Leb. b. Michael Besh]	2.00
Moser, Jacob	1.00
Perscheimer, Jacob S.	2.00
Wolf, J.	

Congregation Ohabei Shalom:
Bayersdorf, Moris
Bensimol, Solomon
Bibo, L.
Blumauer, Leopold
Ehrlich, Moses
Frank, Gerson
Haardt, L. H.
Heineman, Barnard
Lewengood, Louis
Sahlein, William
Schwab, Abraham
Selling, Henry
Strauss, Joseph, Rev.
Wolf, Julius

1861

Congregation Adath Israel · 5.00

Heineman, B.
Hofman, M.
Shoninger, J.
Congregation Ohabei Shalom	50.00
Aaronson, Aaron b. Hillel	1.00
Aaronson, Dober b. Aaron	1.00
Abrahams, Lewis	3.00
Adams, Isaac	5.00
Anonymous	5.00
Anonymous	0.50
Anthony, Henry	3.00
Davidson, David	1.00
Freedman, Israel	0.50
Grahd	0.25
Heiman (?), David b. Mordecai	3.00
Jacob, Benjamin b. Menahem (erroneously Menasseh)	1.00
Jacob b. Joseph	0.50

Kingsbury, William	10.00
Levy, Lewis	1.00
Meir b. Samuel (*Bahur*)	0.25
Mendel b. Israel	0.50
Moses b. Azriel	0.50
Moses, Baruch b. Asher ha-Levi	2.00
Myers, M.	5.00
Nelson, B.	
Pachter, Isaiah b. Samuel (pledges 2.00 annually)	1.00
Rose, Solomon b. Samuel	2.00
Sahlein, D.	1.00
Sidi, Alexander	10.00
Silberstein, I[saac]	1.00
Stranger, A.	0.50
Zuckerman, Simon b. Wolf	1.00

	1867-69
Congregation Adath Israel	7.00
Phillips, John	
Shoninger, J.	
Congregation Mishkan Israel	5.00
Strecker, Judah Leib	1.00
Strecker, Moses	1.00
Congregation Ohabei Shalom	—
Nelson, B.	—

SPRINGFIELD	1867-69
Congregation Ohab Zedek	5.00
Kaufmann, Jachsel [Ezekiel]	

Michigan

DETROIT

	1867
David Zevi b. Judah	2.00
Judah b. Meir	3.00
Littman, Abraham b. Isaac	1.50
Meyers, Mr. & Mrs.	2.00
Moses b. Nathan Neta	6.00
(promises annual donation)	

	1876-79
Congregation Bnei Israel	10.00
Brown, Jacob	1.00
Cash	1.00
Cohen, M.	1.00
Danegger, Louis	2.00

Fisher, Rene E. K.	1.00
Frankenstein, F.	1.00
Ginsburg (?), S.	2.00
Heavemich Bros.	5.00
Newsalt, A.	1.00
Schlon Bros. & Simon	5.00
Simon, David	

Mississippi

JACKSON	1867-69
Congregation Beth Israel	10.25
Asher, G.	0.50
Bear, M.	0.50
Beck, G.	0.50
Cohn, J.	1.00
Feigenbaum, M.	0.75
Goetz, E.	0.25
Hart, John	0.50
Hart, P.	0.50
Hunt, J.	2.00
Kaufman, N.	1.00
Levy, B.	0.25
Ries, J.	1.00
Schwartz, S.	0.50
Steinberg, E.	0.50

MERIDIAN	1867-69
Rosenbaum & Co. ⎰ Wolff, A. ⎱	21.10

Missouri

ST. JOSEPH	1876-79
Leichtman, Isaac, Dr.	1.00

ST. LOUIS	1867-69
United Hebrew Congregation	20.00
Spiro, Michael	—
Weiner, Max	—
Aaronson, Cash	1.00
Berg	2.00
Bienenstock	2.00
Bloch, H. (A?)	3.00
Dallenberg	5.00
Davis, L.	3.00
Ehrlich, M.	5.00
Falk	1.00
Garfunkel, B. M.	3.00
Horwitz	3.00
Johnson	1.00
Kroner, F. H.	1.00

Kutner, Henry	2.00
Levy	1.00
Levy, Adolph	2.00
Lichtenstein, L.	3.00
Liebreich	2.00
Nichols	3.00
Peltz, M.	1.00
Phillips	1.00
Pulvermacher	1.00
Roshbain, M.	1.00
Saragon (?), M.	1.00
Silberstein	1.00
Unterberger, M.	1.00
Winters, L.	1.00

Nebraska

OMAHA	1876-79
Elgutter, Morris	1.00

Nevada

VIRGINIA CITY (?)	1867-69
Nevada Hebrew Society	10.00
Barut [Baruh], H.	—

New Jersey

JERSEY CITY	1867-69
Baum, K.	5.00
Fox, Joseph	2.00
55 Newark Avenue	
Katz, W.	
46 Jersey Cty	
Krause, S.	5.00
4 Newark Avenue	
Oppenheimer, N.	5.00
135 Panama Avenue	
Stern, I.	5.00
16 Newark Avenue	
Syman, Morris	5.00
53 Newark Avenue	

NEWARK	1867-69
Congregation Benai Abraham	
Hannoch, M.	
Congregation Benai Jeshurun	
Lehman, Isador	
Congregation Oheb Shalom	
Stein, Joachim	

PATERSON	1867-69
Congregation Bnai	
Jeshurun	28.50
Barnert, Meir	0.50
Barnert, Nathan	1.00
Brown, Joseph	0.50
Burgauer, Philipp	1.00
Cah (?)	1.00
Cohen, Marks	1.00
Edelman, Jacob	5.00
Goldstein, M.	1.00
Gutther, Jacob	0.50
Hark (?), L.	0.50
Kingsbury, Moses	0.50
Kleinert, Semel	1.00
Kleinert, Viktor	0.50
Levi, Henry	0.50
Levy, Jacob	1.00
Reishler (?), Simon	1.00
Simon, A.	0.50
Simon, L.	1.00
Steckheimer (?)	0.50
Stein, Maier Abraham	1.00
Summer, N. per Wertheim	1.00
Vogel, Jacob A. Dupl.	5.00
Wertheim, David b. Joseph	1.00
Wollenberg, M.	1.00
Wollenberg, Nathan	0.50
?, Lazarus	1.00

New York

ALBANY	
	1850
Congregation Beth-El:	
Shulz, Ferdinand	
Wise, Isaac M., Rev.	
	1861
Congregation Beth El	25.00
Adler, Sigmund	
Congregation Beth El	
Jacob	14.00
Levi, S.	

BROOKLYN	
	1861
Hyman, Samuel	50.00
	1867-69
Congregation in Williamsburg:	
Kessel, M.	
151 South 8 St.	

Shool Beith Israel
Bass
   43 Atlantic St.

BUFFALO

                          1850

Fridenberg Collection:
Abrahams, D.
Ansell, A. Rev. and child
Barnet (?), A.
Barnet, I.
Bernheimer, E.
Bligh, Mr.
Cosstelder, S.
Drucker, I.
Frank, G.
Frank, I.
Fridenberg, Dena
Fridenberg, Isaac
Fridenberg, Lewis
Fridenberg, Micthel (?)
Fridenberg, Rachel
Fridenberg, Solomon
Funk, R.
Getski, I. M.
Graf, Jos.
Graustein, M.
Grunwaler, A.
Hiams, Saul [b. Ḥayyim]
Hyams, Ess.
Hyman, E.
Jacobs, A[braham]
Jacobs, W.
Kurtz (?), D.
Laterstok (?), I.
Lessler, Jos.
Levy, A.
Lichtenstein, S.
Marks, M.
Mautner, I.
Morretz, M.
Phillips, S.
Strass, A.
Strass, Abr.
Strass, I.
Strass, Jos.
Van Baalers

                          1861

Congregation Beth El   25.00
Black, Isaac
Greenberg, Zevi Hirsch b. Israel
Hyman, B.

Isaac b. Sender ha-Levi
   [Black?]
Congregation Scheeris Israel
Rosenthal, A. B.
Westhofen, Aaron

                      1867-69

Congregation Ansche
   Chesed   5.00
Congregation Beth El   7.37
Alexander, H.   1.00
Baruch b. Zeeb   2.00
Hyman, Abraham b. Baruch 5.00
Hyman, Baruch   5.00
Hyman, Mrs.   3.00
Israel   2.00
Judah Leb b. Abraham   3.04
Ruza, Lady   2.00
Segal, Meir b. Simon   2.65
Warenski, Israel   10.00
Congregation Brith Shalom 1.54
Alpern, N. (Menaḥem
   Nahum b. Jacob
   Koppel)   5.00
Brown, M.   0.50
Cohen, A. F. (1867, 13.00;
   1869, 15.00)   28.00
See also ELMIRA
Cohn, H.   1.00
Davis, L.   1.00
Davis, Rosenberg   2.00
Dettelbach   —
Freidman, M.   2.00
Harris, John   0.50
Harris, Samuel   0.50
Hofeller, Descker & Co. 1.00
Hyman, N.   1.00
Israel b. Moses and Früme
   b. Röte   10.00
Mossman   2.00
Scwartz, L. & Co.   1.00
Segal, Zeeb Abraham 2.00
Weber, W. [Zeeb Pinhas
   b. Joseph]

                1876-79

Congregation Berith Sholom:
Cohen, Harris   2.00
Cohen, Moses b. David
Einoch, Harris (Zevi b.
   Yehiel)   2.00
Fridenberg, Israel Oser (?) 1.00
Collection at Fridenberg's
   home   2.59

Galiner, Jacob	0.25
Gotthelf, Mr.	1.00
Grodzenski, Isaac	1.00
Grodzenski, Moses	1.00
Gumbinski, Littman Abba	2.00
Hyman, N.	1.00
Kloneck, Isaac	1.00
Lichtenstein, Meir	3.00
Meyerberg, Jacob Zevi	1.00
Rapperstein, Joseph	1.00
Rubinstein, Aryeh Zeeb	1.00
Sussman	1.00
Congregation Bnai Israel	5.00

ELMIRA 1867-69

Bush, L.	0.50
Bush, Wolf	1.00
Erlich, Barney	0.25
Fellner, B.	0.25
Frankenstein, E.	0.50
Gladki, Joseph	3.00
Happe, Nathan	1.00
Jacobs, J.	0.50
Keyser, Jos.	0.25
Levy, Maurice	0.50
Pale, I. [J.?]	0.25
Salner, I. [J.?]	0.25
Schwartz, F.	1.00
Sittenfeld, Salmon b. Joseph	1.00
Strauss & Samuel	0.50
Tuck, Morris	1.00
Congregation Bnai Israel	5.00
Anhalt, A.	0.25
Ansorge, Mrs.	1.00
Ansorge, Mrs. Hodes	3.00
Bush, Wolf	1.00
Cohen, A. F. (cf. also BUFFALO)	20.00
Deitz, Isaac	1.00
Ehrlich, David Beer	1.00
Frankenstein, A.	1.00
Friedman, Hirsch	0.22
Hoffe, Fryde	0.60
Isaac b. Zevi	1.00
Jacob, Samuel	2.00
Moses b. Simhah Leser	1.00
Raden, J. R.	0.50
Rosenbaum, A.	1.00
Rosenbaum, Mrs.	1.00
Rosenthal, N.	0.50
Rubin, Isaac	3.60
Samuel, A.	1.00

Sittenfeld, Selig b. Joseph	3.00
Sittenfeld, Solomon Zalman b. Joseph	2.00
Stahl, Jacob Joseph, Rev.	1.00
Strauss, Louis	1.00
Todman, Jochebed Yachne	1.00
Todman, Mayer	0.25
Todman, Mrs.	1.00
Tuch, Moritz	1.00
Wittenberg, Joseph	3.00
Wittenberg, Mrs.	1.00
Wolheim, Mrs. A.	0.25
Wolheim, Solomon	0.50
Zamie, Abraham	0.50

HORNILLSVILLE 1867-69

Congregation Ahavas Achim	2.00
Corn, Jacob	
Ehrlich, Israel	10.00
Harris, J.	1.00
Harris, Jacob Joseph	1.00
Joel ha-Kohen	1.00
Ossowski, S.	1.00
Samuel b. Isaac	0.25
Sheftel	0.75
Unger, Louis	0.25
Wile, Benjamin	10.00

NEW YORK

1849-50

Abrahams, Simeon	
Goldsmith, Henry, Sec'y B'nai Jeshurun	
Isaacs, Samuel Myer, Rev.	
Leo, Ansel, Reader of Elm St. Synagogue	
Lyons, Jacques Judah, Rev.	
Micholl, Morland	
Noah, Mordecai M.	
Noot, Simon C.	
Raphall, Morris Jacob, Rev.	

1850

Congregation B'nai Jeshurun:
Ainrich, Louis	1.00
Barnett, Michal	1.00
Barnstein, L.	1.00
Cohen, Sam	2.00
Davis, Jno.	0.50
Devries, Benjamin	1.00
Goldberg, H. L.	5.00
Goodman, Ali	3.00

Grodheim (Goodheim?),
Michal — 1.00
Isaacs, Lazarus — 1.50
Isaacson — 1.50
Joseph, M. — 0.50
Kaufman, W. — 0.25
Leo, Amsel, Rev. — 1.00
Levi, Mrs. — 0.50
Levi, Alexander — 0.25
Levi, Philip — 2.00
Lichtenstein, M. — 3.00
Marks, H. — 0.50
Meyers — 1.00
Raphael, Isidore — 5.00
Roats, David — 2.00
Salomons, Jonas — 1.00
Solomons, Israel — 1.00
Swart, E. M. — 1.00
Swart, M. A. — 0.50
Weinburgh — 1.00
Weinburgh, Jr., & Co. — 2.00
Goldberg Collection:
Goldberg, Judah Hirsch
Aaron b. Michael Moses
Abraham Abba b. David
   (a Bahur)
Abraham Elijah b. David Katz
Abraham b. Judah ha-Kohen
Abraham b. Naphtali
Abraham Raphael b. Ezekiel
Abraham Zevi b. Jacob
Alexander b. Judah
Aryeh b. Meir
Azriel b. Shemariah
Benjamin b. Naphtali
David b. Nathan
David b. Sishi
David b. Solomon
Eliezer b. Isaac Michael
Eliezer b. Nissan
Elijah (?) b. Jacob
Elijah b. Raphael ha-Kohen
Ezekiel b. Nahman
Gershon b. Solomon
Hayyim b. Abraham
Hillel b. Nahman ha-Kohen
Isaac b. Abraham Raphael
Isaac b. Baruch
Isaac b. David
Isaac Isaiah b. Judah
Isaac Michael b. David
Isaac b. Mordecai

Isaac b. Moses
Isaac b. Samuel
Israel b. David
Israel Meier b. Ephraim
Issachar b. Zeeb
Jacob b. David
Jacob b. Kalonymos
Jacob Moses b. Solomon
Judah b. Solomon
Meier b. Abraham
Meier b. Samuel
Meir b. Simḥah
Menaḥem b. Jacob
Menaḥem b. Samuel
Michael b. Zevi
Mordecai b. Joseph
Mordecai b. Zevi ha-Levi
Moses Abraham b. Israel
Moses b. Isaac ha-Levi
Moses b. Nathan
Moses Samuel b. Zevi
Moses b. Samuel
Moses b. Schraga
Moses Zeev b. Zevi
Nahum b. Zevi
Nathan Neta b. Baruch
Nathan Neta b. Moses
Oser b. Menahem Jacob
Peretz b. Gershon
Samuel b. Meir
Samuel b. Moses
Samuel Nissan b. Baruch
Saul b. Zevi
Schraga Feiwel b. Azriel
Selig b. David
Solomon Elimelech b.
   Abraham Katz
Solomon b. Isaac
Solomon Zalman b. David Katz
Zeeb b. Aaron
Zevi b. Abraham
Zevi b. Joseph ha-Kohen
Zevi b. Mordecai Katz
Zevi b. Moses
Other sponsors:
Cohen, Samuel
Falkenau, Jacob M.
Isaacs, S. J.
Khursheedt, Israel B.
Lazarus, Samuel
Moses, Henry
Schwarts, Abraham

Simson, Sampson
Weinschenk, Jacob
Other Contributors:
Blankenstein, Moses Samuel 3.98
Feiwel b. Azriel 0.75
Katz, Heschel b. Joseph 1.00
Makowe, Meir b. Abraham 2.00
Menahem b. Samuel 0.43
Prague, Moses 0.25
Salomon, Mrs. 0.18
Strauss 0.37½
Werkstein, Samuel 1.25

1861
Congregation Ansche Chesed
Congregation Beth
Hamedrash Adas
Jeshurun 20.00
Brody, H.
Congregation Beth
Hamedrash Hagodol 87.13
Boyer, John
Rosentopf, Pesach b.
Gedaliah, Rev. (also
erroneously Rosenthal)
Congregation Beth Israel
u-Bikur Cholim 62.25
Joseph, Ellis
Levy, Isaac 13.50
Congregation B'nai Jeshurun
Congregation Rodef
Sholem 150.00
Hyman, Solomon
Kohn, Hezekiah
Schutz, Meyer
Congregation Shaarey
Tefila 109.84
Congregation Shaarey
Zedek 25.00
North American Relief
Society for Indigent
Jews in Jerusalem
annually 700.00
Abrahams, Simeon
Dob Eliezer 4.50
Friedländer, David b.
Mordecai 0.50
Isaacs, Samuel Myer, Rev.
Leo, Sampson Simeon 5.00
Marks, H. 1.00
Raphall, Morris Jacob, Rev.

1867-69
American Board of Delegates
American Relief Committee
for Jerusalem:
Cowen, N.
Danneberg, M.
Isaacs, S. M., Rev.
Lasky, D.
Messing, A., Rev.
Raphall, M. J., Rev.
Rosenthal, J.
Congregation Beth Israel
u-Bikur Cholim 140.00
Cowen, N.
Messing, A., Rev.
Congregation B'nai
Jeshurun 500.00
Congregation Schary
Rachmim
Danneberg, M.
Congregation Shaaray
Tefilla 5.80
Solomons, B. L.
Isaacs, Samuel Myer, Rev.
North American Relief
Society
Abrahams, Simeon
Isaacs, S. M.
Levy, Louis
Osterman, Rosanna
Other Contributors:
Dreyfus, D. A. 1.00
Gottschall, Abraham, of
Antipoli 1.50
Hernstadt, R. H. 1.00
Mendelson, Joseph } 6.70
Pearlman, Eliezer, Rev. }

1876-79
American Board of Delegates
Joachimsen, Philip J., Judge
Congregation Beth
Hamedrash Hagodol 133.50
Raffel, A.
North American Relief Society:
Cohen, Samuel
Cohen, Sol L.
Isaacs, Meyer S.
Joseph, Israel
Kohn, Hezekiah
Louisohn, Leonard
Myers, Lawrence

Isaacs, S. M.
Marks, Harry H.
Schiff, Jacob H.
Trustees of Palestine Relief:
Barnett, Isaac
Kantrowitz, J. H.
Raphel, S.
Friedman, Perez b. Jacob   1.00
Harris, A.   2.00
Harris, J.   1.00
Nartofsky, David   1.50
Nussbaum, Isaac   1.00
Schwan, Esther   1.00
Wilkowisker, Solomon b.
 Hayyim   1.00
Zabludowski, Eliezer Isaac   1.00
Zeeb Wolf Menahem b.
 Jacob Senior   1.00

OSWEGO   1867-69
Congregation Berith
 Sholem
Abraham Jacob b. Moses   1.00
Kollmeyer, M.   1.00
Leopold, Henry   1.00
Meyer, Gershon   1.00
Weichselbaum, Abraham   1.00

ROCHESTER
    1850
Congregation Bnai Brith:
 Treumann, S.
 Tuska, Mordecai
    1861
Congregation Berith
 Kodesh   25.00
Ettenheimer, Elijah b.
 Solomon   3.00
Hays, Moses
    1867-69
Congregation Berith
 Kodesh   10.00
Adolph, W.   —
Bretenstool, H.   2.00
Caufman, Joseph   1.00
Ettenheimer, Jacob   5.00
Jacob b. Meir   1.50
Katz   1.00
Lempert   1.00
Meyer   0.50
Oberfielder   0.50

Rice, I.   1.00
Rosenberg, Henry   2.00
Rosenblatt, Samuel   2.00
Rosenthal, A.   1.00
Savage, M.   1.00
Stern, A.   2.00
Wile, G.   2.00
Wile, I.   3.00
Wolff, Elias   2.00
"Minyan" of Polish Jews: 2.00
Baruch b. Abraham Moses
David Solomon b. Ezra

    1876-79
Congregation Berith
 Kodesh   5.00
Congregation Beth Israel   3.00
Asher b. Zebulon (?)   1.00
Avner, Hayyim b. Israel
 Joseph   1.00
David b. Ephraim and 5
 children   1.00
Ettenheimer, J.   1.00
Ettenheimer, Solomon   3.00
Goldwater, N.   1.00
Greenstein, Meyer   2.00
Hellman, M.   1.00
Jacob b. Meir   1.00
Joshua b. Joseph ha-Levi   1.00
Levy, Barnet   2.00
Moses b. Nissan   1.00
Moses b. Yehiel David   1.00
Nussbaum, Aaron   2.50
Nussbaum, Meir   6.00
Perez b. Aryeh   1.00
Rosenberg, Henry   4.00
Rosenberg, Sender b. Zevi
 ha-Kohen   1.00
Rosenbloom, M. M.   1.00
Sampson b. Joseph ha-Levi   1.00
Simon, Jacob   1.50
Zevi Leser b. Meir

ROME
    1867-69
Grouse, J.   1.00
Repinski, M(?).
Tekulski, L.   2.00

    1876-79
Aaron, Samuel   1.00

Benjamin b. Süsse and
Zadok ha-Levi and his
wife Surel b. Freida and
Jacob Joseph together with
daughter Blume and son
Judah Ḥayyim 3.00
Cohen, Nathan 1.00
Goldstein, A. 3.00
Grouse, A. I. 1.00
Herz, Rachel 1.00
Isaac and Leah 1.00
Joseph 1.00
Katz (?), Aaron Ḥayyim ... 2.00
Kriensohn, Eliezer Mordecai
b. Nahum 1.00
Levy, A. 1.00
Loeb, Solomon 1.00
Mintz, Israel Moses,
wife Reva Ḥavah, } 2.00
son, Abraham,
daughter, Rachel
Name erased 1.00
Phillip, Hirsch Welwil 3.00
Steinfass, Schöne and
husband Elijah 1.00
Weinberg, Zipporah b.
Nissan 1.00

SCHENECTADY ... 1861

Congregation Shary
Shomaim 9.50
Levy, Pfeifer
Marks, David
"Minyan," local 5.00

SYRACUSE

1850
Anfenger 0.50
Angust, Gottfried 1.00
Benditson (?) Jacob (?) ... 1.00
Buchaus (?) Emanuel A. ... 2.00
Garson (?), Isaac 1.00
Garson (?), Leopold 1.00
Gershon b. Moses 1.00
Goldstein, Moses Aaron ... 1.00
Herschberg [Hirschberg],
Moses 1.00
Isaacs, Alfred A. 2.00
Külsheimer, D. 1.00
Lichtenberg, Benjamin 1.00
Mendes, George 2.00
Nathan, Perre J. 1.00

Rothschild, M. 2.00
Schloss, Joseph 1.00
Silberman, Joel Zevi 1.00

1861
Congregation of Syracuse ... 50.00
Aryeh b. Zevi 0.25
Bamberger, S. 0.50
Elsnes, Judah Leib 1.00
Gershon b. Moses 1.00
Goldschmidt, Mordecai b.
Judah 0.50
Herson, Israel b. Michael
Israel b. Dob
Jacob, Joseph 0.50
Pincus, Meir b. Moses
Rosenbaum, Abraham
Judah b. Mattathias
per annum ... 3.00
Shochet, Israel b. David
Solomon b. Yeḥiel
ha-Kohen 0.25
Weissman, Benjamin 0.50
Wendel, Moses b. Menaḥem

1867-69
Brillman, Isaac 0.50
Eisenbadt, Abraham Judah
b. Mattathias 3.00
Fried, Zevi Hirsch b. Aryeh
Leb 1.00
Goldman, Moses Joseph b.
Jacob 1.00
Hershon, Israel b. Michael ... —
Lesser, Aaron Eliezer b.
Simḥah 1.00
Rollstein, Menaḥem b.
Abraham 1.00
Eisenbadt and Hersohn
collected 10.00

TROY ... 1861

Congregation Ansche
Cheset 10.00
Cohen, T.
Laub, Levi

UTICA

1850
Eliezer b. Samuel Israel ... 1.00
Elsner, Judah Loeb, Rev. ... 1.00
Feldman, Joseph b. Hayyim
Fogel yearly ... 3.00

Hayyim b. Mordecai	1.00
Herschfeld, Aaron b.	
Abraham	2.00
Herschfeld, Zevi b.	
Abraham	1.00
Israel b. Samuel	1.00
Kaiser, Judah	1.00
Katz, Aryeh b. Lapidus	1.00
Katz, Zevi b. Aryeh	1.00
Kern, Aaron	2.00
Levitsky, Meir	1.00
Pincus, Abraham	2.00
Pincus, Raphael Mordecai	1.00
Schwarz, Judah	1.00
Schweig, Joseph b.	
Mordecai	2.00
Segal (?), Moses b. Isaac	
yearly	1.00

1861

Congregation Beth El	20.00
Dob Berush b. Solomon	1.00
Elijah b. Solomon Zalman	
Friedman, Meir	
Judah Leib b. Yehoash	1.50
Rosenthal, Charles	
Wakman, Isaac b. Dob	

1867-69

Goldsmith, S.	2.00
Joseph b. Menahem	2.00

North Carolina

WILMINGTON 1867-69

Baar, Saul, & Bro.	4.00
Bear, Meyer	1.00
Blumenthal & Levy	2.00
Cahen, A.	1.00
David, A.	1.00
Fischer, S.	1.00
Gottberg, N.	5.00
Greenberg, R.	1.00
Hart, Godfrey	1.00
Jacobs, Nathaniel	2.50
Liebman, Alexander	1.00
Lowenstein, A.	1.00
Marcus, H.	1.00
Neuman, Philip	1.00
Reichman, Felix	1.00
Rheinstein, F.	1.50
Rosenthal, G.	3.00
Rudman, A.	1.00

Samson, H.	2.00
Shatz (?), M. M., Co.	4.00
Solomon, J., & Bro.	3.00
Sternberger, Jos.	1.00
Wronski, A.	2.00

Ohio

CINCINNATI

1849-50

Banee (?), Samuel
Gutheim, James Koppel, Rev.
Harris, Abraham
Leitz, Henry Hart
Malzer, Nathan
Mayer, David
Solomon, Seixas
Ullmann, Daniel

1861

Hirschberg, Jacob ⎱	
Holzman, Joseph ⎰	15.95
Melzer	
Moses, Hyman	
Wise, Isaac M.	

1867-69

Heller, Asher	
Heller, Solomon W.	220.00
Isaacs, S.	
Lilienthal, Max, Rev.	
Moses, Hyman	
Wise, Isaac M., Rev.	

1876-79

Lilienthal, Max, Rev.
Moses, Hyman
Wise, Isaac M., Rev.
Union of American Hebrew
Congregations

CLEVELAND

1861

Elhana b. Feiwel	
Shalom b. Shraga	3.50

1867-69

Congregation Beth Israel	8.00
Frank, Isaac Joseph	2.00
Frank, Jacob	2.00
Goldschall, Abraham	1.00
Heiman, L.	1.00

Mann, S.	1.00
Specter, Abraham Joseph	3.25
Saul b. Meir	—
Hebra Kadisha	
Jacobs, M. [Schachna b. Feiwel]	

TOLEDO

1867-69

Shalom b. Zalman

	1876-79
Cohen, Philo	1.00
Livay, Chatzkel	1.00

YOUNGSTOWN   1867-69

Congregation Rodef Sholem	15.00
Guttman, E.	
Theobald, D.	

Pennsylvania

ERIE

1867-69

Becker, B., & L. Rosenzweig	1.00
Becker, Leon	0.50
Goldsmith & Marx	1.00
Loeb, Shuster, Strauss & Kussel Kahn	2.50

	1876
Gans, Moses	1.00
Simon, A.	1.00
Schuster, William	1.00

PHILADELPHIA

1849-50

Adler (?), S.
Hart, Abraham
Leeser, Isaac, Rev.
Lilienthal, Max, Rev. see also
   CINCINNATI, O.)
Rosenbaum, Joseph

1861

Leeser, Isaac Rev.

	1867-69
Board of Ministers:	50.00
Cohn, M.	
Fränkel, J.	
Jastrow, M.	
Leeser, Isaac	

Morais, S.
Papé, G.

PITTSBURGH   1861

Congregation Rodef Sholem	40.75
Arnthal, C. D.	
Frank, William (Alexander b. Eliezer)	

TITUSVILLE   1876-79

Karo, Yente b. Zevi	2.00

South Carolina

CHARLESTON

1849

Abrahams, Abr. [Alexander?]
Abrahams, A. H.
Benjamin, S. A.
Berlin, B. (R.?)
Cohen, David D.
Detterhan, I.
Davis, Henry
Ehrlich, M.
Engelberg, M.
Hart, Hyam N.
Hart, S., Jr.
Hart, S. M.
Jacobs, J. S.
Loryea, Isaac
Levy, Moses A.
Mahn, Reub.
Mairs, L.
Mairs, Levy
Moses, Isaiah
Nathans, M. H.
Nathan, Nathan
Rosenfeld, Jacob
Seckendorff, Isaac
Sommers, E.
Triest (?), Lat.
Triest (?), M.
Valentine, Samuel
Woolf, G.
Zachariah, J.

	1867-69
Congregation Beth Elohim	
Anonymous	1.00
Asher of Gainsville	2.00
Blank, Mrs.	1.00

Brown, L. (S.?)	1.00
Cash	1.00
Chumaciero, Joseph H. M., Rev.	3.00
Cohen, Louis	1.00
David, R. L.	1.00
Fass, I.	4.00
Flaum, J.	1.00
Iser	3.00
Israel, N.	1.00
Kaplan, T.	1.00
Levinson	6.00
Lewitt, E. J.	1.00
Mantone, J.	2.00
Pincuson (?)	2.00
Porelstein, T.	5.00
Preuer, George	1.00
Shapira (?)	1.50
Schatz, Isaac	1.00
Strauss, S.	1.00
Wyman, C.	1.00
Dan Lodge No. 93 I. O. B. B.	5.00
Kaplan, J.	
Spring, B.	
Other Contributors:	
Endel, Moses	2.00
Falk, A.	2.00
C. S. (?)	1.00

MARION   1867-69

Congregation Bnai Rahmanim	27.00
Barnett, M.	1.00
Brown, J.	5.00
Clarke, H.	1.00
Clarke, L.	1.00
Cronheim, H.	1.00
Goldsmidt, B.	1.00
Hartz, H.	1.00
Iseman, J.	4.00
Iseman, M.	4.00
Mitcover, A.	1.50
Mitcover, S.	1.50
Steel, Henry	5.00

Tennessee

MEMPHIS   1867-69

Hebrew Relief Society	10.00
Cash	1.00

Cohen, Julius	2.00
Feldman, F.	5.00
Hesse, Sol	—
Hesse, Levy & Co.	5.00

NASHVILLE

1867-69

Committee:	
Cohen, S.	
Heyerhardt (?), D. J.	
Schwartz, Mical	
Goldstein, B.	1.50

1876-79

Congregation Ohavai Shalom:	
Rosenspitz, Alex, Rev.	
Hebrew Ladies Benevolent Society	5.00
Marks, Mrs. Elias	4.00
From various others	22.10
Various others	14.00

SHELBYVILLE   1867-69

"All Laydis"	4.50
Cohn, G.	3.00
Frankel, H.	2.00
Glick & Loveman	0.25
Greenbaum, L.	2.00
Lyons, E.	0.50
Rosenheim, F.	0.50
Rothschild, S.	2.00
Strassmann, A.	2.50
Wolfson, H.	1.00

Texas

GALVESTON   1876-79

Congregation Bnai Israel	
Bernstein, J.	5.00
Bloom, H.	5.00
Cohn, M.	2.00
Feldman, M.	3.00
Haff, Fr.	2.00
Jacob Moses b. David	3.00
Jacobs, A.	3.00
Kempner, H.	3.00
Koppert, M.	5.00
Maker, Reuben Wolf	2.00
Rigaye (?), Joseph Leb	2.00
Rosenfeld, M.	3.00

MARSHALL   1876-79

Israelson, M.	1.00

266 | *Steeled by Adversity*

Utah

SALT LAKE CITY   1876-79

Auerbach & Bros.   2.00
Ladies Hebrew Benevolent
  Society: 10.00
Popper, Lotte

Virginia

ALEXANDRIA   1867-69

Calham (?), D.   2.00
Eichberg, Isaac   1.00
Ginzberger, L.   1.00
Grash, G.   1.00
Kaufman, Jos.   1.00
Kronheimer, S.   0.25
Waterman, Simon   1.00

NORFOLK   1867-69

Congregation Ohef
  Sholom   56.61
Frankfurt, M.
Hofheimer, L.

RICHMOND

                        1849

Ezekiel, Jacob

                        1865

Congregation Beth Ahabah
Congregation Beth Shalome
Goldsmit, E.
Schriver, I.
Winstock, S. A.
Congregation Keneseth Israel

1867-69

Congregation Beth
  Shalome:
Lazarus, Abraham,   } 17.30
  Ezekiel, Jacob
Keneseth Israel:
  Gundersheimer, J.

Nelson, N. W. and   21.00
  others
Milhiser, M.

1876-79
Abraham, Esther R.   1.00
Clark   0.50
Cohen, P.   Paid
Goldberg, G.   1.00
Goldstein, Mrs. S.   2.00
Herman, Mrs.   1.00
Levy, Ezekiel J.   5.00
Levy, Isaac   1.00
Scho . . . ler (?), B. 0.75

West Virginia

WHEELING   1867-69

Pollock, Augustus   5.00
*Other contributors possibly
  from Wheeling:*
Arch, Marcus A.   3.00
Cantoni, Salvatore, Colón,
  U.,C.S.   5.00
Cash   1.00
Millingan, Joseph   3.00
Moodis, J. M.   1.00
Rosenthal, C.   5.00
Steinfeld, Jacob   1.00

Wyoming Territory

CHEYENNE   1876-79

Gottstein, M.   2.00
Hafon, J. F.   1.00
Simons, Joe   1.00

III
Climax of Immigration

10 *United States 1880–1914*

In the relatively brief span of thirty-four years, 1880 to 1914, the face of the United States and even more of its Jewish community changed profoundly. The industrial revolution, which had received new impetus after the Civil War, had but briefly been interrupted by the panic of 1873. In the single year of 1883, the completion of such transcontinental railroads as the Northern Pacific, the Southern Pacific, and the Atchison, Topeka, and Santa Fe, as well as the Canadian Pacific, opened up the whole continent to a vast, increasingly rationalized agricultural production. The industrial changes were even more startling. In the decade from 1880 to 1890 the output of pig-iron doubled and surpassed that of Great Britain. In 1907 the United States produced more steel and pig-iron than Great Britain, France, and Germany combined. These new economic opportunities attracted millions of immigrants from the Old World. Although, as we shall presently see, beginning with 1882, growing legal restrictions started curtailing the free flow of new arrivals, these thirty-four years marked the peak of the influx of foreigners into the United States. American Jewry's ratio of growth was even more startling.[1]

Population

Unfortunately, our information about the number of Jews residing in the United States in any period, but especially since the

enormous increase at the turn of the twentieth century, is conjectural. The decennial censuses of population, taken by the
government, with ever increasing scope and reliability since 1790,
are of little assistance, since the enumerators were not allowed to
inquire about religious affiliation. Even the so-called censuses of
religious bodies, conducted under governmental auspices but
largely dependent upon varying denominational interpretations,
have yielded only partial data concerning the Jewish population.
The censuses of 1880, 1890, 1906, and 1916 are very informative
concerning the growth of Jewish communal groups, particularly
synagogues. But their figures so obviously represented but a
minority of the Jewish inhabitants that the Jews themselves, in
1926, persuaded the government to replace the old criteria by
an entirely novel approach. Even then much was left to arbitrary
"guestimates" of local leaders. In the ultimate sense, it was
left to the Jewish community itself to ascertain the size of its membership. The first effort in this direction was made in 1878 by
the Board of Delegates and the newly formed Union of American
Hebrew Congregations. Subsequently the methods were somewhat
refined. The application, especially, of the so-called "Yom Kippur
method" (which counted the absences from schools on the Day
of Atonement and contrasted them with the average absences during the rest of the school year and then multiplied the difference
by the ratio of the school population to the general population),
however crude and inadequate, offered at least a partial mathematical formula for the computation of any local Jewish population. Later were added other hypotheses derived from death
records, and even actual enumeration in selected localities. While
these improved methods may have served to refine the results
since the 1930s—even now they still leave much to be desired—
they can but slightly help us revise the figures reached in the
earlier computations.[2]

Nor are the comparative data between the Jewish and the general population quite reliable, since the decennial censuses of religious bodies between 1880 and 1916 did not always coincide with
the regular censuses. The religious census of 1880 has never been

abstracted nor published. Only in 1890, therefore, did the two censuses run closely together. The next religious censuses of 1906 and 1916 occurred in the middle of these decades between the general censuses. Hence the figures given for the general population in those years are based upon approximations, however close, of the U.S. Census Bureau. Subject to these reservations we may cite here the statistical data complied by Harry S. Linfield in the following table:

TABLE I

Number of Jews of United States, Principal Communities, and Congregations, 1877-1917.

Year	Total Population	Jews	Per-cent	Increase in ten years	Princi-pal Commu-nities	Congrega-tions
1877	43,661,968	250,000	0.52	—	174	277
1897	72,106,120	937,800	1.31	—	336	850
1907	88,787,058	1,776,885	2.00	89.47	426	1,769
1917	103,690,473	3,388,951	3.27	90.72	580	1,901

It may be noted that the figures given for the principal communities and congregations in 1897 are those of the census of 1900 and have to be somewhat reduced for 1897.[3]

As may be seen from these data, American Jewry in that period grew much faster than the general population, whose decennial increases were actually declining from 30.1 percent in the decade ending in 1880, to 24.9 percent in that of 1890, 20.7 of 1900, 21.0 of 1910, and 14.9 of 1920. In the Jewish case the population almost quadrupled in the twenty years from 1877 to 1897; it almost doubled in the following decade, and nearly doubled again between 1907 and 1917. This difference, of course, arising from the Jewish mass immigration rather than the natural growth, accounted for the tremendous increase in the ratio of the Jewish population from about 0.5 percent in 1877 to more than 3 percent forty years later.[4]

Because of the impact of immigration, there also was a difference in the geographic distribution of the Jewish population. It was natural for immigrants to remain, at least for a time, in the cities where they first landed. Since many newcomers received aid from previous settlers, particularly relatives or fellow-townsmen, it was also natural for them to stay in their sponsors' places of residence. As pointed out by Joseph Jacobs, the North Atlantic division, which included the large communities of New York, Philadelphia, Boston, and Baltimore, increased its percentage of the Jewish population from 50.64 in 1877 to 70.80 in 1905. At the same time all the other divisions sustained relative losses, all the while they were gaining in absolute numbers. Thus the North Central division, which included Chicago and St. Louis, saw its ratio reduced from 20.24 to 17.77. The South Atlantic division dropped from 9.23 to 4.13 percent; the South Central division from 10.41 to 3.98; and the Western division from 9.32 to 3.30. Despite all efforts of the Jewish community to attain a better distribution this trend continued also in the following decade, and was reversed only after the stoppage of mass immigration and the subsequent increase in the western migration in the last several decades.[5]

Of equal significance was the growing urbanization, in fact metropolitanization, of the American Jewish population. Outstanding in this respect was the growth of the New York community. Although the first organized Jewish community in North America, New York had witnessed but a slow growth to the beginning of the nineteenth century. As late as 1836, it is estimated, the city then numbering 270,000 population embraced only 2,000 Jews. But twenty years later its Jewish community reached 30,000. By 1877 its Jewish population (including that of Brooklyn) was estimated at 73,000, while in 1905 it reached 672,000, and five years later its Yiddish-speaking population alone was counted in the U.S. census as numbering 861,980. Less startling but quite considerable also was the growth of other Jewish communities, such as Chicago, a city which had grown rapidly since the 1840s. It is said to have reached 10,000 Jews in 1877, 80,000 in 1905, and 200,000 in 1912.[6]

Once again, Jews merely showed in more intensive form the

trends characteristic of the United States as a whole. Assuming, with the Census Bureau, that localities exceeding 2,500 inhabitants could be counted as urban, it has been found that America's urban population had increased from three-tenths in 1880 to four-tenths in 1900. It further increased to 46.3 percent in 1910 and 51.4 percent in 1920, then for the first time outnumbering the rural population. However, in the Jewish case, the majority of Jews living in the United States in 1916 resided in metropolitan areas of 1,000,000 population or more, while only a negligible minority lived in localities of less than 2,500 inhabitants. This tremendous process of urbanization, which incidentally affected also the majority of other immigrants most of whom like the Jews had come from small European communities, had far-reaching social and ideological effects in almost all phases of their life which, in part, still await further exploration.

We are even less well informed about various other population factors. No detailed figures, for example, can be given for the sex and age distribution in the Jewish community except insofar as it is reflected by the data concerning immigration which will presently be discussed. But because of the family type of immigration the balance between the two sexes doubtless was much better maintained among the Jews than among their non-Jewish neighbors.[7]

Of interest in this connection would also be the rate of intermarriage among Jews. In other countries of Jewish Emancipation intermarriage became a major biological factor; it sometimes contributed greatly to the deceleration of Jewish population growth, especially in the twentieth century. In the United States, too, this factor may have played a significant role in the earlier periods, when the Jewish population was very small and there was an insufficient selection of mates. In the period here under review, however, it seems to have been relatively rare. At least a study made in New York by the Federation of Churches showed that among 9,668 Jewish families only 78 had non-Jewish partners. The ratio was doubtless much higher in the Middle West and Far West where assimilatory trends were stronger and the Jewish communities much smaller. However, as in more recent decades, for which some data are available, intermarriage did not necessarily result in substantial population losses to the Jewish community. A considerable proportion of non-Jewish mates, particularly of non-Jewish wives of Jews, actually joined the Jewish community. At any rate, the apprehensions frequently voiced by Jewish leaders that intermarriage would lead to the speedy absorption of Jews by the Christian majority which inspired, for instance, Rabbi Bernard Felsenthal of Chicago to advocate that admission of proselytes be facilitated and that rabbis officiate at mixed weddings, did not wholly materialize.[8]

Other vital statistics of Jews leave equally much to be desired. Since most Jews had come from areas with little birth control, and since, like other immigrants, most of them belonged to the age brackets where the death rate was slight and reproduction high, Jews seem to have had a more than average natality and a rather low mortality. A study conducted in 1903 in New York showed that Protestant families averaged 1.85 children, Catholic families 2.03 children, while Jewish families counted on the average as many as 2.54 children each. Another partial investigation of a New York ward produced an even higher ratio of 2.9 children per Jewish family. Other partial studies have shown a remarkably low death rate. For instance, one conducted in Boston in 1895 showed that Russian Jews in the city had a mortality rate of only 6.09 per thousand. However, the next generation had a death rate of 15.95 which was much closer to the general national average of the period.[9]

Migrations

Between 1880 and 1914, the character of the Jewish population of the United States and its geographic concentration changed profoundly as a result of the unprecedented wave of Jewish immigration which exceeded that of any other recorded period in Diaspora history. This was the time when almost 30 percent of the entire Jewish people changed its residence from one continent to another, principally to the United States. Many migrants reaching England, France, or Canada had used these countries merely as way stations toward their final goal, the land of "unlimited possibilities." Needless to say, some of these temporary residents in other countries established there personal and family connections or found good economic opportunities and stayed on. But many succeeded in reaching their ultimate destination. On the other hand, there were some who could not get adjusted to American life and, for one reason or another, decided to return to their native country or to move elsewhere. Not a few were refused admission by the immigration authorities, or else were deported because they came into conflict with the existing laws. But, as we shall see, the number of Jewish reemigrants or, for that matter, of émigrés from among the older Jewish residents was extremely small; in fact, smaller than that of any other major ethnic group recorded in the official statistics.

Reasons for the Jewish mass emigration from Europe were manifold. But from the standpoint of the Jewish influx to the United States, we must principally bear in mind the following factors: (1) the fluctuations in the American economic conditions which at times favored or discouraged prospective Jewish immigrants; (2) the growing concentration of earlier Jewish arrivals who then attracted relatives and friends; (3) increasingly well organized Jewish charitable organizations which helped newcomers to earn a livelihood; (4) the growing ease, safety, and speed of transportation across the Atlantic Ocean with many steamship companies actually sending out agents to solicit travelers from the Old World; (5) the psychological impact of the migrations themselves which, talked about for many years, created a predisposition, especially among younger people, to imitate their predecessors; (6) the new political ideologies, particularly as represented by the Zionist, Socialist, and Am Olam movements, which made acceptance of the accustomed narrow and oppressive ways of living less palatable and stimulated the quest for a new life under freedom.

Understandably, some major events like the Russian pogroms on the one hand, or wars on the other hand, contributed their share to stimulating or retarding such a flow of migrants. Dramatic events of this kind stirred the imagination of contemporaries and often also misled scholars into considering them the most decisive factors. As a matter of record, however, these may be considered but highly significant episodes within certain basic lines of evolution which had been under way on independent grounds.

In our particular case Jewish migrations to the New World had been accelerating for many years before the Russian pogroms of 1881. Just as the Revolution of 1848 marked only a phase in the story of the German Jewish immigration which reached its peak in 1854 and after and, except for the interruption during the Civil War which entailed many hardships for both residents and new arrivals, continued in the late 1860s, so also did the Russian massacres of 1881, the May Laws of 1882 (extended to Russian Poland in 1891), and the pogroms of 1903 and 1905 furnish only additional stimulants to reinforce long existing trends.[10]

As a result of the unsuccessful Polish uprising of 1863, a famine in Lithuania in 1867-69, and a cholera epidemic in Poland in 1869, the economic pressures upon Russo-Polish Jewry to seek a livelihood elsewhere mounted from year to year. In 1869, a leading rabbi, Bernard Felsenthal of Chicago, had suggested that many Jews should be settled in the then young states of Kansas, Iowa, and Nebraska. The communal leader, Simon Wolf, added the Shenandoah Valley and Washington Territory which at that time was administered by a Jew, Edward S. Solomon, as good places to direct Jewish immigrants. These discussions merely underscored the historic fact that emigration from Russia to the United States increased from 673 in 1871 to 7,997 four years later. [11]

In fact, the number of new arrivals was increasing so rapidly and their problems of adjustment were becoming so serious that the leading Jewish organizations, including the Board of Delegates, opposed further indiscriminate admissions. The New York leaders considered the activities of the so-called Koenigsberg Committee, established by the Alliance Israélite in 1869, as not sufficiently selective and, in their appeal to Jewish congregations and charitable societies of April 27, 1870, they contended that "notwithstanding our urgent remonstrances against indiscriminate emigration from West Russia, hundreds of Israelites are here, despatched by the Koenigsberg Committee, and utterly penniless." As a matter of record the Committee had been quite cautious and had chosen only youthful and vigorous immigrants. For example, from July 1870 to July 1871, no less than 5,000 had registered in the Koenigsberg office, but only 300 were actually sent to America.[12]

We have no exact figures for the percentage of Jews among the emigrants from Russia and Austria-Hungary in the 1870s, but it has been estimated that among the Austrian arrivals 25 percent were Jewish, while the ratio among the Russians and Poles averaged 60 to 70 percent. The rapid increase of emigration from those areas between 1869 and 1880 may be seen in the following figures: in 1869, 343 Russians, 184 Poles, and 1,495 Austro-Hungarians entered the United States. In 1880 these numbers increased to 4,854 Russians, 2,177 Poles, and about 17,000 Austro-Hungarians. In all, the immigration from Austria-Hungary amounted to some 63,000 and from Russia and Poland together to some 52,000 in the decade from 1871 to 1880.[13] Assuming the above Jewish percentages, it appears that some 45,000 Jews hailing from these two Empires entered the United States during that decade. This was a sharp increase from the preceding half a century of 1821-70 when, it is estimated, only little more than 7,000 Jews originating from eastern Europe had settled in America, that is, considerably less than arrived in the single year of 1875 or 1880. This acceleration would naturally have continued after 1880 even if Russia had not witnessed those dramatic changes, which followed the assassination of Alexander II and the rise of Konstantin Pobedonostsev to power.

Of course, the immediate psychological impact of the pogroms and the growing agitation for Jews to depart from the Russian Empire were in part responsible for the sudden increase of Russian Jewish arrivals in America from 3,125 in 1881 to 10,489 in 1882, but their number dropped off to 6,144 in 1883, to increase rapidly from 1885 on. At the same time non-Jews were likewise leaving Russia for America in increasing numbers. As a matter of fact, while in absolute figures Jewish emigration from Russia to the United States increased speedily in the three decades from 1881 to 1910, the Jewish ratio in the total Russian emigration actually declined from 63.9 percent in 1881-90, to 44.1 percent in 1901-10.

TABLE II

Total Immigration from Russia and Jewish Immigration from Russia, 1881 to 1910, by Decade, and Jewish Percentage of Total

Decade	Total Immigrants	Jewish Immigrants	Percent of Total
1881-1890	213,282	135,003	63.3
1891-1900	505,280	279,811	55.4
1901-1910	1,597,306	704,245	44.1
TOTAL	2,315,868	1,119,059	48.3 [14]

Somewhat different were the trends of Jewish immigration from Austria-Hungary, as may be seen from the following data:

TABLE III

Total and Jewish Immigration from Austria-Hungary, 1881-1914

Decade	Total Immigrants	Jewish Immigrants	Percent of Total
1881-1890	353,719	44,619	12.6
1891-1900	592,707	83,720	14.1
1901-1910	2,145,266	158,811	7.4
TOTAL	3,091,692	281,150	9.1 [15]

Evidently, Austro-Hungarian Jewry, especially that from Galicia and Hungary, if measured by the relative population strength, was leaving its native habitat in even larger numbers than its Russian coreligionists. Economic pressures, even if not intensified by political persecution and dramatic assaults, sufficed to set in motion even more powerful migratory movements there. It must be borne in mind, moreover, that Galician and Slovakian Jews leaving for Vienna or Budapest were at the same time changing their accustomed habitat no less than those who went overseas.

In Russia, on the contrary, the Pale of Settlement effectively prevented such extensive inner migration and directed almost the entire flow outwardly into other countries, particularly the United States.

Among other countries of Jewish emigration to the United States we need but mention Rumania and, because of its major role as a country of transmigration, Great Britain. Persecution was a permanent concomitant of Rumanian Jewish life even before the country achieved total independence in 1878. In 1874 Leon (Aaron Yehudah Leb) Horowitz, after a journey to Rumania in the preceding year, published a Hebrew volume under the telling title *Rumaniah va-Ameriqah* (Rumania and America: A Book Containing My Travels in Rumania, the Goodness of the United States, and a Guide for Going to America). Nevertheless Rumanian Jewry was quite slow in taking the road to America. In the entire decade of 1881-90 only 6,967 Jews left Rumania for the United States (but 10.4 percent of the total Rumanian emigration). In the following decade their number nearly doubled to 12,789 and 19.1 percent, respectively, reaching full dimensions only in 1901-1910 when 47,301, or the huge percentage of 70.5, reached American shores. That exodus dropped off to a mere 7,896 in the years 1911 to 1914, a figure exceeded by the single year of 1903. Great Britain, which had been an important source of Jewish emigration to the United States through most of the nineteenth century—it ranked second to Germany in the period before the onset of the mass migration from eastern Europe—now became a major country of Jewish immigration and absorbed a multitude of East-European settlers. As late as 1899 to 1902, only a small number of Jews, ranging from 13 to 82, were recorded as having entered the United States from Britain. True, these figures are incomplete because they do not include first-class passengers. But the number of such better situated arrivals, though greater than from most other countries, could not have been very large. After the sharp curtailment of immigration to England in 1903, however, the number of Jewish émigrés from that country to the United States suddenly increased to 14,299 in the single year of 1905, and in the following nine years ranged from a minimum of 3,385 in 1909 to a maximum of 7,032 in 1907. In all, during the decade of 1905-1914 no less than 58,005 British Jews were recorded among the immigrants to the United States.[16]

Of course, there also were Jewish immigrants from other lands. For instance, the Sephardim, who had pioneered in building the colonial Jewish communities, received considerable reinforcement from new immigrants, especially from the Balkans and the Middle East. By 1914, there were many more Sephardic Jews in the United States than ever before.[17] These and other arrivals swelled the total number of Jewish immigrants, estimated at 193,021 in 1881-90, 393,516 in 1891-1900, 976,263 in 1901-1910, and 411,199 in 1911-14. In short, no less than 1,973,999 Jews entered the United States in the thirty-four years here under review.

As against these nearly 2,000,000 Jews who entered the country, but few left. Unfortunately, our data about such departures during the earlier periods are very incomplete. But figures for 1908-14 show that in this respect Jews were at the very bottom of all ethnic groups recorded in the official statistics. Only 53,150 Jews left the country, amounting to but 7.14 percent of the number of entrants during that period. The next lowest ethnic group, the Irish, had 9.36 percent, the ratio rising steeply to 44.71 percent among southern Italians, and 57.6 among the Hungarians. Even the Poles, who shared with the Jews the oppressive regime of the Tsars, showed a reemigration quota of 29.10 percent. Nor was that small Jewish percentage of 7.14 duplicated again in the subsequent years when it dropped to 1.55 in 1915-24. In fact, during the very depression years of 1931-35, when every one of the other ethnic groups showed a surplus of émigrés from the United States over new entrants, whose admissions had been severely curtailed, the Jews alone still had a rate of immigration several times larger than that of departures.[18] Obviously, Jews arriving in the United States came with the intention to stay, whereas many other immigrants sought to accumulate some savings and then return to their native lands.

Similar conclusions may be reached from the sex and age distribution of the Jewish immigrants compared with that of other ethnic groups. It has been estimated that between 1886 and 1898, 41.6 percent of all Jewish immigrants over 16 years of age were women. In some years the percentage was even higher. In 1893, it was supposed to have been 47 percent; in 1895, 49.3 percent; in 1894 even 51.3 percent. More reliably after 1899, when the classification of "Hebrews" made more exact data possible, the reports of the Commissioner-General of Immigration show that, in the fifteen years 1899-1914, females averaged 44.03 percent of all Jewish immigrants. Again in some years this percentage was higher, reaching 47.9 percent in 1906. Among the various ethnic groups only the Irish had in that period a higher percentage of females, namely 51.29 percent, undoubtedly because many Irish girls secured easy and remunerative household employment in the United States. After a few years many accumulated enough resources to return to their home country or else to marry some Irishman from among the offshoots of the earlier mass immigration which had started in the 1840s. More directly relevant are the comparative data with the Jews' European neighbors. Between 1899 and 1914 Polish, Russian, and Rumanian women constituted 32.97, 13.95, and 13.09 percent of their respective ethnic groups.[19]

Even more pronounced was the ethnic disparity in the immigration of children. According to the Commissioner-General's data, the average number of children below fourteen in the years 1899-1910 was 24.9 percent of all Jewish immigrants. In some years this average was exceeded, reaching 26.5 percent in 1902 and 1909, and 28.4 percent in 1906. The other ethnic groups in 1899-1909 averaged only 12.3 percent of children. Among Poles the ratio fell to 9.5 percent; among Russians to 7.5 percent; Magyars, 8.8 percent; Rumanians, 2.2 percent, and so forth.[20] All of this meant, of course, that Jewish immigration was largely a family migration; Jews arrived with their wives and children and with the intention to stay. This does not necessarily mean that the entire families traveled together. Frequently, young men arrived first and, after establishing themselves in the new country, sent for their wives and children or their fiancées. This may help explain why in certain years the number of women equaled or even exceeded that of men. But on the whole, most family groups were reunited sooner or later.

Changing Attitudes

Until 1882 the attitude of the American government as well as the American public was quite friendly to immigration. Typical of these early views are various statements by James Madison; for instance, in his letter to Dr. Jacob de la Motta acknowledging the receipt of a copy of De la Motta's discourse delivered at the anniversary of the Savannah synagogue (July 21, 1820). This sympathetic attitude also continued in the following decades when the number of Jews had grown considerably. For example, in an editorial entitled "Hebrew Immigration," the *New York Herald,* of September 27, 1869, referred to a new immigration society established by San Francisco Jewry to encourage the entry of European Jews to the United States. "This, we think," the newspaper declared, "is good. The Israelites prosper in this great and free country. In no country in the world, since they lost their own land, have they found so much of a home as they have found here. . . . Let our rich Israelites bring their oppressed brethren to this new land of promise."[21]

Needless to say, sympathies for immigrants were even stronger among Jews and the other ethnic minorities. Nevertheless, the ancient Jewish traditions of communal responsibility for the plight of coreligionists were subjected to severe tests upon the arrival of a multitude of distressed and unskilled immigrants. The existing organizations and their moderate budgets were speedily overtaxed by the new needs. In Boston, for example, where according to a correspondent to the *Asmonean* of 1849, there had been not a single Jew on relief, the sudden arrival, in June, 1882, of 415 Russian refugees sent there by the Mansion House Fund of London so startled the leaders of the newly organized local Hebrew Emigrant Aid Society that they "promptly refused to accept them, and shipped them to New York as soon as they arrived." But the community early realized that effective relief was needed, if for no other reason than to spare its wealthy members the annoyance of a multitude of individual beggars. The presence of a host of destitute Jews on the streets, the occasional intervention of non-Jewish charities, some of which were ready to advance funds particularly for the return of the Jews to Russia, likewise served as stimulants to ever more effective Jewish relief activities. From 1895 on, moreover, the earlier arrivals from eastern Europe, who had interveningly established themselves in their new habitat, took an ever more active part in helping more recent immigrants. Apart from their individual efforts in behalf of relatives and friends, they placed much of their manpower and financial resources at the disposal of communal agencies. In their growing press, literature, and theater they also found effective media to stir up the conscience of the entire community whose organs, moreover, had learned, through an arduous process of trial and error, more effectively to cope with the recurrent emergencies. Ultimately, the entire community made valiant efforts to get coreligionists admitted to the United States. It had an effective lobbyist in Simon Wolf. "If we ever miss him," declared Charles Nagel, Secretary of Commerce and Labor in 1911, "we think the world is going to stop. I frequently inquire about eleven o'clock, 'Has Wolf been here?' "[22]

In the 1880s the generally friendly attitude of the American public began changing to one of widespread hostility. This antagonism was not aimed at Jews as such but rather at the new type of immigration in general. Until the 1880s the bulk of immigrants had been recruited from the British Isles, Germany, and the Scandinavian countries. These immigrants, except for the Irish, were considered akin to the predominantly Anglo-Saxon and Protestant population of the country. In the 1880s, on the other hand, the immigration from Austria-Hungary, Italy, and Russia, in that order, increased from year to year. It has been estimated that these three countries supplied but one percent of the total immigration in 1869, but that that ratio increased to 10 percent in 1882, and reached the huge proportion of 87 percent in 1907. Stimulated by the opposition, particularly of Americans living on the West Coast, to the growing Chinese and Japanese immigration, the United States public began increasingly thinking in terms of restricting immigration in such a way as to maintain the traditional Anglo-Saxon supremacy. Economic considerations likewise reinforced these anti-immigration trends. The vast open frontier in the western United States was apparently being filled by native Americans, while the incipient labor movement began viewing newcomers as competitors likely to depress wages. Even the Jewish labor leader, Samuel Gompers, himself an immigrant from London, came to believe in the 1890s that immigrants, by creating a constant surplus of labor, were undermining the wage structure of American workingmen and hampering their struggle for economic betterment. These apprehensions were deepened by the effects of the depression of the 1890s.[23]

Not surprisingly, some American scholars and publicists began to be affected also by the new racialist theories which were gaining ground in Europe from the days of Count Joseph Arthur Gobineau. Houston Stewart Chamberlain, especially, was widely read in America, too. While his impact on American antisemitism was still rather slight, he nevertheless contributed much to the "Nordic" superiority feeling of many Americans and their rejection of the Mediterranean and East-European immigrants. Madison Grant, an anthropologist for the American Museum of Natural History, Lothrop Stoddard, and others wrote influential books stressing the undesirability of the new type of immigration. Grant argued before the President's Commission on Immigration and Naturalization that "new immigrants were . . . the weak, the broken, and the mentally crippled of all races drawn from the lowest stratum of the Mediterranean basin and the Balkans, together with hordes of the wretched submerged population of the Polish Ghettoes." As early as 1903, Gustave Michaud contended that, as a result of the new immigration, the average American's stature had become shorter, his skull abbreviated, and his complexion darker. Michaud warned that mental changes for the worse would speedily follow. "The most conclusive of these, perhaps, will be a decline of that enterprising spirit which has been called the American push." Even without such racialist preconceptions, many observers noted a decline in the morality of Jewish immigrants occasioned by the hardships of adjustment to a new environment, widespread unemployment, living in crowded and unsanitary tenements, and the absence of the effective social restraints of the traditional community. As early as 1894, the social reformer, Jacob A. Riis, wrote with abandon:

> *If it is true of the Jew who through eighteen centuries of oppression and tyranny preserved in him the patriarchal home idea . . . that in a single generation in New York's tenements—always the filthiest and darkest and most crowded to be found anywhere— he breaks down; that his daughters become immoral and his sons thieves to an alarming degree—then what share in it had this tenement that does ever and everywhere violence to the home ideal?*

As a confirmed opponent of slum life, Riis may have exaggerated the extent of Jewish criminality, as did later New York's Police Commissioner, Theodore A. Bingham, who, in an article published in September 1908, claimed that "alien" Jews, amounting to only 25 percent of the city's population, furnished 50 percent of all criminals—a claim which he later withdrew as unfounded. But the nexus between mass immigration and the spreading city slums, with all their adverse social consequences, appeared undeniable.[24]

Even the standard argument of the protagonists of free immigration that the masses of new arrivals increased the population of the United States, and thus contributed to its economic prosperity and political power, was controverted by General Francis A. Walker, who served as chief of the United States Census Bureau and was considered America's leading statistician. By a curious tour de force Walker figured out that the birth rate had declined in America all through the nineteenth century. In the census area of 1790, roughly covering the original thirteen states, there had been 1,900 white children under 16 for every 1,000 white females over 16. By 1850, that ratio declined to 1,400 and by 1900 it fell further to 1,000. Walker claimed that it was the influx of immigrants, themselves still procreating rapidly, which had caused that constant decrease in the birth rate of the original native population. Further pointing out that between 1790 and 1830 the American population had increased from 4,000,000 to 13,000,000, or by 227 percent, he contended that in the following thirty years "in spite of the incoming of 2,500,000 foreigners . . . our population differed by less than 10,000 from the population which would have existed without reinforcement from abroad." Hence "if the foreigners had not come, the native element would long have filled the places the foreigners usurped."[25] The obvious conclusion was that the closing of the gates to further mass immigration would result only in few population losses, while it would assure the supremacy of the white, Protestant, Anglo-Saxon group.

The anti-immigration forces, led by the so-called Immigration Restriction League, understandably aroused much public discussion. Since some of these opponents also used a variety of anti-semitic arguments—we shall see that anti-Jewish feeling was intensified in the three decades before the First World War—the Jews closed their ranks. No longer did one hear Jewish leaders preaching restraint and a strictly selective immigration. In fact, unlike their predecessors before 1881, the immigrants from Russia and Rumania now appeared to the American Jewish public as victims of religious persecution who had a special claim upon the sympathy and support of their American coreligionists. The psychological transformation in Emma Lazarus is quite typical. The poetess who, but a short time before, had declared, "I am proud of my blood and lineage, but Hebrew ideals do not appeal to me," was stirred to her depths by the sight of the new arrivals and the news of the Russian atrocities. She was soon inspired to write her famous sonnet, *The New Colossus*, which was inscribed on the

pedestal of the newly erected Statue of Liberty. Untold multitudes
of immigrants and travelers in the New York harbor have since
been greeted by her stirring lines,

> Give me your tired, your poor,
> Your huddled masses yearning to breathe free,
> The wretched refuse of your teeming shore,
> Send these, the homeless, tempest-tost to me.

We shall, indeed, see that much of the communal effort was now
concentrated on aiding immigrants to come to the United States
and to get adjusted to the new life. Family groups and *Landsmannschaften* were even more deeply interested in helping their relatives
and fellow-townsmen to come to America. According to reports
at Hearings before the Industrial Commission on July 24, 1899,
some 40-55 percent of all immigrants arrived on prepaid tickets.
In addition 10-25 percent, who had paid for their own tickets, had
used funds sent them from America. In all, according to Edward
F. McSweeney, Assistant Commissioner of Immigration at the
Port of New York, 65 percent of the new arrivals had thus been
assisted. These statistics, applying to all immigrants, would probably have shown a still higher Jewish ratio. In short, American
Jewish opinion was practically united against any immigration
restrictions.[26]

Naturally the government could not remain unaffected. Congress instituted hearings where the opposing parties presented their
views. Note had to be taken also of a similar agitation in England
which, after several years of parliamentary debates, had resulted
in the restrictive Aliens Act of 1905. These opposing views led,
for instance, Senator Chandler to declare that Russian Jews were
not "desirable immigrants" and to suggest, in 1892, a one-year
suspension of immigration on account of the outbreak of another
cholera epidemic in eastern Europe. Simon Wolf answered him in
the influential *Washington Post*. These debates even colored some
of the diplomatic memoranda submitted by the American State
Department *in behalf* of the Jews persecuted in Russia and Rumania (for instance, John Hay's well-known dispatch of July 17,

1902, cited below). However, there were as yet few tangible legislative results before 1914. True, the first acts of 1875 and 1882 excluded paupers, criminals, and diseased persons, while the Chinese Exclusion Act of 1882 reduced the oriental immigration to a minimum. But only the elaboration, in 1891, of the term "paupers" and the interpretation thereof by Charles Foster, Secretary of the Treasury, as excluding "assisted immigrants," that is, those helped by organizations to come to America, opened threatening vistas. Yet the Administration could not controvert the fact, pointed out to it by four Jewish organizations, that the numerous Russian Jews who had arrived in the preceding decade "have been assimilated in the mass of citizenry and, so far as can be ascertained, not a single one has become a public burden."[27]

Less threatening was the 1891 expansion of the category of "criminals" who were to be refused admission, a category which excluded those convicted in their home countries for political offenses; the addition, in 1903, of anarchists and persons advocating the overthrow by violence of the government of the United States or of all governments; and the introduction in 1903 and 1907 of the new category of persons having committed a crime or misdemeanor involving moral turpitude and of those whose ticket had been paid for by any private organization or government. The exclusion of anarchists, stimulated by the assassination of President McKinley, could have been used to bar a number of Russian Jewish radicals. But these provisions were not seriously enforced until after the First World War. Nor was the regulation aimed at financing immigration by foreign governments or private associations, which tried to stem the practice of the preceding century to dump many undesirables on American shores, in any way to interfere with Jewish immigrants who arrived with tickets prepaid by relatives, friends, or fellow townsmen of the same *Landsmann-schaft*. Probably more important was the gradual extension of the limits for the deportation of aliens unlawfully admitted from one to two and, later, to three years; "persons who are supported by or receive in whole or in part the proceeds of prostitution" could be deported without any time limit. This extension doubtless enabled the government to get rid of a larger number of Jewish immigrants than might otherwise have been the case. But none of these restrictions could, or was intended to, stop the main flow of legitimate Jewish immigration. In short, not until the enactment of the literacy test in 1917, and the even more stringent Immigrations Acts of 1921 and 1924, were there any serious legal barriers placed in the way of most Jewish entrants whose number was restricted mainly by economic and other social factors.[28]

Agricultural Colonization

Mass immigration of this scope required profound economic adjustments. It was realized quite early that such masses could not be accommodated in the traditional Jewish occupations, particularly in petty commerce. Moreover, for more than a century ideological factors tended to induce Jews to leave these "unproductive" occupations for agricultural and industrial pursuits. Ever since the middle of the eighteenth century Jewish societies had tried to stimulate such transformation toward productivity, while autocratic governments, including that of Tsar Nicholas I of Russia, used less gentle means in placing Jews on the soil. Yet, despite progress in some areas, the economic stratification of the Jewish people, particularly in its largest concentration in eastern Europe, remained quite "abnormal," when compared with that of its neighbors. In the 1870s and 1880s these trends reached a climax in the early Zionist and Am Olam movements and, by 1891, generated, through the Jewish Colonization Association founded by Baron Maurice de Hirsch, the first large-scale endeavor not only to transplant Jews from eastern Europe to the New World, but also to reshape them into productive tillers of the soil, craftsmen, and industrial workers.[29]

Among the new countries, the United States seemed to hold out special promise for Jewish agricultural colonization. The western frontier had opened up and was attracting more and more pioneers from the Eastern Seaboard. For one example, Kansas, which had a total population of about 330,000 in 1870, grew to nearly 1,000,000 in 1880, and almost 1,500,000 in 1890. The territories further west were just being developed. Jews could participate, it was argued, in that western migration and utilize the good will of both the government and people of the United States to rebuild their lives in the vast open spaces of the Middle and Far West. General American Jewish policy, too, aimed at the dispersal of immigrant masses all over the country, rather than their concentration in the few major eastern cities. Only few leaders fully realized the tremendous difficulties involved for large numbers of untrained immigrants to settle on the soil, and to work in a strange environment with the climate, language, and mores of which they were unfamiliar. These difficulties appeared minimized by the effort to establish regular Jewish colonies where the inhabitants could more freely pursue their accustomed ways of life, while acquiring new skills. Hardly anyone mentioned, however, the fact that this Jewish "return to the soil" ran counter not only to the world-wide progress of industrialization, but also to the prevailing trends in the United States, despite its rise in that period to the position of the world's leading agricultural producer. The constant relative shrinkage of the agricultural versus industrial work force—in the single decade of 1900-1910 the percentage of male workers in agricultural pursuits had dropped from 39.6 percent of all gainfully employed males to 35.8 percent—should have served as a warning. Jewish leaders might also have remembered the failure of an earlier agricultural experiment at the beginning of the mass immigration of German Jews. In 1837, an association *Zeire Hazon* (Tender Sheep) of New York had circulated an appeal for colonizing new arrivals "in some part of the Western Section of this country." A group of thirteen Jews, led by one Moses Cohen, had actually left New York City and established a Jewish colony in Wawarsing, Ulster County, New York, under the name of Sholom (Peace). The usual difficulties, however, intensified by the great economic crisis after 1837, had defeated all these good intentions and, after approximately five years, the colony had folded up.[30]

Probably the leaders of the Am Olam movement in Russia knew

nothing about this failure. In October 1881, thirty-five Jewish families from Kiev and twenty-five from Elizavetgrad arrived in New York with the intention of settling on land. Led by the poet and publicist Herman Rosenthal (1843-1917), who later headed the Slavonic Department of the New York Public Library, and financially aided by a New York Committee representing the Alliance Israélite Universelle of Paris, this group established a Jewish agricultural colony on Sicily Island, in the eastern part of Louisiana. Having acquired some 5,000 acres, the 173 colonists divided themselves into three groups and began clearing the land, erecting buildings, and preparing for their new career. Unfortunately, already in the spring of 1882, that entire region suffered from one of the recurrent floods of the Mississippi River which washed away buildings, implements, and cattle and practically eliminated the entire investment of some $20,000, as well as the labor put in by the colonists. Undaunted, Rosenthal headed up a new group of twenty Russian families and established a colony in what later became South Dakota. This colony, named Cremieux in honor of the leader of the Alliance, had ample land at its disposal. Each colonist was assigned between 160 and 640 acres. The location was badly chosen, however, insofar as the nearest railroad station was fourteen miles away and the water supply was unstable. This time the colonists, some of whom had participated in the Louisiana experiment, suffered from the opposite misfortune, a prolonged drought. Combined with a wheat bug which they did not know how to combat, the drought eliminated any possibility of their making a living and, after three years, even the hardiest settlers gave up. Similar failures closed down the colonies of Bethlehem-Yehudah, established in the vicinity of Cremieux; New Odessa in Oregon founded by a socialist group from Russia; and Painted Woods near Bismarck, North Dakota. All of these colonies were founded in 1882, but went out of existence within two to five years despite the assistance of neighboring Jewish communities, such as that of St. Paul, Minnesota.[31]

More promising were the efforts undertaken by Michael Heilprin (1823-88) and his associates, first through the Hebrew Emigrant Aid Society, organized in 1881 but disbanded two years later, and subsequently through the Montefiore Agricultural Aid Society established in 1884. Heilprin, theretofore a retired scholar and littérateur with little involvement in Jewish communal work, now became a most arduous worker in behalf of the East-European immigrants. A native of Piotrków, Poland, he had participated in the Hungarian Revolution of 1848 and later had made a name for himself in New York as an editorial writer for the *Evening Post* and the *Nation*. Now he devoted the last years of his life to help the new arrivals. Among the earliest schemes of the Hebrew Emigrant Aid Society was the establishment, in May 1882, of a Jewish agricultural colony in Cotopaxi, Colorado. Although the fifteen families were each allotted 160 acres from government land, only 100 acres in all were found fit for cultivation. In the spring they were endangered by floods, the rest of the year by the shortage of water. They soon had to give up. The same story, more or less, might be told about the various efforts to establish Jewish colonies in Kansas, such as Beersheba, founded in 1882 with the aid of the Jewish community of Cincinnati; Sir Moses Montefiore, founded in 1884; and Hebron, one of the first to be aided by the Montefiore Agricultural Aid Society. Even the colonies established closer to the Eastern Seaboard in Michigan, Virginia, or Connecticut, failed to prosper.[32]

More enduring were the colonies established in New Jersey particularly in the southern part of the state. The earliest of these, named Alliance, was established in May 1882 by twenty-five families aided by the Alliance. It was soon followed by the colonies of Rosenhayn and Carmel, for which Heilprin was particularly responsible. After Heilprin's death in 1888, Carmel suffered but managed to continue. So did the newly established settlement of Garton Road. According to a statistical account of 1901, Alliance (together with the neighboring Jewish colony of Norma) had a population of 151 adults and 345 children. The figures for Rosenhayn were 64 and 158; Carmel, 55 and 133; Garton Road, 27 and 94. Between them these four (or five) colonies owned 4,259 acres, of which about two-thirds had been cleared by that time.

Together with the buildings, equipment and cattle, these farms were valued at the respectable total of $262,250.[33]

Perseverance of these colonies was in part owing to a new factor: the entry of the Baron de Hirsch Fund into the program of Jewish colonization in America. True, Maurice de Hirsch had at first had serious reservations. Although he had retired relatively early from his very successful banking business and devoted himself to philanthropy—he always spoke of the duty arising from great wealth and once declared, "It is my innermost conviction that I must consider myself as only the temporary administrator of the wealth I have amassed"—he feared that "to increase to any great extent the already enormous number of Jews in the United States would be of advantage neither to the country itself nor to the exiled Jews." For this reason he wished to concentrate on the large-scale transfer of Jews to Argentina, Canada, Australia, and other then underdeveloped countries with small Jewish populations. Nevertheless, when approached by Oscar S. Straus who had received an eloquent plea from Heilprin, he consented to collaborate with a United States committee on projects for permanent reconstruction. Overwhelmed as they were by the immediate needs of immigrants, the American leaders stressed the relief tasks. But De Hirsch, supported by the Alliance and its brilliant secretary, Isidore Loeb, insisted on the primacy of the permanent rebuilding of the shattered fortunes of the immigrants. A compromise was finally reached, by virtue of which up to 40 percent of the funds could be used for short-term purposes. De Hirsch himself never wavered in his long-term program. He publicly declared in 1891,

What I desire to accomplish, what, after many failures, has come to be the object of my life, and that for which I am ready to stake my wealth and my intellectual powers, is to give to a portion of my companions in faith the possibility of finding a new existence, primarily as farmers, and also as handicraftsmen, in those lands where the laws and religious tolerance permit them to carry on the struggle for existence as noble and responsible subjects of a humane government.[34]

Having learned from the disastrous experiences of the 1880s, the Baron de Hirsch Fund now decided to embark upon a new method of settling Jews on land. Since farming alone was not likely to produce sufficient revenues to maintain a substantial number of families, the Trustees of the Fund conceived the idea of combining farming with industrial endeavors and of founding a township where the farmers' wives and children could secure gainful employment while the men worked on the soil. The availability of a larger number of consumers on the spot and of better marketing facilities for their produce might also obviate some of the difficulties encountered by the other pioneers. In 1891, the Fund acquired 5,300 acres with good railroad facilities in Woodbine, New Jersey, and attracted a clothing manufacturing firm, and other industries. In 1895 it established there the Baron de Hirsch Agricultural School which was to train young Jewish farmers for Woodbine and other settlements. Led by an enthusiastic, yet realistic, principal, Professor Hirsch Leib Sabsovich (1860-1915), the school and the community at large, made considerable progress despite numerous difficulties with its often idealistic and individualistic and, hence, at times quite unruly members. Even the school had to weather several strikes. Moreover, while its main objective was to train Jewish farmers, it found that in actual operation the pupils, the majority of whom did not even finish their course of studies, turned to other occupations. Boris D. Bogen, a former principal of that school, later reminisced, "After working a due period as laborers in the fields, our graduates began to look beyond the horizon, and reached for the less laborious stations of the agricultural industry. They went to agricultural laboratories, they entered higher institutions of agricultural learning, they sought positions in the Department of Agriculture at Washington; some deserted agriculture altogether." Among the distinguished graduates was Jacob G. Lipman (1874-1939), a leading soil chemist and bacteriologist, who later served as Dean of the New Jersey State College of Agriculture. With all these difficulties, the community continued to grow and, by 1901, had a population of 2,500, only 400 of whom were considered farmers. The 52 farming families owned 785 acres (500 under cultivation) valued at $50,000. In time the community also attracted non-Jews. By 1919, the total population consisted of 280 Jewish and 70 non-Jewish families. As elsewhere the First World War, by enormously raising the prices of agricultural products, reinforced also Jewish farming in Woodbine and other localities, although the Agricultural School had to be closed in 1916.[35]

Nevertheless the efforts of the agricultural school were not in vain. A survey, conducted in 1914, showed that of the 762 students who had attended the school for six months or more, 285 or 37 percent were still engaged in agricultural pursuits, though not necessarily in Jewish colonies. It thus gave stimulus to individual Jewish farming, which soon displaced colonization as the major objective of the Jewish communal efforts as well. Another Jewish agricultural school, the National Farm School in Doylestown, Pennsylvania, propagated especially by Rabbi Joseph Krauskopf of Philadelphia, likewise trained young Jewish farmers. Opened in 1897, it reached its maximum dormitory capacity of forty-five pupils within seven years. These schools, as well as the training obtained by individual colonists, laid the foundation for the entry of numerous Jews into individual farming, mostly in the vicinity of larger cities. Jewish farmers often concentrated on dairy and truck farming, finding markets in neighboring metropolitan areas such as New York or Philadelphia. Frequently they supplemented their incomes by accommodating summer guests, or by part-time industrial work. Many received initial aid and guidance from the new Jewish Agricultural and Industrial Aid Society, founded in 1900 as an offshoot of the Baron de Hirsch Fund. Learning from previous mistakes, the Society established a model farm and assisted would-be farmers with loans, technical advice, and other businesslike methods. As a result, Jewish participation in American farming, grew both numerically and qualitatively. The enthusiastic comment in the Society's *Report* for 1900-1924 had some validity for the period before 1914 as well:

There is no branch of farming in which Jews have not achieved signal success. . . . They are among the largest producers [of tobacco in the Connecticut River Valley] and they raise a product of the highest quality. . . . In the Geneva [Ohio] grape district Jewish farmers, although in the minority, raise more than half of the crop. A Jew is known as the "Grape King.". . . Jewish farmers are in the front rank of the truck growers in the vegetable sections of South Jersey and Long Island. . . . [A Jew] has developed the "Spiegel" type of Gladiola, regarded by judges as one of the finest varieties. . . . The largest New Jersey potato farm is worked by a Jew. . . . A 30,000 acre wheat farm in Kansas, a truly gigantic enterprise, is in the hands of a Jew. . . . This man's service to the agriculture of the region was fittingly recognized in a celebration in his honor in which high state officials participated. . . . The day of celebration was declared a legal holiday.

One such East-European businessman-farmer of California, David Lubin (1849-1919), achieved international recognition, when under his incessant prompting, delegates from forty nations organized, in 1905, an International Institute of Agriculture, of which he served as director to the end of his days. Thus after much trial and error, Jews established themselves in American agriculture perhaps to the extent of two percent of their total population. Other Jews contributed more indirectly, as when Nelson Morris, an immigrant from Bavaria, helped to develop the great meat-packing industry in Chicago after the Civil War.[36]

Industry and Labor

Numerically far more significant and psychologically equally revolutionary was the Jews' entry into American labor at the turn of the century. The d sparity between the two groups could be seen already at the ports of debarkation. According to the official statistics for 1899-1910, to be sure, no less than 45.1 percent of all Jewish immigrants were listed as persons without occupation. But this figure, by far the largest among the eighteen major ethnic groups in the report and considerably exceeding the average of 26.2 percent, is fully understandable because of the greater ratio of women and children in the Jewish immigration. Moreover, in the old countries of eastern Europe many Jews made a living from a variety of uncertain occupations and, arriving in Castle Garden or Ellis Island, they could not conscientiously list a particular classification. On the other hand, those who did indicate their previous occupation claimed to have been "skilled laborers" to the extent of 67.1 percent, other laborers, 11.8 percent, and servants, 11.1 percent. Such a vast disproportion of skilled laborers, more than a third of them "tailors," hardly reflected actual realities. It stands to reason that many expressed wishes for the future, rather than past experience. Characteristically, only a small percentage of 1.9 claimed to have been farm laborers, and 0.2 farmers.[37]

Upon arrival in the United States most of these immigrants, if they did not become peddlers and petty traders, entered the labor market. Needless to say, even those who brought some useful skills with them required retraining for American methods of production. The majority had to begin from scratch.[38] Most immigrants were attracted particularly to the needle trades. This was the era of great expansion of the entire American clothing industry. By using increasingly efficient mass production methods and thereby constantly lowering the prices of individual garments, it succeeded in creating a genuine mass market. But largely operated by small manufacturers, the industry was often plagued by "cut-throat" competition, unexpected shifts in supply and demand, and frequent bankruptcies. The division of labor had likewise progressed very far, with manufacturers often employing directly only skilled cutters, while delegating the management of the so-called sweat-shops to contractors. Unskilled work, often subdivided and reduced to very simple repetitive motions, was usually conducted in old and unsanitary tenements. Exploitation of these lowly workers, particularly women, often defied description, yet they had to hire themselves out for almost any wages, since the constant influx of new immigrants created an almost inexhaustible "industrial reserve army." These conditions often inspired poets, writers, and publicists to vehement accusations which enlisted much sympathy for the workers not only in the Jewish public but also in the growing group of Christian "settlement workers" led by Jane Addams and other socially minded members of the middle classes.

Clearly, there were also exaggerations on the part of both the working masses, who contrasted their daily experiences with the glittering expectations they had nurtured before they had left their home countries as a result of letters received from earlier arrivals, and the writers and publicists, many of whom had come to the United States as confirmed socialists and anarchists. The critical literary descriptions found, moreover, a responsive echo in the American public which had at that time developed a growing appetite for the "muckraking" type of literature. Only rarely were voices heard which counseled moderation and a better sense of perspective. For example, Isaac Max Rubinow (1875-1936), a physician turned social worker, who had arrived from his native Poland in 1893, informed his Russian coreligionists in a series of articles published in the *Voskhod* in 1903 that the average wages of a Jewish worker amounted to $10-15 a week. Such incomes not only appeared fantastically high when compared with the wage scales in contemporary Russia, but even under American conditions made the lot of the worker far more tolerable.

At the same time [Rubinow added] I must express my conviction (which will evoke protest among the intelligentsia in New York) that the Jewish masses are better off economically than the other immigrants, and extreme poverty in New York is not prevalent in the Jewish section. I think that I am familiar with the horrors of dire poverty. As a medical inspector of the New York Board of Health I had to spend several months in the poor sections of Brooklyn. When I beheld the privations of the Irish, the Italians, the Negroes and others, I had to admit that the condition of the Russian-Jewish masses is more or less satisfactory. The reason for it is their diligence and self-discipline which prevent the Jew from sinking to the lowest depths.

True, the Jewish workers were not prepared to accept such comparative standards and Rubinow himself admitted that there were many "shortcomings of the economic status of the Jewish and the non-Jewish worker and [a] difference between the existing wage scale and the one which he deserves." Newcomers, in particular, as well as women workers often had to suffer years of deprivation, before they reached a tolerable mode of existence.[39]

Only one remedy seemed promising: a better organization of the clothing workers. The American labor movement, although dating back to the 1820s, was still unfolding and the Jews found themselves confronted by the conflicting approaches of the Knights of Labor and the American Federation of Labor, the latter led by their own coreligionist, Samuel Gompers. Although a union of Jewish tailors was organized in New York in 1877, it did not last long. No more successful were the Jewish and other needle workers in Rochester which at that time became a major center of the men's clothing industry. As in New York, and later also in Chicago, and other localities, Jews, primarily of German ancestry, were quite prominent among the manufacturers. This fact facilitated the entry of Jewish immigrants into these trades, although there was much antagonism between the Americanized employers and the newcomers. The few new Jewish arrivals in Rochester seem to have joined in a strike of a small group of clothing workers in 1882. Although the strike was not authorized by the Knights of Labor and the union of clothing workers never got off the ground, some successes were recorded in the subsequent years until 1890, when twenty-one manufacturers organized a so-called Rochester Clothiers' Exchange with the Jewish manufacturer, Henry Michaels, as president, and Attorney Sol Wile as the moving spirit. In 1891, the Exchange successfully staged a lockout which not only weakened the status of the clothing workers, but also undermined the strength of all organized labor in the city. As a reward one of the leaders of the Exchange, Max Brickner, was elected president of the Rochester Chamber of Commerce.[40]

In the same year, however, an eight-week strike of Jewish workmen in New York, although entailing major sacrifices while it lasted, secured an increase of wages which in turn strenghtened the union. Two years later another strike brought about an association of the manufacturers similar to that in Rochester. Curiously, the manufacturers acceded to the union's demand for payment of back wages, but immediately instituted criminal proceedings against the union's secretary, Joseph Barondess, who later became a prominent civic leader. Barondess was sentenced, but he was ultimately pardoned by the Governor. In all these matters the weakness of the Jewish trade union movement lay not only in the objective difficulties generated by the surplus of labor, but also in the extremely individualistic traits of the Jewish workers, who reluctantly accepted union discipline, and the belief of many members that sooner or later they themselves would become the "bosses." Occasional instances of strong-arm men seizing control of some unions and exploiting both management and members for their private benefit helped to undermine the latter's trust in their leadership. John R. Commons, a leading student of American labor history, pointed out some of these difficulties in the study, prepared in 1901 for President McKinley's Industrial Commission.

> The Jew's conception of a labor organization [he wrote] is that of a tradesman rather than that of a workman. In the manufacture of clothing, whenever any real abuse arises among the Jewish workmen, they all come together and form a giant union and at once engage in a strike. They bring in ninety-five per cent of the trade. They are energetic and determined. They demand the entire and complete elimination of the abuse. The demand is almost unanimous and is made with enthusiasm and bitterness. They stay out a long time, even under the greatest of suffering. . . .
>
> But when once the strike is settled, either in favor of, or against the cause, they are contented, and that usually ends the union, since they do not see any practical use for a union when there is no cause to fight for. Consequently, the membership of a Jewish union is wholly uncertain. The secretary's books will show 60,000 members in one month, and not 5,000 within three

months later. If, perchance, a local branch has a steady thousand members from year to year, and if they are indeed paying members, it is likely that they are not the same members as during the year before. A German union, on the contrary, will have the same members year after year, well or ill, with little change. The Jew joins the union when it offers a bargain and drops it when he gets, or fails to get, the bargain.

Commons also considered it a weakness of the Jewish labor movement that its leaders thought in abstract terms, rather than with respect to concrete issues of the day.[41]

What Commons considered as a practical weakness turned out, in the long run, to be an important source of strength and a mainspring for a major Jewish contribution to the American labor movement and American society as a whole. East-European Jews had not only grown up under traditions of social justice enjoined by Bible and Talmud, but had lived in self-governing Jewish communities which had long been inured to peaceful cooperation and more or less amicable adjustment of disputes between employers and workers. Even the so-called *din torah* (the rigid requirements of Jewish law) had rarely been resorted to; its place was usually taken by a *pesharah* (a compromise settlement) often suggested by communal or rabbinic mediators. Without necessarily spelling out such arrangements, East-European Jewish artisans and artisan guilds had long managed to secure fairly tolerable living conditions within the limitations imposed by the existing economic realities. Although class struggle was far from absent from the old ghettos, the communal machinery, abetted by public opinion, for the most part succeeded in blunting the sharpness of controversies and in reaching more or less amicable solutions. With the general instability of Jewish wealth and the solidarity generated by outside hostilities, Jews were also prone to deal with one another on a more egalitarian basis. Transplated to America, these psychological attitudes generated a certain social equilibrium, even a measure of solidarity between management and workers. Early in the twentieth century these traditional attitudes were readjusted to the new needs, rather than abandoned by the newly arriving socialistically and anarchistically oriented intellectuals from Russia. Many new arrivals had been members of the Russian Jewish Bund, founded in 1897, or had otherwise participated in the Russian Revolution of 1905. These leaders saw in labor unions not only a means for the increase of wages and improvement of working conditions of their members, but also a vehicle toward the ultimate attainment of a reign of social justice through the victory of the proletariat.

None of these factors operated at that time in the very large American trade unions embracing workers on railroads, coal or iron mines, or the oil fields, where a handful of captains of industry wielded almost unlimited power. In the greatly subdivided needle trades, on the contrary, where the employers themselves sharply competed with one another and where the ups and downs of the business cycle were felt most acutely on either side of the bargaining table, these psychological and traditional values often reasserted themselves. Particularly so, since the interests of the entire Jewish community often were at stake, and ill will generated by any miscarriage of justice strengthened the hand of the ever more vociferous opponents of the New Immigration. Moreover, as time passed more and more employers had themselves risen from the ranks of recent immigrants and still were trying, like their employees, to get adjusted to the American way of life without wholly abandoning the traditions of their old communities.[42]

Matters came to a head in the famous New York and Chicago strikes of 1909-11. They began with a stoppage of work by some 20,000 waist and dress makers of the International Ladies' Garment Workers Union (founded in 1900) which lasted from November 1909 to February 1910. This self-imposed idleness was followed in July 1910 by a more general strike of some 60,000 cloak makers, many of whom were later affiliated with the Amalgamated Clothing Workers of America (1914). These strikes, which entailed much suffering, attracted wide attention. Socially conscious society women often personally intervened at police stations, lest some imprisoned girl strikers be maltreated. The unfavorable comments appearing in the metropolitan press and elsewhere and aimed at both the employers and the strikers, caused great anxiety among the leaders of the Jewish community. The University Settlement in New York evinced sufficient interest in the "Shirtwaist" strike to institute a special investigation headed by the Jewish social worker, Charles S. Bernheimer. Especially the American Jewish Committee, founded but a few years previously and led by the influential attorney, Louis Marshall, felt that a prolongation of that strike would entail considerable injury to the Jewish community at large. Acting upon a suggestion advanced by Louis Kirstein, a leading Boston businessman and philanthropist, Marshall persuaded the parties to the dispute to invite Louis Dembitz Brandeis, a prominent Boston lawyer known for his liberal views in labor matters, to mediate the controversy. The strike was settled, in July 1910, with the adoption by both parties of the so-called "Protocol of Peace" which provided for a Board of Arbitration, a Board of Grievances, and a Joint Board of Sanitary Control as instruments for settling not only the existing difficulties but also for helping forestall future strikes. In fact, Brandeis, in charge of the Board of Arbitration, applied this instrument only in exceptional cases, preferring the simpler methods of mediation and amicable persuasion which usually proved quite effective.[43]

Provisions for sanitary controls, on the other hand, the need of which was increasingly felt in the needle industries (although other industries, too, suffered severely from health hazards), paved the way for an ever-increasing social welfare program. The unions began providing for their members' relief in distress, more and more educational facilities, seniority rights, and other protective devices which went far beyond the usual contractual safeguards concerning wages. It was in this area that the Jewish unions pioneered, thus setting the pace for the whole American labor movement and finally influencing the entire New Deal legislation of the 1930s. Sidney Hillman (1887-1946), in particular, who, as a cutter in the then leading clothing manufacturing firm of Hart, Schaffner and Marx in Chicago, had cooperated with Joseph Schaffner, the socially minded employer, in settling in 1911 a strike along progressive lines and had subsequently distinguished himself as leader of the Amalgamated Clothing Workers of America, became one of President Franklin D. Roosevelt's closest labor advisers and left his mark on the social legislation of the United States.[44]

Out of the Board of Arbitration there developed the concept of an "Impartial Chairman," jointly selected by management and labor, to settle detailed disputes and ultimately even to assist the very employers in securing new markets and thereby achieving prosperity for themselves and their employees. The nimble-minded Jewish labor leaders, partly influenced by their Marxist ideology which envisaged the proletariat as the ultimate guide in all productive processes, departed also from the accepted patterns of American labor policy and tried to speed up the "Second Industrial Revolution." While other labor leaders saw in the rationalization of industry a threat to job opportunities, the officials of the predominantly Jewish needle trades, on the contrary, tried to help their employers to mechanize, to utilize more efficient business methods, and even to adjust the psychology of the workers to the new conditions. Ultimately, they were in a position to advance funds to employers in critical periods and thus salvage their businesses together with the workers' jobs, without, however, taking over direct management and responsibility. By thus compromising with the basic principles of capitalism and private enterprise, and yet retaining a dose of socialist egalitarianism, these labor leaders left a permanent imprint on the whole American labor movement. Not the slightest contribution of these needle trade unions thus was the training of outstanding labor leaders. In short, there was not much overstatement in the comment by two enthusiastic writers in 1930 that

> these Jewish tailors have immeasurably enriched America. For while their fellow workers—diggers of coal, forgers of steel, weavers of cloth—are still widely denied a collective voice, the masses in the needle trades have been revealing what free, responsible citizens can contribute toward the development of life and industry.[45]

Apart from the needle trades, Jews were found in considerable number also in the fur, cigar, typographical, building, and several other unions. In July 1914, 300 Jewish bricklayers in New York, offended by some slurring remarks in their union's picnic journal, proposed to organize a union of their own. On the other hand, few Jews belonged to the large craft unions in the heavy industries. Nonetheless, next to the Germans, as observed by David J. Saposs, the Jews were the only ethnic group to develop a rounded-out labor movement. Their unions of Fur Workers, United Hatters, Cap and Millinery Workers, and others used Yiddish as their official language. As early as 1888, they were able to organize an association of Jewish unions called the United Hebrew Trades. They also went far beyond their purely professional concerns in trying to promote their political and cultural interests. By founding, in 1892, the *Arbeiter-Ring* (Workmen's Circle) they succeeded in spreading their Yiddishist and socialist ideas among the masses of their members and even in indoctrinating the youth through a network of Sholem Aleichem schools. We shall also see that the union leadership, as well as the rank and file, played a certain role in general American political life before and after the First World War.[46]

Apart from the Jewish laborers and employers in the needle trades, there were numerous Jewish craftsmen, especially tailors, shoemakers, carpenters, painters, and others, most of whom ran their own shops with the assistance of members of their own families and a few, if any, employees. Unfortunately occupational statistics concerning the American population at large for that period are quite unsatisfactory. As far as Jews were concerned hardly any solid work was done in this field before 1914. The few earlier investigations, moreover, were more concerned with Jewish commerce than manufacture. However, enough information is extant to assert that there also was a considerable concentration of Jews outside the garment and building industries. But there is no way of even approximating their percentage in any particular occupation. The only safe generalization is that, already in the period here under review, Jews contributed much beyond their share to the physical upbuilding of the American metropolitan areas and to providing the masses of the American population with a variety of inexpensive garments of fair quality.

Fewer Jews, however, found their way into the heavy industries, particularly the mining of iron, coal and oil which in that period supplied the sinews for the great industrial revolution. One major exception was Meyer Guggenheim, an immigrant from Switzerland. Together with his sons Daniel, Murray, and Solomon, he was, more accidentally than by design, led to the exploitation of copper, lead, zinc, and silver deposits. Before long this closely knit family dazzled the world when, in 1901, it took over the control of the rich American Smelting and Refining Company by owning $45,000,000 in its stock. Under Daniel's able leadership the Guggenheims entered world mining on a large scale and were dubbed the "copper kings" of the period. Their epochal promotion of the nascent aviation industry and their philanthropic foundations spread their fame all over the world at a time when their attachment to Judaism grew weaker and weaker.[47]

Commerce and Professions

Not surprisingly, the large majority of Jews continued in their traditional mercantile occupations. In the United States many an immigrant began by making a living as a peddler. To be sure, an investigation conducted in 1890 by the then newly founded Baron de Hirsch Fund in three New York wards showed that of the 22,647 gainfully employed Russian-Jewish immigrants residing there 76.3 percent were engaged in industrial pursuits and only 15.3 percent made a living through peddling, shopkeeping, and the like. However, there is no way of checking the methods and reliability of that study (the Fund's decision not to publish it may, indeed, have been owing in part to the authors' diffidence in the dependability of its results) and its findings certainly did not reflect the occupational distribution of all New York Jewry. It was even less representative of conditions in the rest of the country.[48]

While the great era of American peddling had passed with the Civil War and the spread of railroad travel, enough opportunities were still left for individuals to invest small amounts of money, often advanced to them by friends or some charitable organization, in merchandise and to try to dispose of it in the city or in neighboring villages. Few peddlers now ventured into great distances and were away from home for weeks or months on end. Yet, Isaac Mayer Wise's vivid description still held true in the period after 1880 for the dwindling number of these perambulating merchants. In 1896 a Jewish Peddlers Protection Society was organized to safeguard the rights of its ninety-two members, particularly against mischievous attacks by street urchins. As late as 1917, there still existed a League of Citizen Peddlers of Greater New York with a reported membership of 300. Incorporated in 1912, it was presided over by Sam Dictor, a dealer in pickles, then aged thirty-two, who had immigrated to the United States but twelve years before. The League's avowed purpose was "to work for mutual aid in social as well as business matters."[49] In the long run, however, peddling was definitely on the decline. The place of peddlers was gradually taken by a host of traveling salesmen, mostly in the employ of wholesale houses and manufacturers.

Most peddlers, however, usually graduated into petty shopkeeping. Here they joined a host of coreligionists who had previously established themselves in small groceries and clothing stores. Hardly a branch of merchandising in the larger cities was without some Jewish representatives. Many others served as business agents or other intermediaries. Still others found employment as clerks, bookkeepers, and sales personnel in larger stores, especially the growing variety and department stores and, before long, also in chain stores. A small, but influential, minority joined the entrepreneurial class on the higher level; some actually acquired department stores or other major establishments as owners or coowners. For example, R. H. Macy and Company was taken over, in 1896, by Isidor and Nathan Straus, who developed it into the largest department store in the country. Many other large stores in New York, Boston (Filene, etc.), and other cities were now owned by Jews, while Julius Rosenwald of Chicago, on assuming in 1909 the presidency of Sears, Roebuck and Co., converted it into the biggest mail-order house in the world. Many opportunities for the employment of Jewish capital and ingenuity also opened up in the real estate business with its numerous ramifications from the erection of residential and industrial buildings to the purely commercial acquisition of property for resale. It was actually a source of pride for Isaac Markens and other Jewish apologists to stress these Jewish contributions to the American economy. Segments of the American press were likewise quite outspoken in their praise. For example, the *New York Sun* commented on May 31, 1891: "Of late years also they [the Jews] have become conspicuous for investments in landed property. Some of the most notable of the purchasers at the Real Estate Exchange are Jews." The same was largely true in the city of Boston where Robert A. Woods observed: "The increase of Jewish ownership in real estate during the past ten years has been amazing. . . . In the North and West Ends in 1900, estates with a total assessment valuation of $6,544,700 were charged to persons of names unmistakably Jewish."[50]

Real estate transactions rapidly multiplied in the first three decades of the twentieth century in line with the general increase in population, the expansion of production, and the growth of the cities, both big and small, in which Jews resided. Not even the crisis of 1907 stopped that process. In fact, by forcing previous landowners to dispose of their property, that emergency played into the hands of the new real estate owners and speculators, among whom Jews occupied a prominent place.

None of this was new to the East-European Jews, except perhaps the fact that they found here much more competition from non-Jews than they had experienced before. Even in peddling they had encountered all along much rivalry from native Yankees, as well as other immigrant groups. Shopkeeping, too, had been a traditional American occupation and Jews predominated only in certain areas, particularly the preeminently Jewish quarters, or in such peculiar "Jewish" branches as clothing stores. In time, Jewish clothing workers, gradually being displaced by newer waves of immigrants, particularly Italian, entered the retail trade on their own. Also employees of retail stores sometimes succeeded in establishing themselves on the entrepreneurial level even if economically such transformation might have entailed certain temporary or permanent sacrifices. Of course, some individuals were more successful than others. Unfortunately, no exact statistical accounts are available. Not even the attempts made later in the 1920s can be considered accurate and scientific enough for more definite backward reconstructions. However, already in 1888, Markens ventured an estimate of the Jews in the wholesale trade in the city of New York and their annual turnover. While one cannot accept his figures uncritically, the following estimates of the annual transactions may give us an approximation of the growing importance of the Jews in the various lines of business in the American metropolis.

Manufacturers of clothing	$ 55,000,000
Jobbers of jewelry	30,000,000
Wholesale butchers	25,000,000
Wines, spirits and beer	25,000,000
Jobbers of leaf tobacco	15,000,000
Manufacturers of cigars	15,000,000
Manufacturers of cloaks	15,000,000
Importers of diamonds	12,000,000
Leather and hides	12,000,000
Manufacturers of overshirts	10,000,000
Importers of watches	6,000,000
Artificial flowers and feathers	6,000,000
Importers and jobbers of furs	5,000,000
Manufacturers of undergarments	5,000,000
Lace and embroidery importers	4,000,000
Manufacturers of white shirts	3,000,000
Manufacturers of hats	3,000,000
Manufacturers of caps	2,000,000
	$ 248,000,000

In addition Markens estimated Jewish holdings of New York real estate at $150,000,000.[51]

Two years later one Max Cohen attempted another estimate based upon a very limited sample. Studying the Jewish names recorded in the R. G. Dunn and Company reports for 1870 and 1890 Cohen came to the conclusion that the Jews had progressed considerably in these twenty years not only in absolute figures, but also in their ratio within the respective branches of industry and commerce. True, Cohen's methods were very crude, but one can hardly disagree with his general conclusion. More scientific was the aforementioned survey by John S. Billings who had examined a fairly representative sample of 10,620 families, comprising 60,630 persons spread over the country, who had answered his questionnaire at the end of 1889. His conclusion that 80.4 percent of all Jewish males between 15 and 44, and 79.9 percent of those in the older brackets were engaged in either wholesale or retail trade or banking, as entrepreneurs or employees, probably approximated the truth. More detailed, though still avowedly incomplete, breakdowns were attempted in 1924 by the so-called American-Jewish Economic Commission of the Aleph Zadik Aleph (B'nai B'rith Youth Organization) which investigated 36 cities, and in 1925 by Rabbi Edward Israel and associates in behalf of the Central Conference of American Rabbis who examined ten other cities. Their main conclusions are shown in the table opposite. These figures are unreliable and contradictory. One might still somehow try to explain the disparity between 47.4 and 30.8 percent in trade, but the contrast between 16.3 and 42.8 in manufacturing is explicable only if one assumes that the investigators had started from totally divergent approaches. But even if these estimates were more dependable, they would still tell us little about the conditions before 1914, since the great transformations of the First World War and the following years, combined with the sharp decline of immigration, must have greatly altered the occupational distribution of American Jewry.[52]

Most startling was the dichotomy between American and East-European Jewish banking. In many areas of Russia, Poland, Ga-

TABLE IV
Percentage Distribution of Gainfully Employed Jews in 46 Cities, 1924-25

Occupations	A.Z.A. Group (36 cities)			Israel Group (10 cities)
	Total	Male	Female	Total
Total	100.0	100.0	100.0	100.0
Trade	47.4	51.1	35.4	30.8
Manufacturing	16.3	18.6	8.8	42.8
Professions	10.1	10.7	8.0	9.6
Clerical	16.8	9.5	40.8	8.4
Domestic and Personal	5.0	5.4	4.0	6.7
Transportation and Communication	2.2	2.2	2.1	1.0
Public Service	2.0	2.3	0.9	—
Other	0.2	0.2	—	0.7

licia, and Rumania Jews had for generations almost monopolized petty moneylending and their leaders had also played a prominent role in the top echelons of the banking profession. The latter held true also in the other Continental countries even where, as in Italy, Jews constituted but a small segement of the population. Not so in the United States, where the immigrants of the post-Civil War era found a strongly entrenched banking system both of the corporate and private kind. All American townships of any size had had for a long time small banks of their own. Even the larger banks were rarely prepared to employ immigrants. In time more conscious discrimination was practiced against Jews in the very employment of tellers or bookkeepers on the part of the giants in American banking. Nevertheless, the German-Jewish immigration had brought forth, especially after the Civil War, a number of families which, in part continuing the line of business they had previously pursued in Germany, had entered private banking with considerable success. "Lazard brothers, hailing from Alsace; the Speyer family, descendants of the old distinguished Frankfort Court Jews of that name; the Seligmans from Bavaria, where early in the century Aaron Elias Seligmann (Baron von Eichstädt) had been the leading banker; the Lehmanns from Württemberg; the Belmonts from Frankfort, for a time representatives of the Rothschild interests—have all won a high position in American banking." By 1888 Markens contended that, in New York City alone, Jewish banking represented an invested capital in excess of $100,000,000.[53]

The most important Jewish banking firm was Kuhn, Loeb and Company. Founded by Abraham Kuhn and Solomon Loeb, it achieved great eminence after 1875 under the leadership of Jacob Henry Schiff (1847-1920), who was also a prominent philanthropist and Jewish communal leader. Competing with a number of leading Christian firms such as John Pierpont Morgan, Kuhn and Loeb contributed greatly both to the development of American railroads and to the placing of foreign loans in the New York market. It has been estimated that between 1881 and 1920, the firm had a leading share in the underwriting of no less than $1,000,000,000 in loans for the Pennsylvania Railroad Company alone. In 1900, at the time when the United States was just emerging from the status of a debtor, to that of a creditor nation, Kuhn, Loeb and Company floated the first German loan in the amount of 80,000,000 marks. During the Russo-Japanese War of 1904-1905 Schiff, propelled in part by his resentment of the Tsar's anti-Jewish policies, took a leading part in lending Japan a total of £55,000,000 which doubtless went far in helping Japan vanquish the Russians. In 1908, a large loan of 460,000,000 Mexican dollars was underwritten by Schiff, the amount was to be used for the consolidation of Mexico's two main railroads. Under Schiff's leadership, Kuhn and Loeb was on the way toward primacy in the private banking system, when the First World War gave Morgan and other pro-Allied bankers a tremendous advantage. Jews also entered some of the larger corporate banks, especially the Manufacturers Trust Company. After 1914, even the unions took up fairly large-scale banking through the Amalgamated Bank controlled by the Jewish needle trades workers. But all these were merely beginnings which, greatly expanding during and after the First World War, were sharply reversed during the depression of 1929-32. This was the time, moreover, when private banking generally was losing ground in relation to the powerful corporate entities.[54]

We know even less about the Jews in the liberal professions and the civil service. The percentages quoted above from the surveys by the A.Z.A. and the Central Conference appear fairly acceptable not only for the mid-1920s but, to a somewhat lesser extent, also for the period before 1914. Admission to the practice of medicine and law, the two professions to which Jews flocked in all countries of Emancipation, still was relatively easy. Many immigrants could earn a living during the day and attend night school in order to secure legal training. Medical schools, too, were at that time much less exacting and less discriminatory than they became after the First World War. Well-informed Doctor Rubinow accepted, in 1903, the estimate that Jews then constituted fifty percent of the 5,000-6,000 physicians in New York City. These Jewish doctors, who included a number of eminent surgeons and other specialists, had among their patients many non-Jews of diverse ethnic origin. More than half the students enrolled in the College of the City of New York at that time were Jews, holding out prospects of even greater participation in the liberal professions, which indeed materialized in the following years. A considerable number of Jews, both male and female, also entered the teaching profession, whether in the ever-expanding Jewish educational system, or in the general public and private schools. Even universities began receiving a sprinkling of Jewish teachers. Less pronounced was Jewish participation in such professions as engineering, architecture, and the arts and letters, although a number of individuals found their way into these occupations as well, some enjoying an excellent reputation in their chosen fields. Of course, the Jewish press, the Yiddish theater and literature furnished employment to a good many Jewish professionals, just as the religious needs created a class of rabbis, cantors, and other synagogue officials. However, we are at a complete loss at numerically assessing the percentages of Jews engaged in the civil service on all levels before 1914. Probably the Jewish ratio was, if anything, smaller than the proportion of Jews to the general population, although this still was the period of a relatively small American bureaucracy and a slowly expanding professional class.[55]

Legal Status and Public Affairs

By 1880 the battle for equality of the Jews in the United States had long been won through the egalitarian provisions of the Constitution and its subsequent amendments. True, the particular structure of American government and the diffusion of sovereignty between the Federal and state governments made possible the persistence, in state constitutions and local laws, of numerous detailed provisions which opened the door for religious and racial discrimination. Moreover, many laws which remained on the statute books had long gone into disuse by the sheer lack of enforcement. But it is noteworthy that not until 1868 was formal equality established in North Carolina, while New Hampshire removed its final discriminatory clause in 1877. Yet many loopholes were left open for some discrimination. For example, after the victory had been won in the protracted struggle for Jewish emancipation in Maryland in 1826, the law demanded that an office holder must take an oath declaring that he "believed in a future state of rewards and punishments." This law was still enforced in the twentieth century; it excluded not only Buddhists and other religious groups not believing in the Hereafter, but also agnostic and atheistic Christians and Jews. Similarly, when in 1847 at the motion of Dr. Joshua I. Cohen the Maryland Legislature passed a law amending the previous regulation, which had prevented Negroes from testifying against white Christians, to include all white persons, Jews gained only at the expense of the Negroes. Technically, certain old laws required that Jews be legally married only in Christian churches, a provision which was not formally removed until 1927. In fact, as late as 1924 a new Maryland Blasphemy Act still provided for a six-months' imprisonment, or $100 fine, or both for anyone denying the divinity of Christ and the Holy Trinity.[56]

Such examples can readily be multiplied in this and many other areas. An American magazine made it its business in recent years to publish in each issue examples of laws still on the statute books in one or another state of the Union which had long gone into oblivion. True, their very presence makes them liable to resuscitation whenever a court or public opinion is ready to enforce them. But public opinion, if strong and persistent enough, can with equal ease bring about the enactment of a totally new law or even push through, with some difficulty, a basic constitutional amendment. The only major legal discrimination against which Jews sometimes raised their voices arose from the Sunday Laws. These "Blue Laws" for the most part outlawed holding stores open on Sunday, forcing many observant Jews to close their shops on two successive days of the week; a genuine hardship, indeed, alleviated only in such states as New York and Indiana by statutory provisions that anyone observing another weekly day of rest was not to be prosecuted under the Sunday legislation. A similar bill submitted by a Jewish member, S. H. Borofsky, was adopted by the Massachusetts House of Representatives but was defeated in the Senate. Though constantly debated and often attacked as a violation of the principle of separation of state and Church, these laws were frequently upheld by the courts as legitimate police measures within the framework of state or municipal legislation. Yet in many parts of the country these laws were largely observed in their breach by both Jews and Christians. Writing to the *Occident* in 1856, a correspondent insisted "that it has been found impossible to collect a fine for laboring on Sunday in Iowa; and its strikes us that a similar result would follow in all the States if the attempt were made to enforce the collection of a fine, as in the present case."[57]

Gradually Jews also entered the stream of American politics and civil service. In this respect the Russo-Polish and Rumanian Jews differed greatly from their German and Galician coreligionists. Coming from countries without free parliamentary institutions, the former viewed the state merely as an organ of oppression and wished to have as little to do with it as possible. Only a minority, especially if imbued with socialist or anarchist ideals, was prepared for political action. In fact, the socialist movement in the United States, in part generated by German Jewish immigrants in the mid-century, received much reinforcement from the eastern intellectuals. Not surprisingly, in the growing socialist movement before and after World War I, Jews played a significant role not only as thinkers and writers, but also as practical organizers. It was no accident that the first socialist to be elected to the American Congress was a Jew, Victor L. Berger (1860-1929), sent to the House from Milwaukee in 1911. He was followed four years later by Meyer London (1871-1926) from New York City. Soon thereafter a well-known labor leader, Morris Hillquit (1870-1933), received a very substantial vote for Mayor of New York City on the socialist ticket. Otherwise, most East-European Jews were quite apathetic in both national and local elections. The usual methods of campaigning at the time, with free beer and promises of governmental jobs, held little attraction for Jewish immigrants having insufficient command of English and hence seeking a living in other domains. Only the older immigrants took a more active interest in politics.[58]

None the less, by 1914, the number of Jewish officeholders was quite substantial. Even the highest elective body, the United States Senate, had occasional Jewish members. In our period Benjamin Franklin Jonas served as senator from Louisiana in 1879-85, Joseph Simon represented Oregon in 1897-1903, and Isidor Rayner (1850-1912) was elected from Maryland in 1905. Seven years later he was proposed as candidate for president of the United States by no less a figure than William Jennings Bryan, the silver-tongued orator and himself three times Democratic candidate for the presidency. There were also several Jewish governors including those of Idaho (Moses Alexander) and Washington Territory (Edward Solomon). Before Simon Bamberger was elected governor of Utah in 1916, his campaign speeches were well received by the Mormons who preferred to listen to a Jew than to a non-Jewish "Gentile." But none of these were elected in their capacity as Jews. In fact, with the exception of Maryland and, to a lesser extent, Louisiana, none of these states had large Jewish communities. Only occasionally was a Jewish congressman elected in a Jewish district and he often appeared as a spokesman for Jewish interests. For example, Henry M. Goldfogle represented a predominantly Jewish New York constituency and he often spoke up in Congress on the passport question which, as we shall presently see, greatly agitated the minds of Jews. There also were, of course, Jews active in municipal affairs (for instance, B. Lewin who was elected mayor of Chicago in 1893), or assisting various governmental organs with their specialized knowledge in conducting surveys or in the preparation of important acts. One such outstanding figure was Simon Sterne (1839-1901) who, as Secretary of the "Committee of Seventy," in 1870-71, helped to overthrow the notorious Tweed Ring in New York City, and in 1894 again aided in the election of an anti-Tammany candidate for the mayoralty. In the same year he was appointed by President Cleveland as Commissioner to "review the relation of railways and state in western Europe," just as he had seven years earlier taken an important part in drafting the Interstate Commerce Act.[59]

Actually, the problem of a "Jewish vote" created an issue. East-European Jews, especially those who were nationalistically minded, expected the Jews to act as a bloc in political affairs. On the other hand, the older Jewish settlers viewed with misgivings any such separatism along religious or racial lines. Typical of the latter point of view was Louis Marshall's reaction to Benjamin Marcus's suggestion before the national election of 1912 that he join a committee to organize Jewish Taft clubs all over the United States. In his reply of March 8, 1912 Marshall, widely recognized as a leading Jewish spokesman, stated,

> While I am strongly in favor of the renomination and the re-election of President Taft, I am utterly opposed to any plan whereby the Jewish people shall segregate themselves from the remainder of the citizens of this country for political purposes. We have no political interests which are different from those of our fellow-citizens. We would subject ourselves to just criticism if we organized political clubs of our own. There is no such thing as a Jewish Republican or a Jewish Democrat. We are either Republicans or Democrats. The sooner it is understood

that we do not recognize a wall of separation as between our-selves and those who advocate the same causes, and do not con-tribute to the creation of one, the better it will be for all of us.

Formally, this represented the prevailing attitude, although in practice politicians running for office always recognized the need of special appeals to the various major ethnic and religious groups in their districts.[60]

Among the appointive officials the highest rank was held by Cabinet members. Joseph Seligman, who, as we recall, had rendered signal services during the Civil War, was offered by his friend, President Ulysses S. Grant, the post of Secretary of Treasury, but he declined. Later, Oscar Solomon Straus (1850-1926) was first appointed in 1887 by President Grover Cleveland to serve as Minister to the Ottoman Empire; he was again sent to the same post by President McKinley in 1897, as "the only man in the United States who could save the situation" created by the Armenian massacres. He was dispatched to Constantinople for the third time in 1909 by President Taft to meet another emergency. In fact, because of the religious problems, both Jewish and Christian, arising in the Ottoman Empire, a Jew was often selected thereafter to head the American legation in Constantinople. Interveningly, under President Theodore Roosevelt, Straus occupied the post of Secretary of Commerce (1906-1909) and served for several terms as the American member of the Permanent Court of Arbitration in The Hague. Incidentally, unlike Seligman who became one of the founders and longtime president of the Ethical Culture Society, Straus was actively interested in Jewish affairs, particularly in immigration, the defense of Jewish rights and the promotion of Jewish historical studies. He served as first president of the American Jewish Historical Society and wrote books on religious liberty.[61] There also were, of course, a host of lesser officials. This situation was dramatized in 1896, when a well-known German antisemite, Hermann Ahlwardt, visited New York. Apprehensive of reprisals on the part of the large Jewish community, he asked for police protection. Theodore Roosevelt, then

New York's Police Commissioner, acceded to his request by assigning to him several Jewish members of the police force.[62]

Jews also fulfilled their military duties. Some 5,000 Jews enlisted during the Spanish American War, which represented a somewhat higher ratio than their percentage in the population. Among the Jewish combatants in that war a few had graduated from the West Point Military Academy, while several hundred served as noncommissioned officers. When the battleship *Maine* was sunk in Havana harbor in 1898, 15 Jewish sailors lost their lives. Several Jews were also among the "Rough Riders" led by Colonel Theodore Roosevelt in his famous attack on San Juan Hill near Santiago, Cuba. A number of Jews distinguished themselves also in the naval battles, among them graduates of the Naval Academy of Annapolis. One, Edward D. Taussig, retired in 1909 with the rank of Rear Admiral, while a much younger Joseph Strauss reached that rank during the First World War and served in 1921-22 as Commander-in-Chief of the Asiatic Fleet. Jewish patriotism was fully recognized by the government and outstanding leaders of public opinion. Theodore Roosevelt, then President, voiced a widely held view when, in his letter of November 16, 1905 to the celebrants of the 250th Anniversary of the settlement of the Jews in the United States, he wrote,

I am glad to be able to say, in addressing you on this occasion, that while the Jews of the United States, who now number more than a million, have remained loyal to their faith and their race traditions, they have become indissolubly incorporated in the great army of American citizenship, prepared to make all sacrifice for the country, either in war or peace, and striving for the perpetuation of good government and for the maintenance of the principles embodied in our Constitution. They are honorably distinguished by their industry, their obedience to law, and their devotion to the national welfare. They are engaged in generous rivalry with their fellow-citizens of other denominations in advancing the interests of our common country. This is true not only of the descendants of the early settlers and those of American birth, but of a great and constantly increasing proportion of

*those who have come to our shores within the last twenty-five
years as refugees reduced to the direst straits of penury and
misery.*[63]

Intergroup Tensions

Not all Americans, however, shared this point of view. We recall that the mass immigration at the end of the nineteenth century had created much antagonism which soon assumed a racialist
coloring. The earlier Irish mass immigration had evoked an outpouring of anti-Catholic literature, including Maria Monk's *Awful
Disclosures* (1835) which allegedly reproduced reminiscences of a
former nun about the debauchery and murders in Catholic con-
vents. It later brought forth such forgeries as the alleged oath of
the Knights of Columbus and a papal encyclical which purportedly
proved that Catholics could not be good citizens. Similarly now
the new mass immigration from eastern and southern Europe
generated a literature aimed at the immigrants from the Mediterranean and Slavonic countries, including Jews. Some anti-immigration writings have already been mentioned. The classic of that
literature, Madison Grant's *The Passing of the Great Race*, was
not to appear until 1916. However, many earlier writers anticipated
his exclamation that "whether we like to admit it or not, the result of the mixture of two races, in the long run, gives us a race
reverting to the more ancient, generalized, and lower type. The
cross between a white man and an Indian is an Indian; . . . and
the cross between any of the three European races and a Jew is a
Jew." Such racialist concepts, streaming over from Europe where
the antisemitic movement had celebrated ever new victories since
1873, were reinforced on the popular level by the great transformations which had taken place in the United States after the Civil
War. A society, overwhelmingly rural and traditionalist in outlook,
witnessed a sudden spurt in industrial production, the growth of
metropolitan centers, and the rise of a new financial oligarchy
which dominated public life. Not only direct victims of that

transformation, but most observers were bewildered by that speed of change. Even Henry James, returning to America in 1907, was astonished by how alien many American cities looked to him. He was particularly impressed by "the extent of the Hebrew conquest of New York," which he called a new Jerusalem. He conceded that the newly emerging culture might "become the most beautiful on the globe and the very music of humanity," but it would be totally different from the "English" culture he and others had been accustomed to consider genuinely American.[64]

Apart from these racial differences the older religious and economic controversies were now revived. The religious antagonisms arising from the Gospel narratives had lost much of their sharpness for generations raised upon the doctrine of mutual toleration. But the idea of a Jewish world conspiracy and the Jews' alleged drive for world domination through capitalist exploitation was gaining ground rapidly, despite the realistic observation that even American banking was dominated by non-Jews. Not surprisingly, some American socialists echoed the old Fourierist line of Alphonse Toussenel's *Les Juifs rois de l'époque*. A leading protagonist of revisionist socialism, Laurence Gronlund, wrote: "Our era may be called the *Jewish age*. The Jews . . . long ago . . . infused in our race the idea of one God and now they have made our whole race worship a new true God: the Golden Calf. . . . 'Jewism,' to our mind, best expresses that special curse of our age, *Speculation*." The raging controversies over bimetallism and William Jennings Bryan's famous exclamation, "You shall not crucify mankind upon a cross of gold!" added fuel to the hatred of Jewish financial power. Typical of some Populist opinions was a utopian novel by Ignatius Donnelly, *Caesar's Column*, published in 1891. Utilizing the then fashionable Darwinian concept of the survival of the fittest, the novel depicted a period in which the aristocracy of the world would be almost exclusively of Hebrew origin. Precisely because of the severe persecutions they had undergone, only the fittest Jews had survived. "Only the strong of body, the cunning of brain . . . the man with capacity to live where a dog would starve survived the awful trial." Now Jews have been placed in a position to accumulate riches and to be "as merciless to the Christian as the Christian had been to them."[65]

All these publications still were relatively mild. But a host of other books, pamphlets, and newspaper articles more nearly approximated the level of the vulgar antisemitic literature then prevalent in Europe. Representative of this type of literature were the writings by one Telemachus Thomas Timayenis, son of a Smyrna high school teacher, who in the United States had a rather checkered career as John D. Rockefeller's confidential agent, owner of a publishing house from which he reputedly embezzled funds, a cigarette manufacturer, short-term Greek consul in Boston accused by the Greek community " as a traitor to Greek interests in this country," and editor of a Boston monthly. His three anti-Jewish works, *The Original Mr. Jacobs*, *The American Jew*, and *Judas Iscariot*, were published in quick succession in 1888-89 by his own Minerva Publishing Company of New York. He rehearsed here the usual antisemitic generalizations based upon the new pseudo-scientific racial theories. He contended, for instance, that

> the Jew is a born trafficker, a born liar, full of cunning and intrigue. The Aryan is enthusiastic, heroic, chivalrous, frank and confident. The Jew sees nothing beyond the present. The Aryan is the child of Heaven, constantly preoccupied with superior aspirations. . . . The Jew has no creative faculty. . . . Not one invention was made by a Jew.

He repeated the antisemitic clichés of a special Jewish odor, lust for money, and enmity toward mankind. Glibly disregarding the growing Jewish labor class, he claimed that Jews were not workers. "Imagine a Jew," he exclaimed, "with his thin long fingers, shaped for theft, with his shaky crooked legs and his flat feet, handling a plough or a spade!" The popular mind bent upon generalization often viewed the Irish, Scotch, and other immigrants in such stereotypes. Timayenis's description of the principal Jewish traits, "the famous hooked nose, the restless eyes, the close-set teeth, the elongated ears, the square nails (instead of being tapered in the shape of an almond), the flat foot, the round knees, the soft hands, almost melting with the hypocrisy of the traitor. Often they have one arm longer than the other," mirrored a widely accepted image and often appeared in popular cartoons. In fact, *The American Jew* was provided with a series of antisemitic illustrations by the talented Russian cartoonist, Valerian Gribayédoff, who worked under Joseph Pulitzer's direction on the *New York World*. Somewhat less viciously, the same types of caricatures appeared also in many other popular journals, often intended for fun rather than hostile propaganda. It even penetrated the Jewish circles themselves, especially the comic magazine, *Der Yiddisher Puck*, published by the Yiddish journalist, N. M. Schaikevitch.[66]

Beyond literary antisemitism, there was a growth of anti-Jewish feeling among the populace. In this respect there was a basic change in the attitude of the American public, particularly in the provinces. While in the earlier periods Jews were often admired as descendants of the biblical patriarchs, now there was a growing resentment of their economic successes, combined with their occasional conspicuous display and what to reticent Anglo-Saxons appeared as raucous behavior. Before long, manifestations of popular prejudice began to multiply. In the 1870s and 1880s with the increase in immigration, there was a noticeable reluctance in some Christian circles to admit Jews to their social gatherings. In 1872, a stir was created by one B. F. Waterman who had enlisted in the New York National Guard. After having been sworn in, he was informed by the captain of his company "that a law was passed three years ago, prohibiting from admission in the company any person, either of foreign or American birth, who should be of the Jewish persuasion." Waterman complained about this action in a letter to the editor of *The Jewish Times* but, apart from some comments in the press, apparently nothing happened to remedy the situation.[67]

Even less could be done when, in 1876, an advertisement by a New Jersey hotel in the New York *Tribune* contained the clause that "Jews are not admitted." On the other hand, in the following year the exclusion of Joseph Seligman from the Grand Union Hotel in Saratoga attracted wide attention because of the eminence of both Seligman and the hotel owner, Judge Henry Hilton. Saratoga, to be sure, had already begun to decline as the great summer center of business and politics as well as recreation, but the Seligman incident accelerated its decline. Jews retaliated not only against Hilton personally, by boycotting his New York department store, A. T. Stewart, which in 1896 was sold to John Wanamaker, but also by buying up several Saratoga hotels. (Hilton died in 1899.) By 1887, about half the summer population of Saratoga was Jewish. At that time a reporter, Alice H. Rhine, after reviewing the situation in the Catskills, claimed that the local summer resorts were about equally divided between those with an exclusively Jewish clientele and others which admitted no Jews. Curiously, she pointed out that the most frequent discrimination was found in the cheaper boarding houses charging $5 to $10 per week. From summer resorts social discrimination spread, especially after 1900, to many other walks of social life. Even Freemasons now refused membership to Jews; as a result, Jews formed their own lodges. Another widely debated incident occurred when the Century Club of New York rejected the application of the renowned scientist, Jacques Loeb. More serious was the growing discrimination in admission to private schools and colleges. This was not always the result of anti-Jewish administrations; often the latter merely respected the wishes of a school's Christian clientele. Sometimes when a renowned school admitted a large number of Jews, Christian parents ceased sending their children to that school, whereupon it lost its attraction to Jewish parents as well and was forced to shut down. Finally, the government had to take cognizance of these antisocial manifestations. Under pressure of the American Jewish Committee, the New York legislature passed a civil rights bill, prohibiting places of public accommodation to advertise refusals to admit persons because of race, creed, or color. This law, signed by Governor William Sulzer in 1913, was emulated by several other states, partly as a result of the agitation of the Anti-Defamation League of B'nai B'rith. In certain major cities there also occurred occasional attacks by rowdies on Jewish passers-by, intimidation also being employed in keeping Jews out of certain districts. None of which, however, prevented the spread of Jews into ever new metropolitan areas and summer resorts. But it was not until after the Second World War that these forms of social discrimination began losing some of their virulence.[68]

The frequency of such incidents ought not to mislead us into believing, however, that most of the American public and its intellectuals were thoroughly antisemitic. In fact, some of the outstanding intellectual leaders, including Mark Twain, Oliver Wendell Holmes, the agnostic Robert Ingersoll, the philosopher Josiah Royce, and others publicly stated their opposition to anti-Jewish hostility. The Saratoga incident induced the famous preacher Henry Ward Beecher to denounce the hotel management's behavior in a sermon which was extensively commented upon at that time. Another leading clergyman, Charles Henry Parkhurst, likewise took up the cudgel for good will and mutual toleration. An eminent publicist like Charles Anderson Dana spoke up for the Jews, as did United States Senator Zebulon B. Vance, whose *The Scattered Nation* belongs to the classics of the philosemitic literature of that period. Often repeated as a public lecture over two decades, it made an even greater impression when it appeared in print in 1904 and, again, in 1916 and 1936. These examples could readily be multiplied. Certainly this group was far more prestigious and influential than the obscure antisemitic pamphleteers. It was not, indeed, until the rise of the Nazi propaganda in the 1930s that antisemitism became a serious public issue with threatening implications for Jewish survival.[69]

International Relations

As American Jewry grew into maturity and became a major center of Jewish life, it also assumed increasing responsibility for the Jews of other lands. The United States government at that time still had few imperial ambitions and responsibilities and was little involved in the power politics of the "European Concert."

Hence it could serve more effectively as a champion of general humanitarian principles. While it recognized the rule of non-interference in the inner affairs of other states, it nevertheless ventured time and again to lend expression to the voice of outraged humanity. In general, the nineteenth century had a far more humanitarian and liberal approach to international relations than was possible in the increasingly virulent imperialist clashes in the era before and after the two World Wars.

American interventions in behalf of oppressed Jewry were not always the results of Jewish initiative; they began at a time when the Jewish community in the country was still extremely small and far from influential. The first major episode occurred during the Damascus Affair of 1840 when, on order of President Van Buren, Secretary of State John Forsythe instructed the American Consul at Alexandria to use his good offices with the government of Mehmet Ali in behalf of "these persecuted people, whose cry of distress has reached our shores." Remarkably, this intercession was ordered on August 14, 1840, even before the President had received any communication from the Jewish community concerning the Blood Accusation in the Syrian city. It was followed by other negotiations and good offices in various countries, for example, in the Mortara Affair of 1858; for the most part, to be sure, by mere rhetoric. Only in the case of the treatment of American Jewish citizens abroad could the United States government intervene more forcefully and claim to be an interested party. The protracted controversy with Switzerland, in particular, in which the United States government had been anticipated by similar moves from France, the Netherlands, and England, led to a signal success. Since Switzerland had to yield to these combined pressures and begin treating the emancipated Jewish citizens of these countries on a par with the non-Jewish citizens, the Swiss found themselves induced to extend in 1874 equal treatment to their own Jewish subjects as well.[70]

In the period here under review, the United States government was particularly involved in diplomatic negotiations concerning the Jews of Russia, Rumania, and the Ottoman Empire including

Palestine. Minor incidents, to be sure, occurred also in other countries. For example, when in 1885 Grover Cleveland appointed Anthony M. Keiley of Virginia United States envoy to Vienna, Secretary T. F. Bayard merely informed the Austrian minister in Washington of this appointment without awaiting the usual confirmation that Keiley was a *persona grata* with the Austrian government. This omission was seized upon by the Austrian Minister of Foreign Affairs, Count Gustav S. Kalnóky, to try to stop Keiley from reaching Vienna. To his envoy in Washington Kalnóky referred, in particular, to Mrs. Keiley's Jewishness and declared that "the position of a foreign envoy wedded to a Jewess by civil marriage would be untenable and even impossible in Vienna." However, Bayard denied any precedents for the United States' seeking previous consent from the governments to which it wished to accredit its ministers and insisted that the faith of a prospective envoy's lawfully wedded wife could play no role in its decisions. In his letter of May 18, 1885, to the Austrian envoy, Baron Schaeffer, Bayard emphasized, "It is not believed by the President that a doctrine and practice so destructive of religious liberty and freedom of conscience, so devoid of catholicity, and so opposed to the spirit of the age in which we live can for a moment be accepted by the great family of civilized nations or be allowed to control their diplomatic intercourse." Realizing that its position had become untenable even in its own country, the Austrian government now explained its refusal by reference to Keiley's speech in 1871, at a public meeting of Virginia Catholics, in which the diplomat had urged their support for a resolution denouncing the invasion of the Papal States by King Victor Emanuel. Since Keiley's earlier appointment as American envoy to Italy had to be rescinded for this reason, the Viennese Foreign Office alleged, Austria could not offend the sensitivities of a friendly neighbor by accepting Keiley as a minister to its court. This argument, though evidently fabricated for the occasion, could not easily be repudiated and the United States withdrew Keiley's assignment to Vienna.[71]

Different issues were raised in connection with Rumania. Even before the constitution of the Rumanian Kingdom by the Treaty of Berlin of 1878, the mistreatment, both governmental and popular, of Jews attracted widespread attention. Seeking to obviate future persecutions and legal discrimination, the powers gathered at the Congress of Berlin inserted into the Rumanian Treaty an article (XLIV) providing that any difference of religious allegiance was not to serve as a ground for exclusion from "the enjoyment of civil and political rights, admission to public employments, functions, and honors, or the exercise of the various professions and industries in any locality whatsoever." The United States, though not a signatory to the Treaty, felt entitled to raise its voice in behalf of any suffering segment of humanity. In fact, in 1870 President Ulysses Grant who, as general of the Northern Armies for the District of Tennessee had issued, on December 17, 1862, the notorious antisemitic order No. 12, which he later sincerely regretted, appointed Benjamin F. Peixotto, Grand Master of the Order B'nai B'rith, as American consul in Bucharest.[72]

With considerable hesitation the United States government joined the European powers in recognizing the new kingdom, knowing that Great Britain had inserted into its note of recognition a clear censure of Article VII of the new Rumanian Constitution which required individual naturalization from the Rumanian Jews. Subsequently, the American government repeatedly suggested to the Rumanian authorities the conclusion of a mutual treaty of naturalization, but Rumania refused. Finally, on July 17, 1902, Secretary of State John Hay, at the direction of President Theodore Roosevelt, informed the American envoys to the signatory Powers of the Treaty of Berlin that the United States could not brook any distinction between citizens on the basis of religion and that, on grounds of humanity, it could not countenance religious persecution of any kind. The pledges of Article XLIV, in particular, Hay contended in this famous dispatch, had been largely nullified by Rumanian legislation and municipal regulations which started from the arbitrary premise that the local Jews domiciled there for centuries were "aliens not subject to foreign protection." Realizing that, in some respects, he was thus interfering in the inner affairs of another country, Hay argued American self-interest.

> Putting together the facts [he declared] now painfully brought home to this Government, during the past few years, that many of the inhabitants of Roumania are being forced by artificially adverse discriminations to quit their native country; that the hospitable asylum offered by this country is almost the only refuge left to them; that they come hither unfitted by the conditions of their exile to take part in the new life of this land under circumstances either profitable to themselves or beneficial to the community, and that they are objects of charity from the outset and for a long time—the right of remonstrance against the acts of the Roumanian Government is clearly established in favor of this Government. Whether consciously and of purpose or not, these helpless people, burdened and spurned by their native land, are forced by the sovereign power of Roumania upon the charity of the United States. This Government cannot be a tacit party to such an international wrong.[73]

These exertions remained without noticeable effect. Similarly, eleven years later, after the conclusion of the Balkan Wars which had resulted in the transfer of about a quarter million Turkish Jews to Rumania and her allies, the American government unsuccessfully tried to secure from the peace conference guarantees for the equality of all citizens in these areas. The American minister in Bucharest received only verbal assurances from the Rumanian government that "the Jewish inhabitants of the territory about to be transferred to Rumanian sovereignty will be accorded the same rights and privileges as are given to persons of other races and religions." Rumania lived up to that pledge as little as to her obligations under Article XLIV. In fact, in that very year 1913, Rumania's Minister of Interior, Take Jonescu, performed some juridical acrobatics to prove that, with the recognition of Rumania's independence, the provisions of the Treaty of Berlin had ceased to be part of international law. "The question of the Jews in Rumania became a question of internal law." The Rumanian government unwaveringly continued its discriminatory policy also after the Senate and the House of the United States had passed a resolution on October 10, 1913, asking the signatory powers of the Treaty of Berlin to "compel Rumania to observe the stipulations" of that Treaty with respect to Jews.[74]

Even more protracted were the American intercessions in Russia. Here no international treaty could be invoked, nor was Russia expected to be amenable to purely humanitarian appeals. The main controversy raged, therefore, about the interpretation of the pertinent clauses in the Commercial Treaty between Russia and the United States concluded in 1832 by the American Minister, James Buchanan, and Russia's Chancellor, Count Charles Robert Nesselrode. The first article of that treaty guaranteed reciprocal liberty of commerce and navigation and the free entry of the inhabitants of both states. The latter were to enjoy "the same security and protection as natives of the country where they reside, on condition of their submitting to the laws and ordinances there prevailing."[75]

Clearly, neither Buchanan nor Nesselrode had in mind the exclusion of Jews from such equal treatment. But in time complications arose when Russian Jews naturalized in the United States tried to revisit their native land. Basically, there was the same difference in interpretation of the doctrine of reciprocity which bedeviled the American relations with Switzerland. According to the United States' view, there could be no legal distinctions in the rights enjoyed by American citizens abroad according to their religious persuasion. The Russians, on the other hand, contended that the American Jews were subject to the same laws as their Russian coreligionists, this being the meaning of the aforementioned "condition of their submitting to the laws and ordinances there prevailing." Russia adhered to that interpretation even after she had negotiated new commercial treaties with France, Austria, and Germany in 1904-1905, which had specifically provided, to quote the German Treaty, that the terms were applicable also to "German commercial travelers of the Hebrew faith." In fact, as the controversy continued unabated, from 1864 on, Russia's attitude hardened. She advanced the additional arguments that many naturalized American citizens had failed, before their naturalization, to fulfill their military duties in the Tsarist Empire, and that, by giving up their Russian citizenship without special permission from the Russian government they had all committed an unlawful act. Hence they could not be readmitted without a special permit from the Tsarist administration. In fact, the Russians sometimes refused admission also to Catholic priests and Protestant missionaries. Ultimately, the Russian Foreign Office actually suggested that, to avoid future embarrassment, the American government not issue passports to Jews intending to travel to Russia. While most American administrations sharply repudiated the implied suggestion that they inquire about the faith of applicants for passports, no lesser an international jurist than Elihu Root, while serving as Secretary of State, sent on May 28, 1907 a circular letter to Russian natives applying for passports, stating that "this Department will not issue passports to former Russian subjects or to Jews who intend going to Russian territory, unless it has assurance that the Russian Government will consent to their admission." This inconsistency was speedily remedied, however, when on Louis Marshall and Edward Lauterbach's objections, the text was amended to their satisfaction.[76]

Few new arguments were added to the course of the three decades since July 29, 1881, when Secretary of State James G. Blaine had eloquently and persuasively stated the American position in his dispatch to the American minister in St. Petersburg, John W. Foster, who was later to succeed him in the Department of State. But behind these legal subtleties there loomed a fundamental difference between the increasingly anti-Jewish Russian regime and the democratic convictions of the various American administrations, both Republican and Democratic. This was the period of the recurrent Russian pogroms which, as was suspected at that time and fully confirmed by documents from the Russian secret archives after the Revolution of 1917, had been instigated by the Russian government itself. Moreover, it was the period when

Count Vladimir Nikolaevich Lamsdorf, Russia's Minister of Foreign Affairs, tried to persuade the Tsar that the Revolution of 1905 had been "actively supported and partly directed by the forces of universal Jewry," led by the Alliance Israélite in Paris, "which possesses gigantic pecuniary means, disposes of an enormous membership and is supported by Masonic lodges of every description." The count suggested a confidential exchange of views with both the Kaiser and the Pope, in order to organize joint supervision and, ultimately, an active struggle against this common foe of Christianity and the monarchical order. Lamsdorf must have resented particularly the power of the American Jewish bankers, especially Jacob H. Schiff who, in retaliation for the governmental maltreatment of Russian Jewry, was instrumental in securing large loans for Japan in America and thus helped that upsurging Asiatic country to win the Russo-Japanese War. In a letter to Lord Nathaniel Meyer Rothschild of April 4-5, 1904, Schiff had indeed boasted, "I pride myself that all the efforts, which at various times during the past four or five years have been made by Russia to gain the favor of American markets for its loans, I have been able to bring to naught." Lamsdorf doubtless also knew that, despite their own class interests, the western Jewish bankers were in favor of a revolution in Russia and hence were even sympathetic to that country's socialist movements.[77]

Under these circumstances, any concession to the American demands for more liberal treatment of former Russian Jews would have entailed, in the Russian statesmen's opinion, not only loss of prestige but also a departure from their basic objective of harassing Jews so that they more speedily leave the country. Of course, as in all other areas of Russia's public life, individual exceptions were frequently made, particularly in favor of wealthy or well-connected businessmen who knew how to scale bureaucratic barriers. But, in principle, the government unwaveringly adhered to its interpretation and it consistently rejected the United States' reiterated suggestions that a new treaty replace the outworn instrument of 1832.

On the American side, too, the issue was viewed from broader perspectives. Secretary Blaine betrayed his deeper involvement in this matter when, on November 22, 1881, he instructed James Russell Lowell, the American minister at the Court of St. James, to explore with the British government the possibility of some international action to improve the conditions of Russian Jewry, native as well as foreign. "He felt that it would be a terrible thing to behold a return of the Ghetto of the Middle Ages, and hoped to initiate a movement which might also include other powers and which would influence Russia to ameliorate the condition of the Jews." Jewish leadership, too, entertained more far-reaching hopes, particularly in view of the effect upon Switzerland of its yielding to foreign pressures. Jacob H. Schiff spelled out this hope in his letter to Adolph S. Ochs, the publisher of the *New York Times*: "The moment Russia is compelled to live up to its treaties and admit the foreign Jew into its dominion upon a basis of equality with other citizens of foreign countries, the Russian government will not be able to maintain the Pale of Settlement against its own Jews."[78] These were, of course, but pious wishes which were to be realized only under the entirely altered conditions of the First World War and the two Russian Revolutions of 1917.

American public opinion became ever more deeply agitated. During the presidential elections of 1904 and 1908, both the Republican and the Democratic parties included in their platforms pledges to work toward "the removal of these unjust discriminations." In his acceptance speech as Republican candidate, William Howard Taft, promised that a Republican administration, if elected, would "continue to make every proper endeavor to secure the abolition of such distinctions which, in our eyes, are both needless and opprobrious." As President, Taft soon held conferences in 1909 and 1910 with Judge Mayer Sulzberger, Jacob H. Schiff, and Cyrus Adler as representatives of the American Jewish Committee. Despairing of Russia's willingness to modify the provisions of the earlier treaty, Jewish leadership now launched a campaign for its termination. The opening shot was fired by Louis Marshall in a closely reasoned and well-documented ad-

dress delivered before the Union of American Hebrew Congregations on January 19, 1911. As a result, resolutions to this effect
were introduced in both Houses of Congress. After its Committee
on Foreign Affairs had held public hearings in February and December, 1911 (these hearings assembled documentation frequently
alluded to here) the House passed, on December 13, 1911, with
a vote of 300 to 1 a resolution that the treaty "ought to be terminated at the earliest possible time." The Senate followed suit.
Since Russia remained adamant, the American ambassador in St.
Petersburg was ordered to give notice to the Russian government
that, in accordance with Article XII of the Treaty of 1832, the
United States declared its abrogation to take affect on January
1, 1913. This cancellation was approved by the three party conventions before the election of 1912, including that of the Progressive Party which nominated Theodore Roosevelt, and went into
effect on the stated date. As a result, the American Treasury
Department withdrew the minimum tariff accorded, under the
most favored nation clause, to Russian imports, particularly wood,
pulp, and paper. Of course, the American exports to Russia likewise suffered. But even American Big Business, which at that time
exerted considerable political influence, submitted more or less
graciously to the will of the aroused public. This acceptance was
the more remarkable as European opinion even in France and
England, then influenced by the Entente with Russia, largely
repudiated the American position.[79]

Less dramatic, but in the long run equally significant, were the
American government's exertions in behalf of the Jews of Persia,
Morocco, and the Ottoman Empire, including Palestine. In Persia
it was particularly a riot in Hamadan occasioned by a Jewish convert to Christianity having taken refuge in the house of an American missionary in 1894 that called forth the intervention of
Vice-Consul General, John Tyler. The masses had evidently been
aroused by fanatical Muslim preachers who adhered to the old
Islamic law, promising protection to Jews and Christians provided
they remained in their ancestral faiths. The Persian government
actually welcomed the American intervention which reinforced

its own resistance to the preachers. In Morocco United States representatives, working together with Levi A. Cohen, sent there by the Board of Delegates of American Israelites, sought to ameliorate the general conditions of oppressed Jewry in 1880-81. In 1906, during the international conference at Algeciras, Spain, devoted to the political future of Morocco, Elihu Root instructed the American delegation to investigate the restrictions upon Moroccan Jews reported to him by Jacob Schiff. The Secretary expected that the powers assembled at Algeciras would recommend the amelioration of these conditions. Curiously, the secretary of the American delegation, Lewis Einstein, at that time serving as assistant secretary of the American Embassy in London, tried to lean backward and in his report asserted that "Moroccan Jews stand today in no need of a special solicitude." But he was overruled by the head of the delegation, Henry White, American ambassador in Rome, who offered a pertinent motion. The Conference as a whole went no further than to secure from the Sultan's delegate the declaration that the ruler "would be happy to keep up the system inaugurated by his father by treating the Jews with fairness."[80]

The Turkish-Palestinian issues were far more complicated. On the one hand, the usual humanitarian considerations had, as early as 1840, aroused the interest of the American public in the victims of the Damascus Blood Accusation. Refugees streaming from Russia to Constantinople and other parts of the Ottoman Empire became objects of solicitude on the part of the American envoys as when Laurence Oliphant, acting as agent of the Mansion House Fund in 1882, acquainted General Lewis Wallace, author of *Ben Hur*, then serving as American minister to Constantinople, with their pitiful situation. Of more direct American concern was the condition of American Jewish citizens residing in Palestine. While other Jewish groups found ready support from the *ḥalukkah* represented by their national *kollelim* (relief centers), American Jews had no such agency of their own, although funds had long been collected in the United States for general Palestine relief. On more than one occasion American consuls in Jerusalem had to report home about the miserable conditions of their compatriots and appeal for help to American Jews. Matters were more complicated insofar as many of these "American" Jews had been natives of Russia who, after a relatively brief sojourn in the United States, had acquired American citizenship and subsequently settled in the Holy Land.[81]

Nor was the Turkish government very cooperative; it was concerned about the constant rise of Zionist tendencies in Europe and the United States long before the first Zionist Congress of 1897. Certainly, the Ottoman suspicions of a movement, which was aimed at wresting from it control over a province so strategically located as Palestine, were not allayed by such moves as those initiated by American Christians in 1891. Led by Rev. William E. Blackstone, many of their leaders submitted on March 5, 1891, a petition to President Benjamin Harrison, asking for major steps to counteract the persecution of the Russian Jews.

> *Why not give [they asked] Palestine back to them [the Jews] again? According to God's distribution of nations it is their home —an inalienable possession from which they were expelled by force. . . . Why shall not the powers which under the treaty of Berlin, in 1878, gave Bulgaria to the Bulgarians and Servia to the Servians, now give Palestine back to the Jews? . . . We believe this is an appropriate time for all nations, and especially the Christian nations of Europe, to show kindness to Israel. A million of exiles, by their terrible sufferings, are piteously appealing to our sympathy, justice and humanity. Let us now restore to them the land of which they were so cruelly despoiled by our Roman ancestors.*

The petitioners suggested that the President ask Queen Victoria, William II, the tsar, the pope, and other European potentates to convoke an international conference for the purpose of securing Palestine for the Jews. This petition carried the more weight, as its signatories included the Chief Justice of the United States Melville W. Fuller, Speaker of the House Thomas B. Reed, the later President William McKinley, Cardinal Gibbons, the leading financiers John Pierpont Morgan and John D. Rockefeller, the outstanding social worker Russell Sage, and many others.[82] The Turkish government reacted to this threat to its sovereignty by limiting the admission of Jewish pilgrims to a period of one and, later, to three months and by prohibiting Jews from acquiring real estate of any kind.

Of course, these discriminatory laws affected some American Jews as well. This situation understandably led to many protracted, if not very fruitful, negotiations. It happened that in that period Oscar S. Straus served as American minister in Constantinople and, with redoubled zest, intervened with the Porte against the new regulations. The Ottoman administration has gone so far as to suggest that foreign governments issuing passports to would-be Jewish pilgrims should certify that the latter were "going to Jerusalem in the performance of a pilgrimage and not for the purpose of engaging in commerce or taking up residence there." Only passports provided with such a certificate would be granted a Turkish visa. Learning of this suggestion, Secretary Bayard instructed Straus on March 5, 1888, to inform the authorities of the Porte that a certificate of this kind "would be utterly repugnant to the spirit of our institutions and to the intent of the solemn proscription forever by the Constitution of any religious test as a qualification of the relations of the citizen to the Government." To illustrate that position Bayard sent Straus a copy of his aforementioned note to Baron Schaeffer in regard to the Keiley appointment. The prohibition for foreign citizens to acquire land was likewise brought to the attention of the American government; this time by an injured party, Hyman J. Roos, who owned some real estate in Jerusalem, but could not sell it. Failing to obtain relief from the American Consul because of an agreement of 1847 between the two governments which had placed all land transactions outside the consul's jurisdiction, Roos appealed directly in 1893 to the Secretary of State W. Q. Gresham. After some negotiations, Roos secured permission to sell his property, the Turkish authorities claiming that they had merely wished to prevent land speculation. On one occasion, Saïd Pasha, the Turkish

Minister of Foreign Affairs, even tried to play on the Christian feelings of the American minister, A. W. Terrell, by telling him, "We believe that Jesus Christ was a great prophet, and if the Jews get control of Jerusalem they will steal the sepulchre of Christ and destroy everything that can remind people of him." This spurious argument impressed neither the minister nor Gresham, who insisted upon the rights of American Jews to visit Palestine for more than ninety days. In 1901, John Hay likewise roundly refused any American cooperation in helping the Turkish authorities to deport Jews who had overstayed their term.[83]

All these were but preliminary skirmishes. Not long thereafter the battle royal was fought by the Allies against the Ottoman Empire during the First World War which led to the British occupation of Palestine and the establishment of the Mandate.

Reviewing the entire series of American interventions, we may indeed agree in retrospect with John W. Foster when, on December 30, 1880, he reported home his conversation with Russia's Foreign Minister N. K. de Giers. In this exchange the American minister observed,

> That while the object of the interview was to obtain proper recognition of the rights of American Jews, my Government took a deep interest in the amelioration of the condition of the Jewish race in other nations, and I was satisfied that it would be highly gratified at the statement of the Minister that a commission was now considering the question of the modification in a liberal sense of the Russian laws regarding the Jews. The experience of the United States had amply shown the wisdom of removing all discriminations against them in the laws, and of placing this race upon an equal footing with all other citizens.[84]

Apart from outright diplomatic interventions, the reaction of American public opinion in favor of oppressed Jews abroad carried considerable weight. The Russian persecutions, in particular, evoked the more responsive an echo in the United States, as the Russian Jewish population itself had increased there by leaps and bounds and as the anti-immigration forces were raising a hue and cry about the dangers arising from Russia's policies for the American society. Even those favoring restricted immigration viewed with horror the reported Russian atrocities against Jews; some of them not so much for humanitarian reasons as out of the realization that each pogrom increased the pressure on the United States to admit Jewish refugees. That is why the Kishinev pogrom of 1903, coming at the height of the Russian immigration, evoked an almost unanimous sharp condemnation of the Tsarist government. The mass meetings held in various cities, editorials and letters to editors appearing in papers, large and small, throughout the country, and sermons by preachers of various denominations sounded in unison the outraged "voice of America." The B'nai B'rith had no difficulty in assembling a vast number of signatures to a petition which was to be presented to the Tsarist government. The American Minister, Robert S. McCormick, to be sure, was at first hoodwinked by the Russian authorities. In reply to an inquiry by Secretary of State John Hay, concerning the need of financial aid and supplies to be sent to the sufferers, he wired on May 9, 1903, that it was "authoritatively denied that there is any want or suffering among Jews in Southwestern Russia and aid of any kind is unnecessary." Not surprisingly, when he later wished to transmit to the Russian government the American petition couched in very moderate terms, the Russian Foreign Office refused to accept it. Yet on this occasion the American government as such declined to take a stand, although Simon Wolf had doubtless argued in Washington, as he did in his letter to a protest meeting in Baltimore on May 17, 1903, that "it is high time that it behooves them [our government and the American people] to take active part in bringing about reforms in Russia to prevent these outrages and inhumanities, for every outbreak in Russia swells the army of refugees that will inundate our country, making it so much harder not only upon the victims, but upon those who by kinship are compelled to care for them on their arrival." True, Wolf supported this suggestion by reference to the principles enunciated in John Hay's aforementioned note to Rumania of 1902. But Russia was not Rumania. Apart from the absence of treaty obligations like those assumed by Rumania at the Congress of Berlin, Russia was a great power. The American government considered it, therefore, a better part of wisdom not to intervene directly. It merely allowed public opinion to exert whatever pressure it could on the recalcitrant Tsarist ministers, some of whom, like the later Finance Minister Count Serge Witte, fully realized the damage caused by such acts of barbarism against Jews to both Russia's economy and prestige.[85]

Even less direct was the American government's involvement in the Dreyfus Affair in France. At first, in 1895-96, the American public, too, took in its stride the condemnation of an unknown French captain for espionage, but it reacted ever more sharply when the miscarriage of justice became increasingly evident. It is truly remarkable, comments Rose A. Halpern, that despite the deep preoccupation with the turbulent developments at home, "when the Dreyfus Case came to the forefront, the American people were just as keenly interested as if it directly concerned them." It was especially Emile Zola's *J'accuse* and the ensuing trial of the famous novelist which deeply stirred the American public. Only a segment of the Catholic press took the side of the Boulangists and the other assailants of the French Republic. The *Church Progress* of March 5, 1898 wrote menacingly:

> The peculiar interest that the Jewish papers, even in this country, have been taking in the Zola trial and the amount of sympathy they have displayed with the malodorous novelist and the convicted spy whom he championed, tend to confirm certain charges that have been going the rounds. . . .

On the other hand, several Catholic bishops and many laymen favored a new trial for Dreyfus. Some Jews and their friends agitated for a boycott of French goods. Rumor had it that, in 1899, Senator Stewart of Nevada planned to introduce a resolution in the Senate asking for the withdrawal of the United States from the forthcoming Paris Exhibition. This agitation was cut short, however, when the French government extended a pardon to Captain Dreyfus and the latter accepted it.[86]

Community Life

Meeting its increasing responsibilities, the American Jewish community established ever new institutions and devised new methods of cooperation. From the outset it differed from most European communities inasmuch as its control over its members was entirely voluntary. At no time did it enjoy the backing of public law and possess the power of enforced taxation, such as was the rule in European lands down to the twentieth century. In fact, at first, after its entry to New York in 1654, American Jewry had to fight every inch of its way when it wished to build a synagogue or establish a cemetery, the two institutions which were taken for granted in Europe wherever Jews were tolerated at all. Less unusual, except for its being spelled out, had been the obligation assumed by the first Jewish arrivals on the American soil to take care of their own poor. This voluntary nature of the community was reemphasized after the rise of the United States and its constitutional provisions for the separation of state and Church, which ruled out any governmentally backed legal enforcement of the communal will. Yet American Jewry, like the other religious denominations, demonstrated to the world that religious life could prosper without governmental buttresses. What in 1837 so greatly impressed a European visitor, Harriet Martineau, was even more true of Judaism than of Christianity. "The event," she wrote, "has fully justified the confidence of those who have faith enough in Christianity to see that it needs no protection from the state, but will commend itself to human hearts better without."[87]

In the Jewish case, to be sure, this freedom was in danger of being abused. The endless proliferation of organizations in the period here under review threatened to submerge all organized forms of Jewish life in total anarchy. Until the synagogues began splitting up in Philadelphia in 1802 along Sephardic or Ashkenazic ritualistic lines, and until B'nai Jeshurun, because of internal dissensions, broke away from Shearith Israel in New York in 1825, all communal activities were grouped around the synagogue. Soon

thereafter there emerged not only a number of rivaling congregations but also some new, wholly independent organizations which
caused the synagogue to drop to a position of but one of many
communal institutions. In 1878, we recall, a letter writer observed
"that of the large number of Jews in this city [New York] only
a small percent joined regular constituted synagogues" because of
the high fees charged for synagogue membership and the sudden
changes in ritual then characteristic of the militant Reform movement. There also was little inducement, he claimed, for joining
a congregation, since "mutual benefit societies provide[d] burial
grounds and funeral expenses, besides other benefits, and cost less,"
and rabbis could easily be secured to officiate at weddings for
small fees. The only tangible benefit, therefore, derived from
congregational membership consisted in Sunday Schools for the
children of members. This declining role of the synagogue exerted
a debilitating influence on Jewish community life as a whole; the
more so because outwardly the Jewish people constituted but one
of America's numerous religious denominations and its synagogue
continued to be regarded by the non-Jewish world as its focal
communal institution. Many synagogues, moreover, particularly
outside New York, were the main instrumentality for the collection of charitable dues. Describing the religious activities in Chicago at the beginning of the twentieth century, an informed
observer claimed that almost all charitable organizations in the
West Side, where most new immigrants had settled, could trace
their origin to the congregation Ohave Sholom Mariampol,
founded in 1872. Subsequently, too, all the West Side synagogues
contributed their share to the upkeep of the charitable activities
by taxing their members.

> In addition to synagogue dues there are dues for the *Talmud
> Torah* (Hebrew Free School); the *Hachnosis Orchim* (Shelter for
> strangers); the *Beth Moshav Zkeinim* (Home for the Aged); the
> *Lechem L'rovim* (Bread for the Hungry); the *Gomley Chesed
> Shel Emeth* (Association for the Free Burial of the Poor); the
> free loan associations which loan money to those in need and

charge no interest; the yeshibahs or strictly orthodox advanced schools of Jewish learning in this city and in Russia; the Palestine chaluka or charity for indigent Jews of the Holy Land. Before Pesach, or Passover, a fund is raised to supply the poor with matzoth (Passover cakes) and other necessaries, and when winter sets in coal is given to poor families.[88]

Under the accelerating tempo of immigration at the end of the century communal differentation progressed rapidly. Each group of immigrants brought with it different habits and outlooks, even different synagogue rituals and Hebrew or Yiddish dialectal varieties. The simultaneous rise of the Reform Movement which, while revealing numerous internal variations in that period of its greatest creativity, was in sharp conflict with all traditional forms of Jewish life, be they Sephardic, German, or East-European, likewise militated against any effort to unify the communal activities around a religious core. At the same time the need for charitable support of the incoming masses and their economic and cultural adjustment became so overwhelming that most communal energies had to be expended on these noncontroversial tasks. Regardless of their national origins and religio-cultural orientation all Jews could readily cooperate on alleviating the misery of the old, sick, and the orphans, or of the newly arrived immigrants. Thus philanthropies assumed a more focal position in the American community than in any other country of Jewish settlement, although far-reaching communal responsibility for social welfare had long featured much of the people's communal history. This situation led to the growth of a ramified communal structure, which was both quantitatively and qualitatively unprecedented.[89]

Not surprisingly, the plethora of existing organizations led to frequent duplication of effort and, ultimately, in some areas to totally chaotic conditions. In the sphere of philanthropic endeavor, which generally appeared least controversial, the best remedy was offered, as we shall presently see, in the "federation movement" which unified endeavors on the local scene and in the end achieved significant results on the national scale as well. It was far more difficult to unify the defense and community relations agencies, often split along ideological and social lines. But this became a major communal problem only after 1914.[90]

Outstanding among the relief organizations was that called the United Hebrew Charities in New York. It had arisen in 1874, at an inauspicious moment because of the panic of the preceding year, from a merger of the old Hebrew Benevolent Society organized in New York in 1822 and the German Hebrew Benevolent Society, established in opposition thereto by the German immigrants in 1844. Yet in the very first fiscal year it raised the substantial sum of $37,007 owing to its active board, headed by Henry Rice who served as president until 1908. When the large influx of East-European immigrants in the 1880s started to overtax even the United's resources (in the single year from 1882 to 1883 new applications rose by 53 percent to 4,955 and the expenditures by 64 percent to $9,000), some of its leaders feared the total diversion of its funds from the long-established local needs and warned that their Society's functions were "to care for the needy of New York City and not of the world." It actually sent protests to the European leaders against their alleged promotion of an indiscriminate immigration. Yet it could not evade the issue, particularly when the specially organized Hebrew Immigrant Aid Society suspended its activities after but fifteen months (in March 1883). Before long the United Hebrew Charities had a permanent agent at the port of entry, established a temporary shelter for the newcomers, and bent every effort to help them to move to other American cities. The growth of the latter activity is well illustrated by the number of railroad tickets it distributed which grew from 300 in 1882 to 4,030 ten years later. At the same time it had to assist a great many persons who remained in New York and could not find employment; in 1896 no less than 8,000 unemployed Jews received aid from the society. It also helped establish a home for chronic invalids, formed the first visiting nurses service, founded a legal aid society and, in 1890, brought into being a special Russian Refugee Committee. Data for 1904-1905 show that among its 10,015 applicants nearly a third (3,229) sought relief because of illness. The next largest group (2,050) came from women having no male support. Lack of work and insufficient earnings represented a total of 2,422 cases. Old age was advanced by only 471 applicants, whereas 360 requested aid for transportation. There were also quite a few cases arising from insanity, intemperance, or imprisonment of a family's chief wage earner—170 cases in all. These needs were constantly increasing in the subsequent years to the outbreak of the First World War.[91]

Philanthropic societies of this kind existed in many other communities. In fact, quite early Jewish and non-Jewish leaders realized that the great concentration of immigrants on the Eastern Seaboard created many problems not only to themselves but also to American society at large. The organization, under the auspices of the Baron de Hirsch Fund, of the Jewish Agricultural and Industrial Aid Society in 1900 was in part prompted by the expectation that it would help remove some Jews from the congested eastern centers. As an outgrowth of that Society the Industrial Removal Office was organized in 1901 to cooperate with the B'nai B'rith and other groups in settling new arrivals throughout the country. Nearly 2,000 persons were relocated to 250 places at an average per capita cost of $12.50 during the first year. In the following year the Office added the "Ellis Island" experiment whereby immigrants were met at the New York harbor by persuasive agents, including a well-known rabbinical orator, who tried to induce them to proceed westward immediately. Difficulties, particularly with the Chicago branch, soon convinced the leaders, however, that they had to be more selective in sending to other cities only those immigrants holding out the promise of becoming self-supporting. As a result of the financial crisis of 1907, moreover, the work suffered severely, and in 1909 fewer persons were removed than in any previous year since 1902. Nevertheless, the organization continued to function and, in 1912, no less than 6,000 persons were removed from New York, the majority of whom had lived there three years or more. In all, some 100,000 persons, or nearly 7 percent of all new Jewish arrivals, were "removed" between 1901 and 1914.[92]

An important variant was the so-called Galveston Movement. The initial suggestion had come from Frank Pierce Sargent, United States Commissioner-General of Immigration, to Jacob H. Schiff. At the same time Israel Zangwill, who had broken away from the World Zionist Organization and founded the Jewish Territorial Organization, became amenable to helping promote among the prospective émigrés from Europe the idea of settling in diverse parts of the United States. On August 24, 1906, Schiff wrote to Zangwill,

> It appears to me that in this existing emergency the Jewish Territorial Organization, if for the time being it will occupy itself with something which is immediately practicable and sidetrack its cherished project of finding a separate land of refuge where the Jew can live under autonomous conditions, can be of very great service to the momentous and pressing cause which we all have very much at heart.

Schiff proceeded with the organization of a Jewish Immigrants Information Bureau and donated $500,000 to start the work. After mature consideration, Galveston, Texas, was selected as the best port of entry from which Jews could readily and inexpensively be sent north and northwest to the sparsely populated Jewish communities of the western United States. As director of the Bureau in Galveston, Morris D. Waldman enjoyed the full cooperation of the local rabbi, Henry Cohen. The work was inaugurated with great éclat and the news of the arrival of the first group of immigrants in July 1907 was given world-wide circulation. The group was officially welcomed by the Mayor of Galveston, one of the new arrivals replying, "the Mayors of our [Russian] cities would take absolutely no notice of us or of any people of our station. . . . There may be a time when the American people will need us, and then we will serve them with our blood!" These grandiloquent gestures could not conceal the inherent difficulties, however. Many immigrants were reluctant to go into what they considered the American wilderness, where they could not expect Yiddish-speaking friends to greet them. There also was growing resistance on the part of American labor which had suffered much unemployment in the wake of the crisis of 1907. Under its pressure, the government likewise changed its mind. Originally, Theodore Roosevelt had welcomed the opening of "a new door to immigration into the United States." But in 1910 Secretary of Labor Charles Nagel contended that, because the Society and its allied organizations were defraying the transportation costs and placing the new arrivals in prepared jobs, they were violating the Federal contract labor laws. While the first rejections of some newcomers by a special Board of Inquiry were overruled on appeal, a shipload of one hundred immigrants was refused admission in August 1910. Nonetheless, by December 1912, some 5,000 immigrants had passed through Galveston at the average cost of some $30 to the Bureau. Yet sharp criticisms continued to be voiced also in the Yiddish press until the outbreak of the First World War which put an end to the entire experiment.[93]

Many other Jewish charitable organizations and institutions, such as hospitals, orphanages, homes for the aged, likewise spread rapidly throughout the United States. The first Jewish hospital was established in New York in 1852. Renamed in 1866 the Mount Sinai Hospital, it gradually developed into a major center of medical training as well. In 1884 followed the Montefiore Hospital for Chronic Diseases which was extolled later by the New York City Commissioner of Hospitals as "a pioneer in the scientific treatment" of these diseases. Several other Jewish hospitals in New York and other cities, including the Michael Reese in Chicago, Beth Israel in Boston, Mount Sinai in Cleveland, likewise achieved an international reputation. In view of the then wide prevalence of tuberculosis the National Jewish Hospital and the Jewish Consumptives' Relief Society were established at Denver, Colorado, in 1899 and 1904, respectively. Like most other Jewish hospitals, these Denver institutions, though supported by Jewish funds, were also open to non-Jewish patients who, in more recent times, outnumbered the Jewish. Insofar as they served kosher food, however, they were particularly useful to stricken orthodox Jews. In periods of anti-Jewish discrimination, young

Jewish doctors also found the facilities of Jewish hospitals of considerable assistance in securing internships, residencies, and other
opportunities for specialized research.[94]

We can merely mention here in passing the numerous other
benevolent societies and institutions established in the various
Jewish communities. Before long their number became so great
as to cause much duplication of effort and incessant competition
for funds. Contributors often tired of the innumerable appeals
from Jewish as well as general charities.[95]

Understandably, there gradually grew a movement to combine
these efforts which often were both costly and inefficient. To be
sure, many organizations and their boards of directors were jealous
about preserving their complete independence. They also feared
that any central fund-raising organization possessing the power of
the purse would ultimately try to dictate their policies. Others expressed apprehensions that donors interested only in a particular
charity would fail to contribute to a general fund even if assured
that donations could be earmarked for special purposes. More
convincingly, the opponents argued that wealthy contributors who
had therefore yielded to entreaties by various friends interested
in many societies would contribute lesser lump sums to a federation. Nevertheless the need of pooling resources became so imperative that, beginning with Boston in 1895 and Cincinnati in
1896, federations began spreading throughout the country. Not
surprisingly, the greatest resistance was offered by the multifarious
charitable groups in New York. None the less, in 1917 ninety-one
organizations banded together to establish the New York Federation of Jewish Philanthropies. The federation movement thus
came to full fruition only during the period of consolidation following the cessation of the mass immigration after 1914.[96]

Fraternal Groups

A host of other groups met a variety of other social needs. The
United States had long been a "nation of joiners" with a "passion
for associational activity [which] became a sovereign principle of

life." The well-known humorist, Will Rogers, was to quip later that "two Americans can't meet on the street without one banging the gavel and calling the other to order." Jews, too, found it convenient to form all kinds of social and cultural associations. We recall that, as early as 1761, seven Jewish families living in Newport, Rhode Island, had organized a purely social club in which any discussions of synagogue affairs was strictly forbidden.[97] As immigration increased in the nineteenth century, and the differentiation of Jewish life in speech, mores, and religious outlooks rapidly progressed, the need for such voluntary clubs grew in geometric progression. The German immigration of the mid-century, particularly, which included many freethinkers unwilling to seek the satisfaction of their social needs in the synagogue, stimulated the quest for new forms.

A major fraternal group which emerged during that period was the Independent Order of B'nai B'rith, founded in 1843 by Henry Jones and eleven German Jewish associates in New York. According to its constitution,

> B'nai B'rith has taken upon itself the mission of uniting Israelites in the work of promoting their highest interests and those of humanity; of developing and elevating the mental and moral character of the people of our faith; of inculcating the purest principles of philanthropy, honor and patriotism; of supporting science and art; alleviating the wants of the poor and needy; visiting and attending the sick; coming to the rescue of the victims of persecution; providing for, protecting and assisting the widow and orphan on the broadest principles of humanity.

A quarter century later the Order numbered more than 20,000 members under six Grand Lodges in New York, Cincinnati, Philadelphia, San Francisco, Baltimore, and Chicago. It then underwent a reorganization under the leadership of Julius Bien of New York, who served as President from 1868 to 1900. He was succeeded by Leo N. Levi of New York (1900-1904), Simon Wolf (1904-1905), and Adolph Kraus (1905-25). By the end of the century the number of District Grand Lodges had increased to ten, including three abroad (Germany, Austria, and Rumania) which, beginning in 1882, had followed the American example.[98]

At first the Order had certain Masonic rituals. Like its Christian counterparts (not all of which admitted Jews to membership), it invested its proceedings with an aura of secrecy. In time, however, the secret rites were abandoned, partly because they exposed the Jews to suspicions by unfriendly neighbors of hatching some secret cabales in these mysterious assemblies. Many Jews must have felt, as Louis Marshall did in 1924 when he wrote, "I have always opposed Jewish secret organizations, and, I do not say because of my action, but in consonance with my views, the B'nai B'rith has gradually dropped all of its secret ceremonials." On the other hand, yielding to the preeminent pressures of philanthropic needs, the various District Lodges assumed more and more responsibility for supporting such major charitable institutions as orphan asylums in Cleveland, Atlanta, and New Orleans, a Home for the Aged in Yonkers, and the aforementioned National Jewish Hospital for Consumptives in Denver. Nor did the Order abstain from political action. As early as 1870 its Grand Sar, Benjamin F. Peixotto (1834-90), was appointed United States Consul in Bucharest, but since the United States' budget had made no provision for such a consular office, his expenses had to be defrayed by the B'nai B'rith for more than five years (Peixotto subsequently served as American consul in Lyons, France, in 1877-85 on the government payroll). B'nai B'rith also collaborated with the Board of Delegates of American Israelites and, later, with the Union of American Hebrew Congregations in various political intercessions, particularly in behalf of immigrants. By 1913, it organized its own Anti-Defamation League, designed to combat antisemitism in all its forms. This branch was soon put to severe tests because of the rise of anti-Jewish discriminatory practices and ideological attacks which reached heights of frenzy in the 1930s. To a lesser extent the Order also promoted cultural efforts. This phase, too, was to expand greatly after 1945.[99]

The B'nai B'rith was followed by various other lodges. Most important of these was the Order B'rith Abraham founded in 1859.

Because of internal dissensions, a new order calling itself Independent Order B'rith Abraham was formed in 1887 and, before long, outstripped the parent body. In 1913 these two orders claimed a membership of 73,000 and 182,000, respectively. Somewhat older was the Independent Order Free Sons of Israel, founded in 1849. In 1879 East-European arrivals, who felt discriminated against by the largely German oriented existing lodges, organized the Order of Sons of Benjamin which, within eleven years, grew to a membership of more then 12,000, forming 135 regular and 12 ladies' lodges. In the period here under review twenty-three new Orders were added. The largest among the new groups was the Independent Order Ahawas Israel which, though founded only in 1890, claimed twelve years later a (doubtless exaggerated) membership of more than 120,000, organized in 124 lodges. A more reasonable figure of 21,000 was quoted in 1913. There also were many splinter groups such as that bearing the picturesque Hebrew name *Kesher shel Barzel* (Link of Iron), founded in 1860, and regional orders such as the Independent Order Western Star, centered in Chicago since 1894. With the rise of the Zionist movement there also was room for a special Zionist lodge. Founded in 1908 by Judah L. Magnes and associates, it was named Order Sons of Zion. Several of its lodges subsequently conducted all their business in Hebrew. Most of these organizations published bulletins and other periodicals of their own.[100]

Even less is known about another form of social organization which, despite its ancient antecedents reaching back to the Roman Empire, assumed unprecedented scope and vigor in the United States. As immigrants arrived from various parts of Europe, they often banded together in *Landsmanschaften* where they could meet with like-minded members of their former communities for social, cultural, and religious purposes. Some of these *Landsmanschaften* maintained synagogues and cemeteries for their members, extended help to new arrivals, and even helped to get some of them out of their East-European domicile. Little was known about the number and membership of these organizations until 1938, when the Works Progress Administration of the American government sponsored, among many other intellectual make-work projects, one devoted to a survey of the variegated groups going under that name in New York City. To the surprise of even informed persons, it turned out that New York alone had at one time some 3,000 groups falling into this category. One of them, a Dutch society, dated back to 1859. Others, beginning in 1862, often assumed the Hebrew name *Anshe* (Men of) followed by the name of the locality from which the members had come. These were predominantly synagogue groups, no less than 290 still being counted in 1938, by which time their heyday had passed, their majority having been founded in the quarter century of climactic Jewish immigration of 1890-1914. Quite a few had gone out of existence before 1938. Not infrequently, the membership of a New York *Landsmanschaft* numerically exceeded the total number of Jews who had remained in the original *Shtetl*. In time, many organizations got together to form federations of Polish, Galician, Rumanian, or Hungarian Jews without, however, in any way giving up their autonomy. An interesting variant was the so-called family society uniting members of the same family; sometimes offspring of the same patriarchal couple which had first set foot on American soil. For the most part these family groups catered not only to the sociocultural needs of their members, but also provided joint cemetery plots which, under the anarchical conditions of the Jewish burial customs in many of America's metropolitan areas, were a decided boon to their members.[101]

Related to both the fraternal and city-of-origin groups were the various workmen's groups which also provided some occupational aids and counseling. The most important of these was the Jewish Workmen's Circle (Arbeiter Ring) which, after tentative beginnings reaching back to 1892, was incorporated in 1905. Permeated with a socialist ideology of the type represented by the Russian-Jewish *Bund*, this Circle grew rapidly both before and after the First World War. Its first president, Samuel Shapiro (1904-1905), had as his second successor the outstanding labor leader Joseph Weinberg (1908-1909) who intermittently occupied the presidency for many years after 1923. From 1911 on, the Circle published its own Yiddish monthly, *Der Fraind,* and other periodicals. In its activities it combined a variety of social, welfare, and cultural programs. It founded a special sanatorium for consumptives (1910), and a number of dwellings for workers, as well as many libraries and a publishing firm. To its members it offered lectures, concerts, and other cultural services. Its most important cultural contribution was, as we shall see, a ramified Yiddish school system which included grammar, secondary, music schools, and a teachers' seminary. In the 1920s no less than 7,000 children were enrolled in these schools, which then employed 120 teachers. Because of ideological differences, an independent Zionist group was formed in 1911 under the name of the Jewish National Workers Alliance. Among its early leaders was, in particular, the statistician and publicist, Isaac A. Hourwich (1860-1924).[102]

Quite early Jews organized also literary societies. The first was founded in Philadelphia in 1850 and bore the characteristic name, Young Men's Hebrew Literary Association, while the first American Young Men's Christian Association was not organized until December 1851. The need for such literary circles seems to have been keenly felt particularly among the German-Jewish immigrants, about whom, as previously stated, Francis Lieber had testified in 1869 that "the German Jews in America gain in influence daily, being rich, intelligent, and educated or at least seeking education. They read better books than the rest of the Germans, the booksellers tell me."[103]

Before long, the East-European Jewish immigrants likewise began making extensive use of the new societies, many of which went under the name of Young Men's (later also Young Women's) Hebrew Associations. The first institution of this type, founded in New York in 1874 under the presidency of Lewis May, had varying fortunes during the first twenty years of its existence. But it succeeded in establishing a "downtown" branch on the East Side, from which after 1891 gradually unfolded the important Educational Alliance with its memorable services for a multitude of immigrants. After its reorganization in 1897, however, the "Y," now actively supported by Jacob Schiff, began to prosper. Its new building on Lexington Avenue, erected in 1900, was soon equipped with a substantial library, a gymnasium, and an auditorium where lectures and regular evening classes were held. According to a report of 1905, 166,289 persons had attended the various programs during the preceding year. The New York "Y" was emulated in other cities, such as Philadelphia, New Orleans, St. Louis, and San Francisco. In fact, quite a few institutions of this type were established in smaller communities such as Savannah, Georgia; Nashville, Tenessee; Ft. Worth, Texas; and Milwaukee, Wisconsin. When this spontaneous growth and the general freedom of association threatened to submerge the movement in unrestrained anarchy some of its far-sighted leaders got together and organized, in 1913, the Council of Young Men's Hebrew and Kindred Associations. The Council was still in the throes of its initial experimentation, when the First World War intervened. Needs of the Jewish combatants led to the organization of the Jewish Welfare Board, into which the Council was soon merged. Thenceforth that Board assumed the main responsibility for the direction of the ever-expanding Jewish Center movement, while the individual organizations, whether retaining the old designations of "Y's" or called Community Centers and the like, retained full autonomy.[104]

An interesting variant of such sociocultural organizations were the Jewish academic fraternities and sororities which began developing in our period. As more and more Jewish students entered colleges and universities on a full-time basis, many began appreciating the benefits of membership in one or another of the Greek-letter fraternities. However, precisely because their numbers increased so rapidly, they found that many of these organizations shut their gates to them. Many bore a distinctive denominational character. It was natural, therefore, for the Jews, too, to conceive of special Jewish fraternities. The first professedly Jewish fraternity was Zeta Beta Tau, the Greek letters representing the abbreviation of *Zion Be-mishpaṭ Tippadeh* (Through Justice Shall Zion Be Redeemed; Isa. 1:27). The main protagonist of that organization, dating back to 1898, was Richard J. H. Gottheil (1862-1936),

Professor of Semitic Languages at Columbia University, who served as Nasi or Supreme President of the new fraternity in the years 1911-20. The first national Jewish sorority, the Iota Alpha Pi, was organized at Hunter College in New York in 1903. Chapters of these organizations spread throughout the country. Other fraternities, such as Pi Lambda Phi, established at Yale University in 1895, or Phi Epsilon Pi, founded at the College of the City of New York, started as nonsectarian groups, but before long had an exclusively Jewish membership. Other Jewish fraternities were organized along professional lines (medicine, law, and so forth). Within a quarter century there existed some thirty-six national Jewish college and professional fraternities with a membership of about 75,000 students.[105]

There was far less inducement for Jews to organize separate sportive associations, although many young Jews were attracted to the games and sports which dominated the American scene. Individual Jewish players distinguished themselves, indeed, in American baseball, college football, boxing, as well as in chess. However, there was little advantage for them to organize separate Jewish clubs, since there was very little, if any, discrimination in this field. "The truth is," observes a student of Jewish sports, "that Jewish players were so sought after that when Andy Cohen broke into the Giant [New York baseball club] lineup, national weeklies gave him a six-page spread and [Manager] John McGraw chortled happily. Managers sought Jewish players as though they were more valuable than diamonds." Only with the spread of the Zionist movement and the growing appreciation of "muscular Judaism" among Jewish youth came also the formation of some Jewish sport associations bearing for the most part the names of Maccabees or Hakoah. But this development essentially belongs to the period after 1914.[106]

American Jewish Committee and New York Kehillah

Progressive organizational diffusion made any concerted action increasingly difficult. Even in the relatively idyllic conditions of

the mid-nineteenth century, when a small number of congregations embraced the overwhelming majority of Jews, the need for
unification was strongly felt by such enlightened leaders as Isaac
Leeser and Isaac Mayer Wise. These leaders, even if they had
not themselves been ministers of the faith, could conceive of
such unity only in terms of a representative body uniting the
religious congregations. The very Board of Delegates of American
Israelites, formed in 1859 in response to the Mortara Affair principally for defense purposes, could be organized only through such
congregational cooperation. When in 1878, Wise finally succeeded
in organizing the Union of American Hebrew Congregations it
was fairly natural for the Board of Delegates to be merged into
the new organization.[107]

Before very long the growth of both Orthodoxy and secularism
in the American Jewish community removed whatever semblance
of unity had been given it by Wise's Union. The latter now became merely the exponent of Reform Judaism and, as such, the
representative of a minority even among religious Jews. The growth
of particular interests, demonstrated by the expansion of various
philanthropic and fraternal organizations, merely accentuated the
existing divisions. Some new national organizations, too, contributed to the further diversification of the community. For example,
the new National Council of Jewish Women was intended to
foster country-wide cooperation of Jewish women in response to
woman's generally growing public responsibilities and emancipa-
tory trends. In fact, the impetus to the organization was given by
the World Parliament of Religions held in Chicago in 1893, which
included a number of denominational congresses; among them,
one of Jewish women. The latter's chairman and secretary, Hannah G. Solomon and Sadie American, sounded the clarion call for
a permanent Council of Jewish Women which was finally organized in 1896. As defined in its constitution, its objectives were:

> To serve the best interests of Judaism, to bring about closer
> relations among Jewish women; to furnish, by an organic union,
> a medium of communication and a means of prosecuting work

of common interest; to further united efforts in behalf of the
work of social reform by the application of the best philanthropic
methods.

In these activities the women were to shun any affiliations with
either Orthodoxy or Reform. The Council's speedy progress was
attested by its third triennial meeting in 1902, when it already
embraced seventy sections with 7,000 members and fifteen junior
sections with 500 members. Like the B'nai B'rith it was speedily
emulated in other countries, beginning with an English group
founded in London in 1899.[108] But from the standpoint of American Jewry's unity its end effect was to increase further the existing
organizational diversity and to compound the difficulties of nation-
wide cooperation.

Once again it required some external stimuli to awaken the
feeling of urgency for uniting the scattered efforts. The Russian
pogroms of 1903 and 1905, combined with the effects of the
Russian Revolution upon the then largest Jewish community in
the world, demonstrated that necessity. Independently, such
rabbis as Judah Leon Magnes, Jacob Voorsanger, Henry Pereira
Mendes, as well as the Central Conference of American Rabbis
and the B'nai B'rith—all suggested action along similar lines.
Their activities were superseded, however, by a new group of lay
leaders who organized the American Jewish Committee. The idea
was originally broached in a private gathering of the "Wanderers,"
an informal group of friends who for some time had been meeting for intellectual exchanges in one another's homes. After some
preliminary discussions, Louis Marshall (1856-1929) issued, in
December 1905, invitations to a number of influential leaders,
both lay and rabbinic, throughout the country for a conference
which met in New York in February 1906 and launched the new
organization. Understandably, it had to overcome considerable
resistance from various quarters. Adolf Kraus, then President of
the B'nai B'rith, viewed it as a rival to his own organization. Others
resented the self-appointive character of the initial group and
demanded democratic election. Marshall conceded the validity

of the latter argument and declared in his letter to Henry S. Stix of January 16, 1907, "It is our design to ultimately make the movement democratic in every sense of the word, so that our successors will be elected by the Jewish communities, and the criticism that ours is a self-appointed committee will be without foundation." For the immediate future, however, he and his associates were convinced that direct elections by the far-flung membership of the various congregational and secular groups, or even a meeting of delegates dispatched by such groups would not only create a cumbersome machinery, but in any case would also result in the participation of but a small minority of American Jews. Under the existing conditions such a meeting might actually prove extremely harmful. As Marshall expressed it in a letter to Magnes in the following year, such a congress would merely open the gates to a flood of "indiscreet, hot-headed, and ill-considered oratory [which] might find its way into the headlines of the daily newspapers inflicting untold injury upon the Jewish cause." He also feared all sorts of half-baked sensational schemes which would attract public notice by their very eccentricity. Certainly the spokesmen of the then flourishing radical movements among American Jews, would not have hesitated to champion some extreme measures which could not possibly meet with the approval of the established wealthy leadership, and thus led to open dissension, rather than unity.[109]

Hence only fifty-eight persons were invited to the February 1906 meeting. After considerable discussion, which extended over several months, the Committee was organized. Judge Mayer Sulzberger (1843-1923) of Philadelphia, who at first hesitated to join any group other than a Russo-Jewish relief organization which might subsequently take up matters of wider concern, was won over to the cause and became the Committee's first president. But Louis Marshall remained its guiding spirit and, in 1912, he formally assumed the presidency, calling it his "principle and favorite office." In 1911, he secured for it a charter of incorporation from the legislature of the State of New York, in which the objectives of the corporation were defined as follows:

to prevent the infraction of the civil and religious rights of Jews, in any part of the world; to render all lawful assistance and to take appropriate remedial action in the event of threatened or actual invasion or restriction of such rights, or of unfavorable discrimination with respect thereto; to secure for Jews equality of economic, social and educational opportunity; to alleviate the consequences of persecution and to afford relief from calamities affecting Jews, wherever they may occur; and to compass these ends to administer any relief fund which shall come into its possession or which may be received by it, in trust or otherwise, for any of the aforesaid objects or for purposes comprehended therein.

Notwithstanding the refusal by Adolf Kraus and Rabbi Emil G. Hirsch to participate and the more vociferous objections raised by segments of the Yiddish press, the tangible achievements of the Committee, and especially its success in securing the abrogation of the American treaty with Russia, gradually silenced most of the opposition. Only the great new complications arising from the First World War revived the demands for a more democratic representation.[110]

Another factor which greatly contributed to the stemming of the opposition was the role played by the Committee and Marshall in stimulating the New York *Kehillah* movement. Their active participation in this first effort to organize the inchoate masses demonstrated that they were not opposed to democratic processes as such. In fact, the very acceptance of the idea of a *Kehillah*, a counterpart to the traditional unified East-European community under which most new immigrants had grown up, represented in many ways a major concession on the part of the older Jewish families used to the free and easy ways of American communal life. Here, too, the immediate stimulus was given by an external event. In an article, published in the September 1908 issue of the *North American Review*, the New York Police Commissioner, Theodore A. Bingham, had contended, as we recall, that 50 percent of all the crimes committed in New York City had been perpetrated by Jews. The Jewish communal leaders easily enough assembled reliable data to disprove this contention and, ultimately, Bingham himself publicly apologized for his error. But this incident pointed up not only the presence of crime and vice within the Jewish community which the leaders considered necessary to combat, but also underscored the inadequacy of available statistical and sociological data concerning the Jews of America. Some far-sighted leaders, such as Judah Leon Magnes (1877-1948) also saw in this incident another illustration of how harmful to the Jewish community was the absence of a permanent representative organization which could speak in its behalf.

Magnes and several associates, recruited chiefly from among the new arrivals in the "Downtown" community (Joseph Barondess, Bernard Semel, Otto A. Rosalsky, and others) issued, on October 11, 1908, a call in English and Yiddish for an all-embracing conference at Clinton Hall. They claimed, "We Jews are almost a million strong in this city, and yet our position is so exposed and so weak that we are almost powerless against attacks from without and dissolution from within. Is this largest Jewish Community of the world to continue a prey to the foe within and without our ranks?" A constituent assembly, at which 222 organizations were represented, met in February 1909, and elected an executive committee under Magnes's chairmanship. The objectives of the new organization were very broad. They embraced a variety of economic and social welfare activities, including an employment bureau, arbitration, conciliation and mediation of industrial disputes. A rabbinical council was to supervise *kashruth*, Sabbath observance, and other religious matters, which were then in an extremely chaotic condition. The *Kehillah* also anticipated overall cooperation of the various charitable organizations and established for that purpose a special Welfare Committee in 1912. Above all it sought to introduce some order into the anarchical system of Jewish education. After a survey prepared by the Palestine-born, Samson Benderly of Baltimore, it established in 1910 a Bureau of Education, headed by Benderly, which, as we shall presently see, left a permanent imprint upon Jewish education in America. A special Bureau of Social Morals was to endeavor to improve the ethical conduct of the Jews, efforts which drew eloquent praise from the New York Mayor, William Gaynor, in August 1913. Doubtless assisted by other social changes, the long-range effects of the *Kehillah* activities purportedly reduced the percentage of Jewish juvenile delinquents from 30 to 14 in the years 1913 to 1933. To understand properly the whole gamut of organized Jewish life in the city and the better to plan for its amelioration, the organization decreed that a Bureau for Research compile a complete listing of all the existing Jewish communal organizations in the city.[111]

Almost immediately a decision had to be made concerning the relationship between the new Community and the American Jewish Committee. Because of Magnes's personal influence the Committee from the outset strongly supported the movement. Finally, Marshall and Magnes agreed that the members of the *Kehillah's* Executive Committee, elected by its constituent bodies, should simultaneously serve as the New York representatives on the national board of the American Jewish Committee. Ultimately, Louis Marshall himself, who had interveningly become Magnes's brother-in-law, on May 4, 1912 wrote a letter to the editor of the *American Israelite* which had attacked the sponsors of the *Kehillah* as demagogues and men "who are given to fads and religious and social extravagances." Within its brief compass, Marshall's letter became an eloquent apologia for, and succinct summary of, the activities of the *Kehillah*.[112]

When the First World War had begun in Europe American Jewry had thus achieved a strong leadership in both the American Jewish Committee and the New York *Kehillah* and had influential exponents in both Marshall and Magnes. The war, however, created new conditions and needs which ultimately brought about a certain weakening of the Committee and a total eclipse of the *Kehillah*. But these developments are beyond the confines of the present essay.

Education

Perhaps the most important legacy left behind by the defunct *Kehillah* movement was its Bureau of Jewish Education and the reforms in the educational structure of the Jewish community it initiated. Its influence was felt far beyond the confines of New York City, and ultimately helped both the educators and the Jewish public at large to rethink Jewish educational problems in many other countries of the dispersion.

Originally Jewish education was intimately connected with the synagogue. In fact, the public school system was rather late in coming to the United States and almost all education, other than in private homes, bore a denominational character and was administered by the religious bodies themselves. The first American Jewish school on record was the Polonies Talmud Torah, founded in 1809. But even that school was only part and parcel of the Spanish and Portuguese Synagogue in New York.[113]

With the growth of the public school system in the mid-nineteenth century, however, more and more Jewish children attended the public schools. This trend was reinforced by the large increase of the Jewish population, the intensifying struggles between Reform and Orthodoxy, the diffusion of communal and congregational controls, and the presence of a fairly substantial unsynagogued, even agnostic, group of Jews. The Jewish community, moreover, confronted with increasingly burdensome tasks in relief and immigrant adjustment, simply was not in a financial position to maintain sufficiently large and effective day schools to accommodate the rapidly growing Jewish school population, even had the leaders desired to do so.

Most decisively, the very will of the community was undermined by the ever more powerful drive toward "Americanization" of the immigrants. Theoretical and practical considerations combined to persuade the Jewish leaders that giving the immigrants opportunities to learn English and become familiar with American institutions, as well as retraining them for their new occupations, would facilitate their struggle for existence and at the same time help to remove some major objections voiced by the swelling chorus of the anti-immigration propagandists. The older Jewish settlers, predominantly of German descent, independently resented the Yiddish speech and the "ghetto" ways of life of their new compatriots, and tried to reshape the latter's mentalities in their own image. In these efforts they received all the sympathy and cooperation from the American public at large. It is small wonder, then, that "Americanization" of the Jewish immigrants began to be preached with semireligious fervor; it appealed to both the patriotic and the charitable instincts of the outstanding leaders in the Jewish community. Many Jewish fraternal orders, though organized for other purposes, included various Americanization programs in their activities. Ultimately, whether consciously or unconsciously, the very Yiddish press contributed much to that process of integration of the newcomers into the larger American community.[114]

Of course, the main agency of Americanization was the public school. Partly under Jewish influence, the public school extended its activities more and more also to adult groups by arranging for evening classes which could be attended by immigrants employed during the day. In the earlier years, however, the only instruction adults could receive was from private agencies. Here the Jewish community stepped in vigorously and, particularly with the aid of the Baron de Hirsch Fund, established, or subsidized, a number of institutions in such major centers as Philadelphia, Baltimore, Boston, Pittsburgh, St. Louis, and Chicago. Understandably, the greatest effort was made in New York. Here the so-called Neighborhood Guild, later renamed the University Settlement, had been started in 1886. Under the guidance of Lillian D. Wald (1867-1940), the Henry Street Settlement, although mainly concerned with health and social welfare problems—Miss Wald first introduced the idea of the school nurse (1902) and was ultimately instrumental in putting across that of a Federal Children's Bureau—likewise had its share in the Americanization of the immigrant.[115]

In 1891, the Hebrew Institute, two years later renamed the

Educational Alliance, was organized. Its scope was defined by the leaders as being "of an Americanizing, educational, social and humanizing character." It attracted the support of the leading Jews and it could boast of such eminent scholars as Caspar Levias and Max L. Margolis among its teachers. An interesting innovation consisted in its advanced English courses for *melammedim* of the various Hebrew schools, intended to bridge the gap between the Yiddish-speaking teachers and their Anglicized pupils. In many ways, however, these classes functioned as preparatory schools for colleges. It turned out, for example, that of one such class of eighteen Hebrew teachers, eight later entered medical schools, five became lawyers, and four studied for other skilled professions. Less frequently mentioned, but no less significant, was the effect of the Educational Alliance on narrowing the chasm which was opening between the older generations of immigrants and their own children. Apart from the usual revolt of youth, one of the saddest by-products of the latter's speedy Americanization was its frequent rejection of its "backward" parents. Hutchins Hapgood was not wrong in seeing in the work of the Educational Alliance an opportunity "to combine the American and Hebrew elements, reconcile fathers and sons by making the former more American and the latter more Hebraic, and in that way improve the home life of the quarter."[116]

At first, however, the stress was almost exclusively laid on the program of Americanization, which understandably elicited considerable resistance on the part of many immigrants who feared that the new school would estrange their pupils from Orthodoxy. In fact, some opponents equated it with such Christian schools as the Five Points Mission Schools which indeed engaged in far-flung proselytizing activities among Jews. It became necessary, therefore, to send out visitors to attract pupils from the Lower East Side. In time, however, under its much-admired superintendent, David Blaustein, during the years 1898-1907, the Educational Alliance, with its diversified classes, well-stocked reading room, and social activities, became so widely accepted that many immigrants proceeded to enroll in it as soon as they disembarked from the boats. In 1901, the aggregate attendance at its hundreds of classes, lecture programs, and clubs exceeded 2,051,000. It even became necessary to limit admissions and to shift many pupils to the public schools as soon as possible. By 1900, more than 5,500 children had been sent on from the Baron de Hirsch classes to the public schools. In addition there were many adult classes in English, American history and citizenship, as well as in stenography, bookkeeping, dressmaking, and other vocational skills. In 1910, special classes were organized for mothers. Only with the decline of immigration after 1914 and the enhanced role played by the public school system in adult education as well, the impact of the Educational Alliance and its sister institutions began to weaken markedly.[117]

On the other hand, many schools, old and new, were exclusively devoted to Jewish education, although as enrollment in the public schools increased, the additional hours devoted to Jewish subjects were constantly reduced. Most synagogues ran so-called Sabbath schools which often met on both Saturdays and Sundays, later on Sundays alone. The Reform movement, in particular, with its growing emphasis on prayers in English, considerably reduced the interest of both parents and children in the acquisition of a good knowledge of Hebrew. Even Orthodox circles were often satisfied with the children's ability to recite Hebrew prayers by rote and cared little for their comprehension. Individual parents often hired incompetent teachers to give instruction at home, or else sent their children to one of the growing number of Ḥadarim. This traditional institution, sharply criticized at that time even in Europe, revealed in the United States all its European weaknesses and few of its traditional advantages. Under the metropolitan conditions in New York and other vastly expanding American cities such Ḥadarim often met in unbelievably crowded and unsanitary quarters. Many teachers were completely unprepared for their tasks; they often were men who had failed in other occupations and turned to teaching. Few of them knew English, whereas more and more children attending the public schools could not follow their instruction in Yiddish. And yet at the beginning of the twentieth century there were some 400 such *Ḥadarim* in New York City alone; their number increased to some 500 a decade later. Of course, one or another *Ḥeder* had both better facilities and more dedicated and competent teachers. But few parents, deeply preoccupied with earning a living and getting adjusted to the new country, really cared much if their children acquired no more than a minimal knowledge of prayers and customs. The problems of the then existing Jewish educational system were graphically described in a 1910 address by Samson Benderly. He stated:

> The difficulties are as numerous as they are far-reaching. We lack financial means. We cannot count upon the time of the children which is occupied by general education. Economic considerations make it impossible for the Jewish school to keep the children for more than a few years. Our literature which should be the content of our education is defective. Neo-Hebraic literature is, at bottom, a campaign literature and incomprehensible to children who have been reared in an entirely different environment. Not even the Bible can be fully appreciated by our children, unless given them in a pedagogic form suited for them. The main question of the Jewish school however is not so much the amount of knowledge obtained, as in the creation of a Jewish atmosphere.

Moreover, a great many children of the period received no Jewish instruction at all. A survey of 181 schools in the five boroughs of New York conducted in 1917 showed that only 14.9 percent of Jewish children attended regular Jewish schools, while perhaps 10 percent more received instruction in either one or another *Ḥeder* or from private tutors. In other words, some three-quarters of all Jewish children of school age received no training in Jewish subjects at all.[118]

Much more orderly, but no more effective, was the instruction given throughout the country in the Sabbath schools. Organizationally, these schools, such as the one started by Temple Emanu-

El in New York, in 1854, were far superior, especially after the establishment of the Hebrew Sabbath School Union of American Hebrew Congregations in 1886. With its main object of "advancing common methods and discipline in Jewish Sabbath schools," the Union gathered information concerning the existing schools in the country, proposed a universal course of study, published textbooks, and screened teachers. On the other hand, its educational expectations were very small. According to the resolution of its convention of 1886, an ordinary school's curriculum was to embrace the following subjects: "a. Instruction in the principles, doctrines and precepts of Judaism; b. reading of the Bible in the vernacular translation; c. the Hebrew language at least to the extent of understanding Hebrew prayers, and appropriate portions of the Bible; d. Jewish History covering Biblical and Post-biblical periods; e. music, with a view to prepare the children to participate in services." These objectives were to be attained in five years of weekly sessions of at least three hours. In addition the school was to maintain confirmation classes and two-years of post-confirmation instruction. Needless to say, only very few schools attained even these limited objectives. From 1905 on, the School Union was wholly integrated into the Union of American Hebrew Congregations as one of its departments. Like the Reform movement in general, the Sabbath school was most effective in those geographic areas where there was a higher ratio of older American settlers and where the inner clashes within the Jewish community were less sharp. Unfortunately, this and other phases of Jewish education outside New York City are known to us only from sporadic local surveys or later studies which are neither comprehensive enough nor fully comparable with one another.[119]

Much more ambitious were the programs of the Talmud Torahs. These schools, originally combining philanthropic with educational aims, long accommodated only children of poor parents. But when their instruction proved much superior to that available elsewhere, some wealthy parents, beginning with

368 | *Steeled by Adversity*

the directors of the schools themselves, began enrolling their children in them. The earliest enduring institution of this type was founded in 1862 by Rev. Pesach Rosenthal of New York. After a two-year intermission, it was reorganized in 1881-1883 under the name of *Machzike Talmud Torah* (Supporters of Talmud Torah). In the 1890s followed the so-called Downtown and Uptown Talmud Torahs, another named after Montefiore, and one, later called the School of Biblical Instruction, in Brooklyn. Typical is the program of the *Machzike*, whose constitution of 1885 provided that "the object of this School shall be to instruct poor Jewish children gratis in the Hebrew language and literature and to give them a religious education. The instruction shall be conducted on strictly orthodox principles." The children were to attend classes from 4 to 8 o'clock every weekday afternoon except Friday, from 2 to 5 P.M. on Saturday, and from 9 A.M. to 3 P.M. on Sunday, to achieve "fluent reading [of Hebrew] in accordance with the rules of Hebrew grammar" and to study the *Shulḥan 'Arukh*. Still more intensive was the instruction given in various Yeshivas. While in Europe the Yeshiva usually was a more advanced school for adolescent youth, most American institutions were but elementary schools dedicated to concentrated study of Jewish lore. The first Yeshiva of this type was called *Etz Chayim* and was incorporated as the Etz Chayim Talmudical Academy in 1886. In daily sessions from 9 A.M. to 4 P.M. the pupils were to study Bible, Talmud and the *Shulḥan 'Arukh*. Three additional hours were to be devoted to the study of the English, Hebrew, and Yiddish languages. Started by enthusiasts, this school had great financial difficulties—according to an early participant, there was not enough money to buy copies of a talmudic tractate for each of the three teachers; so only one copy was acquired for 90 cents and torn into three parts for independent use. Its religious orientation was made clear by the constitutional provision, further elaborated by the Board, that it was to "be guided according to the strict Orthodox and Talmudical Law and the custom of Poland and Russia." At one session, the minutes inform us, the Board decided, by oath and by everlasting pledge, which shall not be altered, that all the directors of the Yeshibah shall conduct themselves, only according to the customs of Poland and Russia, in accordance with the customs of our fathers and our forefathers. And if, God forbid, any one of the directors shall suggest any matter or any subject which shall contain an admixture or inkling of any change or alteration or deviation, even from the smallest and least of the customs of Poland, either nominal or actual, even if the matter which is thus proposed shall be considered right by the majority of the Board, we the Board of Directors, hereby agree and accept upon us, that even a single member of the Board, whether he be small or great, poor or rich, may prevent such action.

Other *yeshivot* which followed were less stringent. One of the largest, renamed the Rabbi Jacob Joseph School in honor of the chief rabbi of that time, became a leading Jewish day school, combining intensive Hebrew-rabbinic with secular education.[120]

At the other extreme were the so-called national radical schools which usually met only on Saturdays and Sundays and taught Jewish culture in Yiddish. Begun in 1911, they became a battlefield between Yiddishists and Hebraists until a compromise was reached in 1915, whereby Hebrew was to be taught, but each school was to decide by itself in which grade and how intensively that instruction was to be given. Within a few years three other schools arose in New York City and thirty-one more thoughout the country. Between these extremes was the Zionist school. Nationalistic and secularist in nature, it pursued intensive studies of modern Hebrew, but it also taught Bible with commentaries and Talmud as part of Jewish culture. The first of these schools, called Shaarey Zion School, was founded in 1893 and several more were added in New York and elsewhere after 1905.[121]

Such diversity of approaches naturally obstructed any efforts at unification. It was much easier for the Hebrew Education Society of Philadelphia, established in 1848, or for the similar Hebrew Free School Association, organized in New York in 1864, to offer a more or less uniform Jewish education to the children. But in 1917, despite an intervening slight improvement, the conditions in New York City were altogether chaotic. Of the 275,000 Jewish children attending the eight grades of grammar school, only some 65,000 (including 16,000 girls) or but 23.5 percent were receiving any kind of Jewish education at all. Some 17,000 of these children, observes Samson Benderly, "are taught in miserable holes, known as Chedarim. These are located in cellars, in vacant stores, in meeting rooms, in the rear of saloons, and in garrets. About 10,000 children are taught in their homes, the place of instruction being the kitchen, the dining-room, the parlor or one of the bedrooms." The contrast between these "holes" and the well-constructed, clean, and well-lit public schools which these children normally attended unavoidably helped to lower the prestige of Jewish instruction in their eyes. The sponsorship of the existing schools and their curricula likewise varied greatly. Apart from the 500 Ḥadarim, there were some 181 better organized schools, of which 67 were community weekday schools, 50 congregational weekday schools, 37 congregational Sunday schools, and so forth. Only four schools were of the type of parochial or day schools. This anarchical situation prevailed, despite several years of strenuous efforts on the part of the newly organized New York *Kehillah*, which from the outset realized that some sort of coordination of Jewish educational efforts was imperative. We recall the establishment by it of the Bureau of Education of the Jewish Community of New York led by Benderly. A major part of the Bureau's effort consisted in the unification of the Talmud Torahs whose representatives formed, in 1909, a Central Board of Jewish Education. But all these were mere beginnings which, while holding out great promise, were quite slow in introducing order into the chaos. The Board continued to function even after its parent body, the *Kehillah*, went out of existence. From New York similar Boards of Education spread to other communities, but most of their achievements were to come decades later.[122]

All these schools required teachers and advanced teacher training became an important communal task. For the most part it was found convenient to attach such teacher training institutions to existing seminaries; only after 1914 several independent Teachers Colleges in such centers as New York, Boston, Baltimore, and Pittsburgh tried to bridge the gap between the different religious orientations avowedly represented by these schools of higher learning.[123]

On the highest level the seminaries became the leaders in the educational efforts not only through the instruction they imparted to their pupils, but also through the research and scholarship of their faculties which made of them major centers of Jewish learning. In the nineteenth century several sporadic attempts had been made to establish a school for the training of Jewish ministers and teachers. The earliest proposal came from one Moses Elias Levy of Florida in 1821. Although it elicited the support of such influential leaders as Mordecai Manuel Noah and Rev. Moses Levy Maduro Peixotto, spiritual head of the Spanish and Portuguese Congregation in New York, this project never materialized. Subsequently it was Isaac Leeser and Isaac Mayer Wise who reiteratedly advocated the founding of a central institution as part of their independent calls to Jewish unity. Apart from those short-lived experiments as that of Sampson Simson to establish a Jewish Theological Seminary and Scientific Institute in 1852, or that of an Emanu-El Theological Seminary Association organized by Temple Emanu-El in New York in 1865, the most serious effort was made by Leeser when he founded in 1867 the Maimonides College in Philadelphia which endured for six years and pointed the way for all future endeavors. The Maimonides College also laid the foundation for the building of a major Jewish scholarly library in the country. True, the call of the editor of the *Jewish Messenger* of June 26, 1868, that a collection of some 3,000 Hebrew books which was going on sale in Amsterdam be acquired for the College apparently went unheeded. But a year and a half later the Board entrusted Mayer Sulzberger with the purchase for it of some books at a similar New York auction of works of Amsterdam provenance. The 318 volumes acquired on this occasion not only formed a small nucleus for a future

Jewish library, but this transaction doubtless stimulated Sulzberger to become a major book collector in his own right and, subsequently after the formation of the Jewish Theological Seminary, to contribute to the upbuilding of its library which ultimately owned the largest assemblage of Jewish books and manuscripts in history.[124]

Isaac M. Wise, who had agitated for a "Zion College Association" as early as 1854, finally succeeded in founding the Hebrew Union College in Cincinnati in 1875. In 1883, the first four rabbis were publicly ordained by the College. After Wise's death in 1900, Moses Mielziner and, from 1903 to 1921, Kaufmann Kohler served as presidents. Conservative Jewry likewise felt the need of building a central institution of higher learning. In 1887, the Jewish Theological Seminary of America was established in New York under the presidency of Sabato Morais. According to the announcement, "the students will be subjected to practical exercises according to their intention of becoming teachers, readers or preachers." There was an interval in the presidency after Morais' death in 1897, but in 1901 Solomon Schechter was called from Cambridge and Jacob Schiff, Louis Marshall, and others helped develop the institution into a major center of learning. In 1903, special classes for teachers were established, out of which developed six years later, the Seminary's Teachers' Institute. It took Orthodoxy considerably longer to establish a similar school of higher learning. From a nucleus, in 1897, of the Yeshivat Yitzchak Elchanan, arose ultimately through a merger with the older Yeshivat Etz Chayim, the Rabbi Isaac Elchanan Theological Seminary under the presidency of Bernard Revel from 1915 on. Curiously, the original intention of giving only advanced rabbinical instruction had to be abandoned after a "strike" of students in 1908, who felt that they could not pursue a rabbinical career in America without the knowledge of English and secular subjects. Ultimately, this theological school expanded by adding a regular Yeshiva College and still later the existing ramified Yeshiva University.[125]

Religious Conflicts

Much of that duplication of effort and general disorganization was owing not only to the free competitive system in which any group was able to erect its own educational structure, but also to the sharp ideological divisions which separated these groups. Apart from the conflict between Americanization and the cultivation of Jewish values and from the natural distinctions between countries of origin, there were also sharp contrasts in religious and political outlooks which kept the Jewish community in permanent turmoil. In general, this was a period of great intellectual creativity. Strong individuals appeared on the scene and clashes between personalities added to the general confusion.

In the 1870s and 1880s the Reform movement still largely controlled the major communities of the United States and held almost undisputed sway in the smaller provincial centers. Even German Jews, who had at home adhered to a more or less rigid orthodox ritual, were inclined, upon arrival in the United States, to join the more prestigious and influential Reform congregations. For example, Jacob H. Schiff, who had spent his early years in Frankfort in the orthodox environment of Samson Raphael Hirsch's congregation, after settling in New York in 1865, became an influential member of the Reform temples Beth-El and Emanu-El. True, all his life he retained a certain modicum of ritualistic observance and, in time, played a role in the upbuilding of the Conservative Jewish Theological Seminary. But he was preeminently a member of the Reform group.[126] The same holds true of Louis Marshall who could simultaneously preside over the Boards of both Temple Emanu-El and the Seminary. But these were relatively rare exceptions even among laymen.

Reform's domination of the American scene is well illustrated by the governmental census of religious bodies of 1890, the only such enumeration seeking to distinguish between Reform and Orthodox Jewish congregations (the Conservative movement still was in its early stages of evolution). Although by that time the new immigrants of the last two decades, together with their off-spring, easily outnumbered the American-born families, the supe-riority of Reform in the size of its structures and their seating capacity was undeniable. Of the 217 Reform congregations counted in that census, 179 possessed edifices of their own with an approximate seating capacity of 92,397. Only 38 congrega-tions met in halls and other temporary accommodations with a seating capacity of 3,630. The total number of communicants or members was reported as 72,899. In contrast, the 316 Orthodox organizations had only 122 edifices with a seating capacity of 46,837, whereas 193 met in halls with a capacity of 24,847 seats. Their total number of communicants, as given was only 57,597. True, the Orthodox membership was undoubtedly larger. As in the case of other denominations, the smaller and poorer congrega-tions often failed to report. Yet the preponderance of Reform, particularly outside the Eastern Seaboard, was incontrovertible. While in New York State the Orthodox membership of 29,064 considerably outnumbered the 16,743 Reform communicants, al-ready neighboring Pennsylvania counted 5,582 Reform members as against 2,447 Orthodox. In the Middle West, Far West, and the South the numerical disparity was even more pronounced. Ohio, in particular, where Cincinnati was a major center of the Reform movement, had a ratio of 6,575 to 2,313 in favor of Reform. In South Carolina, the locale of the earliest Reform ex-periment in 1824, the reports mentioned no Orthodox counter-parts at all to the 800 Reform Jews. At the same time, however, many new congregations, founded by pioneers venturing into new regions, followed an Orthodox ritual. We recall the story reported to the London *Jewish Chronicle* of March 1850 relating to the New York group proceeding to California, "taking with them a shoḥet and Sefer Torah." Thus in the census of 1890 the states of Alabama, Iowa, Montana, North Dakota, Texas, Ver-mont, and Washington reported the presence of an Orthodox Jewish congregation each; of course, without any permanent reli-gious edifice. On the other hand, only one Reform congregation without a permanent building was reported in New Mexico, whereas the single Reform congregations in Colorado, the District of Columbia, Oregon, and Utah—all boasted of edifices of their own.[127]

In the 1880s the founders of the American Jewish Reform movement were at the height of their influence. Only David Einhorn (1809-79), the most distinguished theologian among them, had passed away. Max Lilienthal (1814-82), Samuel Hirsch (1815-89), Samuel Adler (1809-91), Bernard Felsenthal (1822-1908), and particularly Isaac Mayer Wise (1819-1900), were all at the acme of their reputation. While many of them did not see eye to eye, and, for instance, Einhorn's Reform was on the whole more radical than that of Wise, they all agreed on certain fundamentals with respect to the changes needed to adjust the Jewish religion to modern life in America. Notwithstanding individual reservations, they cooperated in the rabbinical conferences which met in Cleveland in 1855, Philadelphia in 1869, and Cincinnati in 1871. Perhaps the most memorable of these assemblies, at least from the ideological point of view, was the Pittsburgh Conference of 1885 which formulated a sort of credo for the Reform movement. Although not formally considered a catechism of American Reform and in certain teachings repudiated by some Reformers themselves, the Pittsburgh platform furnished the most succinct summary of the Reform outlook for decades to come. Its eight principles contended that Judaism had best preserved the God idea of Scriptures "as the central religious truth for the human race" (Art. I); recognized that the Bible, while reflecting certain primitive ideas of its own age, was nevertheless a potent instrument of religious and moral instruction (Art. II); considered Judaism "a progressive religion, ever striving to be in accord with the postulates of reason" (Art. VI); and subscribed to the doctrine of the immortality of the soul, but not to that of bodily resurrection and reward and punishment in the Hereafter (Art. VII). The other four articles may be cited here in full:

We recognize in the Mosaic legislation a system of training the Jewish people for its mission during its national life in Palestine, and to-day we accept as binding only its moral laws, and maintain only such ceremonies as elevate and sanctify our lives, but reject all such as are not adapted to the views and habits of modern civilization [Art. III].

We hold that all such Mosaic and rabbinical laws as regulate diet, priestly purity, and dress originated in ages and under the influence of ideas entirely foreign to our present mental and spiritual state. They fail to impress the modern Jew with a spirit of priestly holiness; their observance in our days is apt rather to obstruct than to further modern spiritual elevation [Art. IV].

We recognize, in the modern era of universal culture of heart and intellect, the approaching of the realization of Israel's great Messianic hope for the establishment of the kingdom of truth, justice, and peace among all men. We consider ourselves no longer a nation, but a religious community, and therefore expect neither a return to Palestine, nor a sacrificial worship under the sons of Aaron, nor the restoration of any of the laws concerning the Jewish state [Art. V].

In full accordance with the spirit of Mosaic legislation, which strives to regulate the relation between rich and poor, we deem it our duty to participate in the great task of modern times, to solve, on the basis of justice and righteousness, the problems presented by the contrasts and evils of the present organization of society [Art. VIII].

Probably the main spiritual father of this declaration was Kaufmann Kohler (1843-1926), who had come to the United States in 1869. As a successor to his father-in-law, Einhorn, in Temple Beth-El in New York from 1879 on, he exercised considerable influence on the Reform movement from the pulpit and, from 1903 on, also as President of Hebrew Union College.[128]

General resolutions of this type, even if they were unflinchingly subscribed to by the whole Reform rabbinate and laity, could not obviate differences of opinion in details. Each congregation remained autonomous and, while yielding to the pressures of the more or less united rabbinate, could deviate on various occasions. There was a particularly obvious difference between large segments of the laity, which saw in the movement merely an opportunity for getting rid of a number of burdensome ritualistic requirements, and some of the Reform rabbis who were convinced that they demanded from their public a different type of, but no less genuine a piety, than did their Orthodox colleagues. Emil G. Hirsch's exclamation may, indeed, be accepted as a sincere expression of his faith and that of many of his associates. "My Radicalism," he contended, "and it is that which I imbibed at the feet of my own father and found in the instruction of my master Geiger, both of blessed memory, the Radicalism of Einhorn and Samuel Adler, intends to be more Jewish than ever was official orthodoxy. We hunger for more Judaism, not for less of it."[129]

A number of particularly touchy and controversial problems, however, revealed how little the generally conceived theories met some of the living needs and strong sentiments of the generation. Among them were the questions of circumcision, especially of newly proselytized adults, intermarriage, and Sunday services. Beginning with the Frankfort *Reformverein* of 1843, extreme Reformers had demanded the elimination of the "barbarous rite" of circumcision along with many other traditional rituals. The predominant feeling was, however, that this "Abrahamitic rite" ought to be retained. Matters came to a head in 1877 and 1890 when Rabbis M. Spitz of Milwaukee and Henry Berkowitz of Kansas City, Mo., respectively, were confronted with such a situation. In each case a young Christian wished to marry a Jewish girl and, though prepared to adopt Judaism, he refused to submit to circumcision. When the two rabbis consulted their colleagues the problem led to extended discussions. Ultimately, the Central Conference of American Rabbis resolved by a vote of 25 to 5 that any officiating rabbi, with the approval of two associates and the consent of his congregation, could receive into the covenant of Israel "any honorable and intelligent person, who desires such affiliation, without any initiatory rite, ceremony or observance whatever, provided such person be sufficiently acquainted with the faith, doctrine and religious usages of Israel." The Conference merely demanded that the prospective proselyte sign a document

378 | *Steeled by Adversity*

declaring his or her intention to adhere to the fundamentals of Judaism (1892 and 1896). Understandably, problems of this kind added impetus to the constantly renewed endeavors to define these fundamentals.[130]

Even more vexatious was the problem of intermarriage, since a purportedly universalist religion had difficulty in denying the permissibility of mixed unions. In fact, the German Rabbinical Conference, which had met in Brunswick in 1844, had permitted mixed marriages under the condition that the children be brought up in the Jewish faith. Most Reformers, however, including the radical David Einhorn (though not Samuel Hirsch), were opposed to it. In the decisive session of the Central Conference of 1909 Ephraim Feldman read a comprehensive paper, "Intermarriage Historically Considered." While stressing that the universalistic ideal of Samuel Hirsch indeed favored intermarriage, he pointed out a certain inconsistency in David Einhorn's emphasis upon the Jewish mission in the period of Emancipation when most Jews were trying hard to become integrated in the body politic of the majority peoples. "We will have to bear in mind that to strain every fibre to become like somebody else, and at the same time talk about our mission to *convert* that somebody else, i.e., to make him like ourselves, who are all the time aching to be like him, is to say the very least—amusing. We are liable to wake up some fine day and find that sensible people are laughing at us." Yet the arguments presented by the opposition, especially by Samuel Schulman (1864-1955) were shared by the large majority of the members. The rabbi contended that the "complete union of souls" required by marriage could not be attained when the couple differed on religious matters and also that mixed marriages threatened the survival of the Jewish minority. The Conference resolved "that mixed marriages are contrary to the tradition of the Jewish religion and should therefore be discouraged by the American Rabbinate." This resolution did not prevent individual Reform rabbis, however, from officiating at weddings between Jews and Christians.[131]

No less inconsistent with the theory, but based upon hard

realities, was the equivocal attitude of the Reform rabbinate to the transfer of the Sabbath services to Sunday. The facts of life were such that the traditional Sabbath observance had given way to the economic needs of a large majority of Jewish businessmen and workers even outside the Reform group. Attendance at Saturday morning services was reduced to a small fraction of the male members. The enlargement of the services on Friday night was an insufficient substitute and conflicted with the cultivation of the traditional Sabbath practices at home. It is small wonder, then, that many congregations tried to supplement the Saturday services with those held on Sundays. But the public at large, although finding Sunday services quite convenient, could not escape the feeling of its being primarily a Christian holiday. The resulting quandary was well expressed by Rabbi Jacob Voorsanger who, at the Conference session of 1902, led the discussion on the Sabbath question. "Our position is just at present," he declared, "that, on the one hand, our Sabbath is being killed by non-observance and that, on the other, we do not want another Sabbath." Finally after long debates in and outside the Conference, the latter adopted a resolution in 1905 in which it declared "itself in favor of maintaining the historical Sabbath as a fundamental institution of Judaism and of exerting every effort to improve its observance." However, this resolution was adopted by a vote of only 23 to 9, while the large majority of Conference members, then numbering 163, were not heard from. Later the Conference made clear that it did not oppose Sunday services which, after all, could be considered on a par with any weekday service of the traditional ritual. As expressed by Kaufmann Kohler these services, held in many cities by eminent preachers, helped to "bring the message of Judaism home to thousands that would otherwise be strangers to the house of God and to the influence of religion."[132]

Equally unresolved was the frequently debated problem of convoking a Jewish synod. The idea of such an assembly was in line with Wise's constant exhortation to unify the American Jewish communal efforts, but the differences between the various wings of American Jewry were too great to make such a meeting feasible and effective. Reform Judaism proceeded, therefore, with the building up of its own central organizations, the Union of American Hebrew Congregations, the Hebrew Union College, and the Central Conference of American Rabbis. The Union was organized in 1873 with an initial membership of 28 congregations. By 1914 this membership had grown to 186. As we recall, in 1876 the Union had absorbed the Board of Delegates of American Israelites. Paying attention to the growing influence of women on the American scene, the Union helped organize a Federation of Reform Sisterhoods in 1913. Apart from devoting its attention to the Sunday school and forming in 1886 the aforementioned Hebrew Sabbath School Union, the Union, from 1906 on, started working among Jewish university students. In 1903, it also organized a Department of Synagogue Extension devoted to establishing new congregations throughout the United States and Canada. The need for such "circuit preaching" was pointed out, for example, by the report from Sioux City, Iowa, that a leading Jew of that city had joined the directorate of the Unitarian Church because of the absence of Jewish services in the city (1895). In addition to the then existing 115 member congregations that Department tried to service, through visiting rabbis and regional meetings, the numerous communities which had no permanent congregations of their own. The Union's publication department distributed a considerable number of textbooks and apologetic treatises, mainly addressed to laymen. Not being a rabbinical organization, the Union attracted many influential laymen, such as its first presidents, Morris Loth who held office from 1873 to 1889, and Julius Freiberg from 1889 to 1903. Both took an active part in many Jewish public affairs. Of importance were also the permanent secretaries, especially the first secretary, Lipman Levy, who served for 44 years until 1917. The Central Conference, too, founded in 1889, became a more enduring and permanent association of rabbis than any other in the modern world. Apart from regularly publishing its *Year Book*, which recorded the proceedings at the various conferences and included a number of scholarly papers of general interest, it issued in 1894-95 the *Union Prayer Book* in two volumes which replaced the theretofore existing enormous variety of rituals among the Reform congregations. True, there was some opposition even within the rabbinic ranks and, for instance, the Cleveland rabbi, Moses J. Gries, a future president of the Central Conference (1913-15), thought so little of the new compilation that he contemplated preparing another. Yet subject to subsequent revisions (in 1918-22, etc.) this prayer book is still generally used in the Reform congregations. Partly under the impact of Walter Rauschenbusch's Social Gospel movement, the Reform rabbis placed social justice increasingly into the focus of their preaching. Understandably, the Conference from its inception also paid some attention to the professional interests of its members, beginning in 1890 with a fund to support indigent colleagues. Regular pension funds, however, could not be launched until 1917, when a program was started with a gift of $100,000 from Jacob H. Schiff.[133]

Nothing comparable from the organizational standpoint existed among the Orthodox Jews. Their members were increasing by leaps and bounds. Even those who were not willing or able to live up to the full demands of Orthodoxy often had guilt feelings about their own nonobservance and believed that such observance was really part and parcel of Judaism. The majority was prepared to join one or another Orthodox synagogue, despite the relatively high cost of the membership dues and related expenses which constituted a severe drain on the already overstrained family budgets. Typical of many other communities was the situation in Chicago and its twenty-five West Side synagogues with a total membership of some 2,000 early in this century. "These congregations," writes a contemporary observer, "are self-supporting, members contributing annual dues, ranging from $6 to $12. Permanent or life seats are from $100 to $150 each. Yearly rentals are from 50 cents to $5, entitling the holder to a seat for himself and in the gallery for his wife or other female relative."[134]

Internally, however, the differences between the Orthodox

groups stemming from various countries of origin, as well as the general lack of organizational interests among the East-European immigrants, militated against any form of cohesion. That is why even when a Union of Orthodox Jewish Congregations of America was finally organized in New York in 1898, it embraced only a minority of the Orthodox congregations in the country. In contrast to Reform, the Orthodox Union was to "advance the interests of positive Biblical, Rabbinical, traditional and historical Judaism" and it pledged its adherence to the authoritative rabbinic interpretations contained in the Talmud and the rabbinic codes. It, too, ultimately had its rabbinic counterpart in the Rabbinical Council of America which, in its present form, arose from a merger, in 1930, of the Rabbinical Council of the Union, founded in 1924, and the Rabbinical Association of the Rabbi Isaac Elchanan Theological Seminary consisting of the alumni of that Seminary. Independently there existed, ever since 1902, an organization of Orthodox rabbis of the older East-European variety, called the Union of Orthodox Rabbis of the United States and Canada, or *Agudath Harabbanim.* The two orthodox unions often cooperated, but together they reached only a limited number of Orthodox congregations. Many of the latter, particularly the numerous temporary assemblies meeting in halls organized for worship on High Holidays, joined no central organization whatsoever.[135]

An interesting attempt at unifying a number of Orthodox congregations at least on a local level was made in the agitation for the election of a chief rabbi in New York in 1877-88. In the 1850s Max Lilienthal had simultaneously served as the rabbi of three German congregations in New York, preaching in each on alternate Sabbaths. But this arrangement did not work out; Lilienthal retired and later went to Cincinnati. Isaac Leeser, the perennial protagonist of unity, began demanding the election of a chief rabbi for the whole United States along the patterns of the English chief rabbinate. A step closer to the fulfillment of that idea was made in 1877-79 when the leading East-European congregation, the Beth Hamedrash Hagodol, during a vacancy in its rabbinic post, decided to invite the distinguished Bible commentator and talmudic scholar, Meir Löb b. Yeḥiel Michael Malbim (1809-79) of Rumania. Temporarily Rabbi Malbim seemed available because of his expulsion by the Rumanian authorities. However, he was then seventy years old, had accepted a call to Kremenchug, and had died on the way to this new post in 1879.[136]

More serious was the effort begun after the death, in 1887, of Rabbi Abraham Ash of the Beth Hamedrash Hagodol. In a Hebrew volume on the Jews of New York Rabbi Moses Weinberger severely criticized the low religious and educational status of the atomized community, suggested that the one hundred thirty existing Orthodox congregations be consolidated into ten to twelve larger groups, and that the latter be united in a congregational association which would establish a chief rabbinate and a supreme tribunal serving them all. Under the leadership of the Beth Hamedrash Hagodol fifteen congregations joined forces and demonstrated their active interest in the matter by financial contributions. Out of these negotiations arose an Association of the American Orthodox Hebrew Congregations which secured from the State of New York a certificate of incorporation on December 2, 1887. Its purposes were here defined as follows:

> To encourage, foster and promote the observance of the Orthodox Jewish Religion, to spread and disseminate the doctrines and learning of the said religion, to improve and elevate the moral, social and spiritual condition of the Jewish people, to designate, support and maintain a Chief Rabbi and such other officers as may be deemed necessary or advisable, and to do, perform and effect all such other charitable and benevolent acts and purposes, as may be specified in the Constitution and By-Laws of the said Society or Organization.

When it came to the choice of a chief rabbi the leaders were subject to pressures from friends and associates of the revered Rabbi Isaac Elchanan Spektor of Kaunas, Lithuania, that they invite Spektor's son, Zvi Hirsch, who was at that time in financial difficulties. Nevertheless the New York group turned to Rabbi

Elijah Ḥayyim Meisels of Łódż and, when the latter replied in very uncertain terms, to Rabbi Jacob Joseph, a communal preacher of Vilna. Jacob Joseph accepted and, in July 1888, arrived in New York. Although a fine scholar, good preacher, and active organizer, the new Chief Rabbi could not overcome the centrifugal forces in the community. Within five years signs of his eclipse were fully noticeable. When in 1897, Jacob Joseph was stricken with paralysis and died five years later, the New York chief rabbinate and, with it, all attempts at spiritual unification of history's largest Jewish community came to an abrupt end. Only in Philadelphia, under the vigorous leadership of Rabbi Bernard L. Leventhal (1865-1952), who in 1891 succeeded his father-in-law, Eleazar Kleinberg, as rabbi of the Congregation B'nai Abraham, did the United Orthodox Hebrew Congregations maintain more than a semblance of unity.[137]

Needless to say, Orthodoxy was not a monolithic entity in America. There were the old differences between Sephardic and Ashkenazic orthodoxy, although these distinctions carried far less weight in the United States than in England or Holland. As a matter of fact the Spanish-Portuguese synagogues of both New York and Philadelphia not only freely accommodated Ashkenazic members but, almost from the outset, frequently had an Ashkenazic majority. Yet there were sufficient ritualistic and cultural differences between the two groups to make cooperation less intimate. Another dichotomy carried over from the Old World, namely *Mitnagdim* and *Ḥasidim*, and even between the respective ḥasidic schools themselves, likewise served as a disturbing factor. The small but vocal group of German Neo-Orthodox from the school of Samson Raphael Hirsch injected still another element of discord. Most importantly, in addition to these internal divisions carried over from Europe, there gradually emerged the difference between the old-type orthodoxy which tried to preserve intact the European folkways and the new more or less Americanized congregations whose fairly modern rabbis preached in English and which generally sought adaptation to American ways of life. Some of the most influential Orthodox leaders of the early twentieth century such as Zevi Hirsch Masliansky (1856-1943), Judah David Eisenstein (1854-1954), or Ephraim Deinard (1846-1930) represented different approaches to Orthodox Judaism, particularly in its attitudes to the problems then facing the American Jewish community.[138]

Gradually there emerged also an intermediate movement between Orthodoxy and Reform which, in some respects following the patterns developed in Germany by the Frankl-Graetz school of "positive-historical" Judaism, came to be known as "Conservative" in the United States. At first quite a few less staunchly Orthodox occupants of American pulpits were prepared to join a moderate type of Reform. But as the Reform movement became increasingly radical and as Wise's organizing ability succeeded in molding it into a more or less unified whole, some of these rabbis became hesitant. Among them were men of such distinction as Sabato Morais (1823-1902), Marcus Jastrow (1829-1903), both of Philadelphia, and Henry Pereira Mendes (1852-1937) of the Spanish and Portuguese Congregation in New York. More resistant was a relatively recent arrival in the United States, Alexander Kohut (1842-94). When he assumed his pulpit in New York in 1885, he was a recognized scholar and a man of determined views. In a series of sermons, later published under the title *Ethics of the Fathers*, he immediately threw down the gauntlet to all opponents of the unbroken chain of tradition from Moses to the late rabbis. "On this tradition," he declared, "rests our faith, which Moses first received from God on Sinai. On this foundation rests Mosaic-rabbinical Judaism today; and on this foundation we stand. He who denies this . . . on principle, disclaims the bond of community that united the house of Israel. . . ." The challenge was immediately taken up by Kaufmann Kohler and, in the subsequent exchange between the two leaders, the theological divergence of the burgeoning Conservative movement became quite clear.[139]

Out of this controversy grew the realization that the more conservative elements ought to become organized for common action. In 1886, as we recall, the Jewish Theological Seminary of

America was established in New York under the presidency of Sabato Morais, with the active cooperation of Kohut and other scholars. But the Seminary did not really begin flourishing until 1902, when Solomon Schechter (*ca.* 1847-1915) was brought over from Cambridge, England. Schechter, a dynamic personality, equally distinguished as a scholar and teacher, became the spokesman of the new movement. Above all he emphasized modern Jewish learning, according to the best standards of the *Wissenschaft des Judentums*, of which he remained a life-long faithful disciple. On various occasions he tried to impress his Seminary pupils not to yield to the pressures of their congregants who often wished to see the rabbi "do things," rather than devote himself to study. In his address at the Seminary Commencement of 1910, Schechter referred to the assertion of more than one former disciple that "the rumor of his being 'addicted to Jewish learning' will bring him into disrepute and will only prove injurious to his career," and insisted that rabbis disregard such counsels of despair because "what is life without thought, and, least of all, what value has Jewish religious life without Jewish religious thought?" For the sake of learning he even spoke at the dedication of the new buildings of Hebrew Union College in Cincinnati in 1913. While stressing the differences between his views and those of "His Majesty's opposition," he nevertheless firmly believed in the need for Jewish scholarly research, "a work in which both parties, realizing the nature of the problem, can work together."[140]

Nevertheless the gulf separating the new movement from Reform Judaism deepened perceptibly under Schechter's guidance. Perhaps the most succinct summary of these differences is found in the preamble to the constitution of the United Synagogue of America, which Schechter helped to organize in 1914. It read:

> Recognizing the need of an organized movement for advancing the cause of Judaism in America and maintaining Jewish tradition in its historical continuity, we hereby establish the United Synagogue of America, with the following ends in view:
> To assert and establish loyalty to the Torah and its historical exposition,

To further the observance of the Sabbath and the Dietary Laws,
To preserve in the service the reference to Israel's past and the
hopes for Israel's restoration,
To maintain the traditional character of the liturgy, with Hebrew
as the language of prayer,
To foster Jewish religious life in the home, as expressed in traditional observances,
To encourage the establishment of Jewish religious schools, in
the curricula of which the study of the Hebrew language and
literature shall be given a prominent place, both as the key to
the true understanding of Judaism, and as a bond holding together the scattered communities of Israel throughout the world.
It shall be the aim of the United Synagogue of America while
not endorsing the innovations introduced by any of its constituent bodies, to embrace all elements essentially loyal to traditional Judaism and in sympathy with the purposes outlined
above.

Schechter was also quite vehement in opposing the Reform idea
of a Jewish universal mission. He did not believe that "this
bourgeois religion of ours," deficient in enthusiasm and with its
main virtue consisting in its adaptability, would be calculated to
convert the world. Himself a child of eastern Europe, he constantly combated the snobbery of the German-Jewish upper
bourgeoisie, although at the same time he and his associates tried
to introduce more decorum into their religious services. Schechter
also consistently opposed the idea of a synod because, as he admitted in private letters, he simply did not trust the contemporary
American rabbis to adopt reasonable and moderate reforms. At
the same time he and the other conservative leaders were dedicated
to fostering the unity of the community. In his inaugural address
at the Seminary of November 20, 1902, Schechter declared, "The
ultimate goal is union and peace in American Israel. Although the
Conservative spirit permeates it, the Institution is not to become
a place of polemics, but rather a spot where Heaven and earth
kiss each other." Borrowing a phrase from Joseph Jacobs, he
preached throughout his active life the basic unity of "Catholic
Israel."[141]

Religious relations with the various Christian denominations likewise assumed new forms in the United States. Of course, the impact of Protestant ideas and rituals upon the Reform movement had made themselves strongly felt already in Germany, but in the freer American society imitation of non-Jewish neighbors encountered far fewer obstacles. In fact, not even Conservatism and Orthodoxy could entirely escape the influence of the American patterns of worship in externals and even in some such important religious performances as the sermons. From the outset, Jews often faced the necessity of converting former churches into synagogues. Because of the mobility of all congregational membership, such buildings were at times freely available, and their construction made them easily adaptable for synagogue use. Even Orthodox leaders must have set aside whatever compunctions they may have had against putting to use such ready-made structures, when they learned that two distinguished European rabbis had expressly permitted this practice. In 1858, Rabbi Judah Mittelman (Middleman) inquired from Rabbi Joseph Saul Nathanson of Lwów as to whether his congregation (probably the one called Beth Hamidrash livne Yisrael yelide Polin) was free to acquire the Welsh-Scotch Methodist Church in New York and to convert it for synagogue use. Mittelman pointed out that, since the previous worshipers had been Protestants, the church did not have crucifixes. Nathanson answered in the affirmative, buttressing his point of view with the curious argument that "with the advent of the Messiah all nations will serve the one God and all churches will turn into synagogues." A similar answer was given by Rabbi Jacob Ettlinger of Altona to another New York inquiry from Rabbi Abraham Joseph Ash of the Beth Hamedrash Hagodol. It is small wonder, then, that when the catastrophic Chicago fire of 1871 destroyed four or five synagogues, the predominantly Orthodox worshipers did not hesitate temporarily to hold services in churches, according to reports which reached the ears of the European public. Before long some Reform rabbis and Protestant pastors actually exchanged pulpits, which was considered the acme of goodwill in a religiously pluralistic society, where Judaism was one of the major denominations among the scores listed by the Census of Religious Bodies.[142]

Such rapprochement, naturally enough, stimulated missionary appetites among Christian churchmen. The idea of mission among Jews had often been propagated already in the colonial period. But in the nineteenth century a number of organized groups tried to emulate the London Society for the Promotion of Christianity amongst the Jews. Perhaps the most important of these organizations bore a very similar name, the American Society for Meliorating the Condition of the Jews. Organized in 1820 by Joseph Samuel Levy, who had been renamed after his conversion Christian Frederick Frey, this society functioned for half a century without much success. Several other missionary groups opened offices within the crowded Jewish quarters. Despite their charitable contributions and their political propaganda for Jewish rights (for instance in 1887, four years before he approached President Harrison with his famous memorandum, William E. Blackstone had founded his Chicago Hebrew Mission; see below), the success of their missionary efforts was quite limited, and the Jewish papers in the United States and abroad often had a field day in ridiculing their work. However, a number of converts found their way to the baptismal font, just as, more exceptionally, a few Christians were converted to Judaism, calling forth the aforementioned discussions among the Reform rabbis about the requirement of circumcising adult proselytes.[143]

Zionism and Diaspora Nationalism

Apart from these religious movements, Zionism gradually began to mold the spiritual outlook of American Jewry. The difficulties inherent in the American scene were illustrated by Schechter's somewhat ambivalent attitude to it in the first years of his residence in the United States. Intrinsically, Schechter's outlook had always been close to the Zionist ideals. In a letter of 1897 commenting on the Basel Congress, he expressed the view that "with all its material drawbacks it [Palestine] has its spiritual advantages,

390 | *Steeled by Adversity*

just to form an idea and an ideal." But he was frequently discouraged by the irreligiosity of Zionist leaders and felt that without religion the Jewish nationality could not survive. "I have spent," he wrote to a friend in 1898, "nearly fifty years on the study of Jewish literature and Jewish history; I am deeply convinced that we cannot sever Jewish nationality from Jewish religion." He was also far from certain that Palestine under the existing conditions would be the best home for the Jews and exclaimed, "Let us first have Zion at home, and maintain Jewish institutions wherever we can and then prepare for the great day." Two years after these words were written in 1903, however, Schechter reconsidered. In December 1905, he joined the Zionist Federation and soon thereafter published his *Zionism: a Statement*, which in both its English and Yiddish versions made a great impression on the Jewish and non-Jewish public.[144]

Otherwise the Zionist ideal found a generally receptive audience even among American Christians. Long before the rise of political Zionism, American literature had reflected considerable interest in the Holy Land. According to a recent analyst, three main approaches colored the regnant American views on Palestine during the two and a quarter centuries preceding 1867; the "metaphysical" concept of the Holy Land in the original theological thinking of the seventeenth century was replaced by a "metaphorical" concept in the subsequent political period of eighteenth-century American letters. The latter was soon supplemented, and later overshadowed, by the "millenarian" concept. All three approaches were, of course, based on Christological assumptions. In general there was sufficient sympathy for the idea of Jewish restoration to Palestine to generate some practical implications for the present. In the case of one visionary, Warder Cresson (1789-1860), scion of a well-to-do Quaker family in Philadelphia, this sympathy led to his conversion to Judaism and his settlement in Palestine in 1852. Although his appointment as American consul in Jerusalem in 1844 was canceled almost immediately after his departure from the United States, Cresson maintained his interest in the country and its Jewry. As a successful farmer, he looked forward to a large-scale Jewish agricultural colonization in Palestine, believing that "agriculture is to be Israel's vocation, when restored to their own land." Pro-Zionist sentiments of this kind were particularly widespread in certain American sects, such as the Mormons. Following in the footsteps of Joseph Smith, Brigham Young and his associates published, in 1845, a "Proclamation of the Twelve Apostles of the Church of Jesus Christ of Latter-Day Saints to All the Kings of the World, To the President of the United States of America," and so forth. This enunciation of principles included the following passage:

> And we further testify that the Jews among all nations are hereby commanded, in the name of the Messiah, to prepare to return to Jerusalem in Palestine, and to rebuild that city and Temple unto the Lord. And also to organize and establish their own political government, under their own rulers, judges and governors, in that country.

In 1879, Wilford Woodruff, an influential Mormon leader and later president of the sect, testified "that the time is not far distant when the rich men among the Jews will be called upon to use their abundant wealth to gather the dispersed of Judah, and purchase the ancient dwelling places of their fathers in and about Jerusalem, and rebuild the holy city and temple." The widely publicized views of such English writers as George Eliot and Laurence Oliphant found a responsive echo across the Atlantic Ocean. Among the American Jews it was particularly Emma Lazarus who enthusiastically reacted in a series of articles entitled "An Epistle to the Hebrews" which appeared in the *American Hebrew* in 1882-83. Finally, as we recall, the Chicago businessman, William E. Blackstone, marshaled an array of outstanding Americans for his petition to President Harrison in 1891.[145]

On their part the Jews, too, had always evinced a deep interest in helping their coreligionists to live in the Holy Land, often believing that study and prayers offered by Jews there somehow accrued to the benefit of the whole people. Ever since the eighteenth century when Rabbi Isaac Ḥayyim Carigal had visited the American colonies, messengers from Palestine were frequently collecting funds for Palestine relief among American Jews. As elsewhere, such visitors indirectly contributed to keeping alive the interest in Palestinian Jewry among the local communities. A characteristic recommendation for one such messenger, Aaron Selig, was written by Isaac M. Wise while he served as rabbi in Albany. In this recommendation, dated February 5, 5610 (1850) and doubly noteworthy because of his later stand on Zionism, Wise wrote: "It is a lamentable feature of the total absence of national love among our brethern the remnents of Israel, that even the rich, whom God has blessed with abundance, withdraw their hands from the needy and poor watchmen, that God's mercy allowed to remain in the sacred vineyard חרפה שברה לבי ואנושה. I hope that other Congregations and individuals will do more for the house of Israel." With the aid of a bequest of $10,000 from Judah Touro the North American Relief Society was organized in 1854 to dispatch annual subsidies to the Palestinian poor. Apart from fund raising, however, the Holy Land carried sufficient appeal to the American Jews for a number of them, for the most part fairly recent immigrants, to give up their United States residences and settle in Jerusalem. These Americans were often poverty stricken and, as such, not infrequently engaged the attention of American consuls.[146]

More directly relevant for the history of Zionism became the American offshoot of the Lovers of Zion movement in the 1880s. Not since the much-debated appeals of Major Noah did the Zionist idea occupy so many minds in the United States. At first, to be sure, the movement was almost entirely limited to fairly recent arrivals. The first Ḥovevei Zion group was organized in New York in 1882 under the presidency of M. Bernstein. Its Yiddish organ, the *Shulamit*, well described its initial difficulties.

The very religious consider us heretics, who wish to bring on the redemption before its time. The liberals look upon us as fanatics, who obscure the light of civilization with this new-

fangled idea. The "Know Nothings" (she'eno yode'a litten) are against us from sheer inertia. And where are the critics, the tomer farkert (maybe it's the other way around) Jews, who are not in favor of this nor that, but nevertheless think it necessary to find fault with anything and everything?

Despite these objections the movement gradually spread to other cities and, by 1889, had eight branches. To safeguard themselves against the accusation of heresy, some Lovers of Zion emphasized time and again that their "national pride is not nationalistic but religious." They also stressed the insecurity of the future of Judaism in America and claimed that "only Palestine can save our children from apostasy." The Ḥovevei tried to encourage actual settlement in Palestine by American Jews, a task more specifically undertaken by another group, the *Shovei Zion* (Returnees to Zion), organized in 1891 by a popular orator and publicist, Moses Mintz. The latter pursued less religious ideals—in fact, Mintz was accused of having sponsored some of the ill-famed Yom Kippur balls—but indulged in various colonization schemes, whose financial lack of soundness became a ready target for the opposition. Among his opponents was Isaac Blaustein, president of one of the Lovers of Zion branches, as well as a leading orthodox publicist, Kasriel H. Sarasohn, then publisher of the important Yiddish daily, the *Tageblatt*. In 1892 Sarasohn temporarily reversed himself, however, and Chief Rabbi Jacob Joseph joined the organization.[147]

As elsewhere, the Zionist movement in America entered a new phase with the appearance of Theodor Herzl. The various smaller groupings now banded together and in 1897 organized the Federation of American Zionists under the presidency of Richard J. H. Gottheil of Columbia University. The Federation attracted a more substantial following and in 1900 its membership rose to 8,000. But even in 1918, despite the tremendous upsurge of the Zionist sentiment during the First World War and the vigorous leadership of Louis D. Brandeis, it still was decidedly but a minority movement. Internally, too, the Federation at first had to overcome the resistance of the older "Lovers of Zion" who resented the new leadership of westernized and largely Reformed Jews and in 1902 actually secured from the Inner Actions Committee of the World Zionist Organization the permission to remain an independent federation. But after a few years this splinter group was absorbed by the general group. More enduring were the fundamental ideological divisions. Not only the numerous Orthodox who objected to political Zionism as a travesty of the old messianic ideal, but even the Orthodox members of the Zionist movement frequently resented its secular character and the irreligious life of many leaders. The Federation itself assisted, therefore, in the formation, in 1903, of the American section of the Mizrachi organization. Two years later another autonomous group emerged from among the socialist adherents to Zionism who had earlier formed little clubs of their own, two of them bearing the name Poale Zion, in 1900 and 1901. At first both the Mizrachi and the Poale Zion were under the Federation's jurisdiction. But in 1907, the World Zionist Congress passed a resolution, allowing each party marshaling 3,000 shekel-paying members throughout the world to form its own interterritorial faction independent of the regional federations. Thenceforth, the three organizations worked independently but, although internally remaining divided along ideological lines, they often cooperated in pursuing their common goal.[148]

The rupture caused in Zionist ranks by the Uganda offer of the British government in 1903 was reflected also in the United States. Some American leaders had long believed in the feasibility of Jewish colonization outside Palestine. They were particularly attracted to the Mesopotamian project, advocated since 1892 by Professor Paul Haupt of Johns Hopkins University. Cyrus Adler, Haupt's pupil, and Richard Gottheil called it to Herzl's attention in 1896-97. When Zangwill split with the Zionist organization on Uganda and formed the Jewish Territorial Organization, Haupt's scheme was revived and attracted the powerful support of Jacob Schiff and Mayer Sulzberger. Within the Labor Zionist movement there also existed a difference of opinion between Ber Borochov and Nachman Syrkin, the two leading theorists who for a time resided in America. The majority of Zionists, nevertheless, staunchly adhered to the Palestinian ideal, and tried to foster the World Zionist Organization's newly adopted program of practical work in Palestine. A dedicated individual like Simon Goldman of St. Louis was able to propagate the idea of *Haachuza*, that is, the establishment by American Jews of self-supporting settlements in the Holy Land. Ultimately, he himself settled in Poriah, Lower Galilee, the first American Zionist colony in Palestine. In 1912, Henrietta Szold attracted not only many Zionist women, but also non-Zionists interested in philanthropy, to organize the *Hadassah* which developed a health program for the *Yishuv*. A number of youth groups, particularly among college students, cultivated both political Zionism and a renaissance of Jewish culture. All these efforts were reported, and in many ways coordinated, by the Zionist press, especially *The Maccabaean*, a monthly founded in 1901 under the able editorship of Jacob de Haas and Louis Lipsky. Here Zionism was propagated in the broadest terms of a cultural and democratic movement but with an unwavering focus in the ultimate erection of a Jewish state in Palestine.[149]

Understandably, a movement of so vast a scope also created much opposition. Many Reform spokesmen saw in it a denial of Judaism's basic principles. While individual leaders like Felsenthal, the two Gottheils, young Stephen Wise, and Max Heller enthusiastically embraced the Zionist idea, the majority of the Reform rabbinate and laity sharply condemned it. After a scathing attack by Isaac Mayer Wise, the Central Conference of American Rabbis adopted in 1897 a resolution which sounded the keynote for the Reform movement until after the First World War. It read:

Resolved, That we totally disapprove of any attempt for the establishment of a Jewish state. Such attempts show a misunderstanding of Israel's mission which from the narrow political and national field has been expanded to the promotion among the whole human race of the broad and universalistic religion first

proclaimed by the Jewish prophets. Such attempts do not benefit, but infinitely harm our Jewish brethren where they are still
persecuted, by confirming the assertion of their enemies that
the Jews are foreigners in the countries in which they are at
home, and of which they are everywhere the most loyal and
patriotic citizens.

So determined was the leadership to combat Zionism, that, although it had generally tried to adhere to the German academic
practice of *Lehrfreiheit*, it could not tolerate the expression of
Zionist opinion by members of the faculty of Hebrew Union College. A much-discussed controversy led in 1907 to the resignation
of Professors Henry Malter, Max L. Margolis, and Max Schloessinger, the former two soon joining the faculty of Dropsie College.
While Kohler tried to explain these resignations on other grounds,
the public at large believed Margolis when he quoted Kohler as
saying: "The College was not an academic institution where
mooted questions might be freely discussed and the students
trained to think for themselves and arrive at their own conclusions." Only the upheavals of the First World War, the establishment of the Mandate, and the mass entry of the College's alumni
of East-European parentage into the Reform rabbinate transformed the pro-Zionist minority into a majority group. Among the
Orthodox, on the contrary, the anti-Zionist group, though quite
articulate, seems always to have represented a minority opinion.
Though no statistical data of any kind are available, it appears
that the rank and file of Orthodox congregants were not particularly inclined to follow even those of their leaders who joined the
Agudas Israel movement when it was founded in 1911. Most
Orthodox Jews readily contributed to the new Zionist appeals, as
well as to the old *ḥalukkah*. Quite a few must have sympathized
with a leading New York Orthodox rabbi, M. Z. Margulies, when
he defied a wide-spread prejudice and hung a portrait of Theodor
Herzl on his wall.[150]

Despite the vigor of this nationalistic sentiment, Diaspora Nationalism made little headway in America. Even after the Bund

and the other socialist groupings in eastern Europe had been converted to the idea of Jewish minority rights after 1903, their
American counterparts failed to advocate similar legislation for
the Jews of the United States. The very Chaim Zhitlowsky who,
in 1892, had sounded the clarion call for Jewish minority rights
in Russia, greatly modified these demands during his sojourn in
America in 1904-1906, and again from 1908 to the end of his
life in 1943. The twenty-one volumes of his *Collected Works*,
which notwithstanding their large compass form only a selection
from his writings, clearly reflect that process of modification. Only
some European thinkers could demand the consistent application of the same principle to American Jewry, as Nathan Birnbaum did in 1906 when he visited the United States. As late as
1937, the distinguished historian Simon Dubnow felt that such
demands in the United States were perfectly in order.[151] Little
did these thinkers realize that, under the American conditions,
minority rights, if achieved, would principally have led to the
establishment of "equal but separate" public schools for Jewish
children, a procedure bitterly opposed by liberals and the vast
majority of Jews when applied to Negro children in the southern
states.

Cultural Renaissance

During the three and a half decades before the First World
War American Jewry witnessed an upsurge in its intellectual creativity which surpassed any legitimate expectations. In the field
of Jewish studies along the lines of the German *Wissenschaft des
Judentums* America entered the ranks quite suddenly and with
considerable distinction. True, most of the scholars active in this
field had been born abroad, but they caught some of the spirit of
American scholarship and began contributing to world Jewish
learning in a somewhat special way. Similarly, the Orthodox rabbis
coming from eastern Europe continued writing their responsa and
homilies in the traditional vein. Yet even here one might detect
some American overtones. But most astonishingly there was a

revival of Hebrew and, even more, of Yiddish letters which, almost overnight, placed American Jewry in the forefront of world Jewish literary creativity. Understandably, there was much confusion and duplication of effort; many disparate tendencies came to the fore; ambitious or hungry individuals often tried to outshout one another by popular sloganeering. But out of that turmoil grew a literature and, allied with it, a press and a theater of unprecedented quality. At the same time individual Jews, particularly from amidst the earlier settlers entered the stream of general American culture and began significantly contributing to American science, humanities, and the arts. Understandably, reference can be made here only to a few highlights of that noteworthy creativity.

Scholars often reflected the American spirit by banding together in joint enterprises. Although the ideological divisions between them were sharpened by the growing acerbity of Reform-Orthodox-Conservative-Zionist debates, they nevertheless found common ground in certain undertakings which they felt were needed by all. One of the first such collaborative enterprises was the Jewish Publication Society, organized in 1888. A need for such a publishing firm had long been felt and one, bearing the same name, had functioned for five years in Philadelphia until a fire destroyed all its stock in December 1851. A second society had been founded in 1871 in New York but, after publishing five volumes, it had to abandon its ambitious projects as a result of the panic of 1873. The one, organized on the initiative of Joseph Krauskopf and Solomon Solis-Cohen in 1888, finally proved enduring. Aided by two $5,000 donations from Jacob Schiff and Meyer Guggenheim, it dedicated itself to "the publication and dissemination of literature, scientific and religious works." Not surprisingly, it focused its interest on history and began with the *Outlines of Jewish History* by Lady Katie M. Magnus. This was followed, from 1891 on, by the publication of the English translation of Heinrich Graetz's *History of the Jews* in six volumes. Although the translation was not made from the main work by Graetz but from an abridged edition, it proved very serviceable, particularly by the addition of an Index volume prepared by Henrietta Szold. At first there was a dearth of original materials and the Society had to be satisfied with publishing translations of belles lettres, as well as scholarly works. Before long, however, it issued Israel Zangwill's *Children of the Ghetto*, Louis Ginzberg's *Legends of the Jews* (beginning in 1909), laid the foundations for the Schiff Library of Jewish Classics, and, jointly with the Central Conference of American Rabbis, prepared from 1908 on a new English translation of the Bible, a project which had been under discussion for seven years previously and had resulted in the publication of the *Book of Psalms* translated by Kaufmann Kohler. This undertaking was completed in 1917. Another enduring legacy of those years was the *American Jewish Year Book*, begun under the editorship of Cyrus Adler in 1899. The *Year Book* pursued the practical purpose of supplying directories of national and local organizations, of Jewish periodicals published in the United States, and reviews of current events. But it soon started including articles on special subjects of general interest and has thus accumulated over the years data of considerable value for historians. After the formation of the American Jewish Committee the latter assumed editorial responsibility for the volume, while the Publication Society continued to serve as the publisher. This arrangement has proved valuable to both partners ever since.[152]

Another important collective enterprise was the American Jewish Historical Society, organized in 1892 under the presidency of Oscar S. Straus. To be sure, at first apologetic tendencies predominated and the Society stressed particularly the Jewish contributions to general American history. In describing its objectives the leaders stated bluntly, "The object of this Society is to collect and publish material bearing upon the history of our country." Citing examples of Jewish participation in the discovery of America and in the early settlements in several colonies, as well as the part played by Jews in the Revolutionary War and subsequent governmental activities, they expressed the hope that the achievements of these Jewish individuals would materially contribute to the knowledge of American history. In short, "the objects for which this Society was organized are not sectarian but American." Not a word was mentioned about the relations of these researches to, and their relevance for, general *Jewish* history. In time, however, the internal logic of the situation reasserted itself and the Society's *Publications* became hospitable also to writings about the history of Jews in other lands; most studies, moreover, stemmed from the pens of students of Jewish history rather than from those concerned with American history who were but tangentially interested in the destinies of the Jewish minority. At any rate, the Society pioneered in what its constitution called "the collection, preservation and publication of material having reference to the settlement and history of the Jews on the American Continent." In its yearbook called *Publications*, of which twenty-two volumes and an Index to Vols. I-XX appeared between 1893 and 1914, scholars could find the first accumulation of serious studies in this field.[153]

Perhaps the most astounding achievement of American Jewish scholarship at the beginning of this century was the *Jewish Encyclopedia*. The need for such a comprehensive reference work had been felt in the Old World for many decades, and a full prospectus for one had been prepared by Moritz Steinschneider and David Cassel as early as 1844. But despite the great vigor with which Germany and other European countries pursued Jewish studies during the last decades of the nineteenth century, it was left to an American group to bring this project to its first and so far unsurpassed fruition. It owed much of its success to the dedication and singleness of purpose of Isidore Singer, its managing editor, and the business-like methods employed by the non-Jewish publisher, Funk and Wagnalls Company. A member of that company, I. K. Funk, a scholar in his own right, brought to this undertaking his earlier experiences as editor-in-chief of the *Standard Dictionary of the English Language* and other publications. Funk and Singer assembled a strong editorial board consisting of Cyrus Adler, Gotthard Deutsch, Louis Ginzberg, Richard Gottheil, Joseph Jacobs, Marcus and Morris Jastrow, Kaufmann Kohler, Frederick de Sola Mendes, and Crawford Howell Toy, the latter replacing George Foot Moore. These editors were supported by both an American and a foreign board of consulting editors, which included some of the best names in Jewish scholarship of the period. The enormous amount of work put into this undertaking led to the publication of twelve substantial volumes in New York, 1901-1906. The *Encyclopedia*'s program "to give, in systematized, comprehensive, and yet succinct form, a full and accurate account of the history and literature, the social and intellectual life, of the Jewish people—of their ethical and religious views, their customs, rites, and traditions in all ages and in all lands," was thus accomplished with relative success and served as a model for all subsequent works of this kind, including the first Hebrew encyclopedia, *Oṣar Yisrael*, edited in ten volumes by Judah David Eisenstein, New York, 1907-1913.[154]

Apart from these collective undertakings American Jewry found its scientific voice in the publications of individual scholars particularly those grouped around the major schools of higher learning. In addition to those mentioned in connection with the *Encyclopedia*'s Board of Editors, one ought to mention the names of Alexander Kohut, Alexander Marx (1878-1953), Israel Davidson (1870-1939), and Mordecai M. Kaplan (1881-   ) of the Jewish Theological Seminary; Moses Mielziner, David Neumark (1866-1924), and Jacob Z. Lauterbach (1873-1942) of Hebrew Union College; Max L. Margolis (1866-1932), and Henry Malter (1867-1925) of the same institution, later of Dropsie College, where they were joined by Benzion Halper (1884-1924), and a number of others. With the transfer, in 1910, of the *Jewish Quarterly Review* from England to Dropsie College in Philadelphia, American scholarship had a local outlet for some of its researches. The old-type Jewish learning likewise had a good many devotees ever since the publication of the aforementioned scholarly Hebrew book by Joshua Falk which appeared in 1860. A fairly complete listing of the scholarly studies which appeared in Hebrew in that period and soon thereafter was compiled by Ephraim Deinard in 1926.[155]

More popular Anglo-Jewish journals likewise frequently carried articles of scholarly interest. The *Jewish Review*, in particular, edited by Max Lilienthal and later by Kaufmann Kohler in 1880-82, included some more technical essays. Otherwise, too, Jewish journalism in the English language, which had had a fairly long history since Isaac Leeser started issuing the *Occident* in Philadelphia in 1843 (it lasted until 1868), had many distinguished representatives in New York and other cities. Among the leading weeklies of the period here under review were: the *American Hebrew*, established in New York in 1879; the *American Israelite* founded by Isaac Mayer Wise in Cincinnati in 1854; the *Chicago Advocate* since 1891; the *Boston Jewish Advocate* since 1900, and so forth. It may be noted that a weekly *Jewish Times and Observer* had appeared in San Francisco in 1855, but a few years after the gold rush. In fact, there was hardly any major Jewish community in the United States which did not have a journal of its own. Some of these were both enduring and of respectable quality. In addition, the national organizations published periodicals of their own, such as the *B'nai B'rith Magazine*, later called the *National Jewish Monthly*, since 1886; the aforementioned *Maccabaean* since 1901; the *Young Judean* since 1911, and others.[156]

Hebrew and Yiddish Letters

The decades before the First World War also witnessed the flowering of a Hebrew press. East-European immigrants had to some extent been accustomed to reading Hebrew journals in their home countries and it was natural for them to continue that practice in the New World. Energetic individuals overcame many financial and organizational difficulties in issuing Hebrew weeklies, none of which, however, endured for very long. One of the longest-lived was the earliest called *Ha-Zofeh ba-Areṣ ha-Ḥadashah*, edited by Zvi Hirsch Bernstein (1846-1907) and Mordecai Jalomstein in New York, 1870-76. Shorter-lived Hebrew periodicals proliferated in the last two decades of the nineteenth century. Among the score of new ventures was the *Ha-Pisgah*, a Zionist journal, edited by W. Schur successively in New York, Baltimore, and Chicago in 1890-99 and continued for another year under the name of

Ha-Teḥiyah. A Hebrew weekly, *Ha-'Ibri*, of a more general political and literary character was issued by Gershon Rosenzweig in New York in 1892-1902. Ḥayyim Enowitz made several attempts to establish Hebrew periodicals in the 1890s. Most ambitious and successful from the literary angle was the *Ha-Toren*, founded in 1913 and continued for about a dozen years. It indirectly benefited from the First World War which not only stimulated interest in international Jewish affairs, but also turned the United States into a haven for a number of distinguished Hebrew writers and publicists. However, the more costly undertaking of a Hebrew daily, issued under the title *Ha-Yom* in 1909, lasted only for a few months. All these journals appealed to the relatively small intellectual elite among the newcomers, deeply divided along ideological and party lines. The Hebrew press encountered, moreover, the competition of the general English and Anglo-Jewish press, as well as of the growingly large and influential Yiddish periodical literature. Certainly almost all Hebraists and Yiddishists could also peruse English magazines. In fact, as we shall presently see, many Hebrew writers themselves turned to the Yiddish press with their own intellectual output.[157]

In these journals most of the creative Hebrew writers found the best opportunities for self-expression, since the market for Hebrew books was even more limited. Yet some early pioneers persevered and from time to time published collections of poems in an environment which was not altogether favorable to poetry in general. Among these protagonists was the erratic but gifted Naphtali Herz Imber (1856-1909), whose *Hatikvah* before very long became the national anthem of the Zionist movement and of the State of Israel; Menaḥem Mendel Dolicki (1856-1931) and Isaac Rabinowitz (1846-1900). More numerous were the prose writers, particularly publicists like those connected with the Hebrew press, essayists, and scholars. Apart from the aforementioned students like Kohut, Eisenstein, Deinard, and Davidson, one might mention the brilliant, if not completely disciplined, Bible scholar, Arnold B. Ehrlich (1848-1919); the talmudic scholar and translator of the Babylonian Talmud, M. L. Rodkinson (Frumkin, 1845-1904); the journalist and popular historian, Perez Wiernik (1865-1936), who was to serve for years as the editor of the Yiddish *Morning Journal*; the brothers Max (1881-1953) and Jacob S. Raisin (1878-1919); and the encyclopedist, Abraham Ḥayyim Rosenberg. All of them were widely read in Europe also. In the last years before the First World War, Reuben Brainin (1862-1939), himself a distinguished essayist and editor, served as a catalyst and general stimulant for Hebrew literature in America. Of course, there was constant exchange also with writers abroad, including many visitors to the United States, such as the Zionist leader, Shemarya Levin (1867-1935). For a time there appeared a possibility that Ahad-Haam (Asher Ginzberg) would accept a call to Hebrew Union College. On the whole, however, the American climate was even less conducive to the development of Hebrew literature on a grand scale than it was to that of the Hebrew press.[158]

With the growth of Zionism in the United States, interest in the Hebrew language spread beyond the circle of the old *Maskilim*. Many younger people, some of them born in America, became interested in Hebrew as a living language. True, few of these newcomers mastered the language sufficiently to become writers and publicists. If, in 1900, Bernard Drachman enthusiastically spoke of the contemporary neo-Hebraic literature in America as being "so surprisingly rich and varied in its content that the only proper manner of giving a conception of its extent and variety is by classifying its production according to the department of literature to which they belong," this assertion evidently referred almost exclusively to émigré authors, including a considerable number of rabbis cultivating the traditional genres of rabbinic letters. In 1902, an organization called *Mefiṣei sefat ʿever ve-sifrutah* was founded in New York for the purpose of propagating the knowledge of Hebrew and its literature throughout the country. This organization lasted till 1913 and generated such important offshoots as the *Ivriah* in 1906 and the *Achiʿever* in 1909, which contributed both to the formation of Hebrew-speaking clubs and the stimulation of Hebrew publications. Public libraries, too, now began accommodating Hebrew readers and, according to one statistical account, there were, in the years 1905-1915, 84,956 withdrawals of Hebrew books (as against 462,852 Yiddish books) from the New York Public Library alone. However, only after the organization of the various Hebrew teachers colleges and the formation, in 1916, of the overall organization called the *Histadruth Ivrith*, did the Hebrew movement receive some solid underpinnings.[159]

Yiddish literature likewise developed in America first through journalistic endeavors. Ever since the issuance of the first journal, *Di Post*, by Zvi Hirsch (Henry) Bernstein and Zvi (Henry) Gersoni (1844-97) in 1870, most Yiddish writers earned a living by their contributions to magazines and newspapers, rather than through their books. On the other hand, because of its intimate connection with belles lettres the Yiddish press offered much more of a literary and scholarly fare to its readers than was customary in the contemporary English press. Short stories, even full-length novels, poems, literary criticisms and essays, which in the general press appeared, as a rule, only in weekly supplements, were daily features in Jewish journalism. At the same time practical advice to new immigrants, as well as counsel in family matters and the lovelorn, often appearing in letters to newspapers printed as a column called *Bintele Brief*, added much of human interest to the news items. These letters furnish interesting source material for the daily life of the Jewish masses in America. This is not the place to describe in any detail the efforts of the pioneering publishers in this field in the 1870s. Suffice it to say that Kasriel Hirsch (Zvi) Sarasohn (1835-1905) who, as early as 1872, established a weekly, *Di New Yorker Yidishe Tseitung* succeeded, after many vicissitudes and the foundation of a new paper, *Di Yidishe Gazetn*, in 1874, in issuing in 1885 the first Yiddish daily in the world under the name *Yidishes Tageblatt*. The *Gazetn* continued as a weekly supplement. Conservative in their attitude to social problems and Orthodox in their religion, these papers did not satisfy the yearnings of the growing number of immigrants permeated with radical tendencies. To meet these new needs the Jewish Anarchists and Socialists published a series of periodicals of their own, among which the *Arbeiter Tseitung,* founded in 1890, is particularly noteworthy. More ambitious was the work of Abraham Cahan who had already established for himself an enviable reputation as an English journalist and novelist. Beginning in 1897, he edited the *Forverts* (The Jewish Daily Forward) which, through its mass circulation, became the most successful venture in the history of Jewish journalism. Its socialist orientation appealed in particular to the multitude of Jewish workers, but it was also widely read by members of other classes.[160]

A third Yiddish paper, the *Yidisher Morgen Zhurnal* (*The Jewish Morning Journal*), established by Jacob Saphirstein in 1901, added a morning paper to the afternoon *Yidishes Tageblatt* to represent the conservative point of view. Finally, in 1914, *Der Tog* (*The Day*) was established by Herman Bernstein; soon thereafter it absorbed *Di Wahrheit* and other contemporary publications. Outside New York it was particularly Chicago which contributed much to Yiddish journalism ever since 1897, when the *Israelitishe Presse* was founded. Its daily *Der Jüdischer Courier* established in 1887, had an enduring career. By 1922 there were nine Yiddish dailies in the United States with a total circulation of 452,567. These papers gave extensive coverage to general American and European news, less than 40 percent being devoted to items of specific Jewish interest, about equally divided between Europe and America. Understandably, the latter loomed much larger in the weeklies and other magazines, whether they were of a general literary nature or served as organs of one or another political party. Among the monthlies *Di Zukunft,* published with some interruptions since 1891, has had a long and enduring literary impact. An anarchist monthly, *Di freie Gezelshaft,* published by M. Leontiev and M. Katz from 1895 to 1902, gave way to *Di freie Arbeiter Shtime,* more or less regularly published since 1899. Its anarchist orientation was toned down into a more socialist attitude in the course of years. A distinguished Labor-Zionist weekly, *Der Yidisher Kempfer,* has maintained a high standard of journalism since its foundation in 1905. There also appeared more specialized periodicals, such as the aforementioned *Farmer's Journal* to teach the colonists various farming techniques; the *Grocery Man*, published by Alexander Shaikevich in 1908-1912; or *Der Groisser Kundes*, a weekly devoted to Jewish humor founded by Jacob Marinoff in 1909 (it was to last until 1927).[161]

Around these periodicals of the 1880s and 1890s gathered a group of distinguished writers, who gradually displaced the authors of the widely read low-brow stories of the dime-novel variety. These stories had appealed to the cruder tastes of the nearly illiterate masses to whom they opened new vistas of romance and high living, as well as of crime and prostitution. Their authors, including A. Tannenbaum, M. Seifert, and the old hand, N. M. Schaikevitch (Shomer; 1849-1905), who had already achieved a certain notoriety in this field in Russia, ran off lengthy novels in frequent 16-page installments. For instance, the *Men-schenfresser* or *Cannibals* by Isaac Rabinowitz appeared in no less than 266 such pamphlets, which kept the naive readers in a state of extended suspense. Apart from thus offering some solace and escape into unreality to the downtrodden laboring masses, these cheap novels ultimately paved the way for a truly high-class novelistic literature particularly by forcing the hands of publishers of the daily press to include in their papers short stories and serialized novels, often two or three in each number. They thus attracted a considerable array of writers some of whom had arrived from eastern Europe with well-developed artistic tastes and talents, while others were newly discovered after their settle-ment in America. While in some cases the impact of the great Yiddish classicists of the period, Mendele, Sholem Aleichem (who spent the last two years of his life, 1914-16, in the United States), and I. L. Peretz, made itself clearly felt, others revealed the influence of the great Russian writers, especially Tolstoy and Turgenev, or of the French realists, particularly Émile Zola. Realism was, indeed, the outstanding characteristic of the Yiddish novel of the period. It was often pushed to an extreme and made to serve propagandistic, rather than artistic purposes. Abraham Cahan's Yiddish novels, for instance, were little more than socialist tracts clad in fictional form. "The difference between Cahan's belles lettres in Yiddish and in English is so great that it is difficult to believe that the same author could write in so different a vein; in Yiddish Cahan is a preacher, in English an artist." His socialism did not blind him, however, as it did many others, to the faults of the laboring classes and, in his novel *Di Neshomo Yesere* (The Special Soul), he realistically depicted the weaknesses of both the labor movement and the religious life of American Jewry. More distinguished and searching were the prose writings by B. Gorin (pseudonym for Isaac Goido, 1868-1925), a protégé of Peretz while still in Europe, Jacob Gordin (1853-1909), who was to become better known as a playwright than a novelist, and particularly Leon Kobrin (1872-1946), who not only wrote a number of distinguished novels where eroticism alternated with idyllic descriptions, but also translated for the benefit of the Yiddish reading public many foreign classics, including Maupassant. Less sophisticated, but equally popular, were the plays and stories by Solomon (Z.) Libin (pseud. for Israel Hurewitz; 1872-1955) who had himself been through a sweatshop and described proletarian life in simple but persuasive colors.[162]

While none of these novelists reached the heights of achievement of the classical trio in eastern Europe, whose impact on world Jewry was heightened, however, by their early enthusiastic acceptance in the United States, many American poets set the tone for Yiddish poetry the world over and even entered the stream of world literature. Beginning with a modest volume of poetry in Hebrew and Yiddish published in New York in 1877 by Jacob Zvi Sobel (1831-1913), poetry served as vital and diversified form of expression, through both lyrics and plays. The Yiddish lyrics of the time were increasingly refined into a major art form. Eliakum Zunser (1836-1913), who arrived in America in 1889, still remained to the end of his life the unsophisticated folk poet of the older East-European variety. But more and more of the American lyricists joined the phalanges of America's social reformers. Among the outstanding lyricists of the period was

Morris Rosenfeld (1862-1923) whose publications, beginning in 1886, immediately struck a responsive echo and achieved an international reputation. His poem "The Sweatshop," for instance, reflecting his own experiences as a needle-worker, was filled with a combination of resentment with quiet resignation which deeply impressed readers in many lands. A typical stanza reads:

> Oh, here in the shop the machines roar so wildly
> That oft, unaware that I am, or have been,
> I sink and am lost in the terrible tumult;
> And void is my soul . . . I'm but a machine.
> I work and I work and I work, never ceasing;
> Create and create things from morning till e'en;
> For what?—and for whom?—Oh, I know not!
> Oh, ask not!
> Who ever has heard of a conscious machine?

Even in their English rendition by Rose Pastor Stokes and in their German translation, which had been issued with beautiful woodcuts by Ephraim Moses Lilien, these poems made a deep impression upon Jews and non-Jews alike. More directly propagandistic, and hence perhaps somewhat less appealing to other classes, were the poems of Morris Winchevsky (1856-1933). Upon arrival from London in 1894, Winchevsky came with a fine reputation of a publicist and poet in both Hebrew and Yiddish. In New York and Boston he untiringly championed the cause of socialism, though not in its extreme revolutionary form as then advocated by Daniel de Leon. In his articles, feuilletons, as well as in his poems, bitter denunciations of social oppression alternated with battle songs calling the proletarians to gather around the socialist flag. Other distinguished radical poets included David Edelstadt (1866-92) and Joseph Bovshover (1872-1915). More deeply steeped in the Jewish tradition, on the other hand, were the lyrics of the distinguished playwright David Pinski (1872-1959) and the essays of the publicist Abraham Lyessin (Wald, 1872-1938), who brought to bear on them the fruits of the talmudic learning they had acquired in their youth. Another great poet of that generation, Yehoash (Solomon Blumgarten or Bloom-garden, 1871-1927), whose first volume of collected songs was published in 1907, became one of several writers, both Hebrew and Yiddish, who were attracted to the Indian lore in America. He translated Longfellow's *Hiawatha* into Yiddish. Later defying an incurable disease, he undertook single-handedly the extra-ordinary task of translating the entire Hebrew Bible into literary Yiddish. In preparation, he spent several years in Palestine and Egypt where he learned enough Arabic to translate parts of the Quran into Yiddish. He returned to America, however, at the outbreak of the First World War and in protracted labors of another dozen years completed the Bible translation, most of it appearing posthumously. Another leading poet and prose writer, whose greatest fame was to be achieved after 1914, was Abraham Reisin (1876-1953), who arrived in the United States as a mature writer and with predilection turned back to the themes of his youth in eastern Europe.[163]

Many of these poets and prose writers distinguished themselves also in the Yiddish theater in America. In the two decades before the First World War the Yiddish stage carried great appeal to the Jewish masses. The father of the Yiddish theater, Abraham Goldfaden (originally Goldenfodim, 1840-1908), stimulated the growth of the American-Jewish theater by his own visits to the United States, especially after 1903 when he returned to New York after an absence of sixteen years. Goldfaden's music was no less attractive than his simple and naive, but very popular plots, some of which also glorified major events in Jewish history. Many needle-workers, to while away the boredom of their repetitious motions, often sang in unison popular folk songs as well as tunes from Goldfaden's plays. Among these workers was Boris Tomashef-sky, later a renowned actor, who, endowed with a good voice, had at first earned some extra money by singing in a synagogue choir. On Tomashefsky's urging a troupe was brought over from London which, together with some newly discovered local talent, performed in 1882 Goldfaden's musical *Kolddunya*. In the same year Sigmund

Mogulescu arrived with a company from Rumania and, in 1883, Jacob P. Adler brought to America members of his family, some of whom soon developed into eminent actors. Other performers who made Jewish theatrical history included David Kessler, Morris Moscowitch, who later became a star on the British stage, and Bertha Kalish. These actors worked hand in hand with gifted playwrights, the most prolific of whom was Jacob Gordin (1853-1909). In addition to such original plays as *Mirele Efros; Der yidisher Kenig Lear; Gott, Mensh un Taifel;* and *Elisha ben Avuya,* he translated and adapted many other plays to the Yiddish stage, some seventy in all. Most of the aforementioned lyrical poets also tried their hands at playwriting, Perez Hirschbein (1880-1948) and David Pinski achieving an international reputation. Some of Pinski's dramas were produced by Max Reinhardt in German. At first many authors wrote their plays with specific actors in mind. But as the technical skills of the Jewish performers increased and their appeal to the masses in New York and other American cities rapidly grew, they ventured to present Shakespearian and other world dramas in competition with the English stage. Clearly, some works were shoddy and keyed to the inferior tastes of naive workers and shopgirls; and playwrights turned out plays with reckless speed. Yet, on the whole, there was an aura of dedication in some theatrical circles which permeated both the performance and the audience reaction with a semi-religious fervor. After his visit to the United States in 1904, the famous German historian, Karl Lamprecht, compared his impressions of the New York Yiddish theater and the emotional intensity of its audience with his experience at the Cologne Cathedral. "In ancient Hellas, too," he concluded, "they must have played theater with such religious consecration."[164]

In the following years, however, the growing commercialization of the Yiddish stage, Americanization of the immigrants which opened to them the gates of the English theater, and particularly also the rise of the motion picture theater, in which Jews were to play such an outstanding role as both entrepreneurs and entertainers, gradually diverted the stream of the more educated and zealous Jewish public from the Yiddish stage. The majority of the Yiddish devotees now preferred melodrama and low-caste comedy, as well as vaudeville, to the more artistic plays.

Contributions to General Culture

In time the Yiddish theater served as a training ground for artists who ultimately made a career on the English stage in which Isaac Harby and Mordecai Manuel Noah as playwrights and Adah Isaacs Menken as actress had played a certain role earlier in the nineteenth century. This evolution was to come to fruition particularly after the First World War, but its beginnings were noticeable long before 1914. Jews left an imprint on the American theater as a whole as producers even more than as playwrights or actors. Some, of course, combined two or three of these talents, David Belasco for a while performing in all three capacities. More permanently influential were the brothers Charles and Daniel Frohman. Although primarily a businessman, Charles was to some extent, as George Bernard Shaw claimed, "the most wildly romantic and adventurous man of my acquaintance." Even more pronounced was the Jewish contribution to the development of the new theatrical medium, the motion picture. Almost all the pioneers in that industry including Marcus Loew, Adolph Zukor, Carl Laemmle, William Fox, and Samuel Goldwyn (Goldfish) were Jews. Jewish domination lasted unquestioningly until the depression of 1929 which temporarily transferred the controls to other hands.[165]

Less prominent was the Jewish share in other arts and belles lettres. Only a sculptor of the rank of Sir Moses Jacob Ezekiel, born in Richmond, Virginia, in 1844, achieved international fame. Although for the last forty-four years of his life he lived as an expatriate in Rome, his remains were brought back to the country of his birth and have since rested in the Arlington National Cemetery alongside other distinguished American patriots. Ezekiel found worthy successors in Jo Davidson and Jacob Epstein. The latter, born in New York in 1880, made his career, however, almost entirely in Europe. The great era of American Jewish painters did not come until after the First World War. Yet Bernard Berenson had already embarked on his brilliant career as an art historian when he moved to Italy in 1900. Similarly, with the exception of Emma Lazarus, there were few Anglo-Jewish poets and novelists of distinction until after 1914 when the children of immigrants, having become fully acclimatized to the American scene, began taking their places among the foremost American littérateurs of that period. However, such authors as Ludwig Lewisohn, Edna Ferber, and Louis Untermeyer had already made their literary debuts before the First World War and were achieving growing recognition. Of earlier vintage was the significant role played by Jewish musicians, including the brothers Frank and Walter Johannes Damrosch. Equally far-reaching was the Jewish contribution to journalism, exemplified especially by Joseph Pulitzer (a half-Jew), and Adolph S. Ochs, publisher of the Chattanooga *Times* and, from 1896 on, of the *New York Times* which he converted into a foremost world daily. As the son-in-law of Isaac Mayer Wise he permanently retained a deep interest in Jewish religious and philanthropic endeavors.[166]

Equally widespread was the growing Jewish participation in the various sciences and humanities. Little would be gained within the confines of this chapter to list a vast array of names. Suffice it to say that the first Nobel prize given to an American, other than the Peace prize bestowed upon President Theodore Roosevelt in 1906, was that in physics awarded to Albert A. Michelson for his studies in light and the invention of the interferometer in 1907. His computation of the velocity of light, made at the age of twenty-six, was widely accepted. Abraham Jacobi, Joseph Goldberger, members of the Friedenwald family in Baltimore, and Simon Baruch, father of the well-known statesman, Bernard Baruch, are only some of the better known Jewish physicians who significantly contributed to medical theory and practice in the United States. The anthropologist, Franz Boas, the physiologist Jacques Loeb, his namesakes, Morris and James

Loeb, sons of the banker Solomon Loeb, the former a chemist and the latter a classicist of distinction and founder in 1912 of the series of Loeb Classics, the scientific organizers and educators, Abraham and Simon Flexner, and others left a permanent mark on their respective fields of activity. Among the outstanding economists of that period was Edwin R. A. Seligman, whose studies of taxation had a practical as well as theoretical import. Another member of a Jewish banking family, Paul M. Warburg, is widely considered one of the fathers of the Federal Reserve Act of 1913. There also were Jewish inventors like Emile Berliner. All these mark merely the beginnings, however, of the mass entry of Jewish intellectuals into various academic fields which was to reach its climax in the development of the atomic and hydrogen energies during and after the Second World War.[167]

IV

Twentieth Century Problems

11 *Impact of Wars on Religion**

The Second World War seems to have brought about a wide-spread religious revival, at least in so far as it relates to politics. Many continental countries have been dominated by parties emphasizing their allegiance to religious doctrine. The De Gasperi regime incorporated the main provisions of the Lateran Treaty of 1929 into the democratic constitution of postwar Italy. The Catholic orientation of the French Popular Republican party and the religious coloring of Adenauer's Christian Democratic following are likewise uncontested. One need but add the influence of religiously oriented parties in the Low Countries and the evident strengthening of the religious element in the public life of such "neutrals" as Spain and Portugal, to note the far-reaching effects of this religious revival on the political structure of almost all continental Western Europe.

During the Second World War, and in the postwar years, even the Soviet Union has greatly toned down its antireligious policies. Although the "peoples' democracies," under the impact of Soviet imperialism, have for the most part seen fit to persecute the Catholic Church and its hierarchy, indeed to view the Vatican as one of the world's major anti-Communist forces, the Soviet regime has long since made peace with its Russian Orthodox Church. This reconciliation, under way ever since the first war

* Reprinted with permission from the *Political Science Quarterly*, 67 (December 1952), 534-72.

clouds had begun gathering on Russia's horizon after Hitler's rise to power, reached its climax in the installation of the new Patriarch of the Russian Church in 1945. This installation, performed with great pomp in Moscow with the participation of leading ecclesiastics of most Eastern churches, received the full blessing of the Stalin regime. In fact, Patriarch Alexis was soon thereafter encouraged to make a pastoral tour through the Balkans and the Middle East, a tour which was to serve Russia's imperialist aims as much as the ecclesiastical interests of its national Church.

In the Anglo-Saxon countries the political impact has been less noticeable, although even in the United States observers have noted many signs of weakening of the rigid separation between state and Church. All students, moreover, agree that whatever its political influence, the revived interest in religion has made itself felt in education, literature, the arts, and many walks of social life.

While some sort of religious revival is thus uncontested, its extent and duration remain debatable. One is readily reminded of the early years of the great American depression, when many observers claimed to have noted an intimate correlation between economic adversity and increased attendance at church services. This observation may have been colored, however, by the often postulated nexus between religion and "hard times," inherited from medieval ascetics and modern Puritans. Perhaps there is some merit in the suggestion, yet to be fully explored, that there are periodic swings in religious attitudes as there are in economic life. "Probably there is a cycle," remarked Rev. Romanzo Adams of Honolulu, "in the changes that take place in the religious experience of a people, but it covers a much longer period than does the business cycle."[1]

Are we, then, merely in another phase of that spiritual cycle which happened to coincide with World War II and its aftermath? Or is it a very special constellation which has made living Western man despair of the rational and humanistic solutions because of his keen disappointment with the millennial promises held out either by nineteenth-century liberalism or by twentieth-century communism, fascism, or Nazism? True, many thinking persons have been impressed by the resistance offered by churches under totalitarian regimes. They saw how quickly the press, the universities, and the labor unions surrendered to the Hitler regime in 1933 and were *gleichgeschaltet* almost with no opposition, and how the churches alone, both Catholic and Protestant, put up a struggle; not to mention members of the Jewish faith, those tragic victims of the Nazi onslaught. This struggle, though not as strong and consistent as some outsiders may have wished it to be, was nevertheless a significant deterrent to the all-embracing uniformity of Nazi totalitarianism. Obviously, religion was not altogether that "private affair of the individual" which many liberals and socialists had long thought it to be.

Answers to these complex problems could be given only by the intensive collaboration of scholars from different fields, using refined sociological and psychological techniques, alongside of the more traditional methods of literary and theological disciplines. These combined efforts must be supported by comprehensive historical investigations which alone will enable us to discern how much of the new findings are but the result of a special concatenation of contemporary circumstances and how much is the more or less permanent effect of interrelations between war and religion.[2]

Nature of Conflict

We must always bear in mind the important difference between wars among belligerents of the same faith and such as were fought by nations professing different religions. In the latter case religion itself often became an instrument of war, since by fanning religious fanaticism each state could hope to increase its army's will to fight. In ancient times, particularly, armed conflicts between nations were considered also combats between their respective deities. A victorious nation usually claimed that its gods, too, had been victorious and sometimes demanded the religious, as well as the political, surrender of the vanquished population.

Even more emphatic was the religious conflict in outright wars of religion. Initiated, as it seems, by the Maccabean Wars, these ideological, as well as political, struggles generated the idea of religious martyrdom superimposed upon that of death on the battlefield in fulfillment of a patriotic duty. This blend of political and religious sacrifice was refined by Mohammed, and deeply permeated the conquering hosts of expanding Islam. In reaction thereto the great European Crusades likewise became wars of religion in which the propelling political and economic forces appeared totally submerged under the religious façade. Later, the Thirty Years' War quickly uncovered the mutual jealousies among the Protestant Powers and their wish to benefit from the discomfiture of their coreligionists. Before long a cardinal (Richelieu) led his Catholic country into an alliance with the Protestant enemies of the Catholic Habsburgs. Nevertheless, here too it was the flame of hatred fed by religious intolerance which threatened to consume all of Germany in unprecedented devastation. Clearly, the reciprocal effects of such wars on contemporary religious beliefs and practices were equally profound.

More relevant to our inquiry are, therefore, wars among adherents of the same faith. Such were the hostilities between Israel and Judah, those between the Greek city-states or between countries within the orbits of either medieval Christendom or Islam. True, each Greek city-state had patron deities of its own, but so great was the overriding unity of the Hellenic religion that even the Peloponnesian War had none of the earmarks of a religious conflict. Thucydides, the great historian of that war, may have deplored the death of one Nicias who "least deserved to meet with such calamity, because of his course of life that had been wholly regulated in accordance with virtue," and admitted that by crossing a frontier one was immediately placed under another god, but he did not allow the religious element to infringe upon his purely secular explanation of the factors operating during the war.[3] Perhaps it was this very absence of intense religious feelings during that great conflict which induced its famous narrator to give a purely secular interpretation of history, and thereby to depart from Herodotus and all other known predecessors. This new approach, as we know, revolutionized all subsequent historical writing.

Similarly, the endless wars among medieval states professing the same Catholic religion were not fought over principally religious issues despite medieval man's overriding concern with matters pertaining to his faith. Modern romantics to the contrary, medieval wars recurred with distressing regularity. Spring was often called the season in which kings went to war. The devastating Hundred Years' War, exceptional even then, was not condemned as a matter of principle but, on the contrary, produced one of the greatest patriotic saints in history, Joan of Arc.[4]

Contemporary rationalizations are, therefore, of very great interest. Heinrich Finke, the distinguished historian of medieval Spain, once claimed that Christianity was the first to introduce the idea of a "just" war into the world. This theory is debatable, for we find an early Jewish distinction between wars "in fulfillment of a commandment" as opposed to "wars of choice," and many Graeco-Roman attempts to justify a particular campaign or even war in general. One may readily admit, however, that "holy" wars became characteristic of the more exclusive medieval monotheistic religions, rather than of the more tolerant and all-embracing polytheistic faiths of antiquity. Justification of war as a "holy" or even "just" war is in the ultimate sense derived from some religious preconception. No wonder, then, that awareness of this problem reciprocally influenced also the religious feelings of combatants.[5]

For the sake of greater clarity, however, most of the illustrations in the following remarks will be limited to three major wars, all of them of a religiously fairly neutral character: (1) the Roman-Jewish War of 66-70; (2) the Revolutionary and Napoleonic Wars; and (3) the First World War. These wars seem to be particularly significant for our theme because they all marked important turning points in history, because they had long-range and enduring effects on religion though the issues involved in them were not primarily religious, and, last but not least, because we have a considerable number of data left behind by contemporaries.

The mixed character of the Roman-Jewish War requires perhaps some further elucidation. On its face this was a religious war between the monotheistic, messianically inspired Jews, led by a religiously fanatical Zealotic party, and polytheistic Romans who likewise cherished a semimessianic belief in the manifest destiny of their empire. Many Jews believed that Daniel's apocalyptic visions of the four beasts applied to the successive empires of Babylon, Persia, Greece, and Rome. They felt that the Roman Empire, "dreadful and terrible, and strong exceedingly," would soon be succeeded by the reign of a son of man whom God would entrust with "dominion and glory and kingdom, that all the peoples, nations, and languages should serve him." On the other hand, most Romans, too, believed, with Pliny the Elder, that Italy had been chosen "by the providence of the gods to make heaven itself more glorious, to unite scattered empires . . . to give mankind civilization, and in a word to become throughout the world the single fatherland of all the races."[6]

The particular encounter of 66 A.D. might well have been delayed, however. Certainly the religious leaders of the Jewish people, whether Pharisee or Saducee, as well as King Agrippa II and his counselors, were all opposed to the revolt against Rome. So were many sectarian groups, including the generally pacifist Essenes and the nascent Christian Church. As a matter of fact, a century and a quarter earlier Judea had been taken over by Pompey almost without resistance. True, even at that time Cicero voiced the regnant opinion of ancient imperialists concerning the divine will which had led to the subjugation of Judea. Four years after Pompey's occupation, the famous Roman jurist pleaded before the Senate,

> Even while Jerusalem was standing and the Jews were at peace with us, the practice of their sacred rites was at variance with the glory of our empire, the dignity of our name, the customs of our ancestors. But now it is even more so, when that nation by its armed resistance has shown what it thinks of our rule; how dear it was to the immortal gods is shown by the fact that it has been conquered, let out for taxes, made a slave.[7]

Nevertheless the War of 63 B.C.E., and even that of 66 to 70 C.E., were principally political conflicts. In the latter, the dissatisfaction of the masses with Rome's fiscal exploitation decidedly overshadowed the religious disparity in importance.

The wars initiated by the French Revolution at times likewise assumed a religious coloring. The religious policies of the Revolutionary government, France's progressive alienation from the Catholic Church, and her increasingly radical reforms climaxed in the Religion of Reason—all contributed much to the bitterness of the struggle. On the other hand, the insolent manifesto issued by the Duke of Brunswick upon his entry into France at the head of the Allied armies added much fuel to the antireligious agitation. Internally, too, the levy of 300,000 soldiers for the Revolutionary armies was the final spark for the revolt in the Vendée, which ultimately broke the back of the antireligious movement. For many years country priests preached against the war as detrimental to both the French religion and society. On the other hand, the interventionist propaganda of French émigrés, particularly from among the so-called refractory clergy, also injected much religious venom into the war. The 8,000 French priests—more than a quarter of all refugee priests—who settled for a time in England, doubtless added fuel to the English people's growing hostility to the Revolution.

Only with the advent of Napoleon and the subsequent Concordat of 1801 between France and the Papacy were the religious problems shoved into the background. They nevertheless continued to color both the French and the Allied domestic and international policies. General August Wilhelm Anton Gneisenau, as well as the theologian, Friedrich Schleiermacher, realized that here was a great ideological conflict cutting across all national boundaries. "Two parties," the latter exclaimed, "seem to oppose each other with undisguised hostility in all states, two historical eras oppose each other among all nations."[8] This clash of ideas, religious and political, flared up anew under the French Restoration and the European system of the Holy Alliance.

Nor was the religious issue quite negligible during the First

World War. Viewed superficially, it should have played no role whatsoever. Predominantly Protestant Germany, Catholic Austria, Greek Orthodox Bulgaria, and Muslim Turkey were allied against practically the entire rest of the world which included the religiously heterogeneous British Empire and Shintoist Japan. Christians of all denominations and Jews fought on both sides at all fronts; and yet, the propaganda machines of all belligerent nations, now put into high gear, exploited to the full the religious differences as well. The Ottoman Empire called for a *jihad* (holy war) against the "unbelieving" Allies, even though the latter included more Muslims in India and North Africa than lived in the Ottoman Empire itself. Although appealing for domestic religious peace with Catholics and Jews, the Russian government tried to rally the Russian Orthodox majority around the "Little Father" in St. Petersburg, head of both their Empire and their Church. Even the Western Allies tried to whip up enthusiasm against the Kaiser's worshipers of the anti-Christian virtue of "blood and iron." Exaggerating certain manifestations of German science and philosophy, they tried to prove that the Germans were really pagans or followers of a pantheistic doctrine, rather than Evangelical or Catholic Christians.

Warrior's Faith

Numerous essays have been written on the influence of war on actual combatants during the two World Wars, though none is based upon objective psychological tests. Even in the United States forces during World War II, where psychological testing reached a high degree of refinement, the usual nine tests did not include any concerning the moral and spiritual make-up of the individual soldier or sailor. Our main sources of information, therefore, remain, next to direct observation, letters sent home from the front. These showed, indeed, that being uprooted from one's customary environment and the imminence of death often produced a religious awakening among previously agnostic or only superficially religious persons. Confirmed believers found their convictions intensified in the crucible of war. Outward conformity, moreover, also in the religious sphere, was promoted by the general military discipline.

In many other cases war produced opposite effects. Constant violence and bloodshed awakened in many men dormant sadistic impulses and helped remove their customary inhibitions. External conformity here often went hand in hand with acts of lawlessness and the breakdown of ethics particularly in the sexual sphere. Already in 1915 Alfred Loisy protested against overoptimistic assertions that there "had come to France a marvelous revival of faith."[9]

Apart from this evident polarity one must bear in mind that letters from the front were generally attuned to the prevailing views at home and were most articulate with respect to emotions and behavior considered laudable by the recipients. One may discount, particularly, the pious assertions intended for the comfort of the families left behind. Moreover, most of the letters examined, particularly those considered worthy of publication, stemmed from the more sensitive, often exceptional, intellectuals. These lent themselves admirably to poetic exaggeration, even outright propaganda, as in the booklet by Maurice Barrès.[10] But they need not have been representative at all of the rank and file of soldiers and sailors. Together with some obvious biases of most investigators, this limitation has proved a serious drawback for the few psychological studies published soon after the First and Second World Wars.[11]

One wishes that studies of this kind were available also for earlier wars. We possess a great many letters from participants in the Napoleonic Wars, including those of that perennial letter writer, Napoleon himself. In one of his epistles, for example, the then young general Bonaparte confessed that constant danger made him a fatalist rather than a believer. "My permanent state of mind," he wrote to his brother Joseph in 1795, "is that of a soldier on the eve of battle. I have come to the conclusion that, since a chance meeting with death may end it all at any minute, it is stupid to worry about anything."[12] Diaries and memoirs could likewise be used to good advantage. If the German pastor, Heinrich Möwes, for example, later reminisced that before the battle at Ligny he had not taken part in any church service, and probably had not prayed at all, his recollection may well have reflected the religiously rather lackadaisical attitude of many German soldiers during the early campaigns.[13]

Beginning with Ernst Ludwig von Gerlach,[14] many observers have also rightly emphasized the importance of another psychological factor, boredom. The dramatic moments of battle are usually preceded and followed by days, weeks, and even months of inactivity during which the soldier's mind is apt to turn to spiritual, as well as to material, preoccupations. This was particularly true in the case of the trench warfare of 1914-18, in which boredom alternated with danger in endless succession.

In many ways different was the attitude of soldiers and sailors stationed behind the lines, or while in training. Here the element of personal danger appeared more remote, although sensitive or fearsome individuals often envisaged the gruesomeness of warfare even more vividly there than while they were in action. Distractions were also more numerous, temptations very great. On the other hand, the military discipline and the pressure of public opinion induced a great many young men who had never gone to church before to attend services and to participate in other religious functions. True, agnostics were not forced into the fold. But, except among socialists and other determined freethinkers, resistance to moderate religious conformity was generally weak.

Here we have to consider the historic role of the military chaplaincy. A comprehensive history of the part played by chaplains in modern armies is much needed by itself and also for the light it would shed on the general impact of religion on war and vice versa. Apart from official chaplains, clergymen and students of theology often served as soldiers themselves. "Yale's records show," Professor Henry Hallam Tweedy informs us, "that there is scarcely a campaign of note, or an important battle in American history, in which her sons among the clergy did not share the hardships and dangers of the soldier's lot."[15] Some countries like the United

States or Austria-Hungary exempted theological students from active service, but others, including Germany and France, entrusted only a minority of the clergy with official chaplaincies, whereas the rest served as regular officers or soldiers. Early in the First World War it was estimated that there were more than 25,000 clerics in French uniform alone. These comrades in arms doubtless influenced their respective coreligionists in a different, but no less direct, fashion.

On the other hand, religious, as well as patriotic, enthusiasm often wore off in the course of a long campaign. "At the beginning of a war," Bertrand Russell warned in January 1915, "each nation, under the influence of what is called patriotism, believed that its own victory is both certain and of great importance to mankind."[16] During the French Revolutionary Wars, to be sure, only the French armies were aroused to patriotic and semireligious—even if at first antireligious—frenzy, whereas the Coalition armies long went about their work matter-of-factly. In the last years of the Napoleonic regime, however, the enthusiasm of the French soldiers, even more of the home front, greatly cooled off, and it was the turn for the Russians during the invasion of 1812, and the Germans during the Wars of Liberation of 1813-14, to be inspired with great national and religious zeal. Once having expelled the enemy from their own country, however, the Russian armies which pursued Napoleon into Germany and France lost much of that zest. The German armies of liberation were perhaps saved from losing their ardent religious, as well as national, fanaticism only by the relatively short duration of the campaign.

In the First World War, the great élan of the first year of war, nurtured in part by the prevailing belief that it would last only a very short time, gradually gave way to a feeling of despondency among millions of Frenchmen, Germans, Austrians, and Russians. In Russia, particularly, the revolutionary agitation within the armed forces assumed a strongly antireligious coloring because of the deep interlocking of the Russian state and the Russian Church. Ultimately, the armed forces themselves overthrew the Tsarist regime, making way, first, for the liberal and, later, for the

428 | *Steeled by Adversity*

Communist Revolution. The latter immediately proceeded to im-
plement its antireligious program which provoked the memorable
outburst of Patriarch Tikhon on January 15, 1918, marking the
definitive break between the Church and the Revolution. Less
dramatically, but no less deeply, the German armies felt an upsurge of antireligious feeling during the last difficult and increasingly hopeless war years.

On the Home Front

The effects of wars on the religious life at home were no less
marked. Many wives, parents, or children of combatants often
found their way to religion even if they had had none before.
True, there were some embittered citizens who, especially during
World War I, queried why religion, and more particularly Christianity, had not prevented the wholesale destruction of human
lives. But, as Dean Charles Reynolds Brown of the Yale School of
Religion remarked, those who thus questioned the integrity of
the churches unwittingly paid a fine compliment to religion. No
one asked, remarked Dean Brown, as to why science, big business,
newspapers, or universities had not prevented the war. Only
Christianity, or religion in general, was held at least theoretically
capable of sufficiently restraining human belligerence.[17] Whether
or not echoing such sentiments, most persons unquestioningly repaired to their churches to pray for their beloved at the front, and
to give vent to their pent-up emotions. In dramatic moments,
before and after decisive battles or at the conclusion of the Armistice, most churches were crowded beyond their capacity.

True, such reports, though attested with a fair degree of unanimity, lack solid statistical support. Before long, war fatigue
began affecting church attendance, too, and, from 1916 on, Evangelical church bodies in Germany voiced increasing concern over
the decline of public participation in services which, in many areas,
had fallen below that of 1914. Certainly observers impressed by
thousands attending churches may easily have overlooked other
thousands who had remained at home. We know how generally

inadequate have been religious statistics of the United States despite the decennial censuses of religious bodies. But even in those countries where data on religious affiliation are included in regular population censuses, statistical studies concerning the ratio of regular or irregular participants in religious functions during war or peace are woefully inadequate. We possess practically no quantitative measurements, extremely difficult but not impossible, to ascertain of the more subtle changes in inward religious emotions at times of crisis.

Fuller studies of the impact of war on inter-faith relations are likewise indicated. As soon as the French Revolution realized that its antireligious policies were greatly undermining its military strength, it quickly made peace with the "refractory" churches. Just as the outbreak of the revolt in the Vendée and adjacent districts can be traced back to the levy of soldiers for the Revolutionary armies, so was their pacification in many ways the direct effect of the war's exigencies. Napoleon's entire policy of reconciliation with the Catholic, Protestant, and Jewish faiths was in the ultimate sense dictated by his military-imperialistic aims.

> My policy is [he declared in 1800] to govern men as the greatest number of them wish to be governed. That is, I think, the way to recognize the sovereignty of the people. It was this principle that made a Catholic of me when I had finished the war of Vendée, made a Mussulman of me when I had established myself in Egypt; made an Ultramontane of me when I had gained the good will of Italy. If I governed a Jewish people, I should reestablish the temple of Solomon.[18]

On the other hand, he was perfectly prepared to make use of inner religious dissensions in enemy countries. In his letter of April 21, 1807 to his Minister of Police, Joseph Fouché, he wrote, "I want you to get up a great agitation, especially in the provincial press of Brittany, Vendée, Piedmont, and Belgium against the persecutions which the Irish Catholics are suffering at the hands of the Anglican church." At the same time he enjoined the minister to speak very tactfully of the Anglican, rather than the Protestant, Church, "for there are Protestants in France, but there are no Anglicans."[19] His grandiose gesture in convoking a Jewish Sanhedrin, some seventeen centuries after the dissolution of that ancient institution, was intended to serve the double purpose of domestic pacification and of undermining the internal cohesion of enemy countries. It so impressed the Austrian and Russian emperors that they forbade their Jewish subjects to send delegates to Paris. In Russia it even led directly to the suspension of the expulsion of Jews from rural districts which was then under way.[20]

Napoleon's daring religious policies baffled his enemies, particularly among the German nationalists. Schleiermacher was convinced that the emperor was toying with the idea of reunion of the two churches. "I should like," he exclaimed in August 1806, "to challenge the most powerful man on earth to try to put this thing over, too, for everything is but a game to him." Four months later, however, he felt that Napoleon, who loathed "Protestantism as much as he hated speculative philosophy," would soon initiate a religious war and encounter the invincible resistance of Northern Germany. This would, indeed, be a holy war for the Germans— not so much for the German states which, not being "cosmopolitan entities," had a foremost duty of safeguarding the interests of their subjects, as for the German people, which would defend its religious and scientific as well as its political ideals. Fichte, too, argued that Napoleon's attempt to establish a universal monarchy ran counter to the divinely ordained national and cultural variations. To an ultranationalist like Ernst Moritz Arndt, finally, Napoleon's empire was the very embodiment of Augustine's *civitas terrena,* to which he sought to oppose "German freedom, a German God, German faith without a scoff."[21]

The First World War started with an effort to unite all national forces. The *Burgfrieden,* proclaimed by the German war administration, contrasted sharply with the previous residua of Bismarck's *Kulturkampf,* the sharp anti-Polish policies in the eastern provinces, and the traditional discrimination against Jews in officers' corps and higher governmental posts. Tsar Nicholas II, too, immediately suspended his administration's traditional anti-Catholic and anti-Jewish measures. He appealed, in particular, to the Catholic Poles, strategically located at the front lines, to let bygones be bygones. He who is said to have spent more than 12,000,000 rubles of his private funds on financing the printing and distribution of antisemitic literature, now, through his mouthpiece, the Generalissimo Nicolai Nicolaievich, appealed in a manifesto addressed "To My Beloved Jews" for the latter's unstinting collaboration in the war effort. Such closing of ranks was characteristic also of France, Great Britain, and the United States.

Of course, actions did not always correspond to the high-sounding professions. As soon as the Tsarist armies entered eastern Galicia in 1914 they began to persecute the leaders of the Ruthenian Uniate Church. They resumed here the old Russian policy of converting the Greek Catholic Ukrainians, or, as they preferred to call them, Little Russians, to the Orthodox faith, thus paving the way for the complete denationalization of the Ukrainian peasantry and its incorporation in the Russian nation. Jews were also harassed by the removal of "hostages" to the interior of Russia and, later, by wholesale deportations from areas threatened by the advancing Austro-German armies. Russian "massacres of Moslems on the Asiatic fronts," wrote M. Philips Price, at that time Special Correspondent of the *Manchester Guardian*, "were no less criminal if less extensive, than the Turkish massacre of the Armenians."[22]

Elsewhere, too, interdenominational peace could not permanently withstand the strains and stresses of a long war. Religious disparity strengthened the national irredentas of Germany's, as well as Russia's, Polish population, which ultimately led to the resuscitation of an independent Poland. Finland's and the Baltic countries' secession from the Russian Empire was likewise stimulated by the revival of old religious animosities. By 1918 Germany's internal peace had so greatly weakened, that the Catholic Center party, and particularly its leader, Matthias Erzberger, now began preparing for a rapprochement with the Allies against the will of the imperial regime.

More overt were the effects of the war on intellectual life and religious thought of the belligerent nations. The impact of the great Roman-Jewish War, particularly, on both Judaism and Christianity has been the subject of extended literary discussion by modern scholars. S. C. F. Brandon has argued (in this writer's opinion, unjustly) against the authenticity of Eusebius' report concerning the departure of all Christians from Jerusalem to Pella in Transjordan in 66 A.D., and denied that the young Christian Church thus publicly proclaimed its neutrality in the armed conflict. Yet there is little doubt that most Christians failed to participate in this crucial encounter and thus definitely broke their ties with the old religion.[23] This attitude of aloofness was the more deeply resented as the equally pacifist Essenes rallied behind the revolutionary leadership in this great emergency of their people, and literally fought to the last man.

The breach was finally sealed by the Bar-Kocheba uprising against Rome in 132-35. This time the overshadowing issue was Hadrian's religious intolerance, and particularly his outlawry of circumcision and Jewish public assemblies. Jewish public opinion, now united in the defense of its cherished religious institutions, viewed the professedly neutral Christian community as an outright fifth column in favor of Rome. Internally, too, the effects of the fall of Jerusalem were manifold and enduring. From there on, the Jewish people, eschewing all sectarian currents, concentrated on the cultivation of its national mores and instilled in its members an exclusive allegiance to the growingly normative talmudic forms.

The impact of the Revolutionary and Napoleonic Wars on religious thought has likewise been deep and enduring. The new religious and political views formulated in France by François René de Chateaubriand, Louis Gabriel Ambroise de Bonald and Joseph de Maistre had a far-reaching influence on French, indeed on all European, literature in the first half of the nineteenth century.

In 1795, at a time when most enlightened Germans were still exalting the liberating effect of the Revolution, the Bremen theo-

logian, Gottfried M. Menken, began preaching a religious crusade
against atheistic France. To him Napoleon's universal empire embodied the principle contrary to God's universal empire.[24] Before
long, the distinguished poet, Novalis (Georg Friedrich Leopold
Freiherr von Hardenberg) contrasted "Christendom or Europe."
In an essay under this title published in 1799, which so sharply ran
counter to regnant opinion that Johann Wolfgang von Goethe, for
example, opposed its inclusion in the *Athenäum*, he preached the
return to the medieval unity of Catholicism. Somewhat later,
Friedrich von Schlegel, after his conversion, actually preached
world unity through the medium of the Catholic clergy. Beginning
with Count Friedrich Leopold Stolberg's conversion in 1800 there
set in a regular stampede of Protestant writers and artists hasten-
ing to join the Catholic faith. Within German Protestantism itself
the new teachings of Friedrich Schleiermacher, August Neander,
and other theologians, buttressed by the related philosophies of
Johann Gottlieb Fichte, Georg Wilhelm Friedrich Hegel and Friedrich Wilhelm Joseph von Schelling, permanently transformed the
intellectual image of German Protestant thought. All these teachings clearly revealed the imprint of the great wars of the period.[25]

No less pronounced were the religious effects of the First World
War on both religious and antireligious thought. From the war
years emerged the great assault on all organized religions set in
motion by the Russian Revolution and climaxed in the ruthless
propaganda of Russia's "godless" societies of the 1920s. On the
other hand, there also was a less publicized, but intrinsically profound, reorientation in the new schools of theology and religious
philosophy. Reacting in part to this agnostic propaganda, Karl
Barth and others writing during the war years called for the return to the more dogmatic and traditional teachings of their
respective churches. In Neo-Reformation theology, Protestantism
found a method of reconciling liberal, at times even radical, social
action with fairly orthodox religious convictions. Reinhold Niebuhr
was not alone to feel, at least during the great economic depression, that "adequate spiritual guidance can come only through a
more radical political orientation and more conservative religious

convictions than are comprehended in the culture of our era."[26] Catholicism, too, unflinchingly adhered to the antimodernist doctrines of Pius X. In fact, "modernism" suffered during the war a defeat from which it has never recovered.

Churches

From ancient times priests were expected to bless arms. Ancient soothsayers were often instrumental in precipitating or delaying the outbreak of hostilities by whatever omens they derived from their particular oracles. Even in the Middle Ages and early modern times, war was so much taken for granted that the collaboration of the religious functionaries under both Christendom and Islam appeared self-evident. Christian theology had some difficulty in squaring this new attitude with the pacifist traditions of the early Church, dating from a time when Christianity was not yet a dominant faith of the empire. As leaders of a persecuted religion, Church Fathers could indulge in such affirmations as that "Christians inhabit their own fatherland as aliens. Each foreign country is their fatherland, and each fatherland a foreign country."[27] But the rationalizations of the new attitude had so long and so thoroughly changed prevailing opinion that religious pacifism hardly was a deterrent to the cooperation of any church with its national leadership in times of war.

During the Roman-Jewish War the priests reflected the deep inner divisions of the people. Like the other upper classes, the priestly aristocracy was averse to the rebellion against Rome. Not only the mercenary high priests of the period but most of their associates at the Temple of Jerusalem had long been active collaborators with the Herodian rulers and their Roman overlords. Mostly belonging to the Sadducean party, they had lost contact with the living currents and particularly the messianic yearnings of their people. They also sensed the rumblings of unrest among the masses and foresaw that any anti-Roman outbreak would signal also the beginning of a social revolution aimed, in part, at the extortionist practices of many priests. Josephus, himself a priest, severely censured, for instance, the high priest Ananias (47-59 A.D.), whose servants "went to the threshing floors and took away tithes that belonged to the priests by violence, and did not refrain from beating such as would not give these tithes to them." Some undoubtedly feared that an unsuccessful revolt would lead to the destruction of the Temple by the Romans. A priest Zadok, the Talmud tells us, had fasted for forty years imploring God to avert this anticipated disaster. No class willingly commits mass suicide. Even a non-officiating country priest, like Rabban Johanan ben Zakkai, allowed himself to be smuggled out from beleaguered Jerusalem to come to terms with the conqueror. He was aided therein by the officiating Levite, R. Joshua ben Hananiah, who was to become one of his chief associates in the postwar reconstruction period.[28]

Other priests, however, collaborated with the "rebels." The very outbreak of the revolt dated from an incident occasioned by the Roman procurator Florus extracting seventeen talents of silver from the Temple treasury. However reluctantly, Josephus assumed the military command over the rebellious forces in Galilee. Other priests more actively supported the uprising and carried on with their Temple services to the very end. They also played a vital role in the subsequent reconstruction of their people and its religion.[29]

Even more deeply divided was the French clergy during the Revolutionary Wars. As the name indicates, the "refractory clergy" refused to cooperate with the new regime. In fact, those of its members who emigrated abroad willy-nilly became protagonists of a crusade against the atheistic republic. The constitutional clergy, however, and later the priests of the new Religion of Reason supported the constantly changing revolutionary governments to the best of their ability. In no other country of the time, however, was there any serious cleavage between the churches and the respective governments.

It was a sign of the growing pacifism and humanitarianism of the late nineteenth and early twentieth centuries that the churches' attitude to war became such a major issue in 1914. A considerable number of conscientious objectors refused to bear arms for their country. Their right to do so was upheld not only by such pacifist sectarian groups as Quakers or Mennonites, but in principle also by all major churches. Only in the Anglo-Saxon countries, however, were such conscientious objections tolerated, with however ill a grace, by the governments. Elsewhere the military usually rode roughshod over all conscientious scruples.

Official church bodies and most of the outstanding ecclesiastical leaders in all countries lent a willing hand in the support of the war efforts. No large-scale collection of war sermons, similar to those compiled for the American Revolution, for the German Wars of Liberation, or for the Franco-Prussian War of 1870-71,[30] has appeared in print. The sermons published during the war bear earmarks of undiluted apologetics, whereas after the war the churches themselves lost all interest in permanently recording these homiletical effusions which, for the most part, no longer squared with their reawakened conscience. Many felt, with Devere Allen, that "the black and sickening record of those years will not bear close retelling. If it could be obliterated, what a blessing it would be!"[31] But enough is known to justify the generalization that, with few exceptions, churchmen of all denominations clung closely to the propaganda line of their respective countries. Individual preachers were more circumspect than others, but few, like John Haynes Holmes or Judah Magnes, dared publicly to invoke the ancient pacifist ideals of their faiths and to defy the prevailing war hysteria.

On the whole, declarations by church bodies were somewhat more restrained. Although in essence they, too, reflected their authors' conviction that their countries fought for a just cause, none went so far as publicly to avow the principle of "right or wrong my country."[32]

Behind these public declarations, however, a great deal of inner soul-searching was going on. Most clergymen deplored the necessity of advocating war. Only in the first months after the entry into the war (1914-15 in Europe, 1917 in the United States) was there much joyous affirmation of patriotism as a supreme religious

duty. In this early period French Catholics, whether of the
orthodox or the modernist variety, were so convinced of the righteousness of their country's cause that they viewed the struggle
against the German war machine as part of their religious obligation to fight evil impersonate. German Catholics, organized in a
special defense committee, replied in kind. "If Harnack [an outstanding Protestant theologian]," commented an English pastor
at that time, "talks of the Czar as desiring the destruction of
Protestant *Kultur* . . . the Archbishop of Cologne speaks of 'schis-
matic Russia' in alliance with 'infidel France' against our 'God-
fearing Kaiser.' "[33]

Formally the relations between the states and their churches
underwent little change, and yet the outbreak of hostilities usually led to the relaxation of existing tensions. Not only did each
nation's concentration on winning the war relegate all divisive
issues to the background, but the growing subtle integration of
the churches in the political fabric of each wartime society reduced
many sources of friction. In France the din of controversy, raging
before and after 1906 over the separation of state and Church,
now died down. Even agnostic groups no longer fulminated against
the very large enrollment of pupils at Catholic schools. Relations
to the Holy See likewise became more intimate. Italy alone persevered in shutting the Vatican out of international conferences,
whereas France and the United States found it to their advantage
to send representatives to the See of St. Peter. The Vatican was too
important a sounding post for the belligerent Powers not to make
use of it despite objections of extreme "separationists."

Wars also influenced the development of foreign missions. Imperialists of all kinds could not resist the temptation to make
use of missionaries for their political purposes. With his customary
frankness Napoleon wrote in 1804, "These monks will prove very
useful to me in Asia, Africa and America. I shall send them there
to collect information on the state of the various countries. Their
habit protects them and helps cover up political and commercial
designs." Just as in his Middle Eastern campaign he restored French
"protection" of the Holy Sepulcher and the Syrian Christians, he

also tried to revitalize the French missions in China, principally, as he admitted, in order "to deprive the English of the management of these missions."[34]

During the First World War, too, the Allied blockade effectively disrupted the communications between the German missions and the home country. As a result many of them withered away even before the direct occupation of the German colonies by Allied troops. At the same time the expanding world-wide hostilities seemed to open new opportunities for Allied missions. An otherwise judicious senior army chaplain of the Church of England suggested that every young cleric be made to serve several years overseas. "The nation," he exclaimed, "that sends its working men to conquer Bagdad and defend the Suez Canal has learnt to think imperially; and the Church that is to hold its allegiance must think imperially, too." Only after the war did some leading missionaries realize how much the internecine struggle among the colonial Powers had undermined the prestige of them all, and fostered the desire for national independence among the colonial peoples.[35]

Religious Minorities

Despite efforts to secure internal peace, many prewar antagonisms were unavoidably sharpened after the beginning of hostilities. In the general witch hunt of alleged or real spies, shirkers, and war profiteers, which became a popular pastime in most belligerent countries, the patriotism of religious, as well as ethnic, minorities was often impugned. Prejudices, long dormant or but timidly voiced before 1914, burst out into all-devouring passions during the hysteria of the first "total" war. Protestants in Catholic countries, Catholics in Protestant or Greek Orthodox lands, and Jews practically everywhere were easy targets. These suspicions stimulated leaders of minority faiths in many countries, especially in the United States, to organize special bureaus to secure denominational statistics of combatants. This gave rise to a vast literature listing not only members of particular denominations serving in the armed forces, but also those who died in battle, received military decorations, or otherwise distinguished themselves in the service of their country. At times such war-born religious statistics became major contributions to the knowledge of denominational divisions in general. Before long these and other denominational war agencies proliferated to such an extent that the Federal Council of Churches had to prepare a directory covering over 300 pages.[36]

The attitude of the minority leaders is well summarized by the declaration of the First Plenary Council of Catholic archbishops and bishops in the United States held in September 1919.

> The traditional patriotism of our Catholic people [the resolution read] has been amply demonstrated in the days of their country's trial. And we look with pride upon the record which proves, as no mere protestation could prove, the devotion of American Catholics to the cause of American freedom. . . . The account of our men in the service adds a new page to the record of Catholic loyalty. It is what we expected and what they took for granted. . . . To many assertions it answers with one plain fact.[37]

Did these minority efforts attain their practical, apologetic objectives? A detailed and fully documented answer to this question would furnish valuable insights into the general long-range efficacy of apologetic literature. For the most part, it appears, these compilations were read by members of each minority group, rather than by outsiders to whom they were addressed. Certainly few deeply prejudiced persons were persuaded by them to change their minds.

In Germany, for example, the rising tide of antisemitism was in no way stemmed by the proofs adduced by Jewish leaders that more than 30,000 Jews, or some 6 percent of the Reich's total Jewish population, had won military decorations during World War I. Subsequently, the Association of German Jewish War Veterans listed the names of over 10,000 Jewish soldiers and sailors who had given their lives for the fatherland. These cold statistical facts were enlivened by a remarkable selection of letters sent home by Jewish combatants from the various fronts.[38] These data showed conclusively that Jews had participated in the German war effort beyond their ratio in the population. And yet the myth of Jewish "shirking" and preponderant share in the legendary "stab-in-the-back" continued to haunt for years the Jewish minority in Germany, and became one of the most powerful propaganda weapons during the Nazi march to power.

Nevertheless, these apologetic efforts were not all in vain. Like most other apologias they eminently served the purpose of strengthening the morale of the writers' own groups. Indirectly, accusations and replies contributed to the general religious awakening. They also promoted many interdenominational activities, such as those initiated in the United States by the Committee of Six, under the chairmanship of Father Burke which, formed at the request of War Secretary Newton Baker, advised the Department on matters of religious concern.

Postwar Effects

For the most part, it appears, war-generated religious revivals carried over into postwar periods—with varying degrees of intensity. The great Judeo-Roman War resulted in the lasting reformulation of Judaism and great intensification of the Christian mission. Although Jewish extremists demanding total abstention from the consumption of meat and continuous national mourning were quickly checked by such moderate leaders as Joshua ben Hananiah, a modicum of mourning became a permanent and characteristic feature of the Jewish religion and way of life during the following centuries. The war helped the Pharisaic-Rabbinic leadership to establish undisputed control over Jewish life, to eschew all sectarian movements and to pave the way for the unification of Jewry in the institutional forms of talmudic Judaism. It also brought about the final separation of Christianity as an independent religion. Forever after, the Christians were persuaded that the fall of Jerusalem had proved that the "sceptre had departed from Judah" because of the Jews' repudiation of Christ.

The Revolutionary and Napoleonic Wars likewise had permanent religious effects. Precisely because the Revolution had been associated in the minds of men with anti-Christianity, even outright atheism, the subsequent revulsion led to strong reaffirmation of the Christian tradition. Politically, the French Restoration and the international system of the Holy Alliance with their strong religious mystique may have proved to be of short duration, but the spiritual forces brought to the fore in the renaissance of French Catholicism, German Protestantism, and such intermediary forms as the Oxford Movement and Puseyism in England strongly reversed the powerful antireligious currents of European Enlightenment. In his anti-Christian crusade Lenin, following Engels, advised his readers to study the antireligious works of French Enlightenment, which he considered more effective than anything written in the nineteenth century.[39]

Instead of being on the defensive, Catholicism reasserted itself after 1815 not only through the writings of such "romantics" as F. R. de Chateaubriand and J. de Maistre or such distinguished converts as Friedrich von Schlegel, Adam Müller, John Henry Newman and Henry Edward Manning, but also through the reformulation of its own doctrine with an ever stronger reaffirmation of its dogmatic and irrational elements. Of course, the great pre-Revolutionary authors continued to be widely read. According to a governmental inquiry, more than half a million copies of Jean Jacques Rousseau's works alone were sold in the years 1817-1824. Nonetheless even French Gallicanism now gave way to the supremacy of the Papacy, whose infallibility was ultimately proclaimed by the Vatican Council, profoundly challenging the basic principles of enlightened rationalism.[40]

Protestantism, too, underwent, through Schleiermacher and others, a reaction against the preeminence of "enlightened" doctrines. Within the very church services there was increasing concentration on prayer, congregational as well as individual, as against the sermon. Not only were the new reactionary governments suspicious of political sermons which some of them had encouraged during the Wars of Liberation—F. Schleiermacher and Johann Heinrich Bernhard Dräsecke were now expressly enjoined by the Prussian administration to devote their sermons only to "pious sentiments"—but the congregations themselves wished to commune more directly with God. Even church architecture reflects for a time this change of emphasis from pulpit to congregational service.[41]

No one will deny that in academic circles historicism, and with it a certain measure of liberal relativism, continued to celebrate ever new victories. As the nineteenth century progressed, radical Bible criticism and philological-historical approaches to Protestant theology and church history dominated all scholarly discussions. At the same time there evolved in the official Church bodies a growing reassertion of the dogmatic and irrational ingredients of the Reformation and a more authoritative control of life within the churches. The revived forms of German pietism, continued growth of Methodism in England and America, and the spread of the various ritualistic and liturgical movements— all testified to the deep reaction among the ecclesiastical intelligentsia against the "shallow" teachings of the Enlightenment era. True, the impact on the masses was far less immediate and widespread. Its uneven diffusion was illustrated in the very vicinity of Paris where, in 1816, of the 1,600 inhabitants of the village of Gallardon only four participated in the Easter communion, while in Champrond only fifteen persons of a population of 800 failed to do so. Curiously, however, when some priests refused ecclesiastical burial to noncommunicants, antiecclesiastical mobs at times forced entry into the churches for such corpses.[42] Toward the end of the nineteenth century, moreover, rationalism raised its head again within the churches themselves. An increasing segment of the population turned its back completely on all organized religion, many joining one or another of the increasingly powerful antireligious movements. However, the postrevolutionary reaction of the early 1800s was still very much alive when the First World War broke out.

In this war, religion as such was not a major subject of controversy and, hence, the war's effects upon it were also more complex and ambiguous. The great religious revival in its early stages was soon displaced by war fatigue and, after the Armistice, by a stampede back to "normalcy." It had been wishful thinking on James Monroe's part when, in his message to Congress of December 3, 1822, he had written:

> It has been often charged against free Governments, that they have neither the foresight nor the virtue to provide, at the proper season, for great emergencies; that their course is improvident and expensive; that war will always find them unprepared, and whatever may be its calamities, that its terrible warnings will be disregarded and forgotten as soon as peace returns. I have full confidence that this charge as far as relates to the United States, will be shown to be utterly destitute of truth.[43]

Alas, in the United States even more than in other countries, 1919, as well as 1946, confirmed the truth of the charge, rather than of President Monroe's optimistic forecast. In an attempt to forget the horrors of the war as quickly as possible, there was an increasing revulsion also to the ideals and institutions which had supported it. Returning veterans at Amherst College were reported in the spring of 1920 to have told their professors, "For God's sake, don't talk to us about ideals! We never want to hear of them again."[44] Precisely because, in the first rush of patriotic enthusiasm, the leading churchmen of all countries had aligned themselves with the powers that were, the ensuing reaction often assumed an antiecclesiastical and antireligious character. The closer the alliance between the Church and the state had been, and the deeper went the disaffection of the masses with the established order, the more did the ensuing revolutionary movements repudiate the Church along with the powers of the state. In Russia the armies themselves supported a revolution which increasingly went beyond the original Leninist program of complete separation of the Church from the state and the school, and finally led to the well-known distinction in the decree of 1929 (also in the Constitution of 1936), establishing "freedom for the conduct of religious worship and freedom for antireligious propaganda." They thus unfurled the flag of universal antireligion or, if we wish, a universal counterreligion.

In Germany, too, spokesmen of the various Socialist parties likewise pointed an accusing finger at the churches and their part in the war. Typical of the growing antireligious mood is the following wartime exclamation of Adolf Hoffmann, the later Socialist Minister of Public Enlightenment in Prussia: "The religion of love for one's neighbors has long since suffered ship- wreck. Battlefield and religion cannot be reconciled. . . . Chris- tianity, financially supported by the state, has never yet vigorously combated the atrocities and bestialities of war."[45] The number of formal withdrawals from church membership jumped from an annual average of some 12,000 before the war to almost 230,000 in 1919, and to 305,584 in 1920, declining gradually in the following years.

On the other hand, the prewar prediction of a leading So- cialist that a world war would spell the end of all organized religion in Germany proved to be mere wishful thinking. Upon seizing power in 1918 the Socialists themselves, partly as a result of surprising electoral successes of the Catholic Center party, had to tone down their opposition to the churches. The new Weimar Constitution provided for separation of state and Church, but this was accomplished in a way which actually accrued to the internal benefit of all major denominations. Although in the Catholic parts of Europe there was some rejoicing about the down- fall of the foremost Protestant Power on the Continent, Protestant churches found themselves, for the first time in German history, liberated from the stifling tutelage of the state. No longer did Catholic monarchs like the emperor of Austria or the king of Bavaria appoint ecclesiastical chiefs for their Protestant subjects. So effective now became the religious teaching of both Protestant denominations (Lutherans and Reformed) that, aided by the population shifts to the large metropolitan areas of northern Germany, they succeeded year after year in converting more Catholics to their faith, than they lost through the conversion of their adherents to Catholicism. In 1920, for example, 11,017

Catholics joined the Protestant faiths, while only 8,565 Protestants entered the Roman Church. It has also been estimated that in the postwar years two-thirds of German children born from mixed Catholic-Protestant unions were reared in the Protestant faith.[46]

At the same time Catholicism, too, rapidly gained ground. In Germany it was relieved from many official restraints and the residua of Bismarck's *Kulturkampf*. Enjoying the new freedoms, the Church rapidly expanded its school system. In the Rhineland, where in 1900 Protestant school teachers outnumbered Catholics 2:1, the ratio was reversed by 1924 to five Catholic teachers for each Protestant teacher. There also was a great resurgence of the monastic orders. In less than a decade after the Armistice the number of German monasteries increased by 711, and that of monks and nuns by 11,354. No wonder that European wags of the early interwar period often asserted that "from the military point of view France had won the war; from the political, England; from the economic, America; from the cultural, the Jew; from the racial, the Slav; from the religious, the Roman Catholic Church."[47]

In the victorious Allied countries the effects in both directions were more moderate. While war fatigue and general disillusionment with the achievements of the peace often nurtured cynicism and antisocial behavior, the negative effect on the churches found expression less in overt attacks than in growing indifference. Large segments of the population once again stayed away from churches, failed to provide for the religious education of their children, or merely paid lip service to their religious allegiance. A clergyman ministering to some 50,000 population in a London suburb during the interwar period complained that "only some 100 or fewer attend our two church halls of a Sunday. They are all working class: the devotion of the little worshipping community (men as well as women) to their Church is amazing. Outside their circle is a vast unapproachable paganism."[48] Other informed observers claimed that in France less than a quarter of the population had any real contact with the

Church. Many, however, who had undergone some deeper religious conversion during World War I continued to cherish this ideal also in the postwar era.

In one respect, the postwar period generated new religious concerns. Revulsion to the nationalist frenzy of the war period awakened increasing consciousness of the humanitarian and pacifist traditions of Christianity. The result was the rise of a new religious universalism which benefited both the Catholic and Protestant churches. Catholic leadership now emphasized the Church's supranational character, condemned the excesses of a man-centered universe, and preached the return to the orderliness and harmony of the Catholic Middle Ages. Many Catholics subscribed to Pope Pius XI's declaration of December 23, 1922 that

> there exists an institution able to safeguard the sanctity of the law of nations. This institution is a part of every nation; at the same time it is above all nations. She enjoys, too, the highest authority, the fullness of the teaching power of the Apostles. Such an institution is the Church of Christ.[49]

Less extremely the Protestant churches found in the ecumenical movement a way of world-wide cooperation to overcome their previous nationalist limitations and the more effectively to preach peace among men. Old antagonisms could not be readily overcome, however. While the Greek Orthodox churches, now decimated by the Russian Revolution, were ready to collaborate with Protestant leadership, the Catholic Church held aloof. An individual Jesuit's *Catholic Plea for Reunion*, published in London in 1934, led to the author's (Albert Gille's) forcible retirement from the Society of Jesus. Even more tragic was the failure of the ecumenical movement to stem the new tide of nationalism and racism loosened by the rise of the Nazi party. Precisely when the ecumenical movement was reaching a certain degree of fruition in the Oxford Assembly of 1938 and the establishment of the World Council of Churches, the new demonic forces were

447 Impact of Wars on Religion

setting in motion that powerful train of events which led to the outbreak of the Second World War.[50]

Not that these energies were completely lost. The lessons of the First World War and the achievements of the interwar period exerted a great moderating influence during the Second War. True, few clergymen could live up to professions made after the First War. At that time Rev. Merle N. Smith of the First Methodist Episcopal Church of Pasadena, California, asserted, "I would be loyal to my country and to Christ. If my country forces me to choose, I will be loyal to Christ." After analyzing the vast and then still growing evidence for the spread of pacifist sentiments among Protestant churchmen, Walter W. Van Kirk predicted, as late as 1934, "that the government in the event of another war, will have to get along without the moral support of many of our larger and more influential Church bodies."[51]

When these words appeared in print, a new storm was quickly gathering momentum. Before long it swept away all such pious expectations. Yet, when World War II finally broke out, the churchmen of all denominations were, as a rule, far more circumspect in their utterances and more anxious to harmonize their convictions as citizens and as believers. They were aided therein by a generally less hysterical frame of mind of the general public. The mood of all countries was far less permeated with the messianic fervor of a "war to end all wars." The previous Nazi onslaught on all churches, moreover, not only dampened the ardor of the German clergy, but also furnished the churches in both the occupied and the Allied countries a genuine religious issue. This time, indeed, the very fundamentals of the Judeo-Christian tradition were under attack. Churchmen of all denominations could not forget Alfred Rosenberg's programmatic enunciation: "Today a new faith is arising: the myth of blood, the belief that by defending the blood, we defend at the same time the divine essence in man. This faith is combined with the clearest knowledge that the Nordic blood represents that mystery which has replaced and overcome the old sacraments."[52] Typical of most contemporary declarations was one issued by 93 leading American Protestants which read, "We abhor war, but upon the outcome of this war depends the realization of Christian principles to which no Christian can be indifferent." To Karl Barth even this statement was not outspoken enough.

> If the realization [he wrote] of the Christian principles depends upon the outcome of this war then there is no point in the assurance that war is abhorrent; for it is surely only unnecessary and unjust wars which are condemned as abhorrent, and among this number the present one is not to be classed.

True, even now there were some such devotees of the idea of nonresistance and the supreme horror of shedding human blood that, before the outbreak of the war, they had urged on Archbishop William Temple "to receive the evil of the Nazi regime into my own soul as a redemptive sacrifice, instead of resisting it." The Archbishop of Canterbury repudiated these suggestions by pointing out what such pacifism would mean to the oppressed Czechs and Poles and even contending that "this notion that physiological life is absolutely sacred is Hindu or Buddhist, not Christian."[53]

All this greatly facilitated the speedy revival of the interwar ideals soon after the cessation of hostilities. In fact, the ecumenical movement and the World Council of Churches resumed in 1945 with renewed vigor where they had left off in 1939.

More far-reaching were the effects of World War I on theological doctrine. In the midst of the First World War Barth had sounded his clarion call for a return to the ideals of the early Church and the Reformation. At the same time, Rev. F. William Worsley, a Church of England chaplain, discussed sin, the sacramental view of life, and the future life as the main "beliefs emphasized by the war," and concluded that "far from needing a lessening of dogmatic teaching this generation needs more than anything else real definite instruction" in these doctrines.[54] From 1918 on, these appeals to "metahistorical" and absolute verities began to multiply in number and insistence. Within Catholicism, too, prewar modernism gave way to Neo-Thomist and other dogmatic affirmations, sometimes combined with outright historic negativism. This new quest for religious absolutes has also been reflected in the belles-lettres of our generation, although not with the same degree of intensity which characterized the Romantic literature of the early nineteenth century.[55] This process is still continuing today. Whatever its outcome, it has already fructified and intensified religious thinking in many domains.

Tentative Conclusions

Of course, effects of wars on religion cannot be isolated from other contemporary factors. We must never forget that the same body of men, often the very same persons, who as church members deeply influence religious affairs, as politicians, businessmen, labor leaders, or scholars guide also the political and economic destinies of their nations. Any "established" church will naturally be subject to the wishes, even whims, of political rulers. In countries of separation of state and Church, the latter will always depend on the voluntary allegiance of a mass membership and the financial contributions, particularly of wealthy members. Here we have natural incentives toward both demagoguery and plutocracy, and frequent submission to an aroused public opinion or to demands of the ruling classes. That is why the religious evolution of any period cannot be understood out of context with contemporary socioeconomic, political and cultural factors.

During the interwar period one often heard—not only from economic determinists—that "wars settle nothing." Clearly, wars themselves are but the result of peculiar political and social situations, created by a concatenation of historical factors. It was argued, therefore, that even without war these factors would have produced essentially the same results.

This assertion is a gross oversimplification. The mere ac-

celeration and intensification of existing trends have often pre-
cipitated decisions previously far from certain. Karl Marx once
called revolutions the "locomotives of history." With equal right
one may so designate wars, too. By speeding up existing social
processes, armed conflicts usually shortened the time of their
maturation and often produced within a few years what would
otherwise have required decades. With the constant change-
ability of human evolution such acceleration has also doubtless
prevented the maturing of some opposing forces, which would
have nullified or modified those earlier factors. In many cases,
moreover, some opposing forces are from the outset more or
less equally strong. Wars, like other dramatic events, by tipping
an often tenuous balance, did indeed "settle" issues which
otherwise would have been resolved in some other way.

In the religious sphere, too, wars as such have had many
permanent effects. Without recourse to ever futile "iffy" questions, we may assert that, in the case of at least two of the
three wars discussed here, religion was affected deeply and endur-
ingly. Both the Judeo-Roman and the Napoleonic Wars resulted
in lasting religious decisions, the effects of which have been felt
in both the religious and the social spheres during all subsequent
generations.

Certainly, the destruction of the Temple in Jerusalem in 70
C.E., with or without Titus' concurrence—this was a moot
question already in that emperor's lifetime—ended once for all
Jewish sacrificial worship. Few Jews in resurrected Israel today
think of rebuilding their sanctuary. Even the most orthodox do
not expect a reestablished priesthood to be entrusted with the
task of again offering animal sacrifices—before the advent of a
supernatural Redeemer. To be sure, the majority of world Jewry
living in the dispersion had long before the year 70 been alienated
from the Temple ritual. In the daily life of the rank and file
of Palestinian provincials, too, the Synagogue had played a
far greater role than the Temple, which they visited on relatively
rare occasions and whose prestige had been undermined by the
abuses of its venal hierarchy. Yet, judging from the general ac-

ceptance of animal sacrifices in the ancient world, the great admiration for the Temple of Jerusalem on the part of such outstanding Diaspora Jews as Philo of Alexandria, and the widespread genuine mourning after its destruction, one must admit that Jewish sacrificial worship still had tremendous vitality. No one can tell how, under what totally different circumstances, and with what totally different results, it would have gone out of existence at some later date.

This victory of the Synagogue over the Temple paved the way for the eventual universal acceptance, throughout the Western World, of the former's daughter institutions, the Church and the Mosque. It also tipped the balance in the struggle between Judeo-Christianity and Paul's Gentile Christianity. Only a few years before the fall of Jerusalem, Paul himself had to acknowledge the supremacy of the Jerusalem Judeo-Christian leadership, and even personally perform certain ritualistic purifications rather inconsistent with his own doctrine. It stands to reason that, without the fall of Jerusalem, the Judeo-Christians would long have retained their position of leadership in the nascent Church. Without the concomitant victory of Pharisaism over all other sectarian groups, they would also have remained members of the formerly latitudinarian Jewish community. No one can gauge the extent to which this development would have retarded the halting progress of the Gentile-Christian mission during the following two centuries, and played into the hands of such competing propagandists as the devotees of Mithraism. The fall of Jerusalem thus indeed became a decisive event in the secular, as well as in the religious, destinies of the Western World.

Less far-reaching, but quite significant, were also the long-range religious effects of the Revolutionary Wars. The antireligious onslaught of French Enlightenment was definitely checked. This is the more remarkable as Enlightenment's other ideals, such as individualism and nationalism, rational and scientific approaches, civil liberties and the dissolution of the feudal order, continued to celebrate one victory after another during the nineteenth century. In all these areas Napoleon's military dictatorship, rather than reversing the Revolutionary program, spread it into other lands. In the religious sphere, however, Napoleon's policies marked a clear reversal of the Revolutionary trends, paradoxically made more complete and peremptory by his defeat.

One may perhaps explain this difference by the fact that only in Voltairian France did the antireligious forces gain real ascendancy, whereas in the Anglo-Saxon countries and in Germany such leading spokesmen of Enlightenment as David Hume, Thomas Jefferson and Gotthold Ephraim Lessing had a far more positive attitude toward religion. One need but compare the effects of the American and French Revolutions. Where the two revolutionary movements agreed, as in the Rights of Man, they really expressed the basic universal trends of the Enlightenment era and, as such, they proved victorious. Where they disagreed, as in the area of religious freedom, France, pursuing her peculiar course, was ultimately defeated. Perhaps because in America separation of state and Church meant freedom *for* religion, while in France and all of nineteenth-century Europe it came to mean freedom *from* religion, the final military defeats of the French armies decisively influenced not only the revival of religion but also that of religious authority, as symbolized by papal supremacy, new ritualistic emphases, romantic yearning for the medieval hierarchy of values, and religious as well as imperialistic Panslavism.

This religious revival wore off toward the end of the nineteenth century. Aided by the spread of popular education and democratic participation in public affairs, religious agnosticism and free thought now attracted far greater mass following than it ever did in eighteenth-century France. Once again a great war, World War I, brought to a head this long simmering conflict. As its result, antireligion triumphed for a time in defeated Russia and, to a lesser extent, in many successor states of the Central Powers. But the war set in motion also the contrary quest for new religious absolutes. Once again there was a widespread resurgence of both religious feeling and submission to religious authority. Catholic modernism and Protestant historicism were now eclipsed by renewed stress on metahistorical truths, on dogma and ritual. The Second World War, finally, in many ways but a climactic continuation of the First, abruptly terminated even the antireligious crusade of the Soviet Union. In any case, taking the entire period of World Wars as a single entity—one may consider it a Thirty Years' War of rivaling nationalisms as opposed to the seventeenth-century Thirty Years' War of rivaling religions— there has been a marked upsurge of religion in 1952 as contrasted with, say, 1912.

12 The Second World War and Jewish Community Life*

During the period of extreme pacifism between the two wars, the shallow slogan that wars produce no change got hold of the minds of many men. This slogan was justified only in the sense that wars do not create the fundamental conditions which bring about the ultimate changes but merely accelerate the realization of existing trends, whether visible or invisible. Moreover, humanity's devious historic career is usually the resultant of many conflicting forces which, often precariously balanced, are brought to a head by a violent explosion, the outcome of which then decides the issues for all time. If Karl Marx once called revolutions the locomotives of history, one might, with equal justice, apply the same designation to wars. Today, when mankind is involved in a war of unprecedented magnitude and, at the same time, is undergoing a world revolution of unpredictable dimensions, our generation finds itself seated behind a locomotive, the size and velocity of which seem to have no parallel in history. That such a war and world revolution are bound to have far-reaching and permanent effects also on Jewish communal life in this country and abroad appears self-evident.

* Address delivered, with considerable variations, at the annual meeting of the Conference on Jewish Relations in New York on May 26, 1942, and as the Harry L. Glucksman Lecture at the National Conference of Jewish Social Welfare in Rochester on June 6, 1942, and published as a *Harry L. Glucksman Memorial Lecture for 1942*; and in the *Contemporary Jewish Record*, V (1942), 493-507.

The First World War

It is enough for us to recollect the transformations in the American Jewish community which took place as a result of the First World War to get an inkling of what changes might be expected from the Second War which is so much greater in the issues at stake, so much more profound in the depth of its upheaval, and so much more encompassing in both area and apparent duration.

To put it in a nutshell, during the years 1914-18, the American Jewish community grew into maturity. Until 1914, despite the tremendous increase in their population and wealth, the Jewries of the Western Hemisphere were largely the recipients of the cultural and political bounty emanating from the Old World. Even the Reform movement, in which American leadership went much further, both ideologically and ritualistically, than anything consistently expounded on the European continent, was largely a European creation. Its protagonists for the most part were born and bred abroad and came here as mature men with definite opinions. While adaptable enough to adjust their views to the new situation as they saw it, they all bear the clear imprint of their earlier training and environment. Orthodoxy and Conservative Judaism were, of course, even more conspicuously a continuation of trends deeply rooted in the old heritage and, until the War, made only relatively minor adjustments to the new milieu.

Politically, too, every important movement from Zionism to extreme assimilation, from Diaspora Nationalism to Bundism and labor unionism, was essentially a carry-over of ideologies and attitudes generated by Old World conditions. Even in those international activities where American Jewry through its Board of Delegates and, subsequently, through its American Jewish Committee proved to be an influential factor, the leadership, except in matters of direct importance to the Jews in the United States (for instance, the abrogation of the Russian Treaty in 1912), rested as a rule with such European organizations as the

Anglo-Jewish Association, the Alliance Israélite and the Hilfsverein. The Zionist Organization, too, though significantly aided by the American Zionist Federation, depended for its ideological and practical progress upon the intellectual resources and manpower of Continental Jewry.

This situation changed suddenly when the European Jews found themselves sharply divided through the belligerence of their respective countries. Within a few days the Jewish masses of the Russian Empire saw themselves cut off from the millions of coreligionists and their leaders residing in Germany and Austria-Hungary. America, long neutral, was thus placed in a position of extraordinary responsibility and had to take over many urgent tasks entirely on its own. For one example, the struggling Palestine settlement, which had theretofore been supported by a primarily European *halukkah* on the one hand and a primarily European Zionist movement on the other, was plunged into misery by Turkey's entry into the war on the side of the Central Powers. Apart from the speedy drying-up of supplies from enemy countries such as Russia, England, and France as well as from the much harassed Jewries of Germany and Austria, the political suspicions of the Turkish administration, and especially of Djemal Pasha, the ruthless and inscrutable commanding general of that area, brought it to the brink of ruin.

At that crucial moment the American community assumed responsibility. The small and powerless American Zionist Federation gave way to the newly organized Provisional Committee for Zionist Affairs, under the leadership of Louis D. Brandeis and Shemarya Levin, who was then in America as the representative of the World Zionist Organization. The immediate result was effective assistance through both relief and political action. To quote a subsequent report of the Zionist administration in Jerusalem, "in spite of all efforts made in Palestine to cope with the situation, the Jewish population would have succumbed had not financial help arrived from America."[1] Moreover, the leadership thus assumed by the American community was corresponsible for the issuance of the Balfour Declaration and for the important decisions made at the Peace Conference and the League of Nations concerning international guarantees for a Jewish homeland in Palestine.[2]

On the European scene, too, it was American initiative in both the economic and political domains which greatly helped to reconstruct vast areas of war-stricken Jewish life. The American Jewish Joint Distribution Committee, a new and in many ways original creation of American Jewry during the First World War, assumed the responsibility first for the immediate relief and, subsequently, for the permanent economic reconstruction of millions of Jews in eastern and central Europe. During the first decade of its activity (1915-24) it spent some $60,000,000 on these two tasks—an enormous sum, indeed, when one considers that it was all raised from purely voluntary contributions.

The effects of the "Joint" upon Jewish life between the two wars cannot yet be fully appraised. Much of the important source material assembled in its archives, important not only for its own organizational history but also for the general history of the Jews during that eventful period, has unfortunately been left behind—if I may be permitted a personal remark, despite my own early and repeated warnings—in areas dominated by Nazi Germany and may never be fully recovered. Nevertheless, there is little doubt that the future historian of Jewish community life in modern times will assign to the foundation of the Joint Distribution Committee its proper significant place in the development of new and vital Jewish organizational forms.[3]

About the same time the American Jewish Congress was called into being. The wartime Congress, organized in cooperation with the American Jewish Committee, was an indubitable expression of the will of a very large section of American Jewry. Led by men like Julian W. Mack, Louis Marshall, and Stephen S. Wise, the Congress undertook to defend Jewish rights the world over regardless of the evident divisions on many issues among the various groups of its constituents. It was Louis Marshall's great historic achievement at the Paris Peace Conference that, despite his own antinationalist bias and his chairmanship of the antinationalist American Jewish Committee, he became the most effective champion of national minority rights for East-European Jewry. He felt that it was not up to the American Jews to dictate to their coreligionists in Poland, Lithuania, and other lands what political and legal status they *ought* to enjoy, but that the Jews of the United States should rather bend all their efforts in assisting these respective national groups abroad to attain their *own* political aims, at least insofar as they were attainable under the stress and strain of the contradictory imperial interests at the Peace Conference.[4]

The transformations brought about by World War I were not limited to international affairs. Called upon to serve in large and significant numbers in the American armed forces, the Jews of America created a new organization, the National Jewish Welfare Board. Primarily designed to serve Jewish soldiers and sailors, this Board soon began to focus in itself the manifold communal functions which had developed in the preceding decades outside the strictly religious and philanthropic services. The "center" movement, building on foundations laid down a few years before the outbreak of the war, soon grew into a primary function of the American community, as is witnessed by the large constituency of the National Association of Jewish Center Workers. The Young Men's and Young Women's Hebrew Associations, too—although in some localities, such as New York, reaching far back into the nineteenth century—now received powerful stimuli through this new superstructure. In short, the Jewish Welfare Board, conceived as an emergency measure, became, together with its affiliated organizations, one of the most creative forms of modern Jewish communal endeavor.[5]

Growing Communal Organization

The decade of the war and early postwar years is unrivaled also from many other aspects of communal history. Although the *Kehillah* movement in New York, started before the war, proved decidedly abortive—it failed to take account of the enormous diversity of origin, habits, and outlook of the then largely immigrant constituency—it nevertheless gave impetus to the unification of many communal undertakings, which has already accomplished a great deal and holds out an even greater promise for the future. It was then that the federation idea, born and acted upon in Boston and Cincinnati before the war, received new stimuli. The largest of all federations known in the annals of Jewish history, that of New York City, was established in 1917 in the midst of the war turmoil. Other federations followed. It was merely as a crowning of that achievement that we witnessed in the last few years the rise of all-embracing local community councils and welfare boards, culminating in the general Council of Jewish Federations and Welfare Funds.

In those years the first professional school for Jewish social work was established and enjoyed excellent graduate standing. Although this institution succumbed in the inhospitable clime of the 1930s, the idea is by no means dead and certainly the school's reestablishment after World War II would encounter far fewer difficulties than did its original foundation. The present National Conference of Jewish Social Welfare may be in direct line of succession to the early conferences of Jewish charities. It nevertheless also testifies, by its very size and the great variety of its interest and functions, to the upsurge given to all fields of communal endeavor by both the enhanced feeling of responsibility and the enthusiastic acceptance by its predecessors a generation ago.[6]

Even in the realm of religion, learning, and culture, where external transformations take effect very slowly over a period of many years, the impact of the last war and the early postwar years is undeniable. During the war the Menorah movement was started; its contributions to the cultural life of American Jewry of that time can hardly be overestimated.[7] In the 1920s such significant institutions of higher learning as the Jewish Institute of Religion in New York and the Hebrew Teachers College in Boston (Roxbury) were founded; others were vastly expanded and enriched in content and vigor. They all added significant hues to the multicolored pattern of American Jewish culture. More, those years saw the emergence of an increasing group of American-born leaders and scholars upon whose shoulders began to rest the ever more important task of synthesizing American and Jewish culture. In other words, the decade of 1915-24 will forever remain in the annals of American Jewish history an era of memorable creativity and of qualitative as well as quantitative expansion.

A *Challenge to American Jewry*

If during the First World War American Jewry came to maturity, the Second War has placed in its hands undisputed leadership of world Jewry, with all the challenges and responsibilities which it entails. Should we live up to these exalted demands in a measure at all comparable with the achievement of our predecessors earlier in this century, we would lay the ground for an even more unique communal structure and earn the gratitude of generations. Should we fail, however, we would fail not only for ourselves but for the Jewish people as a whole and, to a certain extent, be justly called to account by mankind at large.

Not that we may envisage immediate progress. The road to the immediate future is strewn with great difficulties, indeed grave pitfalls. Hundreds of thousands of young American Jews have been, or will be, drafted into the armed forces of the United States. The dislocation of private and family life, occasioned by such a transition from civilian to military life, is bound to affect every phase of communal life as well. The larger, more comprehensive, and more efficient our communal superstructures are, the more they depend upon long-range planning. Under wartime conditions all long-term planning, and especially such as depends in execution on a particular personnel, is well-nigh impossible. All communal activities, particularly those centering around civilian life, are therefore bound to rely on improvised programs and rapid adjustments to changing and usually unexpected situations.

It is an acid test of the quality of our leadership whether or not it proves its mettle in such creative improvisation. Critics of contemporary American Jewish communal life have often contended that its major drawback consists in the growth during the last decades of a communal bureaucracy which has displaced the previously independent, self-sacrificing, and creative leaders. The wartime developments may furnish an answer to these criticisms, and either prove them right or wrong.

This much-needed improvisation will doubtless be further complicated by budgetary uncertainties arising from the new concentration on the war production effort, the increased taxation, and the declining standard of living of communal constituencies. In the long run, however, I sincerely believe that these factors will stimulate rather than detract from the liberality of the Jewish, as well as the non-Jewish, public. It has long been observed that in periods of great stress and insecurity people are more inclined to part with portions of their income or wealth—in the future of which they themselves believe less firmly—than in periods of comparative stability.

Of course, the last few years have also generated many a surprise in the economic reactions to the war—witness Wall Street—and hence one is wary of predictions. One may also anticipate the great competitive pressure of general patriotic causes, such as the U.S.O. and the Red Cross, in which citizens naturally participate to the full extent of their ability. An even more serious complication might arise from the mistaken application of the fine and genuine call to American unity. Many a champion of one or another denominational cause may be misled by his great and justified zeal to contribute to the unitarian effort (for instance, a local war chest) into forgetting the cultivation of his own vineyard, to the permanent detriment not only of his denominational group but, in the ultimate sense, of the American community as a whole.

Nevertheless, if one may venture any guess at all, one might perhaps reasonably expect a diminution of Jewish philanthropic and educational revenue from the few large contributors at the top of the economic ladder, but a substantial increase in contributions from the upper and lower middle class. The term middle class is used here in the economic rather than in the social sense. Many a "proletarian" wage earner in one of the well-paid industrial positions may now, perhaps for the first time, join the ranks of substantial contributors to communal causes, other than those intimately tied up with some specific interest of labor. That this process requires thorough reorientation on the part of both the Jewish communal and the labor leaders is evident. But the acceleration of such reorientation—for a long time an urgent communal necessity—may yet prove to be one of the major gains resulting from the war crisis.

Shifting Conditions and Problems

However this may be, the problems confronting our communal agencies will be vast and complex. The great concentration of communal effort in recent years on international relief and defense against antisemitism is bound to give way under the changed conditions of the war period. Not that there is less need today for relief abroad or that the danger of antisemitic propaganda in this country has passed away. But the considerable difficulties and necessary adjustments in extending actual assistance to Jews in war-stricken areas, the continued decrease in immigration, and the great new needs and opportunities for local philanthropic action will call for radical readjustments in the field of relief.

Above everything else we are now witnessing a tremendous inner migration, one unparalleled in American history since the days of the early pioneers. Millions of Americans have changed their residence since 1940; many more millions are bound to migrate either voluntarily or under the compulsion of an industrial draft. New industrial centers are springing up under our eyes, while, New York, for example, seems to be losing ground in its relative importance on the American scene. These transformations, long adumbrated by the stoppage of large-scale immigration and a certain detachment of America from the European world, which have gradually shifted the center of gravity from the Atlantic border to the Midwest and Far West have been greatly accelerated by the need for strategically located industries, difficulties in transportation, and other natural as well as social factors.

This evolution places the Jewish communal organs before novel and important decisions. For decades observers of American Jewish life have deplored the concentration of the Jewish population in this country in the few northeastern states. The agglomeration of nearly two-thirds of American Jewry within a radius of two hundred miles from Times Square has had many serious implications for its social status. Even before the last war and during it, various "dispersion committees," attempted to distribute Jews more uniformly throughout the country.[8] Their failure at that time may not have been altogether a misfortune. There were decided communal advantages in this great concentration in a smaller area. Even politically, the oft-repeated assertion that large Jewish accumulations have promoted the growth of antisemitism has not been borne out by experience. It is a matter of record that the most virulent antisemitic pamphlets and the most riotous antisemitic groups have often originated from areas with few or almost no Jews, for instance, Montana. On the other hand, the concentration of great voting power in a small area has had some favorable repercussions, at least among those politicians who are dependent on votes.[9] Now, however, the trend is definitely toward dispersal, without dispersion committees.

It will be the task of the communal leaders to watch these migratory trends closely, to investigate the new economic opportunities thus opened to American Jewish youth from both the short-range and the long-range points of view, to rearrange the educational, and especially vocational, programs, and generally to be on guard lest the people be caught unawares. It will also bear thinking ahead on the effects this redistribution of population may have on Jewish family, social, and religious life, and what new communal forms may be necessary to meet the exigencies of the new era. The difficulties experienced and partly overcome by the Resettlement Division of the National Refugee Service may furnish many a valuable clue for communal planning on a far more ambitious scale.[10]

Even more difficult, and far less unanimous, will be communal action relating to the new economic developments. Personal bias and class interest may sharply divide the Jewish public on this issue, as it will divide the American people at large. But one cannot help feeling that Jewish leadership would be remiss in its duty, if it were not to take cognizance of the deep transformations in the economic structure of the whole world, which are taking place under our eyes and which have all the earmarks of permanence. Unless we totally misread the signs of the age, there is hardly any question that humanity, after emerging from the present conflict, will witness the spread of social controls in all countries, including the democratic countries, and may even live under certain regional and world-wide controls transcending the national boundaries of the largest countries.

To be sure, those who for many years have sung the *el male raḥamim* (dirge) over capitalism have been, to say the least, premature. The capitalist order still has great vitality, and its sudden replacement in this country by another order could be accomplished only by a civil war going far beyond the civil-war elements implied in the present world-wide clash. At any rate, those of us who have evolutionary convictions or temperaments will anticipate a more gradual transition. Whatever our personal evaluations, however, we must reckon with the new and ever-increasing government controls over the economy as a permanent feature of our governmental system and should not delude ourselves into believing that they will be swept away by another wave of *laissez faire*, such as followed the emergency measures adopted during the First World War. The only question—in fact the most crucial question confronting mankind today—is the extent to which these powerful social controls can be permanently reconciled with our traditional system of individual liberties, that is with democracy.

The effects of these transformations upon Jewish life will be tremendous. Many of us may regret the passing of the extreme liberal era which seemed to offer such excellent opportunities to countless Jewish individuals. It is probably too early now to draw the balance of the Jewish contributions to the rise and development of modern capitalism or of the influence of modern capitalism on Jewish life. I have taken occasion in an essay on "Modern Capitalism and Jewish Fate,"[11] to discuss briefly these interrelations as they emerge from the mist of ages. One factor seems to stand out above all others, namely, that the capitalist system cannot be treated as a single entity. While in its early and advanced stages, roughly ending at the start of this century, the economic progress of Jewish individuals was quite undeniable—though here, too, one should guard oneself against those obvious exaggerations which emanated from overt or concealed antisemites or over-assertive Jews—this progress was checked by the developments of what is called "late" capitalism, especially in the period between the two wars.

Under this latest economic system, there was such a growth of corporate control, often of corporate monopolies which sometimes formed huge international cartels, that the old "rugged individualism" has long become a beautiful myth. Little chance, indeed, had the small Jewish shopkeeper or artisan in competing with the gigantic chain stores or industrial combines. In this country, moreover, the vast corporations have often evinced positive leanings toward anti-Jewish discrimination. Corporate banking itself, in many other countries open to participation by Jews far beyond their numerical strength, has in the United States—antisemitic assertions to the contrary—been a peculiarly non-Jewish domain. What increased social controls, on the other hand, have in store for Jews both as economic agents and members of their group, still is largely in the realm of speculation. In any case, whatever one believes about the probabilities of the future evolution, its gradual unfolding through successive stages will bear careful watching and require the most intelligent and concentrated communal effort in order to mitigate the unavoidable sufferings of a great many individuals and better to prepare the younger generation for its future struggle for survival.

Ideologically, too, the Jewish community will be called upon to strain all its intellectual resources to meet the difficulties of the new era. The perennial crisis in religion may have been slightly alleviated by the war emergency. There is some evidence of increased churchgoing by the American public, including Jews. Even more pronounced is the religious appeal upon many young men drawn into the armed forces. I have been told on good authority that a great many young Jews, as well as Christians, who had completely lost contact with their ancestral creed have been participating in the religious services and maintaining close personal relations with their religious advisers. Whether this is mere nostalgia for home and one's accustomed environment, or whether it forebodes a deeper dissatisfaction with the rationalist explanations of the mysteries of existence previously accepted, remains to be seen.

Other ideological currents operating in the Jewish community have, on the other hand, evidently forefeited much of their vitality and the enthusiastic allegiance of their members. Zionism, especially, which in many youth groups here and abroad had taken the place of religion in its emotional and messianic strivings, has, partly under the stress of international bickerings and contrasting Arab claims, lost some of its appeal, at least outside its purely utilitarian aspects. Many professed Zionists have become apologetic and, like their non-Zionist confreres, speak of the urgent need of a haven of refuge for uprooted European Jewry, rather than of ushering in a new epoch. Communism, too, which but a few years ago seemed to hold out the great millennial promise to a numerically small but articulate Jewish group, lost much of its appeal to the emotions of its adherents at the time of the unnatural Russo-German collaboration and has never recovered it; not even after the German assault on the Soviet Union. Opportunism and realism, however necessary and rationally understandable, have never been a sufficient substitute for messianism and have never satisfied the emotional yearnings of youth.

A Disillusioned Generation

The result is that we now have a generation perhaps even more disillusioned than any of its predecessors, a generation which has seen its gods fall to dust, but no new ones arising to take their place. This is true of the world at large, perhaps even more true of its democratic than of its totalitarian sections, but it is doubly true of the Jewish group. Despite the ridicule subsequently heaped upon the slogans of World War I by a great many well-meaning persons who misinterpreted motives because of the effects, that conflict *was* fought as "a war to end wars" and in order to "make the world safe for democracy." In 1917-18 these watchwords carried supreme conviction because they so deeply corresponded to the yearnings of mankind. Perhaps the greatest danger to the cause of the United Nations today looms from that much debated "complacency" of their public, which considers the anti-Nazi struggle merely as a "difficult job" which has to be "seen through"—a danger which is but slightly mitigated by the fact that the totalitarian nations, too, entered the war without the great fervor and emotional uplift of 1914. Similarly, the Jewish people, though fighting for its very life in desperation, with its back against the wall, reveals few signs of deep feeling about an immediately dawning messianic era.

This ideological and psychological situation seems far more threatening than some of the obvious socioeconomic difficulties. To handle it adequately will require even more creative thinking, perspicacity, and organizational effectiveness than the social and economic challenge discussed before. What is worse, in looking over the communal scene in America one finds little attention paid to these basic issues. To continue plodding along the daily routine is, under these circumstances, no less dangerous than even a grand failure in some daring, major attempt which, it may readily be admitted, is likely to evoke greater differences of opinion and hence conjure up the much feared phantom of disunity. As if unity in outlook and behavior were at all characteristic of American Jewry!

Planning for Postwar Reconstruction

Beyond these immediate exigencies the American community is called upon to make a major contribution to the "winning of the peace." In fact, the reconstruction of American Jewish life in itself has an immediate bearing on the future of world Jewry since more than one-third of the entire people is concentrated in the United States. With the bulk of the Jews elsewhere economically and socially ruined, and with the largest section living in the Soviet Union having lost contact with the rest of Jewry since 1917, the Jews of the United States together with the smaller groups in Latin America and the British Empire, especially Palestine, will decide in the next few years the course of Jewish history for generations to come.

Unlike during the First World War, American Jewry in 1942 almost stood alone. After 1918, despite its great sufferings, East-European Jewry still commanded important economic and intellectual resources. Though not generally known, it is a fact that for every dollar spent by "foreign" relief in Poland, Czechoslovakia, Rumania, and other countries, several dollars were contributed by the local Jews themselves. In contrast, in the early 1940s, despite the miracles performed daily by the relief agencies of the new ghetto communities created by the Nazis in Poland and elsewhere, one could reckon very little with local resources for reconstruction after World War II. "Foreign" relief itself at that time, though consisting primarily of American disbursements, both communal and private, was substantially shared in the 1920s by Dutch, French, and other European Jews. In contrast, the formerly wealthy German, French, Dutch, and Belgian communities will for a time be among the recipients of bounty rather than among its contributors.

The enormity of the relief and migration problems confronting European Jewry at the end of the hostilities will overtax the resources of the entire Jewish people. This is, of course, not a Jewish problem alone. Undoubtedly some international action of unprecedented magnitude will be required to salvage the hundreds of millions of suffering humanity in Europe and Asia. But the extent to which such international action will take cognizance of the Jewish sufferers will depend largely on American Jewry. Its representatives will not only have to stand guard and serve as permanent reminders for those international organs which will be entrusted with the execution of the plans, but also be prepared to call attention to certain peculiarities of the Jewish situation and to devise remedial action to meet these particular exigencies. Certainly a group exposed to years of relentless extermination by the Nazis and to deep-rooted antagonisms in all Axis-dominated areas will require different treatment than most local majority groups. In addition, American Jewry will have to strain its own resources to a maximum to supplement governmental action and to find new creative ways not only to alleviate the immediate misery but also to help reconstruct the shattered life of European Jewry along permanent lines. The rebuilding of the destroyed religious, educational, and cultural institutions and the reawakening of the vast creative cultural energies of European Jewry will, in any case, remain principally a specific Jewish communal obligation.[12]

Fortunately, unlike 1940,[13] the American Jewish public is far more awake to such need of long-term planning and thorough preparation. The American Jewish Committee, the American Jewish Congress, the Jewish Labor Committee, and others have called into existence special institutes devoted to the study of postwar problems. Together with the Conference on Jewish Relations (since renamed Conference on Jewish Social Studies) and other older organizations, these institutes are now collecting and sifting data so as to offer a factual background for whatever policies might ultimately be adopted by American Jewish leaders. They also cooperate with a multitude of non-Jewish agencies which are devoting much energy, thought, and money to the clarification of many major issues which will confront the rebuilders of the world after the cessation of hostilities.

Nevertheless, it is a matter of common knowledge that we are still far from attaining the necessary information and clarity, and still further from any general agreement in regard to our major aims. However, the confusion and bewilderment of both the public and the leaders, which was characteristic of the early months of the war has given way to greater comprehension and to serious attempts at seeking solutions. We may still be far from the goal, but we are on the road toward it.

Moreover, the absence of a fully formulated and thoroughly discussed program of postwar reconstruction need not be as alarming as it appears. To be sure, this war, which most of us reasonably expect to be very long, has been marked by an unparalleled succession of surprises. We may live to see another surprise, the sudden end of hostilities at a moment least expected by the public and even the respective high commands. Nevertheless, the danger of finding ourselves at such a moment with an unprepared leadership, an unfinished program, and a highly incomplete accumulation of factual data is constantly diminishing not only by the progress in the work done by our communal agencies. There is a widespread belief now that this war will not be followed immediately by a regular peace conference, but by a lengthy intermediate period of reconstruction without a peace treaty. During that armistice period, which may last many years, the preliminary economic and social reconstruction will be accompanied by a process of psychological detoxication, which will make possible ultimate decisions based upon mutual understanding and, hence, hold out greater promise of permanence.

Under these circumstances, American Jewish leadership need not have at its disposal a completely prepared definitive program. It seems most advisable now to work along two lines and to seek clarity for a two-fold program of action: one relating to the intermediary reconstruction period after the war, and the other looking toward more permanent solutions. That the latter is not only ultimately unavoidable and also necessary to safeguard ourselves against surprises, but that it also inherently must give direction to the provisional measures, goes without saying. However, it might save a great many unnecessary efforts if the two programs are clearly understood as differing in both compass and application.

The effect of the war on this phase of American Jewish communal life, already great, is bound to increase the closer we come to its end. Much of the creative élan of the World War I period in the domestic life of American Jewry was due to international fermentation. This may be repeated during the present war. It becomes ever clearer that those in our midst who have tried to persuade themselves and their fellows that American Jewish life can be made secure without reference to the fate of world Jewry, were even more grievously mistaken than the general American isolationists who nurtured the irrational expectation of divorcing the destiny of this continent from that of the rest of mankind. He who preaches American Jewish isolationism—and there are some among us who do it even after December 7, 1941—puts wishful thinking ahead of even intelligent realization of self-interest. On the contrary, the stimuli emanating from a clear recognition of the intimate tie-up between the destinies of America and those of the rest of the world, as well as between the fate of American Jewry and of world Jewry, are bound to fructify communal action greatly in this country itself.

The Need for Courageous Leadership

In conclusion, I may be allowed to repeat the final sentences of my aforementioned address before the National Conference because I believe that, despite the great changes generated by two years of greatest historic significance, the hope then expressed still bears repetition today:

If ever, since the days of the first Exile, the Jewish people has been in need of a far-sighted and courageous leadership, it is in these days of great crisis. If the leaders, in particular of American Jewry, equipped with the knowledge furnished them by the methods of modern social and historical sciences and imbued with the accumulated wisdom of the ages of rabbis and thinkers, will undertake to look courageously into the realities as they are and to adopt measures which they will consider best, regardless of whether or not they meet with the instant approval of the less informed, then they may yet be destined to render a historic service lesser to none performed by their predecessors in other ages of great transformation.

13 *Some of the Tercentenary's Historic Lessons**

From the welter of speeches, articles and books which have appeared in connection with the Tercentenary celebrations there have thus far emerged but few new insights into the processes of the American Jewish historical evolution. True, many new data have been marshaled. Especially the numerous communal studies conducted on a local and regional level have already yielded considerable new information, and are likely to bring forth much more of such detailed knowledge when the researches initiated during the Tercentenary year will be brought to fruition. There is no question but that the growing awareness of their historical heritage by American Jews and its greater appreciation by their non-Jewish neighbors has, for the first time, created a climate of opinion favorable to historical investigations, which in the long run will place the knowledge of American Jewish history on solid scientific foundations. In the meantime, however, some of the historic lessons which can tentatively be drawn from the three centuries of Jewish experience in America must still largely be based upon information accumulated before the Tercentenary year started.

Peculiarities of Jewish Immigration

One such outstanding lesson is the peculiar nature of Jewish migratory movements to and from America, which, as far as can

* Address of the President, delivered at the Fifty-Third Annual Meeting of the American Jewish Historical Society held at the Community Center of The Congregation Shearith Israel, New York, N. Y., February 12, 1955 and published in *PAJHS*, XLIV (1954-55), 199-209.

be seen, more or less always distinguished the Jews from other immigrant groups in this "nation of nations." To begin with, probably already in colonial America, but most certainly in the great migrations of the nineteenth and twentieth centuries Jews, as a rule, arrived here in order to make this country their permanent home. Of course, we know relatively little about the Jewish and general emigration from this country and its causes in the earlier periods. But it is noteworthy that, already in 1872, Judge Daly estimated that of the 300,000 Jews (this figure seems to be decidedly exaggerated) then living in the United States, only "something over one-third" were American born.[1] As in the case of non-Jews there must always have been a certain number of involuntary Jewish émigrés from this country, particularly among those who were deported because of illegal entry or some other conflict with the law. Some insolvent debtors may likewise have chosen to disappear from the country rather than "face the music" on the part of irate creditors. A case of three such Jews, Philip Samuel, Henry Mordecai, and Israel Joseph, who allegedly left for England and Holland in 1760 and whom the creditor, James Beekman, unsuccessfully tried to locate, is known from the latter's papers.[2] There also were numerous voluntary expatriates for economic, emotional, or intellectual reasons. In the 1920s, especially, many Americans felt the attraction of such Old World centers as Paris and London or, for ideological reasons, decided to settle in Palestine. The official statistics of the Mandatory Government in Palestine showed the steep rise of American Jewish immigration into the Holy Land from 65 in 1922, to 570 in 1925. Although the numbers fell off considerably in the subsequent more critical years, they still amounted to a total of 1,817 in the seven-year period of 1922-28.[3] There had existed an American Jewish community of more than fifty persons in Jerusalem as early as 1877, although like most other Palestinian Jews of the period, they depended on the support of charitable coreligionists abroad.[4]

And yet, insofar as immigration statistics are at all available, they showed that such émigrés were but a small fraction of Jews who came into the country. We need cite here only the statistical data from the period of 1908-1927. Owing to the crisis of 1907, the World War and the Immigration Laws of 1924, the number of immigrants had greatly diminished, while the number of maladjusted persons left behind from the previous peak years of immigration and hence also that of re-emigrants was still very high. These data show that in the twenty-year period, 1,040,673 Jews entered the country, but only 53,150 left. Thus altogether only 5.11 percent of American Jewish residents, including immigrants of that and earlier periods, left the country. Even in the six years immediately preceding the First World War, when conditions in the Old World were still tolerable and inducements to return were fairly strong, the percentage amounted to only 7.14. In the entire twenty-year period the excess of immigration over emigration thus amounted to nearly a million Jewish persons, or almost 95 percent.[5]

In this respect, the Jews were an exception. Next to them ranked only the Irish, Scotch, and Germans, whose percentages for re-emigration ranged from 8.58 to 14.53 (in the years 1908-1914, 9.36-19.25 percent). Among the other ethnic groups recorded in the governmental statistics these percentages went up steeply until they reached the staggering total of 78.51 percent of all immigrants from the Balkan countries (Bulgaria, Serbia, and so forth). In fact, after the sharp curtailment of immigration in 1924, the departures from the latter groups far exceeded the number of immigrants (367.11 percent). Even the immediate neighbors of most East-European Jewish émigrés showed a much higher ratio of re-emigration during that twenty-year period. The percentage for Poles was 40.30, Russians 50.61, Hungarians 64.46, and Rumanians 69.06. Here, too, in the years 1915-1927 the number of re-emigrants exceeded that of immigrants especially among the Rumanians. If, in the case of Russians the percentage of returning émigrés had risen to 123.77 percent in 1915-24, but declined to 57.97 percent in the subsequent three years, this reversal is easily explainable in the light of the Revolution of 1917 which, after a temporary flare-up, attracted fewer and fewer residents of the United States. In the prewar years of 1908-14 despite the continued Tsarist oppression which affected the Ukrainians and other minorities furnishing the bulk of non-Jewish immigrants from the Tsarist empire, the ratio of those leaving this country still was 36.94 percent.[6]

During the Great Depression

Even more startling is the comparison during the years of 1931-1935, those dark and tragic years of widespread unemployment, farm foreclosures, and other untold sufferings. Immigration, sharply curtailed by the legislation of 1924, was further reduced by Presidential orders and their rigid application by consular officials all over the world. On the other hand, the declining economic opportunities in this country forced a great many residents to seek a living abroad. Nevertheless, but few Jews felt induced to leave the United States. Only in 1931 there still was a general surplus of immigrants over emigrants. In 1932-1935, however, year after year, we witnessed an excess of emigration from, over immigration into, this country. In fact, each of the major ethnic groups recorded in the official statistics revealed such a surplus. The sole exception were the Jews. Here the percentage of émigrés never exceeded one-sixth of those who arrived (16.41 percent in 1932) and went down to one-fifteenth in 1934 (6.82 percent). In 1936, when the number of admissions once again exceeded departures, Jewish arrivals who by themselves accounted for the reversal of this trend, surpassed the number of those departing in a ratio of more than 20 to 1. In short, during the five years of 1931-1936 the United States lost 103,142 residents through the excess of emigration, while the Jewish community still gained 23,930 members through immigration.[7]

Family Migration

The same tendency is noticeable also in the differing types of Jewish and non-Jewish immigration. While most of the other immigrants consisted of men, some of whom evidently intended to spend but a few years in the United States and then return with their savings to their home countries, Jews migrated largely in family groups, or at least with families following their husbands or fathers at the earliest opportunity. To be sure, in the period of 1899-1927 proportionately more Irish women (50.1 percent of all Irish immigrants) came to these shores, while among the Jews the ratio of women to men was only 45.88 to 54.12. But this circumstance was largely owing to the great demand for Irish girls as household workers before 1914. This situation was reversed during and after the First World War when the ratio of Irish women declined to 49.12 percent in 1915-1924 and 46.39 percent in 1925-1927. At the same time the Jewish ratio of females increased to 52.93, and 54.47 percent, respectively, evidently because more women now followed the heads of households previously settled in this country. All other ethnic groups had a much higher ratio of men, well in excess of 86 percent in the case of Russians, Rumanians, and the Balkan Slavs before 1914. Even the Poles averaged 65.82 percent of males during the three decades of 1899-1927. The same results are obtained if we look at the immigration statistics from the point of view of age groups. The incoming Jewish immigrants show a consistently higher ratio of children under 14 than any other ethnic group—a clear indication of the original intent of the family fathers to stay in the new country.[8]

Of course, Jewish migrations differed from those of most other ethnic groups, inasmuch as the majority of Jews had not left countries in which they had felt completely at home, in order to emigrate to some strange lands. As a rule they merely exchanged the status of an oppressed minority in the Old World for one treated with a fair measure of equality in the New World. For this reason they had very little inducement to go back to the "old country." However, this is basically true also of other oppressed minorities like the Poles in prewar Russia or Prussia.

Moreover, the United States was not the only western country where Jews enjoyed the fruits of emancipation. Jews emigrated, indeed, in vast numbers to other western lands as well. There was a major difference, however; they also left these countries in much larger numbers. For instance, Great Britain or our own neighbor Canada have likewise accommodated a great many Jewish immigrants in the course of the last hundred years, but they also saw at times a considerable Jewish emigration. There were, in particular, a great many East-European Jews who went to England or Canada as middle-of-the-way stations on their way to the United States. Some had to await their American quota, others could not afford passage to the United States. But ultimately many succeeded in reaching their goal. That is why, for example, in 1915-1916, 6,539 Jews are officially recorded as having been admitted to Canada. But in that year no less than 6,450 departed for the United States, leaving a slender balance of 89. In the two postwar years of 1922-1924 almost twice as many Jews left for Canada's southern neighbor as came in from all lands (11,907 against 7,148).[9]

Many of these temporary settlers in England or Canada, however, became so well adjusted to their new country that they converted their stay into a permanent residence. Both countries thus benefited from Jewish migrations to the United States, which already during the Revolution of 1848 had created in central Europe the powerful *Auf nach Amerika* movement.[10] In the 1880s the *Am Olam* ideology aimed at revamping the entire structure of Jewish life by the mass transfer of East-European Jews to American agricultural colonies. On the whole, it seems, that, apart from the State of Israel, the United States has been the only modern country which has consistently and uninterruptedly attracted far more Jewish immigrants than it lost through Jewish departures. Clearly for most Jewish migrants America has marked the end of their journey.

Marrano Background

The nature of Jewish immigration explains also numerous other phenomena in American Jewish history. Many of the early settlers had been Sephardim, directly or indirectly originating in part from

Marrano settlements on the Iberian Peninsula and their ensuing dispersion through western Europe and the New World. As late as 1757, or 260 years after the "expulsion" from Portugal, Aaron Lopez rescued his brother with a wife and three sons from the clutches of the Lisbon Inquisition on "a ship I order'd for the better convenience of their transportation."[11] Aaron himself had probably been born and bred in Portugal. Many other American Jews may likewise have been Marranos in their youth, or their ancestors, living as New Christians in Spain, Portugal, France or their possessions, had long been integrated into Christian society, and had actively participated in its economic, political and intellectual life. Whatever Jewish beliefs they secretly entertained, whatever Jewish rituals they managed to observe in the recesses of their homes, impinged but little on their general life as Spaniards and Portuguese. In fact, in their quest for security against the probing by Inquisitorial agents, a disproportionate number of them had sought refuge in the clerical profession, behind the walls of churches and monasteries.[12] They also played a considerable role in government and army service.

Certainly such people, even after their public reversion to Judaism in Amsterdam, London, or New York were not ghetto Jews inured to a system of discriminatory treatment and living under segregated culture patterns of their own. The very first twenty-three Jews who, in 1654, established the first organized Jewish community of New Amsterdam, had come from Brazil where they had played a great role in both the economy and the public life of the country.[13] Whatever dangers they or their forebears may have faced under Portuguese domination as suspected "Judaizers," they did not suffer from formal legal disabilities. Later, under the Dutch occupation, they had taken an even more active part in the administration and defense of the country.

Upon their arrival in New Amsterdam, therefore, neither they nor other early arrivals were prepared to take the discriminatory policies of Peter Stuyvesant "lying down." Hence came the then unusual spectacle of Jews actively fighting for their legal, even political rights. On April 20, 1657, four New Amsterdam Jews

(Salvador Dandrada, Jacob Cohen Henriques, Abraham de Lucena and Joseph d'Acosta) successfully petitioned the government to "permit us, like other Burghers, to enjoy the Burgher right." They rather sweepingly interpreted the previous decree of the Directors of the West-India Company (of February 15, 1655) as a consent "that we should enjoy here the same freedom as other inhabitants of New Netherlands enjoy."[14]

Public Worship

Some observers have pointed out that Colonial Jews did not carry their staunch struggle for recognition of their rights into the realm of public worship, and were long satisfied with the existing provisions for the private observance of religious rites. But this failure, too, is understandable in the light of their own background, as well as of the nature of Jewish worship as such. Certainly those among them who had Marrano ancestors had been accustomed to private, indeed to utterly secret forms of worship. Even Jews living in countries tolerating the overt profession of their faith did not require any public display of their rituals to meet the requirements of their religious law. From ancient times any ten adult male Jews assembling in any locality constituted the *synagogé*, the congregation of the Lord. They were the *'edah*, the *keneset*, not the much less significant *bet ha-keneset* (house of worship). A service conducted by such ten Jews in a cave or in an open field had exactly the same religious value and standing as that performed in an elaborate synagogue building. The requirement of a Jewish burial ground was somewhat more serious, but by no means vital.

For this reason the early New York Jews could get along for a while even without a separate Jewish cemetery, and did not proceed to erect a synagogue until they were able to raise the necessary funds three-quarters of a century after the establishment of their community. In my 1954 Presidential address I have pointed out how many early American synagogues were built by an intercommunal, if not international, effort.[15] In practice it mattered little whether the community was legally recognized as an "artificial person," or whether it had to acquire title to a synagogue lot under the name of individual trustees. To all intents and purposes, the early Jews of New York or Newport, even before the Naturalization Act of 1740, enjoyed basic equality of opportunity; in fact, equality in all those rights that really mattered to them.[16]

Law vs. Life

Here it may well be worth correcting a widespread popular, even scholarly, misconception. Our historians, particularly those raised on the traditions of Franco-German historiography, have often attached undue significance to formal legal enactments. On the Continent the medieval system of more or less clear-cut formal privileges and disabilities was followed, ever since 1789, by even more clear-cut proclamations of the principle of equality. Viewing all of Jewish history in these Continental terms, historians and public alike have often misunderstood the situation prevailing in Anglo-American lands with its numerous legal ambiguities. The entire evolution of Anglo-American law, often so puzzling to Continental jurists, has made possible also the peculiarly equivocal legal position of Jews in the American colonies where, without any sweeping declarations, they were even allowed to vote. In Europe the exercise of such political franchise was usually considered the acme of emancipation. True, we recall that, when in 1737 the New York Legislative Assembly was confronted with a protested election, it declared that Jews had no right to vote, because they could not participate in elections to the English Parliament. But, as has often been pointed out, Jews continued to vote in New York even after that decision. More, in England herself, as Albert M. Hyamson pointed out, "Jews might be debarred from voting at parliamentary elections, but by the end of eighteenth century very few could remember a returning officer refusing any Jew the right to do so."[17]

Much of the struggle for Jewish emancipation on the Continent was centered around the admission of Jews to occupations theretofore barred to them by their exclusion from the guilds. In America, perhaps even before the Revolution, but certainly in 1786, Myer Myers could without much ado serve as President of the Gold- and Silversmith's Society of New York.[18] On the whole, after an initial period of hesitation, the Jews were allowed to participate fully in the upbuilding of the ever-expanding economy of the various colonies.

In short, here as in most other Anglo-Saxon lands practice was far more significant than the legal theory. But even where we find instances of a discriminatory theory, these can hardly be derived from some specific British or Colonial legislation concerning Jews, but must largely be reconstructed from general regulations relating to religious tests which incidentally affected Jews, too. In very few cases did the legislators have Jews in mind at all, when they enacted these discriminatory provisions.[19]

For this reason the American Revolution and its general proclamations of religious liberty and the Bill of Rights, although not mentioning Jews by a single word, had as much bearing on Jewish emancipation as did the specific enactments concerning the equality of rights to be enjoyed by Sephardic and Ashkenazic Jews which were adopted by the French Constituent Assembly in January 1790 and September 1791. Of course, lack of precision and oblique references in the laws have at times created many ambiguities which sooner or later had to be resolved by the courts. Since even supreme courts have always acted in response to changing social realities, it was once again the legal practice that counted, rather than the theory of law.

Jewish equality of rights in the American Republic was for a time endangered also by the division of powers between the Federal government and the states, which allowed several states to retain for many decades discriminatory provisions against Jews. Best known is the protracted struggle in Maryland. But the widespread assumption that it ended in 1828 with the complete victory of the egalitarian principle is not quite correct. In several keen juridical analyses Benjamin H. Hartogensis has pointed out that, even after 1828, at least non-conforming Jews and Christians, as well as all Buddhists, were excluded from office holding in Maryland by the necessity of signing a declaration that they "believed in a future state of rewards and punishments." Until 1927, Jews were not supposed to be legally married outside the Christian Church. In fact, the new penal code of 1924 provided for severe penalties for uttering profane words against the holiness of Christ and the members of the Holy Trinity.[20] And yet Maryland Jewry has lived under these statutes without any serious concern. The Baltimore Jews, especially, may look back with pride on the record of their achievements during the last century. Nor did Judge Joseph Sherbow in his fine address before the American Jewish Historical Society feel the need of referring to these *possible* sources of discrimination.[21]

Generally, too, the situation today is not entirely devoid of ambiguities. I remember that soon after the enactment of the Nuremberg Laws of 1935, the late Professor Jerome Michael delivered a memorable address at the Conference on Jewish Relations, which has regrettably remained unpublished. In this address the distinguished jurist pointed out that many of these Nazi enactments could conceivably be placed on American statute books as well, if a Nazi-minded party were to control a majority in Congress, or in one or another state legislature. Have not our Negro compatriots suffered from much legal discrimination in several states despite the constitutional provisions for equality? On the other hand, we have also learned to our deep chagrin that no constitutional provision, however express and unequivocal, could withstand such a revolutionary onslaught, as was presupposed in the Michael hypothesis. We recall how quickly the outspokenly liberal constitution of the Weimar Republic was swept away by the Nazi upheaval.

Democratic Vitality

In the long run even the Constitution of the United States, although "written for all times and all ages,"[22] will only offer such effective safeguards for the civil rights of all American citizens as will be dictated by the will of the people. The people will, in turn, be influenced much less by legal formulas, however impressive, than by the genuine vigor of its democratic institutions and the long-range impact of its democratic education. By promoting the mutual understanding among American citizens of diverse faiths and ethnic origins, and by making them all aware of the distinct, and yet complementary, historic strains in their common American heritage, even our Tercentenary celebrations have contributed something to the strengthening of that American democracy.

14 *Some Historical Lessons for Jewish Philanthropy**

Challenges to Jewish philanthropy have been met by the Jewish community since its beginning. The Jewish people has lived through one crisis after another. Today's crisis is perhaps insofar different as it is not derived from persecutions which we faced through the ages, but rather from freedom of choice and decision as well as affluence. I remember an incident of 1946 when I visited Johannesburg, South Africa, and was taken on a tour of the local Jewish orphanage. It happened to be a converted mansion of a mining magnate—a beautiful building with extensive grounds, a tennis court, swimming pool, and so forth. As far as I could see there were more doctors, nurses, teachers, and other employees than children, for the simple reason that there were not enough impoverished Jewish orphans to be taken care of. South African Jewry was, and still is, an affluent Jewish society. Understandably, I inquired what the administration did with these boys and girls after they graduated from the orphanage. Did these youngsters have to rent some small rooms in slum districts while trying to make a living after being accustomed to a life of luxury and abundance? The leaders admitted that this was a genuine problem. This example applies also to American life where the Jewish welfare institutions face the challenge of affluence.

* Reprinted from the *Critical Challenges to Philanthropy; a Symposium*, held on the occasion of the fiftieth anniversary of the Federation of Jewish Philanthropies of New York October 21, 1965 and published by the Federation for private circulation (multigraphed).

Another type of challenge is offered by the Welfare State with its various anti-poverty programs. Now the government itself takes over many functions previously provided by private philanthropies. Perhaps the underlying philosophy about the possibility of eradicating poverty altogether is too optimistic. We must remember the biblical assertion that "the poor shall never cease out of the land" (Deut. 15:11). It appears that there will always be some poor people whether as a result of circumstances beyond their control or because of their unwillingness to work. Moreover, the very definition of poverty is rather arbitrary. What is now considered income on the poverty level would, even in stable dollars, have placed Americans receiving it fifty years ago within the small privileged minority of the population. Such income, and the purchasing power generated by it, may well appear as an unattainable goal to 90 percent of humanity today. Certainly, any society may arbitrarily decide to classify as poor 10, 15, 20, or even 25 percent of its population, whose income falls below a certain level, even if it be objectively high, merely because that of the majority is still higher. In other words, we face a different type of challenge on this score.

Yet, I feel confident that the Jewish community will meet these challenges, too, as it has met other challenges for thousands of years. We do not quite realize how much all of Jewish history is filled with various forms of pioneering, including communal pioneering. It is one of the rather neglected phases of Jewish historiography which has failed to show that one of the keynotes of Jewish historic experience has been that, whenever Jewish communities faced a major challenge, as they often did, they met it creatively in some novel and unprecedented way. They thus pointed the way not only for themselves and their successors, but for the world at large.

In our American Jewish community philanthropy has always played a preeminent role. In the first place, a community of immigrants hailing from different lands and bringing with them different traditions and languages, badly required mutual support. But beyond that, philanthropy was the one noncontroversial aspect of communal cooperation. In religion and political ideology the Jews were deeply divided. They were Orthodox, Reformed or Conservative in their religious views; some were freethinkers. They were Zionists or anti-Zionists, Hebraists or anti-Hebraists. Each even had a certain superiority complex because of his particular country of origin. When I came here in 1926 I was amazed to learn how intense social and even economic discrimination against coreligionists from other lands was in certain Jewish circles.

But all Jews agreed that the sick required care and the poor required support, and so their support became the focal endeavor of the entire community. True, there was no harm in the fact that ideologically Jews were deeply divided, and in this regard I may even quote Thomas Jefferson who, in replying to a Jewish preacher, referred to "the maxim of civil government being reversed in that of religion, where its true form is, 'divided we stand, united we fall.' "[1] The famous Protestant theologian, Friedrich Schleiermacher went further and claimed that religious dissent "always involves the assumption that the judgment of the whole community is wrong."[2] In fact, this country has been built on religious diversity. The 1926 census of religious bodies showed that we had 212 religious denominations in this country. In 1936 the figure was raised to 256. In other words, 44 new denominations appeared in the ten-year period. There were in fact 47 more, but three had disappeared through mergers. So we have specialized in diversity of religion, just as Russia has specialized for a time in ethnic-cultural disparities. But in philanthropy there was general agreement that all could work together. Thus it came about that the Federation of Jewish Philanthropies of New York and other Federations appeared as the most representative overall communal bodies. This consensus lent them superior status which went far beyond their specific accomplishments in the field of charity as such.

If I may indulge in a personal recollection, in the late 1920s at a dinner party at the home of the late Dr. Stephen S. Wise, the president of the New York Federation told us about a project then under discussion. In those years the Federation did not raise any $24,000,000 a year nor did it have a major Capital Fund project. But it raised the substantial sum of $5,000,000 which required a great deal of effort. Hence someone suggested that, instead of going through the annual travail of collecting this amount from some 35,000 members, the Federation should enlist the support of 100 persons in New York City able and willing to subscribe $50,000 annually each. This seemed like an easy way of meeting the $5,000,000 budget without any meetings, public appeals, and the like. I was a rash young man at the time and I asked two questions: 1) "How sure are we of the permanence of our prosperity?" 2) "Is it advisable to drop the large membership in favor of a select group of 100 philanthropists?" In my opinion, the Federation should rather enlist, if possible, another 30,000 members contributing $10 each, even if the cost of collection might be as high as the additional revenue therefrom. I insisted that the Federation, being the overall Jewish communal body in the City, should attract as many Jewish members as it possibly could so as to make them integral partners in our community life. Despite the numerous changes in the intervening period I still believe today that the Federation is performing a great function as a representative body of New York Jewry at large.

A second lesson from history which we may all derive has been the perennial Jewish concentration on self-help. Jews did not wait for the government to help them. Certainly, when Governor Peter Stuyvesant finally consented to the admission of the first Jewish settlers in New Amsterdam (now New York) in 1654, provided that they would take care of their own poor, this condition must have sounded incongruous to these hardy pioneers. They knew that the Jewish communities in all countries had consistently taken care of their impoverished members as well as they could. In fact, at times they supported needy Gentiles "for the sake of peace," but were hesitant to accept charitable donations from non-Jewish philanthropists. Some rabbis actually advised the communal elders graciously to accept such gifts, if refusal might create ill feeling, but to try secretly to distribute this revenue among the Gentile poor.[3] Of course, these "separatist" teachings reflected the segregationist tendencies promoted by both sides at the time and do not apply to an open society like ours. But they reveal the extent to which Jewish self-reliance and mutual self-help were part and parcel of the overall communal responsibility.

In general, Jews were very happy if the respective governments left them alone and did not interfere with their communal affairs. Even in our country it required strenuous efforts to persuade the government to give the Jews permission to build a synagogue. It took eighty years after the settlement of the first group of Jews on the North American Continent before they were able to erect their first house of worship, the Spanish and Portuguese Synagogue in New York. More remarkably, American Jewry had to make an international appeal and most of the money for the New York building, erected and consecrated in the 1730s, came from the West Indies and particularly London, England. As a matter of fact, as late as 1863 the Jewish community of Washington, the national capital, was unable to erect its synagogue without engaging in a large national campaign.

In some respects this national or international cooperation was a sign of growing maturity and of a basic solidarity of all Jews conscious of meeting a major challenge to their survival. By the time of the First World War we Americans had become the more opulent people while the Europeans were impoverished. So we undertook to help needy Jews in all countries. It was a gigantic effort, indeed, which has no parallel in history. The underlying motivation was, of course, the feeling that Jews were responsible for one another and that communal self-help was an obligation hallowed by tradition and the best practical way of meeting the ever-changing needs of various groups. It is well known that Maimonides, the twelfth-century philosopher and jurist, had taught that among the eight different forms of charity the obligation of any individual and the community to help a man to support himself ranked highest: for instance, to lend him money to start a new business, to train or retrain him for a job, and thus make him a proud and self-respecting individual. Another distinguished codifier, Moses of Coucy, considered the economic

490 | *Steeled by Adversity*

rehabilitation of a fellow-Jew the fulfillment of a basic obligation, one of the 248 positive commandments in Judaism.[4]

The obligation to mutual self-help was, indeed, placed so high in the scale of values by the Jewish tradition that rabbinic law even allowed the communal leaders to divert gifts or legacies destined for the building of a synagogue to the erection of a hospital or to any other form of healing the sick. It is small wonder that the name *heqdesh*, chosen for the hospital, which was often combined with a hospice to accommodate strangers, was borrowed from the original designation of offerings for the ancient Temple in Jerusalem.

There are, indeed, many lessons which we may learn from the long-term experience of the Jewish people for the government's anti-poverty program. To illustrate that inherent feeling of communal solidarity, I should like to quote another personal recollection. My late father happened to serve for many years as president of a medium-sized Galician community of some 16–18,000 Jews. It was during the First World War that I returned to my parental home for a Passover holiday. To my surprise on the first holiday morning three Jewish families knocked at our door. They all, parents and children, some twenty persons strong, marched in and took their seats. They had a legitimate grievance: during the First World War all of Austria suffered great shortages of food. Under the existing system of rationing, the government allotted too little flour to the community for its customary distribution of Matzoth among its poverty-stricken members. These three families, and many others, discovered that the ration allocated to them could not possibly see them through the holiday and they came to the president of the community to urge some remedial action. They did not come as beggars but as citizens demanding their rights and staged what may have been one of the first sit-ins. They remained, crowding our home, throughout the day. Yet it never occurred to my father that he might call on the police forcibly to remove these "intruders." All he could do was, despite the holiday, to call the communal board into session and to lead a delegation to the district governor. Their urgent pleas were crowned with a modicum of success and a small, but vital, additional allocation was made from the government's store of flour. Such examples could readily be multiplied.

Another important challenge facing the anti-poverty program is the problem of education. Our American public, including the Federal Government, has for a long time failed to realize the importance of education even for the material well-being of the nation. I personally remember the numerous frustrations I suffered when as a member of the Citizens' Federal Committee on Education I used to come, year after year, to meetings in Washington and found that the United States Bureau of Education was unable to undertake even some of the most important projects for lack of funds. This was true long after the New Deal had been initiated and the nation had assumed increasing responsibilities for helping the poor. Nor were private charities fully cognizant of the integral nexus between philanthropy and education. It required the launching of the Sputnik and our ever more complicated technology for the American people to realize that without a comprehensive educational program any charitable work would remain ineffective. The New York Federation recognized this fact a quarter century ago when it initiated, and included in its budget, support for the Jewish Education Committee.

Jewish history is filled with examples of the recognition of the high value of education, a recognition which went far beyond anything we hear today. When occasionally I listen to a TV appeal urging students not to drop out of school because they thereby impair their chances of securing good jobs, I cannot help feeling that there is too much emphasis on the material aspects of education. True, material benefits had also been stressed by Jewish lore. Since ancient times it frequently happened that a prosperous businessman took on an impoverished scholar as a silent partner for no other purpose than to supply him with a decent livelihood. In early modern Poland it was customary for the large bankers and traders assembled at the two great semi-annual fairs to inquire from the rabbis and communal leaders simultaneously meeting at the sessions of the Council of Four

492 | Steeled by Adversity

Lands whether they knew of any bright and industrious students at their respective academies. Such students, however poor and outwardly unequipped for the competitive struggles of life, were often considered most desirable sons-in-law. These leading financiers were frequently right, the young rabbinic students turning out to be the most effective business leaders of the following generation. Yet above all, education was considered a bonanza in itself because, it was felt, it alone made for a richer and more abundant life and also taught people to learn something about the divine nature and the tragedy of life, or as they styled it, helped each individual in his quest to know the ways of the Lord.

Perhaps an outstanding illustration of the high evaluation of learning was given in a responsum of Solomon ibn Adret, a leading Spanish rabbi of the thirteenth century. Objecting to the spreading custom of some Aragonese Jews to repair in their litigations to state or municipal rather than Jewish courts, the rabbi not only stressed the traditional insistence upon the exclusive Jewish judicial autonomy, but he also argued that if that custom were allowed to become universal, Jewish students might lose interest in studying Jewish civil law. This is indeed a curious reversal. We study law today in order the more effectively to appear at court; according to Ibn Adret, Jews were to cultivate the Jewish courts, in order the more intensively to study the law.[5] In short, it was fully understandable why in discussing the 613 commandments of Judaism the rabbis contended, with a bit of exaggeration, that the one commandment relating to the study of Torah outweighed all the 612 other commandments. Hence it is wholly in line with the Jewish heritage that the New York Federation has enlarged one aspect of education by helping to establish a new Jewish medical school.

Still another challenge facing Jewish philanthropies, indeed all Jewish communal life, today is the problem of long-range planning which cannot be achieved without marshaling a greater amount of knowledge than is now available. It is a strange phenomenon in Jewish life that the same businessmen who in their own offices will not make a single move without consulting all available data about the major trends in their particular branches of endeavor and who will sometimes pay thousands of dollars to establish research departments in their own firms; the same lawyers who will not go to court without familiarizing themselves with every detail of their particular cases and with every precedent established by the courts, will when they appear at four o'clock in the afternoon at a session of a Jewish communal body pass judgment about major aspects of Jewish communal endeavor without having at their disposal any of the vital facts necessary for the understanding of some of these highly complicated problems. What do we know about the Jewish community in America? Do we really know how many Jews there are in America or in New York? At best we have various "guesstimates." We know even less about such demographic facts as the Jewish birthrate or distribution by sex or age. Our information about the Jewish economic stratification is quite minimal.

Years ago we had a ready excuse that so many Jews were unemployed, so many immigrants required aid, and the community had more pressing needs than to engage in research and long-range planning. Fortunately nowadays we have become a rather affluent society and we may indeed indulge the luxury—I believe the necessity—of taking time and funds out for comprehensive research into Jewish communal life.

Nor must we forget that knowledge and understanding have been the mainstays of Jewish existence through the ages. Certainly poverty as an ideal was never espoused by the leaders of Jewish tradition, but neither was wealth praised as a religious achievement. Wealth was considered most beneficial when it served as an instrument of social welfare and as a means for expressing that individual and collective responsibility to which all had to submit.

In conclusion, I wish to state again that, looking back on 3,000 years of Jewish communal history, we view the remarkable spectacle of how, through the ages, the Jewish community has met every challenge facing it effectively and creatively. In doing so it often had to introduce certain unprecedented methods and thereby set an example not only for its own progeny but also for other peoples. I believe that today, too, one of the tasks of the Jewish community is not only directly to help our neighbors, especially the minority groups (our Jewish hospitals have long accommodated more non-Jewish than Jewish patients, and that is fine), but also to engage in new pioneering to set some new examples, to detect new approaches to our novel challenges, and particularly to develop new psychological, sociological, educational, and other methods of treating poverty.

We have already done some of these things with considerable success. I look forward to our doing them even more extensively and better—in line with our age-old heritage.

15 Cultural Pluralism of American Jewry*

There is virtual unanimity among Jews and non-Jews alike with respect to the great need of Jewish self-defense. There hardly exists any difference of opinion concerning the need for Jews to defend themselves whenever they face a mounting tide of anti-semitism and anti-humanitarianism. However, we must increasingly realize—and I feel that we all do to a lesser or greater extent —that antisemitism cannot be solved by any action on the part of the Jews; that antisemitism basically is and has always been a disease of the non-Jewish peoples. It is only through concerted and intelligent action of the non-Jewish world that a remedy may be found for that world-wide, ancient affliction which has accompanied the Jewish people throughout its history in the dispersion.

To be sure, the Jews, too, can, and ought to, do something about it. They may patiently gather and test reliable information to counter the unreliable, vastly exaggerated, or altogether mendacious statements of their opponents. They may be protesting, with firmness and dignity, against the barbarism of their assailants, stimulate the conscience of the outside world; but in no way will any action undertaken by the Jews as such be ultimately decisive. The world can get rid of antisemitism only if all progressive and

* Address delivered at the Annual Meeting of the National Jewish Welfare Board on April 23, 1939 and published, together with an Address by Henry N. MacCracken delivered on the same occasion, as the first Harry L. Glucksman Memorial Lecture (New York, 1939).

humane non-Jews are ready to combat it, not on behalf of the Jews but for the sake of their own deeply threatened interests.

The only major incident of recent history when the struggle against antisemitism was truly successful, occurred during the Dreyfus affair of France. It was not because Jewish leaders, such as Joseph Reinach and a few others, took up the cudgels in the defense of a theretofore obscure captain in the French army, that the latter was eventually released and the cause of justice triumphed. This result was attained only after the progressive forces in the French nation began realizing that it was no longer a question as to whether or not one particular Jewish officer happened to be guilty of espionage, not even a question as to the status of the small Jewish minority under the French republic, but that the very survival of the Third Republic was at stake, and that, under the guise of antisemitism, the forces of reaction threatened to submerge all progressivism and democracy in France. Then Zola came out with his *J'accuse*, not on behalf of the Jews, but on behalf of the conscience of France, and the battle was half won. It was fully won when all of progressive France rallied behind that battle cry.

There also is virtual unanimity among Jews as to the necessity of refugee and other relief work by the organized forces of the Jewish community. Here and there we may differ on questions of method and on the application of particular relief funds, but there is no basic divergence of opinion in regard to the vastness of the relief needs as such and the imperative necessity to pool all communal resources, physical, financial, and intellectual, to meet the emergency. The resolution unanimously adopted by the 1939 assembly of the National Jewish Welfare Board may serve as an illustration of this great unanimity which pervades the Jewish public in America, as elsewhere, concerning the high importance of the various relief undertakings, not only for the purpose of saving a number of individuals but for the good of the entirety of the Jewish community. This unanimity and the considerable success of the efforts in its realization are a shining example of voluntary cooperation. Relief, moreover, and especially relief for people oppressed in other countries, has been a Jewish tradition for millennia. The Jewish people may glory in its great achievement, as far back as the pre-Christian era, of paving the way for a most extensive system of communal charities, and the safeguarding of public welfare.

But when we come to the far more significant, because positive, aspects of Jewish life, Judaism, and Jewish culture, we encounter an endless variety of conflicting interpretations. As a matter of fact, the very term "Jew" has come to connote different things to different men, Jews as well as non-Jews. Nevertheless, a moment's reflection ought to convince everybody that the struggle for self-defense and the relief of temporary needs are but palliatives, incapable of meeting any of the deeper issues of Jewish survival. They evidently are a high price which Jewry is paying because it wants to remain Jewish. In any case, centuries ago, or even decades ago, it was enough for a Jew to become a Christian, or a Muslim, to have his "Jewish" problems immediately solved. Even now we must realize that all our relief activities, all problems of self-defense become really significant only insofar as we regard being a Jew, in other words, the Jewish religion and culture, as truly worth while to both the Jew and to mankind at large.

To be sure, in recent years the opportunity for escape from Judaism through conversion to another faith has no longer been universally available. Today, racial antisemitism, wherever it prevails, makes allegiance to Judaism something final and unavoidable. Generations after an ancestor's conversion to another religion the detection of a single Jewish grandmother or grandfather forces one to proclaim his own belonging to the Jewish group. For the first time in its millennial history Judaism is no longer a matter of voluntary affirmation, but has become—at least in the countries dominated by zoological antisemites—a matter of necessity and inescapability, a sort of natural law which no individual nor group may evade with impunity.

One might venture a paradox that a certain element of inescapability remains even in the eyes of those who deny racial antisemitism. Let us assume, for the sake of argument, that tomorrow all Jews in the world should unanimously decide to adopt the creeds of their environment and to become Catholics, Protestants, or Muslims. Let us assume that an action like that undertaken, in 1799, by David Friedländer on behalf of a small group of Berlin Jews, would be more successful today. At that time Wilhelm Abraham Teller, a Protestant superintendent, blandly refused the offer that the Jews adopt Christianity without believing in the messiahship of Jesus. Let us hypothetically assume, however, that another pastor or group of pastors today would be ready to accept such an offer, or even that all the Jews would unreservedly join the dominant creeds and overnight become Christians, Muslims, or Buddhists. The result, I am afraid, would not be the complete disappearance of the Jewish question, even in those countries which refuse to accept the pseudo-scientific assumptions of racial antisemitism. We probably would witness the rise of a Hebrew Christian Church, or a Hebrew Muslim Mosque, i.e., a new sect within the various sects of Christianity or Islam. The ultimate effect would still lag far behind that postulated complete assimilation and disappearance of the Jew or of the Jewish question. On the contrary, through its artificiality and inner untruth such a contingency which, of course, no one considers as a practical solution, would merely further aggravate the Jewish problem.

If we realize that, we can understand why there are so many Jews in the world today who are Jews without their own will. Some are Jews against their will. For the first time in the history of the Jewish people we witness the rise of a substantial group of persons whom I have ventured to designate as "inverted Marranos." The Marranos professed Judaism in their hearts, even though outwardly they were forced to profess Christianity. Today, we have thousands, maybe hundreds of thousands, of Jews who outwardly profess Judaism but inwardly would like to escape from it. The mental and characterological disequilibrium generated by this inner conflict often converts the people so affected into cultural and religious nihilists.

Cultural nihilism is a grave menace, a menace not only to the persons concerned but a menace to the Jewish group amongst whom they live, indeed, a menace to society at large. Here is a vast area for self-defense which, by its very nature, becomes a primary task for the Jews themselves. All organized Jewish bodies must very carefully consider the serious implications of "inverted Marranism" in all its multicolored forms and ramifications, and most effectively counteract it by making Judaism so much more worth while to their own membership. Judaism must again become a voluntary profession, one for which a man is ready to sacrifice a great deal, even his life, if necessary, as it was during all these centuries and millennia of Jewish life in the dispersion.

Of course, the basic values of Judaism as a religion and culture are not necessarily the same which our ancestors strove to preserve in the past. The Jewish religion, like the Christian religion, has been subjected to violent attacks or, worse yet, to the disintegrating acids of indifferentism. It is well known that perhaps one-half of American Jewry is unsynagogued, at least in the sense of not belonging to any particular congregation. Together with families this total membership may amount to three million persons, contrasted with the more than five and one-half million Jews now living in the United States. While many non-members appear in the synagogue on the High Holy Days, or at a Jewish cemetery in connection with the funeral rites administered to some of their relatives, the participation of the enrolled members in synagogue life often is more nominal than real. There actually are myriads of Jews in America who are not affiliated with any Jewish organization whatsoever, but who are nevertheless considered to be Jewish by themselves as well as by all outsiders. Association with the synagogue, at any rate, is no longer an exclusive criterion for Jewishness. In view of the numerous rivaling ideologies we can no longer regard religion as the sole binding force preserving the unity of Israel.

I am not even discussing the differences between the various types of Jewish religion, between Reform Judaism, Conservatism, or Orthodoxy. These differences loomed very large about half a century ago, but have constantly been losing their sharpness in the postwar period. The cessation of large-scale immigration into the United States combined with the rise of a world-wide Palestinocentric movement has brought American Jews of varying religious convictions much closer to one another. It is perhaps not altogether visionary today to consider the possibility of a new unity on a religious basis, and the cementing of what Solomon Schechter liked to call "Catholic Israel" in America. However, the fact that outside of religious Jews, Orthodox, Conservative, or Reform, there are so many others who avowedly do not belong to any congregation, or are simply indifferent and do not care to partake of any form of religious or cultural life, has served to undermine Jewish culture in a higher degree than any purely external forces. That is why, although we may agree that all generations of men have faced great crises, the Jewish people now happens to be weathering a crisis of extraordinary proportions. In fact, the present crisis in Jewish life is as fundamental and far-reaching as was the crisis of the Babylonian Exile, when the Jews, having lost their national independence, had to adjust themselves to a new life as a permanent minority confronted by varying, often hostile, majorities.

The modern crisis of Jewish life has not begun with Hitler; indeed, is not altogether the result of antisemitism, but in its roots goes much deeper into the entire fabric of Jewish history during the last two centuries. Occasioned by the complex problems of the emancipation of the Jews, it has merely assumed a new guise by the disfranchisement and dissimilation of the Jew attempted by the Hitler regime and its satellites outside of Germany. One of its essential by-products has been the deep fermentation in all domains of Jewish life, and the strengthening of the forces of disintegration. Before long it led to the formation of innumerable groups, each group professing a different type of Judaism.

If President MacCracken has spoken of the chief characteristics of the American civilization consisting in the people's mobility and voluntary cooperation, we can easily find counterparts of both as dominant traits of the history of the Jews in the dispersion. Perhaps there really exists a certain basic affinity between American culture and the culture developed by dispersed Jewry in the course of two millennia, and it may not be a mere accident of history that the United States has exercised the greatest attraction upon modern Jewish migrants and has come to harbor the largest agglomeration of Jews in the world.

Jewish mobility, tragically symbolized in the legend of "The Wandering Jew," has never ceased; in fact, it has increased during the Emancipation era. It was during the one generation from 1890 to 1914 that the migratory movement seemed to have reached its all-time peak in the history of the Jewish people. Fully one-third of the world's Jews changed its residence from one country to another within that single generation. Probably more than another third moved from one locality to another or from one province to another within the same nation or state. Even after the First World War, despite the increasing restrictions of international migration, there was a tremendous transfer of Jewish populations; for example, from the western provinces of the Soviet Union to the centers of the Soviet Republics. A city like Moscow, which had only a few thousand Jews before the War, twenty years after the Revolution included a Jewish population of perhaps 400,000.

While the element of Jewish mobility was fully maintained, the voluntary cooperation among Jews—previously their outstanding feature—has suffered great decline during the Emancipation era. As late as the eighteenth century the Jewish community was one of the most powerful self-governing agencies in the history of governments. The ghetto community united in itself, to put it briefly if not altogether precisely, most attributes of government now shared by the federal government of the United States and by the respective American state and municipal governments. Its authority over its members was further reinforced by all the sanctions of an organized religion. Any violation of the communal laws simultaneously became a criminal offense and a religious sin. Even if it remained undetected and hence unpunished in the lifetime of the offender, the penalty was expected to be imposed upon him when he appeared, after his death, before the divine throne. It is difficult to find a concentration of power of equal comprehensiveness and duration, even among the various known church-controlled states in history, even within Islam, whose great emphasis upon law otherwise offers striking resemblances to the socioreligious structure of Judaism. This powerful Jewish community organization, primarily based on voluntary cooperation even where it was regulated by state law, has broken down in the Emancipation era. Especially in the western countries, a process of dissolution—at least on the organizational basis—has set in, which has threatened the very survival of Jewry.

I repeat, it is not because of Nazism alone, nor because of the rise of antisemitism; it is ever since the eighteenth century that the problem of Jewish communal adjustment has loomed greater and greater for the Jew and for the world at large. If the crisis has been most obvious in the domain of religion, so vital in the entire make-up of the Jewish people, this was due to the rise of strong secularist forces throughout the western world which could not but strengthen the trend toward communal disintegration generated by the political and economic emancipation.

We are accustomed to hear that religion, whether Jewish or non-Jewish, cannot survive our scientific age or the rise of the new radical movements, Socialist or Communist. I must disagree with both of these contentions. Science is no rival of religion, because science essentially appeals to the reasoning element in man; religion appeals to the emotional element in man. Science has not even been able to create sectarian groups in the very small intellectual elite; it has never become a mass movement, whether organized or unorganized.

Even the second contention that the rise of the proletariat in modern times necessarily leads to the elimination of that famous "opiate," religion, seems to me to hold little water. Centuries and millennia of experience tell us that it is the workingman and the farmer who have always been the mainstay of religion. It was the "enlightened" bourgeoisie of the eighteenth century which threatened religion much more seriously than do the new forces of proletarian radicalism. If there ever was a chance for religion to disappear as a major social force, such a chance seems to have

503 | *Cultural Pluralism of American Jewry*

been offered by bourgeois Enlightenment. The French Revolution proclaimed the patriotic and rationalist Religion of Reason, to which many Jews, as well as other Frenchmen, contributed their share. In the city of Paris a synagogue was voluntarily transferred to the Religion of Reason. In the two main sections in the south and the north of France possessing a considerable Jewish population Hebrew books were burned, as were other religious books. In these stages of the French Revolution the atheist leaders persecuted all established religions and their ministers (especially those who refused to take an oath of loyalty to the new creed) no less violently than do the *bezbozhniki* (godless) of Soviet Russia today. There was a much deeper reason for the French people, who during the eighteenth century violently shook off the shackles of feudalism under the leadership of the liberal middle class, to become atheistic, than there is today for the proletarian, essentially religious-minded masses of the Soviet Union, with their profound messianic yearnings for world redemption, and their deep-rooted Russian sectarianism. It is therefore by no means sheer utopia to look forward toward an ultimate reconciliation of Judaism as a religion and traditional culture even with the new civilization, which may emerge from the present socioeconomic turmoil.

I may be permitted to cite the saying of an ancient rabbi quoted in the tractate Shabbat, that every commandment for which Israel has suffered martyrdom in a period of persecution (for example, idolatry and circumcision) is still strictly adhered to; whereas every commandment for which Israel has not suffered martyrdom (wearing phylacteries, for one example) has remained of dubious observance. These words were spoken some eighteen hundred years ago. They are still valid today. The elimination of idolatry, and the adherence to circumcision, although it was outlawed by Hadrian, and deprecated by the medieval churches as a sign of Cain—those beliefs and rituals for which the Jews have suffered grave hardships—have ever since remained a permanent possession of the entire Jewish people; whereas other rituals and other beliefs for which nothing vital was sacrificed in the course of millennia, have often lost their hold on the Jewish masses. Once more staunch adherence and love deepened by sacrifice are likely to preserve the integrity of the Jewish religion and help safely to pilot it through the tempests of our strife-torn era.

It may readily be admitted, however, that the Jewish religion is not the only form of Jewish culture. The multifarious communal, humanitarian, nationalist, and other purely cultural activities of the various Jewish bodies, however "secular" in nature, offer so many opportunities for the assertion of a positive rather than negativistic Judaism, of one arising not from sheer self-defense, but from the sincere conviction of its intrinsic value that for more than half a century rivaling ideologies of "secular" Judaism have been able to dispute the indispensability of religion for Jewish culture.

I am, therefore, quite convinced that we cannot possibly agree as to what Jewish culture is or ought to be. In this period of great social unrest and rapid change, of the greatest dispersion of the Jewish people in history, of the individual Jews being distributed over the various classes in society, sharing their respective interests and biases and subjected to conflicting nationalist jingoisms, there is, of course, no hope for a uniform, consistent, and self-sufficient Jewish culture similar to that which existed in the Middle Ages. At present we can build our future only upon the principle of mutual toleration and the recognition that none of us holds an exclusive brief for the truthfulness of his specific brand of Judaism. Orthodox and Reform Jews, nationalists and anti-nationalists, Hebraists and Yiddishists, religionists and secularists must learn to respect the sincerity of one another's convictions. We must learn the lesson that, under the present conditions, multiformity rather than uniformity of Jewish culture is the only feasible and, in fact, the only desirable counterpart of Jewish reality. Cultural pluralism is and has been greatly enriching American culture. Cultural pluralism must now also become an acknowledged factor working for mutual toleration within the Jewish group as well. Unlike political nationalism, cultural self-assertion is inherently neither mutually exclusive nor totalitarian. One of the great duties of all Jewish organizations, it seems to me, is to help evolve a composite American Jewish culture, one of cultural plurality within and without. It is cultural nihilism which we all have to combat; cultural pluralism is to be welcomed by all.

On this road American Jewry may again build a great synthesis of Judaism and humanitarianism such as was the Hellenistic culture of Alexandrian Jewry, or the Judeo-Arabic culture of the Jewish "Golden Age" in Iraq and Spain. The building of such an integrated, though multicolored, American Jewish culture, and the instilling in American Jewish youth of a creative pride in their American and Jewish heritage is perhaps the paramount task of Jewish leadership at this most critical moment in the destinies of both the Jewish people and the human race as a whole.

16 *Are the Jews Still the People of the Book?**

The name "People of the Book" came to the Jews not from a friend. The man to use it most influentially was Mohammed, who called Jews, as well as Christians, the people of the book, of the book of books, the Bible. Because Jews had been known for many centuries as bearers of a tradition based on Scripture and ready to sacrifice their lives for it, they indeed deserved the designation of the "People of the Book." If one were to ask whether the Jews still are the people of *that* book today, the answer would be far from simple. Many Jews have forgotten their scriptural heritage, and abandoned the living spring of their tradition. I received one of the greatest shocks of my life when I delivered my inaugural lecture at Columbia University in which I mentioned several times some differences between the Old and the New Testaments. After the lecture a young man—as it later turned out, a brilliant young chemist—came to me and, dangling his Phi Beta Kappa key, asked me, "You have spoken all the time of the Old Testament and the New Testament. What is the difference?" The boy had never looked at either.

Fortunately this boy is not typical of the entire generation. Many Jews have not only heard of the difference between the Old and the New Testaments, but have intensively studied at least

* Address delivered at the North Shore Congregation Israel in Glencoe, Illinois on January 14, 1955 and published there as the third Oscar Hillel Plotkin Lecture.

some sections of the former. In fact, in certain Jewish circles in America (not to mention Israel), biblical studies have been on the increase, although the acquaintance with the Bible of the majority still is far from adequate. In this sense certainly the Jewish people at large no longer deserves the name of a "People of the Book."

In speaking of such a people today, however, we have in mind not only the Bible but other books as well. Certainly the Jewish people who produced the Bible may also take legitimate pride in having contributed to civilization much of what was to become the alphabet in most languages. We now know more than we knew but a few years ago about the processes which led to the gradual evolution of symbols reproducing words easily and adequately. We know that the ancient Hebrew script was a vital, perhaps the most vital, link in the evolution of the alphabet.[1] The people which seems to have created the first full-fledged alphabetical system undoubtedly also wrote many books. After all, the Bible itself is but an anthology, a selection of books, which had been written and recited over a period of many centuries. However, books by themselves did not matter; there was effective resistance, then and long after, against books of inferior quality. You may recall the famous exclamation of Ecclesiastes (12:12) against *asot sefarim harbeh en qeṣ* (making many books of which there is no end).

For many centuries of the postbiblical age Jews believed that, next to the written word, they also possessed an extensive oral law, which they considered fully on a par with the written law, for both stemmed from the same divine revelation. Curiously, for the sake of accuracy, Judaism long forbade written scriptures to be recited by heart, and oral traditions to be committed to writing. Oral traditions, it believed, could be recited in oral form only. The ancient rabbis explained this prohibition by saying that, if entrusted to written documents, the Oral Law would be in constant danger of developing a variety of traditions. Experience had taught them that copyists made frequent mistakes, and that ignorant or biased writers often altered the existing readings. Once such new versions arose, the sages warned, they were bound to foster contradictory opinions in Israel. Ultimately, they would lead to endless partisan strife, and even sectarian conflicts over the meaning of certain legal doctrines. The rabbis urged, therefore, that the Oral Law be entirely entrusted to the memory of man, to specially trained memorizers, capable of recording any oral tradition verbatim. They were convinced that only a reliable transmission of this sort from generation to generation, easily controlled at central academies of learning, might prevent serious differences of opinion. It is rather difficult for us today to think of oral tradition being more faithful and more reliable than written documents. And yet this was precisely the case, not only in Judaism, but also in many other ancient and medieval civilizations.

More significant still is the fact that this combination of a fully controlled oral tradition and a rigidly safeguarded "masoretic" Scripture gave Judaism the opportunity for extraordinary selectivity. In the course of time, much that was inferior was simply discarded. Orally transmitted laws which did not enjoy ultimate acceptance were, for the most part, committed to oblivion. What remained was of permanent value. It was studied again and again by one generation after another.

Quality versus Quantity

When we contrast this situation with conditions today, we are amazed at the great outpourings of books, newspapers, and magazines. We have even developed a new oral law communicated to us by radio or television. We have a constant flow of words, millions upon millions of words, said, written, and publicized in one way or another, and broadcast all over the world. But how many of them are of permanent value? How many have quality in addition to quantity? Let me cite a very simple example: Every one of us, I am sure, spends so and so much time daily reading newspapers; for example, a good paper like the *New York Times*. Yet next week, I would not read today's *Times*; a year from now it would be ridiculous for me to read the *Times* of this morning, unless I were to look up some very specific fact or document. And yet, day after day I spend time reading the *Times* or some other paper, each equally ephemeral in nature. My great-grandfather, on the other hand, may not have read any newspaper at all. But when he read, he concentrated on the Bible or Talmud, the Midrash or Zohar, or some other classic of Jewish literature. Similarly the great-grandfathers of some of my Christian friends read the Bible or Josephus, Shakespeare or Tennyson. In other words, they read something that was valuable then and remained valuable a week later, a year later, even a hundred years later. They added to their knowledge from day to day, and from year to year. Clearly, much of our intellectual effort is wasted on ephemeral things, on matters which are alive only for the day.

Such ephemerality is not limited only to our newspapers and magazines, it is characteristic of most of our books as well. Very frequently we are led to believe that nothing succeeds like success. Because a book is successful, it must also be good. Because a book hits the best-seller list, it necessarily is also of high quality. We all, I believe, know better. By definition, a best-seller can only become such if it appeals to the widest circles of readers. The widest circles consist by the nature of things of average persons. Books which appeal to average persons may be presumed to be themselves rather average or mediocre. So one might put up an argument that a best-seller is mediocre by definition. And yet it is the best-seller which establishes reputations, generates wide popular acceptance, and often strongly influences public opinion, at least for the day.

To be sure, the really influential books in history, the real best-sellers, in the long run, have usually been good books. Somebody has figured out that, for example, Shakespeare actually belongs to the greatest employers of all time. He has furnished a livelihood for so many theatrical employees, actors, producers, stagehands, and promoters; so many printers, booksellers, writers, and teachers that if you add up all such persons through the ages you will find that William Shakespeare was a bigger employer than Henry Ford. When we consider the Bible, there is really nothing comparable to the book of books in quantitative output. Already in 1687 an Amsterdam Jewish printer, Joseph Athias, boasted, "For several years I myself printed more than one million Bibles for England and Scotland. There is not a plow boy or servant girl there without one."[2] Today many millions of copies are printed every year in the more than 300 languages and dialects into which the Bible has been translated.

I have heard many people complain especially about American Jews. In connection with the Tercentenary celebrations some people asked, "What have American Jews produced of their own in the realm of Jewish literature? They have been here for three centuries as an organized community, not to speak of individual Jews who had come here earlier, but for two out of these three centuries not one Hebrew book was written and published in America." These questioners do not refer, of course, to prayerbooks or Scriptures reprinted in the United States, but to some novel, original writings. Only in 1860 did an American Jew, himself an immigrant, write the first independent Hebrew work and publish it in this country. Nor was this a particularly important book. Of course, even these carping critics admit that in the third century of Jewish communal life in this country many Hebrew books and magazines were written, and that there was a flowering of Yiddish literature which exceeded much of what had been done in this field in the Old World itself. We have had a Yiddish press and theater, Jewish art, an Anglo-Jewish press and literature, which have been quite respectable.[3] But in these critics' opinions, all this is still but a fragment of what a large community like American Jewry might and should have accomplished.

No one will deny that much more could, indeed, have been achieved. If I may mention a personal experience: Some sixteen years ago, I tried to prepare a technical "Bibliography of Jewish Social Studies" for the years 1938-39.[4] When I started that work I did not know that 1938-39 would become a vital date in the history of the Jewish people; that these years would mark the end of the era of European predominance in Jewish life and that thenceforth the center of gravity would shift from Europe to

America and Israel. When published in 1941, that bibliography became almost immediately, so to say, a monument to the creativity of the Jews before the outbreak of the Second World War. Looking at that bibliography now, I am ever more astonished at the creativity of the Jews in Palestine, Germany, and Poland, in Italy, Holland, and France, a creativity which extended to all domains of life. It sounds almost unbelievable, but it is true that in 1938-39 the Jews of Poland alone produced more rabbinic books of the old type, more responsa, books of ethics, kabbalistic and ḥasidic works, and the like, than had appeared in any two decades of the seventeenth or eighteenth centuries during the heyday of European rabbinic literature. What is more, some of these books are of genuinely high quality; from the point of view of acumen and erudition, they may well take their place alongside some of the more renowned rabbinic works of centuries ago. At the same time, however, Polish Jewry was also active in all domains of Polish literature and science. Polish Jewish émigrés were found among the scientists and littérateurs of many other lands. No lesser a figure than Henri Bergson, for example, one of the great French philosophers of the twentieth century, was born and bred in Warsaw. Polish Jewry thus was creative not only in its own domain, in the rich and variegated fields of Judaism and Jewish culture, but contributed much also to the various sciences, arts, and letters in Poland and elsewhere.

Fundamental Transformation?

Have Jews changed so radically? Was that intellectual creativity limited to European Jewry? Not at all. When some time ago, I delivered an address before the Middle East Institute in Washington on the then recent developments in Israel, I pointed out an example of the new country's literary creativity which bears repetition here. In the 1940s a group of Israeli scholars and writers decided to issue a new comprehensive encyclopedia of the kind of the *Encyclopaedia Britannica*. I certainly do not have to explain the meaning of the *Britannica*, a major landmark in

512 | Steeled by Adversity

human culture. In preparing that Hebrew encyclopedia in twenty-odd volumes, the Israelis decided to include more information about Jews and Judaism than is found in non-Jewish encyclopedias, but at the same time to devote most of the space to sciences, literatures, history, sociology, economics, and other disciplines of a more general nature. I still remember that before the undertaking was launched, the organizers discussed with me in Jerusalem the possibilities of selling such an expensive, multi-volumed work. The publisher told me frankly that he anticipated a sale of at best five or six thousand sets; five thousand in Israel and a thousand abroad. Such sales could not possibly cover the expenses. Everybody agreed that this vast undertaking would require considerable subsidies from public-spirited citizens. Although the publisher secured only a relatively small initial subsidy, he went ahead and published the first volume or two. Now some eighteen volumes are out and several more are under way. From the outset the number of subscribers began increasing at an unbelievably rapid pace. It grew with each volume from five thousand to ten, fifteen, twenty-five thousand. The latter figure held for a while because at that time Israel could not provide the publisher with more printing paper than was necessary for twenty-five thousand copies. No sooner did the paper allotment increase when the list of subscribers jumped to thirty-five thousand with a waiting list of an additional ten thousand subscribers.

Do you realize what forty-five thousand subscribers to a weighty, multi-volume and expensive series means in comparison with the total population and financial resources of Israel? It is tantamount to the *Encyclopaedia Britannica* being issued volume by volume in seven or eight million copies for distribution in the Anglo-American world! This is almost unbelievable! Moreover, while this large encyclopedia is in progress, there appear several special encyclopedias like the *Encyclopedia Biblica*, the *Talmudic Encyclopedia*, a special encyclopedia for the history and topography of Palestine, as well as a great many other books.

Are the Israel Jews any different by nature than American Jews? By no means. At times it was a mere accident which members of the same East-European family emigrated to the United States and which settled in Israel or remained in Europe. They still are essentially the same people. Hence I am not prepared to assume for one moment that American Jewry is intrinsically uninterested or incapable of producing a culture of its own. But we have been confronted by serious difficulties. One very obvious difficulty consists in the competitive pressures of the numerous cultural strains in our general American life. Our educational system has long suffered from our attempt to teach more and more subjects, that is to give our children less and less knowledge about more and more fields of human endeavor. In such an environment Jewish learning is the more likely to be spread thin and to go into superficialities rather than depths, as the Jewish minority struggles to maintain its identity against the overwhelming pressures of the great general American culture.

Another equally serious difficulty, obviously interrelated with the former, is the fact that our community, and especially our Jewish leadership have, for special historical reasons which I cannot explain here, reached a point in their historic evolution in which culture plays but a minor role. I happened to hear one of our great communal executives and fund raisers draw an illuminating comparison between the prevailing Protestant and Jewish attitudes to cultural efforts. On the whole, wealthy Protestants are more interested in contributing funds for a university chair or a research project than for charity. We all know how much money the Rockefeller, Ford, and Carnegie Foundations have been spending on subsidizing research, schools, libraries, museums, and other cultural undertakings all over the world. At the same time Jewish campaigns are largely limited to charitable appeals of one kind or another, nearly all of them essentially directed to philanthropy rather than culture.

This is a very serious shortcoming, indeed. If I may again indulge in a personal recollection, I should like to mention that I had the honor of serving as chairman of the Cultural Advisory Committee of the Conference on Jewish Material Claims Against Germany. You undoubtedly know of the arrangements made with

Germany to pay many millions over some fourteen years for the rehabilitation of victims of Nazi persecution. The largest part has gone to Israel, but a certain portion was to be expended outside Israel also for Jewish cultural reconstruction. One afternoon, I remember, I presided over a meeting of that Cultural Committee which tried to devise a good program for the distribution of approximately $900,000 during the year 1954 for Jewish cultural undertakings relating to victims of Nazi persecution. The same evening I chaired a meeting of the American Jewish Historical Society in which the expenditure of the small sum of $500 for an American Jewish cultural project loomed as a major budgetary item. That paradox has been with us for many years. We have become accustomed to giving money for relief and other undertakings of Jews abroad, rather than for Jews at home. I have been told of a Yiddish author in New York who, in order to publish a book, had to send it to a publisher in Mexico City. The latter solicited funds in New York, and secured them, only because he did not live in the United States. Here you have in a nutshell the deplorable situation in the financing of cultural projects within the American Jewish community.

Turn for the Better

Is that situation permanent? Shall we take it as the final word in the American Jewish cultural evolution? Fortunately, not. Fortunately, the situation has been improving very rapidly. We have before us the example set by the late Oscar Hillel Plotkin in organizing and endowing a library of Jewish knowledge. We see here how one public-spirited citizen can stand up and tell the community that he considers books as valuable as, or even more valuable than, relief. That sentiment is growing. The Council of Federations had, for a number of years, intensely debated the issue of what can, and what should be done to support cultural undertakings in this country. As a result there ultimately emerged the National Foundation for Jewish Culture. Throughout its history the Jewish community has been supporting cultural enterprises with funds and other effective measures. For example, some Jews in six-teenth-century Poland felt the urgent need of publishing a new edition of the Talmud, one of the first editions to appear in print. It was felt, however, that the Jewish communities of Poland, number-ing only about 70,000 at that time, were too small to support such a voluminous and difficult publication. Thereupon the communal leaders of Polish Jewry decided to issue a call—in the nature of a decree, rather than an appeal—to all rabbinical schools in Poland to arrange for the study of a particular talmudic tractate during the following year. This request was heeded all over Poland. Since all the schools had to purchase the same tractate, the printers were assured of a minimum sale of several hundred copies. The follow-ing year the central leadership of Polish Jewry selected another tractate. In the course of years, this concerted effort made possible the publication of the entire Talmud.[5]

This example could not be emulated in distant Yemen, where Jews lived in extreme poverty. With their great intellectual alert-ness, however, they found a way of securing a considerable supply of books for study, without either printing them or acquiring them from abroad. They often imported but one copy of a book printed in Venice or Amsterdam, and had local scribes copy it by hand. The result is that today American libraries are offered outwardly very precious Yemenite manuscripts, which when exam-ined more closely, turn out to be but copies of printed books. That is the length to which a community went in providing for the cultural wants of its constituents.

Sagacious Daring

Examples of such communal actions could easily be multiplied. In America, particularly, the community can see to it that there should be foundations for Jewish research, creative arts, and the publication of good books. To be sure, here we must beware lest there be dictation from above. You cannot manufacture culture, nor impose it on the creative minds. You cannot prescribe to authors what books they should write. That is why whatever cultural foundations may emerge from the American Jewish communal effort, will have to combine a great deal of sagacity with self-restraint, of daring with understanding of individual endeavor, of the individual imagination and creativity of every scholar, writer, musician, and artist. This combination is not easy because it may well mean that communal leaders will consciously have to allocate funds for things which they do not understand, or even disapprove. True of all cultural foundations, such self-restraint may be doubly difficult in the case of an embattled minority, whose leadership is not always internally secure. But in the long run perhaps these very disapproved of publications may prove a greater boon for the preservation of Judaism and the Jewish people than the orthodox and accepted approaches. Books and journals of both kinds, moreover, may well be a greater blessing to the Jewish faith and humanity at large than any of the more secular efforts, charitable, political, and economic in which the American Jewish community is now so splendidly engaged.

Let me say, therefore, in conclusion, that it is not too venturesome to expect that now, after the Jewish community has entered the fourth century of its existence on this Continent, it will feel to have been here long enough, and to have taken deep enough roots in this new environment, to resemble more closely the older Jewries of Europe, or the new Jewry of Israel, in their approaches to culture. I repeat, American Jews are not essentially different from other Jews. They have merely been here a shorter time, as far as the masses of their population are concerned. They have also been exposed to the tremendous pressure of a great civilization to which they first had to adjust themselves. But they already have overcome all sorts of difficulties, already have to their credit significant achievements in the area of Jewish culture. Very likely, however, these initial achievements will be far overshadowed by the great creativity which is yet to come.

I sincerely believe that American Jewry in the fourth and fifth centuries of its communal existence has a real opportunity to develop some vitally new approaches to Jewish culture. Facing the unprecedented challenges of the Emancipation era in its climactic drive under the American democracy, it may, indeed, draw a new cultural synthesis, a new compound of Americanism and Judaism. When this happens, the American Jews will again deserve the honorable designation of the People of the Book.

17 *The Jewish Community and Jewish Education**

Without attempting to offer a sketch concerning the historic responsibility of the Jewish community for Jewish education, it may nevertheless be said here, by way of introduction, that a people, which two thousand years ago had already pioneered with compulsory education for boys and which in its educational endeavor and community sponsorship was far superior to its neighbors, including even such enlightened nations as the Greeks and the Romans, such a people has known for ages that the community at large is responsible for education.

In the last few generations this conviction has penetrated deeply into western civilization and today it is shared by almost the entire world. Nobody, in either a democratic or a totalitarian country, has to be persuaded that the state or the city must assume responsibility for public education. In fact, totalitarian countries make an even greater effort to indoctrinate their youth. Such religious bodies as the Catholic Church have long advocated communal responsibility for education. As late as 1930 a Papal encyclical insisted on the primary responsibility of the Church for the education of youth as preceding even that of the state. We know that in this country nearly half of all Catholic school children go to parochial schools.

* Address delivered on October 19, 1947 at a session of the Board of Governors of the American Association for Jewish Education and published by that Association in New York, 1948. It also appeared in *Jewish Education*, XIX, No. 2 (1948), pp. 7-13, 42.

The rest largely attend public schools. So communal responsibility is almost self-evident, and needs no further persuasion.

Communal responsibility carries, however, many serious implications which are at times quite perplexing. This is particularly the case in America where the religious community is but a voluntary organization.

Communal vs. Individual Responsibility

One major difficulty becomes ever more evident as time goes on, namely the problem as to the extent to which the community at large, as represented by a community council or a welfare fund, should assume the main obligation for Jewish education; and how much, on the other hand, must such responsibility rest with each individual Jew. Historically, a balance has been struck between individual and communal responsibilities which will be dangerous to forsake. All along, from the days of the Talmud through medieval and modern rabbinic literature, we find reiterated exhortations and legal provisions demanding that each individual should seek self-education to the end of his life and that his responsibility for the education of his children ends only with their coming of age.

That is why the situation in the United States appears the more threatening, as far too many individuals are prone to delegate this responsibility entirely to the community or to special communal groups and institutions. A great many adult Jews begin by abandoning all attempts at Jewish self-education and by being satisfied with whatever formal education in Jewish subjects is given their children in a communal school. So happy are they to delegate that responsibility to the school that they are afraid to inquire more deeply about the details of the curriculum or the scholastic progress, if any, made by their children.

We must try, therefore, to reawaken the conscience of the people along the lines of greater responsibility of the parents for the education of children and of each adult for his or her own educational advancement. The community itself must try to stimulate such reawakening of individual efforts because they alone can

assure ultimate success. It must, at the same time, fully assume its
own sphere of responsibility which, ever since the Second Commonwealth, it has always maintained. Curiously, the ancient
schools were established for adults first and for children more than
a century later. Our ancestors during the Second Commonwealth
felt that adults or adolescents, aged 15 or 16, required even more
attention than children, most of whom were for a long time
educated merely at their respective homes.

Historical Role of the Jewish Community

We now know, however, that Jewish public education goes back
to remote antiquity. Owing to recent archaeological excavations,
we have come to realize the extent to which public instruction
existed throughout the Middle East, even before Israel was born,
and still more so after Israel had entered the scene of history. To
mention only one example, in a city like Mari in northern Syria
two regular schoolrooms were excavated before World War II.
Located in the marvelous royal palace they were equipped with
various utensils for writing, with books written on cuneiform
tablets, and everything else needed for effective instruction. These
schoolrooms date from about 1800 B.C.E.[1] A whole library located
in another school for scribes was found in Ugarit (a part of ancient
Canaan) with writings going back to 1400 B.C.E., which have,
in the last four decades, become an inexhaustible source of information for students of biblical literature.

Judaism, going far beyond all its predecessors in both the intensity of its religious devotion and the democratic appeal of its basic
institutions, extended the area of public education in both Palestine
and the dispersion to a theretofore unprecedented degree. Generation after generation re-echoed the Psalmist's glorification of God's
ordained strength "out of the mouth of babes and sucklings."
Both Philo and Josephus boasted of the intellectual superiority of
an average Jewish child before their enlightened Greco-Roman
readers. Centuries later a great rabbi, Yeḥezkel Landau of Prague,
voiced the widely accepted explanation that the existence of a com-

munal "school for children" was the main cause for Jewish survival through the ages of severe persecutions. What is more, unbiased observers will recognize in retrospect the essential validity of this claim.[2]

Today, however, in this country particularly, we are still struggling sometimes with simple principles, with the rudimentary beginnings of communal Jewish education, as if an evolution of two thousand years were completely forgotten and we had to start from scratch. The assumption of communal responsibility, one might expect, would lead to the most obvious conclusion that the community as such should allocate adequate funds for Jewish education. Since the days of Joshua ben Gamala, antedating the second fall of Jerusalem, the Jewish communities all over the world have indeed cheerfully assumed the burden of supplying instruction to children, particularly to those children whose parents could not provide them with teachers. Ever since the days of the Talmud, the legal maxim prevailed that a school was even more "sacred" than a synagogue and that, hence, a house of prayer could be converted into a house of learning but not the other way around. Asher ben Yeḥiel, one of the greatest medieval rabbis, whose decisions often became binding legal precedents, ruled that if someone established a foundation for such religious purposes as a synagogue or cemetery, the community might at any time alter the terms of the foundation and use its funds for educational purposes, even against the will of the donor. But if, on the other hand, the foundation had been established for the sake of Jewish education, it must never be diverted to any other more strictly religious uses. In short, in the hierarchy of values, in the hierarchy of the 613 commandments of Judaism (the *taryag miṣvot*) education was considered on a par with all the other commandments put together.[3]

Priorities in Jewish Communal Program

In the American community, however, this is no longer true. Charitable needs come first. Defense needs come second. All sorts of other needs come long before that most vital of all needs: education. I do not wish to blame any particular person or set of persons. There are good historic reasons for this change in attitude in this country. We have been a people of immigrants. The simple needs of making a living, of getting established in the new environment, long came first. We also were a people of immigrants from various countries, with diverse views and attitudes. The result was that there was little agreement as to what should be the objectives of Jewish education. As against this area of grave disagreement, charities, or even defense against antisemitism, were areas of agreement. All Jews agreed that antisemitism was bad, that sick people ought to be helped. Moreover we could, in the past, delegate a major share of responsibility for Jewish education to other countries, especially Poland, Russia, and Germany. We felt that they could supply us with educators, scholars, rabbis, and so forth, while we were busy with other matters.

The situation has changed. Even before Hitler, immigration constantly diminished, while, on the other hand, American Jews have grown ever more homogeneous. There still are great differences of opinion, we still have divergent ideologies and religious attitudes, but there is a growing basic similarity of outlook among American Jews and particularly among American Jewish youth. We can no longer look to European Jewry as a source of our leadership. We must, therefore, build as quickly as we can, be it through rapid improvisation, our own wholly self-sustaining cultural life.

I am glad to testify that on my numerous journeys all over the country I have noticed a growing awareness of this need in both professional and lay circles. In the last few years "Jewish Culture" (with a capital C) has become almost a fetish. People of all walks of life speak about it. Not only experts and people in a position of leadership but the rank and file have come to realize that the community at large as well as many of its subdivisions must embark upon ever-growing constructive programs in the field of Jewish education.

A group like the American Association for Jewish Education

has been formed as a direct expression of that underlying trend, of that community awareness that something constructive ought to be done soon on a community-wide scale. We all know how often we still run up against the wall, no longer of complete indifference —but rather of an established system of priorities, deeply imbedded in both tradition and vested interests. Nevertheless, the conscience of the public having been so deeply stirred, I believe that the prospects of overcoming that resistance, often more passive than articulate, are very promising indeed.

Some other difficulties are likewise obvious. In any attempt at getting education sponsored communally one has to strike a balance between control and liberty, between authority and license. Although the American Jewish community has been growing ever more homogeneous, it is far from—and I hope it will always remain far from—completely uniform. In a democratic way there always will be differences of opinion among us. One of our major difficulties is that, to prove truly effective, any communally sponsored education must contain a fairly strong dose of some sort of indoctrination. Hitler had it easy, for it is not very hard to instill in youth a Nazi type of single-mindedness through constant repetition and repression of any opposing point of view. Those communists in Russia who are employed in training the Young Communist League also have a relatively easy task, for they too have before them a single, set point of view. In its parochial schools even the Catholic Church has it—or at least had it until the deep divisions following the era of the Second Vatican Council— comparatively easy to present to the pupils a well-rounded, dogmatically buttressed outlook on life. The same held true for our own ancestors several generations back. Old type Judaism had in essence a single set of values, one basic outlook, which could readily be communicated to children. The same textbook could be used in Spain or Germany, Turkey or Poland. The same copy of the Bible or Talmud, the same exegetical and moralistic work could be used for countless generations all over the world, because the Jews of different periods and countries shared essentially the same doctrines and practices.

Old and New Approaches

Today our education must try to reconcile old and new values. Old type Judaism in its pristine purity has little immediate meaning for the majority of our youth. We may deplore the fact, but we must not lightly dismiss it, that now and for generations to come an average American Jewish boy or girl will very likely know much more about Lincoln and Shakespeare than about R. Akiba or Maimonides. Two or three generations ago the opposite was true. Any intelligent young Jew could recite a great many facts about R. Akiba's life or that of Maimonides. He probably had memorized quite a few sayings of both sages. Today, under American conditions, indeed under those prevailing in any country of Jewish Emancipation, we must accept as an educational premise the vast area of both information and indoctrination imposed upon our youth by the public school and the general environment of the country in which they live.

Educationally, therefore, the Jewish element will of necessity be but a supplemental factor; the more deeply significant it is, the more readily will we persuade our youth that such supplementation is essential to its well-being, indeed, the happiest way to its integration into America's democratic society. But we must not teach our youth exclusively matters unrelated to its own experience. We must not place undue stress, for example, on the history or literature of the Polish and Russian ghettos, or even on the persecutions under which the Jews had lived in the past centuries and the compensatory beauties of their internal life which they developed. All this may in itself be very edifying and illuminating, but it will relate itself very remotely to the American youngster's immediate observation of the facts of life in his own environment. I do not say these things with relish. As a historian and a staunch believer in Judaism's historic heritage I should much rather see the multicolored patterns of life of the old ghetto Jews becoming truly meaningful to their more fortunate descendants today. But it would be sheerly utopian and defeat the purposes of Jewish education, if an undue emphasis on these bygone realities would estrange the American, Israeli, and West-European Jewish youth from the realities of today.

Similarly, some of us may deplore the fact that so many of our children are interested primarily in sports. We may readily condemn a public school which allows pupils to bring portable radios to listen to the progress of the World Series during the usual hours of instruction. On the other hand, we ought also to realize that games and, more generally, the cultivation of the playful element in man have been an essential part of many a great civilization. Let us remember the ancient Greeks and their famous Olympic games. Their great stress on athletics did not prevent their civilization from producing eminent philosophers, artists, and scientists, and generally becoming one of the greatest civilizations in the history of mankind. Indeed, next to their "amphictyonic" religious festivals and their common language it was their Olympic games which served as a unifying bond among their politically divided, often mutually hostile city-states and maintained the unity of their great Hellenic civilization, in contrast to the outside "barbarian" world.

To be sure, the ancient Jews, even if they had wished to, could not emulate the Greeks in indulging in athletics as a major national effort, rather than as a pastime. The Greeks, as well as their Roman successors, often had a great many slaves to whom they could delegate the main responsibility for work. Even in the period of their prosperity the Jews never had a plethora of slaves. The vast majority had to work and to toil through endless hours of the day in order to eke out a meager existence from the few occupations open to them. They really had little time and leisure for sports, even if their general religious austerity and their great concentration on the spiritual and ethical aspects of life had not turned their minds into other directions. Today, however, our modern civilization has increasingly developed mechanical slaves which are placing at the disposal of man more and more leisure time; so much, indeed, as to create serious problems of boredom and psychological unrest. Under these circumstances, playfulness has become a widely accepted characteristic of Jewish adults, and is doubly legitimate among children and adolescents. Jewish educators, too, better take cognizance of these facts. Instead of discouraging playfulness, which appears pretty hopeless in any case, they ought to make use of it for Jewish educational purposes. The Jewish center movement, in particular, has already tried to harness this great source of youthful energies into the service of its program of informal education, and the more formal Jewish schools seem to be following suit.

In short, Jewish education appealing to old values, taking in the new values being created daily in Israel, but adding to them constantly the ever-new cultural elements injected into Jewish life by their varying environments in the countries of their dispersion, may ultimately prove effective. When we shall have combined all of these vital ingredients into a new integrated system of Jewish education we may well have found the key to the new successful approach to the instruction of our youth.

Community Program Integrates

I realize that I am proposing a very difficult task. It means courageous pioneering; it means finding some new and wholly unprecedented approaches to Jewish education. This is doubly difficult in the American environment, because it must be designed to superimpose a religious and ethnic type of culture upon a "melting-pot" culture. In some of its aspects this education may ultimately assimiliate many ingredients from the new Jewish life in Israel. But it cannot be oriented completely toward Israel because Israel has its own way of life and faces a variety of its own problems which radically differ from the life and the problems of a Jewish minority in the dispersion. In building an American Jewish educational structure we must also take cognizance of the major trends in Jewish education in the rest of the world. We must not allow the Jewish school system in this country, its educational aims and curricula, to be completely at variance with similar endeavors in Canada, South Africa, or Argentina. We must even stress the similarities rather than the differences, what we have in common with, rather than in what we deviate from, the Jewish educational system once developed in the Soviet Union. Otherwise, we may become a very serious menace to Jewish unity.

If allowed to pass, such a geographically differentiated Jewish education might lead to the development of an American Jewish people which would be very different from an Argentinian or Swiss Jewish people, and these in turn would have completely divergent characteristics from those of a Soviet Jewish people. However well-meaning, our diverse educational systems would thus become a disintegrating force, a force dividing the Jewish people, if not into ideological, into territorially divergent groups. This danger is more tangible than many of us realize. If we want to maintain the unity of the Jewish people—and I assume that most of us want it—we must take full cognizance of the existing menace and of the measures necessary to forestall it. Certainly dangers of this type can be coped with successfully only by the Jewish community at large. They are likely to increase rather than diminish, if the necessary counteraction is left completely to the disparate efforts of individuals or small communal groups.

Community Program Encourages Ideological Differentiation

We have to make many other compromises with reality. While the new system of American Jewish education must prove superior to the stray efforts of individual groups, it yet must leave enough leeway to such individual undertakings. Communally sponsored education means that every constructive effort within the Jewish community must be encouraged. Every element within the community, every synagogue or center, every Hebraic or Yiddish group should be helped by the community to raise the standards of its own Jewish educational program. In fact, it is only through a total community effort that the individual institutions can hope for continued existence. While a community approach may mean diversity of approach, it also means that no single one-sided form of Jewish education must be permitted to run away with the communally sponsored program as a whole. The community's attention must not be diverted from its unifying goal, which is intended to serve the community at large.

Such advice may be easier to follow in discussion than in the practical world of clashes in ideology and vested interests, which any board of education will encounter in its daily business in a local community. Jewish leaders will continue meeting these ideological difficulties, which go the more deeply as they are based upon a long history and existing social differences. Today, many a community, wishing to steer clear of these difficulties, often takes the line of least resistance, that is, it tries to disregard the differences. We must not run away from these difficulties which will haunt us, I am sure, for many years to come. I fully sympathize with the busy communal leader who would like to see them thrashed out somewhere else. However, unlike charities, unlike even defense, both of which are essentially negative forces and in which unity along the lines of least resistance is often quite feasible, education, to be effective, must be based upon a positive philosophy of life. Positive attitudes are necessarily conflicting, for they cannot mean the same thing to every Jew; particularly not at a time of such profound ideological differences as divide the Jewish people today.

Nor am I prepared to state that one should simply follow the majority view. This is but another line of least resistance: "Let us put the matter to a vote and the majority shall have its way." It may be unavoidable in the political sphere, but it certainly is not the best method of adjusting controversies in the realm of the spirit. Montesquieu remarked that in spiritual matters the will of the majority does not necessarily have the presumption of truth on its side. In deciding upon a course of action one must follow the majority, but in matters of the spirit a minority, even a single individual, has time and again proved right against the consensus of a whole generation. In other words, the minority should have its chance. At the same time we ought to give the majority, too, a chance to act along its own lines. Wherever possible, we must use the means of persuasion rather than those of enforcement.

Qualitative vs. Quantitative Approach

Another equally vital compromise seems clearly indicated. I heartily believe that a certain balance must be struck between the quantitative and qualitative approaches to Jewish education. Much too frequently, we find a board of Jewish education judging educational success by statistical figures. This is even truer in the case of the general communal leadership which has to balance educational needs against other communal requirements. Such a quantitative yardstick may be justified in the area of business, for under the existing profit system, the more profits one accumulates the more successful is one's business. One can indeed statistically compute the amount of profit and the general growth of one's enterprise from year to year. To a certain extent the same is true in politics. But it is completely untrue in the spiritual sphere. Neither are the ideas themselves measurable, nor is their ultimate success or failure to be ascertained by a sheer statistical computation.

That is why when I travel through the country and hear complaints that so few Jewish children attend school, that they attend it only during so few hours a week, or that they stop attending at this or that early age, I consider these complaints perfectly legitimate. But if the complainants, indeed, the majority of people derive therefrom the lesson that Jewish education in this country has been a complete failure, I believe that this conclusion is somewhat rash. A great talmudic sage, R. Simon b. Yoḥai observed: "This is the way of the world: a thousand enter the Bible school but only a hundred proceed to the study of the Mishnah; ten of those advance to the study of the Talmud, but only one achieves the rabbinic degree."[4] However, that distinguished sage was by no means discouraged. He believed that a single scholar at the end justified the efforts of the other nine hundred and ninety-nine pupils as well. Unfortunately, I repeat, however much we individually pay attention to quality, our communal endeavor is still largely geared to quantity. If any of us appears before a community council or welfare fund and asks for an allocation for the local school, I am sure that in nine out of ten cases most of the questions hurled at him will be related to such problems as budget, the financial statement for the preceding year, the *number* of children attending school, the *number* of teachers and their respective salaries, the *number* of hours of instruction per child, and so forth. All these are very pertinent questions and, when it comes to a charitable undertaking, they have much justification, although even there they must not be allowed to rule out all other considerations. In an educational enterprise, however, they are decidedly secondary. Under no circumstances must they be permitted to serve as an ultimate criterion for the effectiveness of a local school or of Jewish education at large.

When we speak about the future of the Jews in the United States quality is certainly at least as important as quantity. I have said it before, but I believe that it bears repetition that, if I were assured today that a generation hence we shall have 100 first-rate Jewish scholars, 100 first-rate rabbis, 100 first-rate teachers, 100 first-rate communal leaders and 100 first-rate writers, publicists, and artists—their total number would amount to only 500, which in a population of some five million would be just one-hundredth of one percent—I should feel assured nevertheless of a great future for the Jews in this country. For I would feel confident that these 500 would detect the necessary paths to guide their people through the perplexities of Jewish life under the conditions of modern existence in the Western Hemisphere.

Jewish education must be geared to produce such 500 first-raters. Fifty thousand others, again representing only a total of one percent of the population, would be needed to fill the second and third ranks in American Jewish leadership. Similarly, if someone would guarantee that in the next generation we shall have 50,000 Jews in America speaking Hebrew fluently and engaged in the intensive reading of Hebrew literature, I might protest that this number is not sufficient in comparison to the total Jewish population, but essentially I should still feel reassured. Although I am not ready to surrender more ambitious expectations, I would nevertheless consider 50,000 good Hebraists in the United States a generation hence as a force sufficient to redeem the other 4,950,000

Jews with but a smattering of Hebrew or living in total ignorance of all the original sources of the Jewish heritage. For these 50,000 would be our guarantors of that essential unity of the Jewish people. They would tie American Jewish culture with unbreakable links both with the millennial historic tradition of the people and with contemporary Jewish life in Israel which is going to be permanently Hebraic.

In conclusion, I wish to say that the communal responsibility for Jewish education will require not only much constructive thinking on the part of educators and communal leaders, but also a great deal of hard and painfully slow persuasion of unlike-minded individuals. It will necessitate many patient negotiations with diverse factions in Jewish life. It will mean in particular the overcoming of a long standing tradition that responsibility for Jewish education can be delegated to specialized synagogue, center, or language groups within the community.

While we face all these difficulties, there is good reason for reassurance and genuine confidence that under able professional and lay leadership throughout the country, we will be able to overcome them. Not speedily, not within a year or even five years from now, but in the long run. We are a somewhat impatient people. We like to see results immediately. In the realm of education and culture, however, results are not speedily forthcoming. They require tenacity and perseverance under competent and devoted leadership. I believe that Jewish education in America has clearly revealed signs of great vitality in recent years and that the present impetus may be carried forward to ever-new heights of achievement.

18 *American Jewish Scholarship and World Jewry*[*]

The mantle of leadership has suddenly, perhaps too suddenly, descended on the shoulders of the American Jews. This event was bound to come sooner or later in view of the large number, great cultural diversity, and economic affluence of the American community. However, under normal circumstances this transfer of leadership would have been slow and gradual and for several decades to come European leadership would have shared with America in the task of facing the ever-changing world of emancipated Jewry. Under the best of circumstances the American community could no longer rely on practically all its communal and intellectual manpower being supplied by the Old World, while it could concentrate on its pioneering tasks of exploring new methods of communal organization, collecting funds for the stricken communities anywhere else, and raising its highly audible voice in behalf of oppressed coreligionists of other lands. Unfortunately the stark tragedy of the 1930s and 1940s has to all intents and purposes eliminated the main European partners in those tasks of Jewish reconstruction.

Generally true, this new situation has become doubly marked in the sphere of intellectual leadership. Until quite recently American Jewry could bodily import the main European ideologies and

[*] Address delivered at the Sixty-first Annual Meeting of the American Jewish Historical Society at Hotel Roosevelt, 45th Street and Madison Avenue, New York, N. Y., Sunday evening, April 21, 1963.

even some of their outstanding spokesmen. This is no longer possible today. Even Israel, which has become a prime intellectual center, cannot supply those basic answers which are needed by the communities of the dispersion who, unlike their Israeli brethren, are bound to live as permanent minorities facing diverse majorities; facing them moreover, not as outsiders, as their ancestors had done for two millennia, but as part and parcel of the majority nations. It is small wonder, then, that the American Jews are quite confused and insecure. Many doubt the very possibility of American Jewry ever finding independent answers for the great tasks facing them, as well as the other Jews of the Western Hemisphere, the British Commonwealth, and even Europe, who now look to it for guidance.

On several occasions I have had the opportunity of speaking up against this mood of despair. I feel quite strongly that facing this changed world situation, the Jewish people—and particularly its American segment—as in its long past will reveal its basic pioneering spirit and meet the challenges of the new era independently and creatively.

Effects of the Holocaust

Among the major tasks for American Jewish scholarship, including the members of the American Jewish Historical Society, is the continued cultivation of Jewish history in the older, as well as newer, areas of Jewish settlement. Even the Society, dedicated as it primarily is to the study of American Jewish history, has long realized the historic interdependence of the various Jewish groups and the impossibility of comprehending any particular territorial evolution without reference to their totality. Suffice it to quote our Society's objectives as announced in every issue of its *Quarterly*:

> The object of this Society is to collect and publish material bearing upon the history of America, and to promote the study of Jewish history in general, preferably so far as the same is

related to American Jewish history or connected with the causes
of emigration from various parts of the world to this continent.

Not surprisingly, therefore, some of the best papers published in
the long series of its annual and quarterly publications included
Alexander Marx's "Aims and Tasks of Jewish Historiography," and
Max J. Kohler's "The Jewish Rights at the Congresses of Vienna
and Aix-la-Chapelle," both of which appeared in its *Publications,*
Vol. XXVI. This happened at a time when America's historiographic achievements in general could hardly compare with the
advanced historical research conducted on the other side of the
ocean by both independent Jewish scholars and organized groups.
We need but remember another paper by Alexander Marx submitted to the Society and entitled "Societies for the Promotion
of the Study of Jewish History" which appeared in Vol. XX, pp.
1-9.

Almost all of these societies went under during the Great
Catastrophe. The only significant exception is the Jewish Historical Society of England which, though it sustained very severe
losses in its collections during the bombings of the Second World
War, has recovered its old zeal for careful research into the
medieval and modern history of English Jewry and may be looking
forward now to another rich period of growth and creativity.
Another sister institution, the Yivo Institute for Jewish Social
Research, was fortunate enough to salvage much of its personnel
and library holdings and resume its fruitful activities on this side
of the ocean. French Jewry, too, has been coming into its own.
For a time, to be sure, the *Revue des Etudes Juives*, once a major
tribune for historical research, was able to appear but sporad-
ically, and its main area of concentration was the field of intellectual history of the earlier Middle Ages. But after a few years, it
joined forces with the *Historia Judaica* and resuscitated the dormant forces of historical research into the past of both the French
and other Jewries. Most remarkably, without Jewish sponsorship,
Spain has made some signal contributions to Jewish historical
studies. The Instituto Arias Montano, connected with the Uni-

versities of Madrid and Barcelona, through its quarterly *Sefarad* and numerous other publications, has overshadowed anything done by non-Jewish scholars in the fields of medieval and modern Jewish historical research in any other European country.

The losses far outweigh the gains, however. Neither Germany nor Poland are able now to contribute more than a few occasional monographs or the *Bulletin* of the Jewish Historical Institute in Warsaw, which has devoted most of its attention to relatively recent events. Thus two countries which before the Second World War led the Jewish world in creative scholarship—I need but refer to my own *Bibliography of Jewish Social Studies, 1938-1939*— are now speaking only with muted voices and cannot even take care of the minimal investigations needed to elucidate various phases of the Jewish past in their own countries.

Perhaps even more tragic has been the silencing of all Jewish historical creativity in the Soviet Union. Although still embracing the second largest Jewish community in the world, the Union has long since suspended all possibilities for fruitful Jewish historical research. At the beginning of the Communist regime there still were quite a few scholars of the older vintage who, while placing their historical techniques in the service of the new materialistic conception of history, made some important contributions to the study of the Jewish past. To be sure, from the outset the areas of research were strictly circumscribed. With the main emphasis placed upon the economic evolution, even the few scholars who, like M. Lurie and N. M. Nikolskii, worked in the field of ancient Jewish history, specialized only in its socioeconomic facets. Most other scholars concentrated on the recent period of East-European Jewish history, likewise viewed from the aspect of socioeconomic or, at best, also some literary developments, but totally neglected the two thousand years of intervening history or that of the Jewish past in other lands. Nevertheless we must be grateful to men like I. Sosis, A. Yuditskii, Max Erik, Meir Wiener, and Lev Zinger for a number of searching analyses of both Jewish demography and economic life on the one hand, and of literary history on the other hand. Regrettably, Zinger's *Dos banaite Folk*, published in 1941, is the last important document of Jewish social research published in the length and breadth of the Soviet Union. The other scholars have been silenced even earlier. As a result, during the last decades Russian Jewish scholarship was able to contribute but little to the sum total of Jewish historical and sociological knowledge.

New Responsibilities

Under these circumstances, the burden on American Jewish as well as Israeli scholarship has grown immensely. During the last three decades the most significant contributions to the history of European Jewries have been made by residents of either the United States or Israel. Certainly there is nothing comparable in Germany's own intellectual output in this field to the researches of Selma Stern, Guido Kisch and others assembled around the Leo Baeck Institute in New York, London, and Jerusalem. Similarly Zosa Szajkowski has elucidated, more than any other single individual, many aspects of modern French Jewish history—and he has resided in this country since the early 1940s. The history of Italian Jewry has been told more effectively by Cecil Roth in England, Moses Shulvass in this country, as well as by Attilio Milano and others in Israel. Similarly, most of the research on East-European Jewish history has been carried on in this country (by Abraham Duker, Bernard Weinryb, Isaac Levitats, Isaac Lewin, and others), Israel, or Argentina. While most of the protagonists in this historical drama have been natives of these very European countries and many of them had arrived here as mature and fully trained scholars, a number of younger American students have already arisen in our midst to reveal the potentialities of future development. I am happy to say that one of my own pupils, Lloyd P. Gartner, was able to write one of the best monographs on Anglo-Jewish history published in recent years.

All these are mere beginnings, however. It becomes increasingly imperative for American Jewish scholars to take an active part in the gathering of sources and their careful sifting, in analyzing and systematically integrating these findings into the total picture of the local and universal Jewish historical evolution. True, this task is beset with many difficulties. It was never easy to conduct research from a great distance. As a rule foreign scholars have been able only to supplement some of the information gathered by local researchers who not only had direct access to the archives, libraries and museums of their countries, but also had an unmatched living experience within each particular environment. They may sometimes have lacked historical perspective; they may have been subject to varying local biases. But these deficiencies were usually more than made up by their ability to appreciate the fine points and nuances in the local records. Without such cooperation of local scholarship, foreign researchers are always severely handicapped.

Nevertheless we must not forget that long stretches of human history have been investigated exclusively by such "outsiders." This is not only true of ancient and medieval history which were separated by centuries from the modern investigators, but also of many more recent areas where local scholarship had not yet matured. What would we have known about the history of the Middle East or Africa, were we to rely only on the fruits of local scholarship? It is only in the last several decades that Middle-Eastern scholars have been able to make vital contributions to the historical understanding of their own countries. Before doing so, however, they had to go to western schools and acquire western techniques so as to speak the same lingo as their western predecessors and masters. Native African historical scholarship still is in its infancy today. In some respects research in eastern and central European history by American and Israeli scholars may have to overcome the same difficulties but also yield the same fruitful results as did Arabic, Turkish, or Iranian scholarship developed by Europeans in the nineteenth century.

I am not blind to the practical difficulties of such undertakings. It may be particularly difficult to work in areas behind the Iron Curtain because, despite the toning down of the general xenophobia of the Stalin era, foreign scholars still encounter many serious obstacles in pursuing free and independent research there.

538 | Steeled by Adversity

On the other hand, we now possess certain facilities which were not available to the nineteenth-century students. The mere possibility of Xeroxing or microfilming archival sources, and other great technological advances, have smoothed the task for many investigators who, but several decades ago, had to undertake long, costly, and arduous journeys, copy many records by hand, and otherwise waste a great many energies on merely overcoming the resistance of inert matter.

If these new facilities are symbolic of our space age, so are the methodological changes in our historical and social science research. I shall be the last to disparage the creative potential of individuals working on subjects of their own choice and pursuing their own independent ideas. In the long run, great contributions to historical or any other scholarship will be made by those mysterious ingredients in the gray matter and nervous systems of certain gifted individuals, animated by some unidentifiable inner impulses. However, much of the building material for the erection of great structures can best be assembled through the collective efforts of well-directed groups, provided with the necessary financial means, and dedicated to the pursuit of certain specialized projects. In our era of historiography the greatest results may be expected only from such a constant interplay of extraordinary individual creativity and well-organized cooperative undertakings. It is in this area, I believe, that all historical societies have a great opportunity to play a vital historical role of their own.

We have to beware, to be sure, of another powerful contemporary trend: the emphasis on public relations. This is not only true of the United States, dominated in many phases of its intellectual as well as daily life by the "Mad'son Avenue" ideology, but also of the Soviet Union and many other countries, where propaganda values frequently outweigh all intrinsic merits. There is little basic difference between the "Madison Avenue" approach or the programming of even major religious events with the view to their effect on the press or television, and the methods employed by the Soviet, Nazi, or Fascist propaganda machines. Semblance of reality is often dinned into the masses with such power and persistence that it overshadows reality itself and some-times even alters it. Not necessarily to its advantage! Genuine scholarship must try to steer clear of such fictitious conquests and to penetrate the real heart and substance of the area under in-vestigation.

Another modern penchant for semblance rather than reality is a certain building mania which has afflicted some of the great-est centers of learning. It is a matter of record that universities, research institutes, and academies have found it much easier to interest patrons in donating funds for elaborate buildings than in supplying the necessary means for carrying on significant researches within their walls. The donors often see themselves immortalized in the mortar and stone erected with their money, whereas they personally have little understanding for the complex, often even abstruse lines of research, basic or applied, which alone justify the existence of such facilities. This trend is so overwhelming that even our national administration finds it easier to negotiate with Congress over federal aid to education through grants to building funds or else through the philanthropically tinged student aid than through direct subsidies for raising teachers' salaries and thus helping attract some of the best talents to the academic pro-fession. In this respect, we frightfully lag behind the Soviet Union where the salaries of academicians and research personnel compare favorably with those of the highest executives in govern-ment and state-controlled business. Society at large, and Jewish society in particular, must try to steer clear of such glittering ex-ternals and come to grips with genuine fundamentals.

Nor is this situation entirely new. Ancient philanthropists have likewise often gloried in erecting beautiful synagogues and other communal structures. If I may be allowed to quote a passage from my own *History*, it will best illustrate that dichotomy between the layman's love for display and the scholar's profound interest in the substance of scholarship as such.

When R. Ḥama ben Ḥanina pointed out to R. Hoshaiah II a beautiful synagogue in Lydda in which his ancestors had sunk a lot of money, the latter exclaimed: "And how many souls did they sink here? Were there no men willing to study the Torah?" R. Abin, on similar grounds, reproached a friend for installing a beautiful gate in his large schoolhouse and applied to him the verse, "For Israel hath forgotten his Maker, and builded palaces" (Hos. 8:14; j. Pe'ah VIII, 9, 21b). [SRH, 2d. ed., II, 284].

The most crying need for American Jewish scholarship and particularly historical scholarship today is the development of highly qualified manpower. Because of the lack of support and understanding on the part of the community many talented students of Jewish history have drifted into the rabbinate or other professions or else devoted themselves to the teaching of some general disciplines. They were lost to specialized Jewish historical research. The situation has been improving somewhat in recent years, but we have a long way to go before we shall build up the necessary cadres of young Jewish historians to carry on with even a minimal but indispensable program of research in the vast domain of Jewish history, including that of its American segment.

Here is the great opportunity for the American Jewish Historical Society. Together with other like-minded organizations, it might embark on a comprehensive, well thought out and, despite its staggering difficulties, perfectly feasible program. Its rather obvious components might be:

1) To start a publication series in the field of Jewish history which would not be completely dependent on haphazard offerings by individual scholars but would delineate well-conceived plans for the investigation of significant areas of historic research.

2) To encourage individual researches by grants-in-aid and particularly by opening avenues for the publication of fruits of research, however technical and lacking in popular appeal.

3) To announce substantial prizes for major contributions to historical research and writing.

4) To explore avenues of assembling archival and other historical materials through photostats and microfilms and constant

exchanges with other research organizations, Jewish and non-Jewish, in various lands.

5) To stimulate more indirectly, rather than directly, the public interest in both conserving Jewish historical records and in their utilization.

This program is by no means novel. But the very fact that it has never been genuinely attempted, largely because of unavailable financial means, makes it doubly imperative now that it be adopted and executed at the earliest possible date.

I may conclude by again referring to my belief that, when confronted by a great historic challenge, the American Jews, including their scholarly sector, will, as Americans and as Jews, regain their vigorous pioneering spirit and meet that challenge in a novel and creative way.

19 Can American Jewry Be Culturally Creative?*

The American Jewish community today is seriously concerned about culture. Whereas for the last several decades one heard for the most part the question, "Will American Jewry survive?" nowadays the query is: "Is American Jewry going to be culturally creative?"

This Jewish concern about survival, as well as cultural creativity, is, in my opinion, a decidedly favorable feature. It is essentially in line with the millennial tradition which built its religious life around the concept of ethical monotheism, or what I prefer to call ethical-historical monotheism.

A Pessimistic Mood

At present the prevailing mood in the American Jewish community is that of pessimism. This is a curious reversal: Generations back Jews in America, as elsewhere, spoke of their future in glowing terms, a characteristic they shared with the majority of the American people who optimistically viewed the future of their

* A combination of revised summaries of an Israel Chipkin Memorial Lecture delivered under the auspices of the Alumni Association of the School of Jewish Studies of the Jewish Theological Seminary of America, and published in the *Jewish Heritage*, I, No. 2 (1958), pp. 11-14, 53; and of an address delivered at the 74th Annual Meeting of the Jewish Publication Society of America held in Philadelphia on May 20, 1962, published in its *The Bookmark*, IX, No. 2 (1962), pp. 7-9.

nation or of mankind as a whole—though today that optimism, too, is a bit tempered, if not reversed.

Many reasons can be advanced for this uncertainty, even despair. A major argument often presented is that the Jewish community here has not yet been genuinely creative in the cultural sphere. The Jews were in America from 1654 until 1860, or more than two centuries, before the first Hebrew book was published in this country.

Since that time, to be sure, we have had a very large output of Hebrew books and periodicals. We developed an even greater Yiddish literature, theater, and press which, in certain areas, exceeded the achievements of European Jewry.

Yet, this creativity was essentially an elongation of what had happened in Europe. To a large extent this continuation of Yiddish and Hebrew letters was accomplished in the New World even physically by persons who had come over from the Old World and had brought that culture with them.

In fact, many people ask, not without justice, as to whether one might not view every important ideological movement in American Judaism as a mere continuation of trends which had been fully developed in Europe. Is there, they question, basic ideological novelty in anything American Jewry has produced?

Historical Perspective

However, viewed from the broad historic perspective, it is not at all surprising that American Jewry has not yet produced those great cultural achievements for which we are all hoping.

Suffice it to look back upon the major Jewish cultural centers of past ages—Hellenistic Egypt, Babylonia which created the Babylonian Talmud, Spain with its Golden Age, medieval Germany and France, or modern Eastern Europe. A brief consideration will convince us that it took every one of these communities much longer to develop its particular Jewish culture than the entire duration of Jewish settlement on this continent.

Whether or not we assume that some descendants of the ancient Hebrews who had failed to join Moses in the Exodus still survived underground and joined the newly settled Israelites of the First Commonwealth, there is no question that there has been an uninterrupted Jewish life in the Nile Valley since the sixth or, more probably, seventh century B.C.E. Next to the Jewish military colony in Elephantine, Upper Egypt, there existed Jewish communities in Migdol, Taḥpanhes, Noph (mostly identified with Magdalos, Daphne, and Memphis in Lower Egypt) and "in the country of Pathros" in the days of Jeremiah (44:1). And yet it took three centuries before any sign of intellectual life began burgeoning in this new environment, to come to full fruition only in the days of Philo of Alexandria in the first century C.E. So little did the Jewish people in both Egypt and Palestine remember the more than two centuries of the first Persian domination that a rabbi could claim that the latter lasted only thirty-four years after the erection of the Second Temple.[1] Even the few Hellenistic Jewish writers before Philo might have been completely forgotten, were it not for some pagan collectors and Christian Church Fathers who salvaged a few fragments together with the Greek translation of the Bible, the Septuagint.

Jewish life in Babylonia had blossomed during the Babylonian Exile in the sixth century B.C.E., if not much earlier. Babylonian Jewry was unquestionably creative during that period, but this was only a temporary phenomenon. As soon as the exiles returned to Palestine, the large majority of their fellow Jews who were left behind ceased to function as a great cultural force. In his first book on the Great War, Josephus addressed himself to the Babylonian Jews, whom he speaks of as consisting of "countless myriads."[2] Although it is estimated that more than a million Jews, or one-eighth of the total Jewish population in the world, lived in Babylonia in the days of the ancient historian, they seemed to have failed to create anything culturally significant.

And yet, it was Babylonian Jewry which furnished important cultural manpower for Palestine; this was true time and again, not only in the days of the Exile and Restoration but in later periods as well. A third-century Palestinian sage, R. Simon ben

Lakish, recorded that three times the *Torah* was in danger of being forgotten in the Holy Land, and that each time Babylonian Jews came to the rescue—first, Ezra; the second time, Hillel; and the third time, Rabbi Hiyya.[3] In other words, there existed in Babylonia distinguished scholars and rabbis, but they were inarticulate. If in the year 200 C.E., or eight centuries after the first fall of Jerusalem, that country had suffered from an earthquake or another major cataclysm causing the Jews to disappear from that region, practically nothing of Babylonian Jewish culture would have survived. This despite the fact that the Babylonian community was headed by exilarchs who, it appears with some legitimacy, traced their descent directly to the royal prisoners deported from ancient Israel by the Babylonian conqueror. Many learned men must have lived in Babylonia, some of whom are recorded to have exerted considerable influence in remote Jerusalem. Yet none of them left behind a permanent heritage until Rab (Abba Arikha) founded his academy in Sura (219 C.E.).

A similar situation existed in Spain. This country became a great Jewish cultural center only during the Golden Age, in the tenth to the twelfth centuries, and yet there is cogent evidence of Jewish communities in Spain as early as 300 C.E. and probably earlier. It is even surmised that the Christian apostle Paul planned to visit that country to address Jewish communities and to preach in synagogues. None the less, had a catastrophe occurred and wiped out Spanish Jewry before 900 C.E. there would have been no record of any major Jewish cultural activity. This absence of creativity would have occurred notwithstanding the fact that the Spanish Jews had long been quite numerous, had enthusiastically fought for their religion against intolerant Visigothic kings, had endured two expulsions and forced conversions, and had nevertheless emerged strong and powerful enough to play a significant role in the Moorish conquest of the Iberian Peninsula. But no vestige of cultural activity, no Hebrew book or poem written by a Spanish Jews has survived. Clearly, after six or more centuries of organized communal life, Spanish Jewry was still culturally uncreative. Then all of a sudden, from the tenth century on, a galaxy of great personalities arose, including Samuel ibn Nagrela, Solomon ibn Gabirol, Yehudah Halevi, Moses and Abraham ibn Ezra. The great Golden Age of the Spanish Jews was at hand, the like of which the Jewish people experienced nowhere else in the Middle Ages.

The same thing happened in Germany. In the fourth century, Emperor Constantine the Great addressed two decrees to the Jewish community of Cologne; these decrees were actually incorporated in the official Theodosian Code. Organized Jewish communities had thus existed along the Rhine at least from about 300 C.E. on. Yet, nothing is heard of any German literary creativity before the tenth century, shortly before Rabbenu Gershom "the Light of the Exile." In fact, from 300 to 900, Hebrew literary documents were so completely absent that we might well have doubted the very presence of Jews in Germany at that time were it not for some incidental references in non-Jewish sources. But in the tenth century there was a sudden upsurge of creativity and the production of law books, commentaries, homilies, poems, and chronicles, which made medieval German Jewish history of focal significance to world Jewish culture.

In Eastern Europe, too, we know of the presence of Jews in Khazaria in the eighth and in Kiev in the tenth centuries, the latter even boasting of a "Jewish gate." Nevertheless, Polish and Ukrainian Jews remained culturally inarticulate until they found their voice in the late fifteenth and early sixteenth centuries, when a great cultural outpouring took place. In the middle of the sixteenth century Polish Jewry produced some of the greatest Jewish scholars. From that time on, Poland, like Germany, became a great center of Jewish culture and remained so until the destruction of the Warsaw Ghetto.

What is clear from these five examples is that it takes a very long time for any culture to grow. Centuries must pass before the Jewish community can strike sufficient roots in any new country to get adjusted and develop its own new attitude which can become a basis for its new creativity.

Perhaps we are expecting the American Jews to produce results much too quickly. We must not forget that the real history of the Jews in the United States, as far as the large majority of its population is concerned, had only begun a century and a quarter ago. This is much too short a period of time for any community to take roots and to establish its unique identity in a new environment. None of this proves, however, that the American Jews are not capable of developing a culture of their own.

Effect of Emancipation

True, the differences from past ages are also staggering. Most significantly, we are living in an era of Emancipation in which the Jews are being integrated into society at large. Jews are expected, not to live as a minority facing different majorities, as they did for twenty-five centuries in Egypt, Babylonia, Spain, Germany, Poland, and elsewhere, but to be part and parcel of the majorities themselves. Nowadays we are supposed to be Americans *and* Jews, Englishmen *and* Jews, Argentinians *and* Jews, and so forth.

In short, we are facing a problem of developing a culture which will be both Jewish and Western (or, to take the Soviet Union, both Jewish and Soviet) to embrace a total Jew, a Jew who, for instance in this country, feels himself completely American and completely Jewish at the same time. This is, indeed, a tremendous, in many respects unprecedented, challenge.

Moreover, the very meaning of Jewish culture has undergone a change during the Emancipation era. In Eastern Europe during the twentieth century Jews have been recognized as a nationality among other nationalities. If the Soviet Union had continued along the lines of its first decade during and after the Lenin regime—with the recognition of Jewish national minority rights, with a national school system in Yiddish, a Yiddish press and theater—one might really have witnessed there the emergence of a Judaism devoid of religion, Hebrew, the Zionist-messianic ideal, that is, a purely secular, Yiddishist national entity. Under such conditions, a Russian Jew—as began to be noticeable in the 1920s and the 1930s—could actually look down upon the American

Jew as assimilated, because the latter sent his children to English-speaking schools, himself spoke English, and outwardly lived a purely American life.

If that evolution had developed undisturbedly we might have had by now two types of Judaism, a national secular Yiddish Judaism of Eastern Europe, and the religious, Zionist, Hebraic Judaism of the Western world. Each would claim superiority over the other. Unfortunately, the last thirty years have seen great changes in the Soviet Union, and have put an end to the possibility of the development there of any really flourishing secular Judaism in the foreseeable future.

The main question today really is whether Jews can be culturally creative under Emancipation. Can they be creative within their own, as well as within the majority culture? Certainly, there will be Jewish poets and writers, artists, musicians, scientists, and scholars. If the pattern follows past experience, Jews will undoubtedly contribute to the cultures of their environment more than may be expected from their ratio in the respective populations. But will they have enough cultural energy left creatively to cultivate their own Jewish heritage? We can find no answer in history because history has had no precedent of real Jewish Emancipation.

Sixty years ago, a relatively short time in history, half of world Jewry lived in Tsarist Russia; another significant portion in Rumania, the Ottoman Empire, and North Africa—all under conditions of non-emancipation. Even though one-third of world Jewry lived in the United States and other free countries at that time, most of them had been born and bred under conditions of non-emancipation. They could hardly have been expected to have changed overnight merely because they had left their *Shtetls* in the Ukraine or Poland for Chicago or London. In 1917, with the Russian Revolution, and in 1919 with the Peace Treaties it began to look as though world Jewry might at last be truly emancipated once and for all. The great counter-movement of Nazism, however, arose to deny not only Emancipation but also the very right of Jews to exist.

Consequently, Emancipation really had no chance fully to reveal its good, as well as bad, effects until after World War II. Only in our own day have we had the opportunity to observe the effects of real freedom—in this country and elsewhere. As a result, we have seen a tremendous rate of assimilation, but we have also simultaneously witnessed certain elements of religious and cultural revival which pessimists had previously considered impossible.

Augury for the Future

Looking into the future, we must never lose sight of the fact that cultural values are changeable; they are not the same from generation to generation. We ourselves have often been guilty of comparing American Jewish culture exclusively with the old cultures of the European communities. The underlying assumption was that, in order to be meaningful, American Jewish life would have to be based upon a knowledge of Hebrew and Yiddish letters more or less equal to that of our ancestors and the desire of each individual to conduct himself along what were assumed to be the patterns of living of the best of his forebears. Roughly speaking, we have equated Jewish culture almost exclusively with that developed in the ghetto era of Jewish history.

Of course, we cannot expect to revive that culture of bygone ages. It would be meaningful neither here nor in the Soviet Union, nor even in Israel. The ghetto era certainly had great values of its own, but it represents a way of life of the past and not of the future.

We also must bear in mind that cultural values are not limited to books, nor to ideologies. To be sure, the written word has always been in the very focus of Jewish life; it is also going to play a tremendous role in the future. In this respect the work done by the Jewish Publication Society and, hopefully, its even greater achievements in the future are an inestimable ingredient of the developing cultural life in this land.[4] At the same time, I for one, am prepared to place our charitable contributions high on our list of cultural values. For historic reasons philanthropies have played a unique role in American Jewish communal history and, for some time to come at least, they are going to retain a central position in our communal activities.

It is easy to disparage this great concentration on charities. I myself have often spoken condescendingly of the "checkbook Judaism" which makes many individuals equate their duty toward their community with the writing of a certain number of checks to the order of worth-while organizations. Nor must we overlook certain adverse features inherent in the very philanthropic efforts.

Nevertheless it was this concern for human welfare which has helped American Jewry to erect its magnificent communal structure. The fact that, for many generations past, the American Jews have built much of their own culture around philanthropy is not devoid of deeper long-term implications. In the course of the last century, since the Civil War, our community had to face first a tremendous influx of immigrants coming from many lands in search of new economic and cultural opportunities. The earlier settlers had to concentrate on helping these newcomers to earn a living, as well as to acquire familiarity with the language and mores of their new environment. In this area we have proved ourselves to be really creative and found basic answers to the challenges of that age. During the half-century of 1865 to 1914 most of our basic Jewish institutions and organizations were established in the service of both the new arrivals and the older residents.

Since 1914, with the cessation of the pressure of new immigration, American Jewry raised its sights to embrace the whole Jewish world. It assumed a major responsibility for world Jewry, first for its European segment, and later through its commitment to Israel. We have undertaken a tremendous task, unprecedented in the annals of history—except, perhaps, when the ancient Babylonian community undertook to restore the Second Jewish Commonwealth. This job is not yet finished; we have to continue to extend constant support to the State of Israel, financially, politically, culturally.

We are beginning to realize, however, that, while doing many things for Jews of other lands we must also assume responsibility for our own religio-cultural endeavors. By their very nature religion and culture are personal concerns which cannot be delegated. In its time, the large European immigration has helped us with furnishing the cultural manpower for research, teaching, and communal service. We now realize that the future is up to us.

In conclusion, I can merely say that I feel confident that the same Jewry which has already successfully confronted other great challenges and which has proved vastly creative in devising new means of communal coexistence, will also find some appropriate solutions for our present difficulties. After all, our entire community is in many ways unprecedented. Despite the lack of any form of law enforcement, it has succeeded in answering in a pioneering way the challenges of the constant emergencies which it has faced here and abroad.

Given the time, given the challenge, and most importantly given the understanding of that challenge, American Jewry, I am certain, will also give unprecedented, pioneering answers to its present challenge of creating a novel American Jewish culture.

20 *Reordering Communal Priorities**

We have come together to consider with utmost seriousness the grave challenges now confronting American society at large and the Jewish community in particular. I am not a preacher of fire and brimstone threatening his audiences with dire results if they fail to follow his path to ultimate salvation. On the contrary, I have always been accustomed to look for silver linings on the darkest horizons. Since this particular session is held in connection with my seventy-fifth birthday, you all realize that I have lived through all the great crises of the twentieth century, a century which will be memorable in the history of man for its catastrophic upheavals. Yet, I have remained a firm believer in the vitality and adaptability of man, and particularly of the Jew, and his ability to pioneer along uncharted paths in meeting every new challenge as it arises.

In the preceding essays[1] I have tried to show that the recurrent crises in American Jewish history, which in some respects went back to the very discovery of America by Columbus, have always been met creatively by the respective generations. I have also discussed past Jewish communal pioneering in this country and the enormous debt of gratitude which the present-day magnificent

* Address delivered on November 14, 1970, under the auspices of the National Foundation for Jewish Culture and the Council of Jewish Federations and Welfare Funds at the latter's 39th General Assembly in Kansas City, Missouri. It appears here greatly enlarged and revised substantially in the form published by the Council under the title "Transmitting and Enriching the Heritage of Judaism."

structure of the American Jewish community owes to the enterprising spirit of generations of downtrodden immigrants working along unprecedented lines of endeavor.[2] I cherish, therefore, the deep conviction that, no matter how staggering our difficulties may appear today, no matter how disheartening may be our innumerable frustrations and shattered hopes, we shall once again emerge victorious from the present age of anxiety and continue on the way to a new level of achievement. But this task will require concentrated efforts on the part of the communal leadership as well as the public at large, and will doubtless involve a gradual reorientation of our community programs and a quest for new approaches in both theory and practice.

Changing Priorities

A major share of responsibility for that quest rests with members of the Council of Jewish Federations and the National Foundation for Jewish Culture. It so happens that, for historic reasons, federations of philanthopies have in this country become the nearest approximation to the old-time *Kehillah*. A community, long consisting largely of immigrants stemming from various lands with different speech, different traditions and customs, and even different religious rituals, was badly in need of relicf. Its members, often deeply divided along ideological and party lines, could also best cooperate in the noncontroversial task of helping one another. Self-help and mutual help had indeed become the greatest watchwords for American Jewish communal action. Only thus was it possible for wave after wave of new arrivals to strike roots in this land and to raise themselves, so to say, by their own bootstraps, from extreme poverty to a life of relative affluence.

Times have changed, however. One merely needs enter any of the fine hospitals maintained by Jewish communal funds to notice that the majority of ward patients and of those who seek help in clinics are non-Jews. The same is largely true of many sport facilities offered by Jewish Centers and Y's throughout the country. To be sure, it is a wonderful thing for the Jewish community to be able to help the underprivileged of any faith. This is also in line with Jewish tradition. Medieval rabbis may have debated the problem of whether one ought to accept charitable donations from Gentiles; the majority decided that one ought to do it only when one cannot reject the gift without causing resentment and that, if at all possible, the funds thus obtained should be secretly distributed among the Gentile poor. But all along little objection was raised to Jews helping Gentiles in distress.[3]

The rationale often advanced in recent years that such befriending of non-Jews would permanently enhance the good will of the Gentile neighbors toward the Jewish community has regrettably been disproved by experience. Gratitude is not often found among individuals; on the contrary, many recipients of bounty often develop a deep hatred toward their "rich uncles." To expect gratitude from groups or nations is even less realistic. Our country is learning every day with deep chagrin how little good will has been secured by the billions of dollars of foreign aid distributed by it over the years in Latin America, Africa, and even western Europe. In other words, a general humanitarian attitude to fellow sufferers of other creeds is a perfectly welcome manifestion of the great Jewish pride of being "merciful sons of merciful sires." But primary stress must be laid on helping Jewish individuals and causes, especially in the present historic era when governments all over the world are assuming ever greater responsibilities for the welfare of all their citizens.

The complexities of contemporary life are well illustrated by the hardships caused through the domestic unrest to untold numbers of Jewish shopkeepers and artisans. Many of these Jewish petty merchants and craftsmen have been living and working in the affected areas long before the present residents arrived there en masse. And yet there is unrelenting pressure that they abandon their old habitats, give up their sources of livelihood and, often at a more advanced age, seek new opportunities elsewhere. Certainly, to many members of this new class of Jewish displaced persons, such an exodus spells financial ruin and the abandonment of their cherished way of life.

This tragic concatenation of circumstances has induced one of my friends, a specialist in public administration, seriously to advance the proposal that the Jewish welfare organizations should raise substantial sums to buy up the properties of the prospective displaced Jews and donate them to the racial minorities. Little did he realize that this was the very type of discrimination which was applied in interwar Poland and which rightly created great resentment among the Jews all over the world. After the First World War the rapidly increasing Polish peasant population, unable to make a living in its traditional agricultural pursuits, moved in droves to the cities where, with the aid of government and Polish society, including some Jewish doctrinaires, it began displacing Jewish artisans, shopkeepers, and even factory workers. For one example, the tobacco industry, which had furnished much employment to both Jewish tobacco workers and tobacconists, became a state monopoly under the then existing Polish etatism. Within a few years the numerous Jewish tobacco workers of Warsaw were discharged in order to make room for the incoming Polish peasants. At the same time only those Jewish tobacconists could continue to operate their small shops who found Christian "strawmen" ready to serve as the purported licensed owners against a substantial share in the revenue without any work. It was against such practices that the American and other Jewish communal organs vigorously protested. And yet under different conditions in this country, where the government is but indirectly involved, such policies find an "understanding" audience among Jewish intellectuals and political leaders.

Of course, the Jewish welfare organizations have done a yeoman's job in helping Jews abroad. Fund raising for Israel, in particular, has been and will remain for years to come a primary responsibility of the Jewries of the dispersion, particularly that of the United States. I am saying it not only for ideological reasons but out of the historical experience of many Jewish communities. I still remember an informal discussion in which I participated in 1938 soon after the infamous *Kristallnacht* which followed the assassination of a petty German diplomat by a young Jew in Paris.

In retaliation the Nazi government imposed upon the entire German Jewish community a collective fine of one billion marks, officially worth about $240,000,000. This amount had a purchasing power of more than the $1,000,000,000 which Golda Meir now demands from world Jewry over the next year or two. Moreover, by 1938 the resources of German Jewry, reduced by the Great Depression of 1929-32, were further gravely depleted by the more or less forced emigration of nearly half of its members and the sharply discriminatory laws and policies relentlessly pursued by the German government against it. In our discussion on that occasion we speculated on what might have happened if, ten years earlier, the German Jews, then still at the height of their economic and cultural prosperity, would have voluntarily raised one billion marks for the benefit of the Palestinian *Yishuv*. Aided and abetted by such an enormous infusion of money, the Jewish settlement in Palestine doubtless would have rapidly expanded in the intervening ten years. Even the British Royal Commissions, which successively examined Palestine's "economic absorptive capacity" and invariably came to the conclusion—later proved completely erroneous—that the country could absorb only a small number of Jewish immigrants annually, would have been forced to admit that Palestine could have opened her gates to several hundred thousand Jews over a period of 6-7 years. This means that the country could have accommodated almost all the German Jews able and willing to settle in the Promised Land. This at a time when nearly all other countries had reduced the opportunities for Jewish immigration almost to a vanishing point.

I do not wish to convey the impression that I believe that American Jewry needs, or will need in the near future, such an indirect form of insurance. But quite apart from the need of providing a potential haven of refuge for the multitude of Jews living behind the Iron Curtain the moment they might be allowed to leave, there is considerable evidence that, for the first time in many years, thousands of Americans voluntarily choose expatriation because of their unhappiness over the state of affairs in this land. Among these expatriates, actual and potential, are quite a few Jews, some driven by a similar disaffection with racial strife, the crime wave, drug addiction, and other symptoms of a deep social malady, while others are dominated by more positive idealistic impulses to participate in the upbuilding of the rapidly advancing State of Israel. Certainly, it is not completely unrealistic to consider Israel as a possible haven of refuge even for Jews of one or another country in the Western Hemisphere. But whether for selfish reasons and in the realization of the oft-demonstrated interdependence of fate of the Jewish communities the world over, or because of the ever welling springs of Jewish solidarity, there is no question that the overwhelming majority of American Jews are emotionally involved in the future of the State of Israel and its inhabitants.

New Defenses

The other major preoccupation of American Jewry for the last several decades has been the defense of Jewish rights. In the nineteenth century the main stress was laid on securing and safeguarding Jewish rights abroad. In the first quarter of this century American Jewish leadership faced the additional task of warding off hostile anti-alien legislation which would have barred a great many East-European Jews from entering this country. In the 1930s, however, American Jewry itself felt threatened. Like the rest of world Jewry it was under a savage attack of international antisemitism which, at its peak, found expression in a poll showing that fully 8 percent of the American public approved the Nazi policies against Jews. With the United States' entry into the war against Hitler this threat was greatly modified and, in recent years, most American Jews allowed themselves to be lulled into a sense of security not quite warranted by the facts.

It was, therefore, with a start that many Jews saw themselves suddenly confronted by a new wave of antisemitism now often disguised through anti-Zionist and anti-Israeli slogans. Sponsored by the vast international machinery of Russian communism and spearheaded by the Arab enmity to Israel, this new form of anti-semitism was doubly startling, as it was combined with liberal slogans of anticolonialism, Zionism's alleged alliance with western imperialism, and Jewish exploitation of the underprivileged masses. Jewish liberals, including many leaders of the defense sector of the organized Jewish community, who had just spent years of toil and millions of dollars on the civil rights movement in this country, now found themselves repudiated by the extremists, both black and white.

Most galling has been the vociferous participation of the Jew-ish members of the New Left in this attack on the Jewish com-munity. This was not merely an extension of the revolutionary assault on the existing Establishment, but a specific anti-Jewish stance. If I may be allowed to refer to a personal recollection, I remember meeting Theodor Lessing, the author of the classical work on Jewish self-hatred,[4] at the World Zionist Congress in Prague in 1933. One of the early refugees from Nazidom, Lessing at that time had temporarily settled across the border in Czecho-slovakian Marienbad and was visiting Prague for a day. Our con-versation naturally touched on self-hatred which was then spreading among German Jews overwhelmed by the suddenness of the Nazi deluge. We deplored especially the presence of a small extremist Jewish faction which was prepared to fraternize even with the Nazis, though its approaches were time and again roundly rejected. When we parted company Lessing returned to Marienbad while I proceeded overnight to Vienna. Arriving in the Austrian capital in the morning I learned to my great distress that Lessing had been assassinated during the night by Nazi thugs who had ille-gally crossed the Czechoslovakian frontier and then had safely returned to Germany after committing their heinous act. Such Jewish self-haters are now trying to escape their Jewish heritage by preaching the violent overthrow of the existing order (including the Jewish communal structure) in the name of the liberation of the downtrodden masses of other races and ethnic groups in this country and abroad.

New Assimilation

This is indeed a new form of assimilation. It has been argued that the Jewish New Left cannot be classified as assimilationist because its goal is not to integrate the Jews into American society as it now exists. In fact, it repudiates that society with all that it stands for. None the less, if theirs is not assimilation to American culture at large it is full-fledged integration into one of the American subcultures, namely precisely their own fragmented New Left culture. If in their general outlook they agree more on what they wish to repudiate than on what they wish to replace it with, most of them assert that Judaism is obsolete and that it would somehow be submerged in whatever the new emergent culture might be. As in the case of the old Jewish self-haters, much of that escapism is derived from ignorance of Jewish history, including the tragic experiences of their like-minded predecessors.

Similar misinformation underlies the New Left's interpretation of Israel's domestic policies. It echoes the pro-Arab and anti-semitic allegations about the racial immigration policies pursued by the State of Israel. It points out that, while Jews are freely admitted into the country, other foreigners have to meet certain specific legal requirements. It readily forgets that the State of Israel owes its origin to the idea, confirmed by world opinion as represented by the League of Nations and again by the United Nations, that the Jewish people was entitled to a national home in Palestine and that that country was to serve as a haven of refuge for the oppressed and imperiled Jewries of other lands. For this reason the new State, while generally exercising its usual sovereign rights in regulating the admission of foreign citizens to the country, voluntarily imposed upon itself a partial limitation of that sovereignty by including in its fundamental laws the "Law of Return." It thereby tied its own hands by declaring in advance that it wished forever to admit Jews regardless of their age and their physical or mental capacity. This law has indeed operated for over twenty years and made it possible for the multitude of

Jews ousted from the Arab lands to gain free admission to the country of their forefathers. With respect to all other would-be immigrants Israel merely follows the customary lines of all states in choosing such new settlers as might best serve its own national interest.

No less untenable are the frequent accusations aimed at Israel's treatment of the Arab refugee problem and the related contention that "aggressors" should not be rewarded by any territorial gains acquired by force of arms. It is truly ironical to hear the Iron Curtain countries piously declaim these lofty principles. One merely has to remember that since 1946 the Soviet Union has occupied by force East Prussia with its capital in Königsberg (now renamed Kaliningrad), an area which it had never possessed before nor had any historic claims to. It would also be ridiculous, if it were not so tragic, to listen to the Czechoslovak and Polish spokesmen at the United Nations and elsewhere mouth the sanctimonious phrases about the injustices wrought by Israel on the poor Arab refugees during the War of Liberation of 1948. They readily forget that military campaigns have always set in motion waves of émigrés who sought refuge away from the battlefields. More, Czechoslovakia does not like to be reminded that, not during military encounters, but long after the hostilities had ceased, it decreed the expulsion of some 4,000,000 Germans who for many centuries had lived in the Sudeten and other parts of the country. Similar cold-blooded approaches enabled Poland not only to occupy territories which had been German for centuries but also long after the armistice to issue decrees of expulsion of their German-speaking citizens. The nexus between Poland's expansionist program and the expulsion of the Germans was clearly formulated by Wladyslaw Gomulka, later the ruler of the country. At the Plenary Meeting of the Central Committee of the Polish Workers' Party (Communist), held on May 3-5, 1945, he declared that "if we do not polonize the former German territories, we shall have no grounds for claiming what they already refuse to give us." The effect was that although as late as January 1, 1946, eight months after the cessation of hostilities, the Germans still constituted 60 percent of the inhabitants; they were reduced two years later under peaceful conditions to a mere 3.7 percent.[5] This obvious difference between Palestine and East-Central Europe is never mentioned in the communist world or by its New Left sympathizers. But the fact remains that the Arab refugees ran because of their own fears, actually exacerbated by their own leaders, whereas the Germans of Czechoslovakia and Poland left by virtue of public law and a publicly declared national policy of the two governments under peacetime conditions.

A second, equally obvious, difference consists in the fact that most Arab governments have refused to accept and resettle the Palestinian Arabs whom they claim as fellow members of the great Arab nation; this despite the untold sufferings thus imposed upon the hundreds of thousands of refugees forced to live for more than two decades in refugee camps. In contrast, West Germany, though emerging from the Second World War as a defeated nation with many of its cities in ruins and its citizenry on extremely short rations, immediately opened her gates to her conationals expelled from Czechoslovakia and Poland. By the dint of hard work on the part of both her older and newer citizens, Germany recovered from her wartime debacle and once again became a prosperous and powerful nation. Thus, while the millions of these new citizens greatly contributed to the "economic miracle" of Ehrhardt's Germany, the hundreds of thousands of Arab refugees have been living on doles largely provided for by American money and have become a pawn in Arab power politics.

Nor do the New Leftists, together with many others, hesitate to borrow an accusation, first heard in Zionist circles, against American and other diaspora Zionists who fail to live up to their ideals and settle in Israel. This is a complete misreading of twentieth-century history. Slogans of this type were somewhat justified in the early stages of the Zionist colonization of Palestine when the *Yishuv* cried out for additional Jewish manpower and when the growth of the Jewish population in the country had enormous political and strategic, as well as economic, importance. Today, Israel still welcomes the accession to its manpower especially by immigrants from Western countries, many of whom bring with them some technological know-how which helps the country's economy. If I may indulge in a personal recollection: In 1957 I attended the so-called Ideological Conference in Jerusalem. At that time David Ben-Gurion, as he did on many previous and subsequent occasions, strongly demanded the speedy immigration of 2,000,000 Jews from the dispersion. When, on the following day, I had to initiate the discussion I regretfully pointed out that throughout history mass migrations were mainly the result of economic drives, whether or not these were initiated or reinforced by political and cultural factors. One could not expect that more than a limited number of idealists would expatriate themselves from their respective western lands and accept more primitive ways of living in a distant country.[6]

The situation has since changed greatly. Today immigration to Israel may be sought by persons who never cherished the Zionist ideology. When they arrive in the country their adjustment often entails fewer hardships than those which usually accompany migratory movements. On the other hand, Israel's international position is enhanced precisely by the presence in various lands of many Jews dedicated to the idea of Zion. The latter's economic resources, political contacts, and scientific expertise often prove more helpful to the new country, beset by a permanent state of war against most of its immediate neighbors, when they remain in their old residences than when they settle in Israel.

New Cultural Challenges

Certainly, the prevalence of so many Jewish self-haters, some of them gifted writers and thinkers, offers another challenge to the Jewish community. It is easy to dismiss such an alienation of a substantial number of intellectuals as born from a warped psychology, overpermissiveness by parents and educators, and a misdirected revolt of youth. And yet, the communal leadership cannot allow itself the luxury of doing nothing about it. After all some members of that alienated segment may become influential leaders in the next generation and their negative impact on both society at large and the Jewish minority in particular might undermine further the vitality of the community, beset as it is with tremendous difficulties in maintaining its identity. It simply will not do to preach to that youth along the outworn patterns of thought and behavior. On the other hand, we must not abandon the continuity of the Jewish heritage as the basic guideline for our future.

At the same time, against this gloomy background of the present turmoil we must also consider certain positive aspects of Jewish regeneration. Dire predictions about the future of American Jewry have been heard for generations. Among the strongest impressions I received upon arrival in this country in 1926 was the slow drifting away of many Jewish scholars, writers, and artists from any allegiance to their people, its culture and religion, as well as the growing conviction even among loyal Jews that Judaism's very survival in the United States was deeply endangered. Since that time the conditions have, if anything, substantially improved. Interest in Jewish affairs and in the totality of the Jewish heritage has greatly increased among both Jews and non-Jews. If I may refer to another personal experience, before joining the faculty of Columbia University in the academic year of 1929-30, I raised with my colleagues the anxious question as to what kind of students were likely to register for a course in Jewish history. I could still visualize some undergraduates taking such courses as part of their general cultural education but, since my assignment was in graduate instruction, with but a small sprinkling of undergraduates specifically permitted by their deans to take graduate courses, the query appeared quite legitimate as to which graduate students would choose to devote enough time out of their specialized training in some field of social science, the humanities, or pure science to an "unrelated" study of the Jewish past and present. I still vividly remember a colleague of mine answering my query in a light vein: "If at the beginning of the next semester you come into the classroom and find no students, go home and write a book." But being a young man of thirty-four, equally dedicated to teaching and research, I found that humorous reply deeply disquieting.

Fortunately, our apprehensions proved unjustified then and, more importantly, they would have been even less justified today. In fact, during the last two decades we have seen an unparalleled expansion of teaching and research in Jewish studies at American schools of higher learning. A survey conducted several years ago has shown that at that time no less than 92 American universities and colleges were employing full-time teachers, even entire departments, devoted to instruction in various fields of Jewish studies.[7] At the same time the Jewish schools of higher learning, including the two new Jewish universities of Yeshiva and Brandeis, have greatly broadened the horizons of their concern with Jewish learning. The demand has been constantly increasing and but a couple of weeks ago Professor Leon Feldman of Rutgers University informed me that he had such an unexpectedly large registration for Hebrew courses that at the last moment he had to engage an additional instructor. As a matter of fact, despite the general stringency in the academic budgets the field of Jewish studies is one of the few areas where demand for teaching personnel still exceeds the supply.

On the primary and secondary school levels, too, we have witnessed a similar unprecedented growth of the Jewish Day School. Back in the 1930s many public-spirited Jewish citizens objected, on principle, to Jewish Day Schools because, in their opinion, such schools would tend to segregate the Jewish children from the mainstream of American society and because only in the public schools would Jewish pupils meet a cross section of all classes, races, and ethnic groups inhabiting each particular area. This sounded like a very plausible democratic argument. Even advocates of the Day Schools took cognizance of the fact that their total enrollment at that time did not exceed 2 percent of the Jewish school population. They insisted that, while the large majority of Jewish school children would continue to attend general schools, the ability to train a small Jewish élite by giving it a much more intensive training in Judaism than could be offered by supplementary schools would only be a blessing to the community. Nobody envisaged the possibility that Jewish Day School attendance might ever approximate that of the Catholic parochial schools which at that time attracted nearly half of the Catholic school population.

The situation has dramatically changed since. The general decline of public school instruction in the large cities discouraged many parents from sending their children to them. Nor was the argument that these children would find there a typical cross section of the population valid any longer. The turmoil in many schools, frequent lack of physical security, and the major preoccupation of teachers with disciplinary problems rather than instruction, made the Day School appear as a welcome alternative even to parents whose commitment to Judaism was not very strong. As a result we have noted in recent years a rapid increase in the Jewish Day School system and in its total enrollment even without the intervention of the larger communal bodies. However, the Jewish community at large can accomplish a great deal by using some of its charitable funds in granting full or partial scholarships to deserving pupils whose parents cannot afford the high tuition fees necessarily imposed by all private institutions. It may also initiate, and otherwise support new educational experiments, help to finance forward-looking programs and research projects, which would make the network of Jewish schools a contributory factor to Jewish survival, as well as an enriching element in the American educational system at large.

On a different level there has also been a considerable growth of interest in Jewish books and journals. I am not referring only to general American literature written by Jews, some of whom now are the protagonists in certain areas of American letters and sometimes even produce books of Jewish content of the self-hating variety. I have in mind books of constructive Jewish interest. Not so long ago an author of a Jewish book, however meritorious, could find no publisher because of the alleged lack of interest of the American public in Jewish subjects. At that time The Jewish Publication Society of America, some Hebrew and Yiddish publishing firms, and the Jewish schools of higher learning stood out as the beacons of light saving Jewish writers from total despair and stemming the flight of younger Jewish scholars and authors into general fields of culture. Today, Jewish books have often become best sellers in the American market and the most reputable general publishing firms are often competing with one another in attracting Jewish talent. None the less the existing Jewish publishing enterprises still offer much stimulation to Jewish cultural creativity.

Even they, however, must treat their publishing activities basically as self-supporting business enterprises, which makes it impossible for them to issue many technical works or journals which, by their very nature, appeal only to small circles of readers. Yet it is often such technical publications, representing years of basic research by competent scientists and scholars, which are likely to break new ground and open new vistas on the realities of Jewish life and the most promising avenues for the future. Well chosen sponsorship of specific projects of this kind may, indeed, accomplish much more than the better known and talked about publications.

In general, we hear much less about these scholars and writers, or about the college students dedicated to serious studies because they are not considered newsworthy by the media. Nor do we learn much about the considerable revival of religious feelings among the American Jewish youth. Some twenty years ago I was invited by the American Historical Association to deliver a paper on "The Impact of Wars on Religion."[8] In that paper I contended that the Second World War had, for reasons which need not be explained here, generated a more enduring return to religion among non-Jews and Jews alike. Today, one is not surprised when told that in graduate lecture courses in physics or mathematics at some of our major universities one will find a substantial number of students wearing skull caps for religious reasons. These are, as a rule, very bright, alert, and eager students who give their instructors much more satisfaction than members of some other groups whose exploits fill the pages of our newspapers and hours of our radio and television time.

Not surprisingly, the religious revival has taken many forms. While a great number have pursued the traditional lines of the Jewish religion and, if anything, turned to orthodoxy, even of a militant variety, many others have sought some new ways of religious expression. We have even had some reflections of the Protestant "God is dead" movement. Disregarding such aberrations—all none the less signs of a new quest for religious verities and therefore of religious vitality—the interest of the Jewish youth in religion is definitely much more intensive today than it had been in the 1920s and the 1930s.

Of course, there are many individuals who have little feeling for religion, just as there are many others who have no ear for music. Such persons often find religious beliefs totally incomprehensible, while they view traditional practices as little more than superstitious survivals of bygone darker ages. They naturally misunderstand the true meaning of many religious concepts and easily misinterpret, for instance, certain Hebrew phrases. For example, in questioning why Jews sympathizing with Israel do not choose to live there, they contend that, instead of reciting the traditional formula in the Haggadah *Le-shanah ha-ba'ah bi-Yerushalayim* (next year in Jerusalem), the worshipers should move to Jerusalem which is now open to them. Little do they comprehend that this phrase refers not only to a mere physical transfer to Jerusalem but that it also connotes to a pious Jew the ushering in of the messianic age when the Torah will radiate forth from Zion and when a reign of eternal peace will be established. Such peace is envisaged not only among nations or even individual men and families, but also in nature when "the wolf shall dwell with the lamb" (Isa. 11:6). This kind of a miraculous transformation of the universe, attainable only by supernatural intervention, has, of course, but little meaning for the untutored observers of the contemporary political scene.

Even less mystically inclined persons often look for religious answers to the perplexities of existence. They seek rational, if emotionally colored, interpretations of the various factors involved in the historical evolution. I have long been a believer in the Sci-

ence of Judaism which, by using modern scientific methods, tries
not only to reconstruct the whole course of history, Jewish and
human, but also examines the contemporary socioeconomic, political, and cultural trends in the light of reason. For those of
us who believe in the divine guidance of history—and Judaism
has, in my opinion, pioneered along the lines of historical, as well
as ethical, monotheism—the divine will has often revealed itself
through historical processes. More than thirty years ago I
insisted that "the interpretation and reinterpretation of the history
of the people, a kind of *historic Midrash*, is now to serve as a
guidance for the future. A new divine book has opened itself before
the eyes of the faithful: the book of human and Jewish destinies,
guided by some unknown and [perhaps] unknowable ultimate
Power. This book, if properly understood, would seem to answer
the most perplexing questions of the present and the future."[9]
Of course, such interpretation may diverge in individual cases;
even semisectarian controversies may rage over the lessons to be
derived from any such interpretation, as they may in any other
area of ideological conflict. But out of the welter of contradictory
opinions there may ultimately emerge a consensus concerning
actions to be taken by the community and its leaders.

At the same time we must not lose sight of the serious questioning of all rational approaches from the Right as well as from the
Left. In some cases we can observe an outright reversal of modern
trends and a return to what for generations have been considered
obsolete methods and outlooks. With their insistence upon "relevance" some of our radicals overlook the fact that much of what
appears relevant today is but a fad which becomes completely
irrelevant tomorrow, as against some basic human and Jewish
verities which have in them perennial forces. After all, "today"
is but a moment in history with a long past behind us and an
often unforeseeable future ahead of us and we are all heirs to
age-old traditions. Many a chapter in the Bible or Plato written
two millennia ago, may be much more relevant to us than much
of what appears on the front page of a newspaper this morning.
Yet, the very freedom of inquiry as an ideal is under attack in

large areas of the world today. Under the guise of a quest for national freedom or group equality there have been concerted attacks upon individual freedoms, including the freedom of research. Dogmatist, ideologically predetermined findings have often replaced the results of independent rational inquiry. In their extreme forms totalitarian states, whether Stalinist, Maoist, Mussolinian, or Hitlerite, have on principle denied such freedoms and declared only such research worth while as is aimed at fostering their particular ideologies.

Not far removed from this approach is a certain religious totalitarianism which, with even deeper conviction, searches for absolute truths as opposed to the relativist, and hence often transitory, findings of free inquiry. The *Wissenschaft des Judentums*, too, has in recent years been under attack from certain quarters. They feel that the ever-changeable results attained by fallible human minds can only help confuse issues which had appeared long settled by an absolutely omniscient divine revelation. Such fundamentalist approaches cannot easily be disregarded; they constitute a genuine menace to the pursuit of free research which most of us, I assume, deeply cherish.

There have also occurred major changes in the evaluation of both historical and contemporary phenomena. From my early youth I have been controverting—I do not like to use the term combating—the traditional "lachrymose conception of Jewish history." Instead of concentrating on the history of sufferings and scholarship, modern research has tended to concentrate on the broader socioeconomic, political, linguistic, cultural, and religious movements and trends, treating even great individuals more in terms of their contributions to such movements than in the more accidental phases of their biographies. Religious martyrology, long an eminent means of social control, as well as a major ingredient in the interpretation of Jewish history, has been greatly toned down; this in the face of the greatest martyrdom of the Jewish people which has taken place in our own lifetime.

For a time it looked as if the Jewish martyr were to be replaced by the Jewish pioneer, the *Ḥaluts*, as the most symbolic figure of

Jewish history. Indeed, the Jewish people can take great pride in its pioneering contributions to civilization, beginning with the religion and ethics of the Bible and continuing with many vital economic services and communal innovations throughout the ages. Jewish contributions to the ideas of social justice, in particular, have been in the past and still are today a major factor in the development not only of Jewish society but also of those of the majority peoples.

However, this theme has receded somewhat in recent years, as the growing urbanization, industrialization, and prosperity of Israel has helped push the original pioneers into the background. Moreover, the greatest pioneering today is performed not by hardy builders of roads and stalwart conquerors of deserts, but by "soft" scientists often working in beautiful and airy laboratories and surfeited with the worldly goods around them. Since much of this research, moreover, is animated by the profit motive—allegedly a sordid incentive—pioneering of the brain of this type has lost some of its idealistic glamor and does not seem to carry with it the romantic appeal of the old pioneering, be it of the American covered-wagon variety or the old Israeli *Ḥalutsiut*.

Another symbolic figure emerging in recent decades has been that of the Jewish warrior. For generations past, Hanukkah was a relatively minor holiday in the Jewish calendar, principally commemorating the divine "miracle" of saving the people and rededicating the Temple to divine service. It greatly gained in stature in the popular mind only after the Maccabean heroes were raised to positions of highest eminence in the galaxy of the Jewish "great."

For later periods, too, we have ceased glorifying above all martyrs meekly accepting a divinely ordained fate, as was done by generations of Diaspora Jews from ancient times, and have rather become used to expatiating on the virtues of self-relying resistance fighters against their people's enemies. This change was graphically illustrated to me some years ago when the late Jo Davidson, the eminent sculptor, asked me to view a model he had prepared for a then projected monument for Nazism's six million victims which was to be erected on Riverside Drive in New York. In the sculptor's interpretation, the central figure was not the typical Jewish martyr and sufferer, but the resistance fighter, the member of the Warsaw Ghetto who against tremendous odds defied the Nazis' overwhelming power. The same theme is all-pervasive in the Warsaw Jewish Museum, with the additional variant, however, that this fighter is depicted as having been a communist. The emergence of Israel after its War of Liberation and its subsequent victories in 1956 and 1967 in the face of the imminent danger of total extermination have added glamor to the figure of the Jewish warrior as a most appealing symbol in Jewish life and letters.

At this moment, to be sure, war is not popular among our youth in America and most other western lands. For the last couple of years one could even hear of draft resisters being more highly venerated than heroes on the battlefield. On the other hand, some spokesmen of the New Left, so popular in certain circles of Jewish youth, are admirers of Che Guevara and his ideology of, and practical lessons in, guerilla warfare. I would not at all be surprised if before very long someone were to publish a book on the Maccabean Wars in terms of the great successes attained by that people's guerilla army against the overpowering Syrian hosts. It is generally known that ancient Palestine, with its innumerable caves created by rainwater accumulating under the surface of a geologically predominantly limestone soil, had always offered guerilla fighters excellent opportunities for attacks on unwary enemies and sudden disappearance before the latter were able to react with sufficient force. This situation is somewhat similar to conditions in Vietnam or Bolivia. From all these angles the quiet Jewish businessman and scholar, or even craftsman and laborer, who between them formed the large majority of members of the older Jewish communities, have little to offer to such interpreters. Nor was I surprised when, among some of the self-hating Jewish intellectuals, there have arisen some enthusiastic admirers of the Arab guerilla fighters and "terrorists" in Israel, despite the fact that their bravery was demonstrated almost exclusively in hit and run attacks on defenseless civilians in Israel and abroad, rather than on Israel's armed forces.

Leaving such historical distortions aside, it is clear that even the secularists among us may also derive good lessons from historic experience. If such careful analyses of elements of the Jewish heritage and contemporary relations are buttressed by modern methods of social science and humanistic research, intelligent action may replace the often haphazard approaches now prevailing because of the lack of available information. We all know how difficult rational planning has become in our complex and turbulent world. Yet just as no businessman would venture to write long-range contracts without familiarizing himself with the existing trends in his line of endeavor, and just as no lawyer would dare to submit briefs to the courts without investigating the existing legislation and precedents established by courts many years before, so Jewish communal leadership will increasingly require a solid body of materials concerning the realities and trends in Jewish life to be guided in its intelligent planning for the future. The present comprehensive demographic project sponsored by the Council of Jewish Federations, which will for the first time secure reliable data concerning the Jewish population in all of the United States, and the archival investigation as well as the survey of Jewish studies in American universities and other schools of higher learning undertaken by the National Foundation for Jewish Culture are major steps in the right direction. Of course, much more must be done, on an organizational as well as individual basis, before the requisite body of Jewish information will become available.

In the long run, to be sure, the decisive programs for the restructuring of Jewish life in theory and practice will have to be formulated by some outstanding individuals. But their efficacy will largely depend on the vigorous response of the public and the practical implementation by the active leadership. In short, much has already been accomplished, but much more has yet to be accomplished before Judaism, still suffering from its necessary adjustments to the conditions of the Emancipation era, will again become the vibrant entity that it was in the preceding three millennia.

Abbreviations

AJA	*American Jewish Archives*
AJYB	*American Jewish Year Book*
Baron Jub. Vol.	*Essays on Jewish Life and Thought Presented in Honor of Salo Wittmayer Baron.* Ed. by Joseph L. Blau *et. al.* (New York, 1959).
JC	Salo Wittmayer Baron. *The Jewish Community: Its History and Structure to the American Revolution.* 3 vols. (Philadelphia, 1942).
JCR	*The Jewish Communal Register of New York City, 1917–1918,* published by the New York Kehillah (New York, 1918).
JE	*Jewish Encyclopedia*
JP	*The Jewish People—Past and Present,* especially vol. 4 (New York, 1954).
JSS	*Jewish Social Studies*
PAAJR	*Proceedings of the American Academy for Jewish Research*
PAJHS	*Publications of the American Jewish Historical Society*
SRH	Salo Wittmayer Baron. *A Social and Religious History of the Jews.* 1st ed. 3 vols. (New York, 1937); 2d ed. rev., vols. 1–14 (New York and Philadelphia, 1952–69).
YA	*YIVO Annual of Jewish Social Science*
YB	*YIVO Bleter*
YCCAR	*Yearbook of the Central Conference of American Rabbis*

Notes

Part II

ESSAY 3
American Jewish History: Problems and Methods

1 See the authors' own prefatory references to the contemporary background of their researches. "The time has finally come," Zunz declared, "for the Jews of Europe and particularly of Germany, to be granted right and liberty, in lieu of rights and liberties" (p. iii). He believed that this aim might more readily be achieved by the diffusion of accurate information about Jews and Judaism. Apart from indicating in the title, *Der gerichtliche Beweis nach mosaisch-talmudischem Rechte . . . Nebst einer Untersuchung über die Preussische Gesetzgebung hinsichtlich des Zeugnisses der Juden* (Berlin, 1846), Frankel began his Foreword by stating: "The struggle for equality of rights, for recognition of the Jew as a rightful son of the Fatherland has been fought to exhaustion."

2 Benjamin Sheftall's diary, completed by his son, Mordecai, remained in manuscript until published by Isaac Leeser in his *Occident*, I (1843), 381 ff. On the New York controversy of 1737, see Max J. Kohler, "Civil Status of the Jews in Colonial New York," *PAJHS*, VI (1897), 98 ff.; and *infra*, Essay 5. In general, Jews were not particularly active in electoral campaigns. On the contrary, it seems that Jewish voting constituted so little of a problem that Shearith Israel saw no need of incorporating in its statutes a provision similar to that adopted by the Spanish and Portuguese Congregation in London (which it generally emulated) in 1668 and repeated as late as 1817, forbidding Jews to participate in general elections. See Moses Gaster, *History of the Ancient Synagogue of the Spanish and Portuguese Jews* (London,

1901), p. 88. When in 1783 Haym Salomon and three other Jews protested to the Council of Censors of the State of Pennsylvania against the new formula of oath which, by affirming the divine inspiration of both the Old and New Testaments, barred Jews from taking seats in the Assembly, they stated quite honestly, "Your memorialists cannot say that the Jews are particularly fond of being representatives of the people in assembly or civil officers and magistrates in the State." See Charles Edward Russell, *Haym Salomon and the Revolution* (New York, 1930), p. 302. See in general, also, Abraham V. Goodman, *An American Overture* (Philadelphia, 1947).

3 See, for example, his statement to the Hebrew Congregation of Newport, "All possess alike liberty of conscience and immunity of citizenship," which went as far as he possibly could go. In his letter to the Roman Catholics of December, 1789, Washington could merely express the hope that "as mankind become more liberal, they will be more apt to allow, that all those, who conduct themselves as worthy members of the community are equally entitled to the protection of civil government." See the selection from his letters in Edward Frank Humphrey's *George Washington on Religious Liberty and Mutual Understanding* (Washington, 1932), pp. 10, 22.

4 See Max Vorspan and Lloyd P. Gartner, *History of the Jews of Los Angeles* (Philadelphia, 1970; Regional History Series, II), pp. 225 ff. (the contemporary estimates relate to the metropolitan areas).

5 Only "racialist" historiography, inspired by German prototypes, at times evinced interest in the Jewish past, but it confined its attention to some generalities, even clichés, rather than to detailed factual investigation. See, for example, Edward N. Saveth, "Henry Adams' Norman Ancestors," *Contemporary Jewish Record*, VIII (1945), 250-61; and, more generally, his *American Historians and European Immigrants, 1875-1925* (New York, 1948).

6 See Herman Ausubel, *Historians and Their Craft: a Study of the Presidential Addresses of the American Historical Association, 1884-1945* (New York, 1950; Studies in History of Columbia University, 567).

7 See, for example, George Alexander Kohut, *Ezra Stiles and the Jews* (New York, 1902), pp. 64 ff.; Isaac Pinto's introduction to his English translation of *Prayers for Shabbat, Rosh-Hashanah and Kippur* (New York, 1776); Isaac Rivkind's, Hyman B. Grinstein's and Joshua N. Neumann's essays in *PAJHS*, XXXIV

(1937), 51-116; Grinstein's *The Rise of the Jewish Community of New York* (Philadelphia, 1945), pp. 211 f., 225. We must accept, therefore, with serious reservations the well-known assertion by Rev. John Sharpe who, while pleading in 1712-13 for a School Library in New York, declared, "It is possible also to learn Hebrew here, as well as in Europe, there being a synagogue of Jews, and many ingenious men of that nation from Poland, Hungary, Germany, etc." Perhaps the most noteworthy part of this statement is its glossing over the main cultural element in New York Jewry of that time, the Sephardic Jew. Evidently the Marrano antecedents of many American Sephardim must have further curtailed the ratio of Jewish scholars among them. On the "lachrymose conception" of Jewish history and its venerable antecedents, see my "Ghetto and Emancipation," *Menorah Journal*, XIV (1928), 515-26; *SRH*, 1st ed., III, 5 f. n. 6, 42 f. n. 27, 104 f. n. 14; various essays in my *History and Jewish Historians* (Philadelphia, 1964); and *infra*, Essay 6.

8 The need for some such new approaches to American Jewish history has often been discussed in recent years. See esp. the papers presented at the Conference of Historians held under the auspices of the American Jewish Historical Society on September 13-14, 1954 and published under the title, *The Writing of American Jewish History*, ed. by Moshe Davis and Isidore S. Meyer (New York, 1957; reprinted from *PAJHS*, XLVI).

9 The United States National Archives, *Guide to the Records of the National Archives* (Washington, 1948), p. xi; *Thirteenth Annual Report of the Archivist of the United States* (Washington, 1948), pp. 10 ff.; *How to Dispose of Records: a Manual for Federal Officials* (Washington, 1945); The National Record Management Council, *Your Business Records: A Liability or an Asset?* (New York, 1949). See also American Historical Association, Public Archives Commission, *The Preservation of Local Archives: a Guide for Public Officials* (Washington, 1932); A. Y. Judges, *The Preservation of Business Records* (London, 1936); and Oliver W. Holmes, "The Evaluation and Preservation of Business Archives," *American Archivist*, I (1938), 171-85.

10 The suggestions here made in 1949 may be coming closer to realization in 1970 through the Jewish Archives Advisory Council, appointed by the National Foundation for Jewish Culture.

11 See Ernst Posner, "European Experiences in Protecting and Preserving Local Records," *Archives and Libraries*, ed. by A. F. Kuhlman, Chairman of the American Library Association's Com-

mittee on Archives and Libraries (Chicago, 1940), p. 95. Of course, a mere listing of the available Jewish archives in the country would be a great aid to research. Suffice it to mention here the examples set by the Mississippi State Conference of the B'nai B'rith (Rabbi Stanley R. Brav, Chairman) which jointly with the Mississippi Historical Records Survey Project of the WPA compiled an *Inventory of the Church and Synagogue Archives of Mississippi, Jewish Congregations and Organizations* (Jackson, 1940) and by the Michigan Synagogue Conference (Rabbi Max J. Wohlgelernter, Secretary) which together with a similar Michigan Historical Records Survey Project published an *Inventory of the Church and Synagogue Archives of Michigan: Jewish Bodies* (Detroit, 1940), both mimeographed. See also, *Inventory of Church and Synagogue Archives in Tennessee: Jewish Congregations* (Nashville, 1941), mimeographed.

12 A. S. W. Rosenbach, *An American Jewish Bibliography* (PAJHS, XXX [1926]); Cecil Roth, *Magna Bibliotheca Anglo-Judaica* (London, 1937); Ruth F. Lehmann, *Nova Bibliotheca Anglo-Judaica . . . 1937-1960* (London, 1961); F. M. Brody, "The Hebrew Periodical Press in America in 1871-1931: a Bibliographical Survey," *PAJHS*, XXXIII (1934), 127-70; Jacob Shatzky, ed., *Zamelbuch zu der Geshichte fun der yidisher Prese in Amerike* (Studies in History of the Yiddish Press in America; New York, 1934). As far back as 1905 the American Jewish Historical Society had a committee at work to draw up plans for a complete indexing of at least the major American Jewish periodicals. This committee, headed by Max J. Kohler, submitted a brief report, prepared by Joseph Jacobs and published in *PAJHS*, XIII (1905), xix-xxiii, but its resources evidently proved inadequate for this staggering undertaking. A more limited project conducted in the early 1930s by the Graduate School of Jewish Social Work likewise bogged down. More recently the American Jewish Archives undertook to prepare a general index, the results of which still await publication. On these and other bibliographical data, see also Moses Rischin, *An Inventory of American Jewish History* (Cambridge, Mass., 1956). Of considerable help also are such newly published periodical indexes as those of the *AJYB* (Vols. I-L), prepared by Elfrida C. Solis-Cohen (New York, 1967); *Historia Judaica* (Vols. I-XX), compiled by Kurt Schwerin (New York, 1961); *JSS* (Vols. I-XXV), compiled by Max N. Rothschild (New York, 1967); *PAJHS* (Vols. I-XX, New York, 1915). Jacob Robinson and Philip Friedman's *Guide to Jewish History*

under Nazi Impact, with Forewords by Benzion Dinur and myself
(New York, 1960) also includes much American material. See
also Abraham G. Duker's additional references in his review of
that volume in *JSS,* XXV (1963), 154-56.

13 B. (H. D.) Friedberg, *Bet Eḳed Sepharim* (Bibliographical Lexi-
con of the Whole Hebrew and Jewish-German Literature . . .
Printed in the Years 1475-1900; Antwerp, 1928-31); 2d ed. revised, 4 vols. (Tel Aviv, 1951-56); Ephraim Deinard, *Ḳoheleth
Ameriḳa: Catalogue of Hebrew Books, Printed in America from
1735-1925* (St. Louis, 1926); Jacob R. Marcus and Albert T.
Bilgray, *Index to Jewish Festschriften* (Cincinnati, 1937; mimeographed).

14 See my A *Bibliography of Jewish Social Studies; 1938-39* (Jewish
Social Studies, Publications, I; New York, 1941).

15 See the *Annual Reports* of the American Historical Association
listing "Writings on American History" of different years.

16 Since these lines were originally written, the first part of this
postulate has been fulfilled by Malcolm Stern's *Americans of
Jewish Descent: a Compendium of Genealogy* (Cincinnati, 1960;
Publications of AJA, V). A continuation of such a study, on an
increasingly selective basis, for the later periods still remains a
desideratum. Some biographies of individual leaders will be mentioned in the following notes to this and later chapters. Of considerable value also are such autobiographical records as Jacob
Rader Marcus's *Memoirs of American Jews,* 3 vols. (Philadelphia,
1955-56; The Jacob R. Schiff Library); and other documents reproduced by Joseph L. Blau and myself in *The Jews of the United
States, 1790-1840: a Documentary History,* 3 vols. (New York-
Philadelphia, 1963; new impression, 1969). See also *infra,* Essay
10.

17 There is only a partial substitute in the successive volumes of
Who's Who in World Jewry; the first volume appeared in 1955.

18 See Harry S. Linfield, "Jewish Communities in the United States;
Number and Distribution of Jews of the United States in Urban
Places and in Rural Territory," *AJYB,* XLII (1940-41), 215-66.

19 See Uriah Zvi Engelman, "Jewish Statistics in the United States
Census of Religious Bodies (1850-1936)," *JSS,* IX (1947), 127-
47; Ben B. Seligman and Harvey Swados, "Jewish Population
Studies in the United States," *AJYB,* L (1948-49), 651-90;
Maurice R. Davie *et al., Refugees in America* (New York, 1947);
Mark Wischnitzer, *To Dwell in Safety: the Story of Jewish
Migration in the Past 150 Years, 1800-1947* (Philadelphia, 1948);

and the literature listed there. The pros and cons of the discontinuation of the entry "Hebrew" in immigration records are aired in *The Classification of Jewish Immigrants and Its Implications: A Survey of Opinion*, published by the Yiddish Scientific Institute (New York, 1945). See also Ira Rosenswaike's suggestive study, "The Utilization of Census Tract Data in the Study of the American Jewish Population," *JSS*, XXV (1963), 42-56.

20 In this respect we are far behind even our closest neighbor, Canada, as may be gleaned from Louis Rosenberg's fine volume, *Canada's Jews: a Social and Economic Study of the Jews in Canada* (Montreal, 1939), and several of his other monographs. For valid historic reasons, however, the government of the United States, unlike that of its northern neighbor, has refrained from inquiring into the religious faith and ethnic origin of residents during the regular decennial census and, hence, this main source of information available in Canada has been denied to students of the ethnic and religious divisions in the United States.

21 See *supra*, n. 19.

22 This is not the place to elaborate on this intriguing problem. Suffice it to mention the fact, recognized long ago, that the native-born urban population has generally had a far smaller birth rate than either the native-born rural or the foreign-born urban population. For one example, a statistical account of 1900 showed that 1,000 native white women aged 15 to 44 in cities of over 25,000 population had, on the average, only 296 children aged 1 to 5 years; foreign-born in such cities averaged 612 children; native white women in villages, 522; foreign-born women in villages, 841. American Jews always were a predominantly urban group, and the older settlers among them evidently shared the small birth rate of other native urbanites. In a study made in Buffalo in 1938 it was shown that while the median number of children per Jewish family was 2.4 (contrasted with an average of 4.6 for American Jewry in 1890 according to the *Vital Statistics of Jews* then compiled by the Surgeon General), it was only 1.4 in families of two native-born parents. See Uriah Z. Engelman, "The Jewish Population of Buffalo, 1938" in *Jewish Population Studies*, ed. by Sophia M. Robison (New York, 1941), p. 45. We do not know to what extent and how permanently these unfavorable biological trends have been reversed by the general increase in the American, and probably also the Jewish birth rate since 1940.

23 The transition being so extremely fluid, we may, *faute de mieux*,

accept this year as the starting-point of large-scale German-Jewish, or what I. J. Benjamin II calls the "second immigration of Israelites." See his *Reise in den östlichen Staaten der Union und San Francisco* (Hannover, 1862), pp. 44 f.; or in the English trans. by Charles Reznikoff, entitled *Three Years in America,* with an Intro. by Oscar Handlin, 2 vols. (Philadelphia, 1956), I, 74 ff.

24   Friedrich Gerstäcker, *Amerikanische Wald- und Strombilder* (Leipzig, 1849), cited by Max J. Kohler in *PAJHS,* IX (1901), 97. Of interest is also the advertisement of A. R. Thümmel's *Die Natur und das Leben in den Vereinigten Staaten von Nordamerika, in ihrer Licht- und Schattenseite, nach den Schilderungen von Augenzeugen und den Briefen ausgewanderter Landsleute dargestellt* (Erlangen, 1848), which appeared in the Feb. 5, 1848 issue of the *Literaturblatt des Orients,* col. 96. "The West is treated here with particular consideration," we are told, "for Germany is especially interested in that region toward which is directed the largest stream of its emigration. Since the latter includes a particularly large number of Israelites, they will be grateful to us for turning their attention to this work which is of greatest interest to every émigré." See other data assembled by Rudolf Glanz in "The Immigration of German Jews up to 1880," *YA,* III-IV (1947-48), 81-99; and on the paucity of evidence concerning genuine "Jewish 48'ers in America," see Bertram W. Korn's pertinent article in *AJA,* II (1949), 3-20. See also my studies, "The Impact of the Revolution of 1848 on Jewish Emancipation," *JSS,* XI (1949), 195-248, and particularly, pp. 233 f.; and "The Revolution of 1848 and Jewish Scholarship, I-II," *PAAJR,* XVIII (1948-49), 1-66; XX (1951), 1-100.

25   See the brief supporting data cited in *SRH,* 1st ed., II, 264 ff.; III, 154 f.; and *infra,* Essay 10.

26   See Oscar and Mary F. Handlin, "A Century of Jewish Immigration to the United States," *AJYB,* L (1948-49), 1-84. See also Lloyd P. Gartner, *The Jewish Immigrant in England, 1870-1914* (London, 1960; Studies in Society, IV; a revised Columbia University dissertation).

27   See, for example, the selected bibliography appended to Prescott F. Hall's *Immigration and Its Effects upon the United States* (New York, 1906). Hall, Secretary of the Immigration Restriction League, was interested primarily in anti-immigration literature. But he also quotes, for example, the *Twenty-Seventh Annual Report of the United Hebrew Charities* (New York, 1901), which included the following description of the moral degeneration

among recent arrivals: "The vice and crime, the irreligiousness, lack of self-restraint, indifference to social conventions, indulgence in the most degraded and perverted appetites are growing daily more pronounced and more offensive." Such candor was perhaps possible only when antisemites were not indiscriminately attacking all Jews and when antisemitism was not the great and fearsome specter dominating the discussion of all external and internal Jewish problems which it became in the 1930s.

28 See *infra*, Essay 10.

29 Isaac Markens, *Hebrews in America* (New York, 1888); Editors of Fortune, *Jews in America* (New York, 1936). Of great interest also are such biographies of outstanding business leaders as those by Cyrus Adler, *Jacob H. Schiff: His Life and Letters*, 2 vols. (New York, 1929); Naomi Wiener Cohen, *A Dual Heritage: the Public Career of Oscar S. Straus* (Philadelphia, 1969); and the more popular and hence less well documented story by Stephen Birmingham, *"Our Crowd": The Great Jewish Families of New York* (New York, 1967; also paperback).

30 Henry J. Meyer, "The Economic Structure of the Jewish Community in Detroit," *JSS*, II (1940), 127-48 (summary of an unpublished University of Michigan dissertation); idem, in S. M. Robison, *Jewish Population Studies*, pp. 119 ff. See also such brief general summaries as the Jewish Occupational Council's *Patterns of Jewish Occupational Distribution in the United States and Canada* (New York, 1940); and Nathan Goldberg, *Occupational Patterns of American Jews* (New York, 1947; Jewish Life in America, II).

31 See Gabriel Davidson, *Our Jewish Farmers* (New York, 1943); Samuel Joseph, *History of the Baron de Hirsch Fund* (Philadelphia, 1935); the studies of the Jews in professions undertaken by the Conference on Jewish Relations and summarized, in part, in Melvin M. Fagen's "The Status of Jewish Lawyers in New York City," *JSS*, I (1939), 73-104; Jacob A. Goldberg, "Jews in the Medical Profession—a National Survey," *ibid.*, pp. 327-36; and *Two Hundred Thousand Jewish Collegians*, published by the B'nai B'rith Vocational Service Bureau (Washington, 1948). See also the recent publication by Joseph Brandes in association with Martin Douglas, *Immigrants to Freedom: Jewish Communities in Rural New Jersey since 1882* (Philadelphia, 1971; Regional History Series, III).

32 See *infra*, Essay 10; R. Glanz, "Notes on Early Jewish Peddling in America," *JSS*, VII (1945), 119-36; Lee M. Friedman, "Mod-

ern American Radanites" in his *Pilgrims in a New Land* (Philadelphia, 1948), pp. 277-96, 430-38; Maxwell Whiteman, "The Colonial Jewish Peddler," *Studies and Essays in Honor of Abraham A. Neuman*, ed. by Meir Ben-Horin *et al.* (Leiden, 1962), pp. 503-515; I. M. Wise, *Reminiscences*, trans. from the German by David Philipson (Cincinnati, 1901), pp. 37 ff. See also the fascinating materials assembled by Rudolf Glanz in *The Jew in the Old American Folklore* (New York, 1961).

33   Sylvia Kopald and Ben M. Selekman, "The Epic of the Needle Trades," *Menorah Journal*, XVIII (1930), 314. See E. Tcherikower, ed., *Geshikhte fun der yidisher Arbeiter-bavegung in di Fareynikte Shtaten* (History of the Jewish Labor Movement in the United States), 2 vols. (New York, 1943-45); *Gewerkschaften*, issued by the United Hebrew Trades on the occasion of its 50th anniversary as a trade union central body in Greater New York, edited by Harry Lang and Morris C. Feinstone (United Hebrew Trades of the State of New York, New York City, 1938; in Yiddish and English); E. D. Strong, *Amalgamated Clothing Workers of America* (Grinnell, Ia., 1940); Benjamin Stolberg, *Tailor's Progress: The Story of a Famous Union and the Man Who Made It* (New York, 1944; on David Dubinsky); Samuel Gompers, *Seventy Years of Life and Labor: an Autobiography*, 2 vols. (New York, 1925); Louis Reed, *The Labor Philosophy of Samuel Gompers* (New York, 1930); Abraham Cahan, *Bleter fun mein Leben* [Autobiography], 5 vols. (New York, 1926-31); or in the abridged English trans. of Vols. I-II by Leon Stein *et al.*, entitled *The Education of Abraham Cahan* (Philadelphia, 1969); Judah J. Shapiro, *The Friendly Society: a History of the Workmen's Circle* (New York, 1970). This list could be indefinitely extended; a complete bibliography, in itself a very worthwhile project, would fill a sizable volume. See also *infra*, Essay 10.

34   *New York Sun* of May 31, 1891, cited by N. Goldberg in *The Jewish Review*, III (April, 1945), 3; Robert A. Woods (ed.), *Americans in Process* (Boston, 1903), pp. 112 f., 117, cited by Lee M. Friedman in his *Pilgrims*, p. 304. In this connection we must also bear in mind the great Jewish share in the upbuilding of the suburban communities which, in the years after World War II, have substantially altered the face of America. See Albert I. Gordon, *Jews in Suburbia* (Boston, 1959); and Hyman B. Grinstein, "Flight from the Slums," *Baron Jub. Vol.*, pp. 285-97.

However, much further research is needed before we can do
justice to this epochal transformation.
35 Charles Abrams, "The Segregation Threat in Housing," *Commentary*, VII (1949), 125 f.; Jefferson's letter to Noah of May
28, 1818, reprinted in Simon Wolf's *The American Jew as
Patriot, Soldier and Citizen* (Philadelphia, 1895), pp. 59 f.; and
infra, Essays 5 and 10.
36 See the B'nai B'rith's *Two Hundred Thousand Jewish Collegians*;
Lee J. Levinger, *The Jewish Student in America* (Cincinnati,
1937). Material for communal efforts in this direction is, of
course, widely scattered and its interpretation depends on the
understanding of such broader issues as are analyzed, for example,
in Louis Coleridge Kesselman's study of *The Social Politics of
FEPC: a Study in Reform Pressure Movements* (Chapel Hill,
N. C., 1948).
37 See "The Earliest Extant Minute Books of the Spanish and
Portuguese Congregation Shearith Israel in New York 1728-
1786," *PAJHS*, XXI (1913), 12; David de Sola Pool, *The Mill
Street Synagogue* (New York, 1930), pp. 24 ff.; the Newport
correspondence reprinted in Friedman's *Pilgrims*, pp. 121 ff.;
Grinstein, *The Rise of the Jewish Community of New York*, p.
520 (quoting an excerpt from Lyon's *Scrapbook*, Vol. III, p.
150); continued in Moses Rischin, *The Promised City: New
York's Jews 1870-1914* (Cambridge, Mass., 1962). See also David
de Sola Pool, *Portraits Etched in Stone: Early Jewish Settlers,
1682-1831* (New York, 1952); idem and Tamar de Sola Pool,
*An Old Faith in the New World: Portrait of Shearith Israel 1654-
1954* (New York, 1955); Israel Goldstein, *A Century of Judaism
in New York: B'nai Jeshurun, 1825-1925* (New York, 1930). Of
interest for New York's antecedents also is Arnold Wiznitzer, *The
Records of the Earliest Jewish Community in the New World*
(New York, 1954).
38 One must bear in mind, however, that the lack of public, tax-
supported subsidies also affected the other denominations. At the
time when Shearith Israel circulated its letters of solicitation, the
Lutherans were forced to suspend the building of their church
and even the wealthy Dutch Reformed congregation found itself
in serious financial difficulties. See De Sola Pool, *The Mill Street
Synagogue*. It certainly was difficult to induce lenders to extend
loans on the tenuous security of forthcoming voluntary donations
by members who themselves often suffered sudden financial re-
verses. Did not Aaron Lopez—in 1775 still by far the largest

Jewish taxpayer in his community (he paid £32-9-10 or considerably more than all the other fourteen Jewish taxpayers combined, according to S. Broches's data in his *Jews in New England* [New York, 1942], II, 75)—die seven years later leaving behind debts which his executors could not fully meet?

39   This letter, dated July 8, 1851, appeared with comparative speed in the July 25th issue of the *Chronicle.*

40   *PAJHS,* XXI (1913), 2, 66 f., 74; H. B. Grinstein, *The Rise of . . . New York,* pp. 234 ff.; Henry Berkowitz, "Notes on the History of the Earliest German Jewish Congregation in America," *PAJHS,* IX (1901), 125 f.; S., "The Synagogue Question," *Jewish Messenger,* Oct. 11, 1878, p. 5.

41   Nathan Schachner, *The Price of Liberty: a History of the American Jewish Committee* (New York, 1948); Oscar I. Janowsky's *The JWB Survey* (New York, 1948), pp. 45-156. See also *Unity in Dispersion: a History of the World Jewish Congress* (New York, 1948). Through its headquarters in New York after 1939 (though later transferred to Geneva), its leadership by Stephen S. Wise and its main affiliate, the American Jewish Congress, this organization has been to a very large extent an American institution. On the origins of the American Jewish Congress during World War I, see Oscar I. Janowsky, *The Jews and Minority Rights (1898-1919)* (New York, 1933; Columbia University dissertation), pp. 161 ff.; *infra,* n. 43; and Essay 10.

42   Herbert I. Bloom, "The Dutch Archives, with Special Reference to American Jewish History," *PAJHS,* XXXII (1931), 12. See also, more generally, my *JC,* II, 356 ff.

43   Harry L. Lurie, "Communal Welfare," *AJYB,* L (1948-49), 139. See also idem, *A Heritage Affirmed: the Jewish Federation Movement in America* (Philadelphia, 1961); Robert Morris and Michael Freund, eds., *Trends and Issues in Jewish Social Welfare in the United States, 1899-1952* (Philadelphia, 1966); and such local monographs as Barbara Miller Solomon's *Pioneers in Service: the History of the Associated Jewish Philanthropies of Boston* (Boston, 1956); Joseph Hirsh and Beka Doherty, *The First Hundred Years of Mount Sinai Hospital of New York* (New York, 1952).

44   Harry S. Linfield, "The Communal Organization of the Jews of the United States, 1927," *AJYB,* XXXI (1929-30), 99-254; Maurice J. Karpf, *Jewish Community Organization in the United States* (New York, 1938). See also the earlier "exposition of principles and methods of Jewish Social Service in the United

States" presented by Boris D. Bogen in his *Jewish Philanthropy* (New York, 1917); and the useful data assembled in *JCR*, published by the Kehillah of New York in 1918, including a brief (much too brief!) sketch of the history of that significant communal experiment by Harry Sackler. A more comprehensive study by Arthur Aryeh Goren, *The New York Kehillah, 1908-1928* (New York, 1970; Columbia Univ. dissertation) has recently appeared.

45 See *supra*, n. 37.

46 Edwin Wolf 2nd and Maxwell Whiteman, *The History of the Jews of Philadelphia from Colonial Times to the Age of Jackson* (Philadelphia, 1957); Joshua Trachtenberg, *Consider the Years: the Story of the Jewish Community in Easton, 1752-1942* (Easton, 1944); Barnett A. Elzas, *The Jews of South Carolina from the Earliest Times to the Present Day* (Philadelphia, 1905). Charles Reznikoff (in collaboration with Uriah Z. Engelman) prepared a new history of Charleston Jewry in connection with the bicentenary of the Jewish congregation there in 1950. Other communal histories include: H. T. Ezekiel and G. Lichtenstein, *The History of the Jews of Richmond, 1769-1917* (Richmond, Va., 1917); Stuart E. Rosenberg, *The Jewish Community in Rochester, 1843-1925* (New York, 1954; American Jewish Communal Histories, I); S. Joshua Kohn, *The Jewish Community of Utica, New York, 1847-1948* (New York, 1958; American Jewish Communal Histories, II); B. G. Rudolph, *From a Minyan to a Community: a History of the Jews of Syracuse* (Syracuse, 1970); Selig Adler and Thomas E. Connolly, *From Ararat to Suburbia: the History of the Jewish Community of Buffalo* (Philadelphia, 1960); Philip Pollack Bregstone, *Chicago and Its Jews: a Cultural History*. With an Intro. by Julian W. Mack (Chicago, 1933); Simon Rawidowicz, ed., *The Chicago Pinkas* (Chicago, 1952; includes essays in Hebrew); Morris Aaron Gutstein, *A Priceless Heritage: the Epic Growth of Nineteenth Century Chicago Jewry* (New York, 1953); idem, *The Story of the Jews of Newport: Two and a Half Centuries of Judaism, 1658-1908*. With an Intro. by David de Sola Pool (New York, 1936); and Irving I. Katz's profusely illustrated *The Beth El Story, with a History of the Jews in Michigan before 1850* (Detroit, 1955). More recently, the American Jewish History Center of the Jewish Theological Seminary has embarked upon a major project of describing the history of various Jewish communities in North America. The three volumes thus far published consist of Louis J. Swichkow

and Lloyd P. Gartner, *The History of the Jews of Milwaukee* (Philadelphia, 1963; Regional History Series of the American Jewish History Center, I); and the aforementioned studies of the Los Angeles and rural New Jersey communities (*supra,* nn. 4 and 31).

See also other Jewish communal studies (including some unpublished ones) in Harry L. Lurie's *A Heritage Affirmed,* pp. 475 ff.; and other monographs mentioned in this and other chapters, esp. *infra,* Essay 10 n. 88. A noteworthy analysis of changes which have taken place over three generations is offered by Sidney Goldstein and Calvin Goldscheider in their *Jewish Americans: Three Generations in a Jewish Community* (Englewood Cliffs, N. J., 1968; with reference to the community of Providence, R. I. where a careful communal survey had been conducted by Prof. Goldstein and associates in 1962). Much light on approaches and methods in studying Jewish communal histories has also been shed by the papers and debates in the *Proceedings of the Conference on the Writing of Regional History of the South* (New York, 1956; held under the sponsorship of the American Jewish History Center).

In contrast to the relative proliferation of local histories, those of entire states attracted few investigators. See, for instance, Rudolf Glanz, *The Jews of California: from the Discovery of Gold to 1880* (New York, 1960); idem, *The Jews in American Alaska* (New York, 1953); Allan DuPont Breck, *A Centennial History of the Jews of Colorado, 1859-1959* (Denver, Colo., 1960; The West in American History, I); W. Gunther Plaut, *The Jews of Minnesota: the First Seventy-Five Years* (New York, 1959; American Jewish Communal Histories, III).

In this connection one must mention also such artistic aspects of Jewish community life as are analyzed by Rachel Wischnitzer in her *Synagogue Architecture in the United States: History and Interpretation* (Philadelphia, 1955); and Jeanette W. Rosenbaum's biography of *Myer Myers, Goldsmith, 1723-1795* (Philadelphia, 1954), whose products included some objects of Jewish ritual art, such as scroll bells. On Minneapolis, see also Albert I. Gordon, *Jews in Transition* (Minneapolis, 1949), which is principally concerned with the contemporary sociological changes in the community. Of a different kind is Bernard Postal and Lionel Koppman, *A Jewish Tourist's Guide to the U. S.,* with a Foreword by Jacob R. Marcus (Philadelphia, 1954). Pursuing practical as well as historical aims, the authors sought "to identify, locate and give an account of the thousands of sites, landmarks, shrines, memorials, public buildings and other places whose story is part of the chronicle of three centuries of Jewish settlement in America" (p. ix).

47 The Yiddish Writers' Group of the Federal Writers' Project, *Di yidishe landsmanshaften fun New York* (New York, 1938); B. Rabinowitz, "The Young Men's Hebrew Associations (1854-1913)," *PAJHS*, XXXVII (1934), 221-326, with a good bibliography of local publications. On "Jewish Fraternal Orders in America" see, for example, M. Ivensky's brief Hebrew summary under this title in *Sefer Hashanah li-Yehude Amerika* (The American Hebrew Year Book; New York, 1939), pp. 388-404. Some thirty years ago Miss Helen H. Levinthal undertook, under my direction, a more comprehensive investigation of "The Jewish Fraternal Order, an Americanizing and Socializing Force." But the project has not progressed beyond the scope of an unpublished Master's essay. Once again Detroit is more fortunate than most other large communities in possessing in S. D. Weinberg's *Yidishe institutsies un anshtalten in Detroit* (Jewish Social Service in Detroit. A History of the Welfare Institutions, Agencies and Activities; Detroit, 1940), a fairly comprehensive survey with bibliography. See also *supra*, n. 43.

48 See *infra*, Essay 7.

49 Francis Lieber's letter to Privy-Councillor Bluntschli of March 27, 1869, published in his *Life and Letters*, ed. by Thomas Sergeant Perry (Boston, 1882), pp. 390 f.; Karl Lamprecht, *Americana—Reiseeindrücke, Betrachtungen, Geschichtliche Gesammtaussicht* (Freiburg in B., 1906); Allen Lesser, *Enchanting Rebel* (New York, 1947; on Menken). The enormous wealth of material available to the historian of the Jewish role in American theatrical arts is indicated in Henry W. Levy's brief sketch in the *Universal Jewish Encyclopedia*, X, 223-36. On the Yiddish theater, see esp. the useful reference work, edited by D. Zylbercwajg and J. Mestel, *Leksikon fun yidishen teater*, 2 vols. (New York and Warsaw, 1931-34).

50 Louis Gershenfeld, *The Jew in Science* (Philadelphia, 1934); Solomon R. Kagan, *Jewish Contributions to Medicine in America (1656-1934)* (Boston, 1934); Isaac Goldberg, *Major Noah: American Jewish Pioneer* (Philadelphia, 1936); Max B. May, *Isaac Mayer Wise, the Founder of American Judaism* (New York, 1916); Israel Knox, *Rabbi in America: Story of Isaac M. Wise* (Boston, 1957); Norman Bentwich, *Solomon Schechter* (Philadelphia, 1938), supplemented by Adolph S. Oko's *Solo-*

mon Schechter: a Bibliography (Cambridge, 1938); Norman Bentwich, *For Zion's Sake: a Biography of Judah L. Magnes* (New York, 1954; The Jacob R. Schiff Library); Jacob de Haas, *Louis D. Brandeis: a Biographical Sketch. With Special Reference to His Contributions to Jewish and Zionist History* (New York, 1929); Charles Reznikoff, ed., *Louis Marshall, Champion of Liberty: Selected Papers and Addresses*. With an Intro. by Oscar Handlin, 2 vols. (New York, 1957); Morton Rosenstock, *Louis Marshall, Defender of Jewish Rights* (Detroit, 1965); Stephen S. Wise, *Challenging Years* (New York, 1949); Carl Hermann Voss, *Rabbi and Minister: the Friendship of Stephen S. Wise and John Haynes Holmes* (Cleveland, 1964); and *infra*, Essay 10. Of special interest to American Jewish historiography is the life story of the antiquarian and historian Abraham Simon Wolf *Rosenbach: a Biography* by Edwin Wolf 2nd and John F. Fleming (Cleveland, 1960).

Among the host of other autobiographical and biographical studies we need but mention here the following in alphabetical order: Alexandra Lee Levin, *Vision: a Biography of Harry Friedenwald* (Philadelphia, 1964); Eli Ginzberg, *Keeper of the Law: Louis Ginzberg* (Philadelphia, 1966); David Philipson, *My Life as an American Jew: an Autobiography* (Cincinnati, 1941); Lillian D. Wald, *Windows on Henry Street*, with Drawings from Life by James Daugherty, 4th ed. (Boston, 1937); Robert Luther Duffus, *Lillian Wald, Neighbor and Crusader* (New York, 1938); Sam Cauman, *Jonah Bondi Wise*. With an Intro. by David J. Seligson (New York, 1966); and the collection of excerpts from other *Autobiographies of American Jews*, compiled with an Intro. by Harold Ribalow (Philadelphia, 1965). Of interest also is Hannah R. London's collection of *Portraits of Jews by Gilbert Stuart and Other Early American Artists*, with an Appreciation by A. S. W. Rosenbach and an Intro. by Lawrence Park (New York, 1927).

51 See Beryl Harold Levy, *Reform Judaism in America: a Study in Religious Adaptation* (New York, 1933; Columbia Univ. diss.); *Reform Judaism. Essays by Hebrew Union College Alumni* (Cincinnati, 1949). See also *infra*, Essay 10.

52 Moshe Davis, *The Emergence of Conservative Judaism. The Historical School in Nineteenth Century America* (Philadelphia, 1963); idem, *Yahadut Ameriqah behitpathutah; The Shaping of American Judaism* (New York, 1955); Marshall Sklare, *Conserva-*

590 | *Notes to pages 68–70*

tive Judaism: an American Religious Movement (Glencoe, Ill., 1955); and *infra*, Essay 10.

53 See Lee M. Friedman, *"Biblia Americana:* the First American Attempt at Post-Biblical Jewish History," *Journal of Jewish Bibliography (infra*, Essay 5 n. 11); idem, *Jewish Pioneers and Patriots* (Philadelphia, 1942), p. 99; Mather's prayer as entered in his Diary on July 18, 1699, and published in the *Collections of the Massachusetts Historical Society*, 7th ser., VII, 64; Thomas James Holmes, *Cotton Mather: a Bibliography of His Works*, 3 vols. (Cambridge, Mass., 1940), II, 730 ff.; Max Eisen, "Christian Missions to the Jews in North America and Great Britain," *JSS*, X (1948), 31-65. See also Rabbi David Max Eichhorn's as yet unpublished study, *A History of Christian Attempts to Convert the Jews of the United States and Canada*; and *infra*, Essay 10.

54 We may cite here, for one example, A. Roy Eckhardt's Columbia dissertation, *Christianity and the Children of Israel* (New York, 1948), written from the standpoint of neo-Reformation theology, but furnishing much material on other Christian approaches to the problem of antisemitism.

55 See my review of *The Jewish Theological Seminary of America, Semi-Centennial Volume*, ed. by Cyrus Adler (New York, 1939) in *JSS*, III (1941), 101.

56 Gilbert Klaperman, *The Story of Yeshiva University: the First Jewish University in America*. With an Intro. by Arthur J. Goldberg (New York, 1969). See also *infra*, Essay 10.

57 Joshua Bloch, *Of Making Many Books: an Annotated List of Books Issued by The Jewish Publication Society of America, 1890-1952* (Philadelphia, 1953).

58 Needless to say the impact of the Catastrophe and the rise of the State of Israel on American Jewish history has raised a plethora of new problems requiring scholarly elucidation. Much research and thinking has been under way in American scholarly circles in the quarter century since the end of World War II. See, for instance, Jacob Robinson and Philip Friedman's bibliographical compilations, esp. their *Guide to Jewish History under Nazi Impact* (New York, 1960); and "Papers and Proceedings of the Joint Conference on the Impact of Israel on the American Jewish Community," held in December 1956, *JSS*, XXI (1959), 3-88. See also Moshe Davis, *Beit Yisrael be-Amerikah* (House of Israel in America: Texts and Studies; Jerusalem, 1970).

59 Alexander M. Dushkin, *Jewish Education in New York City*

(New York, 1918). I understand that Dr. David Rudavsky has in 1960 completed a dissertation on *Jewish Education in New York City since 1918* which still awaits publication. See also, for example, Julius H. Greenstone, *Statistical Data of the Jewish Religious Schools of Philadelphia for 1906-1907* (Philadelphia, 1907); and a companion pamphlet on Baltimore and Pittsburgh, for 1908-1909, published in 1909.

60 Among recent studies see for example, Nathan Schachner, "Church, State and Education," *AJYB*, XLIX (1947-48), 1-48; Abraham I. Katsh, "The Teaching of Hebrew in American Universities," *The Modern Language Journal*, XXX (1946), 575-86; Arnold J. Band, "Jewish Studies in American Liberal Arts Colleges and Universities," *AJYB*, LXVII (1966), 3-30; Uriah Z. Engelman, *All-Day Schools in the United States, 1948-1949* (New York, 1949).

61 David de Sola Pool, "Judaism and the Synagogue" in *The American Jew: a Composite Portrait*, ed. by Oscar I. Janowsky (New York, 1942), p. 35; Janowsky's newer collection, *The American Jew: a Reappraisal* (Philadelphia, 1964); Isaac Levitats, "Communal Regulation of Bar Mitzvah," *JSS*, XI (1949), 153-62. Numerous fascinating problems in this field have been analyzed by Abraham G. Duker in his "Emerging Culture Patterns in American Jewish Life: the Pyscho-Cultural Approach to the Study of Jewish Life in America," *PAJHS*, XXXIX (1949-50), 351-88. See also Isaac Rivkind, *L'Ot ul'Zikkaron. . . .* (Bar Mitzvah, a Study in Jewish Cultural History with an Annotated Bibliography; New York, 1942), pp. 46, 62 f., 72-73, 134, 135-36.

62 Even here ever new documentary evidence changes the details, if not the general contours of the picture. The extent to which, for example, the documents relating to the crucial years 1664-74 in New York, acquired by the State Library in Albany (see the State Librarian's announcement in the *New York Times* of July 4, 1949) will cause us to reevaluate our information, remains to be seen.

63 Marnin Feinstein, *American Zionism, 1884-1904* (New York, 1965; revised Columbia Univ. dissertation); Avyatar Friesel, *Ha-Tenu'ah ha-ṣiyyonit be-Arṣot ha-Brit* (The Zionist Movement in the United States, 1897-1914; Tel Aviv, 1970); Samuel Halperin, *The Political World of American Zionism* (Detroit, 1961).

64 Julian P. Boyd, "The Function of State and Local Historical Societies with Respect to Manuscripts," in *Archives and Libraries* (1940), pp. 132 ff.

ESSAY 5
*The Emancipation Movement
and American Jewry*

1 Max L. Margolis and Alexander Marx, A *History of the Jewish People* (Philadelphia, 1927), pp. 603 ff.

2 Lucien Wolf, "The First Stage of Anglo-Jewish Emancipation," in his *Essays on Jewish History* (London, 1934), pp. 117-43.

3 Arthur K. Kuhn, "Hugo Grotius and the Emancipation of the Jews in Holland," *PAJHS*, XXXI (1928), 173-80.

4 See my *SRH*, 1st ed., II, 164 ff.; III, 129 ff.; and my "New Approaches to Jewish Emancipation" in UNESCO's *Diogenes*, No. 29 (1960), 56-81 (also appeared in its French and Spanish editions).

5 See esp. the comprehensive study by Abraham Vossen Goodman, *American Overture* (Philadelphia, 1947).

6 See Samuel Oppenheim, "More about Jacob Barsimson, the First Jewish Settler in New York," *PAJHS*, XXIX (1925), 39-52; Arnold Wiznitzer, "The Exodus from Brazil and Arrival in New Amsterdam of the Jewish Pilgrim Fathers, 1654," *ibid.*, XLIV (1954-55), 80-97; *Report of the Suffolk County Court*, II, 624, cited by A. V. Goodman, p. 17. On the family Gideon, see Lee M. Friedman, *Jewish Pioneers and Patriots* (Philadelphia, 1942), pp. 281 ff.

7 *Public Records of the Colony of Connecticut*, II, 644, cited by A. V. Goodman, pp. 28 f. See also Jacob R. Marcus, *Early American Jewry*, 2 vols. (Philadelphia, 1951-53), I, 35 ff.

8 See the text reproduced by A. V. Goodman in facsimile, p. 132, and his comments thereon, pp. 136 ff.

9 See Morris U. Schappes in his *Documentary History of the Jews in the United States* (New York, 1950), pp. 13 ff.

10 See J. H. Hollander, "Some Unpublished Material Relating to Dr. Jacob Lumbrozo, of Maryland," *PAJHS*, I (1893), 25-39; idem, "The Civil Status of the Jews in Maryland, 1634-1776," *ibid.*, II (1894), 33-44.

11 Lee M. Friedman, "*Biblia Americana*: the First American Attempt at Post-Biblical Jewish History," *Journal of Jewish Bibliography*, III (1942); reprinted in his *Pilgrims in a New Land* (Philadelphia, 1948), pp. 15 ff. See also the chapter on "Cotton Mather's Ambition," reprinted from *PAJHS*, XXVI, in Friedman's *Jewish Pioneers*, pp. 95 ff. (citing Mather's *Diary*, ed. by Worthington Chauncy Ford and published in the *Collections* of

the Massachusetts Historical Society, 7th ser. VII, Part 2, p. 219).

12 See L. M. Friedman's essay, "Judah Monis, First Instructor in Hebrew at Harvard University," *PAJHS*, XXII (1914), 1-24; idem, "Some Further Notes on Judah Monis," *ibid.*, XXXVII (1947), 121-34. See also *infra*, Essay 6.

13 In his pamphlet directed against the dominant church, *Hireling Ministry None of Christ's*, published in 1652; it is cited by Oscar S. Straus in his *Roger Williams: the Pioneer of Religious Liberty* (New York, 1894), p. 178.

14 *Records of the Colony of Rhode Island, and Providence Plantations in New England, 1636-1792*, ed. by John Russell Bartlett, 10 vols. (Providence, 1856-65), III, 160: A. V. Goodman, *American Overture*, p. 39; J. R. Marcus, *Early American Jews*, I, 116 ff.

15 In his book, *Magnalia Christi Americana; or the Ecclesiastical History of New England, from Its First Planting in the Year 1620, unto the Year of Our Lord, 1698*, 7 parts (London, 1702); new ed., 2 vols. (Hartford, 1820).

16 John Locke, *Constitution for Carolina* (London, 1670); Barnett A. Elzas, *The Jews of South Carolina from the Earliest Times to the Present Day* (Philadelphia, 1905), pp. 17 ff. Locke's proposal, to be sure, did not become part and parcel of the Carolinian constitution, but his basic idea exerted great influence on liberal thought in the pre-Revolutionary era.

17 Bolzius' diary published together with an *Extract of the Journals of Mr. Commissary Van Reeck* in London, 1734; and that by one of the Jewish pioneers in that settlement, Benjamin Sheftall, which appeared a hundred years later in the Philadelphia *Occident*, I (1844), 381-84, 486-89. See also the more general survey by Leon Huhner in "The Jews of Georgia in Colonial Times," *PAJHS*, X (1902), 65-95 (reprinted in his *Jews in America in Colonial and Revolutionary Times: a Memorial Volume* [New York, 1959], pp. 43 ff., 53 ff.); and Reba Carolyn Strickland, *Religion and the State in Georgia in the Eighteenth Century* (New York, 1939). It may be noted that in 1733 Sheftall estimated the ratio of Jews among the Georgia colonists as high as one-third—probably an overstatement. See his "Diary" in *Occident*, I, 331 f.

18 On the thrice-told tale about the first decade of Jewish life in New York, which need not be elaborated here, see especially the documents collected by Samuel Oppenheim in his important study, "The Early History of the Jews in New York, 1654-64," *PAJHS*, XVIII (1909), 1-91; and the aforementioned mono-

graphs by A. V. Goodman; and J. R. Marcus. On Asser Levy, see also the brief biographical sketch, "Asser Levy van Swellem," in Lee M. Friedman's *Jewish Pioneers*, pp. 133-40.

19 See *Documents Relative to Colonial History of the State of New York*, 15 vols. (Albany, 1853-87), esp. III, 216 ff. See also Max J. Kohler, "Civil Status of Jews in Colonial New York," *PAJHS*, VI (1897), 81-106; idem, "Phases in the History of Religious Liberty in America, with Particular Reference to the Jews, I-II," *ibid.*, XI (1903), 53-73; XIII (1905), 7-36.

20 The history of that cemetery and the succeeding Jewish burial grounds until 1831, as well as the biographies of the persons buried there, are well described in David de Sola Pool's *Portraits Etched in Stone* (New York, 1952). On the early evolution see also Samuel Oppenheim, "The Jewish Burial Ground on New Bowery," *PAJHS*, XXXI (1928), 77-103.

21 See David de Sola Pool, *The Mill Street Synagogue, 1730-1817, of the Congregation Shearith Israel* (New York, 1930); and, more fully, idem and Tamar de Sola Pool, *An Old Faith in the New World: Portrait of Shearith Israel 1654-1954* (New York, 1955).

22 Abigail Franks' letter published by Leo Hershkowitz and Isidore S. Meyer in their ed. of *The Lee Max Friedman Collection of American Jewish Colonial Correspondence, Letters of the Franks Family (1733-1748)* (Waltham, Mass., 1968), p. 66. Other examples of *The American Synagogue and Laxity of Religious Observance, 1750-1850* have been analyzed by Hyman B. Grinstein in his Columbia University Master's essay under this title (typescript).

23 See Leo Hershkowitz, *Wills of Early New York Jews (1704-1799)*. With a Foreword by Isidore S. Meyer (New York, 1967; Studies in American Jewish History, IV); Jacob R. Marcus, *Early American Jewry*, I, 42 ff.; D. de Sola Pool, *Portraits Etched in Stone*, p. 447.

24 *Ibid.*, p. 199. The text of the London resolution is reproduced in Moses Gaster's *History of the Ancient Synagogue of the Spanish and Portuguese Jews* (London, 1901), p. 45. See also Lionel D. Barnett, *Bevis Marks Records* (Oxford, 1940).

25 *Journal of the Votes and Proceedings of the General Assembly of the Colony of New York* (New York, 1764), I, 710 ff.; Albert Edward McKinley, *The Suffrage Franchise in the Thirteen English Colonies in America* (Philadelphia, 1905; Publications of the University of Pennsylvania Series in History, III), pp. 211 ff.;

M. J. Kohler, "Civil Status," *PAJHS*, VI, 96 ff.; A. V. Goodman, *American Overture*, pp. 109 ff. To be sure, Van Horn's attorney persuaded the New York Legislature not to accept Jewish testimony in this matter. This refusal—it was illegal, for Jewish witnesses were admitted to testify in both England and her colonies —made little difference in this case because apparently no one contradicted the fact that Jews had voted in the election. Nor was the tone of the resolution essentially anti-Jewish. Legally it was difficult to prevent the drawing of comparisons between the English Parliament and the colonial Assembly. As is well known, even in the period of the struggle for Jewish Emancipation in England in the mid-nineteenth century, a Jew as such was not disqualified from being elected; he was merely unable to take his seat because he would not take the oath of office with its customary Christian formula.

26   B. A. Elzas, *The Jews of South Carolina*, pp. 25 f.; A. V. Goodman, *American Overture*, pp. 36 ff., 96 ff., 154 ff.; Peter Kalm, *Travels into North America*, included in an English translation in John Pinkerton, *A General Collection of the Best and Most Interesting Voyages and Travels*, XIII (Rome, 1812), p. 455. Goodman rightly observes that the Rhode Island ordinance of 1665 allowed "all persons with adequate property" to participate in elections. None the less the regulations enacted from 1719-28 spelled out that Jews and Catholics were not included in this privilege. See the text of that ordinance cited by Simon W. Rosendale in his "An Act Allowing the Naturalization of Jews in the Colonies," *PAJHS*, I (1893), 94 ff.

27   See the text, reprinted *ibid.*, pp. 93-98.

28   These figures are cited from Jacob H. Hollander, "The Naturalization of Jews in the American Colonies under the Act of 1740," *PAJHS*, VIII (1897), 102-117. In addition to the names mentioned in these lists there were undoubtedly other Jews who became naturalized, although their names were not properly transmitted to London or had otherwise disappeared from the extant records.

29   Ezra Stiles' diary of March 18, 1762, in *Extracts from the Itineraries and Other Miscellanies of Ezra Stiles*, ed. by Franklin Dowditch Dexter (New Haven, 1916), p. 53. See also George Alexander Kohut, *Ezra Stiles and the Jews, Selected Passages from His Literary Diary Concerning Jews and Judaism*, with Critical and Explanatory Notes (New York, 1902).

30   See Aaron Levy's letter to Isaac Da Costa, dated September 17,

1767, reproduced by Jacob R. Marcus in *Early American Jewry*, I, 139 f.

31 See Abraham Halevi's letter (in a mixture of Hebrew and Yiddish), addressed to Lopez on April 25, 1770, and published by Isaac Rivkind in his "Early American Hebrew Documents," in *PAJHS*, XXXIV (1937), 69 ff.; and, more generally, Morris A. Gutstein, *The Story of the Jews of Newport 1658-1908* (New York, 1936).

32 See the aforementioned study by J. H. Hollander, *supra*, n. 28. See also Israel Solomons, "Satirical and Political Prints on the Jews' Naturalization Bill, 1753," *Transactions of the Jewish Historical Society of England*, VI (1912), 205-233.

33 Count Gabriel H. R. Mirabeau, *Sur Moses Mendelssohn, sur la réforme politique des juifs et en particulier sur la révolution tentée en leur faveur en 1753 dans la Grande Bretagne* (London, 1787; new ed., Leipzig, 1853); Sir John Simon's article in the jubilee issue of the *Jewish Chronicle*, November 13, 1891.

34 Caroline Cohen, *Records of the Myers, Hayes, and Mordecai Families from 1707 to 1913* (Washington, n.d.; privately printed); D. de Sola Pool, *Portraits*, pp. 280 ff., 300 ff.; and Jeanette W. Rosenbaum, *Myer Myers, Goldsmith, 1723-1795* (Philadelphia, 1954). The lack of concern about the Jewish status and the general serenity of life in colonial Jewish households is also illustrated by such private letters as those of the Franks family. See *supra*, n. 22. To be sure, the same largely holds true of a similar collection of Yiddish letters written in Prague and Vienna in the midst of the storms of the incipient Thirty Years' War. See Alfred Landau and Bernhard Wachstein, eds., *Jüdische Privatbriefe aus dem Jahre 1619* (Vienna, 1911; *Quellen und Forschungen* of the Historische Kommission der Israelitischen Kultusgemeinde Wien, III). But fear of censorship and repression by the authorities, which undoubtedly imposed great restraints on the Austro-Bohemian correspondents, was absent from the American scene.

35 See B. A. Elzas's *The Jews of South Carolina*, pp. 68-77; the more recent work by Charles Reznikoff, *The Jews of Charleston* (Philadelphia, 1950), pp. 34 f.; and Leon Huhner, "Francis Salvador: a Prominent Patriot of the Revolutionary War" in his *Jews in America*, pp. 16-31. But it ought to be mentioned that Salvador's children were educated in a Christian school.

36 Simon Wolf, *The American Jew as Patriot, Soldier, and Citizen* (Philadelphia, 1895), pp. 44 ff.; Cecil Roth, "Some Jewish Loy-

alists in the War of American Independence," *PAJHS*, XXXVIII (1948-49), 81-107. The problem of the relative participation of the various denominations in the American Revolution is discussed by Edward Frank Humphrey in his *Nationalism and Religion in America 1774-1789* (Boston, 1924). Not surprisingly, many names considered Jewish by Wolf, turned out to be non-Jewish. But apart from the incompleteness of the extant records we must remember that quite a few Jews bearing non-Jewish names are no longer identifiable as such. See also Cecil Roth, "A Jewish Voice for Peace in the War of American Independence. The Life and Writings of Abraham Wagg, 1719-1803," *PAJHS*, XXXI (1928), 33-75.

37 It should be noted that in his "Jews in America in the Colonial Period" (Yiddish), *Gedank un Lebn*, IV (1946), 46 ff., Rudolf Glanz tries to justify the hypothesis current some fifty years ago that the number of Jews in the United States in 1790 amounted to some 3,000. But his proofs are inconclusive and the contrary estimate of but 2,000 Jews or less appears more justified. See Ira Rosenswaike, "An Estimate and Analysis of Jewish Population in the United States in 1790," *PAJHS*, L (1960-61), 23-67.

38 See M. Sheftall's own description reproduced by George White, in his *Historical Collections of Georgia*, 3d ed. (New York, 1855), pp. 340 ff., and again reproduced from there in M. U. Schappes's *Documentary History*, pp. 55 ff.

39 The economic conditions greatly deteriorated at that time. Even some government officials sought to enrich themselves from the existing emergency. See the vast materials accumulated by Robert A. East in his *Business Enterprise in the American Revolutionary Era* (New York, 1938). The masses of the population, suffering from both galloping inflation and heavy taxes, readily listened to such mutual recriminations. From time to time accusations were hurled at Jews, some of whom liked to display their wealth, as did their coreligionists in other lands. The satirical poem cited in the text was quoted in a contemporary letter published in the *Pennsylvania Gazette* of Philadelphia on March 17, 1790, and reproduced in M. U. Schappes's *Documentary History*, pp. 72 ff.

40 Cited from *The South Carolina and American General Gazette* of December 3, 1778 by B. A. Elzas in *The Jews of South Carolina*, pp. 88 f.; this text is followed by a detailed listing of the local Jewish militiamen and their contributions to the war effort.

41 See Lee M. Friedman's biographical sketch of Moses Michael Hays ("Mr. Hays Speaks Out") in his *Jewish Pioneers*, pp. 141 ff.,

144 f., 391 ff.; and J. R. Marcus, *Early American Jewry*, I, 156 ff. It may be noted that when he died in 1805, Hays left behind an estate valued at $82,000; it also included "22 Hebrew books."

42 George Washington's correspondence with the Jewish community has frequently been reprinted. See, for instance, S. W. Wolf's *The American Jew*. The problem is more fully discussed in Edward Frank Humphrey, *George Washington on Religious Liberty and Mutual Understanding* (Washington, 1932); and Joseph L. Blau and Salo W. Baron, eds., *The Jews of the United States 1790-1840: a Documentary History*, 3 vols. (New York, 1963; 2d printing, 1969), I, 8 ff., 240.

43 *Ibid.*, I, 15 ff., 33 ff., etc.

44 See the summary of Hume's speech in *Hansard's Parliamentary Debates*, 3d ser. XVII, 242 ff.; and in the *Mirror of Parliament*, ed. by John Henry Barrow, both cited by Israel Abraham in his "John Quincy Adams and Joseph Hume," *PAJHS*, XXII (1914), 177-78; Samuel Oppenheim, "Mordecai M. Noah: a Letter to Him, Dated 1822, from Eduard Gans and Leopold Zunz, relating to the Emigration of German Jews to America," *ibid.*, XX (1911), 147-49.

45 See Manuel M. Noah, *Travels in England, France, Spain and the Barbary States in the Years 1813-14 and 15* (New York, 1819), App. pp. xxv f.; reproduced by S. W. Wolf in *The American Jew*, pp. 59 f.

ESSAY 6

From Colonial Mansion to Skyscraper:
An Emerging Pattern of Hebraic Studies

1 Herbert W. Schneider, *The Puritan Mind* (New York 1930; Studies in Religion and Culture. American Religion Ser. I), p. 26.

2 Reproduced in the Intro. to *Bradford's History of "Plimoth Plantation,"* ed. from the Original Manuscript for the Commonwealth of Massachusetts (Boston, 1898), p. viii.

3 John Cotton, *An Abstract of the Lawes of New England* [*Moses, His Judicials*], reprinted in Peter Force's *Tracts and Other Papers, Relating Principally to the Origin, Settlement and Progress of the Colonies in North America, from the Discovery of the Country to the Year* 1776 (Washington, 1844; new impression, New York, 1947), Vol. III, Pt. 9; Ezra Stiles, Election Sermon in John Wingate Thornton's *Pulpit of the American Revolution*

(Boston, 1860), pp. 409 f.; Samuel Langdon, Election Sermon of 1775, *ibid.*, p. 239; Roger Williams' letter to John Winthrop of July 12, 1654, in his *Letters*, ed. by John Russell Bartlett (Providence, 1874; Publications of the Narragansett Club, VI), pp. 261 f. = *The Complete Writings of Roger Williams*, 7 vols. (New York, 1963), VI, 261 f. See also Oscar S. Strauss, *Roger Williams, the Pioneer of Religious Liberty* (New York, 1894); Louis Israel Newman, *Jewish Influence on Christian Reform Movements* (New York, 1925; Columbia University Oriental Series, XXIII), pp. 631 ff.; and my *Modern Nationalism and Religion* (New York, 1947; also paperback, New York, 1960), pp. 128 f., 135.

4 Cotton Mather, *Magnalia Christi Americana*, or *The Ecclesiastical History of New-England, from the First Planting, in the Year 1620, unto the Year of Our Lord 1698*, iv. 1, ed. with an Intro. and Occasional Notes by Thomas Robbins and Translations of the Hebrew, Greek, and Latin Quotations by Lucius F. Robinson, 2 vols. (Hartford, 1853-55), II, 12.

5 David de Sola Pool, "Hebrew Learning Among the Puritans of New England prior to 1700," *PAJHS*, XX (1911), 39 f.; and Isidore S. Meyer, "Hebrew at Harvard (1637-1760). A Résumé of the Information in Recent Publications," *ibid.*, XXXV (1939), 145-70.

6 See the detailed monograph by Ewald Mueller, *Das Konzil von Vienne, 1311-12. Seine Quellen und seine Geschichte* (Münster, 1934); *SRH*, XIII, 160 ff., 390 ff.

7 Michael Adler, "The History of the Domus Conversorum," reprinted in his *Jews of Medieval England* (London, 1939), pp. 279 ff., 334 ff.

8 Cotton Mather, *Diary*, ed. by Worthington Chancey Ford, in the *Collections* of the Massachusetts Historical Society, 7th ser. VII, 200, cited together with other pertinent passages and analyzed by Lee M. Friedman in his "Cotton Mather and the Jews," *PAJHS*, XXVI (1918), 201-10, reproduced under the title, "Cotton Mather's Ambition" in his *Jewish Pioneers and Patriots* (Philadelphia, 1943), pp. 95 ff. See esp. p. 99; and *infra*, n. 21.

9 M. Wigglesworth's *Diary*, cited by Leon Huhner in "Jews in Connection with the Colleges of the Thirteen Original States prior to 1800," *PAJHS*, XIX (1910), 108 n. 25.

10 Jeremiah Mason, "Autobiography," reproduced in his privately printed *Memoirs and Correspondence* (Cambridge, Mass., 1873),

p. 11; Ezra Stiles, *The Literary Diary*, ed. with Notes by Franklin Bowdich Dexter, 3 vols. (New York, 1901), III, 306, and the comments thereon by George Alexander Kohut in his *Ezra Stiles and the Jews: Selected Passages from His Literary Diary concerning Jews and Judaism*, with Critical and Explanatory Notes (New York, 1902), esp. pp. 99 ff. See also Edwin Wolf 2nd, "Ezra Stiles Writes a Hebrew Letter," *Studies and Essays in Honor of Abraham A. Neuman*, ed. by Meir Ben-Horin et al. (Leiden, 1962), pp. 516-46.

11 Herbert W. and Carol Schneider, eds., *Samuel Johnson, President of King's College: His Career and Writing*, 4 vols. (New York, 1929), IV, 115 f. The University of Pennsylvania, too, founded by Quakers rather than Puritans, likewise intensively cultivated Hebrew and Semitic studies ever since 1784. See James A. Montgomery, "Oriental Studies in the University," *The General Magazine and Historical Chronicle of the University of Pennsylvania*, XXXVI (1933-34), 205-16.

12 Herbert I. Bloom, *The Economic Activities of the Jews of Amsterdam in the Seventeenth and Eighteenth Centuries* (Williamsport, Pa., 1937), pp. 49 f.

13 "Harvard College Records, II," *Publications* of the Colonial Society of Massachusetts, XVI (1925), 562 ff., 627 ff.; Isidore S. Meyer in *PAJHS*, XXXV (1939), 165 ff.

14 Wilberforce Eames, "On the Use of Hebrew Types in English America Before 1735," *Studies in Jewish Bibliography . . . In Memory of Abraham Solomon Freidus* (New York, 1929), pp. 481 ff.

15 Harry A. Wolfson, "Hebrew Books in Harvard; Exemplifying the Story of Hebrew Literature," *Harvard Alumni Bulletin*, XXXIV (1932), 886-97, reprinted in *Brandeis Avukah Annual of 1932* (New York, 1932), pp. 651-64.

16 B. B. Edwards, "Reasons for the Study of the Hebrew Language," *American Biblical Repository*, XII (1838), 113-32. See also Joseph L. Blau and Salo W. Baron, eds., *The Jews of the United States, 1790-1840: a Documentary History*, 3 vols. (New York, 1963), II, 419 ff.

17 Simon's work appeared seven years later in London in an English translation, entitled *A Critical History of the Old Testament*. See also *SRH*, VI, 305 f., 483 f. nn. 98-99.

18 See, for instance, Adrianne Koch, *The Philosophy of Thomas Jefferson* (New York, 1943); and, more generally, Herbert M. Morais, *Deism in Eighteenth Century America* (New York, 1934;

new impression, New York, 1960; both Columbia University dissertations).

19 See my "Azariah de' Rossi's Attitude to Life," *Jewish Studies in Memory of Israel Abrahams* (New York, 1927), pp. 12-52; and "La méthode historique d'Azaria de' Rossi," *Revue des études juives*, LXXXVI (1928), 151-75; LXXXVII (1929), 43-78; both (the latter in English trans.) reprinted in my *History and Jewish Historians* (Philadelphia, 1964), pp. 174 ff., 205 ff., 406 ff., 422 ff.

20 See E. André Mailhet, *Jacques Basnage, théologien, controversiste, diplomate, et historien. Sa vie et ses écrits* (Geneva, 1880).

21 Cited by Lee M. Friedman in *"Biblia Americana:* the First American Attempt at Post-Biblical Jewish History and Some Successors," in his *Pilgrims in a New Land* (New York, 1948), pp. 20 ff.

22 Hannah Adams, *History of the Jews*, 2 vols. (Boston, 1812), I, iii f. This work, unsubstantial as it may appear to us, made a considerable impression in its day. Within a few years it appeared in a German trans. entitled, *Geschichte der Juden von der Zerstörung Jerusalems an bis auf die gegenwärtigen Zeiten*, 2 vols. (Leipzig, 1819-20).

23 Stiles himself listed six such rabbinic visitors with whom he had extended learned discussions. See the excerpts from his *Diary*, culled and analyzed by G. A. Kohut in his *Ezra Stiles*, pp. 78 ff., 114 ff. App. ii. On Carigal see also Lee M. Friedman's *Rabbi Haim Isaac Carigal: His Newport Sermon and His Yale Portrait* (Boston, 1940).

24 Rev. John Sharpe cited by Judge Charles P. Daly in his *Settlement of the Jews in North America* (New York, 1893), p. 29, n. 30; Ezra Stiles, *Diary*, I, 97, analyzed by Kohut in his *Ezra Stiles*, pp. 64 f.; Joshua N. Neumann, "Some Eighteenth Century American Jewish Letters," *PAJHS*, XXXIV (1937), 75-106; Hyman B. Grinstein, "A Haym Salomon Letter to Rabbi David Tevele Schiff, London, 1784," *ibid.*, pp. 107-16.

25 Isidore S. Meyer, "Sampson Simson's Hebrew Oration, 1800," *PAJHS*, XXXVII (1947), 430-33, with a facsimile of Simson's MS. An English trans. of that address appeared in "The Lyons Collection: Items Relating to the Simson Family, New York," *ibid.*, XXVII (1920), 374 f.

26 Morris U. Schappes, *A Documentary History of the Jews in the United States 1654-1875* (New York, 1950), p. 72 No. 47.

27 In his Preface to *A Critical Grammar of the Hebrew Language*, 2 vols. (New York, 1838-41), Nordheimer thus defined the main

objective of his work: "It has been the author's constant aim, to analytically investigate and synthetically exhibit and explain, those laws which give rise to the phenomena of formation and inflection presented by one of the most natural and regular of languages; and at the same time incidentally to point out its surprisingly intimate connection, both lexicographical and grammatical, not only with the other Shemitish languages, but also with those of the Japhetish or Indo-European stock,—thereby laying open to the view of the future investigator in this interesting field of research the rich mine of discovery which awaits him." See also David de Sola Pool's brief biography of "Isaac Nordheimer," in the *Dictionary of American Biography*, XIII (1943), 547-48.

28 Isaac Rivkind, "Palestinian Wines Offered for Sale in New York in 1848" (Hebrew), *Mizrahi Jubilee Volume* (New York, 1936), pp. 123-27; David Philipson, *Max Lilienthal: American Rabbi, Life and Writings* (New York, 1915), pp. 58 f.; Ḥayyim Solomon Silberman, *Or Yaʻaqob* (Jerusalem, 1859), Preface, here cited in the English translation by Mendel Silber in his *America in Hebrew Literature* (New Orleans, 1928), pp. 92 f.; Joshua Falk b. Mordecai Cohen, *Abne Yehoshuʻa* (Commentary on *Abot*; New York, 1860). See Ephraim Deinard, *Ḳoheleth Amer-ica*: Catalogue of Hebrew Books Printed in America from 1735-1925 (St. Louis, Mo., 1926), p. 5.

29 Such estimates have been made by various students of higher education including Sidney G. Tickton of The Fund for the Advancement of Education of the Ford Foundation.

30 This is not the place to discuss the depth and durability of the present religious revival. Suffice it to say that many great wars left behind not only a trail of destruction and misery, but also an enduring heritage of that confrontation of many individuals with death which made them wrestle with the fundamental riddles of existence. See, for instance, my "Impact of Wars on Religion," *infra*, Essay 11.

31 Abraham I. Katsh, *Hebrew in American Higher Education* (New York, 1941); idem, *Hebrew Language, Literature and Culture in American Institutions of Higher Learning* (New York, 1950; Monographs of the Payne Educational Sociology Foundation, II). See also his brief but more up-to-date summary of "Hebraic Studies in American Higher Education: an Evaluation of Current Trends," *JSS*, XXI (1959), 15-21.

32 See Arnold J. Band, "Jewish Studies in American Liberal Arts Colleges and Universities," *AJYB*, LXVII (1966), 3-30.

ESSAY 7
American Jewish Communal Pioneering

1 George Washington, *Writings*, edited by Jared Sparks, 12 vols. (Boston, 1834-1837), IX, 137.
2 *Society in America*, 3d ed. (New York and London, 1837), II, 349.
3 Cited by Hyman B. Grinstein in *The Rise of the Jewish Community of New York* (Philadelphia, 1945), p. 335.
4 Henry Berkowitz, "Notes on the History of the Earliest German-Jewish Congregation in America," *PAJHS*, IX (1901), 125 f.
5 R. Wischnitzer, *Synagogue Architecture in the United States* (Philadelphia, 1955).
6 See *infra*, Essay 9.
7 This letter is more fully quoted *supra*, Essay 3.
8 *Occident*, VI, 9 (Dec., 1848), 433.
9 See Albert I. Gordon, *Jews in Suburbia* (Boston, 1959).
10 See Bertram W. Korn, "The First American Jewish Theological Seminary: Maimonides College, 1867-1873," reprinted in his *Eventful Years and Experiences. Studies in Nineteenth-Century American Jewish History* (Cincinnati, 1954), pp. 151-213; and *infra*, Essay 10 n. 124.
11 "What Then Is the American, This New Man?" *American Historical Review*, XLVIII (1942-1943), 243.
12 See my *JC* (Philadelphia, 1942), I, 362 f.; III, 93 n. 16.
13 Letter to Bluntschli in *Life and Letters of Francis Lieber*, edited by Thomas Sergeant Perry (Boston, 1882), p. 390, cited *supra*, Essay 3.
14 See the text of the *Rules*, adopted on November 25, 1761, in Morris U. Schappes, *A Documentary History of the Jews in the United States, 1654-1875* (New York, 1950), pp. 35 ff.
15 *Ibid.*, p. 217.
16 Benjamin Rabinowitz, *The Young Men's Hebrew Association (1854-1913)* (New York, 1918; reprinted from *PAJHS*, XXXVII); Oscar I. Janowsky, *The JWB Survey* (New York, 1948).
17 David de Sola Pool, *The Mill Street Synagogue* (New York, 1930), p. 25.
18 David Philipson, "The Cincinnati Community in 1825," *PAJHS*, X (1902), 98 f.
19 *Occident*, XXI, 6 (Sept., 1863), pp. 273 ff.
20 See "Palestinian Messengers in America, 1849-79," *infra*, Essay 9; and, more generally, Abraham Yaari, *Sheluḥe Ereṣ Yisrael*

(Palestinian Messengers: a History of Missions from Palestine to the Dispersion from the Destruction of the Second Temple to the Nineteenth Century; Jerusalem, 1951); and *infra*, Essay 10 n. 80.

21 *Jewish Chronicle*, VI, No. 15 (Jan. 18, 1850), pp. 115 f.

22 S. A. in *The Asmonean*, I, No. 1 (Oct. 26, 1849), p. 2.

23 Leopold Kompert, "Auf nach Amerika," *Oesterreichisches Central-Organ für Glaubensfreiheit* (1848), pp. 77 f., 89; Guido Kisch, "The Revolution of 1848 and the Jewish 'On to America' Movement," *PAJHS*, XXXVIII (1948-49), 185-234. See also *infra*, Essay 13 n. 10.

24 "The Federation Movement in American Jewish Philanthropy," *AJYB*, XVII (1915-1916), 159-198. See also the literature cited *supra*, Essay 3 n. 43.

25 Bertram Wallace Korn, *American Jewry and the Civil War* (Philadelphia, 1951), pp. 21 ff., 46 f.

26 Jefferson's letter to De La Motta of September 1, 1820, reprinted by Max J. Kohler in "Unpublished Correspondence between Thomas Jefferson and Some American Jews," *PAJHS*, XX (1911), 21. See also Joseph L. Blau and Salo W. Baron, eds., *The Jews of the United States, 1790-1840*, II, 572 ff., 660 f.

ESSAY 8
The Image of the Rabbi, Formerly and Today

1 See Simon M. Dubnow, "Records of the Jewish Crown Diet or the Va'ad of the Four Lands" (Russian), *Evreiskaya Starina*, V (1912), 70-84, 178-86, 453-59, esp. p. 184.

2 See my "Freedom and Constraint in the Jewish Community," *Essays and Studies in Memory of Linda R. Miller* (New York, 1938), pp. 9-23.

3 Herbert I. Bloom, "The Dutch Archives, with Special Reference to American Jewish History," *PAJHS*, XXXII (1931), 12 f.

4 Fritz (Yitzhak) Baer, *Die Juden im christlichen Spanien*, 2 vols. (Berlin, 1929-36), II, 349 f. No. 338.

5 Israel Zinberg, "The Conflict between the Elders and the 'Last Rabbi' of Vilna" (Hebrew), *He-'Abar*, II (1918), 45-74; and other studies cited in my *JC*, III, 129 n. 34.

6 Simon M. Dubnow, ed., *Pinqas ha-Medinah* (The Minutes of the Lithuanian Council of Provinces; Berlin, 1925), pp. 225 Nos. 839-40, 231 No. 882; the Prussian *General-Juden-Reglement* of

1797 cited by Josef Perles in his "Geschichte der Juden in Posen," *Monatsschrift für Geschichte und Wissenschaft des Judenthums*, XIV (1865), 87 ff.

7 Nathan Neta Hannover, *Sefer Yeven Meṣulah* (Chronicle of the Massacres of 1648), reproduced in Abraham Kahana's *Sifrut ha-historiah ha-yisre'elit* (Jewish Historical Literature: an Anthology), 2 vols. (Warsaw, 1922-23), II, 314.

8 Solomon ibn Adret cited by Joseph Karo in his *Bet Yosef* (Commentary on Jacob b. Asher's *Arba'ah Ṭurim* [Code of Law]), *Ḥoshen mishpaṭ*, No. 26 end.

ESSAY 9
Palestinian Messengers in America, 1849–79:
a Record of Four Journeys

1 See the literature cited in my *JC*, III, 213 ff.; and Abraham Yaari, *Sheluḥe Ereṣ Yisrael* (Palestine Messengers: a History of Missions from Palestine to the Dispersion from the Destruction of the Second Temple to the Nineteenth Century; Jerusalem, 1951). On the messengers from Palestine in 1774-1778, see Jacob Rader Marcus, *American Jewry—Documents Eighteenth Century* (Cincinnati, 1959), pp. 100 ff. No. 46.

2 Heb. 904. See B. I. Joel's *Catalogue of Hebrew Manuscripts in . . . Jerusalem* (Jerusalem, 1934), No. 517. From this MS are taken all subsequent quotations for which no other reference is given in the following notes.

3 George Alexander Kohut, *Ezra Stiles and the Jews* (New York, 1902), pp. 83 f., 114 f., and esp. 129 f.; Lee M. Friedman, *Rabbi Haim Isaac Carigal* (Boston, 1940); and in general, David de Sola Pool, "Early Relations between Palestine and American Jewry," *The Brandeis Avukah Annual of 1932*, pp. 536-48; and Isaac Rivkind, "Some Remarks about Messengers from Palestine to America," *PAJHS*, XXXIV (1937), 288-94. Very interesting information culled from unpublished communal sources for the period up to 1860 may also be found in Hyman B. Grinstein's *The Rise of the Jewish Community of New York*, pp. 440 ff.

4 For these and other reasons the Jews of New York organized, in 1833, a special society, the *Terumat hakodesh*, to collect annual contributions from its members without the intervention of visitors from the Holy Land, and to forward them through the mediation of a trustworthy European leader.

5 *The Occident*, VII (July 1849), 220. These comments follow a

number of excerpts from Abrahams's memorandum submitted for publication in the journal. Similar attacks on the messenger system had been frequently voiced before, especially by the chief European exponents of Palestine relief, the *Pekidim* and *Amarkalim* of Amsterdam. See, for example, their appeal of 1834 published by Isaac Rivkind in his "Loose Leaves" (Hebrew) in *Yerushalayim* (in Memory of A. M. Luncz; Jerusalem, 1928), pp. 175 ff.; and the editor's general remarks, *ibid.*, pp. 114 f.

6 *Jewish Chronicle*, V (1848-49), 4, 104, 153; *Jewish Intelligencer*, XIV (1848), 344 f. Apart from the United States Yeḥiel Cohen also visited Jamaica, where on Sept. 13, 1849, Rev. Solomon Jacobs, in a stirring sermon at the Portuguese Synagogue of Kingston, urged his coreligionists to extend liberal support to him. The congregation, though not large, proved very receptive. It is noteworthy that the report of this gathering concludes with the comment: "We must, however, remark that we noticed very few of our Christian brethren there, and we must remind them that the Jews of this community have always evinced great liberality in contributing to the erection of Christian places of worship when called upon." *Jewish Chronicle*, VI (1849-50), 128. There is no way of ascertaining on the basis of the now available sources, to what extent the preceding visit of R. Moses Suze of Tiberias in 1848, who had brought with him 32 barrels of Palestinian wine for sale in behalf of the Palestine relief—he attended for that purpose even a "tea meeting" at the First Wesleyan Methodist Church—had affected the work of these messengers. See Isaac Rivkind, *"Meḳorot ḥiṣṣonim"* in *The Jubilee Volume of the Mizrahi* (New York, 1936), pp. 4 f. See also in general my "Contribution to the History of the German Jews in Palestine" (Hebrew) in *Minḥah le-David* (The David Yellin Jubilee Volume; Jerusalem, 1935), pp. 3 ff., 11; and *infra*, n. 74.

7 *Allgemeine Zeitung des Judenthums*, VI (1842), 645 ff.

8 The fact that the pertinent entry (signed by Yeḥiel Brill) was made in 1860, however, many years after Ashkenazi's return, at a time when the Kolel handed the MS to Ashkenazi's successor on his way to America, leaves considerable room for suspicion.

9 See A. L. Frumkin and E. Rivlin, *Toledot ḥakhme Yerushalayim* (Jerusalem, 1928-30), III, 227 ff., Addenda, p. 68 (Burdaki), 223 f., Add. pp. 66 f. (Nathan Neta), 263 f., Add. p. 75 (Neeman), 220 f., Add. p. 66 (Salant), 243 f., Add. p. 70 (David Tebele). See also my "Contributions to the History of the Jewish Settlement in Jerusalem" (Hebrew) in *Sefer Klausner* (The

Joseph Klausner Jubilee Volume; Tel-Aviv, 1937), pp. 302-312.
10 One wonders whether this was not meant to be a conscious dig in the direction of the rival Sephardic community, with its historic background of Marranism.
11 The text of these credentials has been published, probably from our MS, by Pinchas Grajewski in his *Mi-Ginze Yerushalayim*, II (Jerusalem, 1930), 5 ff.
12 See also A. B. M. Serfaty, *The Jews of Gibraltar under British Rule* (Gibraltar, 1934).
13 *Jewish Chronicle*, V (1848-49), 117 f., 124 f., 132, 140, 156; Sir Moses Montefiore's *Diaries* (Chicago, 1890), II, 31 ff. (giving data for 1853 and only indirectly referring to previous activities). Although Aaron Selig's name is nowhere mentioned, there is little doubt that he must have been in contact with Montefiore and the other Jewish leaders of the British capital, as is evidenced also by his and his supporters' frequent subsequent appeals that the bulk of the contributions be forwarded to Palestine through the good offices of Sir Moses. Such appeals evidently presuppose the philanthropist's acceptance of this rather burdensome duty. There is no way of ascertaining, however, to what extent these renewed negotiations gave him and his wife the final stimulus to undertake another of their memorable journeys to the Holy Land in the summer of 1849. Noah's address, on the other hand, was due to the incentive given by Yehiel Cohen's arrival. Delivered in the Shearith Israel Synagogue of New York, it resulted in "a handsome collection" in behalf of Cohen's objective. See A. S. W. Rosenbach, *An American Jewish Bibliography* (New York, 1926), No. 645. Leeser mentioned both the address and the collection, but expostulated that "the articles demanding admittance this month preclude us from noticing the gentleman's production in extenso"; *The Occident*, VI (Jan. 1849), 525. On Noah's well-known proto-Zionist sentiments, see esp. Isaac Goldberg, *Major Noah*, pp. 189 ff., where, however, the present episode is not mentioned.
14 Raphall had many friends and admirers overseas, where he was soon to move, accepting, on Dec. 23, 1849, a call to the congregation B'nai Jeshurun in New York "at a salary which was commented on as being the most munificent salary received by any preacher in the country." See Israel Goldstein, *A Century of Judaism in New York* (New York, 1930), pp. 110 ff. The *Jewish Chronicle* of Feb. 1, 1850 (VI, 130) likewise commented on the great enthusiasm with which Raphall had been greeted in New

York upon his arrival and upon the "liberal allowance of 2000 Dollars and an adequate retiring allowance when incapacitated" which had been granted to him by the Elm Street Synagogue. See also *The Asmonean*, I (1849-50), 11, 21, 31, 76 f., etc.

15 Unlike Joseph, Raphall, and Isaacs, the last two signers add also their Hebrew signatures.

16 fols. 4b-6a; *Occident*, VI (1848-49), 599. For Isaacs's position in the New York community, see the warm appraisal by the correspondent of the London *Jewish Chronicle* of March 25, 1842 (I, 115 f.). As far back as 1846 he was active in behalf of Palestine relief. See also the *Occident*, IV, 360. His life-long interest in Palestine was eloquently eulogized some thirty years later by Sabato Morais in a funeral address published in the *Jewish Messenger* of May 31, 1878 (XLVIII, No. 21, p. 5). For some reason the B'nai Jeshurun seems to have dissociated itself from the general collection, and to have forwarded £5 directly to Jerusalem. The receipt of this sum was acknowledged by the Jerusalem leaders in an elaborate Hebrew letter, dated 18 Tammuz, 5610 (June 28, 1850), published, as a "specimen of Oriental correspondence," with an English version, in the *Asmonean*, III (1850-51), 156. Another contribution of £9 was sent to Montefiore by Philipp Levi and Samuel Cohen of the same congregation and acknowledged by the latter on Oct. 16, 1850; *ibid.*, p. 84.

17 fols. 6b-7a; the *Occident*, VII, 221 f. Leeser signed his testimonial on the "1st day of Rosh Hodesh Tamus 5609" (June 20, 1849) and added his Hebrew signature.

18 fol. 7a. For Rice's resignation see *Occident*, VII, 178; and Hyman B. Grinstein, *The American Synagogue and Laxity of Religious Observance, 1750-1850* (typescript).

19 fol. 9a; *Occident*, VII, 224. The Hebrew designations read curiously: ק"ק בני ישראל סינגאמע, פו"מ לחזר [?] גבאי צדקה, גבאי בית החיים, גבאי בית החותך while Abraham Harris is described as Treasurer.

20 fol. 9b.

21 fol. 10a. For the seal of the Congregation (reading: The Gates of Mercy Institutions קהל שערי חסד ניו ארליאנס 1828), the story of its founding and of its prominent rabbi see Leo Shpall, "The First Synagogue in Louisiana," *The Louisiana Historical Quarterly*, XXI (1938), 518-31; and "Rabbi James Koppel Guttheim," *ibid.*, XXII (1939), 166-80. See also Bertram Wallace Korn, *The Early Jews of New Orleans*, (Waltham, Mass., 1970; American Jewish Communal Histories, IV).

22 fols. 11-12.

23 fol. 13; *Occident*, VII, 477; VIII (1850), 199; IX (1851), 266; *Asmonean*, I (1849-50), 54. Valentine signs also in Hebrew.

Rosenfeld's blessing for the "accredited Messenger from the Holy City" reads as follows: "May the Almighty prosper his laudable and sacred undertaking, and may he reach his home and family, השם יצליח דרכו ויוליכו למחוז חפצו לחיים ולשלום." See also Barnett A. Elzas, *The Jews of South Carolina* (Philadelphia, 1905), pp. 140, 171, 213, 246.

24 fols. 14-15a; *Occident*, VII, 330. Raphall added to his signature: "of Birmingham, England"; while Isaacs, apart from adding his address at 669 Houston St., New York, signed also in Hebrew. Apart from the $25 (according to Noah, $24) pledged annually by the Shearith Israel, we learn from the congregational minutes that a grant of $20 (here unrecorded) was made directly to Aaron Selig for his traveling expenses. See Hyman B. Grinstein's aforementioned study, *The Rise of the Jewish Community of New York*, pp. 440 ff.

25 fol. 15b.

26 fol. 16a.

27 fols. 16b-17a. The Bat [Beth] Israel congregation, apart from opening with a Hebrew blessing, ה' צבאות יגן עליהם ויברכם יעלה על ראשיהם (?), has also three Hebrew signatures. The first two, evidently representing the congregation, have here been identified by the English names of the first two contributors signing on parallel lines.

28 fol. 17b (the quotation is from Psalms 69: 21); *Occident*, VII, 416 f., where there is also a report of the elections in the Congregation Beth El, with Ferdinand Shulz serving as President.

29 Concerning Rabbi Asher Lemel, see Frumkin and Rivlin, *Toledot*, III, 225 f.

30 fol. 19ab. (The quotation is from Deuteronomy 15:7.)

31 fols. 19b-20a.

32 Indeed, as early as March 1, 1850, the *Asmonean* (I, 149) published Montefiore's letter to Isaacs, in which the British philanthropist acknowledged the remittance from Baltimore of an unspecified amount, and expressed gratification over Isaacs's expectation to send soon nearly $500.00 received "for the holy cause" from Cincinnati, Louisville, and St. Louis. "I am delighted to hear," Sir Moses added, "of the prosperity of our co-religionists in America, and of the lively interest they take in the welfare of our brethren dwelling in the Holy Land. I have recently returned from visiting them, and can in truth assure you that they are in the utmost need of assistance from their more fortunate brethren, and that they are in every respect truly deserving all the aid that can be afforded to them."

33 fols. 20b, 22b, 24ab (the intervening fols. were left blank).

34 The *Asmonean,* II (1850), 4, 20, 29, 124, 172, 180, 188; Grinstein, *The Rise of the Jewish Community,* pp. 142, 144.
35 fol. 25ab.
36 fol. 26ab.
37 fol. 27b.
38 *Asmonean,* IX (1855), 68, 117; X (1850), 60, 84, 109 f., 116, 124, 134, 174, 189; *Occident,* XII (1854-55), 263, 325, 421, 423; XIII (1855-56), 26 f.; *Jewish Messenger,* IV (1856), 28. The tapering off of the donations after Aaron Selig's departure may already be noted in the Committee's announcement of March 7, 1851 (*Asmonean,* III, 156) which combined the communication that it had received from the Amsterdam *Terumat hakodesh* a receipt for $151.20 (of which $104.20 had come from New York alone), with an appeal for further contributions to round up the sum of $50 which it intended to forward to Jerusalem. See also *ibid.,* IV (1851), 177, where mention is made of new Palestinian letters of authorization for Isaacs *as the treasurer,* thus confirming the impression that the breach between him and the messenger had no permanent repercussions in the Holy Land.
39 fol. 28b.
40 *American Israelite,* VII (1860), 66; *Occident,* XVIII (1860-61), 172; *Jewish Messenger,* IX (1861), 22; *Jewish Chronicle* of Aug. 3, 1860 and July 26, 1861. For the effect of the Syrian massacres upon the Jews, see my "The Jews and the Syrian Massacres of 1860," *Proceedings of the American Academy for Jewish Research,* IV (1932-33), 3-31; idem, "Great Britain and Syrian Jewry in 1860-61," *JSS,* II (1940), 179-208. The activities of the Palestine missionaries and the role of James Finn therein are well reflected in the latter's *Stirring Times,* 2 vols. (London, 1878) and in his dispatches to London and Constantinople published by Albert M. Hyamson in *The British Consulate in Jerusalem in Relation to the Jews of Palestine,* 2 vols. (London, 1939-41). See also *Jewish Messenger,* IX (1861), 59 (the editor derides the effects of the Palestinian mission which, according to the Bishop of Jerusalem Samuel Gobat's own report, had succeeded in converting only eight persons at the expense of thousands of pounds; "surely there is more wealth than wisdom in Great Britain"), 194 (reprinting from the Scottish *Witness* an article on "The Jew and His Land" pleading for the Jews' restoration to Palestine).
41 The text of this appeal, too, has been published by Pinchas Grajewski in *Mi-Ginze Yerushalayim,* II. For the signatories see *supra,* n. 9; Frumkin and Rivlin, *Toledot,* III, 246 f., Add. p. 71. Brief

biographical data for Abraham Nissan are to be found *ibid.*, p. 252, Add. p. 71. The text of his credentials of 1855 is available in Grajewski's *Zikkaron le-ḥobebim rishonim*, XIII, 11.

42 *Jewish Messenger*, IX (1861) 20, 52, 76 f. (the former's date of Jan. 20 is undoubtedly erroneous). If the messenger obtained Finn's recommendation before his departure from Jerusalem, he must have traveled speedily and without a stop for him to have been able to hand the letter to Isaacs for publication on Jan. 18, 1861. A year and a half later (June 23, 1862), Finn again intervened in behalf of the Jerusalem Perushim who, at that time, were engaged in the construction of an elaborate new synagogue. In a much publicized letter he heartily recommended "to all Israelites who may read this, to assist in completing this much-wanted and handsome synagogue, the firman for which was obtained by means of the English Embassy in Constantinople"; *ibid.*, XII (1862), 78. See also *ibid.*, XI (1862), 167; and *infra*, n. 46. For Finn's general attitude to the messenger system see his *Stirring Times*, I, 121 ff.

43 fol. 30a. Curiously, in the various issues of the *Jewish Chronicle* of 1861, which list Rev. S. M. Isaacs as its "Agent for the U. S. A.," his address is given consistently as 694 Houlston St., New York. About that time (Feb. 28, 1861) the *Occident* (XVIII, 298), referring to Abraham Nissan's mission, stated that "Dr. Raphall testifies to the genuineness of R. Abraham's papers, who asks nothing for himself, but wishes all gifts to be forwarded to Rev. Samuel M. Isaacs, who has long distinguished himself by his exertions for Palestine." In appealing to the public for contributions, the Editor mentioned another recent letter from Jerusalem, transmitted by the messenger, which complained of the injurious effects of the exportation of foodstuffs from Palestine without a corresponding increase in industrial production.

44 In a separate entry, dated April 3, the officials of Congregation Shaary Zedek pledged themselves to "try all what there is in our power to send yearly funds to Jerusalem for the support of the Synagogue פירושים."

45 fols. 30b-32a; *Jewish Messenger*, IX (1861), 53, 61, 76 f., 84, 100, 108; X (1861), 11; XI (1862), 48; XII (1862), 78. See also Isaacs's financial report below.

46 *Occident*, XIX (1861-62), 273, 524 f.; *Jewish Messenger*, X (1861), 12 f. The distribution of the *ḥalukkah* as given in the *Occident* evidently refers only to such funds as were divided among the Sephardim and Ashkenazim without any allowance for

the German-Dutch (HOD) congregation, which case the writer
mentions later on. Both journals expressed their hope that aid
would be extended to this worthy undertaking. The Board itself,
however, does not seem to have pursued the matter any further
and its Third Annual Report of 1862 contains no reference to
Palestine relief. See *ibid.*, XII (1862), 2. The circular of 1861
undoubtedly had served as a basis also for Leeser's earlier editorial
(of Feb. 1861), in which the value of such hospices was strongly
urged upon his readers. Leeser referred especially to early indorsements of a similar project by James Finn (in a letter dated April
28, 1858) and Solomon Munk (May 18, 1859). In a separate
undertaking, reported in the *Daily Telegraph* of London and,
therefrom, in the *American Israelite* of Aug. 10, 1860 (VII, 45),
a messenger had arrived in Vienna for the purpose of establishing
a joint stock company of owners of the Jerusalem synagogue, so
that it could neither be sold nor mortgaged again. On still another
mission, Mordecai b. Solomon arrived in London in Nov. 1861
in order to raise funds for the completion of the great Ashkenazic
synagogue then under construction; see *Jewish Chronicle* of Nov.
29, 1861, p. 5. This plethora of missions must have cooled the
zest of many an informed reader of the Jewish press.

47 fols. 32b-33b; *Jewish Messenger,* IX (1861), 116, 157. The seal
of the larger congregation reads: Congregation Ohabei Shalom
ק"ק אהבי שלום 1845 Boston, Mass.

48 fol. 34a; *Jewish Messenger,* IX, 141.

49 fol. 34b; *Jewish Messenger,* X (1861), 110.

50 fols. 34b-36a; *Jewish Messenger,* X (1861), 5, 45. Hyman Black
and Boasbergck of Beth El, Buffalo expostulated to Isaacs for the
small contribution, due to the small membership, but mentioned
that "they received the Rabbi kindly, and showed him every attention." The reference to the foundation of Scheeris Israel reads as
follows: ויקומו חדש קהל בשם שארית ישראל בבופאלא בחודש האייר בשנת
תרכ"א לפ"ק.

51 See *supra,* Essay 3 n. 39.

52 fol. 36ab; *Jewish Chronicle,* VII (1850-51), 335; *Jewish Messenger,* IX (1861), 172; X (1861), 13 (the Pittsburgh sender is
here designated as A. Fink).

53 fol. 37ab.

54 fols. 38-39. Henry in his own attestation, as well as in certifying
the copies of the communications by Craner and Choynski, signed
in Hebrew. On fol. 38b there is also a Hebrew entry by Jacob
b. Noah, Reader (ש"ץ) in San Francisco, stating that he had

given Abraham Nissan $20.00 for his brothers-in-law Zanwil and Samuel the sons of Ben Zion. For a Hebrew communication by one Abraham Abba see Appendix III. In the *Jewish Messenger* of Jan. 17, 1862 (XI, 16) Isaacs reported these negotiations in San Francisco in some detail, mentioning that, after a preliminary conference of representatives of various congregations on Nov. 20, a general assembly, meeting on Nov. 25, decided to organize the society *Ohabei Zion* throughout the State of California. Isaacs concluded: "Our California brethren thus have a favorable opportunity of manifesting that active benevolence for which they have so fairly earned a reputation." Three weeks later the *Messenger* (XI, 39) reported the return from California of Abraham Nissan who "speaks in the highest terms of his reception and treatment there. . . . They paid his passage to New York, and altogether evinced a commendable kindness towards the messenger from Palestine."

55 *Jewish Messenger,* XI (1862), 48 f., 160.
56 fol. 40b. Montefiore, in acknowledging, on Dec. 3, 5622 (1861), the receipt of £74 10s, informed Isaacs that he had forwarded this amount to the Perushim in Jerusalem, "and requested them to distribute the same according to the instructions given in your letter dated October 22nd." *Jewish Messenger,* XI, 16, 128.
57 *Ibid.* pp. 45, 112 f., 161. In fact, at the annual meeting of the Society several weeks before in Isaacs's home—Isaacs then served as its Treasurer—the President, Simeon Abrahams, "produced documentary evidence from the Orient, of the good the society was effecting by transmitting large amounts [about $700 annually] for the poor, thus avoiding the deduction caused by traveling expenses, and other items allowed to accredited messengers." *Ibid.,* pp. 70, 115.
58 The failure of the Society's early attempts to collect funds other than those accruing from the investments of the Touro bequest explains in part its self-imposed limitation, which made the dispatch of Palestinian messengers a recurrent necessity. The following entry in its manuscript minutes, dated April 8, 5616 (1856), sheds a characteristic light on the reasons for its aloofness: "Whereas two circulars have been published and sent throughout the United States soliciting members and donations, and no response has been made to such appeals, therefore be it Resolved that the Trustees take upon themselves the sole management of the Society and will henceforth receive gratefully all donations with which they may be entrusted." It was rare for anyone to send

a contribution on his own initiative, as when in 1863 B. L. Solomon, President of the congregation Shaaray Tefilla in New York contributed $5.80 "received by that קהלה as מחצית השקל" (entry *ibid.* dated Feb. 19, 5623), which may well have been a residual amount from the collections initiated by Abraham Nissan. See also *infra*, nn. 63 and 89. (The authors are indebted to the late Mr. Leon Huhner, President of the Society, for kindly placing its early minute book at their disposal.) Of course, such inertia in the long run must have discouraged many potential contributors. No better illustration is needed than the will of the Society's own long-term President, Simeon Abrahams, who died in 1867. Although leaving many generous bequests totaling over $200,000 and ranging from $1,000 to $25,000 to Jewish and non-Jewish charities, Abrahams made no provision whatever in favor of the Society. *Jewish Messenger*, XXI, Nos. 16, pp. 5 f., 17, p. 4. See also for 1864 *ibid.*, XV, 118, 150; XVI, 60, 84, 123, etc.

59 *Ibid.*, XXI, No. 22 (June 7, 1867), p. 1; Herbert T. Ezekiel and Gaston Lichtenstein, *The History of the Jews of Richmond, Va.* (Richmond, 1917), p. 248; Israel Goldstein, *A Century*, p. 173. The Board's appeals were, on the whole, very ineffective. The annual convention of May 17, 1868 must have learned with misgivings that the preceding appeal had evoked but one single donation which, together with the newly accumulated interest, raised the total of the balances of the Palestine Fund to $3,459.83. See *Jewish Messenger*, XXIII, No. 20, p. 4, S. M. Isaacs, in an editorial on the recommendations of the Board in 1867 (*ibid.*, XXI, No. 22, p. 4), likewise urged his readers to "assist well-devised movements for promoting the agricultural and industrial interests of the Palestine Jews. Simple almsgiving should be discouraged— idleness should on no account be invited or rewarded." It is noteworthy that Isaacs himself at that time tried to discourage a New York woman, Mrs. Rachel Cohen, from emigrating to Palestine with her son and two daughters, on the grounds that the country "was not very favorable to afford a home of comfort to any one— unless she was amply provided with funds for permanent support." Claiming that two married daughters—one in New York, the other in San Francisco—had undertaken to provide for her needs, she persisted in going "to live and die on the soil watered by the nation's tears." On the other hand, in an editorial published the very next week (No. 23, p. 1), Isaacs professed to be "somewhat amused" by the proposal of the *Alliance Israélite Universelle* to direct the emigration of the persecuted Serbian Jews to America,

where he asserted, they "would be woefully out of place among the Yankees," and once more advocated their settlement in Palestine, where "the material obstacles have been partially overcome by the Jaffa colonists and would be as nothing to a large body of men determined to make the land subservient to their intelligent will."

60 Abraham Moses Luncz, "The Ḥalukkah, its Origin and Development" (Hebrew), *Yerushalayim*, IX (1911), 46 ff.

61 fols. 41b-42. This letter of authorization has also been published by Grajewski in *Mi-Ginze Yerushalayim*, II, 8 ff. For Notkin, see Frumkin-Rivlin, *Toledot*, III, 272 and the sources cited there. The following elders may be identified among the signers of the letter of authorization: 1) Moses Nehemiah Kahanov of Chaslowitz (*ibid.*, p. 270, Add. p. 78); 2) Jacob b. David Theomim, formerly rabbi of ווילאן and then a leader of the Central Committee (*ibid.*, p. 247, Add. p. 71); 3) [Isaac ?] Joseph Katz (*ibid.*, p. 258, Add. p. 72); 4) Jacob b. Judah Berlin, formerly rabbi of Mir (*ibid.*, pp. 246 f.); 5) Abraham b. Zevi Eisenstein, likewise leader of the Central Committee (*ibid.*, p. 262, Add. p. 76); 6) Zeeb ha-Kohen of Pinsk (perhaps identical with Zeeb Wolfensohn; *ibid.*, pp. 264 f., Add. p. 75); 7) Jacob Judah Levi (or Leb), one of the leaders of the "Warsaw" congregation (*ibid.*, p. 267, Add. p. 76); 8) Isaac David Biedermann (*ibid.*, p. 268, Add. p. 74); 9) Isaac [Oplatka] of Prag (Prager, *ibid.*, p. 268, Add. p. 77); 10) Moses Segal [Hamburger] of Nowemiesto (Neustadt), Hungary, leader of the Hungarian congregation (*ibid.*, p. 270, Add. p. 77); 11) Moses Eliezer Dan b. Aryeh Leb Ralbag (*ibid.*, p. 270, Add. p. 77); 12) Eisig Wunder (Luncz, *Yerushalayim*, IX, 46 ff.); 13) Moses Aaron Leb . . ; 14) Eliezer Zevi Kab ve-naki of Grodno (Frumkin-Rivlin, III, Add. p. 80); 15) Shneur Zalman Epstein (perhaps identical with Schneersohn, a leader of the congregation Ḥabad, *ibid.*, p. 273, Add. p. 77); 16) Zevi David of Tiktin (?); 17) Isaac Zevi b. Moses ha-Levi; 18) Meir b. Asher [Kamaikin] Aniksht (*ibid.*, p. 269, Add. p. 77); 19) Eliezer Nathan (?); 20) Azriel Selig Hausdorff. See also my aforementioned essay in *Sefer Klausner* (*supra*, n. 9). There were also the following congregational seals: 1) Siegel der Israeliten Gemeinde Aschkenazim Perushim in Jerusalem ציון במשפט תפדה ושבי' בצדקה אם אשכחך ירושלם

תשכח ימיני והי' עיני ולבי שם כל הימים פה עה"ק ירושלם תוב"ב חותם חותם ק"ק אנשי פולין מחוז וואירשע (2 הכולל דק"ק אשכנזים פרושים הי"ו המתנדבים לשבת בירושלם ת"ו כותל מערבי ונחם ה' את ציון ובחר עוד בירושלם (3 Sinagogensiegel der deutsch-israelischen Gemeinde in

חותם בי"הכנס אהבת ציון של כולל ילידי דייטשלאנד הי"ו בעיר Jerusalem ו,קודש ירושלם תוב"ב (4) Siegel der israelitischen Gemeinde Aschkenasim . . . in Jerusalem חותם הכולל . . . החכמים החסידים וגאלינער פה עה"ק ירושלם תוב"ב [כי מציון תצא] תורה ודבר ה' מירושלים 5) Siegel der oesterreichische Israeliten Gemeinde aus Galizien in Jerusalem חותם הכולל אנשי עסטרייך ילידי גאליציוא המתנדבים לשבת בעה"ק ירושלם ת"ו שאלו שלום ירושלים.The absence of the signature of Meyer b. Isaac Auerbach, Ashkenazic Chief Rabbi, and main organizer of the Central Committee (see the literature listed by Frumkin-Rivlin, III, 269, Add. p. 77) may have been due to purely extraneous reasons.

62 fols. 45a, 49-50a. It may be noted, however, that while fols. 43-44 have remained unfilled, fols. 46-48 are altogether missing. They might easily have contained general indorsements and statements of larger congregational contributions, similar to those appearing at the beginning of Abraham Nissan's record. Cowen's and Danneberg's entries would then appear only as the tail-end of a long series of recommendations, pledges, or records of actual payments. This assumption is reinforced by the corresponding Philadelphia entries and by the reference to such an indorsement in the appeal of the New York Committee.

63 MS Minutes of the society; *Jewish Messenger*, XXI, Nos. 3, p. 3; 6, p. 3. For other legacies of Mrs. Osterman, for whom a new B'nai B'rith Lodge (No. 84) was named in Cincinnati, see *ibid.*, Nos. 6, p. 5; 7, p. 4. The four laymen who joined the three rabbis on the Committee were active in congregational work. Reference has already been made to N. Cowen, President of the Beth Israel u-Bikur Cholim Synagogue, of which Messing was the Minister.

64 fols. 57b-59a. It may be noted that the seal of one of the three Newark congregations reads: ק"ק אוהב שלום תר"ך לפ"ק Congregation Oheb Shalom Organized 5620 Newark, N. J.

65 A copy of this recommendation is entered in the book (fol. 60a) under date of April 4, 1867 together with a similar recommendation in German which, at that time, was widely used in Jewish congregational life. They refer, especially to the "durch Cholera, Heuschrecken und Missernten schwer heimgesuchten Israeliten Jerusalems und Palästina's."

66 fols. 60a, 61b; *Occident*, XXV (1867), 154 f. Leeser appended his Hebrew signature and added his address (1227 Walnut St.) for the benefit of prospective donors. These statements by Leeser were but another illustration of how he, like other Diaspora leaders, reversed his deep-rooted aversion to the messenger system, as

soon as a messenger appeared upon the scene. Hardly a year had passed since he had published another lengthy editorial on "Aid to Palestine" (*Occident*, XXIV, April 1866, pp. 32 f.) in which he deplored the inadequacy of the distribution of the *ḥalukkah* and suggested the dispatch of an impartial commission of average common-sense delegates (rather than men of the exalted standing of a Montefiore) to investigate conditions on the spot. Referring to Aaron Selig's mission, about whom he could not say "whether he obtained any sum worth naming for his exertions," he stated categorically: "With our ideas on the subject, which are neither of recent date nor were hastily formed, we could not help him greatly, and this would be our course were a hundred special envoys to come hither, under the conviction that the expenses of traveling so great a distance, and those attending on any length of residence here, would utterly consume all that might be gathered up from the charitably disposed. It will be, in all such instances, best to give the messenger at once as much as will carry him home again, and to collect all that is possible, and forward it without his intervention." In his sweeping condemnation of the *ḥalukkah* system, Leeser even went so far as to assert: "A change must come; the Jews should quit Palestine or become self-supporting, and every obstacle should yield before this necessity, even if it deprived men, who, by learning and study, are distinguished above their fellows, of a stipend to which they have been deemed entitled that they might by their meditations and prayers protect their distant brothers." See also *ibid.*, pp. 134 f., 366 f. It is a testimony to Notkin's irresistible appeal, as well as to Leeser's deep emotional attachment to Palestine, that all these objections were silenced once the messenger appeared in Philadelphia.

67 fols. 50b-51a. Eisenbadt and Hersohn, registered their acceptance of office in a lengthy Hebrew entry. They also mentioned as their first official act the payment of $10.00 to the messenger.

68 fols. 51b-52b. Jacobs' two entries: נאום שאכנה בן ר' פייוועל יקאבס side by side with the seal of חברה קדישא and אני הח"מ קבלתי עלי בל"נ לעסוק לטובת ירושלים לקבץ נדבות ולקבוע ביקסעס כפי יכולת וד' נאום ותובב"א הקדושה ירושלים יושבי בזכות לי ועזור M. Jacobs, seem to refer to the same person. The date of the Peoria visit seems to be indicated by the position of the Peoria entries between those of the Chicago Hebrah Kadishah and the Relief Association of the same city.

69 fols. 52b-53a.

70 *The American Israelite,* XVI (1869), Nos. 2, p. 5; 6, p. 3; 17, p. 10; *Jewish Messenger,* XXII (1867), No. 5, p. 4. A year later (Oct. 1868), the *Occident* (XXVI, 336) took occasion to commend Moses's effort by reporting a communication which appeared in the *Jewish Chronicle* concerning his and his wife's benefactions during their short stay in Jerusalem: "Besides giving liberal donations for all worthy purposes, they formed a committee to distribute future gifts which they might forward." Indeed, upon his return to Cincinnati, Moses remained for many years the staunchest and most active supporter of Palestine relief in his city.

71 fols. 53b-55a. The latter page in the MS is frayed and the number obliterated. At about the same time, Montefiore received from "the representatives of the different congregations in Jerusalem," an acknowledgment for £60 sent them by "Mr. King and his friends," which he forwarded on Oct. 3, 5628 (1867) to Isaacs for transmission "to that gentleman." See *Jewish Messenger,* XII, No. 17, p. 4. See also Morris Silverman, *Hartford Jews, 1659-1970* (Hartford, 1970).

72 fols. 55-57b. Some of the officers of the Western congregations and societies signed their names also in their Hebrew forms.

73 *Jewish Messenger,* XXIII, No. 12 (March 20, 1868), p. 4. See also Mordechai Eliav, *Ahavat Ṣiyyon ve-anshe HOD* (Love of Zion and Men of HOD: German Jewry and the Settlement of Eretz-Israel in the 19th Century; Tel Aviv, 1970), pp. 252 ff.

74 *Ibid.,* XXII, No. 24 of Dec. 20, 1867, p. 2; XXIII, No. 3 (July 17, 1868), p. 2. Apparently unable to await the results of his appeal, Beauboucher, on Nov. 14, 1867, addressed another letter of solicitation to Isaacs in behalf of Billah Pincus, an American citizen, who after the death of her husband, wished to return to America, where, as she writes in her accompanying petition, "I have a few friends and shall be able to support myself, which I cannot do here." In the meantime the Consul provided her with free lodging for two months. Isaacs published both the petition and the recommendation, and stated that the Lilienthal matter "can await action until he arrives," but he will be happy to forward the relatively inconsiderable amount needed for Mrs. Pincus's transportation. *Ibid.,* XXII, No. 24, p. 2.—We have no information as to whether any funds were sent to Isaacs for that purpose, nor do we know the effects of the appeal of the American group published in New York in July 1868. At least the early reaction must have been quite unsatisfactory, since we learn that Meyer Koppel, together with his brother Simeon Koppel, addressed to

Isaacs another solicitation, on Nov. 2, 1868, in which they begged him for assistance for themselves personally. They claimed that continual sickness, combined with local discrimination against them as American citizens, made it imperative for them to look for outside support. Beauboucher once more, after having "carefully examined the facts," indorsed their request stating that they were "honest, laborious artisans, worthy of the deepest sympathy, and who will be exposed to misery if succor be not promptly accorded to them." Isaacs merely published the communication and indorsement, and expressed his readiness to forward whatever funds might be sent to him. *Ibid.,* XXIII, No. 24 (Dec. 18, 1868), p. 5. It may be noted that Beauboucher, who in December 1867 had been praised by the *Jewish Messenger* as one "who has evinced the utmost kindness to our coreligionists," was two months later sharply attacked in that paper in a communication from Jerusalem, for his part in forcing a Prussian Jew, L. Marcus, to deliver his ward, a young girl, to her converted sister. The Board of Delegates felt impelled to make representations on this score to the State Department. *Ibid.,* No. 9, p. 4.—These appeals of the American congregation in Jerusalem seem to have had little effect for many years to come. Only in 1900 did it succeed in obtaining an agreement from the Central Committee of the Ashkenazic *ḥalukkah,* whereby it was to receive fully one-third of all general funds collected in the United States. A year later, we learn, it received 27,000 frs. for distribution among its 200 members. See A. M. Luncz, "The Revenue of the Ḥalukkah in Jerusalem and the Methods of Its Distribution," *Luaḥ Ereṣ Yisrael,* VII (1901-2), 171; idem, *Yerushalayim,* IX (1911), 45.

75 fols. 59b-61a. Jacobson signed his name also in Hebrew.

76 fols. 45b, 62a-63a. The interesting joint entry of the Richmond Polish and Portuguese congregations reads as follows:

Richmond June 20ᵗʰ 1868

ב״ה, יום ו׳ עש״ק פ׳ קרח שנת תרכ״ח לפ״ק פה רישמאנד
אנחנו ח״מ קבלנו מן אנשי קהל פאלן הנקראים כנסת ישראל ומן אנשי קהל
פורדיגעזען הנקראים בית שלום ס״ה טו״ב מאלערס ושלושים צענט ומסרנו
להמשולח הרב ר׳ נתן נטע נאטקען בעד אחב״י היושבים לפני ד׳ בעיר ירושלים
עיר הקודש תובב״א
נאום הקטן כהר״ר יעקב גונדרסהיימער
ונאום אברהם בן אליעזר שו״ב

J. Gundersheimer
Abrᵐ Lazarus

77 fols. 53b, 62b, 63b-65b.

78   fols. 53b, 66b-69a. Bendel signed his name also in Hebrew.
79   fols. 67ab, 70a-72a. See Barnett A. Elzas, *The Jews of South Carolina*, p. 292; idem, *Jewish Marriage Notices* (New York, 1917), pp. 34 f.
80   fols. 45a, 72b-73a. Apart from the $20.00 and other individual contributions in Hornillsville, .the Congregation Ahavas Achim, represented by Jacob Corn (?), President, and S. Ossowski, "Curatoren," donated two dollars. In Buffalo, too, the Congregation Beth El, with a contribution of $7.37, once more appears side by side with numerous private donors. It is also possible that some of the undated entries of fol. 45, recording contributions from Utica and Springfield, really belong, together with those of Hornillsville, to Notkin's journey in 1869 rather than to 1867, as listed here in the general order of the minute book. See *supra*, p. 207. Nevertheless, the Hornillsville entries are immediately followed by a Hebrew signature of one שעפטעל dated תרל״ז לפ״ק =1867.
81   The following excerpts from a series of articles on "The Jews of Jerusalem" published by A. M. Luncz in the *Jewish Chronicle* of 1879 may give an inkling of the local situation: "The spirit of progress in the direction of European education, the facilities of traveling and the temptation held out by the *Halukah*, are the principal causes of the increasing immigration to Jerusalem of the Ashkenasi Jews. The Jews of Russia are forced by the special political and economic circumstances. The Ashkenasim may be divided into two classes: Talmudical scholars and Tradespeople. There are 215 merchant families; 362 handicrafts (the number of handicrafts exceeds far the real needs of the place) and 215 laborers families. Among the Ashkenasim as well as among Sephardim there is one class of people enjoying better circumstances than their fellows; it is the generation born in the country."
     "The Ashkenasim are divided into 'Peruschim' and 'Chassidim.' The 'Peruschim' are in respect of the administration of the Haluka divided in different communities, and the total number of those is nine. The Chassidim are divided in five communities, The special communities maintain different synagogues; the enmity existing between the Chassidim and Perushim in Russia is here much softened down. The Chassidim even imitate some of the customs of the Perushim,—235 persons must be added to complete the number of the Ashkenasim, who do not belong to any particular community." *Ibid.*, Nos. 525, p. 6; 527, p. 12. To lower the high prices of food, the Holy Land Relief Committee

of Amsterdam, still the most important Palestine relief agency in the world and soon thereafter the recipient of a legacy of several hundred thousand guilders from M. Abrahamson of Amersfoort, Holland, dispatched 40,000 kilos of various kinds of cereals to Jerusalem. Although this transaction was accompanied by the loss of some 40% of the purchasing price (the Committee had paid in Europe, 10,349 francs and realized in Jerusalem only 6,425 francs), it succeeded in forcing down the price of wheat and other grain in the Holy City by five percent. See *ibid.*, Nos. 548, p. 12; 553, p. 13. All these, however, were but ineffectual palliatives and, in 1883, Major Albert E. W. Goldsmith writing to Emma Lazarus spoke of the task of purifying "an Augean stable" there, "and how foul it is no one that has not been there can imagine." *Letters to Emma Lazarus in the Columbia University Library*, ed. Ralph L. Rusk (New York, 1939) pp. 58 f.

82 The North American Relief Society had, in fact, long insisted upon an equitable distribution of its funds. As far back as Feb. 27, 1862 its minute book records that "Mr. Lawrence Myers was instructed to draw up a letter informing Sir Moses [Montefiore] of the wishes of the Society that all monies forwarded by that Corp. should be divided among the poor Jews of Jerusalem, Hebron, Sephat and Tiberias."

83 The Hebrew text of the petition is published in Grajewski's *Mi-Ginze Yerushalayim*, II, 9 f. The following signatories, incompletely deciphered by Grajewski, appear in the MS: 1) Abraham Ashkenazi, see Frumkin-Rivlin, III, 282 f., Add. p. 83; 2) Moses Benveniste, *ibid.*, p. 311, Add. p. 88; 3) Raphael Meir Panisel, *ibid.*, p. 312, Add. p. 89; 4) Ḥayyim Nissim Baruch, *ibid.*, p. 308, Add. p. 88; 5) Abraham Eisenstein, *ibid.*, p. 262, Add. p. 74; 6) Moses Eliezer Dan Behar-Ralbag, *ibid.*, p. 270, Add. p. 77; 7) Benjamin Yehudah Leb הר״פ בן representing the communities of Safed and Tiberias; 8) Isaac Zevi b. Moses ha-Levi (or I. H. Marcus); 9) Nissan Bax (Berk?), *ibid.*, p. 271, Add. p. 78; 10) Eijah Sorasohn Maggid, formerly rabbi of Szczucin, Łomża, and Suwałki; 11) Moses Graf of Bransk (?); 12) Meir Aniksht, *ibid.*, p. 269, Add. p. 77; 13) Jacob [b. Dober] of Minsk, *ibid.*, p. 258, Add. p. 72; 14) Joḥanan Hirsh b. Mordecai Schlank, *ibid.*, pp. 256 f., Add. p. 72; 15) Solomon Salman Lewin, *ibid.*, p. 272, Add. p. 78; 16) Abraham of Nowemiesto (Neustadt); 17) Joseph Katz, *ibid.*, p. 258, Add. p. 72; 18) Eisig Yafeh of Druyan. For the references here to the grave of Simon the Just see *Jewish Messenger*, XXXIX (1876), No. 15, p. 5, reporting the joint acquisition of that grave

by the Ashkenazic and Sephardic communities, with the support of the Austrian vice-consul, Pascal. Thus an obstacle was removed from the pilgrimages on *Lag be-'Omer.*

84 Montefiore was particularly careful to keep alive the interest of the regular donors. Although, for example, the annual contribution of the North American Relief Society had become a routine matter, on Nov. 7, 5639 (1878) the venerable philanthropist, then ninety-four years old, sent the following acknowledgment to its President, Samuel Cohen, and its new Treasurer, Meyer S. Isaacs, who recorded the text in its minute book: "The enclosed official receipt from the representative of the Holy Land relative to your benevolent Remittance of £140 being the Annual Contribution of your Society for the poor in the Holy Land, has just reached me, and it affords me great pleasure in forwarding the same to you as it contains many blessings, which our Brethren in Jerusalem pray may descend upon yourselves and on your families, likewise on all the esteemed members of your Society the lovers of Jews for having so kindly remembered their deserving poor. I cordially join them in wishing you continued health and lasting prosperity." Moreover, he added a postscript in his own hand: "I beg You dear Sirs to accept my sincere thanks for your zealous, Benevolent exertions for the Relief of our own suffering Brethren."

85 *Jewish Messenger,* XXXIX, No. 13 (March 31, 1876), p. 4; *Jewish Times,* VIII (1876), pp. 4 f., 53 f.

86 *Ibid.,* pp. 74, 197 f., 212; *Jewish Messenger,* XXXIX (1876), Nos. 8, p. 6; 10, pp. 2, 5; 14, p. 2; 29, pp. 4 f. See also the *Jewish Times,* VIII (1876), 676, reprinting from the *Jewish Chronicle* an article on "Secular Education in Palestine," attacking the obscurantism of the local Jewish leaders.

87 fols. 77a-79a; *Jewish Messenger,* XXXIX (1876), No. 21, p. 4. Einoch refers in several instances to money which had come from a contributor's צדקה ביתו. Not improbably this refers to the R. Meir Baal Nes boxes, in which the charitable amounts were gradually accumulating. The late Rochester date may have been but a belated entry similar to those recorded for Elmira, *infra,* n. 88.

88 fols. 79b-86a (fol. 83 is missing). Heiman's Yiddish entry reads as follows:

זייא האבען מתחייב גיוועזען צי געבען יעדווידער יאר ווי א פיל עס וועט
מאכין אין די א צדקה פאר ארץ ישראל יעצט האבען זייע גיגעבין 5 טאלער
פון די א קנגריגיישין בני ישראל פ״ק באלטימאר פרעזעדענטט צאזעפ הייטאן

The time of Notkin's second visit to Elmira is further attested by the Hebrew date 5639.

89 Throughout the years the Society continued to send its annual contribution of $700.00 to Palestine, without making any effort to enlarge the scope of its activities. Its minutes reveal infrequent meetings of the Trustees devoted entirely to such routine matters as reelection, or occasional replacement of deceased officers, reinvestment of capital at the expiration of one or another mortgage and the like. In 1878, with the election of the new Treasurer, M. S. Isaacs and the addition of four new Trustees (Hezekiah Kohn, Leonard Louisohn, Israel Joseph, and Sol L. Cohen), there was a new spurt of activity (June 26). Isaacs was even asked to prepare a new draft of the by-laws which, among other provisions, called for annual elections in May. Nevertheless, the conservatism of the leadership quickly reasserted itself and, to cite the minutes of the session of Dec. 8, 1878, "Sam. Cohen Esq. president addressed the meeting stating the History of the Society, its utility and aim. He eloquently urged the members to adhere to the principals (!) which had guided the founders in their judicious and successful course of management of the funds of the Society. The 'principal' must always be kept intact, by safe investments in Bonds and Mtgs. upon 'unquestionable security.' He said that the aim of the society could all the better be carried out by maintaining it, as it had been, heretofore, viz. a 'close corporation' in order that the funds should always be applied for the purposes intended, viz. for the amelioration and relief of the poor Israelites of Palestine." Apparently the only concession made to the new members, perhaps under the stimulus of Montefiore's aforementioned letter (*supra*, n. 84), was the unanimous adoption, on May 18, 1879, of Hezekiah Kohn's motion "that 3 weeks previous to sending the annual remittance to Sir Moses Montefiore, namely in August of each year, a notice of said intention, should appear in a Jewish public Journal, in order to induce further donations."

90 *Jewish Messenger,* XL (1876), No. 19, p. 6; XLI (1877), No. 21, p. 5; XLII (1877), Nos. 3, p. 2; 5, D. 2; XLIII (1878), Nos. 15, p. 5; 18, p. 4; 20, pp. 4 f.; 21, p. 5; XLIV (1878), Nos. 8, p. 4; 9, p. 1; *American Israelite,* XXVI (1876), No. 3, p. 6; XXVII (1876), Nos. 2, p. 2; 9, p. 6; 17, p. 4. Graetz's memoir, written in May 1872 in cooperation with his fellow-delegates, Asher Levy and M. Gottschalk Levy, has been reprinted by Joseph Meisl in his *Heinrich Graetz* (Berlin, 1917), pp. 142 ff.

91 *Jewish Messenger,* XLI (1877), No. 22, p. 4; XLII (1877), Nos. 2, p. 5; 3, p. 2; 5, p. 2; 7, p. 2; 10, p. 4; 20, p. 4; 23, p. 5; XLIII (1878), No. 21, p. 2; *American Israelite,* XXIX (1877), No. 19,

p. 2. No reason is given by Wilson, or earlier by Beauboucher (see *supra*, n. 74) for their addressing Lilienthal in this matter. In fact, we have no evidence for any sympathetic reaction by Lilienthal to either of these appeals or indeed to the general problem of Palestine relief. It was in these years that the Cincinnati rabbi formulated, as sharply as any reformer, his view on the messianic aspects of the Palestine hope. In his address, delivered at Washington, D.C. in May 1871 he stated, "We have given up all ideas of ever returning to Palestine and establishing there an independent nationality. All our affections belong to this country which we love and revere as our home and the home of our children." See David Philipson, *Max Lilienthal* (New York, 1915), p. 125. While in New York De Hass delivered a lecture at the Y.M.H.A. on Nov. 4, 1876, on "The Land of Israel." This was subsequently published in the *Jewish Messenger*, XL (1876), No. 18, pp. 5 f. The Russo-Turkish war, by playing havoc with the lives and property of thousands of Balkan Jews, created still another diversion to the relief activities in behalf of Palestine. A Jewish committee, organized in Paris by the aged Adolphe Crémieux began soliciting contributions throughout the Jewish world, while in 1878 a New York committee, of which young Jacob Schiff served as treasurer, initiated substantial collections in support of this effort, the Board of Delegates contributing 500 francs from its declining treasury. Isaac M. Wise republished Crémieux's appeal in several issues of the *Israelite* and urged his readers to contribute. All of this must have helped to relegate the Palestine relief activities to a secondary position. See *The American Israelite*, XXIX (1877), Nos. 12, p. 8; 15, p. 6; *Jewish Messenger*, XLIII (1878) *passim.*

92 *Jewish Times*, VIII (1876), 586; *Jewish Messenger*, XXXIX (1876), No. 19, p. 6; XL (1876), No. 23, p. 2; XLI (1877), No. 17, p. 4; XLIII (1878), Nos. 20, p. 4; 21, p. 4; XLIV (1878), Nos. 3, p. 2; 4, p. 4; *American Israelite*, XXVII (1876), No. 11, p. 5; XXVIII (1877), No. 3, pp. 2, 4. Numerous other newspaper reports clearly indicate how much the Palestinian community, though still numerically weak, had become a factor in the international game of power politics. It was not sheer idealism, nor even the wish to gain the goodwill of his newly emancipated Jewish subjects, that induced Emperor Francis Joseph to answer a Hebrew application of Michael Kohen and A. Sussman, publishers of *Ariel*, a progressive organ in Jerusalem (translated into German for the Emperor by Adolph Jellinek)

by a grant of 300 fl. (*ibid.*, XXVI, 1876, No. 15, p. 2). Neither was Baron von Munchhausen, the German consul in Jerusalem, devoid of all imperialistic aims, when he endeavored, with the support of German Jewry, "to introduce German culture and German manner of living among the Jews who enjoy his protection" and when he proposed to send young Jews of Jerusalem to Berlin for further education. The local Jews were, of course, not so easily amenable. They objected that most of their young men were married and could not go abroad for study, and expressed their doubt as to whether those who went to Berlin would ever care to return to Palestine. See *Jewish Messenger*, XLI (1877), No. 20, p. 2; XLII (1877), No. 7, p. 2.

93 fol. 86b. The Trustees appearing here for the first time seem soon to have been headed by Jeruham Zevi (Hirsch) Kantrowitz, to whom, as the "chief officer of the Council of all Kolelim in New York," Isaac Elchanan Spektor addressed, in 1888, his well-known reponsum forbidding the use of charity boxes for any purpose except Palestine relief. See Luncz in *Yerushalayim*, IX (1911), 49.

Part III

ESSAY 10
United States 1880–1914

1 The bibliography for the history of United States Jewry in the crucial three and a half decades before the First World War is enormous and no effort will be made in the following notes to list more than some selected items needed for the documentation of statements made in the text. In fact, even more than in earlier periods of American Jewish history the absence of a bibliographical guide is grievously felt here. See my general observations on "American Jewish History: Problems and Methods," above, Essay 3; Bernard D. Weinryb, "American Jewish Historiography: Facts and Problems," *Hebrew Union College Annual*, XXIII, Part 2 (1950-51), 221-44; Moses Rischin, *An Inventory of American Jewish History* (Cambridge, Mass., 1954); and Abraham G. Duker, "An Evaluation of Achievement in American Jewish Local Historical Writing," *PAJHS*, XLIX (1959-60), 215-53 (listing the main publications by states); with the comments thereon by Selig Adler and Hyman Berman, *ibid.*, pp. 254-64. A good listing of the numerous community studies, published and unpublished, is supplied in the bibliography appended

to Harry L. Lurie's *A Heritage Affirmed: the Jewish Federation Movement in America.* Much information is also readily available in the general histories of American Jewry, especially Rufus Learsi, *The Jews of America: a History* (Cleveland, 1954); and Oscar Handlin, *Adventure in Freedom: Three Hundred Years of Jewish Life in America* (New York, 1954); the essays in *JP*, IV; and the series of biographical sketches presented by Harry Simonhoff in his *Saga of American Jewry 1865-1914* (New York, 1959).

2   An analysis of "Jewish Statistics in the U.S. Census of Religious Bodies (1850-1936)" is offered by Uriah Zvi Engelman in *JSS*, IX (1947), 127-74. Other studies of particular relevance are: *Statistics of Jews of the United States* (New York, 1880); I. Markens, *Hebrews in America* (New York, 1888); David Sulzberger, "Growth of the Jewish Population in the United States," *PAJHS*, VI (1896), 141-49 (quoting and summarizing various previous estimates); Harry S. Linfield, "Jewish Population in the United States," *AJYB*, XXX (1927), 101-198; idem, "Statistics of Jews and Jewish Organizations in the United States: an Historic Review of Ten Censuses, 1850-1937," *ibid.*, XL (1937), 61-84; and on a critique of the methods theretofore employed Sophia M. Robison, ed. (with the assistance of Joshua Starr), *Jewish Population Studies.* See also S. Joseph Fauman and Albert J. Mayer, "Estimation of Jewish Population by the Death-Rate Method," *JSS*, XVII (1955), 315-22. On other more recent refinements, see *supra*, Essay 3. But no systematic effort has as yet been made to utilize these more reliable recent computations for an acceptable revision of the data relating to the earlier periods.

3   Harry S. Linfield, "The Jewish Population of the United States," *AJYB*, XLVII (1945-46), 644. It may be noted that the nearest census totals for the continental United States, exclusive of Alaska, were as follows: 1880—50,155,783; 1890—62,947,714; 1900—75,994,575; 1910—91,972,266; 1920—105,710,620. Dr. Linfield's computations were largely backward projections from the results obtained by him in connection with the censuses of religious bodies in 1926 and 1936. These results have, however, proved to be somewhat exaggerated. See Harry L. Lurie, "Some Problems in the Collection and Interpretation of Jewish Population Data," *Jewish Social Service Quarterly*, X (1934), 263-68; Herman Frank, "Jewish Demography in the United States (Problems, Methods and Results)" (Yiddish), *Yorbuch fun Amopteil*

(Annual of the American Branch of the Yiddish Scientific Institute), I (1938), 155-84; Robison, *op. cit.*, pp. 1 f.; and Ben B. Seligman and Harvey Swados, "Jewish Population Studies in the United States," *AJYB*, L (1948-49), 651-90, esp. 651 n. 3. However, until new comprehensive studies of the growth of the Jewish population since 1880 will have replaced Linfield's estimates, the latter give us at least an approximation, if not of the absolute figures, of the prevailing trends.

4 Not that natural growth as such need be discounted. For example, one Morris Rosenbaum, a Posen Jewish peddler turned Mormon in Utah in 1858, had fourteen children by his first wife. At his death in 1893, he left behind 11 living children, 83 grandchildren, and 13 great-grandchildren. By 1924 his descendants numbered no less than 427 persons. See Leon L. Watters, *The Pioneer Jews of Utah* (New York, 1952; Studies in American Jewish History, II), pp. 24 f.

5 These computations were made by Joseph Jacobs in the article "United States, Section 13: Statistics" in *JE*, XII, 370-78. Jacobs had to base his estimates on the none-too-reliable data assembled by the editors of the *Encyclopedia* in connection with the articles relating to the various states. Yet this pioneer in Jewish statistics had a keen eye for the problems involved and, except for the few cases where he allowed his imagination to fill in the existing gaps, his hypotheses must be taken quite seriously. See also his earlier *Studies in Jewish Statistics, Social, Vital and Anthropometric* (London, 1891); and his later data supplied in his capacity of Director of the Bureau of Jewish Statistics of the American Jewish Committee in "Jewish Population of New York: a Statistical Survey," *Jewish Communal Directory* (New York, 1912), pp. 3-14; and in the essay listed in the next note.

6 Hyman B. Grinstein, *The Rise of the Jewish Community of New York 1654-1860* (Philadelphia, 1945), p. 469; Jacobs in *JE*, X, 372 f.; idem, "Jewish Population of the United States: Memoir of the Bureau of Jewish Statistics of the American Jewish Committee," *AJYB*, XVI (1914-17), 339-78 (see *supra*, n. 5); and, more generally, Jacob Lestshinsky, "The Evolution of the Jewish People during the Last Hundred Years" (Yiddish), *YIVO Shriftn far Ekonomik un Statistik*, I (1928), 1-64.

7 See *infra*, nn. 19-20.

8 See B. Felsenthal's letter to Osias H. Schorr of July 24, 1878, published by Adolf Kober in his "Jewish Religious and Cultural Life in America as Reflected in the Felsenthal Collection,"

PAJHS, XLV (1955-56), 124 f.; Ephraim Feldman, "Intermarriage Historically Considered," *YCCAR*, XIX (1909), 271-307; Samuel Schulman, "Mixed Marriages in Their Relation to the Jewish Religion," *ibid.*, pp. 308-335; and, more generally, Julius Drachsler, *Democracy and Assimilation; the Blending of Immigrant Heritages in America* (New York, 1920); idem, *Intermarriage in New York: a Statistical Study of the Amalgamation of European Peoples* (New York, 1921). See also the more recent discussions of that subject at a 1960 Conference on Intermarriage, ed. by Werner J. Cahnman under the title, *Intermarriage and Jewish Life: a Symposium* (New York, 1963); and Charles B. Sherman, *The Jew Within American Society* (Detroit, 1960).

9   John S. Billings, "Vital Statistics of the Jewish Race in the United States" (Washington, D.C., 1890; XI Census Bulletin, No. 19); with the comments thereon by K. Fornberg in his "Jews in the United States Forty Years Ago" (Yiddish), *YB*, IV (1932), 293-311; F. A. Bushee, *Ethnic Factors in the Population of Boston* (New York, 1904); J. Jacobs in *JE*, X, 377 f.

10   See the interesting collection of 135 excerpts by Rudolf Glanz in his "Source Materials on the History of Jewish Immigration to the United States, 1800-1880," *YA*, VI (1951), 73-156; idem, *The German Jew in America: an Annotated Bibliography, including Books, Pamphlets, and Articles of Special Interest*, with an Intro. by Herbert B. Zafren (Cincinnati, 1969); Elias Tcherikower's brief summary of "Jewish Immigrants to the United States," *YA*, VI, 157-76 (trans. from the chapter in his ed. of *Geshikhte fun der yidisher arbeiter-bavegung in di Fareynikte Shtatn*, I); *infra*, Essay 13; and the literature listed in the forthcoming notes.

11   See J. Ezekiel Lipshitz, "The First Russian Jewish Immigration and the American Jews" (Yiddish), *YB*, IV (1932), 312-29; idem, "An Unsuccessful Attempt of Mass Immigration to the United States; a Contribution to the History of East European Jews in U.S.A." (Yiddish), *Yorbuch fun Amopteil*, I (1938), 39-59; and the biographies of Wolf and Felsenthal cited *infra*, nn. 22 and 128. It may be noted that, upon his arrival in New York in 1852, Simon Berman found more than one hundred coreligionists from his native city of Cracow alone. See his Yiddish *Massa'ot Shimeon* (Masuot Simon; Reisebeschreibung im heiligen Lande; Cracow, 1879), analyzed by Menashe Unger in his "S. Berman and His Project of Colonization of Jews in the United States" (Yiddish), *Yorbuch, ibid.*, pp. 91-111. See also

K. Fornberg's observations on "The Russian-Jewish Immigration to the United States" (Yiddish), *ibid.*, II (1939), 7-31.

12 Morris U. Schappes, ed., *A Documentary History of the Jews in the United States 1654-1875*, pp. 538 f.; Mark Wischnitzer, *To Dwell in Safety: the Story of Jewish Migrations since 1800* (Philadelphia, 1948), p. 34; and, more generally, Narcisse Leven, *Cinquante ans d'histoire: l'Alliance israélite universelle*, 2 vols. (Paris 1911-20). See also Zosa Szajkowski, "How the Mass Migration to America Began," *JSS*, IV (1942), 291-310; and, on the earlier period, Rudolf Glanz, "The Immigration of German Jews up to 1880," *YA*, II-III (1947-48), 81-99.

13 These data have been compiled from lists in Walter F. Willcox, ed., *International Migrations*, 2 vols. (New York, 1929-31), I, 377 ff. See also Zosa Szajkowski, comp., *Yidishe masn-basetzung in di Fareynikte Shtatn* (Jewish Mass Settlement in the United States: Documents and Pictures from the Yivo Archives on Eastern European Jewish Immigration in the Past Hundred Years). Catalogue of an Exhibition Presented on the Occasion of the Fortieth Anniversary of Yivo, 1966 (New York, 1966); other estimates of the size of Jewish immigration before 1880, cited by Moshe Davis in his *Beit Yisrael be-Amerikah* (The Jewish People in America: Studies and Texts; Jerusalem, 1970), pp. 31 f. n. 1; and, in general, the discussions by contemporary observers; for instance, Edward A. Steiner, *The Immigrant Tide: Its Ebb and Flow* (New York, 1909).

14 Samuel Joseph, *Jewish Immigration to the United States from 1881 to 1910* (New York, 1914. Studies in History, Economics and Public Law, Columbia University, 145), pp. 162 ff. Tables IX and XIII. This Columbia University dissertation still is the basic study of this subject.

15 *Ibid.*, p. 170, Table XXIII.

16 Leon Horowitz, *Rumaniah va-Ameriqah* (New York, 1874) with the analysis thereof by Lloyd P. Gartner in his "Rumania and America, 1873: Leon Horowitz's Rumanian Tour and Its Background," *PAJHS*, XLV (1955-56), 67-92; S. Joseph, *Jewish Immigration*, p. 160 Table XVII; Joseph Kissman, "The Immigration of Rumanian Jews Up to 1914," *YA*, II-III (1947-48), 160-79 (trans. from the Yiddish chapter in his *Shtudyes tsu der Geshikhte fun Rumenishe Yidn im 19tn un Onheyb 20stn yorhundert*; New York, 1944); Zosa Szajkowski, "Jewish Emigration Policy in the Period of the Rumanian 'Exodus' 1899-1903," *JSS*, XIII (1951), 47-70; and on the situation in Britain, see

Lloyd P. Gartner, *The Jewish Immigrant in England, 1870-1914* (London, 1960).

17   See David de Sola Pool, "The Levantine Jews in the United States," *AJYB*, XV (1913-14), 207-220.

18   See the statistical data compiled by Michael Traub in his *Jüdische Wanderbewegungen vor und nach dem Weltkriege* (Berlin, 1930), pp. 111 Table XII, 113 Table XIII; "Statistics of Jews, Immigration of Jews to the United States," *AJYB*, XXXVIII (1936-37), 572 Table XIX; and my observations on "Some of the Tercentenary's Historic Lessons," *infra*, Essay 13.

19   *Reports* of the United Hebrew Charities of New York City; and *Reports* of the Commissioner-General of Immigration for the respective years summarized by S. Joseph in his *Jewish Immigration*, p. 176 Tables XXXIII-XXXIV; and by M. Traub in his *Jüdische Wanderbewegungen*, p. 117 Table XVIII.

20   *Reports* of the Commissioner-General of Immigration for the respective years; *Statistical Review of Immigration*, pp. 44 ff., summarized by S. Joseph in his *Jewish Immigration*, pp. 177 ff. Tables XXXV, XXXIX-XLI; and M. Traub in his *Jüdische Wanderbewegungen*, pp. 118 f. Tables XIX-XX.

21   James Madison's reply to De la Motta of August 1820 excerpted from his *Works*, III, 178 f. by Max J. Kohler in his "Notes," *PAJHS*, IV (1896), 219 f. (also reproduced by Morris U. Schappes in *A Documentary History*, pp. 156 f.); the *New York Herald*, cited by M. Wischnitzer in his *To Dwell in Safety*, p. 31.

22   The *Asmonean* of Oct. 26, 1849 (first issue), p. 2; *Boston Hebrew Observer*, of Jan. 26, March 23, and 30, 1883, cited by Jacob Neusner in "The Impact of Immigration and Philanthropy upon the Boston Jewish Community (1880-1914)," *PAJHS*, XLVI (1956-57), 71-85; Charles Nagel's address of Jan. 18, 1911, quoted by Max J. Kohler in *The Immigration Question with Particular Reference to the Jews in America* (New York, 1911), p. 36; Kohler, "Simon Wolf," *AJYB*, XXVI (1924-25), 404-419; Esther and David Panitz, *Simon Wolf: Liberty Under Law* (Washington, 1955). Neusner's analysis of the three phases of the Boston Jewish philanthropic endeavors (1880-90, 1890-95, 1895-1914) applies, with some modifications, also to most other communities outside New York. See also, more generally, Zosa Szajkowski, "The Attitude of American Jews to East European Jewish Immigration 1881-1893," *PAJHS*, XL (1950-51), 221-80; Irving Aaron Mandel, "Attitude of the American Jewish

Community Toward East-European Immigration as Reflected in the Anglo-Jewish Press (1880-1890)," *AJA*, III (1950), 11-36; and M. Wischnitzer, *To Dwell in Safety*, pp. 44 ff., 72 ff., 120 ff. It ought also to be noted that the extremely independent, often sharply critical attitude of many immigrants toward their "benefactors" did not make the latter's task any easier. Typical of many others was Dr. George M. Price, some of whose negative reports appeared in the Russian *Voskhod* and were assembled in an informative volume *Russkiye Yevrei v Amerike* (Russian Jews in America; St. Petersburg, 1893). An excerpt from Price's autobiographical appendix was published in the English trans. by Leo Shpall in "The Memoir of Doctor George M. Price," *PAJHS*, XLVII (1957-58), 101-110. See also *infra*, nn. 27, 88; and Merle Curti and Randall Birr, "The Immigrant and the American Image in Europe, 1860-1914," *Mississippi Valley Historical Review*, XXXVII (1950), 203-230; and, from another angle, Rudolf Glanz, *Jew and Irish: Historic Group Relations and Immigration* (New York, 1966); *Jew and Italian Historic Group Relations and the New Immigration (1881-1924)* (New York, 1971).

23 Samuel Gompers's autobiographical *Seventy Years of Life and Labor*, 2 vols. (New York, 1925), esp. I, 216 f.; II, 161 ff.; Arthur Mann, "Gompers and the Irony of Racism," *Antioch Review*, XIII (1953), 203-214. According to Rowland Hill Harvey, "resolutions against Chinese immigration had been passed with almost mechanical regularity in convention after convention of the Federation [of Labor]." See his *Samuel Gompers: Champion of the Toiling Masses* (Stanford, Cal., 1935), pp. 176 f. See also Florence Calvert Thornes's more recent, equally laudatory biography of *Samuel Gompers, American Statesman* (New York, 1957).

24 Madison Grant in *Hearings before the President's Commission on Immigration and Naturalization*, p. 1840; idem, *The Passing of the Great Race, or the Racial Basis of European History* (New York, 1916); Gustave Michaud, "What Shall We Be?" *Century Illustrated Monthly Magazine*, LXV (1902-1903), 683-90, with a brief reply thereto by Franklin H. Giddings, *ibid.*, pp. 690-92; Jacob A. Riis, *How the Other Half Lives* (New York, 1900); Louise Ware, *Jacob A. Riis* (New York, 1938), esp. p. 104. See the more balanced review of the existing shortcomings of the spreading American ghettos in Charles S. Bernheimer, *The Russian Jew in the United States* (Philadelphia, 1905);

and Hyman B. Grinstein's well-documented analysis of the subsequent Jewish "Flight from the Slums," *Baron Jub. Vol.*, pp. 285-97. Other articles of a racialist character had been written even earlier by Sidney G. Fisher; their titles are self-explanatory. See especially, his "Alien Degradation of American Character," *Forum*, XIV (1892-93), 608-615 (indirectly answered by the preceding pro-immigration article by George F. Parker, *ibid.*, pp. 600-607); and "Has Immigration Increased Population?" *Popular Science Monthly*, XLVIII (1895), 244 ff. See also other data assembled by another leader of the anti-immigration movement, Prescott F. Hall, in his *Immigration and Its Effects Upon the United States* (New York, 1906 and subsequent editions); the opposing views marshaled by Simon Wolf in *The American Jew as Patriot, Soldier, and Citizen*, ed. by Louis Edward Levy (New York, 1895), pp. 544 ff.; and, more generally, *The Influence of Immigration on American Culture: a Dinner Discussion* of the Conference on Immigration Policy (Chairman Harold Fields; New York, 1929); Edward Norman Saveth, *American Historians and European Immigrants* (New York, 1948; Columbia University, Studies in History, 540; Diss. Columbia Univ.); John Higham, *Strangers in the Land: Patterns of American Nativism, 1860-1925* (New Brunswick, 1955); Arthur Mann, "Attitudes and Policies on Immigration: an Opportunity for Revision" in *The Writing of American Jewish History*, ed. by Moshe Davis and Isidore S. Meyer (New York, 1957=PAJHS, XLVI, No. 3), pp. 289-305; *Immigration and American History: Essays in Honor of Theodore C. Blegen*, ed. by Henry Steele Commager (Minneapolis, 1961).

25   Francis A. Walker, *Discussions in Economics and Statistics* (New York, 1899), esp. pp. 422 ff. The spuriousness of this argument was pointed out among others by Isaac A. Hourwich in his *Immigration and Labor: the Economic Aspects of the European Immigration to the United States*, 2d ed. (New York, 1922), pp. 221 ff. which stressed, in particular, the world-wide character of the then declining birth rate. Walker himself, moreover, had on other occasions offered a different explanation of this phenomenon. See Max J. Kohler, *Some Aspects of the Immigration Problem* (Ithaca, N. Y., 1914; reprinted from the *American Economic Review*, IV, 1), p. 12 n. 36.

26   Heinrich E. Jacob, *The World of Emma Lazarus* (New York, 1949); Morris U. Schappes, ed., *The Letters of Emma Lazarus, 1868-1885* (New York, 1949); Eve Merriam, *Emma Lazarus:*

Woman with a Torch (New York, 1956); *Report* of the Industrial Commission on Immigration, Vol. XV (Washington, D. C., 1907), pp. xc f., 95. On the communal efforts, see *infra*, nn. 109 ff. See also Ralph L. Rusk, ed., *Letters to Emma Lazarus in the Columbia University Library* (New York, 1939); and my brief review of that volume in *JSS*, II (1940), 108-109.

27 See the *Official Correspondence Relating to Immigration of Russian Exiles* (Washington, D.C., 1891); and other data succinctly analyzed in M. Wischnitzer's *To Dwell in Safety*, pp. 76 ff.

28 *American Hebrew* of Dec. 9, 1892; Simon Wolf, *Selected Addresses and Papers* (Cincinnati, 1926), pp. 204 ff.; the data analyzed by Jane Perry Clark in her *Deportation of Aliens from the United States to Europe* (New York, 1931; Studies in History, Columbia University, 351), esp. pp. 41 ff., 215 ff. It may be noted that a literacy test had been passed by Congress in 1896, and again in 1909, but it was vetoed by Presidents Cleveland and Taft, respectively. See Clement S. Mihanovich, "The American Immigration Policy: a Historical and Critical Evaluation" in M. Davis and I. S. Meyer, eds., *The Writing of American Jewish History*, pp. 306-336; and Milton R. Konwitz, *The Alien and the Asiatic in American Law* (Ithaca, N. Y., 1946). See also Max J. Kohler's pamphlet, *The Injustice of a Literacy Test for Immigrants* (New York, 1912). Kohler also reproduced a communication by Woodrow Wilson to Cyrus Adler of Oct. 21, 1912 in which, five months before assuming the presidency of the United States, Wilson had declared, "I think that this country can afford to use and ought to give opportunity to every man and woman of sound morals, sound mind and sound body who comes in good faith to spend his or her energies in our life, and I should certainly be inclined so far as I am concerned, to scrutinize very jealously any restrictions that would limit that principle in practice" (p. 5).

29 See Abraham Menes, "The Am Oylom Movement," YA, IV (1949), 9-33 (trans. from his Yiddish chapter in Elias Tcherikower, ed., *Geshikhte*, II). On Zionism, see *infra*, nn. 144 ff. The situation before the mass immigration after the Civil War is analyzed by Allan Tarshish in "The Economic Life of the American Jews in the Middle-Nineteenth Century," *Essays on American Jewish History*, ed. by Jacob Rader Marcus *et al.* (Cincinnati, 1958), 263-93.

30 M. U. Schappes, *A Documentary History*, pp. 195 ff. No. 81;

H. B. Grinstein, *The Rise of the Jewish Community of New York*, pp. 116 ff.; *The Occident*, April 1843. See also M. Unger's aforementioned essay (n. 11); and other data reviewed by Benjamin Steinberg in his "History of Agrarization of Jews in the United States (to 1880)" (Yiddish), *Yorbuch fun Amopteil*, I (1938), 60-90.

31 The first to offer a detailed review of these early attempts was Judah David Eisenstein in a series of Hebrew articles, "A History of the Colonies Founded by Our Brethren the Exiles from Russia" in *Ner ha-Ma'arabi*, II (1898), 8-15, 64-72, 129-36, 179-83. He was followed by many investigators, especially Gabriel Davidson who, as head of the Jewish Agricultural Society, was personally involved in settling many Jews on the land in the twentieth century. Apart from the *Reports* of that Society, see especially Davidson's "The Jew in Agriculture in the United States," *AJYB*, XXXVII (1935), 99-134; and his more comprehensive *Our Jewish Farmers and the Story of the Jewish Agricultural Society* (New York, 1943). See also Martha Clark Silberschutz, *Jewish Agricultural Colonization in the United States 1880-1900* (Master's essay at Columbia University, 1944; typescript); Leo Shpall, "Jewish Agricultural Colonies in the United States," *Agricultural History*, XXIV (1950), 120-46; and the more personal description of later observations by Alfred Werner, "American Jews on the Land," *South Atlantic Quarterly*, XLVII (1948), 342-51.

32 See especially Gustav Pollak, *Michael Heilprin and His Sons: a Biography* (New York, 1912), pp. 205 ff.

33 Philip Reuben Goldstein, *Social Aspects of the Jewish Colonies of South Jersey* (New York, 1921; Diss. University of Pennsylvania), esp. p. 18 Table 1; and J. Brandes's recent study, cited *supra*, Essay 3 n.

34 Maurice de Hirsch, "My Views on Philanthropy," *North American Review*, No. 416, July, 1891; reprinted in Samuel Joseph, *History of the Baron de Hirsch Fund: the Americanization of the Jewish Immigrant* (Philadelphia, 1935), pp. 275 ff. See also *ibid.*, pp. 10 ff.

35 We possess a number of autobiographical records written by participants in the Woodbine experiment. See esp. Hirsch Leib Sabsovich, *The Woodbine Settlement of the Baron de Hirsch Fund* (Woodbine, N.J., 1902); Katharine Sabsovich, *Adventures in Idealism: a Personal Record of the Life of Professor Sabsovich* (New York, 1922); Boris D. Bogen, *Born a Jew* (New York,

1930), esp. pp. 69 f.; and David G. Ludins, "Memories of Woodbine: 1891-1894," *Jewish Frontier*, XXVII, No. 6 (June, 1960), pp. 7-15. Ludins mentions that, by 1959, the Jewish population of Woodbine had dwindled to 300, out of a total number of 2,500 inhabitants. See also Jacob G. Lipman's article on "Woodbine," in *JE*, XII, 558-59; P. R. Goldstein, *Social Aspects*, esp. pp. 22 Table 2; and 29 Table 3; and S. Joseph, *History*, pp. 48 ff.

36   *Report of the Jewish Agricultural Society for 1900-1924*, pp. 46 ff.; Joseph Krauskopf, "National Farm School," *JE*, IX, 187-88; Olivia Rosetti Agresti, *David Lubin* (Boston, 1922); S. Sterling-Michaud, "Un pionnier de l'organisation internationale: David Lubin (1849-1919)," *Schweizer Beiträge zur allgemeinen Geschichte*, IX (1951), 34-67; Allan Nevins, *The Emergence of Modern America* (New York, 1928), pp. 36 f. See also Krauskopf's early address, "Russia and Her Jews," delivered on November 30th, 1890, and published in his *Sunday Lectures*, Series IV (Philadelphia, 1890).

37   S. Joseph, *Jewish Immigration*, pp. 187 ff. Tables LII, LIV, LVI. For an evaluation of these figures see *ibid.*, pp. 140 ff.; M. Traub, *Jüdische Wanderbewegungen*, pp. 50 ff., 68 ff.

38   Bernard D. Weinryb, "The Adaptation of Jewish Labor Groups to American Life," *JSS*, VIII (1946), 219-44. Some of the vocational retraining, which the immigrants had previously received in Europe, proved very useful, however. See Weinryb, *Jewish Vocational Education: History and Appraisal of Training in Europe* (New York, 1948; Jewish Social Research Series).

39   Isaac Max Rubinow, "The Jewish Question in New York City [1902-1903]," translated from the Russian articles in the *Voskhod*, XXIII (May-August, 1903), by Leo Shpall in *PAJHS*, XLIX (1959-60), 90-136, esp. pp. 94 ff. See also Bernard D. Weinryb's remarks in *JSS*, VIII, 219-44; and *infra*, nn. 162-63.

40   Stuart E. Rosenberg, *The Jewish Community in Rochester 1843-1925* (New York, 1954), pp. 125 ff.; Abraham M. Rogoff, *Formative Years of the Jewish Labor Movement in the United States (1890-1900)* (New York, 1945; Diss. Columbia University); and, more generally, Melech Epstein, *Jewish Labor in the U. S. A., an Industrial, Political and Cultural History of the Jewish Labor Movement, 1882-1914* (New York, 1950); and other literature listed in the next notes.

41   John R. Commons in *Report of the U. S. Industrial Commission*, Vol. XV (1901), pp. 319-52; reprinted in his *Trade*

Unionism and Labor Problems (New York, 1905), pp. 316-35.

42 These ideological factors are stressed in Herz Burgin, *Di Geshikhte fun der yidisher Arbeiter-bavegung in Amerike, Rusland un England* (New York, 1915); and particularly in the aforementioned comprehensive *Geshikhte fun der yidisher Arbeiter-bavegung in di Fareynikte Shtatn*, ed. by Elias Tcherikower. This work which, summarized and revised by Aaron Antonovsky, appeared in English under the title, *The Early Jewish Labor Movement in the United States* (New York, 1961), has served as the fountainhead of subsequent publications, including that by Epstein cited *supra*, n. 40, covers only the period to 1890. But it is hoped that three additional volumes, in preparation for many years under the sponsorship of the YIVO Institute for Jewish Social Research, will be completed and published before very long. See the program outlined in the first session of that project's Editorial Advisory Council and reproduced in "Toward the History of the Jewish Labor Movement," YA, IX (1954), 363-96 (also reprint). See also the informative study by B. Weinstein, *Di yidishe unions in Amerike* (The Jewish Unions in the United States; New York, 1929); the statistical data supplied by Hermann Frank in "The Jewish Labor Movement in America (1888-1938)" (Yiddish), *Yorbuch fun Amopteil*, II (1938), 102-132 and the sources listed there; the interpretive essay by Selig Perlman, "Jewish-American Unionism, its Birth Pangs and Contribution to the General American Labor Movement," PAJHS, XLI (1952), 297-337, with the comments thereon by Henry David and Nathan Reich, *ibid.*, pp. 133-55; and the further discussion by David, Perlman, Daniel Bell, and Moses Rischin in the *Writing of American Jewish History*, ed. by M. Davis and I. S. Meyer, pp. 215-32, 257-62.

43 See the succinct descriptions of the "Amalgamated Clothing Workers of America," by its secretary, Joseph Schlossberg, a prominent labor leader and writer, and of "The International Ladies' Garment Workers' Union," by its president, Benjamin Schlesinger, in *JCR*, pp. 1264-69 and 1270-76, respectively, together with the more detailed listing of the then existing locals of these and other unions by Frank F. Rosenblatt in his "Labor Organizations," *ibid.*, pp. 697-715. On their history see the more comprehensive studies by M. Epstein (*supra*, n. 40); B. Weinstein, *Di yidishe unions*, *passim*; and Burgin, *Geshikhte*, *passim*. Credit for the famous protocol has usually been given

to Louis Brandeis. See especially, Alpheus Thomas Mason's biography, *Brandeis: a Free Man's Life* (New York, 1946), pp. 289 ff. However, in his letter of November 29, 1912 to Gertrude Barnum, who had at that time published an article on "How Industrial Peace Has Been Brought About in the Clothing Trade," Louis Marshall stated: "I was called in by the representatives of the contending parties, to act as mediator, and as a result of conferences covering about two weeks, I personally prepared the protocol of peace, and brought about its adoption by both parties. In fact the original document has ever since been in my possession." See *Louis Marshall: Champion of Liberty. Selected Papers and Addresses*, ed. by Charles Reznikoff, II, 1127. This crucial episode in Jewish labor history has been the subject of a detailed monograph by Hyman Berman in his *Era of the Protocol: a Chapter in the History of the International Ladies' Garment Workers Union, 1910-1916* (Diss. Columbia University, 1956; typescript). See also such monographs as Louis Levine, *The Women's Garment Workers: a History of the International Ladies' Garment Workers Union* (New York, 1924), supplemented by Harry Lang's *"62," Biography of a Union* (New York, 1940); Elden La Mar, *The Clothing Workers in Philadelphia: History of Their Struggle for Union and Security* (Philadelphia, 1940); and Benjamin Stolberg, *Tailor's Progress* (Garden City, 1944; on David Dubinsky).

44 See George Soule, *Sidney Hillman, Labor Statesman* (New York, 1939); and Matthew Josephson, *Sidney Hillman: Statesman of American Labor* (New York, 1952); Moses Rischin, "From Gompers to Hillman: Labor Goes Middle Class," *Antioch Review*, XIII (1953), 191-201; idem, *The Promised City*; and on the Jewish communal background of the Hart, Schaffner and Marx strike, Hyman L. Meites, *History of the Jews in Chicago* (Chicago, 1924); and the various English and and Hebrew essays, largely bibliographical in nature, ed. by Simon Rawidowicz in *The Chicago Pinkas* (Chicago, 1952).

45 See Perlman, *supra*, n. 42; John R. Commons observations on the Hart, Schaffner and Marx agreement in his *Trade Unionism and Labor Problems* (New York, 1921, Ser. 2), pp. 543 f.; Sylvia Kopald and Ben M. Selekman, "The Epic of the Needle Trades," *Menorah Journal*, XV (1928), 293-307, 414-27, 526-39; XVIII (1930), 303-314, esp. XVIII, 314.

46 David J. Saposs, "Some Outstanding Features of the Jewish Labor Movement in the American Scene," in the aforementioned

symposium in YA, IX, 366-72; Frank F. Rosenblatt, "The United Hebrew Trades," *JCR*, pp. 1277-80; the essays in English and Yiddish, ed. by Harry Lang and Morris C. Feinstone in *Gewerkschaften Jubilee Book Dedicated to 50 years of Life and Labor of the United Hebrew Trades, 1888-1938* (New York, 1938); A. S. Sachs, *Geshikhte fun Arbeiter-Ring*, 2 vols. (New York, 1925); and *infra*, nn. 121, 160 ff. The gradual decline of Jewish membership in the needle trades unions after the First World War is graphically illustrated in Jacob Loft's review of "Jewish Workers in the New York City Men's Clothing Industry," *JSS*, II (1940), 67-78. See also, more generally, B. Weinstein, *Yidishe unions in Amerike*; and the perceptive analyses by J. B. S. Hardman, "Jewish Workers in the American Labor Movement," YA, VII (1952), 229-54; and Nathan Reich, "The Americanization of Jewish Unionism," *Jewish Quarterly Review*, XLV (1955-56), 540-61; as well as J. J. Shapiro's *The Friendly Society* (*supra*, Essay 3 n.).

47 See Harvey O'Connor's dramatic description, *The Guggenheims* (New York, 1937). Some occupational data of the Jewish entrepreneurial class began to be compiled in the 1920s; they retroactively shed some light on the prewar period as well, and they will be mentioned below. Before 1914, one need refer only to John S. Billings's aforementioned essay (*supra*, n. 9) which more incidentally supplied some data also on the occupational distribution of the Jews in 1890. The lukewarm attitude of the Jewish leaders toward such studies is best exemplified by the Jewish reviewer who called Billings's monograph "one of the eccentricities of the Census Bureau." See his "Jews in the United States," *Reform Advocate*, I, No. 1 (February 20, 1891), 12, cited by Nathan Goldberg in his "Dynamics of the Economic Structure of the Jews in the United States," in M. Davis and I. S. Meyer, eds., *Writing of American Jewish History*, pp. 233-56, esp. p. 234. See also Jesse E. Pope, *The Clothing Industry in New York* (Columbia, Mo., 1905); B. M. Selekman, Henriette R. Walter, and W. J. Cooper, *The Clothing and Textile Industries in New York and Environs* (New York, 1925); and, more generally, Leo Wolman's brief survey of the "Garment Industries" in the *Encyclopedia of the Social Sciences*, VI (New York, 1931), 573-85, with bibliography.

48 The results of the Baron de Hirsch Fund's study were briefly summarized in a correspondence to the *Nedelnaia Khronika Voskhoda* of 1891 No. 17, pp. 489 f., cited by Weinryb in

JSS, VIII, 223. In general, much information on Jewish life in the United States may be culled from the numerous reports appearing in European journals, since particularly the East-European Jewish public avidly read all news coming from the United States. See, for instance, Leo Shpall, "A List of Selected Item of American Jewish Interest in the Russian-Jewish Press," *PAJHS*, XXXIX (1949-50), 87-113. The same holds true for the Hebrew and German periodicals, the London *Jewish Chronicle*, and so forth. A comprehensive project to index pertinent news items and editorials in the foreign as well as the American Jewish press has been pursued by the American Jewish Periodical Center affiliated with the American Jewish Archives in Cincinnati.

49   Isaac Mayer Wise, *Reminiscences*, pp. 37 ff.; *American Israelite*, XLIII (1896-97), Nos. 20, p. 5; 49, p. 2. The story of Jewish peddling in the United States, even in the earlier period, has not been analyzed in the detail it merits. Some data have been supplied, however, by Rudolf Glanz in his "Notes on Early Jewish Peddling in America," *JSS*, VII (1945), 119-36; Lee M. Friedman in "Modern American Radanites" in his *Pilgrims in a New Land*, pp. 277-96, 430-38; Maxwell Whiteman in "The Colonial Jewish Peddler," *Studies and Essays in Honor of Abraham A. Neuman*, pp. 503-515; and *supra*, Essay 3. See also Paul Abelson, "Employers' Organizations in Jewish Trades," *JCR*, pp. 716-23, esp. p. 723 (the list includes associations of Jewish manufacturers as well as merchants).

50   Isaac Markens, *The Hebrews in America: a Series of Historical and Biographical Sketches* (New York, 1888), esp. pp. 139 ff.; *New York Sun*, May 31, 1891, cited by Nathan Goldberg in his "Occupational Patterns of American Jews," *The Jewish Review*, III (1945), 3; Robert A. Woods, ed., *Americans in Process: a Settlement Study by Residents and Associates of the South End House* (Boston, 1903), pp. 112 f., 117, cited by L. M. Friedman in his *Pilgrims*, p. 304. See also Ralph M. Hower, *History of Macy's of New York 1858-1919: Chapters in the Evolution of the Department Store* (Cambridge, Mass., 1943; Harvard Studies in Business History, VII).

51   I. Markens, *The Hebrews in America*, p. 157.

52   Max Cohen, "The Jew in Business," *The American Hebrew*, XLVII, No. 3 (May 22, 1891), pp. 50-53; J. S. Billings, in U.S. Census Bureau, *Census Bulletin*, No. 19; Nathan Goldberg, "Occupational Patterns of American Jews," *The Jewish Review*, III (1945), 3-24, 161-86, 262-90; idem, in M. Davis

and I. S. Meyer, eds., *The Writing of American Jewish History*, pp. 233 ff. Only in the 1930s were foundations laid for a solid investigation of the American Jewish occupational distribution. But our knowledge in this field still is extremely limited and attempts to project the few later data available retrospectively into earlier periods are doubly hazardous, as the tremendous mobility characteristic of the American economy in general was even greater among immigrant groups. See also Henry J. Meyer's interesting attempt to ascertain the trends in "The Economic Structure of the Jewish Community in Detroit" (*JSS*, II, 1940, pp. 127-48) for the years 1890-1935 by consulting the Jewish names appearing in the respective city directories. It ap pears that in the twenty years from 1890 to 1910 the percentage of Jews engaged in manufacturing increased from 19.1 to 23.1, that in the professions nearly doubled (from 2.3 to 4.5), while that in commerce declined from 73.3 to 65.1 and went on declining in the following quarter century.

53 See my *SRH*, 1st ed., II, 269; I. Markens, *The Hebrews in America*, p. 139; Richard J. H. Gottheil, *The Belmont-Belmonte Family: a Record of 400 Years* (New York, 1917). Not surprisingly some of these families had deserted Judaism, for the most part after 1880. The majority remained Jewish, however, Joseph Seligman utilizing his Jewish banking connections in Germany to the best advantage for the American economy and particularly also for helping Abraham Lincoln finance the Civil War. According to William Edward Dodd, the Federal loans negotiated in Europe were scarcely less important than the battle of Gettysburg. See his *Robert J. Walker, Imperialist* (Chicago, 1914), p. 36, applied to Seligman by Max J. Kohler in his "Seligman, Joseph," *Dictionary of American Biography*, XVI, 571-72. See also Stephen Birminghan, *"Our Crowd": the Great Jewish Families of New York* (New York, 1967; also paperback) which, despite its lack of detailed documentation, gives a vivid picture of the life of New York's leading Jewish banking families in the latter part of the nineteenth and early twentieth centuries.

54 See especially Cyrus Adler's biography of *Jacob H. Schiff: his Life and Letters*, 2 vols. (New York, 1929). The story of Schiff's participation in the Japanese loans is graphically described in a memorandum by Baron Korekiyo Takahashi, Japan's chief negotiator and later Prime Minister, reproduced *ibid.*, I, 213-30. Schiff "felt sure," we are told, "that if defeated, Russia would be led in the path of betterment, whether it be revolution or

reformation, and he decided to exercise whatever influence he had for placing the weight of American resources on the side of Japan." *Ibid.*, p. 218. Interesting data on America's high finance were published by Pitirim Sorokin in his "American Millionaires and Multi-Millionaires: a Comparative Study," *Journal of Social Forces*, III (1924-25), 627-40. Although evidently incomplete, his list (p. 635) showed that, while among the 209 deceased millionaires reviewed by him only 9 (4.3 percent) were Jews, among the 195 still living in 1924 there were no less than 30 (or 15.4 percent) belonging to the Jewish group. Obviously that percentage had been much smaller before 1914, but the ascent of individual Jews on the economic ladder must have been quite rapid even then; most of them doubtless through banking and merchandising.

55   Rubinow in *PAJHS*, XLIX, 96 f.; and *supra*, Table IV. On the expansion of Jewish education and religious services, see *infra*, nn. 113 ff., 126 ff.

56   Benjamin H. Hartogensis, "Unequal Religious Rights in Maryland since 1776," *PAJHS*, XXV (1917), 93-107; idem, "Wherein Maryland Is Not a Free State," *The Debunker*, IX (1929), 81-83.

57   *The Occident*, XIII (1856), 558 f.; Frank Rosenthal, *The Jews of Des Moines: the First Century*, with an Intro. by William D. Houlette (Des Moines, 1957), p. 7; Albert M. Friedenberg, "The Jews and the American Sunday Laws," *PAJHS*, XI (1903), 101-115; idem, "Sunday Laws of the United States and Leading Judicial Decisions Having Special Reference to the Jews," *AJYB*, X (1908-1909), 152-89; Jacob B. Lightman, *A Study of Reported Judicial Opinions of the American Courts Regarding the Status of the Jews with Respect to the Sunday Laws* (Master's thesis at the Graduate School for Jewish Social Work; New York, 1933; typescript).

58   See Jacob J. Hertz, *Di yidishe sotsialistishe bavegung in Amerike* (The Jewish Socialist Movement in America; New York, 1954); Bernard H. Bloom, "Yiddish-Speaking Socialists in America: 1892-1905," *AJA*, XII (1960), 34-70 (summary of a rabbinical thesis in typescript at Hebrew Union College, 1957; chiefly concerned with *Di Zukunft*; see *infra*, nn. 160-61); Hillel Rogoff, *An East-Side Epic: the Life and Work of Meyer London* (New York, 1930); Morris Hillquit's autobiographical *Loose Leaves from a Busy Life* (New York, 1934); and Joseph Cohen, *Di yidishe anarkhistishe bavegung in Amerike* (Philadelphia, 1943).

On Berger, see L. J. Switchkow and L. P. Gartner, *The History of the Jews in Milwaukee*, pp. 150, 253 f., etc.

59   L. L. Watters, *The Pioneer Jews of Utah*, pp. 163 ff.; John Foord, *The Life and Public Services of Simon Sterne* (London, 1903). Material on the various Jewish office holders is largely biographical in nature. For the most part it is available in the annual obituaries, as well as in the lists of "Appointments, Honors, and Elections," and directories of Jews in American public service which appeared in successive volumes of *AJYB*. Whatever indifference toward political affairs still lingered among the more recent arrivals gave way, however, under the impact of the First World War and the heated debates concerning the United States' participation in it. See the data assembled by Joseph Rappaport in his *Jewish Immigrants and World War I* (Diss. Columbia University, 1951; typescript); idem, "The American Yiddish Press and the European Conflict in 1914," *JSS*, XIX (1957), 113-28.

60   Louis Marshall's letters, ed. by C. Reznikoff in his *Louis Marshall*, pp. 809 f.; Lawrence H. Fuchs, *The Political Behavior of American Jews* (Glencoe, Ill., 1956); and such more detailed studies as Maurice G. Guysenir, "Jewish Vote in Chicago," *JSS*, XX (1958), 195-214; and Edgar Litt, "Status, Ethnicity and Patterns of Jewish Voting Behavior in Baltimore," *ibid.*, XXII (1960), 159-64. All these studies furnish data based on elections after World War II, but they are suggestive also with respect to earlier periods and raise a number of basic methodological problems. Of course, group voting could be affected by the faith of the candidates, as happened in the presidential elections of 1928 and 1960. See Saul Brenner, "Patterns of Jewish-Catholic Democratic Voting and the 1960 Presidential Vote," *ibid.*, XXVI (1964), 169-78; and Lucy S. Dawidowicz and Leon J. Goldstein, *Politics in a Pluralist Democracy: Studies of Voting in the 1960 Elections*, with a Foreword by Richard M. Scammon (New York, 1963). More directly relevant for the nineteenth century are Stuart E. Rosenberg's "Notes on the Political Attitudes of the *Jewish Tidings*," *JSS*, XVII (1955), 323-28.

61   On his death Seligman was eulogized by, among others, the famous preacher Henry Ward Beecher who had previously delivered a laudatory sermon on his personality in connection with the Saratoga incident. See *infra*, n. 69; H. W. Beecher's necrology reprinted in the *Menorah* of March, 1905; and Linton Wells, *The House of Seligman*, 3 vols. (New York, 1931; type-

script). Oscar Straus's works included *The Origin of the Republican Form of Government in the United States* (New York, 1885); and *Roger Williams: the Pioneer of Religious Liberty* (New York, 1894). Of biographical importance are especially Straus's reminiscences, *Under Four Administrations* (Boston, 1922) and his private diary, of which only a few excerpts have hitherto been published by Moshe Davis in his "The Human Record: Cyrus Adler at the Peace Conference, 1919," *Essays in American Jewish History: To Commemorate the Tenth Anniversary of the Founding of the American Jewish Archives under the Direction of Jacob Rader Marcus* (Cincinnati, 1958), pp. 457-91 (also in Hebrew trans. in his *Beit Yisrael be-Amerikah*, pp. 206 ff.); and by Naomi W. Cohen in "An American Jew at the Paris Peace Conference of 1919" in *Baron Jub. Vol.*, pp. 159-68. Dr. Cohen has also written a full-length biography entitled *A Dual Heritage: the Public Career of Oscar S. Straus* (Philadelphia, 1969; originally Diss. Columbia University). On Straus's relations with Baron Maurice de Hirsch, whose life he briefly described in his article, "Studies of Notable Men; Baron de Hirsch," *Forum*, XXI (1896), 558-65 (also in *JE*, VI, 414-16), see *supra*, n. 34.

62 Theodore Roosevelt, *An Autobiography* (New York, 1922), pp. 186 f. None of this was mentioned, of course, in Ahlwardt's own report on his activities in the short-lived American periodical, *Der Antisemit* of March 21, 1896, in which he claimed that, owing to his efforts, the antisemitic movement had spread widely through the United States. See the summary in Karl Knortz's virulently anti-Jewish pamphlet, *Das amerikanische Judentum* (Leipzig, 1914), pp. 24 ff.

63 *The Two Hundred and Fiftieth Anniversary of the Settlement of the Jews in the United States 1655-1905*, published by the Executive Committee of the New York Co-operative Society (New York, 1906), p. 19. On that gala occasion the former president, Grover Cleveland, delivered an address along similar lines, *ibid.*, pp. 11 ff. On the attitudes of the various presidents of the period, see Simon Wolf, *The Presidents I Have Known From 1860–1918* (Washington, 1918). See also, from another angle, Bertram W. Korn's "Jewish Welfare Activities for the Military during the Spanish-American War," *PAJHS*, XLI (1952), 356-80, reprinted in his *Eventful Years*, pp. 214-37; and, more generally, George J. Fredman and Louis A. Falk, *Jews in American Wars* (New York, 1942).

64 Madison Grant, *The Passing of the Great Race or The Racial Basis of European History* (New York, 1916), esp. pp. 15 f.; Henry James, *The American Scene* (London, 1907), esp. pp. 130 ff. See also, more generally, Edward N. Saveth, *American Historians and European Immigrants* (New York, 1948); Lee J. Levinger, *Antisemitism in the United States. Its History and Causes* (New York, 1925). Saveth also points out some discrepancies between private utterances of even such egalitarian presidents as Theodore Roosevelt and Woodrow Wilson and their official statements as presidents of the United States (pp. 117, 141 f.). On the earlier relations between "The Know-Nothing Movement and the Jews," see Bertram Wallace Korn's pertinent article, reproduced in his *Eventful Years and Experiences*, pp. 58-78.

65 Laurence Gronlund, *The Cooperative Commonwealth in Its Outline: an Exposition of Modern Socialism* (Boston, 1884), p. 50; Ignatius Donnelly, *Caesar's Column: a Story of the Twentieth Century* (Chicago, 1891), pp. 36 f., 111 f., cited by Oscar Handlin in his *Adventure in Freedom*, pp. 174 ff., 182 f., 186 f.; idem, *Dangers in Discord: Origins of Anti-Semitism in the United States* (New York, 1948); idem, "American Views of the Jews at the Opening of the Twentieth Century," *PAJHS*, XL (1950-51), 323-44 (analyzing in particular the American image of the Jew with respect to immigrant stereotypes, financial relationships, and the sense of mystery); and Stephen Bloore, "The Jew in American Dramatic Literature (1794-1930)," *ibid.*, pp. 345-60 (based in part on Edward Davidson Coleman's bibliography of *The Jews in English Drama*; New York, 1943). Alphonse Toussenel's work, *Les Juifs rois de l'époque. Histoire de la féodalité financière*, Paris, 1845, was part of the Fourierist anti-Jewish literature, on which, see especially Edmund Silberner, "Charles Fourier on the Jewish Question," *JSS*, VIII (1946), 245-66; idem, "The Attitude of the Fourierist School towards the Jews," *ibid.*, IX (1947), 339-62; and, more generally, his comprehensive Hebrew volume, *Ha-Soṣialism ha-ma'arabi u-she'elat ha-Yehudim* (Western Socialism and the Jewish Question: a Study in the History of the Socialist Thought in the Nineteenth Century; Jerusalem, 1955).

66 Telemachus Thomas Timayenis, *The Original Mr. Jacobs* (New York, 1888), esp. pp. 6 ff., 21; and his other writings lucidly analyzed by Leonard A. Greenberg and Harold J. Jonas in "An American Anti-Semite in the Nineteenth Century," *Baron Jub.*

Vol., pp. 265-83; Handlin, *Adventure in Freedom*, pp. 178 ff. Caricatures had long been an effective instrument in the political struggles in the United States. Most of them appeared in newspapers and magazines, but some were presented in special publications. See the annotated bibliography by Frank Weitenkampf, *Political Caricature in the United States in Separately Published Cartoons* (New York, 1953). However, this list ends to all intents and purposes in 1888, just before the Jews became a major subject of derision for political cartoonists. We are not surprised, therefore, to find here quite a few anti-Irish cartoons, but none relating to Jews.

67 M. U. Schappes, *A Documentary History*, pp. 559 ff. No. 158. A graphic description of anti-Jewish prejudice spreading on a popular level among the Gentile neighbors of East-European immigrants appeared in the *Sunday Mercury* of Philadelphia on August 10, 1890. It is reproduced under the title "Jewish Immigrant Life in Philadelphia—1890" in *AJA*, IX (1957), 32-42.

68 Alice Hyneman Rhine, "Race Prejudice at Summer Resorts," *Forum*, III (1887), 523-31; Edwin J. Kuh, "The Social Disability of the Jew," *Atlantic Monthly*, CI (1908), 431-39; and numerous other data assembled by John Higham in his informative survey of *Social Discrimination Against Jews in America, 1830-1930* (New York, 1957. Reprinted from *PAJHS*, XLVII). See also idem, *Antisemitism in the Gilded Age* (New York, 1957. Reprinted from the *Mississippi Valley Historical Review*, XLIII); and, more generally, idem, *Strangers in the Land* (New Brunswick, 1955). Sometimes, it may be noted, public protests were heeded, as in Cleveland in 1895 when a landlord retraced his steps and lived up to his agreement with a Jewish family which had rented his house in an exclusive neighborhood. The local *Hebrew Observer* defiantly declared on this occasion that the Cleveland Jews did "not intend to limit themselves to any one street, district or any special location." *Jewish Messenger*, XII (1895), No. 18, p. 4. See also, more generally, Carey McWilliams, *A Mask for Privilege: Anti-Semitism in America* (Boston, 1948); Milton R. Konvitz and Theodore Leskes, *A Century of Civil Rights* (New York, 1961); and other writings listed by Alexander D. Brooks in *A Bibliography of Civil Rights and Civil Liberties* (New York, 1962).

69 See especially, Mark Twain (Samuel L. Clemens), *Concerning the Jews* (1899) in *The Writings* (Author's National Edition), 25 vols. (New York, n. d.), XXIV: Literary Essays, pp. 263-87;

Joshua Bloch, ed., "Beecher's Sermon on the Jews," *Protestant*,
V (1943), 16-25; Zebulon B. Vance, *The Scattered Nation*, 2d
ed. with an Intro. by Marcus Schnitzer (New York, 1916);
Glenn Tucker, *Zeb Vance, Champion of Personal Freedom*
(Indianapolis, 1966); Selig Adler, "Zebulon B. Vance and the
'Scattered Nation,'" *Journal of Southern History*, VII (1941),
357-77; E. Gertz, "Charles Dana and the Jews," *Chicago Jewish
Forum*, VIII (March 1950), 196-203. Much material along
these lines has been assembled by Joseph L. Baron in his two
anthologies, *Candles in the Night: Jewish Tales by Gentile
Authors*, with a Preface by Carl Van Doren (Philadelphia,
1940); and *Stars and Sand: Jewish Notes by Non-Jewish No-
tables* (Philadelphia, 1943).

70 Jacob Ezekiel, "Persecution of Jews in 1840," *PAJHS*, VIII
(1900), 141-45; Joseph Jacobs, "The Damascus Affair of 1840
and the Jews of America," *ibid.*, X (1902), 119-28; Sol M.
Stroock, "Switzerland and American Jews," *ibid.*, XI (1903),
7-52; and, more generally, Cyrus Adler and Aaron M. Margalith, *With Firmness in the Right: American Diplomatic Action
Affecting Jews, 1840-1945* (New York, 1946); Bertram Wallace
Korn, *The American Reaction to the Mortara Case, 1858–59*
(Cincinnati, 1957).

71 See the full documentation in the official publication, *Foreign
Relations of the United States, 1885*; it is reproduced, with com-
ments in C. Adler and A. M. Margalith, *With Firmness in the
Right*, pp. 323 ff.

72 See Lloyd P. Gartner, "Rumania and America, 1873: Leon
Horowitz's Rumanian Tour and Its Background," *PAJHS*, XLV
(1955-56), 67-92; idem, "Rumania, America, and World Jewry:
Consul Peixotto in Bucharest, 1870-1878," *ibid.*, LVIII (1968-
69), 25-117; and the literature cited *infra*, nn. 98 and 107.
Number 12 of Grant's order, usually called Order No. 11, has
been established on the basis of the original record by Nathan
Reingold in his "Resources of American Jewish History in the
National Archives," *PAJHS*, XLVII (1957-58), 186-95, esp.
p. 193 n. 1. On the background of that order, and the subsequent philosemitic attitude of Grant, see Bertram Wallace Korn,
American Jewry and the Civil War (Philadelphia, 1951), pp.
121 ff.

73 John Hay's Note of July 17, 1902 published in *Foreign Relations
of the United States, 1902*, pp. 910 ff.; and reprinted therefrom
by C. Adler and A. M. Margalith in *With Firmness in the Right*,
pp. 120 ff.

74 Max J. Kohler and Simon Wolf, "Jewish Disabilities in the Balkan States," *PAJHS*, XXIV (1916), 89 ff.; *Congressional Record*, 63rd Congress, First Session, Vol. L, Part 6 (1913), 5541; C. Adler and A. M. Margalith, *With Firmness*, pp. 134 ff.

75 See the various other aspects which came up for discussion in James Buchanan, *The Works, Comprising His Speeches, State Papers and Private Correspondence*, ed. by John Bassett Moore, 12 vols. (Philadelphia, 1908-1911), II, 268 ff., 271 ff., 281 ff., 317; Max J. Kohler's remarks thereon in "The Abrogation of the Treaty of 1832 Between the United States and Russia and the International Protection of Religious Minorities," included in the "American Supplementary Chapters" to Luigi Luzzatti's *God in Freedom: Studies in the Relations Between Church and State*, translated from the Italian by Alfonso Arib-Costa (New York, 1930), pp. 705-794, esp. p. 706 n. 2; and, more generally, the literature listed *infra*, n. 79.

76 See "Termination of the Treaty of 1832 between the United States and Russia," *Hearing* before the Committee on Foreign Affairs of the House of Representatives, December 11, 1911, p. 240; Louis Marshall's letters, ed. by C. Reznikoff, I, 50 ff.; and C. Adler and A. M. Margalith, *With Firmness in the Right*, pp. 171 ff., where this documentation is fully analyzed and often reproduced.

77 Blaine's communication to Foster reproduced in *Foreign Relations*, 1881, pp. 1030 ff. and cited in the aforementioned *Hearing*, pp. 129 ff.; and by C. Adler and A. M. Margalith, pp. 195 ff. Count Lamsdorf's memorandum to the Tsar is cited in an English translation in Lucien Wolf's *Notes on the Diplomatic History of the Jewish Question* (London, 1919), pp. 57 ff. On Schiff's hostility to Russia, see Cyrus Adler's biography of *Jacob H. Schiff: His Life and Letters*, I, 213 ff.; II, 122; and *supra*, n. 54. See also Zosa Szajkowski, "Paul Nathan, Lucien Wolf, Jacob H. Schiff, and the Jewish Revolutionary Movements in Eastern Europe (1903-1917)," *JSS*, XXIX (1967), 3-26.

78 Alice F. Tyler, *The Foreign Policy of James G. Blaine* (Minneapolis, 1927), p. 276; James B. Lockey, "James G. Blaine," in *The American Secretaries of State and Their Diplomacy*, ed. by Samuel Flagg Bemis, 10 vols. (New York, 1927-30), VII, 296; Schiff's letter to Ochs cited (without the date) in C. Adler's biography of *Jacob H. Schiff*, II, 151 f. These documents are commented on by M. J. Kohler in "The Abrogation," pp. 710 ff.

79 Louis Marshall's address of January 19, 1911 is reproduced in Luigi Luzzatti's *God in Freedom*, pp. 714-26; and again, to-

648 | *Notes to pages 335–336*

gether with several letters written before and after its delivery, in C. Reznikoff's *Louis Marshall*, I, 57 ff. In a letter to Sulzberger of January 20, 1912, Marshall pointed out that opinions had been divided as to the advisability of his making such a public statement but that he was swayed by Jacob Schiff on the advice of Charles D. Norton, President Taft's Secretary. See Reznikoff, I, 159 n. The subsequent developments are described by M. J. Kohler in "The Abrogation," pp. 726 ff.; and by C. Adler and A. M. Margalith in *With Firmness*, pp. 285 ff. See also the contemporary documentation offered in "The Passport Question," *AJYB*, XIII (1911), 13-128; the analytical studies by J. [Ezekiel] Lipschitz, "A Diplomatic Conflict between the United States and Russia about Jews" (Yiddish), *YB*, XIX (1942), 342-53; Carl G. Winter, "The Influence of the Russo-American Treaty of 1832 on the Rights of the American Jewish Citizens," *PAJHS*, XLI (1951-52), 163-94; and Zosa Szajkowski, "The European Aspect of the American-Russian Passport Question," *ibid.*, XLVI (1956-57), 86-100; and Naomi W. Cohen, "The Abrogation of the Russo-American Treaty of 1832," *JSS*, XXV (1963), 3-41. See also Morton Rosenstock, *Louis Marshall, Defender of Jewish Rights* (Detroit, 1965; Diss. Columbia University).

80 *Foreign Relations*, 1881, pp. 1043 f., 1056 ff.; 1894, pp. 496 f.; 1896, pp. 485 f.; 1905, pp. 680 f.; 1906, pp. 1472 f., 1493 ff.; Joseph Bucklin Bishop, *Theodore Roosevelt and His Time, Shown in His Own Letters*, 2 vols. (New York, 1920), I, 467 ff.; C. Adler and A. M. Margalith, *With Firmness*, pp. 11 ff., 25 ff. In passing one may note how impressed Theodore Roosevelt was when, on his visit to Rome in 1911, he met Mayor Ernesto Nathan and Prime Minister Luigi Luzzatti. "In the Eternal City," he wrote to Sir George Trevelyan on Oct. 1, 1911, "in the realm of the popes, the home of the ghetto, I lunched sitting beside one Jew who was Prime Minister of Italy, and dined as the guest of another Jew who was the head of the Roman Government itself." Bishop, II, 201 f.

81 Margaret Oliphant and W. Oliphant, *Memoir of the Life of Laurence Oliphant and of Alice Oliphant, His Wife* (London, 1891), pp. 213 ff.; *supra*, Essay 9; Abraham Yaari, *Sheluhe Ereṣ Yisrael* (Palestinian Messengers: a History of Missions from Palestine to the Dispersion from the Destruction of the Second Temple to the Nineteenth Century; Jerusalem, 1951); and, more generally, Frank E. Manuel, *The Realities of American-Palestine*

Relations (Washington, D.C., 1949), esp. pp. 48 ff., 89 ff. On the interesting episode of Warder Cresson (1798-1860), a Philadelphia Quaker who, in 1844, emigrated to Jerusalem and there adopted Judaism, see Abraham J. Karp, "The Zionism of Warder Cresson" in *Early History of Zionism in America*, ed. by Isidor S. Meyer (New York, 1958), pp. 1-20.

82 William E. Blackstone, *Palestine and the Jews: a Copy of the Memorial Presented to President Harrison, March 5, 1891* (Chicago, 1891).

83 C. Adler and A. M. Margalith, *With Firmness*, pp. 42 ff.; Frank E. Manuel, *The Realities*, pp. 47 ff., 88 ff.; Naomi W. Cohen, *A Dual Heritage; supra*, nn. 61 and 71.

84 *Foreign Relations*, 1881, p. 998.

85 Cyrus Adler, *The Voice of America on Kishineff* (Philadelphia, 1904; offering a vast assortment of records relating to meetings, sermons, resolutions, editorial articles, relief measures, and the petition), esp. pp. xi f., 18 f.; Simon Wolf, *The Presidents I Have Known*, p. 155; Count Serge J. Witte, *Memoirs*, translated from the Russian by Avram Yarmolinsky (New York, 1921), pp. 190 f.

86 See Rose A. Halpern's unpublished Master's Essay at Columbia University, 1941, *The American Reaction to the Dreyfus Case* (typescript). No one seems to have mentioned on this occasion that some forty years earlier the United States had had a minor Dreyfus Affair of its own in the person of Captain Uriah Phillips Levy (1792-1862). See M. U. Schappes, *A Documentary History*, pp. 375 ff., 672 f. It may be noted, however, that the earlier antisemitic agitation, conducted over many years by the Court Preacher Adolf Stöcker in Berlin, produced no significant reaction in the United States. At the advice of German Jewish leaders, even the Board of Delegates of American Israelites decided to ignore that movement, hoping for the "returning reason of the German people."

87 Harriet Martineau, *Society in America*, 3d ed., 2 vols. (New York, 1837), II, 349. See also, more generally, Evarts B. Greene, *Religion and the State* (New York, 1941); and *supra*, Essay 7.

88 "The Synagogue Question?" (a letter to the editor signed S.), *Jewish Messenger*, XLIV, No. 15 (October 11, 1878), p. 5; Edmund J. James *et al.*, *The Immigrant Jew in America* (New York, 1906; practically identical with Charles S. Bernheimer, ed., *The Russian Jew in the United States*, Philadelphia, 1905), pp. 174 f. As an active social worker, Bernheimer was quite

familiar with the life of the immigrants. See his subsequent reminiscences in his autobiographical *Half a Century of Community Service* (New York, 1948).

Much of Jewish communal history can, of course, be deduced from the histories of individual communities. See *supra*, Essay 3 n. 38 and the literature listed there. While the numerous anniversary volumes of congregations, societies, and the like, which have been appearing over the last several decades, are often devoid of scholarly value, some have preserved significant data, often transcending the bounds of local history. Many historical and sociological studies of American cities include materials, at times even chapters, relating to their Jewish inhabitants. A listing of all pertinent studies would far exceed the confines of this essay. Suffice it to refer here to the monographs listed in our earlier and forthcoming notes, esp. *supra*, Essay 3 n. 46; others mentioned in Rischin's *Inventory*, pp. 51 f. nn. 64-65; and in Abraham G. Duker's "An Evaluation of Achievement in American Jewish Local Historical Writing," *PAJHS*, XLIX (1960), 215-304. A few stray items like the following might likewise be of interest: Arthur Buch, *The Jewish Community of Scranton* (Diss. New School for Social Research, New York, 1952; typescript); A. G. Daniels, *History of the Jews of Boston and New England* (Boston, 1892); Albert Ehrenfried, *A Chronicle of Boston Jewry from the Colonial Settlement to 1900* ([Boston], 1963); Max Heller, *Jubilee Souvenir of Temple Sinai 1872-1922* (New Orleans, 1922); Louis Ginsberg, *Chapters on the Jews of Virginia, 1658-1900* (Petersburg, Va., 1969); S. Winifred Smith, "Plum Street Temple, Cincinnati," *Museum Echoes* of the Ohio State Museum, XXI (1948), 65-70; *Temple Beth-El 80th Anniversary Booklet* (Knoxville, Tenn., 1947); Michael Moses Zarchin, *Glimpses of Jewish Life in San Francisco: History of San Francisco Jewry* (San Francisco, 1952). See also the interesting excerpts compiled by Milton Hindus in *The Old East Side: an Anthology* (Philadelphia, 1969).

Some sociological surveys, though dealing principally with the contemporary situation, often shed light on earlier periods as well. See, for instance, Samuel Koenig, "The Jews of Easterntown: the Genesis of Jewish Community Life in an American Town," *Jewish Review*, V (1948), 1-29 (on Stamford, Connecticut, 1859-1932); Julian B. Feibelman, *A Social and Economic Study of the New Orleans Jewish Community* (Philadelphia, 1941); Lloyd F. Warner and Leo Srole, *The Social System of*

American Ethnic Groups (New Haven, 1945; includes considerable information on the Jewish minority); George Kranzler, *Williamsburg, a Jewish Community in Transition: a Study of the Factors and Patterns of Change in the Organization and Structure of a Community in Transition* (New York, 1961); Nathan Glazer, *American Judaism*, with a Preface by Daniel J. Boorstin (Chicago, 1957; The Chicago History of American Civilization); and the collection of sociological essays, ed. by Marshall Sklare, in *The Jews: Social Patterns of an American Group* (Glencoe, Ill., 1958).

89 See *supra*, Essay 3; Maurice J. Karpf, "Jewish Community Organization in the United States: an Outline of Types of Organizations, Activities and Problems," *AJYB*, XXXIX (1937-38), 47-148 (also reprint); Ben M. Edidin, *Jewish Community Life in America* (New York, 1947). None of these studies is intended to present a history of Jewish communal organizations; they merely furnish historical data in order to illustrate some aspects of the contemporary situation. The same holds true also for the few available statistical monographs, among them the survey conducted in 1927 by Harry S. Linfield and summarized in *The Communal Organizations of the Jews in the United States* (New York, 1930) revised reprint from *AJYB*, XXXI (1929-30). See also Abraham Cronbach, "Jewish Pioneering in American Social Welfare," *AJA*, III, Part 3 (1951), 51-80, likewise furnishing data chiefly for more recent developments.

90 See Robert McIver's *Report on the Jewish Communities Relations Agencies*, Section I (New York, 1951). Although subjected to many relevant criticisms (for instance, by Abraham G. Duker in his *Jewish Community Relation: an Analysis of the McIver Report* [New York, 1952]), this analysis helped to clarify many issues and promote mutual cooperation.

91 *Annual Reports of the United Hebrew Charities,* esp. for the year 1904-1905, and the retrospective analysis of *Fifty Years of Social Service. The History of the United Hebrew Charities of the City of New York. Now the Jewish Social Service Association, Inc.*, published by the Association (New York, 1926). See also Gilbert Osofsky, "The Hebrew Emigrant Aid Society of New York (1881-1883)," *PAJHS*, XLIX (1959-60), 173-87; and, particularly, Mark Wischnitzer, *Visas to Freedom: the History of HIAS* (Cleveland, 1956). This society, it should be noted, declared it to be one of its main objectives: "to check pauperism by discouraging the emigration of persons incapable

of labor." See its Certificate of Incorporation, Osofsky, p. 186. Understandably, the immigrants coming from countries with well-organized communities and used to different methods of social service often complained not only of the insufficiency of the funds granted to them but also of the impersonal nature of the New York organization. See the interesting data assembled by Harold Silver in his *Attitudes of the East European Jewish Immigrants Toward Organized Jewish Charity in the United States, in the Years 1890-1900* (Master's thesis of the Graduate School for Jewish Social Work; New York, 1934; typescript); and M. J. Karpf, "Community Organization," *AJYB*, XXXIX, 79 ff. See also *supra*, n. 13; and, more generally, Boris D. Bogen, *Jewish Philanthropy: an Exposition of Principles and Methods of Jewish Social Service in the United States* (New York, 1924); Harry L. Lurie, *A Heritage Affirmed: the Jewish Federation Movement in America* (Philadelphia, 1961); Robert Morris and Michael Freund, eds., *Trends and Issues in Jewish Social Welfare in the United States: the History of American Jewish Social Welfare Seen through the Proceedings of the National Conference of Jewish Communal Service* (Philadelphia, 1966), esp. pp. 3-157.

92 Joseph, *History of the Baron de Hirsch Fund*, pp. 184 ff.; Rose Margolies, *History of the Industrial Removal Office* (Master's thesis at the Graduate School for Jewish Social Work; New York, 1935; typescript). From its inception in 1874 the leading New York charitable organization, the United Hebrew Charities, tried to persuade new arrivals to move to "more promising fields of residence in the interior." See *Fifty Years of Social Service*, p. 21.

93 Joseph, *History*, pp. 205 ff. See Adler, *Jacob H. Schiff*, II, 94 ff. (reproducing much of Schiff's correspondence on the subject); the reminiscences by Rabbi Henry Cohen in *The Galveston Immigration Movement*. See also Anna Nathan and Harry I. Cohen, *The Man Who Stayed in Texas: the Life of Rabbi Henry Cohen* (New York, 1941), esp. pp. 189 ff.; and Leo Shpall's brief summary of *The Galveston Experiment Spreading the Jewish Migrant in America* (New York, n.d.; reprinted from *The Jewish Forum*). Interesting statistical comparisons with the rest of Jewish émigrés in the United States were drawn by Jacob Lestschinsky in "Die Auswanderung der Juden nach Galveston," *Zeitschrift für Demographie und Statistik der Juden*, VI (1910), 177-84.

94 Notwithstanding the availability of much primary source material, particularly in the *Annual Reports* published by the hospitals
themselves or their sponsoring organizations, few comprehensive
histories of these institutions or of the entire Jewish hospital
movement in the country are as yet available. An anniversary
volume such as Joseph Hirsch and Beka Doherty's *The First
Hundred Years of the Mount Sinai Hospital* (New York, 1952),
is, of course, an inadequate substitute. Only the Denver institutions are historically analyzed against the background of the
local Jewish community in Ida Libert Uchill's story of that
community in her *Pioneers, Peddlers, and Tsadikim* (Denver,
1957). Retrospectively valuable also is the survey by a Sub-
committee of the Conference on Jewish Relations (Reuben
Ottenberg, Chairman) on "Facilities of Jewish Hospitals for
Specialized Training," *JSS*, III (1941), 375-86; IV (1942), 84;
and, more generally, Jacob A. Goldberg, "Jews in the Medical
Profession—A National Survey," *ibid.*, I (1939), 327-36. Interesting studies of "Causes of Death Among Jews in New York
City," by C. Bolduan and L. Weiner, and by David M. Liberson
appeared in the *New England Journal of Medicine*, CCVIII
(1933), 407-416; and *JSS*, XVIII (1956), 83-117, respectively
(the latter article describes the situation in 1953, but sheds light
on earlier conditions as well); and the bibliography cited there.
See also Jacob J. Golub's brief general review of "Diseases
Among Jews," *Jewish Social Service Quarterly*, IV (1927), 144-
55. While these more recent data do not necessarily reflect the
exact ratios prevailing before 1914, they give an inkling of some
differences which had existed even then between Jews and non-
Jews with respect to both the frequency of certain diseases and
mortality rates. Other literature relating, in particular, to mental
illness among Jews is quoted by M. J. Karpf in *AJYB*, XXXIX,
143 nn. 63-66.

95 The vast number of Jewish charitable organizations operating
in New York during World War I is evident from the listing
in *JCR* which covers 131 closely printed pages (999-1129).
This organizational proliferation is the less surprising as even
some of the older communities with much smaller and less
diversified Jewish populations often developed an anarchical
variety of associations. For one example, in Amsterdam, Holland,
a member, B. Cohen, in the early 1800s left bequests for no less
than 210 philanthropic and educational societies to which he
had more or less regularly contributed during his lifetime. See

my *JC*, esp. I, 360 ff. In addition many Jews, particularly among the wealthy, also contributed generously to many non-Jewish philanthropies. Such contributions to general charities were considered important not only on humanitarian, but also on apologetic grounds. Hence Simon Wolf, in his accumulation of data, aimed at an apologia for the Jews of America, also compiled a list of Jewish contributors to non-Jewish causes. See his *The American Jew as Patriot*, pp. 439 ff. See also the biographical accounts of two outstanding Jewish philanthropists of that period by Lina G. Straus, *Disease in Milk, the Remedy, Pasteurization: the Life Work of Nathan Straus* (New York, 1917); and Morris R. Werner, *Julius Rosenwald: the Life of a Practical Idealist* (New York, 1939).

96 Joseph Jacobs, "Federation Movement in American Jewish Philanthropy," *AJYB*, XVII (1915-16), 159-98; Ben M. Selekman, "Federation in the Changing American Scene," *ibid.*, XXXVI (1934-35), 65-87; Herman D. Stein, "Jewish Social Work in the United States (1654-1954)," *ibid.*, LVII (1956), 3-98; and particularly, Harry L. Lurie, *A Heritage Affirmed: the Jewish Federation Movement in America*. Of interest also are such general studies as Robert David Duncan, *A History of Organized Secular Philanthropy in Pittsburgh* (Diss. University of Pittsburgh, 1953; typescript). The Sephardim, it may be noted, maintained in many ways independent organizations which were not completely submerged under those of the large Ashkenazic majority. See Louis Hacker, "The Communal Life of the Sephardic Jews of New York City," *Jewish Social Service Quarterly*, III, No. 2 (1926), pp. 32-40, estimating their number in the city at 40,000, and in the whole country at some 60,000; the latter probably is an understatement.

97 Arthur M. Schlesinger, "What Then Is the American, This New Man?" *American Historical Review*, XLVIII (1942-43), 243; M. U. Schappes, *A Documentary History*, pp. 216 f., 625.

98 See the data regularly published in the Order's organs particularly the *Menorah Monthly*, first edited by Benjamin F. Peixotto. But a fully documented history of the Order still is a major scholarly desideratum. For the time being we must be satisfied with such brief surveys as Bernard Postal's "B'nai B'rith: a Century of Service," *AJYB*, XLV (1943-44), 97-116. More fully descriptive are Helen Hadassah Levinthal's Master's essay at Columbia University, *The Jewish Fraternal Order, an Americanizing and Socializing Force* (New York, 1932; typescript); and the brief Hebrew survey by M. Ivensky, "Jewish Orders in

America," *Sefer ha-Shanah li-Yehude Amerika*, [IV] (5699-1939), 388-404. See also the addresses and biographical data in *Memorial Volume Leo N. Levi I.O.B.B.* (Chicago, 1905); Adolph Kraus, *Reminiscences and Comments: the Immigrant, the Citizen, the Public Officer, the Jew* (Chicago, 1925); and *supra*, n. 16.

99   C. Reznikoff, *Louis Marshall*, I, 394; I. Markens, *The Hebrews in America*, pp. 235 ff.; Max J. Kohler, "Jewish Disabilities in the Balkan States: American Contributions toward Their Removal, with Particular Reference to the Congress of Berlin," *PAJHS*, XXIV (1916); and L. P. Gartner, *supra*, n. 72.

100   These periodicals are, indeed, our main sources of information for most of the orders. Their histories are even less well-known than that of the B'nai B'rith. Their very number is conjectural. It appears that in 1913, their total membership exceeded 520,000 men and women who, together with their families, may have constituted well over a third of the Jews then living in America. See the list compiled by Alexander S. Kohanski in his "Fraternal Orders," *Universal Jewish Encyclopedia*, IV, 419-23; H. H. Leventhal's aforementioned Master's essay (*supra*, n. 98); and, more generally, Charles W. Ferguson, *Fifty Million Brothers: a Panorama of American Lodges and Clubs* (New York, 1937), which also includes a chapter on Jewish Fraternal Orders, pp. 247-62. On Jewish academic fraternities, see *infra*, n. 105.

101   *The Jewish Landsmanshaften in New York*, Prepared by the Yiddish Writers' Group of the Federal Writers' Project (New York, 1938); the general survey, "The Jewish Association in America," by Isaac Levitats in *Baron Jub. Vol.*, pp. 333-49; and Philip Friedman's bibliographical survey of "The Literature of Landsmanschaften in the United States in the Last Ten Years" (Yiddish), *Jewish Book Annual*, X (1951-52), 81-96. In this respect, too, Jews were, perhaps, only slightly more gregarious than other Americans. This subject would likewise merit further monographic treatment.

102   Avraham S. Sachs, *Di Geshikhte fun Arbeiter-Ring, 1892-1925*, 2 vols. (New York, 1925); Maximilian Hurwitz, *The Workmen's Circle: Its History, Ideals, Organizations and Institutions* (New York, 1936), and the collective volume, *Yidish Nationaler Arbeiter Ferband, 1910-1946* (History and Achievements: New York, 1946). See also the lists of the early New York branches of both organizations in *JCR*, pp. 871 ff., 961 ff. See also *supra*, Essay 3 n.

103   Francis Lieber's letter to Johann Kaspar Bluntschli in *Life and*

Letters of Francis Lieber, ed. by Thomas Sergeant Perry (Boston, 1882), p. 390. See also Albert H. Friedlander, "Cultural Contributions of the German Jews in America" and other essays in *Jews From Germany in the United States*, ed. by Eric E. Hirschler (New York, 1955).

104   The first six decades of the "Y" movement have been the subject of a fairly detailed historical monograph by Benjamin Rabinowitz in *The Young Men's Hebrew Associations (1854-1913)* (New York, 1948; reprinted from *PAJHS*, XXXVII), while the early history of the Jewish Welfare Board has been briefly described by Cyrus Adler in "The Jewish Welfare Board—Twenty Years Old," *AJYB*, XXXIX (1937-38), 149-77. See also Oscar I. Janowsky, *The JWB Survey*, with the Report of the JWB Survey Commission by Salo W. Baron and a Foreword by Frank L. Weil (New York, 1948), esp. pp. 47 ff. On the Educational Alliance see *infra*, n. 117.

105   See Maurice Jacobs, "Fraternities, Jewish," *Universal Jewish Encyclopedia*, IV, 423-25. There is no comprehensive history of the fraternal movement among the Jewish college students and professionals, although a good deal of material is accumulated in the official organs of the respective fraternities, such as the *ZBT Quarterly*.

106   Harold U. Ribalow, *The Jew in American Sports* (New York, 1959), esp. p. 9. No reference is made in this volume, however, to specific Jewish sporting associations.

107   Joseph Buchler, "The Struggle for Unity: Attempts at Union in American Jewish Life: 1654-1868," *AJA*, II (1949), 21-46 (summary of Diss. at Hebrew Union College, available in typescript); Max J. Kohler, "The Board of Delegates of American Israelites," *PAJHS*, XXIX (1925), 75-135; Allan Tarshish, "The Board of Delegates of American Israelites (1859-1878)," *ibid.*, XLIX (1959-60), 16-32 (summary of rabbinical thesis in typescript at the Hebrew Union College); idem, *The Rise of American Judaism* (Diss. Hebrew Union College; typescript). On the Union, see *infra*, n. 133.

108   See the *Proceedings* of the National Council of Jewish Women (New York, 1896 and the following years); the regular *Reports* of the Council; the early summary of "The Council of Jewish Women" published by Sadie American in *JE*, IV, 308-309; the more comprehensive description of *The First Fifty Years: the History of the National Council of Jewish Women, 1893-1943* (New York, 1943); and the autobiography of Hannah G. Solomon, *The Fabric of My Life* (New York, 1946).

109 Louis Marshall's letters to Stix and Magnes, ed. by C. Reznikoff in his *Louis Marshall*, I, 25, 33. See also the literature listed in the next note.

110 The annual *Reports* of the American Jewish Committee have regularly appeared in the *AJYB*, beginning with Vol. X (1908-1909). See also the brief "Review of the History of the American Jewish Committee," *ibid.*, XVIII (1916-17), 324-51; the somewhat fuller treatment by Nathan Schachner in *The Price of Liberty: a History of the American Jewish Committee* (New York, 1948); and the forthcoming comprehensive study by Naomi Wiener Cohen. On the Committee's early attitudes to Zionism, see *infra*, n. 149.

111 This compilation, some 1,600 pages long, appeared under the title, *Jewish Communal Register of New York, 1917-1918* (New York, 1918; here frequently quoted under the abbreviation, *JCR*). See also the brief summary, "The Jewish Community of New York City," *AJYB*, XI (1909-1910), 44-54; Norman Bentwich's biography of the *Kehillah's* chief protagonist, *For Zion's Sake: a Biography of Judah L. Magnes* (Philadelphia, 1954), pp. 76 ff.; and, more fully, Arthur Aryeh Goren, *The New York Kehillah, 1908-1922* (New York, 1970). On the Bureau of Education, see also *infra*, n. 122.

112 C. Reznikoff, *Louis Marshall*, I, 39 ff. See also David B. Goldberg, *Attitudes toward the New York Kehillah (Centralized Jewish Community Organization) as Reflected in the Yiddish and Anglo-Jewish Press of New York City, 1908-1913* (Master's thesis at the Graduate School of Jewish Social Work; New York, 1937; typescript).

113 Leon Huhner *et al.*, eds., "The Lyons Collection," *PAJHS*, XXVII (1920), esp. pp. 81 ff.; David de Sola Pool, *Portraits Etched in Stone: Early Jewish Settlers 1682-1831*, esp. pp. 160 f., 341 f., 432, 483 f.; idem and Tamar de Sola Pool, *An Old Faith in the New World: Portrait of Shearith Israel, 1654-1954*, pp. 214 ff.

114 See Charles S. Bernheimer, "Jewish Americanization Agencies," *AJYB*, XXIII (1921-22), 84-111; Isaac B. Berkson, *Theories of Americanization: a Critical Study; With Special Reference to the Jewish Group* (New York, 1920); and Mordecai Soltes, *The Yiddish Press, an Americanizing Agency* (New York, 1924) (both Columbia University dissertations); and, more generally, Edward George Hartmann, *The Movement to Americanize the Immigrant* (New York, 1948). This gradual transformation was clearly reflected in much of the contemporary fiction and auto-

biography such as the widely discussed novel *The Rise of David Levinsky* (New York, 1917) by Abraham Cahan, later editor of the Yiddish *Forverts*, and his own reminiscences in his *Bleter fun mein leben*, 5 vols. (New York, 1926-31). See also Cahan's earlier formulation of his novel, entitled "The Autobiography of an American Jew," *McClure's Magazine*, XL (1913), April, pp. 92-106; May, pp. 73-85; June, pp. 131-52; July, pp. 116-28; Moses Rischin, "Abraham Cahan and The New York Commercial Advertiser: a Study in Acculturation," *PAJHS*, XLIII (1953), 10-36; and Theodore Marvin Pollock's Columbia University dissertation, *The Solitary Clarinetist: a Critical Biography of Abraham Cahan, 1860-1917* (New York, 1959; typescript). Widely read and commented on also was Mary Antin's autobiography, *The Promised Land* (Boston, 1912).

115   See esp. Lillian Wald's own description of *The House on Henry Street* (New York, 1915); and the biographical study by Robert L. Duffus, *Lillian Wald, Neighbor and Crusader* (New York, 1938). From the outset the Settlement Houses evinced a strong interest in immigrants and served as Americanizing agencies. A national survey prepared in 1922 revealed that 283 of the reporting 307 houses, or some 92 percent, were located in immigrant neighborhoods. See Robert A. Wood and Albert J. Kennedy, *The Settlement Horizon* (New York, 1922), pp. 326, 329 f.

116   Hutchins Hapgood, *The Spirit of the Ghetto: Studies of the Jewish Quarter in New York* (New York, 1909; reprinted with Notes by Harry Golden, New York, 1965), pp. 33 ff. On Levias and Margolis and their conflict with Hebrew Union College, see *infra*, nn. 150 and 155.

117   S. Joseph, *History of the Baron de Hirsch Fund*, pp. 253 ff.; Educational Alliance, *Annual Reports*, 1893-1914; Miriam Blaustein, *Memoirs of David Blaustein* (New York, 1913); S. P. Rudens, "A Half Century of Community Service: the Story of the New York Educational Alliance," *AJYB*, XLVI (1944-45), 73-86. See, in particular, Morris Isaiah Berger's comprehensive analysis of *The Settlement, The Immigrant and The Public School: a Study of the Influence of the Settlement Movement and the New Migration Upon Public Education: 1890-1924* (Diss. Columbia University, 1956; typescript), with special reference to the Educational Alliance.

118   Samson Benderly, "The Problem of Jewish Education," an address delivered on Nov. 26, 1910 at the Achavah Club in New

York, and reproduced by Moshe Davis in his "Israel Fried-
lander's Minute Book at the *Achavah* Club," *Mordecai M.
Kaplan Jubilee Volume* (New York, 1953), pp. 188 f. (also
available in a Hebrew trans. in his *Beit Yisrael be-Amerikah,*
pp. 11 f.); and again by Lloyd P. Gartner, together with other
pertinent documents, in his *Jewish Education in the United
States: a Documentary History* (New York, 1969; Classics in
Education, XLI), pp. 127 ff.; Alexander M. Dushkin, *Jewish
Education in New York City* (New York, 1918; Diss. Columbia
University), esp. pp. 63 ff., 154 ff.; Israel Chipkin, "Twenty
Five Years of Jewish Education in the United States," *AJYB,*
XXXVIII (1936-37), 27-116 (also reprint); Leo L. Honor,
"Jewish Elementary Education in the United States (1901-
1950)," *PAJHS,* XLII (1952-53), 1-42; Menahem M. Edel-
stein, "History of the Development of a Jewish Teaching
Profession in America," *Jewish Education,* XXIII, No. 2 (1952),
pp. 45-53, 68; No. 3, pp. 34-48; XXV, No. 2 (1954), pp.
55-66; and, more generally, Leo L. Honor, "Jewish Education
in the United States," in *JP,* II, 151-71; and Zevi Scharfstein,
Toledot ha-ḥinnukh be-Yisrael be-dorot ha-aḥaronim (History of
Jewish Education in Modern Times), 2 vols. (New York, 1947),
esp. II, 155 ff.

119 A. M. Dushkin, *Jewish Education,* pp. 61, 469 ff. App. D. Among
the pioneer Jewish educators before the First World War was
Julius H. Greenstone of Philadelphia who, in 1907, prepared
*Statistical Data of the Jewish Religious Schools of Philadelphia
for 1906-1907* (Philadelphia, 1907); and followed it up two
years later by *Statistical Data of the Jewish Religious Schools
of Baltimore, Maryland, and Pittsburgh, Pennsylvania* (Philadelphia, 1909). A few years later Greenstone also offered a
general review of "Jewish Education in the United States,"
AJYB, XVI (1914-15), 90-127. The story of Jewish education in
other communities had to be painfully pieced together by later
investigators from a few extant sources. See, for instance, H.
Korey, "The Story of Jewish Education in Chicago Prior to
1923," *Jewish Education,* VI, No. 1 (1934), pp. 37-47; Barnett
R. Brickner, "The History of Jewish Education in Cincinnati,"
ibid., VIII, No. 3 (1936), pp. 115-26 (abridged chapter from
a more comprehensive study); Aaron Klein, "A History of Jewish
Education in Buffalo," *ibid.,* XIV, No. 1 (1942-43), pp. 28-32,
35 (digest of a Master's thesis); Nathan M. Kaganoff, "The
Education of the Jewish Child in the District of Columbia 1861-

1915," *ibid.*, XXIX No. 1 (1958-59), pp. 39-49 (summary of a Master's thesis at the Catholic University of America; typescript). Many other articles in *Jewish Education* and its Hebrew counterpart, the *Shebile ha-Ḥinukh*, likewise offer data for a general history of Jewish education in America including the period here under review which, when comprehensively analyzed, will help fill a major lacuna in the communal and cultural history of American Jewry. In the meantime see the literature listed *supra*, n. 118; Alexander M. Dushkin and Uriah Zvi Engelman, *Jewish Education in the United States* (New York, 1959); and, particularly, Judah Pilch and Meir Ben-Horin, eds., *Judaism and the Jewish School: Selected Essays on the Direction and Purpose of Jewish Education* (New York, 1966); and the documents reproduced by Lloyd P. Gartner in his *Jewish Education in the United States.*

120   See A. M. Dushkin, *Jewish Education*, pp. 68 ff., 472 ff. Apps. E and F; and Noah Nardi's brief review of "The Growth of Jewish Day Schools in America," *Jewish Education*, XX, No. 1 (1948), 23-32, covering the period from 1731 to 1948.

121   S. Yefroikin, "Yiddish Secular Schools in the United States," in *JP*, II, 144-50; A. M. Dushkin, *Jewish Education*, pp. 81 ff., 484 App. G. See also Noah Nardi, "A Study of Afternoon Hebrew Schools in the United States," *JSS*, VIII (1948), 57-74.

122   See especially *Fifty Years of the Hebrew Education Society in Philadelphia* (Philadelphia, 1899); Samson Benderly, "Aims and Activities of the Bureau of Education of the Jewish Community (Kehillah) of New York, 1912," reprinted in *Jewish Education*, XX, No. 3 (1949), pp. 92-112; and other essays by and on Benderly included in that issue dedicated to his memory; idem, "The Present Status of Jewish Religious Education in New York City," *JCR*, pp. 349-66; Alexander M. Dushkin, "Prefatory Notes on Jewish Educational Agencies of New York," *ibid.*, pp. 367-99 (includes a list of the existing schools); Israel Konowitz's pessimistic review of "The State of Hebrew Education in America" (Hebrew), *Luaḥ Aḥiasaf*, 1918, pp. 431-65; and Israel Friedlander's judicious discussion of "The Problem of Jewish Education in America," in his *Past and Present* (Cincinnati, 1919), pp. 279-308. An interesting earlier review of the disorganized Jewish education in the 1880s was offered by M. Weinberger in *Ha-Yehudim ve-ha-yahadut be-New York* (Jews and Judaism in New York; New York, 1887). See also Abraham P. Gannes, *Central Community Agencies for Jewish Education* (Philadelphia, 1954; Dropsie College diss.). The

historic background of the ideological and conceptual differences underlying much of that educational diversity is analyzed by Emanuel Gamoran in his *Changing Conceptions in Jewish Education* (New York, 1925).

123 See Samuel Dinin, "Twenty-Five Years of Teacher Training," *Jewish Education*, VII, No. 1 (1935), pp. 25-33; and M. M. Edelstein's essay cited *supra*, n. 118. Of great interest also are the essays, ed. by Oscar I. Janowsky in *The Education of American Jewish Teachers* (Boston, 1967); and Samuel M. Blumenfield, *Ḥevrah ve-ḥinnukh be-yahadut Ameriqah* (Community and Education in American Jewry; Jerusalem, 1965) which, though mainly oriented toward contemporary problems, also sheds light on earlier developments.

124 *Jewish Messenger*, XXIII, No. 25 (1868), p. 4; and other data analyzed by Bertram Wallace Korn in "The First American Jewish Theological Seminary: Maimonides College, 1867-1873," reprinted in his collection of essays entitled, *Eventful Years and Experiences*, I, 151-213 (includes the story of, and documentation for, the earlier projects as well). On the other hand, M. M. Noah's appeal for a Jewish college in 1843, really aimed at the establishment of an "academy" on a primary and secondary level. See his letter to the *Occident*, I (1843), 301-307, reprinted in "The Call for a Hebrew College, 1843," *AJA*, XII (1960), 143-49.

125 See Gilbert Klaperman, *The Story of Yeshiva University, the First Jewish University* (New York, 1969). See also the briefer earlier reviews by Jacob I. Hartstein, "The Yeshivah Looks Back Over Fifty Years," *Jewish Education*, IX, No. 2 (1937), pp. 53-57; idem, "Yeshiva University (Growth of Rabbi Isaac Elchanan Theological Seminary)," *AJYB*, XLVIII (1946-47), 73-84. There is no similar comprehensive study of any other Jewish institution of higher learning and our knowledge is limited to certain general surveys and particularly to the biographies of leaders. See especially David Philipson, *History of the Hebrew Union College* (Cincinnati, 1925; reprinted from *Hebrew Union College Jubilee Volume*, pp. 1-70); Samuel S. Cohon, "The History of the Hebrew Union College," *PAJHS*, XL (1950-51), 17-55; Cyrus Adler, *The Jewish Theological Seminary of America* (New York, 1939); Max B. May, *Isaac Mayer Wise: the Founder of American Judaism, A Biography* (New York, 1916); Israel Knox, *Rabbi in America: Story of Isaac M. Wise* (Boston, 1957); Norman Bentwich, *Solomon Schechter, A Biography* (New York,

1938); Cyrus Adler, *I Have Considered the Days* (Philadelphia, 1943; an autobiography). Understandably, Adler also frequently refers to another Jewish school of higher learning, Dropsie College, which he helped to found in Philadelphia. See also Herbert Parzen, "New Data on the Formation of Dropsie College," *JSS*, XXVIII (1966), 131-47. Hebrew studies were also cultivated in non-Jewish schools of higher learning, particularly theological seminaries and Semitic departments of universities. See *supra*, Essay 6; and *infra*, n. 140.

126 Cyrus Adler, "Jacob Henry Schiff, a Biographical Sketch," *AJYB*, XXIII (1921-22), 21-64, esp. pp. 36 ff.; idem, *Jacob H. Schiff*, I, 3 ff.; II, 44 ff. Judah D. Eisenstein testified that he had seen Schiff on the *Jahrzeits* of his parents regularly attend services at the Orthodox Beth Hamedrash Hagodol. See Eisenstein's *Oṣar Zikhronotai* (Memoirs; New York, 1930), pp. 24 f. On Schiff's relations to the Jewish Theological Seminary see Moshe Davis, *Yahadut Ameriqah be-hitpathutah*: The Shaping of American Judaism (New York, 1951), esp. pp. 243 ff., 286 f.

127 U. Z. Engelman, "Jewish Statistics," *JSS*, IX, 134 ff. Some aspects of the Jewish religious situation may be explained by the growing concentration of Jews in the largest cities. On this aspect see the parallel, but also different, developments in the Catholic Church which were analyzed by F. Houtat in his *Aspects sociologiques du catholicisme américain. Vie urbaine et institutions religieuses* (Paris, 1957). See also Moshe Davis's general review of *Jewish Religious Life and Institutions in America: an Historical Study* (Tel Aviv, 1953).

128 The Pittsburgh Proceedings, reported in the *Jewish Reformer* of January 15, 1886 and reproduced by David Philipson in *The Reform Movement in Judaism*, new and revised ed. (New York, 1931), pp. 355 ff. Much information can be gathered also from the works by and on the leading Reformers. See especially: (1) David Einhorn, *Ausgewählte Predigten und Reden*, ed. by Kaufmann Kohler (New York, 1881); his monthly, *Sinai* (in German, 1856-62); Kaufmann Kohler, ed., *David Einhorn's Memorial Volume: Selected Sermons and Addresses* with a Biographical Sketch by K. K. and a Memorial Oration by Emil G. Hirsch (New York, 1911); and Kohler, "David Einhorn, the Uncompromising Champion of Reform Judaism: a Biographical Essay," *YCCAR*, XIX (1909), 215-70; (2) David Philipson, *Max Lilienthal, American Rabbi: Life and Writings* (New York, 1915), supplemented by Hyman B. Grinstein, "The Minute

Book of Lilienthal's Union of German Synagogues in New York,"
Hebrew Union College Annual, XVIII (1943-44), 321-52; (3)
Samuel Adler, *Jewish Conference Papers* (New York, 1880);
idem, *Qobeṣ 'al Yad. Sammlung einiger in Zeitschriften zerstreu-
ten wissenschaftlichen Artikel* (New York, 1898); Joseph Silver-
man, "Samuel Adler," YCCAR, XIX (1909), 415-23; (4)
Bernard Felsenthal, *Jüdische Fragen* (Chicago, 1896); idem,
The Beginnings of the Chicago Sinai Congregation (Chicago,
1899); Emma Felsenthal, *Bernard Felsenthal, Teacher in Israel*
(New York, 1944); (5) Isaac M. Wise, *Reminiscences*, ed. by
David Philipson (Cincinnati, 1901); idem, *Selected Writings*,
ed. Philipson and Louis Grossman (Cincinnati, 1900); May's
and Knox's aforementioned biographies; (6) Ella M. Mielziner,
Moses Mielziner (New York, 1931); (7) Richard Gottheil, *The
Life of Gustav Gottheil: Memoir of a Priest in Israel* (Williamsport, Pa., 1936); (8) Kaufmann Kohler, *Hebrew Union College
and Other Addresses* (Cincinnati, 1916); idem, *Studies, Addresses and Personal Papers* (New York, 1931; includes essays on
"The Faith of Reform Judaism," pp. 320 ff.: "What Does the
Hebrew Union College Stand For?" pp. 439 ff; and "Personal
Reminiscences," pp. 469 ff.); *Studies in Jewish Literature, Issued
in [K. Kohler's] Honor* (Berlin, 1913; includes a biographical
sketch by Max J. Kohler and a bibliography of Kohler's writings
by Adolph S. Oko); Hyman G. Enelow's obituary of "Kaufmann
Kohler," *AJYB*, XXVIII (1926-27), 235-60; (9) Bernard Martin, "The Religious Philosophy of Emil G. Hirsch," *AJA*, IV
(1952), 66-82; idem, "The Social Philosophy of E. G. H.," *ibid.*,
VI (1954), 151-65; (10) David Philipson, *My Life as an American Jew: an Autobiography* (New York, 1941). There is, of
course, a mass of additional biographical, homiletic, and publicist material pertaining to the Reform movement before 1914,
particularly anniversary issues of various congregations (see *supra*,
n. 88) but this is not the place to present a comprehensive
bibliography.

129 Emil G. Hirsch, *My Religion*, Compilation and Biographical Introduction by Gerson B. Levi (New York, 1925), p. 294. See
also, for example, Hyman B. Grinstein, "Reforms at Temple
Emanuel of New York, 1860-1890," *Historia Judaica*, VI (1944),
163-74.

130 See especially the debates summarized in YCCAR, *passim*. In
time even the certificate of conversion came under discussion
and its form had to be prepared by a special Conference com-

mittee. *Ibid.*, XX (1910), 65 ff., 106 ff.; XXI (1911), 29, 63. The difficulties of the Reform position may readily be understood in the light of the old nexus between assimilation and Emancipation and between the latter and the Reform movement, the honest reservations by Abraham Geiger and others notwithstanding. For one example, Rabbi Max Landsberg of Rochester who, in 1894, was to deliver the Conference sermon on "The Duties of the Rabbi in the Present Time," had some twenty years earlier declared, "Non-Jewish brethren can come here [to his synagogue] and hear us pray and be surprised at how little difference there is between them" and the Jews. *Ibid.*, II-IV (1892-95), 121-30; Stuart Rosenberg, *The Jewish Community in Rochester*, p. 91; and, more generally, my *SRH*, 1st ed., II, 249 f.

131 Ephraim Feldman, "Intermarriage Historically Considered," YCCAR, XIX (1909), 271-307; and the debate between Samuel Schulman and his colleagues, *ibid.*, pp. 308-35. See also the succinct analyses by Beryl Harold Levy in his *Reform Judaism in America: a Study in Religious Adaptation* (New York, 1933; Columbia University diss.), pp. 86 ff.

132 Jacob Voorsanger, "The Sabbath Question," YCCAR, XII (1902), 103-123, followed by a lengthy discussion, *ibid.*, pp. 123-52; XIII (1903), 96-101, 138-71; Kaufmann Kohler, *Jewish Theology, Systematically and Historically Considered* (New York, 1918; also in the new impression with an Intro. by Joseph L. Blau [New York, 1968]), p. 459. These debates, too, are briefly reviewed in Beryl Harold Levy's *Reform Judaism in America*, pp. 92 ff. See also, more broadly, Joseph L. Blau, "The Spiritual Life of American Jewry 1654-1954," *AJYB*, LVI (1954-55), 99-170; idem, *Modern Varieties of Judaism* (New York, 1966; Lectures on the History of Religion. Sponsored by the American Council of Learned Societies, VIII). One must not overlook in this context the unrelenting pressure of the Reform laity which sought as close a rapprochement as possible with its Gentile neighbors. Typical of its attitude is the praise showered in 1874 by the trustees of the Cleveland congregation Tifereth Israel upon its departing rabbi, Jacob Mayer, who "by his liberal views regarding the Jewish religion . . . [had] elevated Judaism in the eyes of our Christian fellow citizens and removed, to a great extent, the barriers of prejudice." See the report in the *Jewish Times*, VI (1874), 407.

133 Report from a trip through the State of Iowa published in the

American Israelite of May 30, 1895 reproduced by Frank Rosenthal in the *Jews of Des Moines: the First Century* with an Intro. by William D. Houlette (Des Moines, Iowa, 1957), pp. 43 ff. The fullest information on these interrelated organizations is available in the respective *Year Books* of the Union and the Central Conference. A general review of the latter's activities during the first twenty-five years was submitted by David Philipson in his "The Principles and Achievements of the Central Conference of American Rabbis," YCCAR, XXIV (1914), 191-223, followed by a "Symposium," *ibid.*, pp. 224-45. A brief history of these organizations in their formative period is presented by Allan Tarshish in *The Rise of American Judaism: a History of American Jewish Life from 1848-1881* (Diss. Hebrew Union College; Cincinnati, 1938; typescript). Much material on the Reform movement and its institutions in the latter part of the nineteenth century has also been assembled by Moshe Davis in his *Yahadut Amerika, passim.* On the *Union Prayer Book*, its antecedents and subsequent revisions, see YCCAR, III-IV, *passim;* XXIV (1914), 125 f., etc.; B. H. Levy, *Reform Judaism*, pp. 38 ff.; and, on Rabbi Gries's opposition, see the unpublished minutes of the Tifereth Israel Congregation in Cleveland. See also Leonard J. Mervis, "The Social Justice Movement and the American Reform Rabbi," *AJA*, VII (1955), 171-230 (summary of diss. at the University of Pittsburgh; typescript).

134 E. J. James *et al.*, *The Immigrant Jew in America*, p. 174.

135 No history of these Orthodox groups is as yet available. Even the primary sources consisting in reports of the major organizations have not always appeared in print and are often inaccessible. A good scholarly analysis of their activities would certainly help fill a major lacuna in the history of the American Jewish community. See, however, the publications listed *infra*, n. 138.

136 D. Philipson, *Max Lilienthal*, p. 51; Isaac Leeser, "Rabbinical Authority," *The Occident*, XXIII (1865-66), 193-203; Judah D. Eisenstein, "The History of the First Russian-American Jewish Congregation: the Beth Hamedrosh Hagodol," *PAJHS*, IX (1901), 63-74.

137 Moses Weinberger, *Ha-Yehudim ve-ha-yahadut, passim;* Judah D. Eisenstein, "A History of the Association of American Orthodox Hebrew Congregations" (Hebrew), *Ner ha-Ma'arabi*, I, Nos. 11-12 (1897), pp. 1-28, 41-47; and the biographical sketches of the respective candidates in Benzion Eisenstadt, *Dor,*

rabbanav ve-soferav, 4 vols. (Warsaw, 1895-Vilna, 1902). The story of these negotiations is fully analyzed by Abraham J. Karp in his "New York Chooses a Chief Rabbi," *PAJHS*, XLIV (1954-55), 129-98, also reproducing in the Appendix (pp. 188 ff.) several documents, including the certificate of incorporation of the Association, cited in our text. On Levinthal, see the jubilee volume, *Kebod ḥakhamim*, published on his seventieth birthday in Philadelphia, 1935.

138 See especially the autobiographical accounts by Z. H. Maslian-sky, *Zichroines: Fuftzig yor lebn un kempfen* (New York, 1924); Bernard Drachman, *The Unfailing Light: Memoirs of an American Rabbi*, with an Intro. and Notes by the editor [Julian Moses Drachman] (New York, 1948); Israel Shapiro, "Ephraim Dein-ard," *PAJHS*, XXXIV (1937), 149-63; and Benzion Eisenstadt's comprehensive *Sefer Dorot ha-aḥaronim: a Biographical Diction-ary of Orthodox Leaders of Recent Generations*, 2 parts (Brook-lyn, 1937-40). Emanuel Rackman's succinct review of "Ameri-can Orthodoxy: Retrospect and Prospect" in *Jewish Life in America*, ed. by Theodore Friedman and Robert Gordis (New York, 1955), pp. 23-36, deals mainly with the situation in the mid-twentieth century.

139 Alexander Kohut, *Ethics of the Fathers*, translated into English by Max Cohen and edited by Barnett A. Elzas (New York, 1920); Kaufmann Kohler, *Backwards or Forwards* (New York, 1885). On this debate see especially Moshe Davis, *Yahadut Amerika*, pp. 233 ff.; and B. H. Levy, *Reform Judaism*, pp. 57 ff. Davis also offers detailed biographical sketches with extensive biographical documentation on Morais, Szold, Jastrow, Pereira Mendes, and quite a few others, pp. 38 ff. See also his "Sabato Morais: a Selected and Annotated Bibliography of His Writ-ings," *PAJHS*, XXXVII (1947-48), 55-93; William Rosenau, *Benjamin Szold* (Baltimore, 1902); Alexandra Lee Levin, *The Szolds of Lombard Street: a Baltimore Family, 1859-1909* (Philadelphia, 1960); and David de Sola Pool, *H. Pereira Mendes* (New York, 1938). Interesting data on Kohut are available also in his wife's, Rebekah Kohut's, autobiographical *My Portion* (New York, 1925); and in the essays included in *Semitic Studies in Memory of Alexander Kohut*, ed. by his son, George A. Kohut (Berlin, 1897).

140 Solomon Schechter, *Seminary Addresses and Other Papers* (Cin-cinnati, 1915), esp. pp. 195 ff., 239 ff. Interesting light on Schechter's dedication to scholarly pursuits is also shed by his

Iggerot (Epistles) to Samuel Abraham Poznanski, ed. from his autographs by Abraham Yaari (Jerusalem, 1943); and Meir Ben-Horin's ed. of "Solomon Schechter to Judge Mayer Sulzberger. Part I: Letters from the Pre-Seminary Period (1895-1901); Part II: Letters from the Seminary Period (1902-1915)," *JSS*, XXV (1963), 249-86; XXVII (1965), 75-102; and "Supplement" thereto, *ibid.*, XXX (1968), 262-71.

141   The United Synagogue of America, *Constitution* in its *Report* of 1913, p. 9; and the data assembled by N. Bentwich in his biography of *Solomon Schechter*, esp. pp. 198 ff., 281 ff. Needless to say, even during Schechter's lifetime the Conservative movement was not a monolithic body. Many of its leaders diverged in both theological views and ritual practices. These divergences became more pronounced after Schechter's death in 1915. Yet the movement has retained its basic continuity because of its great pliability and the very refusal to spell out in detail its doctrines and observances. Hence a sociological study by Marshall Sklare of *Conservative Judaism: an American Religious Movement* (Glencoe, Ill., 1955; originally Diss. Columbia University) sheds a good deal of light also on the social background on that movement's formative years before 1914. See also the succinct review of "Jewish Tradition in 20th Century America: The Conservative Approach," by Theodore Friedman in *Jewish Life in America*, ed. by him and R. Gordis, pp. 37-53. It should also be noted that after the First World War an offshoot of Conservative Judaism was founded by Mordecai M. Kaplan and associates under the designation of the Reconstructionist Movement. See esp. Kaplan's *Judaism as a Civilization* (New York, 1934); and *The Future of the American Jew* (New York, 1948).

142   Joseph Saul Nathanson, *Sho'el u-Meshib* (Responsa), 3 vols. (Lwów, 1865-79), III, No. 72; Jacob Ettlinger, *Binyan Siyyon* (Responsa, Altona, 1868), fol. 28, No. 63, both cited with an English summary by Mendel Silber in his *America in Hebrew Literature* (New Orleans, 1928), Hebrew section, pp. 61 ff.; English section, p. 34; the reports in the European press cited by Jacob R. Marcus in "European Bibliographical Items in Chicago" in the *Chicago Pinkas*, ed. by S. Rawidowicz, pp. 177-95, esp. *s.v.* Tolerance.

143   See Max Eisen, "Christian Missions to the Jews in North America and Great Britain," *JSS*, X (1948), 31-66; David Max Eichhorn, *A History of Christian Attempts to Convert the Jews*

of the United States and Canada (Diss. Hebrew Union College, Cincinnati; typescript). See also such autobiographical accounts of converts as Edward A. Steiner's *From Alien to Citizen* (New York, 1914); or Samuel Freuder's *My Return to Judaism* (New York, 1922); Ira O. Glick, "The Hebrew Christians: a Marginal Religious Group," in Marshall Sklare, ed., *The Jews: Social Patterns of an American Group* (Glencoe, Ill., 1958); and, more generally, Clarice Edwin Silcox and Galen M. Fisher, *Catholics, Jews and Protestants: a Study of Relationships in the United States and Canada* (New York, 1934), which also sheds some light on conditions two or three decades earlier; Gustavus Myers, *History of Bigotry in the United States* (New York, 1943); and *supra*, n. 68.

144 This statement is reproduced in Schechter's *Seminary Addresses*, pp. 91 ff. See also Norman Bentwich's fairly full analysis of Schechter's long hesitant attitude in his *Solomon Schechter*, pp. 309 ff.; and, more generally, Herbert Parzen's analysis of the relations between "Conservative Judaism and Zionism (1903-1922)," paper submitted to the *Second Conference on the History of Zionism in America*, sponsored by the Theodor Herzl Institute in New York, 1957 (typescript).

145 See the informative essays assembled in the *Early History of Zionism in America*, ed. by Isidore S. Meyer (New York, 1958), especially "The Zionism of Warder Cresson" by Abraham J. Karp (pp. 1-20); "Palestine in the Literature of the United States to 1867" by Samuel H. Levine (pp. 21-38); "The American Press and Restoration during the Nineteenth Century" by Milton Plesur (pp. 55-76); "Emma Lazarus and Pre-Herzlian Zionism" by Arthur Zeiger (pp. 77-108); and "Zionism Comes to Chicago" by Anita Libman Lebeson (pp. 155-90). The latter refers also to a privately printed biographical study by Beth M. Limberg, *A God-filled Life: the Story of William E. Blackstone* (Chicago, n.d.). On "Zionism and the Mormon Church" see the data assembled by Eldin Ricks in his paper submitted to the *Second Conference* of the Herzl Institute (typescript). See also, more generally, Rudolf Glanz, *Jew and Mormon: Historic Group Relations and Religious Outlook* (New York, 1968); and Leon L. Watters, *The Pioneer Jews of Utah.*

146 See especially David de Sola Pool, "Early Relations between Palestine and American Jewry," *The Brandeis Avukah Annual of 1932*, ed. by Joseph Shalom Shubow (New York, 1932), pp. 536-48; *supra*, Essay 9; Leon Huhner, *The Life of Judah Touro*

(*1775-1854*) (Philadelphia, 1946), pp. 123 f., 133 f.; and, more generally, Abraham Yaari's aforementioned *Sheluḥe Ereṣ Yisrael*. See also Myer S. Isaacs, "Sampson Simson," *PAJHS*, X (1902), 109-17, esp. pp. 114 f.

147 See Shlomo Noble, "Pre-Herzlian Zionism in America as Reflected in the Yiddish Press" in I. S. Meyer's *Early History*, pp. 39-54. Interesting material was assembled by one of the active members of this movement, Dr. Joseph Isaac Bluestone. See Hyman B. Grinstein, "The Memoirs and Scrapbooks of the late Dr. Joseph Isaac Bluestone of New York City," *PAJHS*, XXXV (1939), 53-64; and Abraham Goldberg, "American Zionism up to the Brandeis Era: a Chronicle of Its Early Development," *The Brandeis Avukah Annual*, ed. by Shubow, pp. 549-75. See also Marnin Feinstein's comprehensive study of *American Zionism, 1884-1904* (New York, 1965; a revised Columbia University dissertation); and Avyatar Friesel's more recent monograph, cited *supra*, Essay 3 n.

148 See Joseph Tabachnik's brief "Report on the American-Jewish Reaction to the First Zionist Congress," and Milton Plesur's "Zionism in the General Press, 1897-1914: From Basle to Sarajevo," both submitted to the *Second Conference* of the Herzl Institute (*supra*, n. 144); Herbert Parzen's general review of "The Federation of American Zionists (1897-1914)" in *Early History*, edited by Meyer, pp 245-74; C. Bezalel Sherman, "The Beginnings of Labor Zionism in the United States," *ibid.*, pp. 275-88; Hyman B. Grinstein, "Orthodox Judaism and Early Zionism in America," *ibid.*, pp. 219-27; Baruch Zuckerman, "The Zionist-Socialist Movement" (Yiddish) in *Gewerkschaften*, ed. by H. Lang and M. G. Feinstone, pp. 155-68, esp. pp. 161 ff.; and, more fully, Samuel Rosenblatt, *The History of the Mizrachi Movement* (New York, 1951); L. Spyzman *et al.*, *Geshikhte fun der tsiyonishtisher arbeiter bavegung in Tsofn Amerike* (A History of the Zionist Labor Movement in North America), 2 vols. (New York, 1955). Gradually some of these movements also developed youth groups of their own. See Samuel Grand, *A History of Zionist Youth Organizations in the United States from Their Inception to 1940* (New York, 1958; Diss. Columbia University; typescript). Much informative material is preserved in the journals published by these factions, as well as in the biographical or autobiographical records of some of the leaders. See especially the aforementioned biographies of Felsenthal, Gustav Gottheil, and Schechter (*supra*, nn. 128, 141 and 144);

Stephen S. Wise, *Challenging Years: the Autobiography* (New York, 1949); Bernard Horwich, *My First Eighty Years* (Chicago, 1939); and Louis Lipsky, *Thirty Years of American Zionism* (New York, 1927). Additional bibliographical material is readily available in Moses Rischin, *An Inventory of American Jewish History*, pp. 3 n. 3, 54 n. 70.

149 See esp. Moshe Perlmann, "Paul Haupt and the Mesopotamian Project, 1892-1914," *PAJHS*, XLVII (1957-58), 154-75, with reference to Haupt's *Über die Ansiedlung der russischen Juden im Euphrat und Tigrisgebiete; ein Vorschlag*, published in Baltimore, 1892; Naomi W. Cohen, "The Maccabaean's Message: a Study in American Zionism Until World War I," *JSS*, XVIII (1956), 163-78; Rose G. Jacobs, "Beginnings of Hadassah," *Early History*, ed. by I. S. Meyer, pp. 228-44. See also Marvin Lowenthal, *Henrietta Szold: Life and Letters* (New York, 1942); Rose Zeitlin, *Henrietta Szold: Record of a Life* (New York, 1952; see also *supra*, n. 139); Ber Borochov, *Nationalism and the Class Struggle* (New York, 1937); Nachman Syrkin, *Essays* (Yiddish), 2 vols. (New York, 1925-26); and, more generally, Arthur Hertzberg, *The Zionist Idea: a Historical Analysis and Reader* (New York, 1959; also paperback), especially pp. 329 ff., 440 ff., 494 ff. Before 1914, it may be noted, the American Jewish Committee took no official stand on Zionism, although it had to reject in 1912 the reservation of the Federation of American Zionists that, in affiliating with the Committee, the latter could not be bound by any decisions opposed to the policies of the international Zionist organization. See Moses Rischin, "American Jewish Committee and Zionism (1906-22)," *PAJHS*, XLIX (1959-60), 188-201. An interesting combination of Zionism, or rather territorialism, with social reform of Henry George's variety was represented by Joseph Fels, a well-known soap manufacturer and philanthropist who spontaneously offered Israel Zangwill $100,000 for a Jewish colony established on a single-tax basis. See Arthur P. Dudden, "The Single-Tax Zionism of Joseph Fels," *PAJHS*, XLVI (1956-57), 474-91; and the full-length biography of *Joseph Fels: His Life and Work*, by his wife and ardent collaborator, Mary Fels (New York, 1916).

150 Naomi Wiener Cohen, "The Reaction of Reform Judaism in America to Political Zionism (1897-1922)," *PAJHS*, XL (1950-1951), 361-94 (a summary of a Columbia University Master's essay in typescript); Melvin Weinman, "The Attitude of Isaac

Mayer Wise toward Zionism and Palestine," *AJA*, III, Part 2 (1951), 3-23 (summary of a rabbinical thesis at Hebrew Union College; typescript); and the additional data assembled, with somewhat contradictory interpretations, by Joseph P. Sternstein in his "Attitude of Reform Judaism toward Zionism as Evinced in the 'American Israelite' 1895-1904," and by Herschel Levin in "The Other Side of the Coin," papers delivered at the afore-mentioned *Second Conference* of the Herzl Institute. On the controversial background of the resignation of Margolis, Malter and Schloessinger from the faculty of Hebrew Union College in 1907, see the literature cited by Robert Gordis in his bio-graphical introduction to the volume, *Max Leopold Margolis: Scholar and Teacher*, ed. by him (Philadelphia, 1952), p. 6 n. 2. On the attitude of Conservative Judaism to Zionism, see *supra*, n. 144. No comparable study for the Orthodox atti-tudes, particularly those of the opposition, is as yet available.

151 Chaim Zhitlowsky, "A Jew to Jews," reproduced in Yiddish in his *Gezamelte Shriften*, 10 vols. (New York, 1912-19), esp. Vol. VI; idem, *Zichroines fun mein leben* (Memoirs), Vols. I-III (New York, 1935-40); Nathan Birnbaum's New York lec-tures of 1908 reported in *The Maccabaean*, XIV (1908), 75 (see N. W. Cohen in *JSS*, XVIII, 173); Oscar I. Janowsky, *The Jews and Minority Rights* (New York, 1933; Diss. Colum-bia University), esp. pp. 62 ff.; Simon M. Dubnow's Yiddish review of my *SRH*, 1st ed., in *Di Zukunft*, XLII (1937), 765-768.

152 Most of the data are available in the Society's *Reports* annually published in *AJYB*. A good bibliographical review of its pub-lications has been compiled by Joshua Bloch in his *Of Making Many Books: an Annotated List of the Books Issued by the Jewish Publication Society of America, 1890-1952* (Philadelphia, 1953). Beyond the confines of that Society see some of Amer-ica's rarer books included in the "tricentennial" exhibition at the New York Public Library of October to December 1954 and described by Joshua Bloch in *The People and the Book: the Background of Three Hundred Years of Jewish Life in America* (New York, 1954).

153 See the successive volumes of *PAJHS*, and particularly Vol. I of which a second edition appeared in 1905. See also John J. Appel's suggestive study of "Hansen's Third Generation 'Law' and the Origins of the American Jewish Historical Society," *JSS*, XXIII (1961), 3-20.

154 See the informative introduction to Volume I of *JE*. The full story of the *Encyclopedia* still remains to be written, however.

155 See Ephraim Deinard, *Kohelet Amerika* (An American Hebrew Bibliography; New York, 1926). As in his other writings, Deinard injected here many polemics against contemporary writers and was, in general, quite pessimistic in his evaluation of the state of Jewish scholarship in the country. On his other writings, which despite their bias shed considerable light on the cultural developments of American Jewry before and soon after the First World War, see Israel Schapiro's succinct observations in *PAJHS*, XXXIV (1937), 149-63. Apart from the aforementioned biographical studies of Kohut, Kohler, and Schechter, see also the obituaries of Henry Malter by Alexander Marx in *AJYB*, XXVIII (1926-27), 261-72; of Benzion Halper by Cyrus Adler, *ibid.*, XXVI (1924-25), 459-71; Max L. Margolis by Adler, *ibid.*, XXXV (1933-34), 139-44; Richard J. H. Gottheil, by Louis I. Newman, *ibid.*, XXXIX (1937-38), 29-46; Israel Davidson by Louis Finkelstein, *ibid.*, XLI (1939-40), 35-56; Cyrus Adler by Abraham A. Neuman, *ibid.*, XLII (1940-41), 23-144; as well as Carrie Davidson, *Out of Endless Yearnings: a Memoir of Israel Davidson* (New York, 1946); the aforementioned memorial volume for *Max Leopold Margolis*, ed. by R. Gordis; and the jubilee volumes in honor of Louis Ginzberg, Alexander Marx, and Mordecai M. Kaplan published respectively in New York 1945, 1950, and 1953. See also Ismar Elbogen, "American Jewish Scholarship: a Survey," *AJYB*, XLV (1943), 47-65; Joshua Trachtenberg, "American Jewish Scholarship," *JP*, IV, 411-55; and Guido Kisch, "The Founders of 'Wissenschaft des Judentums' and America," *Essays in American Jewish History*, pp. 147-70.

156 There is no comprehensive history of American Jewish journalism, especially in the vernacular languages. Brief reviews are included in the respective encyclopedias, particularly under the entry "Periodicals." See *JE*, IX, 602-40; and the *Universal Jewish Encyclopedia*, VIII, 437-57. See also A. A. Roback, "The Anglo-Jewish Press in America" (Yiddish), *YB*, II (1931), 85-95; and the rich data recorded by a leading Anglo-Jewish publicist, Philip Cowen in his *Memoirs of an American Jew* (New York, 1922). On Jews in the general American press, see *infra*, n. 166.

157 A comprehensive bibliography is available in F. M. Brody, "The Hebrew Periodical Press in America in 1871-1931: a Bibliographical Survey," *PAJHS*, XXXIII (1934), 127-70. Unfor-

tunately, a number of bibliographical questions are still moot, especially since the very preservation of many Hebrew journals leaves much to be desired. There also is a dearth of monographic literature on individual publications such as Moshe Davis's study of *"Ha-Zofeh ba-Arez ha-Ḥadashah:* a Source for the History of East-European Jews in America" (Hebrew) in *Alexander Marx Jubilee Volume,* 2 vols. (New York, 1950), Hebrew vol., pp. 115-41. See the brief review of "Seventy-Five Years of The Hebrew Press in America" (Hebrew) by A. R. Malachi in *Sefer ha-Shanah* (American Hebrew Yearbook), VIII-IX (1947), 662-76. Much can also be learned from the more extensive literature on the history of the Yiddish press in the United States, on which see *infra,* nn. 162-63. See also the more general review by J. Lin, *Die hebräische Presse. Werdegang und Entwicklungstendenzen* (Berlin, 1928; Schriften der jüdischen Sonderschau der Pressa).

158 No comprehensive history of Hebrew literature in America has as yet been written. But the basic data are readily available in Abraham Epstein's *Soferim 'ibrim be-Ameriqah* (Hebrew Writers in America; New York, 1952); and in Meyer Waxman's *A History of Jewish Literature. From the Close of the Bible to Our Own Day,* 5 vols., revised ed. (New York, 1960), Vols. IV-V. More detailed bibliographical data were assembled in E. Deinard's *Kohelet Ameriqah.* A number of critical evaluations were published by contemporaries such as Bernard Drachman in his "Neo-Hebraic Literature in America," *Proceedings* of the Biennial Convention of the Jewish Theological Seminary Association (New York, 1900), pp. 53-139; Mordecai Z. Raizin, "The Hebrew Language and Literature in America" (Hebrew), *Ha-Shiloaḥ,* VIII (1901), 175-80; Daniel Persky, "The Story of Our New [Hebrew] Literature in America" (Hebrew), *Sefer ha-Yobel shel Hadoar* (Hadoar Jubilee Volume), ed. by Menaḥem Ribalow (New York, 1927), pp. 323-52; and Eisig Silberschlag, "Recent Trends in Hebrew Literature," *JSS,* II (1940), 3-22; idem, "Hebrew Literature in America: Record and Interpretation," *Jewish Quarterly Review,* XLV (1955), 413-33. See also A. R. Malachi, "The Beginnings of Hebrew Poetry in America" (Hebrew), *Sefer ha-Shanah* (American Hebrew Yearbook), II (1935), 296-311; and Jacob Kabacoff's general survey of "Hebrew Culture and Creativity in America" in *Jewish Life in America,* ed. by T. Friedman and R. Gordis, pp. 170-96. Of interest also is Max Raisin's *Dappim mi-pinkaso*

shel 'Rabbi' (Leaves from a Rabbi's Notebook; contains autobiographical and other essays; Brooklyn, 1941); and Ephraim E. Lisitzky's autobiography, *Eleh Toledot Adam,* or in the English trans. by Moshe Kohn and Jacob Sloan, entitled *The Grip of Cross Currents* (New York, 1959).

159 Bernard Drachman in *Proceedings* (see n. 158), p. 69; Edward Yehezkiel Kutscher, "The Role of Modern Hebrew in the Development of Jewish-Israeli National Consciousness," *Publications* of the Modern Language Association of America, Supplements, LXXII, No. 2 (1957), pp. 38-42; Nathan Goldberg, "The Jewish Book in the Public Libraries" (Hebrew), *Sefer ha-Shanah* (American Hebrew Yearbook), VI (1942), 462-73; and the two informative listings in *JCR:* Zevi Scharfstein, "Hebrew-Speaking Clubs in America" (pp. 564-71); Reuben Brainin, "The Hebraic Movement in America and the Histadruth Ibrith in New York" (pp. 1214-20). See also the succinct analyses by Eisig Silberschlag, "Zionism and Hebraism in America (1897-1921)" in *Early History of Zionism,* ed. by I. S. Meyer, pp. 326-40; and by David Mirsky, "Hebrew in the United States: 1900-1920" in *Second Conference* of the Herzl Institute (typescript). On the progress of Hebrew Education, see *supra,* nn. 119 ff.

160 Some intimate glimpses on these early pioneering efforts are given in Sarasohn's autobiographical notes reproduced by Moses Starkman in his "The Memoirs of the Sarasohns (A Contribution to the History of the Yiddish Press in America)" (Yiddish), *Yorbuch fun Amopteil,* I (1938), 273-95; Starkman's reproduction of the Yiddish text of "The Constitution of the 'Arbeiter Tseitung' (1890)," *ibid.,* pp. 338-48; Abraham Cahan's autobiography (*supra,* n. 114); reminiscences by Jacob Milch, *Di Antshtayung fun Forverts* (The Origins of the Forward and Its Struggles with the Evening Paper; New York, 1936); and other data listed in Starkman's "Source Materials for the History of the Yiddish Press in America (1870-1900)" (Yiddish), *Pinkas,* I (1927-28), 312-20. See also his "Contributions to the History of the Yiddish Socialist Press in America" (Yiddish), YB, IV (1932), 354-87; Kalmon Marmor, *Der Onhoib fun der yidisher literatur in Amerike* (The Birth of Yiddish Literature in America, 1870-1890; New York, 1944); and the literature listed *supra,* nn. 42-43, 158; and *infra,* nn. 161-62.

161 See the essays assembled in Jacob Shatzky, ed., *Zamelbuch zu der geshikhte fun der yidisher prese in Amerike* (Studies in

History of the Yiddish Press in America; New York, 1934);
and in a second *Zamelbuch* (Jubilee Volume in Commemoration of the Two Hundred and Fiftieth Anniversary of the Yiddish Press, 1686-1936; New York, 1937), which included esp.
Moses Starkman, "The Jewish Press in America, 1875-1885"
(pp. 115-35); and A. Goldberg, "Yiddish Professional Journalism in America" (pp. 233-49). See also Mordecai Soltes, *The
Yiddish Press: an Americanizing Agency* (Philadelphia, 1925;
previously printed in *AJYB*, XXVI [1924-25], 165-372; 2d ed.,
New York, 1950); Jacob S. Glatstein and Hillel Rogoff, *75 yor
yidishe prese in Amerike* (75 Years of the Yiddish Press in
America, 1870-1945 [New York, 1946], reviewing the leading
papers and magazines); and, more generally, Samuel L. Zitron
(Citron), *Geshikhte fun der yidisher prese*, Vol. I: 1863-1889
(Warsaw, 1923). The statistical references are taken from A.
Reisin's note on "The Yiddish Press in the United States"
(Yiddish), *Bleter far yidishe demografie*, III (1923), 206-208.
See also Nathan Goldberg "The Jewish Press in the United
States, 1900-1940" (Yiddish), *YB*, XVIII (1941), 129-57;
idem, "The Circulation of the Yiddish Newspapers in the
United States, 1919-1943" (Yiddish), *ibid.*, XXIV (1944), 338-
47, 424; and such personal memoirs as Kalmon Marmor's
Main Lebensgeshichte (My Autobiography), Vols. I-II (New
York, 1959).

162   See Elias Schulman, *Geshikhte fun der yidisher literatur in
Amerike* (A History of Yiddish Literature in the United States,
1870-1900; New York, 1943), esp. pp. 104 ff., 117 ff.; Kalmon
Marmor, *Der Onhoib, passim*; Zalman Reisen, *Leksikon fun
der yidisher literatur, prese un filologie*, 2d ed., 4 vols. (Vilna,
1926-30); and the more recent *Leksikon fun der nayer yidisher
literatur* (Biographical Dictionary of Modern Yiddish Literature), ed. by Samuel Niger and Jacob Shatzky *et al.*, Vols. I-II
(New York, 1956-58; covers the first four letters of the alphabet). See also Leo Wiener, *The History of Yiddish Literature
in the Nineteenth Century* (New York, 1899), esp. pp. 216 ff.;
and A. A. Roback, *The Story of Yiddish Literature* (New York,
1940), esp. pp. 192 ff.; the biographical data offered in Leo
Kobrin's *My Fifty Years in America* (New York, 1946); S.
Libin's "Materials for My Biography" (Yiddish) in his
Geklibene Shriftn (New York, 1912), pp. 3-10; Hillel Rogoff's
Nine Yiddish Writers (New York, 1931); and the literature
listed *supra*, nn. 114, 160, 161, and in the forthcoming notes.

163   See, for instance, the biographical studies by Sol Liptzin,

Eliakum Zunser: Poet of His People (New York, 1950; based in part on Zunser's *biografie*—*A Jewish Bard: Being the Biography of Eliakum Zunser Written by Himself* and Rendered into English by Simon Hirsdansky; New York, 1905); and (in Yiddish) by Kalmon Marmor; *Morris Winchevsky: His Life and Works* (New York, 1927) in Winchevsky's *Gezamelte Shriftn*, I; idem, *David Edelstadt* (New York, 1950); idem, "Joseph Bovshover (1872-1915)," *Yorbuch fun Amopteil*, II (1939), 32-101; and N. B. Minkoff's comprehensive analysis and illustrations of *Pionern fun yidisher poezie in Amerike* (Pioneers of Yiddish Poetry in America; the Social Poem), 3 vols. (New York, 1956). See also Noah Steinberg, *Yung Amerike* (New York, 1917); and, more generally, Samuel Niger, "Yiddish Literature in the Past Two Hundred Years," *JP*, III, 165-219; and other publications listed in the last note and in Waxman's *History* (*supra*, n. 158). An interesting anthology of Yiddish poetry was compiled in 1919 by Zisho Landau (1888-1937), himself a poet of no mean distinction and member of the *Yung Amerike* circle, under the title, *Antologie*—*Di yidishe dikhtung in Amerike biz yor 1919* (New York, 1919). A different type of anthology is now available in Nachman Mayzel's selection, *Amerike in yidishen vort* (America in Yiddish Literature: an Anthology; New York, 1956), which gives interesting material for the image of America as reflected in Yiddish poetry from decade to decade. Both anthologies would have benefitted, however, if the compilers had chosen to furnish fuller biographical data and critical appreciations of the excerpts submitted. This deficiency is remedied in part, however, by N. B. Minkoff's aforementioned *Pionern*. A fine selection of American Yiddish poems in English rendition is available in Joseph Leftwich's *The Golden Peacock: an Anthology of Yiddish Poetry*, trans. into English verse (London, 1939). Of interest also is the contrast to the Yiddish literature of the period after the First World War which is analyzed by Samuel Niger (Charney) in his "New Trends in Post-War Yiddish Literature," *JSS*, I (1939), 337-58.

164 Karl Lamprecht, *Americana*—*Reiseeindrücke, Betrachtungen, geschichtliche Gesammtansicht* (Freiburg i.B., 1906), p. 61. As usual, much of the available material is biographical or autobiographical. See, for instance, the autobiographies of the actors, Bessie and Boris Tomashefsky, both entitled, *Mayn Lebnsgeshikhte*, and published in New York, 1916 and 1937, respectively. On the leading playwrights see esp. Perez Hirschbein's

Im gang fun lebn (Zikhroines) (New York, 1948). Of interest also is Pinski's early compilation of the Yiddish theatres operating during the First World War in New York which he published with a succinct introduction in *JCR*, pp. 572-79; and Aaron B. Seidman, "The First Performance of Yiddish Theatre in America," *JSS*, X (1948), 67-70. See also the comprehensive work by George C. D. Odell, *Annals of the New York Stage*, Vols. I-XV (New York, 1927-49); Jacob Shatzky, ed., *Hundert yor Goldfaden* (A Centenary of Abraham Goldfaden, 1840-1908; New York, 1940), esp. A. R. Malachi's "Goldfadeniana" (pp. 64-87); and, more generally, B. Gorin's standard work *Di Geshikhte fun yidishen teater*, 2 vols. (New York, 1918); A. Mukdoni "Memoirs of a Yiddish Theater Critic" (Yiddish), *Arkhiv tsu der geshikhte fun yidishn teater*, 1930, pp. 321-41; the more comprehensive works by Ignacy (Yitzhak) Shiper (Schipper), *Geshickhte fun der yidisher teater kunst*, 3 vols., Warsaw, 1923-28; and *Leksikon fun yidishen teater*, ed. by Zalmen Zylbercwaig, 3 vols. (New York, 1931-59).

The tremendous impression made upon outsiders is also evidenced by the comments of Hutchins Hapgood in *The Spirit of the Ghetto*, pp. 113 ff. On the other hand, there were also many seamy sides to the American Jewish theater and the sharp critique voiced by Jacob Mestel in 1927 held true, at least to some extent also, for the pre-1914 period. See his "Yiddish Theater in America" (Yiddish) in the *Yidish teater kvartal buch*, 1927 (Warsaw, 1928), pp. 300-312. It was dissatisfaction with the deterioration of the Jewish theatrical arts which led Maurice Schwartz in 1918-21 to establish his Yiddish Art Theater. See also Louis Lipsky's earlier observations on "The Future of the Yiddish Theater" *The Maccabaean*, XVI (1909), 134-38.

165   The story of the Jewish contribution to general American theatrical arts has yet to be written. For the time being we are limited to a popular and none-too-accurate survey by George Cohen, *The Jews in the Making of America* (Boston, 1924; with an introductory essay on "The Racial Contributions to the United States" by Edward F. McSweeney), esp. pp. 144 ff., as well as to such biographical studies as Allen Lesser, *Enchanting Rebel: the Secret of Adah Isaacs Menken* (New York, 1947); William Winter, *The Life of David Belasco*, 2 vols. (New York, 1918); the somewhat less uncritical biography by Craig Timberlake, *David Belasco* (New York, 1954); Isaac F. Marcosson, *Charles Frohman: Manager and Man* (New York,

1917); *Daniel Frohman Presents: an Autobiography* (New York, 1935); George Blumenthal, *My Sixty Years in Show Business: a Chronicle 1874-1934. As Told . . . to Arthur H. Menkin* (New York, 1936); Rudolph Aaronson, *Theatrical and Musical Memoirs* (New York, 1913); *Upton Sinclair Presents William Fox* (Los Angeles, 1933); John Drinkwater, *The Life and Adventures of Carl Laemmle* (New York, 1931); Will Irwin, *The House That Shadows Built* (Garden City, N.Y., 1928; on Adolph Zukor); and, more generally, Benjamin B. Hampton, *The History of the Movies* (New York, 1931). The economic aspects of the Jewish share in the motion picture industry were discussed later, with some apologetic bias, by the editors of *Fortune* in *The Jews of America* (New York, 1937). See also the earlier study by J. Klinow, "Jews in the Film Industry" (Yiddish) in Yivo's *Ekonomishe Shriftn*, II (1932), 142-57. Apart from being authors and performers on the stage, Jews were often also the subjects of various plays, sympathetic or antipathetic to them. This topic is briefly treated by Gilbert Seldes in "Jewish Plays and Jew-Plays in New York," *Menorah Journal*, VIII (1922), 236-40; and Stephen Bloore, "The Jew in American Dramatic Literature (1794-1930)" *PAJHS*, XL (1950-51), 345-60. See also *supra*, n. 65; and Joseph Mersand, *Traditions in American Literature: a Study of Jewish Characters and Authors* (New York, 1939).

166 Once again the absence of an analytical history forces one to concentrate on the few biographies of outstanding individuals or institutions. See, for instance, David Philipson, "Moses Jacob Ezekiel," *PAJHS*, XXVIII (1922), 1-62; Jacob Epstein, *Let There Be Sculpture* (New York, 1940); Bernard Berenson, *Sketch for a Self-Portrait* (New York, 1949); Sylvia Saunders Spriggs, *Berenson: a Biography* (Boston, 1960); Louis Untermeyer, *From Another World: the Autobiography* (New York, 1939); Edna Ferber, *A Peculiar Treasure* (New York, 1939); Adolph Gillis, *Ludwig Lewisohn, the Artist and His Message* (New York, 1933); Walter Damrosch, *My Musical Life* (New York, 1923); James W. Barrett, *Joseph Pulitzer and His Work* (New York, 1941); Meyer Berger, *The Story of the New York Times* (New York, 1951); Gerald W. Johnson, *An Honorable Titan: a Biographical Study of Adolph S. Ochs* (New York, 1946). On Emma Lazarus, see *supra*, n. 26. See also Ludwig Lewisohn, "A Panorama of a Half Century of American Jewish Literature," *Jewish Book Annual*, IX (1950-51), 3-10; Nissan

Touroff, "Jewish Plastic Arts in America" (Hebrew), *Sefer ha-Shanah* (American Hebrew Yearbook), X-XI (1949), 529-69; Karl Schwartz, *Jewish Artists of the 19th and 20th Centuries* (New York, 1949); Abraham W. Binder, "Jewish Music," *JP*, III, 324-76, esp. pp. 344 ff.; Alfred Sendrey, *Bibliography of Jewish Music* (New York, 1951); and George Cohen's observations in *The Jews in the Making of America*, pp. 163 ff., 182 ff.

167 Only the Jewish contributions to American medicine have found careful investigators in Solomon R. Kagan and others. See his *Jewish Contribution to Medicine in America* (Boston, 1931); and such special monographs as S. J. Goldowsky, "Jews in Medicine in Rhode Island," *Rhode Island Jewish Historical Notes*, II (1957), 151-92; Rhoda Truax, *The Doctors Jacobi* (Boston, 1952); Robert P. Parsons, *Trail to Light: a Biography of Joseph Goldberger* (Indianapolis, 1943). Less informative for American Jewish scientists is Louis Gershenfeld, *The Jew in Science* (Philadelphia, 1934); and Bernard Jaffe's more general review of *Men of Science in America* (New York, 1944). Of interest are the following individual biographies and autobiographies: Melville J. Herskovits, *Franz Boas* (New York, 1953); T. W. Richards, *The Scientific Work of Morris Loeb* (Cambridge, Mass., 1913); Abraham Flexner, *An Autobiography*, with an Intro. by Allan Nevins (New York, 1960); Frederick W. Wile, *Emile Berliner: Maker of the Microphone* (Indianapolis, 1926). See also George Cohen, *The Jews*, pp. 196 ff. Materials for fuller studies are, of course, available, most readily in the various encyclopedias and the *Who Is Who in American Jewry*, the first edition of which published in New York, 1926, furnishes at least skeletal biographical data for creative Jewish personalities in various fields of endeavor, including those who had already made significant contributions before 1914.

Part IV

ESSAY 11
Impact of Wars on Religion

1 In a private letter to Samuel C. Kincheloe, communicated in the latter's "Research Memorandum on Religion in the Depression,"

Social Science Research Council Bulletin, 33 (New York, 1937), p. 57.

2 Unfortunately the historian is confronted simultaneously by a bewildering richness and variety of primary sources and monographs on related subjects and an extreme dearth of studies directly relevant to our inquiry. On the one hand, in *The War and Religion: a Preliminary Bibliography of Material in English,* Marion J. Bradshaw listed almost 2,000 items relating to the First World War alone and published before January 1, 1919. Similarly prolific had been the output in French, German and other languages, and of course a great deal more was added since 1919. On the other hand, only the following three monographs have proved directly helpful to the present writer: Karl Holl, "Die Bedeutung der grossen Kriege für das religiöse und kirchliche Leben innerhalb des deutschen Protestantismus," *Gesammelte Aufsätze zur Kirchengeschichte* (Tübingen, 1928), III, 302-84 (concentrating on the Thirty Years' War and the German Wars of Liberation and their impact on German literature and German-Protestant theology); Otto Baumgarten *et al., Die geistigen und sittlichen Wirkungen des Krieges in Deutschland* (New Haven, 1927); and Ray H. Abrams, *Preachers Present Arms* (New York, 1933) (both relating only to the First World War). Despite his attempt at a purely sociological inquiry, however, Abrams has presented evidence mainly for an indictment of the vast majority of the clergy for their surrender to war hysteria. Like Baumgarten and his associates, moreover, Abrams is more concerned with what religious leaders had done for the war than with what war had done to religion.

3 See Thucydides, *The History of the Peloponnesian War,* II, 71; VII, 86, in the English translation by Charles Forster Smith (London, 1919-23), I, 389-390; IV, 177.

4 See Alfred Vanderpol's detailed analysis of *Le Droit de guerre d'après les théologiens et les canonistes du moyen-âge* (Paris, 1911).

5 Mishnah Soṭah VIII, 7; Sanhedrin I, 5; Heinrich Finke, *Der Gedanke des gerechten und heiligen Krieges in Gegenwart und Vergangenheit* (Freiburg i. B., 1915), p. 15. A modern Catholic apologist enumerated seven criteria of a "just war"; John Eppstein, *The Catholic Tradition and the Law of Nations* (London, 1935), p. 331. Cf. also Robert Regout, S. J., *La Doctrine de la guerre juste de Saint Augustin à nos jours* (Paris, 1935).

6 Daniel 7: 7, 14; Pliny, *Historia naturalis,* III, 5.39, in the English

translation by H. Rackham (London, 1938), II, 31 f. See also Albert Zwaenepoel, "L'inspiration religieuse de l'impérialisme romain," *Antiquité classique*, XVIII (1949), 5-23; and my *SRH*, 2d ed., II, 89 ff.

7   Cicero, *Pro Flacco*, XXVIII, 69, in his *Speeches*, translated by Louis E. Lord (Cambridge, Mass., 1946), p. 441.

8   Friedrich Daniel Ernst Schleiermacher, *Predigten* (Berlin, 1843), IV, 675. See also Friedrich Meinecke, *Weltbürgertum und Nationalstaat* (Munich, 1928), p. 176.

9   See the judicious analysis in Alfred Loisy's *Guerre et religion* (Paris, 1915), pp. 82 ff. Similar conclusions were reached by the German pastor, W. Veit, the English chaplain, F. R. Barry, and others. *Cf.* W. Veit's "Busse" in *Die Religion im Krieg, Frankfurter Vorträge* (Frankfurt, 1914), p. 23; and F. R. Barry's "Faith in the Light of War" in *The Church in the Furnace*, ed. by F. B. Macnutt (London, 1918), p. 35. These experiences were confirmed by observations during the Second World War, reported by John E. Johnson in "The Faith and Practice of the Raw Recruit" in *Religion of Soldier and Sailor*, ed. by William L. Sperry (Cambridge, Mass., 1945), pp. 42-67.

10 Maurice Barrès, *The Faith of France: Studies in Spiritual Differences and Unity*, translated by Elisabeth Marbury, with a Foreword by Henry Van Dyke (Boston, 1918).

11 See, for instance, Raymond Dreiling, *Das religiöse und sittliche Leben der Armee unter dem Einfluss des Weltkrieges: Eine psychologische Untersuchung* (Paderborn, 1922); *Religion among American Men: As Revealed by a Study of Conditions in the Army* (New York, 1920); and W. L. Sperry, ed., *Religion of Soldier*.

12 *Mémoires et Correspondance politique et militaire du roi Joseph*, compiled by A. Du Casses (Paris, 1953-54), I, 141; in the English translation by J. M. Thompson in his selection of *Letters of Napoleon* (Oxford, 1934), pp. 17-18.

13 "The solemnity of the battle," Möwes wrote, "did not drive me to Him. I do not recollect even offering up one prayer. We were called up before the engagement to receive the sacrament. I let my friend, whose side I had never before left, go up without me. I could not then comprehend of what use it could be to me." Cited in *Memoir of the Late Rev. Henry Möwes*, with an introduction by Rev. J. Davies (London, 1890), p. 7.

14 Ernst Ludwig von Gerlach, *Aufzeichnungen aus seinem Leben und Wirken 1795-1877*, ed. by Jakob von Gerlach (Schwerin, 1903), I, 64.

15 Henry Hallam Tweedy, "The Ministry and the War" in *Religion and the War*, ed. by E. Hershey Sneath (New Haven, 1918), pp. 88-89.

16 Russell, *Justice in War Times* (Chicago, 1916), p. 23.

17 Charles Reynolds Brown, "Moral and Spiritual Forces in the War" in Sneath, *Religion and the War*, p. 12.

18 Boulay de la Meurthe, *Documents sur la négociation du concordat . . . en 1800 et 1801* (Paris, 1891), I, 77; Henry H. Walsh, *The Concordat of 1801* (New York, 1933), p. 85 n. 17.

19 J. M. Thompson, *Letters of Napoleon*, p. 193. On the same day Napoleon ordered his Minister of Cults, Jean Etienne Portalis, to find a bishop who would recommend to the churches "to institute prayers for our brethren, the persecuted Irish Catholics, and that they may enjoy the liberty of their worship." *Correspondance de Napoléon Ier* (Paris, 1858-70), XV, 126. See also his earlier letters to the Pope and the Minister of War, Gen. Bertier, dated Jan. 13, 1804, *ibid.*, pp. 194 ff.

20 N. M. Gelber, "La Police autrichienne et le Sanhédrin de Napoléon," *Revue des études juives*, LXXXIII (1927), 1-21, 131-45; S. M. Dubnow, *History of the Jews in Russia and Poland*, English translation (Philadelphia, 1916), I, 346 ff.

21 Schleiermacher, Addendum to the 2d ed. of his addresses, *Ueber die Religion* (Berlin, 1806), p. 371; his letter to Georg Reimer of Dec. 20, 1806 in *The Life of Schleiermacher as Unfolded in His Autobiography and Letters*, English translation by Frederica Rowan (London, 1860), II, 73; Johann Gottlieb Fichte, *Reden an die deutsche Nation* in his *Sämmtliche Werke*, ed. by J. H. Fichte (Berlin, 1845-46), VII, 467; Ernst Moritz Arndt, *Katechismus für den deutschen Kriegs- und Wehrmann*, ed. by Max Haber (Dresden, 1913), pp. 18 ff. See also Heinrich Laag, *Die religiöse Entwicklung Ernst Moritz Arndts* (Halle, 1926); and, more generally, my *Modern Nationalism and Religion* (New York, 1947; also paperback), pp. 42 ff., 136 ff.

22 Price, *War and Revolution in Asiatic Russia* (London, 1918), p. 271.

23 Eusebius, *Ecclesiastical History*, III, 5, 2-3; and S. C. F. Brandon, *The Fall of Jerusalem and the Christian Church* (London, 1951), pp. 168 ff. See also Heinz Joachim Schoeps, "Die Tempelzerstörung des Jahres 70 in der jüdischen Religionsgeschichte," *Coniectanea neotestamentica*, VI (1942), 1-45, reprinted in his *Aus frühchristlicher Zeit* (Tübingen, 1950), pp. 144-83.

24 See Gottfried M. Menken's widely read *Glück und Sieg der Gott-losen*, in his *Schriften* (Bremen, 1858).
25 This transformation may be illustrated by the changing attitudes to war itself on the part of Kant, Fichte, Hegel and Schleiermacher. Kant alone, after publishing in 1795 his famous essay on perpetual peace under the impact of the French Revolution, remained true to his convictions in the remaining nine years of his life. Fichte who lived to 1814, Hegel and Schleiermacher who died in 1831 and 1834, respectively, all began as ardent admirers of the Revolution. Even in his later *Philosophy of History* (English translation by J. Sibree, New York, 1905, p. 558) Hegel still spoke of that "glorious mental dawn," acclaimed by all thoughtful persons of the period. Yet before long they all became ardent protagonists of the Wars of Liberation. As early as 1802-1803, Schleiermacher entered in his diary, "The view that all action consists in war, can be demonstrated even in a religious discourse with reference to Christ's words: 'I came not to send peace, but a sword'" (Matt. 10:34). Of course, the great Berlin preacher agreed with Fichte that only a "true war" was justified, namely one which met the requirements of "history." But in the ultimate sense, he believed, "all history is religious history, and religion itself must by its very nature be historical." Cf. his *Tagebuch* of 1798; and, more generally, Wilhelm Braun, *Der Krieg im Lichte der idealistischen Philosophie vor hundert Jahren und ihrer Wirkung auf die Gegenwart* (Gütersloh, 1917).
26 Niebuhr, *Reflections on the End of an Era* (New York, 1934), p. ix.
27 *Epistola ad Diognetum* in Migne's *Patrologia graeca*, II, 1173.
28 Josephus, *Antiquities*, XX, 9, 2.206-7 (Whiston's translation); Babylonian Talmud, Giṭṭin 56a.
29 *SRH*, 2d ed. rev., II, 110 f., 116 f., 375.
30 John Wingate Thornton, *Pulpit of the American Revolution* (Boston, 1860); Friedrich Julius Winter, ed., *Geistliche Weckstimmen aus der Zeit der Erniedrigung und Erhebung unseres Volkes: Zeitpredigten* (Leipzig, 1913); P. Piechowski, *Die Kriegspredigt von 1870-71* (Leipzig, 1917).
31 Allen, *The Fight for Peace* (New York, 1930), p. 43.
32 See, for example, the 1917 declaration of the Federal Council of Churches of Christ in America, reprinted in the interesting chapter on "What the Church Learned in the War" in William Adams Brown's *The Church in America* (New York, 1922), pp. 97 ff.

33 Charles Edward Osborne, *Religion in Europe and the World Crisis* (London, 1916), pp. 163-64. See especially *The German War and Catholicism*, ed. by Alfred Baudrillart, rector of the Catholic Institute of Paris, with an introductory letter by Cardinal Amette, Archbishop of Paris (Paris, 1915); Loisy, *Guerre et religion*; and the replies from Germany entitled *Der deutsche Krieg und der Katholizismus*, ed. by A. J. Rosenberg *et al.* (Berlin, 1915); and *German Culture, Catholicism, and the World War*, ed. by Georg Pfeilschifter, Professor of Theology at the University of Freiburg, English translation (St. Paul, 1916). The latter volume, in which some such outstanding leaders of German Catholicism as the later Cardinal Michael Faulhaber participated, was clearly designed for foreign propaganda as much as for the allaying of the scruples of German Catholics. From the outset French, Dutch, Italian, Portuguese and Spanish translations, as well as that English translation, were planned, principally for distribution in neutral countries.

34 Letters to the Pope and the Archbishop of Paris of August 28, 1802. It was an acknowledgment of defeat of his overseas plans when in a letter to his uncle, Cardinal Joseph Fesch, dated October 8, 1809, he conceded that he had abandoned the foreign missions to the British. *Correspondance de Napoléon Ier*, VIII, 7-8; XIX, 560-61; and J. M. Thompson, *Letters of Napoleon*, pp. 84, 252-53.

35 Philip C. T. Crick, "The Soldier's Religion" in *The Church in the Furnace*, ed. by F. B. Macnutt, p. 367; *The Missionary Outlook in the Light of the War*, prepared by the Committee on the War and the Religious Outlook, and published in New York, 1920.

36 *War-Time Agencies of the Churches: Directory and Handbook*, ed. by Margaret Renton (New York, 1919).

37 Peter Guilday, *The National Pastorals of the American Hierarchy, 1792-1919* (Washington, 1923), pp. 235, 294 ff.

38 Reichsbund jüdischer Frontsoldaten, *Die jüdischen Gefallenen des deutschen Heeres, der deutschen Marine und der deutschen Schutztruppen, 1914-1918: Ein Gedenkbuch* (Berlin, 1932); idem, *Gefallene deutsche Juden: Frontbriefe 1914-1918* (Berlin, 1935).

39 N. Lenin, "Socialism and Religion" in his *Selected Works* (New York, 1932-38), XI, 658, 661; Friedrich Engels, *Internationales aus dem Volksstaat, 1871-75* (Berlin, 1894), p. 44.

40 Albert Schinz, *Etat présent des travaux sur J.-J. Rousseau* (New York, 1941), p. 14; Auguste Viatte, *Les Interprétations du catholicisme chez les romantiques* (Paris, 1922).

41 See the data assembled by Karl Holl in his *Gesammelte Aufsätze zur Kirchengeschichte*, III, 377 ff.

42 Adrien Dansette, *Histoire religieuse de la France contemporaine de la Révolution à la Troisième Republique* (Paris, 1948), pp. 266-67.

43 *Annals of the Congress of the United States*, 17th Cong., 2d sess., 1855, pp. 20-21.

44 Lucien Price, "Between Two Wars" in *Religion of Soldier and Sailor*, ed. by William L. Sperry, pp. 21-22.

45 Cited from the Socialist *Vorwärts* of February 28, 1917 by Karl Holl in his "Luthers Anschauung über Evangelium, Krieg und Aufgabe der Kirche im Lichte des Weltkrieges" (1917), reprinted in his *Gesammelte Aufsätze zur Kirchengeschichte*, III, 147.

46 Adolf Keller and George Stewart, *Protestant Europe: Its Crisis and Outlook* (New York, 1927), pp. 160 ff.

47 *Ibid.*, pp. 157, 168, 171.

48 Guy Kendall, *Religion in War and Peace* (London, n.d.,), p. 118.

49 Pius XI's encyclical *Ubi arcano Dei* in *Principles for Peace: Selections from Papal Documents*, ed. by Harry C. Koenig (Washington, 1943), p. 347.

50 See my *Modern Nationalism and Religion*, pp. 155 ff., 299 n. 39, 316 ff.

51 Walter W. Van Kirk, *Religion Renounces War* (Chicago, 1934), pp. 13, 44.

52 Alfred Rosenberg, *Der Mythus des 20. Jahrhunderts* (Munich, 1937), p. 114.

53 Karl Barth, *The Church and the War* (New York, 1944), pp. 29-30; William Temple, *Thoughts in War-Time* (London, 1940), p. 29. See also *ibid.*, pp. 31 f.

54 See F. William Worsley's essay in *The Church and the Furnace*, ed. by F. B. Macnutt, pp. 69-96.

55 See Halford Edward Luccock, *The Questing Spirit: Religion in the Literature of Our Time* (New York, 1947).

ESSAY 12
The Second World War and Jewish Community Life

1 See also Selig Adler, "The Palestine Question in the Wilson Era," *JSS*, X (1948), 303-334.

2 Nathan Gelber, *Haṣharat Balfour ve-toledotehah* (History of the Balfour Declaration; Jerusalem, 1929), pp. 125 ff.; Frank E. Manuel, *The Realities of American Palestine Relations* (Washington, D.C., 1950).

3 See *supra*, Essay 3.

4 Even before his negotiations at the Conference itself, Marshall had written to President Wilson on November 14, 1918, asking him to support constitutional safeguards for the Jews of reconstituted Poland. These included provisions that "(4) The Jews shall be accorded autonomous management of their own religious, educational, charitable and other cultural institutions (5) Those who observe the Jewish Sabbath shall not be prohibited from pursuing their secular affairs on any other day of the week so long as they shall not disturb the religious worship of others." In Paris, as chairman of the Committee of Jewish Delegations, he espoused outright Jewish minority rights. See Charles Reznikoff, ed., *Louis Marshall, Champion of Liberty*, II, 593 ff.; and Oscar I. Janowsky, *The Jews and Minority Rights 1898-1919*. With a Foreword by Julian W. Mack (New York, 1933; diss. Columbia University).

5 Oscar I. Janowsky, *JWB Survey*, with my letter of transmittal to Frank L. Weil (New York, 1948).

6 See Robert Morris and Michael Freund, comps., *Trends and Issues in Jewish Social Welfare in the United States, 1899-1952* (Philadelphia, 1966).

7 See the early issues of *Menorah Journal*; and some of the articles reproduced in the *Menorah Treasury: Harvest of Half a Century*, ed. by Leo W. Schwarz (Philadelphia, 1964).

8 See *supra*, Essay 10.

9 *Ibid.*

10 See the *Annual Reports* of the National Refugee Service, Inc. (from 1946 on United Service for New Americans, Inc.); and the bibliography appended to Aryeh Tartakower and Kurt R. Grossmann, *The Jewish Refugee* (New York, 1949).

11 *Menorah Journal*, XXX (1942), 116-38; reprinted in my *History and Jewish Historians* (Philadelphia, 1964), pp. 43-64.

12 The cultural re-awakening of East-Central European Jewry may, indeed, prove to be unexpectedly speedy and profound. In compiling my *Bibliography of Jewish Social Studies, 1938-1939,* I have marveled at the great creativity, qualitative as well as quantitative, of Polish Jewry in the last two prewar years. Even the output of the new rabbinic authors (responsa, homilies, old-type commentaries) during those two years doubtless exceeded that of any decade in the seventeenth or eighteenth centuries—the heyday of the ghetto community. Such elemental vitality is likely to survive several years of Nazi oppression and to reemerge triumphant after the defeat of Nazism with a modicum of assistance from more fortunate coreligionists.

13 See my address of May 25, 1940 on "Reflections on the Future of European Jewry" published in the *Proceedings of the National Conference of Jewish Social Welfare (Jewish Social Service Quarterly,* XVII, Sept. 1940, pp. 5-19). It also appeared under a slightly modified title and with minor variations in the *Contemporary Jewish Record,* III (1940), 355-69.
[Postscript: Unfortunately, the optimistic hope expressed in this and the preceding note in 1942 was frustrated by the catastrophic Nazi Holocaust raging during that and the following years. While many refugees from Nazi-occupied Europe in Israel, the United States, and elsewhere have demonstrated their great cultural élan and have left a permanent imprint on the countries of their settlement, the large majority remaining behind fell victim to the Nazi genocidal mania. See esp. *infra,* Essay 18.]

ESSAY 13
Some of the Tercentenary's Historic Lessons

1 Charles P. Daly, *The Settlement of Jews in North America,* ed. by Max J. Kohler (New York, 1893), p. 97.
2 See *Beekman Mercantile Papers,* ed. by Philip White (New York, 1955), pp. 649 ff.
3 *Statistical Abstract for Palestine,* compiled by David Gurevich (Jerusalem, 1930), p. 41. In 1936, no less than 94 American Jews, out of a total of 308 expatriates are recorded to have left for Palestine. See "Immigration of Jews to the United States," *AJYB,* XXXIX (1937-1938), 762.
4 See the interesting letter, addressed in their behalf by the United States Consul J. G. Wilson to Rabbis Samuel M. Isaacs

in New York and Max Lilienthal in Cincinnati on October 10, 1877, and reproduced in the *Jewish Messenger*, XLIII No. 21 (1878), p. 2; and in the *American Israelite*, XXIX No. 19 (1877), p. 2. See also *supra*, Essay 9, n. 91.

5 See the convenient statistical Tables xii-xiii in Michael Traub's *Jüdische Wanderungen vor und nach dem Weltkriege* (Berlin, 1930), pp. 111, 113.

6 *Ibid.*

7 These data have been culled from the aforementioned essay in *AJYB*, XXXIX, 767.

8 M. Traub, *Jüdische Wanderungen*, pp. 116 ff., Tables xvii-xx.

9 Louis Rosenberg, *Canada's Jews: a Social and Economic Study of the Jews in Canada* (Montreal, 1939), p. 136, Table 92. To some extent these mass departures were also repeated in the 1930s. In the seven years of 1931-1938 Canada lost 83 more Jews to her southern neighbor than she took in from all countries. Of course, many Jews entered Canada *via* the United States. But these evidently were for the most part real transients who landed first at United States debarkation points, whereas relatively few avowed immigrants to the United States arrived *via* Canadian ports.

10 Guido Kisch, "The Revolution of 1848 and the Jewish 'On to America' Movement," *PAJHS*, XXXVIII (1948-1949), 185-234 (largely reproducing statements in the *Oesterreichisches Central-Organ* of 1848); and my essay on "The Revolution of 1848 and Jewish Scholarship, II," *PAAJR*, XX (1951), 23 ff.

11 Jacob Rader Marcus, *Early American Jewry* (Philadelphia, 1951-1953), 2 vols., I, 139.

12 See the illustrations cited in my *SRH*, 1st ed. (New York, 1937), II, 66 ff.

13 See Herbert I. Bloom, "A Study of Brazilian Jewish History, 1623-1654," *PAJHS*, XXXIII (1934), 43-125; Arnold Wiznitzer, *The Records of the Earliest Jewish Community in the New World* (New York, 1954).

14 Samuel Oppenheim, "The Early History of the Jews in New York, 1654-1664," *PAJHS*, XVIII (1909), 36. The petition seems to have been occasioned by the unsuccessful application of Asser Levy, who himself may have been an Ashkenazi. See Lee M. Friedman, *Jewish Pioneers and Patriots* (Philadelphia, 1942), pp. 133 ff. However, here, as well as in his famous struggle for the right to stand guard, he and Jacob Barsimson, who was indubitably an Ashkenazi, were probably swayed by the

Sephardic leadership which permanently impressed its outlook on the entire community. Curiously, the four leaders, who wrote in behalf of the community, apparently did not belong to the famous twenty-three arrivals. Cf. Arnold Wiznitzer's "The Exodus from Brazil and Arrival in New Amsterdam of the Jewish Pilgrim Fathers, 1654," *PAJHS*, XLIV (1954-1955), 80-97. However, whether they had come from Brazil or from Amsterdam, the Marrano background of much of their communal life appears certain. It was this proneness of the Spanish-Portuguese Jews to participate in the public life of their countries, which induced the elders of the Spanish and Portuguese Congregation in London to adopt in 1688 an *escama* forbidding members, under the threat of excommunication, to take any part in political questions or to vote in any political contest of the kingdom. See Moses Gaster, *History of the Ancient Synagogue of the Spanish and Portuguese Jews . . . in Bevis Marks* (London, 1901), p. 88. This provision was repeated as late as 1819 in the English rendition of the by-laws (Art. XXIII). Of course, English Jews had to be doubly careful in avoiding political animosities because of their well-known twilight position before the law.

15 See *supra*, Essay 7.

16 See *supra*, Essay 5.

17 Albert M. Hyamson, *The Sephardim of England* (London, 1951), p. 199; and *supra*, Essay 5.

18 See David de Sola Pool, *Portraits Etched in Stone* (New York, 1952), p. 300; and Jeannette W. Rosenbaum, *Myer Myers, Goldsmith, 1723-1795* (Philadelphia, 1954), p. 48.

19 This problem is more fully discussed *supra*, Essay 5.

20 Benjamin H. Hartogensis, "Unequal Religious Rights in Maryland since 1776," *PAJHS*, XXV (1917), 98 f.; and his *Studies in the History of Maryland* (Baltimore, n.d.), especially pp. 28 and 36 ff.

21 Cf. Joseph Sherbow, "The Impact of the American Constitution upon the Jews of the United States," *PAJHS*, XLIII (1954), 159-169.

22 William O. Douglas in "The Dissent: a Safeguard of Democracy," *Journal of the American Judicature Society*, XXXII (1948), 106; cited by Judge Sherbow, in *PAJHS*, XLIII, 161.

ESSAY 14
Some Historical Lessons for Jewish Philanthropy

1 Thomas Jefferson's letter to Dr. Jacob de la Motta, of September 1, 1820, reproduced by Max J. Kohler in *PAJHS*, XX (1911), 21. See *supra*, Essay 7, n. 21.
2 Friedrich Schleiermacher, "Die christliche Sittenlehre" in his *Sämmtliche Werke*, 33 vols. (Berlin, 1835-64), XII, 489.
3 Jacob ben Asher, *Arba'ah Turim* (Code of Laws), Yoreh De'ah, 245, 247, and the commentaries thereon; and my *JC*, II, 347.
4 See Abraham Cronbach, "The Gradations of Benevolence," *Hebrew Union College Annual*, XVI (1941), 163-86.
5 See *JC*, I, 213 f.

ESSAY 16
Are the Jews Still the People of the Book?

1 See the literature on this highly complicated and controversial subject in *SRH*, 2d ed., I, 307 n. 13.
2 See J. S. da Silva Rosa, "Joseph Athias (1635-1700), ein berühmter jüdischer Drucker," *Soncino Blätter*, III, Parts 3-4 (1930=*Festschrift für Heinrich Brody*), pp. 107-111 [183-88].
3 See *supra*, Essay 10.
4 (New York, 1941; Publications of Jewish Social Studies, I.)
5 See Israel Halperin, "The Council of Four Lands and the Hebrew Book" (Hebrew), *Kirjath Sepher*, IX (1932-33), 367-94; and my *JC*, I, 325, 331; II, 95; III, 81 n. 37, 83 n. 41, 133 n. 45.

ESSAY 17
The Jewish Community and Jewish Education

1 See G. Dossin *et al.*, eds., *Archives royales de Mari*, Vols. I-X (Paris, 1941-67).
2 Yehezkel b. Yehudah Landau, *Derushe ha-ṣelaḥ* (Homilies; Warsaw, 1899), fol. 5b.
3 See my *JC*, II, 125, 185 f., 266, and the sources cited there.
4 Kohelet rabbah on Eccles. 7:28.

ESSAY 19
Can American Jewry Be Culturally Creative?

1 *Seder 'Olam* (World Chronicle), xxx, ed. by Ber Ratner (Vilna, 1897), pp. 141 f. See my *SRH*, 2d ed., I, 199, 386 n. 44.
2 Josephus, *Antiquities*, XI, 5, 2.133; *SRH*, 2d ed., I, 168, 370 ff. n. 7.
3 Bab. Talmud, Sukkah 20a; *SRH*, 2d ed. II, 206, 405 n. 38.
4 See *supra*, Essay 10 n. 152.

ESSAY 20
Reordering Communal Priorities

1 See especially Essay 1: "Ages of Anxiety."
2 See *supra*, Essay 7.
3 See *JC*, I, 136; II, 347; III, 218 n. 68
4 Theodor Lessing, *Der jüdische Selbsthass* (Berlin, 1930).
5 Cited from the unpublished Protocol of that meeting by Krystyna Kersten in her "The Transfer of German Population from Poland in 1945-1947 (On the Example of West Pomerania)," *Acta Poloniae Historica* (published by the Polish Academy of Science), X (1964), 27-47.
6 See my "The Dialogue Between Israel and the Diaspora." *Forum*, Vol. IV (1959=Proceedings of the Ideological Conference Held in Jerusalem, 1957), 236-44.
7 See *supra*, Essay 3 n. 60.
8 *Supra*, Essay 11.
9 See my *SRH*, 1st ed., II, 457.

Index*

Compiled by Paula Kasper

---

* Most persons mentioned only in Essay 9 are listed in Appendix II thereto, pp. 246 ff.
The text is fully indexed. A name/author index is provided for the Notes.

Congregations (*cont.*)

Jeshurun (Paterson), 210; Bene Israel (Cincinnati), 165; Berith Kodesh (Rochester), 196, 234; Berith Sholem (Oswego), 212; Beth Ahabah (Richmond), 206; Beth El (Albany), 175-76, 195, 203; Beth El (Buffalo), 196; Beth-El (Jerusalem), 162; Beth El (Utica), 195; Beth El Jacob (Albany), 195; Beth Elohim (Charleston), 224; Beth Hamedrash (N.Y.), 202; Beth Hamedrash Adas Jeshurun (N.Y.), 191; Beth Hamedrash Hagodol (N.Y.), 190, 233, 382-83; Beth Hamidrash (San Francisco), 200; Beth Hamidrash livne Yisrael Yelide Polin, 388; Beth Israel (Boston), 175; Beth Israel (Cleveland), 213; Beth Israel (Hartford), 174, 216-17; Beth Israel (Jackson), 222; Beth Israel (Macon), 222; Beth Israel (N.Y.), 178; Beth Israel (Rochester), 234; Beth Israel u-Bikur Cholim (N.Y.), 191, 203, 208, 209; Beth Jacob (Albany), 176; Beth Shalom (Richmond), 172, 220-21; Beth Shalome Portuguese (Richmond), 206; Birmingham Hebrew, 165; B'nai Abraham (Philadelphia), 384; B'nai Israel (Elmira), 234; B'nai Israel (Galveston), 236; B'nai Jeshurun (N.Y.), 56, 130, 167, 191-92, 206, 341-42; B'nai Sholom (Chicago), 213; B'nai Israel (Detroit), 235; B'nai Kodesh (Rochester), 213; Chevra B'nai Yisroile (Balto.), 236; Children of Israel (Augusta), 222; Elm Street (N.Y.), 167; Fels Point Hebrew Friendship, 170; German and Dutch (Jerusalem), 181, 192; German and Polish (Montreal), 216; Hebrew (Cincinnati), 138; Hebrew (Indianapolis), 198; Hebrew (Marion, S.C.), 224; Hebrew (Montgomery), 171; He-

brew (Washington, D.C.), 220; House of Israel (Philadelphia), 167-68; Keneset Israel (Richmond), 206, 220; Hebrew Benevolent (Atlanta), 222; Mikve Israel (New Haven), 174; Mikve Israel (Philadelphia), 168; North Shore Israel (Glencoe, Ill.), 506; Nefuzoth Yehudah (New Orleans), 223; Ohabei Shalom (Boston), 175, 193, 203, 216; Ohave Sholom Mariampol (Chicago), 342; Oheb Shalom (Newark), 210; Oheb Sholom (Norfolk), 221; Old Seel Street (Liverpool), 165-66; Reim Ahubim (Stockton), 218; Rochester Hebrew, 203; Rodef Sholem (Philadelphia), 181; Rodef Sholem (N.Y.), 190; Rodef Sholem (Pittsburgh), 197; Rodef Sholem (Youngstown, O.), 222; Rodeph Shalom (Phila.), 59, 130-31; Schary Rachmim (N.Y.), 208; Shaaray Tefilla (N.Y.), 167; Shaare Chesed (New Orleans), 223; Shaare Shamaim (Mobile), 171; Shaare Tefila (N.Y.?), 181, 190, 203; Shaarey Hashamaim (N.Y.), 181; Shaarey Shomaim (Schenectady), 194, 203; Shaarey Zedek (N.Y.), 181, 190, 191; Shari Chesed (New Orleans), 171; Shearit Israel (Charleston), 172; Shearith Israel, *see* Shearith Israel Cong. (N.Y.); Shearith Israel (San Francisco), 199; Spanish and Portuguese (London), 92; Spanish and Portuguese (Philadelphia), 384; Temime Derek (New Orleans), 223; Temple Beth-El (N.Y.), 373; Temple Emanu-El (N.Y.), 366-67, 371, 373; Troy Hebrew, 203; United Hebrew (St. Louis), 213

Connecticut, 292

Connolly, Thomas E., 586

Conservative Judaism, 67, 132, 142, 385, 455; emerges from Reform,

London (*cont.*)
Jews help build synagogue in N.Y., 489; and Palestinian relief, 179
London Society for the Promotion of Christianity amongst the Jews, 187, 389
Lopez, Aaron, 57, 78, 138, 479, 584, 596; denied naturalization, 94-95
Lopez, Moses, 95
Lord, Louis E., 681
Los Angeles, 249; its Jewish population, 30, 133-34; and Notkin visit, 218
Loth, Morris, 380
Louisiana, 223, 291, 316
Louisohn, Leonard, 623
Louisville, Kentucky, 170-71, 178, 252
Lovers of Zion, 49, 392-93
Lowell, James Russell, 333
Lowenthal, Marvin, 670
Lubin, David, 296, 635
Luccock, Halford E., 685
Lucena, Jacob, 27, 84
Ludins, David G., 635
Lull, Raymond, 110
Lumbrozo, Jacob, 27, 85
Luncz, Abraham Moses, 615, 619, 620, 625
Lurie, Harry, 585, 587, 626, 652, 654
Lurie, M., 535
Luzzatti, Luigi, 647, 648
Lyessin, Abraham, 409
Lyons, Jacques Judah, 167, 584

Maccabaean, 395, 402
Maccabean Wars, 419-20
Maccabees, 355
McCormick, Robert S., 339
MacCracken, Henry N., 495, 500
Machzike Talmud Torah, 368
McIver, Robert, 651
Mack, Julian W., 457, 586, 686
McKinley, Albert Edward, 594
McKinley, William, 300, 336
Macnutt, F. B., 681, 684, 685
Macon, Georgia, 251

McSweeney, Edward F., 287, 677
McWilliams, Carey, 645
Madison, James, 23, 282, 630
Maggid, E. S., 621
Magna Bibliotheca Anglo-Judaica, 39
Magnes, Judah Leon, 67, 351, 357, 436, 657; and *Kehillah*, 360-61
Magnus, Katie M., 398
Mailhet, E. André, 601
Maimonides, Moses, 489, 524
Maimonides College (Phila.), 134, 371
Malachi, A. R., 673, 677
Malbim, Meir, 383
Malki, Moses, 160
Malter, Henry, 396, 401, 671, 672
Malthus, T. R., 23
Manchester, England, 182, 247
Mandel, Irving Aaron, 630
Mann, Arthur, 631, 632
Manning, H. E., 441
Mansion House Fund (London), 282, 335
Manuel, Frank E., 648, 649, 686
Manufacturers Trust Co., 312
Marbury, Elisabeth, 681
Marcosson, Isaac F., 677
Marcus, I. H., 621
Marcus, Jacob, 587, 605, 633, 667; (Early American Jewry), 592, 593, 594, 596, 598, 688; (Index), 39-40, 579
Marcus, L., 619
Margalith, Aaron M., 72, 646, 647, 648, 649
Margolies, Rose, 652
Margolis, Max L., 80-81, 364, 395, 401, 658, 671, 672
Mari, 520
Marion, S. C., 224, 265
Markens, Isaac, 43, 48, 582, 626, 639, 640, 655; and economics, 308, 309-10, 312
Marks, Harry H., 230-31
Marmor, Kalmon, 674, 675, 676
Marranos, 478-79

Mill St. Synagogue (N.Y.), 56, 137.
  See also Shearith Israel
Miller, John, 90
Milton, John, 108
Milwaukee, Wisc., 316
Minkoff, N. B., 676
Mintz, Moses, 393
Mirabeau, Gabriel, 96, 596
Mirsky, David, 674
Mishmeret ha-kodesh, 177, 188
Missionaries, 68, 389; and Hebrew
  lang., 110-11; and Palestine, 187;
  and war, 437-38
  See also Conversion
Mithraism, 451
Mitnagdim, 384
Mittelman, Judah, 388
Mizrachi, 394
Mobile, Ala., 171, 223, 236, 248-49
Mobility, and Jewish historiography,
  29-30, 35; of Jews, 500; and W.
  W. II, 462-64
Mogulescu, Sigmund, 410-11
Mohammed, 420, 506
Monetary Gazette, 240
Mongliano, Rabbi of Bologna, 237
Monis, Judah, 68, 86, 112
Monk, Maria, 320
Monroe, James, 443
Montagu, Samuel, 229-33
Montefiore, Moses, 205, 292, 608,
  609, 613, 617, 618, 621, 622, 623;
  his *Diaries*, 607; and Montagu-
  Asher report, 230; and Palestine
  relief, 169-75, 178, 182-85; and Pal-
  estinian messengers, 164-65, 166,
  168, 180, 181, 196, 203, 204
Montefiore Agricultural Aid Society,
  292
Montefiore Hospital for Chronic Dis-
  eases, 347
Montefiore Testimonial Fund, 192,
  230-33
Montesquieu, C. L. de Secondat, 528
Montgomery, James A., 600
Montgomery, Ala., 171, 222, 249
Montreal, 216, 246

Moore, John Bassett, 647
Moore, Noel Temple, 228
Morais, Herbert M., 600
Morais, Sabato, 372, 385, 386, 608,
  666
Mordecai, Henry, 474
Mordecai b. Solomon, 612
Morgan, J. P., 312, 337
Mormons, 391
Morning Journal, see *Yidisher Mor-
  gen Zhurnal*
Morocco, 335
Morris, Nelson, 296
Morris, Robert, 585, 652, 686
Mortality, *see* Vital statistics
Mortara Affair, 326, 356
Moscow, 501
Moscowitch, Morris, 411
Moses, Henry, 181
Moses, Hyman, 197, 211-12, 618; and
  Notkin visit, 236-37; (quoted) on
  Palestine relief, 214-16
Moses of Coucy, 489-90
Motion pictures, 411-12
Mt. Sinai Hosp. (Cleveland), 347
Mt. Sinai Hosp. (N.Y.), 347
Möwes, Heinrich (Henry), 426, 681
Mucata, Abraham de, 56
Muckraking, 298
Mueller, Ewald, 599
Mukdoni, A., 677
Müller, Adam, 441
Munchhausen, Baron von, 625
Munk, Solomon, 612
Mutual self-help, *see* Community life
Myers, Gustavus, 668
Myers, Lawrence, 621
Myers, Myer, 97, 587
Myers, Solomon, 91

Nagel, Charles, 283, 347, 630
Napoleon, Bonaparte, 425, 682; and
  missionaries, 437-38; and religion,
  429-30
Napoleonic Wars, impact on religion,
  421, 423, 432-33, 441, 451-52
Nardi, Noah, 660

Nashville, Tenn., 222, 235, 236, 265
Natality, *see* Vital statistics
Nathan, Anna, 652
Nathan, Eliezer, 615
Nathan, Ernesto, 648
Nathan, Neta b. Mendel, 163, 606
Nathanson, Joseph Saul, 388, 667
Nation, 292
National Assn. of Biblical Instructors, 123
National Assn. of Jewish Center Workers, 458
National Assn. of Professors of Hebrew, 123
National Conf. of Jewish Social Welfare, 60, 62, 454
National Council of Jewish Women, 356-57, 656
National Farm School, 295
National Foundation for Jewish Culture, 514, 552, 553, 572
National Jewish Hospital (Denver), 347, 350
National Jewish Monthly, 402
National Jewish Welfare Board, 60, 354, 458, 495, 496-97
National radical schools, 369
National Records Management Council, 37, 577
National Refugee Service, 141, 464, 686
National Socialist German Workers Party, 42, 325, 555-56
Naturalization Act (1740), 93-96, 481
Naval Academy, 319
Nazis, *see* National Socialist German Workers Party
Neander, Friedrich, 433
Nebraska, 234, 276
Needle trades, 297-304, 410
Neeman, Yerahmeel, 163, 606
Negroes, 314, 483
Neighborhood Guild, 363
Nesselrode, Charles R., 330
Neuman, Abraham A., 672
Neumann, Joshua, 576, 601

Neumark, David, 401
Neusner, Jacob, 630
Nevada, 217
Nevins, Allan, 635, 679
New Amsterdam, 83, 88, 90, 128, 479-81
New Hampshire, 314
New Haven, 174, 250-51
New Jersey, 108, 292
New Left, 558-62, 571
New Odessa, 291
New Orleans, 138, 171, 223, 235-36, 252-54
New Testament, *see* Bible; Old Testament
New York City, 52, 63, 345, 357; adult educ. centers, 363; clothing industry strikes, 299-300, 302-304; crime, 285, 359-60; elects chief rabbi, 383-84; establishes literary assns., 135; Federation movement, 142, 345, 459, 487-88, 491, 492; history of Jews in, 27, 310, 312; and Jewish educ., 365-66, 370; and Jewish equality, 27, 93, 315; and *Kehillah*, 458-59; its *Landsmannschaften*, 351-52; national radical schools, 369; and Palestinian messengers, 172, 177, 181, 189, 201, 208, 224, 233-34, 258-61; and peddlers, 307; population (Jewish), 43, 272, 274; synagogues, 5, 130, 341-342; teachers colleges, 371
New York Herald, 282
New York National Guard, 323
New York State, cemeteries, 129, 341; civil rights bill, 324; Jewish vote, 481; its Jews, 77, 87, 88-91, 97, 103; synagogues, 5, 129
New York Sun, 52, 308, 583
New York Times, 333, 413
New York Tribune, 165, 323
New York University, 120
New York World, 238, 323
New Yorker Yidishe Tseitung, 405
Newark, 210, 256
Newman, John Henry, 441

Newman, Louis Israel, 599, 672
Newport, 87; Jews during Amer. Revol., 102; Jews estab. social club, 136, 349; and synagogue building, 56, 76, 95, 138
Newspapers, *see* Press; specific newspapers
Nicolaievich, Nicolai, 431
Nicolls, Gov. Mathias, 89
Niebuhr, Reinhold, 433, 683
Niger, Samuel, 675, 676
Nikolskii, N. M., 535
Nissan, Abraham, 185-89, 208, 225, 611, 613, 614, 616; *Ohabei Zion*, 200, 217; review of contributions received, 202-203; travels in U.S., 189-204
Noah, Mordecai Manuel, 24, 53, 67, 104, 105, 412, 598, 607, 609; Ararat project, 78; and Palestine relief, 174; and Selig mission, 166-167, 179, 181
Noble, Shlomo, 669
Nonez, Benjamin, 99
Nordheimer, Isaac, 120, 601
Norfolk, Va., 221, 266
Norma (colony), 292
North American Relief Society, 185, 204, 205, 209, 236
North American Review, 359, 392
North Carolina, 103, 314
Norton, Charles D., 648
Notkin, Nathan N., 620, 622; first visit, 206-225; his *record book*, 207-208, 225; second visit, 225-242; as *spokesman for entire Yishuv*, 225-28
Novalis, 433
Nuremberg Laws, 483

Occident (Philadelphia), 161, 402, 593, 603; (quoted) on Palestine relief, 173, 186, 192-93, 210-12; and Selig mission, 166, 170
Occupational distribution, 49-50
Ochs, Adolph S., 333, 413, 647
O'Connor, Harvey, 638

Odell, George, 677
Odessa, 139
Oko, Adolph, 588, 663
Old Testament, 109, 116. *See also* Bible
Oliphant, Alice, 648
Oliphant, Laurence, 335, 391, 648
Oliphant, Margaret, 648
Oliphant, W., 648
Omaha, Neb., 234, 256
[Oplatka], Isaac, 615
Oppenheim, Samuel, 592, 593, 594, 598, 688
Or Ya'acob, 121
Oral law, 507-508
Oregon, 291, 316
Orphanages, 347, 350
Orthodoxy, 455; in Europe, 384; in U.S., 131, 141-42, 365; *attempts to unify*, 382-84; and *Census of Religious Bodies*, 373-75; *differences* among, 381-82, 384-85; *history* of, 67, 132, 381-88; and Yeshiva Univ., 372; and Zionism, 394, 396
See also Conservative Judaism; Reform Judaism
Oṣar Yisrael, 401
Osborne, Charles Edward, 684
Osofsky, Gilbert, 651, 652
Ossowski, S., 620
Osterman, Rosanna, 209, 616
Oswego, New York, 261
Ottenberg, Reuben, 653
Ottoman Empire, 79; international relations, 238, 335-38; World War I, 424
See also Palestine
Oxford, 107, 109
Oxford Assembly, 446
Oxford Movement, 441

Pachter, Isaiah, 193
Pacifism, 435-36, 454
Painted Woods, 291
Palestine, 79, 160-62, 186-88, 229-233; immigration, 556; Mandate,